FOURTH EDITION

Henretta Brody Ware Johnson

Selected Historical Documents to Accompany

America's History

Volume 1 TO 1877

David L. Carlton

Vanderbilt University

Bedford/St. Martin's

Boston • New York

Manufactured in the United States of America.

6 5 4 3 2 1
f e d c b a

For information, write:
Bedford/St. Martin's, 75 Arlington Street, Boston, MA 02116   (617-399-4000)

ISBN: 0-312-19388-2

Preface

Volume 1 of the *Selected Historical Documents* brings together over 170 primary source documents to enrich the study of *America's History.* It is our goal that this reader enhance the educational experience of both students and instructors by adding breadth and depth to many facets of American history that deserve a closer look. In addition to key speeches, laws, contemporary accounts, letters, oral histories, autobiographies, and other written documents, the collection includes political cartoons, statistical tables, and figures that shed light on all aspects of political, social, economic, and cultural history.

Following the chapter organization of *America's History,* the documents in each chapter of this reader are grouped into three or four sets corresponding to the main headings of the textbook chapter. Each set begins with an introduction that places that group of documents in their wider historical context. The individual documents follow, each with its own headnote and questions, allowing instructors the flexibility to focus on an individual document or explore a particular section in depth. The wide array of readings enriches a student's learning experience, offering interesting comparisons and contrasts to specific features in the textbook itself. Many of the document sets also present pieces with opposing views meant to stimulate debate in the university classroom. For increased accessibility to students, the spelling in various selections has been clarified. The document set concludes with Questions for Further Thought designed to help students recognize connections among the documents and realize how the documents illustrate or exemplify larger themes.

Putting together the Fourth Edition of the *Selected Historical Documents* to *America's History* has required the efforts of a great many people over a considerable period of time. First and foremost, I would like to acknowledge those who edited and contributed to the first three editions, especially Cathy Matson, John K. Alexander, and Louis S. Gerteis, the editors of the Third Edition. They provided a sound base upon which their successors could build, and I can only hope that my successors will say the same of my efforts. Katherine Kurzman, Executive Editor for History at Bedford/St. Martin's, initiated this project, and bore up well under the grief of working with an author with a number of other balls in the air. Edith Trost Kirkland, Vanderbilt's Bedford/St. Martin's sales representative, has been an ever-ready help in frequent times of need, and by far the best publisher's rep I have ever had the pleasure to work with. Gretchen Boger at Bedford/St. Martin's helped get this project off the ground. Jennifer Rush, her successor, did a superb job as editor, advisor, critic, and goad. That this project made it into final form at all owes enormously to her expertise, hard work, and determination that it be as stimulating and as useful and appealing to undergraduates as we could possibly make it. William J. Lombardo provided the bulk of the new study questions with a fine ear for the significance and context of the material. Emily Berleth, the production editor, did wonderful service in translating frequently messy copy into the readable form you have before you.

Here at Vanderbilt University my Chair, Simon Collier, graciously allowed space, time, and resources, while Brenda Hummel, Lori Cohen, and Vicki Crowthers pitched in when the going got rough. Samuel T. McSeveney, my colleague and the author/editor for the second volume of this set, was, as he has been throughout the years, a never-failing font of wisdom, experience, and support. Others of my colleagues in the department of history, notably Jane Landers and Marshall Eakin, contributed at critical times. My graduate assistant, Mr. Tycho de Boer, was a marvel. Tycho was wonderfully resourceful at tracking down appropriate documents, often with only the most general instructions to go on; his experience as a discussion leader in the U.S. history survey course made him an indispensable source of insights into the sorts of documents that work and don't work in discussions. He truly deserves a credit as coauthor. Other teaching assistants, too numerous to mention, have shared with me over the years their experiences in using primary sources to engage students and meet the larger purposes of the introductory U.S. history course. Last, I have to thank the undergraduates I have taught over the years for their efforts to keep me down to earth; for their endless ability to challenge the clichés and shibboleths of academic historians; for their insistence that history be made meaningful to real American students trying to make sense of it in the context of their own lives and experiences; and, occasionally, for reminding me why I wanted to spend my life doing this in the first place.

David L. Carlton

Contents

PART **2**

The New Republic, 1775–1820

★   ★   ★

CHAPTER 6

CHAPTER 9

The Quest for a Republican Society, 1790–1820

P A R T *3*

Economic Revolution and Sectional Strife, 1820–1877

★   ★   ★

CHAPTER 10

The Economic Revolution, 1820–1860

CHAPTER *1*

Worlds Collide: Europe and the Americas, 1450–1620

★   ★   ★

Native American Worlds

Until late in the fifteenth century, unbreachable oceans bordered the Europeans' world. Totally unknown to them were the two continents of the Western Hemisphere with their more than 40 million inhabitants. Those indigenous peoples were the descendants of Asian migrants who had traveled across the temporary land bridge spanning the Bering Strait during the last great Ice Age (see text pp. 6–7).

After 1492, contact with Europeans proved devastating to the inhabitants of the "New World." Lacking a natural immunity to European diseases such as smallpox, measles, and influenza, native Americans were powerless to resist them. Document 1-1, Graph 1, shows the precipitous decline in the American Indian population north of Mexico in the five centuries after contact with the Europeans. From an estimated 5 to 7 million people, the native American population shrank to about a quarter million by 1900.

Disease made it easier for the Spanish to conquer the indigenous civilizations of Mesoamerica, but technological superiority was equally important, as the classic eyewitness account of Bernal Díaz del Castillo (Document 1-2) demonstrates.

Well before 1492, native Americans had developed civilizations and societies of great complexity and variety (see text pp. 7–11). Europeans were amazed—and often affronted—by the sharp cultural differences they encountered, but they also made some effort to understand these differences (Document 1-3). In fact, Europeans often found the indigenous cultures admirable in their differences from the less attractive features of Old World culture (Document 1-4).

1-1   Indian and Non-Indian Population Charts, 1492–1980

Two parabolic lines on the graphs below tell the story of North American population trends after 1492. One part of the story is tragic: the calamitous decline in native American numbers primarily as a result of the impact of European disease. The other part could be deemed a "success story": the startling increase in the population of non-Indian peoples, which was due primarily to high fertility rates and massive immigration. These graphs refer only to populations in what is now the United States. There is no full consensus among scholars as to the figures underlying Graph 1; in particular, the size of the indigenous population of the New World at the time of contact is a matter of dispute, and indeed may be unknowable. Nonetheless, no adjustments to Graph 1 would alter the fundamentals of the story it tells. This is the greatest known demographic catastrophe in human history.

Source: From *American Indian Holocaust and Survival: A Population History since 1492* by Russell Thornton. Copyright © 1987 by the University of Oklahoma Press. Reprinted by permission.

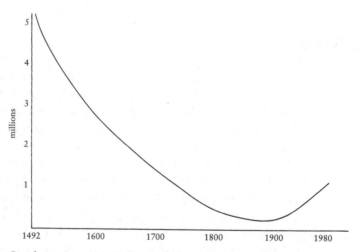

Graph 1   *American Indian Population Decline and Recovery in the United States Area, 1492–1980*

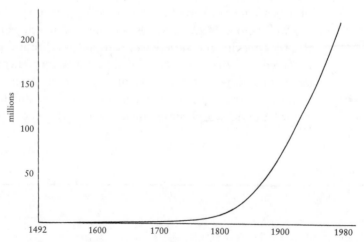

Graph 2   *Non-Indian Population Growth in the United States Area, 1492–1980*

Questions

1. Put this rate of decline in perspective by thinking about a family, a clan, or a tribe. Speculate about the social impact. Imagine a state—say, Wisconsin, with a population of about 5 million in 1990—losing 95 percent of its people. How would the survivors feel? How could they maintain their economic activities?
2. In which years were Indian and non-Indian populations even? Why did rapid Indian decline occur *before* the arrival of many non-Indians?
3. The non-Indian population rose dramatically after 1800, and the Indian population recovered after 1900. Why?

1-2   Discovery and Conquest of Mexico (1517–1521)

Bernal Díaz del Castillo

Most of the precontact hieroglyphic writings of the Aztecs and Maya were destroyed by Spanish priests, and we have learned about these cultures mainly through European eyes. Bernal Díaz del Castillo, who was born in 1492, accompanied Hernando Cortés on the march to Tenochtitlán and the conquest of Mexico. His firsthand account offers many glimpses of Mexican customs and societies and fascinating hints about Cortés's military strategies. Most subsequent histories of the conquest employ Díaz's reminiscences (see text pp. 7–8, 22–24, and especially Map 1.3).

Cacique is a Caribbean term, adopted by the Spanish, meaning a native chief. For Díaz's "Montezuma" read "Moctezuma."

Source: Excerpts from Bernal Díaz del Castillo, *The Discovery and Conquest of Mexico, 1517–1521,* trans. A. P. Maudslay, 102–105, 119, 156–157. Copyright © 1956 by Farrar, Straus & Cudahy. Copyright renewed © 1984 by Farrar, Straus & Giroux, Inc. Reprinted by permission of Farrar, Straus & Giroux, Inc.

We slept the night in those huts, and all the caciques bore us company all the way to our quarters in their town. They were really anxious that we should not leave their country, as they were fearful that Montezuma would send his warriors against them, and they said to Cortés that as we were already their friends, they would like to have us for brothers, and that it would be well that we should take from their daughters, so as to have children by them; and to cement our friendship, they brought eight damsels, all of them daughters of caciques, and gave one of these cacicas, who was the niece of the fat cacique, to Cortés; and one who was the daughter of another great cacique was given to Alonzo Hernández Puertocarrero. All eight of them were clothed in the rich garments of the country, beautifully ornamented as is their custom. Each one of them had a golden collar around her neck and golden earrings in her ears, and they came accompanied by other Indian girls who were to serve as their maids. When the fat cacique presented them, he said to Cortés: "Tecle (which in their language means Lord)—these seven women are for your captains, and this one, who is my niece, is for you, and she is the señora of towns and vassals." Cortés received them with a cheerful countenance, and thanked the caciques for the gifts, but he said that before we could accept them and become brothers, they must get rid of those idols which they believed in and worshipped, and which kept them in darkness, and must no longer offer sacrifices to them, and that when he could see those cursed things thrown to the ground and an end put to sacrifices that then our bonds of brotherhood would be most firmly tied. He added that these damsels must become Christians before we could receive them. Every day we saw sacrificed before us three, four or five Indians whose hearts were offered to the idols and their blood plastered on the walls, and the feet, arms and legs of the victims were cut off and eaten, just as in our country we eat beef brought from the butchers. I even believe that they sell it by retail in the *tianguez* as they call their markets. Cortés told them that if they gave up these evil deeds and no longer practised them, not only would we be their friends, but we would make them lords over other provinces. All the caciques, priests and chiefs replied that it did not seem to them good to give up their idols and sacrifices and that these gods of theirs gave them health and good harvests and everything of which they had need. . . .

When the Caciques, priests, and chieftains were silenced, Cortés ordered all the idols which we had overthrown and broken to pieces to be taken out of sight and burned. Then eight priests who had charge of the idols came out of a chamber and carried them back to the house whence they had come, and burned them. These priests wore black cloaks like cassocks and long gowns reaching to their feet, and some had hoods like those worn by canons, and others had smaller hoods like those worn by Dominicans, and they wore their hair very long, down to the waist, with some even reaching down to the feet, covered with blood and so matted together that it could not be separated, and their ears were cut to pieces by way of sacrifice, and they stank like sulphur, and they had another bad smell like carrion, and as they said, and we learnt that it was true, these priests were the sons of chiefs and they abstained from women, and they fasted on certain days, and what I saw them eat was the pith of seeds of cotton when the cotton was being cleaned, but they may have eaten other things which I did not see. . . .

I remember that in the plaza where some of their oratories stood, there were piles of human skulls so regularly arranged that one could count them, and I estimated them at more than a hundred thousand. I repeat again that there were more than one hundred thousand of them. And in another part of the plaza there were so many piles of dead men's thigh bones that one could not count them; there was also a large number of skulls strung between beams of wood, and three priests who had charge of these bones and skulls were guarding them. We had occasion to see many such things later on as we penetrated into the country for the same custom we observed in all the towns, including those of Tlaxcala. . . .

Cortés then took these Caciques aside and questioned them very fully about Mexican affairs. Xicotenga, as he was the best informed and a great chieftain, took the lead in talking, and from time to time he was helped by Mase Escasi who was also a great chief.

He said that Montezuma had such great strength in warriors that when he wished to capture a great city or make a raid on a province, he could place a hundred and fifty thousand men in the field, and this they knew well from the experience of the wars and hostilities they had had with them for more than a hundred years past.

Cortés asked them how it was that with so many warriors as they said came down on them they had never been entirely conquered. They answered that although the Mexicans sometimes defeated them and killed them, and carried off many of their vassals for sacrifice, many of the enemy were also left dead on the field and others were made prisoners, and that they never could come so secretly that they did not get some warning, and that when they knew of their approach they mustered all their forces and with the help of the people of Huexotzingo they defended themselves and made counter attacks. That as all the provinces which had been raided by Montezuma and placed under his rule were ill disposed towards the Mexicans, and that as their inhabitants were carried off by force to the wars, they did not fight with good will; indeed, it was from these very men that they received warnings, and for this reason they had defended their country to the best of their ability.

The place from which the most continuous trouble came to them was a very great city a day's march distant, which is called Cholula, whose inhabitants were most treacherous. It was there that Montezuma secretly mustered his companies and, as it was near by, they made their raids by night. Moreover, Mase Escasi said that Montezuma kept garrisons of many warriors stationed in all the provinces in addition to the great force he could bring from the city, and that all the provinces paid tribute of gold and silver, feathers, stones, cloth and cotton, and Indian men and women for sacrifice and others for servants, that he [Montezuma] was such a great prince that he possessed everything he could desire, that the houses where he dwelt were full of riches and [precious] stones and chalchihuites which he had robbed and taken by force from those who would not give them willingly, and that all the wealth of the country was in his hands.

Then they spoke of the great fortifications of the city, and what the lake was like, and the depth of water, and about the causeways that gave access to the city, and the wooden bridges in each causeway, and how one can go in and out [by water] through the opening that there is in each bridge, and how when the bridges are raised one can be cut off between bridge and bridge and not be able to reach the city. How the greater part of the city was built in the lake, and that one could not pass from house to house except by draw-bridges and canoes which they had ready. That all the houses were flat-roofed and all the roofs were provided with parapets so that they could fight from them.

They brought us pictures of the battles they had fought with the Mexicans painted on large henequen cloths, showing their manner of fighting. . . .

Questions

1. What "unusual" customs or rituals did Díaz del Castillo observe?
2. Díaz del Castillo emphasizes the strange and the bizarre. Can you spot any similarities between the native American and Spanish cultures?

3. Do you think Cortés could have conquered Mexico without Indian allies? Why or why not?

1-3 Confessionario (1613)

Francisco Pareja

Frey Francisco Pareja (d. 1628?) was born in Spain and came to Florida in 1595 as a Franciscan missionary. Based at the Mission of San Juan del Puerto on the northeastern coast of Florida (near present-day Jacksonville), he traveled extensively among the Timucuan peoples of what is now Florida and southeastern Georgia, mastering their language and recording it using the Latin alphabet. Pareja became a leading figure among the Florida Franciscans, serving for a time as *provincial,* or head of the Florida Province; more importantly, he became the community's foremost scholar, writing numerous works in both Spanish and Timucuan, the latter being the earliest known surviving works in a North American Indian language.

The document included here was a handbook designed to be used by Catholic priests when taking the confessions of their Timucuan parishioners; the original was written in both Spanish and Timucuan. Because the Franciscans were concerned with bringing their communicants into accord with Christian doctrine, they were eager to stamp out much of the older Timucuan culture. To do that properly, Pareja needed to make careful observations of that culture, including the behavior and the world views of the Timucuans. Thus the structure of the *Confessionario* consisted of questions concerning both the actions and the thoughts of the confessant, interspersed with the prescribed responses of the priest. Used with care, this document provides a remarkable window on the culture of an eastern North American indigenous culture.

Source: Jerald T. Milanich and William C. Sturtevant, eds., *Francisco Pareja's 1613 Confessionario: A Documentary Source for Timucuan Ethnography,* trans. Emilio F. Moran (Tallahassee: Florida Division of Historical Resources, 1972), 23–35.

English Translation and Ethnographic Notes

CEREMONIES, OMENS, AND SUPERSTITIONS THAT ARE STILL USED BY SOME.

When someone is possessed, have you believed in what he said?

Have you believed that when the blue jay or another bird sings and the body is trembling, that it is a signal that people are coming or that something important is about to happen?

Have you believed that lighting a new separate fire will cure illness?

Being ill, have you had to light a separate fire so that your meal can be cooked, because if you don't, you will die, have you believed this?

When some woman has given birth, have you avoided coming near the fire, have you considered this sinning?

Have you consented to be cured by some herbalist by praying with words to the Devil?

Toward this end, have you offered in the door of the house maize to the Devil as you used to?

The ceremony of the laurel that is made to the Devil, have you made it?

When collecting acorns or other fruits, did you consider it a sin to eat the first fruits that were cut?

In the clearing or field of maize, when lightning strikes them, have you considered it a sin to eat it or advised that no one else eats it, considering it a sin?

Have you considered it a sin to eat the first maize from a new clearing?

The first fish that enters the new fish traps, have you said not to put them in hot water, otherwise no more will be caught?

The first fish that enters the new fish trap, have you put it near the trap, saying that it will bring plenty of better fish?

Placing a new fish trap, have you desired that the prayers pray to it, believing that many more fish would enter?

In the interior of the country instead of *Ichali* they say *puye* or *jusere,* which is fish trap?

When the owl or barn owl sings, have you believed it to be a prognostication and omen of evil?

When encountering any snake in the road, field, or in the house have you believed it to be a prognostication and omen of evil?

When the eyebrow twitches, have you said or believed that it is a sign of happiness, or of another bad thing that will happen?

That the eyes tremble is a sign of a situation that causes crying, have you believed this?

When the fireplace fire pops, have you said this is a sign of war?

My mouth trembling is a sign that something bad is going to come to me, that they are saying something about me, or that there is going to be food?

Belching, have you said that this is a sign that I want to die, or that there will be much food, have you said this or have you believed that this will be?

Have you held your dreams to be true, believing them?

DOCUMENT AND ADVICE

Son, as one thinks during the day, thus he dreams at night; if he thinks good things then he will dream good things, and if bad, these will also be represented in his dreams; if the dream is about good things he should try to put them into practice, and if bad, don't pay any attention to them because the Devil is the stoker and cause of bad dreams and no matter what form they take, never give any credit to those dreams.

Having had intercourse with a woman, have you said and believed that if you enter the fish trap, no more fish or eels will enter?

When some kin has died or your spouse, have you said I will not eat that which he sowed or of his land which he used to sow, and thus following your superstition, have you given it to another to eat or have you not wanted to eat that which was sowed in an old field?

During your menses have you made a separate fire?

Have you consented that when someone is sick in your house they pray for the counsel of the Devil?

When some relative has died, have you cut your hair?

Have you buried someone with something placed inside of the shroud?

After having been to the burial of someone, have you washed or for some time have you refrained from eating fish?

Having walked in some village of infidels, have you neared where they make some ceremonies with the intention of learning them, or some prayer, or something else that is made to the Devil?

ADVICE AND DOCUMENT

If he has done or consented to any of the above mentioned, it will be said to him: Son, from now on do not do these things or consent to them, only with the herbs and baths cure yourself, because they have virtue in that God gave and created them to heal us, and all other things that you do and pray for are not of benefit, but instead harm us since they are sins.

DOCUMENT ON ALL THAT HAS BEEN SAID

Son, all these abuses and tremors of the body and signs of birds and animals, none of it is to be believed.

FOR CHIEFS AND LEADERS

Before going hunting, have you first made a prayer using tobacco?

To go hunting deer and to burn a pile of straw to hunt them, have you made six arrows and six splinters of oak and mixing a *yaquila* all between a woven cloth, and singing all night, and then you will go hunting and that you will catch many, have you said this?

And arriving at the forest, have you had all the arrows gathered and had an old man say a prayer over them for your use?

The first deer that they kill, have you said that it be given to the above mentioned old sorcerer?

To fish in the lake, have you said that they pray to the lake first?

In the same manner, have you said that these fish that you have caught, in order to eat them, that they were prayed to by the sorcerer and one half of them should go to him?

The first fish that is caught, have you said that they be prayed to and then barbecued?

In order to begin the digging of a field, have you prayed the ancient ceremony to the prayer?

The first maize from this digging, have you held it to be a sin not to pray to it?

The first time that the storehouse is opened, have you made flour, and once you made it, in order to eat it, have you prayed to it?

To gather the nuts and palm berries, have you made with the laurel [and] praying that ceremony that you used to do?

Have you said that you will not eat the fruit of the forest without prayng?

Any other fruit that has been prayed to, have you desired to eat it?

FOR THOSE THAT DIG AND SOW

The first maize from the digging or sowing, have you not eaten it? The maize from the new clearing, have you not eaten it?

When the owl sings, have you believed that it will have pity on you?

When the woodpecker sings, have you said: don't make noise, that blood will come from the nose?

When the owl or red owl sings, have you said not to scare it, that something awful will come to you?

When winter comes, have you held it to be a sin to eat the small chicken?

HUNTERS

When some little goat baas, have you said that if I don't take some herb in the nose, they will crack, and thus with this thought you have sneezed, and having come to the house, you have taken a bath with water of the herb, and not doing this, have you believed for sure that you will die, have you believed this?

Have you said or done, fixing the *coz* for the hunt, some ceremonies, abstaining from eating the deer that you killed, believing that otherwise you would not kill another?

The liver and the lung of the deer have you said not to throw them in cold water to cook, otherwise I will not be able to shoot another?

Having shot a deer and not having killed it, have you prayed to the arrow, believing that thus praying again it will die the next time you shoot it?

The broth of the deer or the wild chicken, have you said not to spill it, otherwise the snare will not catch another?

Have you said that the bones of what was hunted: do not throw them out, otherwise more will not enter the trap, hang them by the ankles or put them in the thatching of the house?

To hunt some deer, have you taken the antlers of another deer, have you prayed to them the ceremony of the Devil?

In none of these things should you believe nor trust that with the prayers of the Devil you will get the prey; instead pray the things of God, and He being served, with His will you will hunt them, having left the prayer of the Devil you can hunt and trust yourself to God.

Having had the doctor cure you and already convalescing, did you make cakes or pap or something else, and did you invite the doctor that cured you, believing that if you did not act in this manner that your illness would return?

Have you said that no one should go up to the maize storehouse without first praying to the Devil?

In order to seek and take the turtle, did you pray?

Crossing with the canoe some sandbar or obstacle, and there being a choppy area, have you whistled to it, believing that you would not turn over?

Have you whistled to the storm believing that it would stop?

When you are in such distress, you will say the holy name of Jesus so that he will help you.

OTHER CEREMONIES OF WAR

When you saw lightning, did you believe that there was war?

To go to war, did you bathe with the juice of certain herbs?

DOCUMENT AND ADVICE

Know, my son, that no matter how much you bathe or rub yourself with this herb, that it will not prevent the arrow from wounding you unless God protects you.

SORCERERS

Have you prayed to the new maize?

Have you looked with the Devil's arts to see if war approaches?

In what way or with which herb did you do this?

Have you searched for something lost with the art of the Devil?

Son, these things that you do to make the things you lost appear and say that it is in this or that place or that such person stole, this the Devil tells you in order to take your soul; do not believe it, abandon it, this is a grave sin.

Have you made rain?

If God does not wish it, no matter what you do it will not rain, abandon this which is a grave sin.

QUESTIONS FOR WOMEN

During your menses have you held it to be a sin to eat fish or deer?

Having given birth recently have you considered eating these things as sinful?

To this end, have you made a new fire or did you make it during your menses?

Annointing the head with bear grease, have you considered it a sin to eat fish for a certain number of months?

Have you eaten charcoal, or dirt, or bits of pottery, or fleas, or lice?

Don't eat charcoal, or dirt, nor bits of pottery, they make a person sick, and because of the harm they do to you, it is a sin.

Your husband having left you, did you bathe with certain herbs, believing that with this he will return to you?

Have you said perfume the *guano* with certain herb and he will not leave me?

And thus perfuming, have you put on the dress skirt?

Have you believed that perfuming *guano* with this intention, that someone will take a liking to you?

Have you fasted with this intention?

And thus with someone did you go on to the night, and in order to eat and drink, did you make the ceremony?

All these abuses and ceremonies and many more which are not included because they have left them already and because in some villages there are some of them; these here are so that the confessor will be forewarned so that when he hears them he will understand them; and in each province they have different ceremonies that because of their tediousness are left out.

Have you made some pregnant woman have a bad birth [miscarriage] with a blow, herb, or with fright or in any other manner?

Have you counseled or wished her to have a miscarriage?

FOR THOSE THAT ARE PREGNANT

Being pregnant, have you killed the unborn child or wished to kill it by taking some drink or striking yourself or squeezing your belly to choke it as you used to do?

By lying badly across the bed and putting your arm on top, have you suffocated the unborn child?

TO MAKE GRAVER THE SIN OF ABORTION AND OF THE GOOD THAT IS TAKEN AWAY FROM THE CHILD, AND SO ON

Daughter, to make another woman have a miscarriage is a grave sin for it is homicide, and because it deprives that unborn child of such a great benefit as it is to receive the waters of the Holy Baptism, through which he could go to enjoy the eternal richness and be united with the powerful God and His saints and angels, and much more than this you make it lose; you and your kin lose the prayers that he could have said from heaven if he had died a Christian, and because you killed him, he went into limbo where he will always be sad without light and contentment, without seeing God, disconsolate and sighing.

If she were single and it is known that she is pregnant, it is to be said to her that she is not to abort or choke the unborn child as they are accustomed to do. My daughter,

although you have fallen into mortal sin, beware that you will fall into an even more serious one if you have brought about a miscarriage, don't commit such a grave sin even if it means shame, bear the sin in God's name.

It is also to be said to her about the good that she will cause the unborn child to lose, as was indicated above, and you will read about the horrible case . . . about a woman that killed the unborn child and was damned.

FOR DOCTORS, HERBALISTS, AND SORCERERS

Are you a doctor?

Did you cure someone badly in such a manner that they had to call you again and give you something more?

In order that they pay more, have you said: if you don't give me something, the sickness that you have will return?

Have you cured anyone with prayers to the Devil or with the ceremony of adulation?

Have you cured some person, entreating the Devil to improve him and doing and saying those things that he commands be taken out and done, have you done this?

Have you produced a new fire or made a fire apart to cure someone?

Have you believed that with these prayers and superstitions a person can be cured?

When they are running for some prize or stake, have you made someone in the race faint with some herbs?

Have you taken an herb to run faster than the other in order to take the bet or the prize that they put up?

After someone ill has given you something to be cured, have you not returned until he pays you more?

FOR BOTH HERBALISTS AND MIDWIVES

Have you made someone late in delivering so that they will call you and pay you well because with this herb you can make her give birth quicker?

Calling you to aid in delivery, did you do it in such a manner that until they gave you the amount that you desire, you did not help her, but instead made her suffer, did you do this?

Someone being in labor, have you prayed those words that you used to say to the Devil?

Leave that evil prayer because it is perverse, cure only with medicine.

FOR SORCERERS

Are you a sorcerer?

Have you bewitched someone?

Have you taken the herb with the intent of bewitching someone?

Have you given the spell to another in order to do evil to him?

Have you advised someone else so that they could bewitch?

Did the spell work?

Did the spell that you gave to the other person take effect?

If he has bewitched someone, it should be said to him to take the antidote and cure him in order to undo the evil done, and when he is cured, to return and he will be absolved, etc.

And if he has given the spell to another or advised that they do it or given instructions for it, the following is to be said to him:

Have you conjured a rain storm or a thunder storm with superstitions?

Thundering, have you blown toward the heavens in order to stop the clouds or water with your evil prayers?

Have you made the ceremony of rain?

Son, don't make this ceremony any more, for do what you will, be aware that it will not rain unless God our Lord is served.

In order to begin to take out the food out of the storehouse, have you prayed?

Have you taken the skin of the poisonous snake or of the black snake and with black *guano* and other herbs have you tried to bewitch someone or have you bewitched them or wished to do so?

And to do the above, have you considered it a sin to eat fish and to paint yourself and to sleep with your wife; but once the person is dead, have you begun to do the things that you were abstaining from, after a bath?

The bewitched person not having died from that evil spell, did you say that then I must die?

And in order to do a similar thing [another ceremony for causing death], have you gone to question the other, and taking water and moss and other things, have you made this evil spell?

Have you told them that they must give you something, otherwise you will kill all of them, and with this fear did they give you something?

Have you made the marriage ceremony, praying over them? And if they did not pay you, did you do something evil?

Have you taken a woman out of her house by singing your charms?

Have you put some herb in the mouth of some woman so that she will love you a lot?

Have you injured anyone with herbs?

Have you ruptured someone?

Have you injured someone in the legs or feet?

In curing someone, have you placed in front of the sick person white feathers and new chamois and the ears of the owl and arrows which are stuck in, and then said that you will take out the evil and sickness?

About the strength of these superstitions many of which are more fears and tremblings than real ceremonies and nonsense, he is to be told that having left all these things (for in them does not lie health nor the obtaining of what is attempted) that he is to heal only with herbs and medicines, since God made them for our health and our illnesses without mixing them with useless words and words from the Devil.

And if he is poor, cure him for the love of God, that such is good pay indeed, thus you are to act.

Another counsel by which one can undeceive those who cure in this way, that what he shows in the palm of his hand after having placed one [there], as if a leech sucking with his mouth (that usually is a little piece of coal, at other times a small lump of dirt and other unclean things, things alive or as if alive) that it cannot be, since no hole is left in the body through which that can exit, and naturally there was deception and some substance where that was, or else the Devil must have managed it subtly, and this can be believed since from as hard a part as the forehead and arms and head and spine or back of the neck it is not possible, it is a secret that has not been comprehended until now; when asked about such things they say with a look of surprise I do not know how this is done, they answer; and it is true, they do not have any treaties or pacts with the Devil, as our sorcerers.

That to begin to cure with the name of Jesus and the sign of the cross, that thusly God willing he will cure, etc. And that if He is not served by this, no matter what he does it will be of no avail.

QUESTIONS TO PLAYERS

Have you defeated someone by stealth?

Have you lied in games?

Did you count more points than there were?

What you won by cheating must be returned to its owner, since something badly won is like something stolen.

Have you played so long that you have lost all that you had in your house?

If the answer is yes: Son, do not do this again, and be sorry for it, because it is a sin.

Have you won something knowing it was stolen?

Playing and having lost, have you said bad words with anger or have you fought with anyone and so insulted him, and affirming what you said not being the truth, swearing by God or by the saints?

Have you obtained something from someone who can't play it?

CEREMONIES OF THE GAME

To win over someone, have you taken some herb and rubbed your hands with it?

Have you taken this herb with the intention of winning over the other person?

That which is this badly won should be returned to its owner like a stolen thing.

Have you played with the intention of winning, and having lost, not paying?

Did you pay what you lost?

If he says no, you must pay because you would want them to pay you.

If a case of restitution arose, the following is to be said: Know that what is stolen is to be returned to its owner, at least restore it when you can because that helps your soul more than any material thing, etc.

In the section below he is to say what he has taken.

Do you still have what you took?

If he says yes, then return it to its owners, or in having it the manner should be suggested how he can honorably return it, etc.

And if it were a Spaniard to whom restitution will be made, the manner of so doing is to be suggested, and do so without attracting attention.

Have you wished that someone die soon, so that you can inherit?

Have you desired someone else's goods?

Have you eaten meat on a day of abstinence?

How many times in a day did you eat it?

QUESTIONS FOR THE CHIEFS

Have you taken more tribute or other things from your vassals, more than you used to take or carry?

Have you taken the daily wages of those that work for you?

Have you occupied your vassals in some work and asked them to miss Mass?

Have you made someone work without permission of the priest on a fiesta day?

Without prayers by the sorcerer have you said that no one should open or go up to the storehouse?

The new maize or other new fruits, have you said that it will not be eaten until the sorcerer tastes it first?

Have you arranged that someone be married according to the Indian ways without first giving notice to the parish priests?

Have you consented that your slaves sleep together?

Have you some slave or servant as your mistress?

Have you consented that in your village someone bringing herbs pray words to the Devil with them?

Have you made some sorcerer look for something lost by the arts of the Devil?

After having eaten bear, have you said that you be given a drink from another shell, and that otherwise you will become sick?

Because they don't come to dance, have you ordered that some woman be affronted or that the penalty be taken to her?

For the beginning of the sowing, have you had fixed a pot of *gacha,* and that six old men eat from it, and etc?

FOR THOSE THAT INHERIT CEREMONIES FOR CHIEFS-TO-BE

Having become a chief, have you ordered a new fire to be made for six days in the community house, and that it be daubed with laurel or with something else?

Have you desired that the chief dies in order to become his heir?

FOR ALL, CHIEFS, AND LEADERS

Being sick, have you made a new house, saying here I will remain and die, etc?

COMMANDING-CHIEFS AND LESSER CHIEFS

Not because of work, but because you are angry, have you ordered that someone be punished by having his arm broken?

Without having any reason except that you were angry, have you punished anyone?

Questions

1. What, in Pareja's view, distinguished Timucuan religion from Christianity?
2. What can you determine from this excerpt about the ways in which Timucuan society was organized?
3. What do you notice about the document that suggests that the European observer might be inserting his own preconceptions into his efforts to render Timucuan culture "objectively"?

1-4 An Account of Huron Society (1721)

Pierre de Charlevoix

Pierre de Charlevoix, a Jesuit, came to New France as a French spy in 1720. He traveled up the Saint Lawrence River, through the Great Lakes, and down the Mississippi to New Orleans. During his travels he kept a journal, cast in the form of letters, that was first published in 1744. Charlevoix's careful observations reveal a social structure that seemed extraordinary to Europeans (see text p. 12). Among the Huron, he tells us, women played an important role in a democratic decision-making process. The historian James Axtell calls Huron society a "gynecocracy," or a government ruled by women.

Source: P[ierre] de Charlevoix, *Journal of a Voyage to North-America* (London, 1761), 2: 23–27. From *The Indian Peoples of Eastern America: A Documentary History of the Sexes,* edited by James Axtell (New York: Oxford University Press, 1981), 150–153. Copyright 1981 by Oxford University Press. Used by permission of Oxford University Press, Inc.

In the northern parts, and wherever the Algonquin tongue prevails, the dignity of chief is elective; and the whole ceremony of election and installation consists in some feasts, accompanied with dances and songs; the chief elect likewise never fails to make the panegyrick of his predecessor, and to invoke his genius. Amongst the Hurons, where this dignity is hereditary, the succession is continued through the women, so that at the death of a chief, it is not his own, but his sister's son who succeeds him; or, in default of which, his nearest relation in the female line. When the whole branch happens to be extinct, the noblest matron of the tribe or in the nation chuses the person she approves of most, and declares him chief. The person who is to govern must be come to years of maturity; and when the hereditary chief is not as yet arrived at this period, they appoint a regent, who has all the authority, but which he holds in name of the minor. These chiefs generally have no great marks of outward respect paid them, and if they are never disobeyed, it is because they know how to set bounds to their authority. It is true that they request or propose, rather than command; and never exceed the boundaries of that small share of authority with which they are vested. Thus it is properly reason which governs, and the government has so much the more influence, as obedience is founded in liberty; and that they are free from any apprehension of its degenerating into tyranny.

Nay more, each family has a right to chuse a counsellor of its own, and an assistant to the chief, who is to watch for their interest; and without whose consent the chief can undertake nothing. These counsellors are, above all things, to have an eye to the public treasury; and it is properly they who determine the uses it is to be put to. They are invested with this character in a general council, but they do not acquaint their allies with it, as they do at the elections and installations of their chief. Amongst the Huron nations, the women name the counsellors, and often chuse persons of their own sex.

This body of counsellors or assistants is the highest of all; the next is that of the elders, consisting of all those who have come to the years of maturity. I have not been able to find exactly what this age is. The last of all is that of the warriors; this comprehends all who are able to bear arms. This body has often at its head, the chief of the nation or town; but he must first have distinguished himself by some signal action of bravery; if not, he is obliged to serve as a subaltern, that is, as a single centinel; there being no degrees in the militia of the Indians.

In fact, a large body may have several chiefs, this title being given to all who ever commanded; but they are not therefore the less subject to him who leads the party; a kind of general, without character or real authority, who has power neither to reward nor punish, whom his soldiers are at liberty to abandon at pleasure and with impunity, and whose orders notwithstanding are scarce ever disputed: so true it is, that amongst a people who are guided by reason, and inspired with sentiments of honour and love for their country, independence is not destructive of subordination; and, that a free and voluntary obedience is that on which we can always rely with the greatest certainty. Moreover, the qualities requisite are, that he be fortunate, of undoubted courage, and perfectly disinterested. It is no miracle, that a person possessed of such eminent qualities should be obeyed.

The women have the chief authority amongst all the nations of the Huron language; if we except the Iroquois canton of Onneyouth [Oneida], in which it is in both sexes alternately. But if this be their lawful constitution, their practice is seldom agreeable to it. In fact, the men never tell the women any thing they would have to be kept secret; and rarely any affair of consequence is communicated to them, though all is done in their name, and the chiefs are no more than their lieutenants. . . . The real authority of the women is very small: I have been however assured, that they always deliberate first on whatever is proposed in council; and that they afterwards give the result of their de-liberation to the chiefs, who make the report of it to the general council, composed of the elders; but in all proba-bility this is done only for form's sake, and with the restric-tions I have already mentioned. The warriors likewise con-sult together, on what relates to their particular province, but can conclude nothing of importance which concerns the nation or town; all being subject to the examination and controul of the council of elders, who judge in the last resource.

It must be acknowledged, that proceedings are carried on in these assemblies with a wisdom and a coolness, and a knowledge of affairs, and I may add generally with a pro-bity, which would have done honour to the areopagus of Athens, or to the senate of Rome, in the most glorious days of those republics: the reason of this is, that nothing is re-solved upon with precipitation; and that those violent pas-sions, which have so much disgraced the politics even of Christians, have never prevailed amongst the Indians over the public good. Interested persons fail not, however, to set many springs in motion, and apply an address in the exe-cution of their designs, we could hardly believe barbarians capable of; they also all of them possess, in the most sover-eign degree, the art of concealing their real intentions: but generally speaking, the glory of the nation and motive of honour, are the chief movers in all enterprizes. What can never be excused in them is, that they often make honour consist in satiating a revenge which knows no bounds; a fault which Christianity alone is able to correct, and in which all our politeness and religion are often un-successful.

Each tribe has an orator in every town, which orators are the only persons who have a liberty to speak in the pub-lic councils and general assemblies: they always speak well and to the purpose. Besides this natural eloquence . . . they have a perfect knowledge of the interests of their employ-ers, and an address in placing the best side of their own cause in the most advantageous light, which nothing can exceed. On some occasions, the women have an orator, who speaks in their name, or rather acts as their interpreter.

Questions

1. What role did women play in Huron decision making?
2. Was their power real or merely a mask for male supremacy?
3. Ideally, Hurons suppressed their "violent passions" for the sake of the public good. Would this be realistic in any society?

Questions for Further Thought

1. A demographic catastrophe and a brutal conquest of another culture: should we pay more attention to American history before European settlement? Why or why not?
2. Note that the three preceding accounts were all by Europeans and based on Euro-pean observations. Do they nonetheless contain reliable information about the peoples they discuss? How do you judge?
3. Do these authors *uniformly* assume superiority to their subjects? Or are they am-bivalent about them, in some ways even admiring of them?

Traditional European Society, 1450–1550, and Europe and the World, 1450–1550

Even before 1450 "traditional" European society was growing and changing. The pop-ulation increased, farming techniques improved, and towns and trade expanded. Eu-rope flexed its muscles by looking outward to the Holy Land, which it sought to re-Christianize by conquest, and to new trade routes to Africa and the East. At the same time many Europeans worked toward the spiritual purification of the continent. Much still remained "traditional," including the ties of most people to the land and the supremacy of the Christian faith. Secular rulers rose and fell; wars and anarchy occurred frequently; famine and disease remained an omnipresent threat; and the Black Death, or bubonic plague (roughly 1347–1400), seemed to be an example of God's inexplicable ways. Social conditions changed everywhere, although not at the same time.

The Renaissance, which began early in the fourteenth century in Italy, transformed Europe, and a transformed Europe discovered America (text pp. 22–27). This "rebirth," or renewal of intellectual inquiry and human knowledge, offered limitless possibility for learning and creativity. Renaissance humanism liberated Europeans from the spiritual and hierarchical dogmas of the past. It celebrated secular and individual characteristics: willpower, activity, the unlimited potential of human nature, creative talent, and *virtù*. By *virtù*, Italian scholars meant the application of the "manly" powers in the secular pursuits of war, statecraft, and the arts.

Portugal, a small and remote European nation that for fifty years had set its sights on the East, paved the way for the discovery of America (see text pp. 20–22). The Portuguese pioneered new navigational techniques that were eagerly studied by the young Christopher Columbus, who lived in Portugal from 1476 to 1485. Columbus was looking for a quick route to the East when he encountered the unknown American landmass in 1492. The Atlantic Ocean, long a barrier to Europeans, became a bridge to the New World.

Quickly Portugal and Spain began Europeanizing the globe, dividing the new lands between them. In 1498 Vasco Da Gama landed on the Malabar Coast of India, establishing an Asian empire of trade and commerce backed by sea power, war, and plunder. Spain established sugar plantations in the Caribbean that soon were worked by African slaves. Cortés conquered the Aztec in Mexico; Pizarro, the Incas in Peru.

The documents in this section explore both continuity and change from the eleventh century through the Renaissance. Document 1-5 recounts the recurring problem of famine. Document 1-6 reveals the goals of the Portuguese. Document 1-7 describes the moment of first contact between Europeans and native Americans.

1-5   An Account of Famine (c. 1040)

Raoul Glaber

Tens of thousands of people still die of famine in the modern world, and their stories often goad the machinery of international relief into action. Imagine a time when the causes of famine were almost wholly natural rather than political, no national or international support system existed, and people were left to their own devices (see text pp. 13–15). The monk Raoul Glaber was a member of the Cluniac monastic order in France. For leadership, the Cluniacs looked exclusively to the pope in Rome rather than to a secular ruler, but on this subject no leadership was forthcoming. Here Glaber describes the effects of the great European famine of 1032–1034.

Source: Eugen Weber, *The Western Tradition,* 4th ed., vol. 1, *From the Ancient World to Louis XIV* (Lexington, Mass.: D. C. Heath, 1990), 250–251. Copyright 1990 by D. C. Heath and Company. Reprinted by permission of McDougal Littell, Inc.

The famine started to spread its ravages and one could fear the disappearance of the human race almost whole. The weather became so bad that none could find the right time for any sowing and that, especially because of the floods, there was no way of harvesting. . . . Continual rains had steeped the whole earth to the extent that during three years one could not dig furrows that would harbor the seed. By harvest time weeds and inauspicious tares had covered all the surface of the fields. In those parts where it gave the best results, a hogshead of seed would produce a harvest of about twelve bushels [about one-fifth of the original seed], and this in turn produced hardly a handful. If by chance one found any food on sale, the seller could exact an excessive price at his will.

Meantime, when the savage beasts and the birds had been eaten, men began, under the empire of a devouring hunger, to gather in order to eat, all kinds of carrion and of things horrible to tell. Certain among them had recourse to escape from death to the roots of the forests and the weeds of the rivers. In the end one is seized by horror at the tale of perversions which then reigned over the human race. Alas! Oh, woe! A thing rarely heard of in the course of ages, a maddening hunger made that men devoured human flesh. Travellers were carried off by those stronger than they, their members cut up, cooked on the fire and devoured. Many of the people who were going from one place to another to flee the famine and who had found hospitality on the way, were slaughtered during the night and served as nourishment for those who had welcomed them. Many, by showing a fruit or an egg to children, lured them into isolated places, massacred and devoured them. The bodies of the dead were in many places torn from the earth and served equally to appease hunger.

There was then tried in the region of Macon an experiment which had not, to our knowledge, yet been attempted anywhere else. Many people drew from the ground a white soil similar to clay, mixed it with what they had of wheat or bran, and made of this mixture bread, on which they relied so as not to die of hunger. However this practice brought merely the hope of salvation and the illusion of relief. One saw only pale and emaciated faces: many presented a skin distended by swellings; the human voice itself became shrill, similar to the little cries of dying birds. The corpses of the dead, whose multitude forced the living to abandon them here and there without burial, served as pasture to wolves who continued for a long time thereafter to seek their pittance among men. And as one could not, as we said, bury everyone individually because of the great number of dead, in certain places the men, fearing God, dug what was commonly known as charnel houses, in which the bodies of the dead were thrown by the five hundreds and more as long as room remained, pell mell, half naked or without any covering. The cross roads, the edges of the fields, also served as cemeteries. If some heard say that they would be better if they moved to other regions, many were those who perished on the way for want of food.

Questions

1. What does this account tell us about the state of transportation and communication in eleventh-century Europe?
2. Short of outside aid, is there any possible human remedy for the situation described here?
3. Do you think the clay eaters were driven by physical or mental urges?

1-6   On Prince Henry of Portugal (1453)

Gomes Eannes de Azurara

Prince Henry "the Navigator" (1394–1460) founded a center for exploration and the study of ocean navigation. He sent Portuguese vessels farther and farther south along the western coast of Africa, until in 1488 Bartolomew Diaz rounded the Cape of Good Hope and entered the Indian Ocean, an event comparable in its contemporary significance to Columbus's discovery of new islands in the Atlantic (see text pp. 20–21). In this account Gomes Eannes de Azurara, the chronicler of Prince Henry's achievements, lists Henry's six principal motivations for exploration. "Lord Infant" is a translation of Prince Henry's Portuguese title, *Infante*, or "(royal) child."

Source: Gomes Eannes de Azurara, *The Chronicle of the Discovery and Conquest of Guinea*, trans. Charles Raymond Beazley and Edgar Prestage (London: The Hakluyt Society, 1896), 1: 27–30.

We imagine that we know a matter when we are acquainted with the doer of it and the end for which he did it. And since in former chapters we have set forth the Lord Infant as the chief actor in these things . . . it is meet that in this present chapter we should know his purpose in doing them. And you should note well that the noble spirit of this Prince, by a sort of natural constraint, was ever urging him both to begin and to carry out very great deeds. For which reason, after the taking of Ceuta he always kept ships well armed against the Infidel, both for war, and because he had also a wish to know the land that lay beyond the isle of Canary and that Cape called Bojador, for that up to his time, neither by writings, nor by the memory of man, was known with any certainty the nature of the land beyond that Cape. . . . And because the said Lord Infant wished to know the truth of this,—since it seemed to him that if he or some other lord did not endeavour to gain that knowledge, no mariners or merchants would ever dare to attempt it—(for it is clear that none of them ever trouble themselves to sail to a place where there is not a sure and certain hope of profit)—and seeing also that no other prince took any pains in this matter, he sent out his own ships against those parts, to have manifest certainty of them all. And to this he was stirred up by his zeal for the service of God and of the King Edward his Lord and brother, who then reigned. And this was the first reason of his action.

The second reason was that if there chanced to be in those lands some population of Christians, or some havens, into which it would be possible to sail without peril, many kinds of merchandise might be brought to this realm, which would find a ready market, and reasonably so, because no other people of these parts traded with them, nor yet people of any other that were known; and also the products of this realm might be taken there, which traffic would bring great profit to our countrymen.

The third reason was that, as it was said that the power of the Moors in that land of Africa was very much greater than was commonly supposed, and that there were no Christians among them, nor any other race of men; and because every wise man is obliged by natural prudence to wish for a knowledge of the power of his enemy; therefore the said Lord Infant exerted himself to cause this to be fully discovered, and to make it known determinately how far the power of those infidels extended.

The fourth reason was because during the one and thirty years that he had warred against the Moors, he had never found a Christian king, nor a lord outside his land, who for the love of our Lord Jesus Christ would aid him in the said war. Therefore he sought to know if there were in those parts any Christian princes, in whom the charity and the love of Christ was so ingrained that they would aid him against those enemies of the faith.

The fifth reason was his great desire to make increase in the faith of our Lord Jesus Christ and to bring to him all the souls that should be saved, understanding that all the mystery of the Incarnation, Death, and Passion of our Lord Jesus Christ was for this sole end—namely the salvation of lost souls—whom the said Lord Infant by his travail and spending would fain bring into the true path. For he perceived that no better offering could be made unto the Lord than this; for if God promised to return one hundred goods for one, we may justly believe that for such great benefits, that is to say for so many souls as were saved by the efforts of this Lord, he will have so many hundreds of guerdons in the kingdom of God, by which his spirit may be glorified after this life in the celestial realm. For I that wrote this history saw so many men and women of those parts turned to the holy faith, that even if the Infant had been a heathen, their prayers would have been enough to have obtained his salvation. And not only did I see the first captives, but their children and grandchildren as true Christians as if the Divine grace breathed in them and imparted to them a clear knowledge of itself.

But over and above these five reasons I have a sixth that would seem to be the root from which all the others proceeded: and this is the inclination of the heavenly wheels. For, as I wrote not many days ago in a letter I sent to the Lord King, that although it be written that the wise man shall be Lord of the stars, and that the courses of the planets (according to the true estimate of the holy doctors) cannot cause the good man to stumble; yet it is manifest that they are bodies ordained in the secret counsels of our Lord God and run by a fixed measure, appointed to different ends, which are revealed to men by his grace, through whose influence bodies of the lower order are inclined to certain passions. And if it be a fact, speaking as a Catholic, that the contrary predestinations of the wheels of heaven can be avoided by natural judgment with the aid of a certain divine grace, much more does it stand to reason that those who are predestined to good fortune, by the help of this same grace, will not only follow their course but even add a far greater increase to themselves. But here I wish to tell you how by the constraint of the influence of nature this glorious Prince was inclined to those actions of his. [Here Azurara describes Prince Henry's horoscope.] And the fact of his being accompanied by the sun, as I said, and the sun being in the house of Jupiter, signified that all his traffick and his conquests would be loyally carried out, according to the good pleasure of his king and lord.

Questions

1. According to Azurara, what motivated Prince Henry to explore the African coast?
2. Was the prince a medieval or a modern figure? Explain your answer.
3. Were the prince's motives scientific or practical? Explain your answer.

1-7   Columbus's Landfall (1552)

Bartolomé de las Casas

In 1492 a Genoese mariner in the pay of Spain set out from Palos for the Canary Islands and thence for Asia (see text pp. 22–23). He had accepted early Renaissance miscalculations of the width of the Eurasian continent, the distance from China to Japan, and the breadth of a degree of longitude. At the end of his 3,000-mile voyage, Columbus thought he had reached Asia; instead, he had landed in the Bahamas. However, great events are measured by their consequences. Christopher Columbus "discovered" America for the Europeans, and the world has not been the same since.

The following passage from Columbus's journal, which includes the brief remarks on the native Bahamians appearing in the text on p. 23, describes the first recorded encounter of Europeans with "America." The "journal," you will note, is not Columbus's own, but is rather the work of the Dominican missionary and historian Bartolomé de las Casas (see also Document 2-1), who quoted parts of Columbus's log, paraphrased others, and inserted new information.

Source: Bartolomé de las Casas, *The Journal of Christopher Columbus (1847/1870),* trans. Cecil Jane, rev. and annotated by L. A. Vigneras (London: The Hakluyt Society, 1960), 19–41.

Thursday, October 11th. He navigated to the west-southwest; they had a rougher sea than they had experienced during the whole voyage. They saw petrels and a green reed near the ship. Those in the caravel *Pinta* saw a cane and a stick, and they secured another small stick, carved, as it appeared, with iron, and a piece of cane, and other vegetation which grows on land, and a small board. Those in the caravel *Niña* also saw other indications of land and a stick loaded with barnacles. At these signs, all breathed again and rejoiced. On this day, to sunset, they went twenty-seven leagues. After sunset, he steered his former course to the west; they made twelve miles an hour, and up to two hours before midnight they had made ninety miles, which are twenty-two leagues and a half. And since the caravel *Pinta* was swifter and went ahead of the admiral, she found land and made the signals which the admiral had commanded. This land was first sighted by a sailor called Rodrigo de Triana, although the admiral, at ten o'clock in the night, being on the sterncastle, saw a light. It was, however, so obscured that he would not affirm that it was land, but called Perro Gutierrez, butler of the King's dais, and told him that there seemed to be a light, and that he should watch for it. He did so, and saw it. He said the same also to Rodrigo Sanchez de Segovia, whom the King and Queen had sent in the fleet as *veedor* [comptroller], and he saw nothing since he was not in a position from which it could be seen. After the admiral had so spoken, it was seen once or twice, and it was like a small wax candle, which was raised and lowered. Few thought that this was an indication of land, but the admiral was certain that they were near land. Accordingly, when they had said the *Salve,* which all sailors are accustomed to say and chant in their manner, and when they had all been gathered together, the admiral asked and urged them to keep a good look out from the forecastle and to watch carefully for land, and to him who should say first he saw land, he would give at once a silk doublet apart from the other rewards which the Sovereigns had promised, which were ten thousand maravedis annually to him who first sighted it. Two hours after midnight land appeared, at a distance of about two leagues from them. They took in all sail, remaining with the mainsail, which is the great sail without bonnets, and kept jogging, waiting for day, a Friday, on which they reached a small island of the Lucayos, which is called in the language of the Indians "Guanahaní." Immediately they saw naked people, and the admiral went ashore in the armed boat, and Martin Alonso Pinzón and Vicente Yañez, his brother, who was captain of the *Niña*. The admiral brought out the royal standard, and the captains went with two banners of the Green Cross, which the admiral flew on all the ships as a flag, with an F and a Y, and over each letter their crown, one being on one side of the . . . and the other on the other. When they had landed, they saw very green trees and much water and fruit of various kinds. The admiral called the two captains and the others who had landed, and Rodrigo de Escobedo, secretary of the whole fleet, and Rodrigo Sanchez de Segovia, and said that they should bear witness and testimony how he, before them all, took possession of the island, as in fact he did, for the King and Queen, his Sovereigns, making the declarations which are required, as is contained more at length in the testimonies which were there made in writing. Soon many people of the island gathered there. What follows are the actual words of the admiral, in his book of his first voyage and discovery of these Indies.

"I," he says, "in order that they might feel great amity towards us, because I knew that they were a people to be delivered and converted to our holy faith rather by love than by force, gave to some among them some red caps and some glass beads, which they hung round their necks, and many other things of little value. At this they were greatly pleased and became so entirely our friends that it was a wonder to see. Afterwards they came swimming to the ships' boats, where we were, and brought us parrots and cotton thread in balls, and spears and many other things, and we exchanged for them other things, such as small glass beads and hawks' bells, which we gave to them. In fact, they took all and gave all, such as they had, with good will, but it seemed to me that they were a people very deficient in everything. They all go naked as their mothers bore them, and the women also, although I saw only one very young girl. And all those whom I did see were youths, so that I did not see one who was over thirty years of age; they were very well built, with very handsome bodies and very good faces. Their hair is coarse almost like the hairs of a horse's tail and short; they wear their hair down over their eyebrows, except for a few strands behind, which they wear long and never cut. Some of them are painted black, and they are the colour of the people of the Canaries, neither black nor white, and some of them are painted white and some red and some in any colour that they find. Some of them paint their faces, some their whole bodies, some only the eyes, and some only the nose. They do not bear arms or know them, for I showed to them swords and they took them by the blade and cut themselves through ignorance. They have no iron. Their spears are certain reeds, without iron, and some of these have a fish tooth at the end, while others are pointed in various ways. They are all generally fairly tall, good looking and well proportioned. I saw some who bore marks of wounds on their bodies, and I made signs to them to ask how this came about, and they indicated to me that people came from other islands, which are near, and wished to capture them, and they defended themselves. And I believed and still believe that they come here from the mainland to take them for slaves. They should be good servants and of quick intelligence, since I see that they very soon say all that is said to them, and I believe that they would easily be made Christians, for it appeared to me that they had no creed. Our Lord willing, at the time of my departure I will bring back six of them to Your Highness, that they may learn to talk. I saw no beast of any kind in this island, except parrots." All these are the words of the admiral.

Questions

1. What personal characteristics of Christopher Columbus are revealed in this excerpt?
2. Why did Columbus believe he was in Asia?
3. Can you discover Columbus's motives for making his journey? What were they?

Questions for Further Thought

1. What characteristics of the Renaissance can be discerned in the European voyages of discovery? (See Document 1-6.)
2. Was Europe in 1492 modern or medieval? Progressive or backward? Explain your answer.
3. We know that Columbus's landfall (Document 1-7) was disastrous for native Americans. Should we celebrate it? Why or why not?

The Protestant Reformation and the Rise of England, 1500–1620

In the sixteenth century Catholicism helped fuel the Spanish conquest of America, but the Protestant Reformation reshaped England and delayed that country's exploration of the New World. When Martin Luther published his Ninety-five Theses in 1517 (see text p. 27), England was not prepared politically or economically to join the Iberian countries in the race for empire. John Calvin's emphasis on predestination and congregationalism (see text p. 30) appealed to many people in England and Scotland. When Henry VIII declared himself the head of the Church in England (see text p. 30), he inaugurated more than a half-century of religious turmoil. During the long reign of Elizabeth I (1558–1603), the compromise later known as Anglicanism was hammered out, considerably Protestant in content but unacceptable to either Roman Catholics or ardent Calvinists (see text pp. 30–31). Many religious dissenters sought refuge in America.

Not only religion but also economics reshaped England. A series of economic changes, including a massive rise in inflation, the beginnings of capitalism, and the transition from a local to a national economy, affected the island (see text pp. 32–34). Spain imported vast amounts of gold from America, which it then spent in Europe. The resulting inflation benefited merchants and landowners who were dependent on rents. Mercantilism brought an emphasis on payment in bullion and government aid to merchants. The English colonies became sources of raw materials, conveniently distant havens for political and religious dissenters, and markets for manufactured goods. England's new wealth made possible a military buildup that led to the defeat of a Spanish invasion in 1588 (see text p. 32).

Document 1-8 addresses the serious social difficulties created by enclosure in England. In Document 1-9 Separatists define their differences with the Anglican Church. Document 1-10 reproduces Richard Hakluyt's arguments in favor of colonization in America.

1-8   Objections against Enclosure (1548)

John Hales

Two economic factors challenged sixteenth-century England: a dramatic rise in population and a shortage of agricultural jobs. England's population had shrunk drastically during the Black Death in the fourteenth century. By 1550 it had made good the loss; after that time, people increased their numbers faster than the economy was able to absorb them. The shortage of agricultural jobs was caused partly by enclosure, the large-scale conversion of arable land to sheep pasturage, and the consequent eviction of tenant farmers (see text pp. 33–34). Modern scholarship has minimized the actual extent of enclosure, but to contemporaries it symbolized all the economic problems they had to endure. In 1548 John Hales, an opponent of enclosure, conducted a commission of inquiry in the Midlands (central England) and vented his wrath.

Source: J. Strype, *Ecclesiastical Memorials* (London, 1721), vol. 2, Appendix of Documents, Document Q, in G. R. Elton, *Renaissance and Reformation, 1300–1648* (New York: Macmillan, 1963).

As by natural experience we find it to be true that if any one part of man's body be grieved . . . it is a great pain to all the whole body . . . so ought we to consider and remember in the state of the body of the realm. If the poorest sort of the people, which be members of the same body as well as the rich, be not provided and cherished in their degree, it cannot but be a great trouble of the body and a decay of the strength of the realm. Surely, good people, methinks that if men would know how much this ungodly desire of worldly things, and the unlawful getting and heaping together of riches, were hated of God, how hurtful and dangerous for the commonwealth of the realm it is, and what a virtue the mean in all things is, these laws nor a great many more that be needed not. God's Word is full of threats and curses against these kind of greediness. . . . When men in a commonwealth go about to gather as much as they can, and to get it they care not how; not considering whether by their gain any hurt should come to their neighbours or to the commonwealth; not only others, but they themselves should shortly perish. What avails a man to have his house full of gold and be not able to keep it with his force against his enemies? So what shall all our goods avail us if we be not able to defend us from our enemies?

The force and puissance [power] of the realm consists not only in riches but chiefly in the multitude of people. But it appears, good people, that the people of this realm, our native country, is greatly decayed through the greediness of a few men in comparison, and by this ungodly means of gathering together goods, by pulling down towns and houses, which we ought all to lament. Where there were [a few years ago] ten or twelve thousand people, there be now scarce four thousand. Where there were a thousand, now scarce three hundred, and in many places, where there were very many able to defend our country from landing of our enemies, now almost none. Sheep and cattle, that were ordained to be eaten of men, has eaten up the men, not of their own nature but by the help of men. Is it not a pitiful case that there should be so little charity among men? Is it not a sorrowful hearing that one Englishman should be set to destroy his countrymen? The places where poor men dwelt clearly destroyed; lands improved

to so great rents, . . . that the poor husbandman cannot live. All things at this present . . . be so dear as never they were—victual and other things that be necessary for man's use. And yet, as it is said, there was never more cattle, specially sheep, than there is at this present. But the cause of the dearth is that those have it that may choose whether they will sell it or not, and will not sell it but at their own prices. . . .

To declare unto you what is meant by this word, enclosures. It is not taken where a man does enclose and hedge in his own proper ground where no man has commons. For such enclosure is very beneficial to the commonwealth: it is a cause of great increase of wood. But it is meant thereby when any man has taken away and enclosed any other men's commons, or has pulled down houses of husbandry and converted the lands from tillage to pasture. This is the meaning of the word, and so we pray you remember it.

To defeat these statutes [laws banning enclosure] as we be informed, some have not pulled down their houses but maintain them; howbeit, no person dwells therein, or if there be it is but a shepherd or a milkmaid; and convert the lands from tillage to pasture. And some about one hundred acres of ground, or more or less, make a furrow and sow that, and the rest they till not but pasture with their sheep. And some take the lands from their houses and occupy them in husbandry, but let the houses out to beggars and old poor people. Some, to colour the multitude of their sheep father them on their children, kinsfolk and servants. All which be but only crafts and subtleties to defraud the laws, such as no man will use but rather abhor. . . .

Besides, it is not unlike but that these great fines for lands and improvement of rents shall abate, and all things wax better cheap—20 and 30 eggs for a penny, and the rest after the rate as has been in times past. And the poor craftsmen may live and set their wares at reasonable prices. And noblemen and gentlemen that have not improved nor enhanced their rents, nor were sheepmasters nor graziers but lived like noblemen and gentlemen, shall be the better able to keep good hospitality among you, and keep servants about them, as they have done in time past. . . .

Questions

1. In Hales's opinion, was enclosure a religious or an economic problem? Why?
2. Do you think moral strictures alone would have been sufficient to reverse the enclosure movement? Why or why not?
3. Does Hales elucidate any underlying economic reasons for enclosure? If so, what are those reasons?

1-9   A Petition: The Separatists State Their Case (1604)

Two groups of Protestant dissenters were among the first English people to immigrate to the New World. The Separatists, who founded the Plymouth colony in 1620, sought total withdrawal from the Anglican Church to establish independent congregations. The non-Separatists wanted to reform the Church of England from within. Non-Separatists (Puritans) founded a settlement at Massachusetts Bay in 1629.

In the 1580s a small group of Separatists left England for the Netherlands, where they could worship freely. When James I succeeded Elizabeth I in 1603, the Amsterdam Separatists (Pilgrims) petitioned the new king for permission to return to England. Their unsuccessful petition spelled out fourteen points of difference between Separatism and Anglicanism.

Source: "The Points of Difference between Congregationalism and the Church of England (1603)," in Williston Walker, *The Creeds and Platforms of Congregationalism* (Boston, 1893; reprint, Philadelphia and Boston: Pilgrim Press, 1960), 75, 77–80.

THE POINTS OF DIFFERENCE

1. That Christ the Lord hath by his last Testament given to his Church, and set therein, sufficient ordinary Offices, with the maner of calling or Entrance, Works, and Maintenance, for the administration of his holy things, and for the sufficient ordinary instruction guydance and service of his Church, to the end of the world.

2. That every particular Church hath like and full interest and power to enjoy and practise all the ordinances of Christ given by him to his Church to be observed therein perpetually.

3. That every true visible Church, is a company of people called and separated from the world by the word of God, and joyned together by voluntarie profession of the faith of Christ, in the fellowship of the Gospell. And that therfore no knowne Atheist, unbelever, Heretique, or wicked liver, be received or reteined a member in the Church of Christ, which is his body; God having in all ages appointed and made a separation of his people from the world, before the Law, under the Law, and now in the tyme of the Gospell.

4. That discreet, faithfull, and able men (though not yet in office of Ministerie) may be appointed to preach the gospell and whole truth of God, that men being first brought to knowledge, and converted to the Lord, may then be ioyned togeather in holy communion with Christ our head and one with another.

5. That being thus ioyned, every Church hath power in Christ to chuse and take unto themselves meet and sufficient persons, into the Offices and functions of Pastors, Teachers, Elders, Deacons and Helpers, as those which Christ hath appointed in his Testament, for the feeding, governing, serving, and building up of his Church. And that no Antichristia Hierarchie or Ministerie, of Popes, Arch-bishops, Lord-bishops, Suffraganes, Deanes, Arch-deacons, Chauncellors, Parsons, Vicars, Priests, Dumb-ministers, nor any such like be set over the Spouse and Church of Christ, nor reteined therein.

6. That the Ministers aforesaid being lawfully called by the Church where they are to administer, ought to continew in their functions according to Gods ordinance, and carefully to feed the flock of Christ committed unto them, being not inioyned or suffered to beare Civill offices withall, neither burthened with the execution of Civill affaires, as the celebration of marriage, burying the dead etc. which things belong as well to those without as within the Church.

7. That the due maintenance of the Officers aforesaid, should be of the free and voluntarie contribution of the Church, that according to Christs ordinance, they which preach the Gospell may live of the Gospell: and not by Popish Lordships and Livings, or Iewish Tithes and Offerings. And that therefore the Lands and other like revenewes of the Prelats and Clergie yet remayning (being still also baits to allure the Iesuites and Seminaries into the Land, and incitements unto them to plott and prosecute their woonted evill courses, in hope to enioy them in tyme to come) may now by your Highnes be taken away, and converted to better use, as those of the Abbeyes and Nunneries have been heertofore by your Maiestyes worthie predecessors, to the honor of God and great good of the Realmc.

8. That all particular Churches ought to be so constituted, as having their owne peculiar Officers, the whole body of every Church may meet togeather in one place, and iointly performe their duties to God and one towards another. And that the censures of admonition and excommunication be in due maner executed, for sinne, convicted, and obstinatly stood in. This power also to be in the body of the Church wherof the partyes so offending and persisting are members.

9. That the Church be not governed by Popish Canons, Courts, Classes, Customes, or any humane inventions, but by the lawes and rules which Christ hath appointed in his Testament. That no Apocrypha writings, but only the Canonicall scriptures be used in the Church. And that the Lord be worshipped and called upon in spirit and truth, according to that forme of praier given by the Lord Iesus, Math. 6. and after the Leitourgie of his owne Testament, not by any other framed or imposed by men, much lesse by one traslated from the Popish leitourgie, as the Book of common praier etc.

10. That the Sacraments, being seales of Gods covenant, ought to be administred only to the faithfull, and Baptisme to their seed or those under their governement. And that according to the simplicitie of the Gospell, without any Popish or other abuses, in either Sacrament.

11. That the Church be not urged to the observation of dayes and tymes, Iewish or Popish, save only to sanctify the Lords day: Neyther be laden in things indifferent, with rites and ceremonies, whatsoever invented by men; but that Christian libertie may be reteined: And what God hath left free, none to make bound.

12. That all monuments of Idolatry in garments or any other things, all Temples, Altars, Chappels, and other place, dedicated heertofore by the heathens or Antichristians to their false worship, ought by lawfull aucthoritie to be rased and abolished, not suffered to remayne, for nourishing superstition, much lesse imploied to the true worship of God.

13. That Popish degrees in Theologie, inforcement to single life in Colledges, abuse of the study of prophane heathen Writers, with other like corruptions in Schooles and Academies, should be removed and redressed, that so they may be the welsprings and nurseries of true learning and godlinesse.

14. Finally that all Churches and people (without exception) are bound in Religion not only to receave and submit unto that constitution, Ministerie, Worship, and order, which Christ as Lord and King hath appointed unto his Church: and not to any other devised by Man whatsoever.

Questions

1. How did the Separatists define their religious beliefs and practices?
2. In what way was the Church of England too Catholic for Separatists? (Hint: Look for the word *Popish*.)
3. The Church of England was a *territorial* church; that is, all English subjects had to be members. How did the Separatists criticize this practice?

1-10   A Discourse to Promote Colonization (1584)

Richard Hakluyt

By the end of the sixteenth century, England's economic and imperial aspirations had led inexorably to colonization. Explorers such as Martin Frobisher and Humphrey Gilbert had reconnoitered the Atlantic coast of North America. The first Roanoke voyage took place in 1584 (see text p. 34), the year in which Richard Hakluyt (1552–1616) issued his *Discourse Concerning Western Planting*. Hakluyt, a clergyman and travel writer (although he never traveled), was an effective pamphleteer and propagandist for colonization. The *Discourse* was written at the request of Sir Walter Raleigh and contains virtually every positive argument for settlement that would be advanced over the next century. Its purpose was to persuade Queen Elizabeth I to put the English state squarely behind American ventures.

Source: Richard Hakluyt, *A Discourse Concerning Western Planting*, in Charles Deane et al., eds., *Documentary History of the State of Maine* (Collections of the Maine Historical Society, 1869–1916), 2: 152–161.

Chapter XX. A brief collection of certain reasons to induce her Majesty and the state to take in hand the western voyage and the planting there.

1. The soil yields and may be made to yield all the several commodities of Europe. . . .

2. The passage thither and home is neither too long nor too short, but easy, and to be made twice in the year.

3. The passage cuts not near the trade of any prince, nor near any of their countries or territories, and is a safe passage, and not easy to be annoyed by prince or potentate whatsoever.

4. The passage is to be performed at all times of the year, and in that respect passes our trades in the Levant Seas within the Straits of Gibraltar, and the trades in the seas within the King of Denmark's Strait, and the trades to the ports of Norway and of Russia, etc. . . .

5. And where England now for certain hundred years last passed, by the peculiar commodity of wool, and of later years, by clothing of the same, has raised itself from meaner state to greater wealth and much higher honour, might, and power than before, to the equalling of the princes of the same to the greatest potentates of this part of the world; it comes now so to pass that by the great endeavour of the increase of the trade of wool in Spain and in the West Indies, now daily more and more multiplying, that the wool of England, and the cloth made of the same, will become base, and every day more base than [the] other; which, prudently weighed it behooves this realm, if it mean not to return to former old means and baseness, but to stand in present and late former honour, glory, and force, and not negligently and sleepingly to slide into beggary . . . were it not for anything else but for the hope of the sale of our wool. . . .

6. This enterprise may stay the Spanish king from flowing over all the face of that waste firmament of America, if we seat and plant there in time. . . And England possessing the purposed place of planting, her Majesty may, by the benefit of the seat, having won good and royal havens, have plenty of excellent trees for masts, of goodly timber to build ships and to make great navies, of pitch, tar, hemp, and all things incident for a navy royal, and that for no price, and without money or request. How easy a matter may it be to this realm, swarming at this day with valiant youths, rusting and hurtful by lack of employment, and having good makers of cable and of all sorts of cordage, and the best and most cunning shipwrights of the world, to be lords of all those seas, and to spoil Philip's Indian navy, and to deprive him of yearly passage of his treasure to Europe, and consequently to abate the pride of Spain and of the supporter of the great Anti-christ of Rome, and to pull him down in equality to his neighbour princes, and consequently to cut off the common mischiefs that come to all Europe by the peculiar abundance of his Indian treasure, and this without difficulty.

7. This voyage, albeit it may be accomplished by bark or smallest pinnace for advice or for a necessity, yet for the distance, for burden and gain in trade, the merchant will not for profit's sake use it but by ships of great burden; so as this realm shall have by that means ships of great burden and of great strength for the defence of this realm. . . .

8. This new navy of mighty new strong ships, so in trade to that Norumbega and to the coasts there, shall never be subject to arrest of any prince or potentate as the navy of this realm from time to time has been in the ports of the empire, in the ports of the Low Countries, in Spain, France, Portugal, etc., in the times of Charles the Emperor, Francis the French king, and others. . . .

9. The great mass of wealth of the realm embarked in the merchants' ships, carried out in this new course, shall not lightly, in so far distant a course from the coast of Europe, be driven by winds and tempests into ports of any foreign princes, as the Spanish ships of late years have been into our ports of the West countries, etc. . . .

10. No foreign commodity that comes into England comes without payment of custom once, twice, or thrice, before it comes into the realm, and so all foreign commodities become dearer to the subjects of this realm; and by this course to Norumbega[1] foreign princes' customs are avoided; and the foreign commodities cheaply purchased, they become cheap to the subjects of England, to the common benefit of the people, and to the saving of great treasure in the realm; whereas now the realm becomes poor by the purchasing of foreign commodities in so great a mass at so excessive prices.

11. At the first traffic with the people of those parts, the subjects of this realm for many years shall change many cheap commodities of these parts for things of high value there not esteemed; and this to the great enriching of the realm, if common use fail not.

12. By the great plenty of those regions the merchants and their factors shall lie there cheap, buy and repair their ships cheap, and shall return at pleasure without stay or restraint of foreign prince; whereas upon stays and restraints the merchant raiseth his charge in sale over of his ware. . . .

13. By making of ships and by preparing of things for the same, by making of cables and cordage, by planting of vines and olive trees, and by making of wine and oil, by husbandry, and by thousands of things there to be done, infinite numbers of the English nation may be set on work, to the unburdening of the realm with many that now live chargeable to the state at home.

14. If the sea coast serve for making of salt, and the inland for wine, oils, oranges, lemons, figs, etc., and for making of iron, all which with much more is hoped, without sword drawn, we shall cut the comb of the French, of

---

[1]*Norumbega:* A legendary kingdom, reputedly located somewhere along the northeastern seaboard of the present United States and Maritime Canada, and allegedly inhabited by a highly civilized people akin in spirit to the ancient Greeks and Romans. Hakluyt uses this term to suggest that the proposed site for his colony was a land overflowing with milk and honey, an earthly paradise prepared for occupation by Europeans.

the Spanish, of the Portuguese, and of enemies, and of doubtful friends, to the abating of their wealth and force, and to the greater saving of the wealth of the realm.

15. The substances serving, we may out of those parts receive the mass of wrought wares that now we receive out of France, Flanders, Germany, etc.; and so we may daunt the pride of some enemies of this realm, or at the least in part purchase those wares, that now we buy dearly of the French and Flemish, better cheap; and in the end, for the part that this realm was wont to receive, drive them out of trade to idleness for the setting of our people on work.

16. We shall by planting there enlarge the glory of the gospel, and from England plant sincere religion, and provide a safe and a sure place to receive people from all parts of the world that are forced to flee for the truth of God's word.

17. If frontier wars there chance to arise, and if thereupon we shall fortify, it will occasion the training up of our youth in the discipline of war, and make a number fit for the service of the wars and for the defence of our people there and at home.

18. The Spaniards govern in the Indies with all pride and tyranny; and like as when people of contrary nature at sea enter into galleys, where men are tied as slaves, all yell and cry with one voice, *Liberta, liberta*, as desirous of liberty and freedom, so no doubt whensoever the Queen of England, a prince of such clemency, shall seat upon that firmament of America, and shall be reported throughout all that tract to use the natural people there with all humanity, courtesy, and freedom, they will yield themselves to her government, and revolt clean from the Spaniard. . . .

19. The present short trades cause the mariner to be cast off, and often to be idle, and so by poverty to fall to piracy. But this course to Norumbega being longer, and a continuance of the employment of the mariner, doth keep the mariner of idleness and from necessity; and so it cuts off the principal actions of piracy, and the rather because no rich prey for them to take comes directly in their course or anything near their course.

20. Many men of excellent wits and of diverse singular gifts, overthrown by suretyship, by sea, or by some folly of youth, that are not able to live in England, may there be raised again, and do their country good service; and many needful uses there may (to great purpose) require the saving of great numbers, that for trifles may otherwise be devoured by the gallows.

21. Many soldiers and servitors, in the end of the wars, that might be hurtful to this realm, may there be unladen, to the common profit and quiet of this realm, and to our foreign benefit there, as they may be employed.

22. The fry of the wandering beggars of England, that grow up idly, and hurtful and burdenous to this realm, may there be unladen, better bred up, and may people waste countries to the home and foreign benefit, and to their own more happy state.

23. If England cry out and affirm that there are so many in all trades that one cannot live for another, as in all places they do, this Norumbega (if it be thought so good) offers the remedy.

Questions

1. What are Hakluyt's arguments for colonization? Do they seem persuasive after four hundred years? Why or why not?
2. Which of Hakluyt's arguments pertain to England's internal conditions? Which have an imperial cast?
3. Are Hakluyt's proposed colonies more important as sources of raw materials or as markets? Why?

Questions for Further Thought

1. In what ways did religious and economic motivations for colonization reinforce each other?
2. Were English colonists driven out of their country by adverse conditions, or were they drawn to America primarily by the promise of progress? Explain your answer.
3. Did England consider America a dumping ground for undesirables? Why or why not?

CHAPTER 2

The Invasion and Settlement of North America, 1550–1700

★　　　★　　　★

Imperial Conflicts and Rival Colonial Models

Early Spanish efforts at colonization and exploration were centered in the Caribbean and Mesoamerica. The Spanish conquistadors were primarily interested in finding precious metals and establishing domination over subject peoples, although sometimes that led to their extermination (Document 2-1). Few Spaniards were interested in living in the New World; Spain's empire, by and large, did not consist of settler colonies. At first only isolated expeditions penetrated North America, motivated mainly by the search for gold and missionary activity. In the latter part of the fifteenth century, however, the Spanish treasure fleet came under attack from English and French privateers, who used the South Atlantic coast as a base of operations. In response, Spain expanded its military presence in Florida, establishing St. Augustine. Similar security concerns led Spanish friars to the northern borderlands of Mexico, or "New Mexico."

Like the Spanish, the French were uninterested in settling their New World holding, Canada, with colonists. Rather, as French adventurers explored the St. Lawrence and Mississippi waterways, they established an extensive fur trade with the native inhabitants, while Jesuits sought Indian conversions to Christianity. The Dutch interest in the New World was even more commercially (and less religiously) oriented than the French interest (Document 2-2); few Dutch came to New Netherland, but the colony attracted a diverse population even before being conquered by the English in 1664 and renamed New York.

The English were different. While their earliest colonies, like those of the French and Dutch, were established by private commercial enterprises with support from the Crown, the first of these, the Virginia Company, floundered about aimlessly in its first years (Documents 2-3 and 2-4). It soon discovered, though, that the best way to make its enterprise successful was to expand its concerns and become a settler colony of the sort advocated by Richard Hakluyt (Document 1-10). While the company itself subsequently lost control of its creation, Virginia began to prosper as a *settler colony*, in which white planters and their indentured servants expropriated land from the native inhabitants and developed a plantation economy built around tobacco.

2-1   History of the Indies (1552)

Bartolomé de las Casas

Fray Bartolomé de las Casas (1474–1566) was born in Seville; his father, a merchant who fell upon hard times, became associated with Christopher Columbus. The younger las Casas went to the New World in 1502 to serve as a priest and missionary to the indigenous peoples. In the following years he both proselytized and prospered as a landowner and gold miner, largely using forced Indian labor. In 1514, however, he experienced a conversion that led him to renounce his old life and dedicate himself to exposing the atrocities visited upon the native peoples. In the remaining half-century of his long life he worked assiduously on both sides of the Atlantic to reform Spanish treatment of the indigenous peoples. Among his numerous writings was *History of the Indies,* begun in Hispaniola in the 1520s and published in Seville in 1552. Las Casas's writings were undertaken in the interest of reform and were animated by his deep Catholic piety; yet they were read all over Europe, and, especially among the English, unintentionally helped bolster a "Black Legend" of a peculiarly cruel—and Catholic—Spanish dominion.

Source: From Bartolomé de las Casas, *History of the Indies,* trans. and ed. Andrée Collard (New York: Harper and Row, 1971), 77–82, 154–159. Copyright © 1971 by Andrée M. Collard, renewed 1999 by Joyce J. Contrucci. Reprinted by permission of Joyce Contrucci.

Once the two caravels on which Comendador Bobadilla[1] was sending Columbus and his brothers as prisoners to Castile had sailed, he [Bobadilla] tried to please the 300 Spaniards who remained on the island. This was the number Columbus had informed the King as being necessary to subjugate the island and its natives; therefore, the King had ordered the admiral to maintain this force. It was more than enough not only to keep the Indians pacified, had they treated them differently, but also to subdue and kill them all, which is what they did. Indeed, twenty or thirty horses were enough to tear them to pieces, especially since they had trained dogs for this purpose and one Spaniard with one dog felt as safe as if accompanied by fifty or a hundred Christians. This is clear even to the dullest minds. How can a people who go about naked, have no weapons other than bow and arrow and a kind of wooden lance, and no fortification besides straw huts, attack or defend themselves against a people armed with steel weapons and firearms, horses and lances, who in two hours could

pierce thousands and rip open as many bellies as they wished? This proves Oviedo's[2] error (*History,* Bk III, Ch. 4) when he says that the Christians would have perished if Columbus, on his way to discover Paria, had not dispatched three ships from La Gomera Island to Hispaniola, and when he presents as a fact that the reinforcement saved the lives of Spanish men as well as their hold on the island, since they said they dared not leave the town or cross the river.

Here and elsewhere Oviedo exaggerates in order to justify Spanish tyranny and accuse the poor and forsaken Indians. Endless testimonies and the above argument prove the mild and pacific temperament of the natives, as well as the fact that we surpassed them in arms so that, had we lived among them as Christians, we would have had no need of weapons, horses or fierce dogs to attract them to us. But our work was to exasperate, ravage, kill, mangle and destroy; small wonder, then, if they tried to kill one of us now and then (the only way to catch a group of even thirty of us was if that group was fast asleep). This is a fact: Indians seldom killed groups of fifty or forty men

---

[1]*Bobadilla:* Francisco de Bobadilla (d. 1502), was sent by the Spanish Crown to Hispaniola (Santo Domingo) in 1500 as chief justice and royal commissioner to deal with grievances of the Spanish colonists against Christopher Columbus and his two brothers. On arrival, Bobadilla found the three brothers brutally suppressing a rebellion; he promptly arrested them and returned them to Spain. He died in a shipwreck two years later.

[2]*Oviedo:* Gonzalo Fernández Oviedo y Valdés (1478–1557), author of *The General and Natural History of the Indies* (1535), a pro-colonialist work generally regarded at the time as authoritative. Oviedo depicted the Indians as inferior to Europeans and as bloodthirsty savages, leading las Casas to attack the veracity of his work.

anywhere in the Indies, especially if they had horses and sentries. So then, a group of 300 could certainly defend itself and kill all the Indians on this island, and this was their number before the arrival of Columbus's reinforcement. He brought more men, not because they were needed, but because he had to dispose of the weak, the sick and those homesick for Castile, as I have already said.

But to return to the point, Comendador Bobadilla wanted to please the 300 men who remained on the island, and his first decision dealt with the trial of those men condemned to be hanged. As far as Francisco Roldán[3] and his followers were concerned, I saw them a few days later, as if nothing had happened, safe and sound, happy and living as honored members of the community. I heard nothing about their having been punished in any way because in those days I took no notice nor did I care to know about them. Comendador Bobadilla granted the 300 men liberties and privileges. He taxed their gold at only 1 peso on 11 and they, having no mind to work and excavate, asked him for Indian labor both for the mines and the making of bread. He ordered—rather, he advised—them to form partnerships of two to share all the profits and assigned Indian tribes to them, thus making them very happy. You should have seen those hoodlums, exiled from Castile for homicide with crimes yet to be accounted for, served by native kings and their vassals doing the meanest chores! These chiefs had daughters, wives and other close relations whom the Spaniards took for concubines either with their own consent or by force. Thus, those 300 hidalgos lived for several years in a continuous state of sin, not counting those other sins they committed daily by oppressing and tyrannizing Indians. They called these women servants and shamelessly spoke of them to one another as "My servant so and so" and "X's servant," meaning "My wife so and so" and "X's wife." The comendador didn't give a straw for all this; at least he took no measures to remedy or avoid the situation. He would frequently tell them: "Take as many advantages as you can since you don't know how long this will last"; he cared even less for the hardships, afflictions and deaths of the Indians. The Spaniards loved and adored him in exchange for such favors, help and advice, because they knew how much freer they were now than under Columbus.

The admiral, it is true, was as blind as those who came after him, and he was so anxious to please the King that he committed irreparable crimes against the Indians. However, if he did not report the harm that certain Spaniards caused them, and if he assigned a tribe of Indians to Francisco Roldán and a few others to do work for them or find gold, it seems the occasions were very, very rare, and he

acted as if forced to it by his own men, on account of past rebellions. At least he did abominate the free and easy life of those sinners who called themselves Christians. Sin leads to sin, and for many years they lived unscrupulously, not observing Lent or other fasts and, except at Easter, ate meat on Fridays and Saturdays. They saw themselves as masters of lords, served and feared by tribes of nobles and common people who trembled at the sight of them because of past cruelties renewed in the present whenever they felt the whim, and who especially trembled if the chief's wife, daughter or sister was thought to be a Spaniard's "wife." Thus they grew more conceited every day and fell into greater arrogance, presumption and contempt toward these humble people. They no longer felt like walking any distance. Having neither mules nor horses, they rode the backs of Indians if they were in a hurry; if they had more leisure, they traveled as if by litter, stretched on a hammock carried at a good speed and with relays. In this case they also had Indians carry large leaves to shade them from the sun and others to fan them with goose wings. I saw many an escort follow them loaded like a donkey with mining equipment and food, many of them with scars on their shoulders like working animals. Whenever they reached an Indian village, they consumed what to fifty Indians would represent abundance, and forced the chief to bring them whatever he had, to the accompaniment of dances. Not only were they exceedingly vain in these matters, but they had other women as well who would serve in other capacities such as chambermaid, cook and similar offices. I once knew an organ maker who had such maids.

There were two kinds of servants. One, all the boys and girls taken from their parents on their plundering and killing expeditions, whom they kept in the house night and day; these were called *naborías*, meaning "servants" in the vernacular. And two, seasonal workers for the mines and the fields, who returned to their own homes starving, exhausted and debilitated. And it was a laughing matter to see the Spaniards' presumption, vanity and air of authority when they had not even a linen shirt to their names, nor cape, coat or trousers but wore only a cotton shirt over another shirt from Castile if they had it; if not, they wore their cotton shirt over bare legs and instead of boots they had sandals and leggings. To console them for their services, they beat and insulted the Indians, hardly calling them anything but "dog." Would to God they treated them as such, because they would not have killed a dog in a million years, while they thought nothing of knifing Indians by tens and twenties and of cutting slices off them to test the sharpness of their blades. Two of these so-called Christians met two Indian boys one day, each carrying a parrot; they took the parrots and for fun beheaded the boys. Another one of these tyrants, angry at an Indian chief, hanged twelve of his vassals and eighteen others all in one house. Another shot arrows into an Indian in public, announcing the reason for punishment as his failure to deliver a letter with the speed he required.

---

[3]*Roldán*: Francisco de Roldán (1462–1502), a Spanish colonist in Hispaniola whom Columbus appointed as chief justice before returning to Spain in 1496. He subsequently led a rebellion against the Columbus brothers that was settled when Christopher Columbus agreed to the *encomienda* system, which granted territory (and the Indians living on it) to each colonist. Bobadilla openly took Roldán's side against Columbus.

Cases of this sort are infinite among our Christians. Having failed in their attempts to defend themselves, these gentle and patient people fled to the hills but, since experience had taught them the impossibility of escaping from Spaniards anywhere, they suffered and died in the mines and other labors in desperate silence, knowing not a soul in the world to whom they could turn for help. And this is at the root of the doubt as to whether they were animals or human beings. Soulless, blind and godless, these Spaniards killed without restraint and perversely abused the patience, natural simplicity, goodness, obedience, gentleness and services of the Indians. They should have admired and pitied them and tempered their own cruelties; instead, they despised and belittled them, discrediting their humanity and believing them to be nonrational animals, and so it was thought throughout the world. The lamentable error to believe them incapable of Catholic indoctrination sprang from this first error and may he who persists in it burn for such beastly heresy.

There were other improprieties, such as saying the Indians needed tutors like children because they could not govern themselves and because, if left to their own resources, they did not work but died of starvation, and all this was said in order to keep power over them. Since nobody spoke on their behalf, but rather ate of the same dish, this pernicious infamy took such roots that for years Castilian kings, their councils, and all manner of men believed it and treated them like animals, until God gave them someone [i.e. Las Casas] who enlightened them and the world as to the truth that lay behind the lethargy—after he had ascertained the stupidity and falseness of that opinion, as well be shown below.

The falseness in itself was not so obscure as to require miraculous light—any rustic mind could have seen it and taken pride in telling others. But having found greed as the prime mover—vehement greed, blind, wild and the root of all evils—it became apparent that the original tyrants and all who followed in their damnable beliefs, confirmed by dismal actions, had been numbed by greed; and a glimmer of hope of stopping it became possible, what learned person does not know that the minds of the wisest and most generous men can degenerate to pusillanimity when subjected to harsh and lasting servitude? Oppressed, afflicted, threatened, tormented and mistreated in various ways, unable to raise their thoughts above their bitter misery, they can forget their own humanity. And this is the first plan of tyrants: in order to sustain themselves on usurped territory, they continually oppress and cause anguish to the most powerful and to the wisest so that, occupied by their calamities, they lack the time and courage to think of their freedom; thus the Indians degenerated into cowardice and timidity, as I amply demonstrated in Chapters 27 and 36 of my *Apologetical History*. Well then, if the wisest of the wise, whether Greek or Roman (history books are full of this), often feared and suffered from this adversity, and if many other nations experienced it and philosophers wrote

about it, what could we expect from these gentle and unprotected Indians suffering such torments, servitude and decimation but immense pusillanimity, profound discouragement and annihilation of their inner selves, to the point of doubting whether they were men or mere cats? And who, down to the lowest idiot, will not think blind and downright malicious those who dared spread this belief and defame so many people, saying Indians need tutors because they are incapable of organization, when in reality, they have kings and governors, villages, houses and property rights, and communicate with one another on all levels of human, political, economical and social relations, living in peace and harmony?

Finally, the following argument makes even more apparent the evil design of those deceivers and counterfeiters of truth. They say that without tutors Indians would not work and would die of starvation; let us ask, then, if Spain sent food to the Indians all those thousands of years people lived there and if, when we got there, we found them wanting and thin? Also, did we give them the means to find food—since they lived on air and we brought food to them all the way from Castile—and did we satiate them or, on the contrary, did they satisfy our own hunger and free us from death many times by giving us not only the bare essentials but many superfluous things as well? Oh, vicious blindness! Wicked, insensitive and detestable ungratefulness! So consequently, these first sowers of destruction are responsible for the infamous lie which spread throughout the world that harmed the cause of multitudes of men, the sons of Adam, without cause and without reason by misinterpreting their natural goodness, gentleness, obedience and simplicity. They should have loved and praised the Indians, and even learned from them, instead of belittling them by publicizing them as beastly; instead of stealing, afflicting, oppressing and annihilating them, making as much of them as they would a heap of dung on a public square. And let this suffice to account for the state of affairs on this island under Bobadilla's government, after he had sent Admiral Columbus as a prisoner to Castile. . . .

When the Spaniards saw how fast they were killing Indians in the mines, plantations and other endeavors, caring only to squeeze the last effort out of them, it occurred to them to replenish the supply by importing people from other islands and they deceived King Hernando with a crafty argument. They notified him either by letter or by a special court representative, presumably with the comendador's consent, that the Lucayo or Yucayo Islands close to Cuba and Hispaniola were full of an idle people who had learned nothing and could not be Christianized there. Therefore, they asked permission to send two ships to bring them to Hispaniola where they could be converted and would work in the mines, thus being of service to the King.

The King agreed, on the blind and culpable recommendation of the council, acting as if rational beings were timber cut from trees and used for buildings or a herd of sheep or any other animals and nothing much would be lost if they died at sea. Who would not blame an error so great: natives taken by force to new lands 100 and 150 leagues away, however good or evil the reason may have been, much less to dig gold in mines where they would surely die, for a King and foreigners they had never offended? Perhaps they sought justification by deceiving the King with a falsehood, that is, that the Lucayo Indians would be instructed in the Faith: which, even if it were true was not right—and it wasn't true, for they never intended anything of the kind nor did anything in that direction. God did not want Christianity at that cost; God takes no pleasure in a good deed, no matter its magnitude, if sin against one's fellow man is the price of it, no matter how minuscule that sin may be; and this is a fact all sinners, especially in the Indies, deceive themselves into ignoring. In total condemnation of this lie, let it be remembered that the Apostles never expatriated anyone by force in order to convert them elsewhere, nor has the universal Church ever used this method, considered pernicious and detestable. Therefore, the King's council was very blind and, consequently, because its members are scholars, it is guilty before God, since ignorance cannot be adduced.

The King's permission arrived and ten or twelve residents from Concepción and Santiago gathered 10,000 or 12,000 gold pesos, bought two or three ships and fifty to sixty salaried men, and raided the Indians who lived in the Lucayos in peace and security. Those are the Lucayo Indians I spoke of at length in Book I and in my *Apologetical History,* so blessed among all Indians in gentleness, simplicity, humility and other natural virtues, it seems Adam's sin left them untouched. I haven't found any comparable nation in the world in ancient history, except perhaps the Seres of Asia, who are a peace-loving and gentle people (Solinus, Ch. 63), who love justice (Pomponius Mela, III, 6), and who know not how to kill or fornicate, have no prostitutes, adulterers, thieves or homicides and adore no idols (Eusebius, *Praeparatione Evangelica,* VI, 8). To this kind of people the Spaniards did the following. They say that the first harvesters of Lucayo Indians, fully aware of their simplicity and gentle manners (they knew this from the report of Christopher Columbus), anchored their ships and were received as they always are before our deeds prove the contrary, that is, as angels from Heaven. The Spaniards said they came from Hispaniola, where the souls of their beloved ones were resting in joy, and that their ships would take them there if they wanted to see them, for it is a fact that all Indian nations believe in the immortality of the soul. After death, the body joins the soul in certain delightful places of pleasure and comfort; some nations even believe that the souls of sinners first undergo torment. So then, with those wicked arguments, the Spaniards deceived the Indians into climbing on board ship, and men and women left their homes with their scant belongings.

On Hispaniola, they found neither father, mother nor loved ones but iron tools and instruments and gold mines instead, where they perished in no time; some, from despair at seeing themselves deceived, took poison; others died of starvation and hard labor, for they are a delicate people who had never imagined such type of work even existed. Later, the Spaniards used every possible wile and force to trick them into ships. At the landing sites, usually Puerto de Plata and Puerto Real on the north shore facing the Lucayos, men, women, children and old people were thrown helter-skelter into lots; the old with the young, the sick with the healthy—they often fell ill in the ships, and many died of anguish, thirst and hunger in the hottest and stuffiest holds—without any concern for keeping man and wife, father and son together, handled like the basest animals. Thus the innocent, *sicut pecora occisionis,* were divided into groups and those who had contributed their share in the raiding expedition drew lots. When someone drew an old or sick one he protested, "Give that old man to the devil, why should I take him? To feed and bury him? And why give me that sick dog? To cure him?"

Sometimes, it happened that Indians died on the spot either from hunger, debilitation, sickness or the pain of a father seeing his son or a husband seeing his wife bought and taken away. How could anyone with a human heart and human entrails witness such inhuman cruelty? Where was the principle of charity, "Thou shalt love thy neighbor as thyself," in the minds of those who, forgetting that they were Christians or human beings, performed such "humanity" upon human beings? Finally, to cover the cost and pay the salaried men, they agreed to allow the sale of allotted Indians at not more than 4 gold pesos per piece—they referred to them as pieces as if they were heads of cattle. And they thought selling and transferring so cheaply was an honorable thing to do, while in truth, had the price been higher, the Indians would have received better treatment as valuable items and would have lasted longer.

As I said, the Spaniards used many ways to draw the Lucayos from their homeland where they lived as in the Golden Age, a life of which poets and historians have sung such praise. Sometimes, especially at first, they won their trust because the Indians did not suspect them and, living off guard, received them like angels. Sometimes they raided by night and other times in the open, *aperto Marte* as they say, knifing those who, having more experience of Spaniards, defended themselves with bow and arrow, a weapon ordinarily used for fishing and not for war. They brought more than 40,000 people here in a period of four or five years, men and women, children and adults, as Pedro Martyr[4] mentions in Chapter 1 of the seventh *Decada.* . . .

He also mentions the fact that some killed themselves from despair, while others, who were stronger, hoped to

[4]*Pedro Martyr:* An Italian by birth, Martyr (1457–1526) became a Spanish courtier, soldier, and academic. He was the earliest historian of what he called the "New World," devoting much of his life to a massive chronicle entitled *De Orbe Novo.*

escape and return to their land and thus endured their hopeless lives, hiding in the northern mountains closer to home and hoping to find a way to cross over. Once—and Pedro Martyr records this in the same chapter—one of these Indians built a raft from a very large tree trunk called *yauruma* in the vernacular (the penultimate syllable is long), which is a light and hollow wood, tied logs to it with *liana,* which is a type of extremely strong ropelike root, placed some corn from his harvest in the hollow of the logs and filled gourds with fresh water; then, closing both ends with leaves, he took off with another Indian and a few women of his family, all great swimmers like all the Lucayos. Fifty leagues from the coast, they unfortunately met a ship coming full speed from their place of destination; they were captured and returned to Hispaniola in tears and lamentations and perished there like the rest.

We do not know, but it is believable that others made the same attempt, and if so, it was to no avail, since the Spaniards were continually raiding those islands until not one single Indian remained. They chose the rockiest and most inaccessible island to corral all the Indians taken from the neighboring islands; and there they left them in charge of a Spanish guard, after breaking their canoes to prevent escape until the ship returned for another load. Once they had 7,000 Indians and seven Spaniards guarding them like shepherds and, the ships being delayed, they ran out of cassava, which is all the food they ever gave Indians. As two ships laden with provisions neared the coast, a terrible gale storm sank them all and the islanders died of starvation; I do not remember what I heard about the fate of those shipwrecked. Nobody thought to attribute these disasters to divine punishment for sins committed here; rather, they attributed them to chance, as if there were no Rector in Heaven to see and register such cruel injustice.

I could have found out, and I could consequently now relate, the particulars of many more cruelties inflicted upon this innocent flock, if in those days of my residence in Hispaniola I had cared to question the men who performed such things. But I want to tell what one of them told me in Cuba. He had come to Cuba in an Indian canoe, perhaps as a runaway from his captain or to escape danger or again from a sense of guilt and a desire to leave such

reprobate ways. He told me they used to stuff shipholds with hundreds of Indians of both sexes and all ages, pack them like sardines and close all the hatchways to prevent escape, thus shutting off air and light. And, since ships carried food and water only for the Spanish crew, the Indians died and were thrown into the sea, and the floating corpses were so numerous that a ship could find its course by them alone, without need of a compass, charts or the art of navigation. Those were his words. This is certain: no ship ever raided the Lucayos that did not for the above reasons have to throw overboard one-third or one-fourth of its human cargo, and this inhumanity went on sometimes more and sometimes less but it is a fact that it went on. This arrangement, if such a thing can bear that name, brought to Hispaniola over a million souls over a period of ten years— men, women, children and elderly; a few shipments were made to Cuba also, and they all perished in the mines from overwork, anguish and exhaustion.

Pedro Martyr declares that according to his information there were 406 Lucayo Islands, from which the Spaniards enslaved 40,000 Indians to work the mines, and, from all the islands they had a total of 1,200,000. . . . He adds that the Lucayo Indians sometimes killed Spaniards. This happened when a small group of Spaniards were caught off guard because, when they realized the Spaniards meant to destroy them, the Indians used bows and arrows invented for fishing to kill their killers. But it was all in vain since they never succeeded in killing more than a handful. As to what Martyr says about the number of Lucayo Islands, he is including those called Jardin de la Rena and Jardin del Rey, which is a string of small islands south and north of the Cuban coast. The Indians there shared the natural goodness of the Lucayos. However, by Lucayos we refer only to the larger islands that go from Hispaniola to Florida away from Cuba, and these number between forty and fifty, large and small. Pedro Martyr also adds that he kept his information constantly up to date, and this was possible because at that time he was a member of the council of the Indies which he joined in 1518 and I was there when he presented his credentials to the council. The Emperor gave him this post in Saragossa almost immediately after the coronation ceremonies.

Questions

1. What is las Casas's position on the accuracy of previous accounts of the Spanish settlement of the Americas?
2. According to las Casas, what reasons did the Spanish settlers give to justify their treatment of the native Americans?
3. From your reading of the document, does las Casas believe the Spanish king to be knowledgeable about the behavior of the Spanish settlers?

2-2   The Dutch Buy Manhattan Island (1624)

Pieter Jansen van Schagen

In the early seventeenth century, the small country of Holland was the leading commercial power in Europe. This maritime empire almost monopolized the Atlantic slave trade with its "castles" on the Guinea coast of Africa and its plantations in Brazil and the Caribbean. Money was also to be made from furs in North America. The river discovered by Henry Hudson offered the deepest navigable penetration of any coastal river, and a commercial enterprise, the Dutch West India Company, soon established trading posts at New Amsterdam and Albany.

The following letter, written to the Dutch States-General (parliament) by Pieter Jansen van Schagen, its representative to the Dutch West India Company, reports the arrival of one of the company's ships from New Netherland. The cargo was worth forty-five thousand guilders—a handsome profit, given that the company had to date spent twenty thousand guilders on the colony. Less noticed at the time was the real estate purchase Van Schagen reported: at sixty guilders, Manhattan was a steal.

Source: Pieter Jansen van Schagen to the States-General at The Hague, 5 November 1626, in John A. Kouwenhoven, *The Columbia Historical Portrait of New York* (New York: Harper and Row, 1953), 29.

High Mighty Sirs:

Here arrived yesterday the ship The Arms of Amsterdam which sailed from New Netherland out of the Mauritius [Hudson] River on September 23; they report that our people there are of good courage, and live peaceably. Their women, also, have borne children there, they have bought the island Manhattes from the wild men for the value of sixty gilders, is 11,000 morgens in extent. They sowed all their grain in the middle of May, and harvested it the middle of August. Thereof being samples of summer grain, such as wheat, rye, barley, oats, buckwheat, canary seed, small beans, and flax. The cargo of the aforesaid ship is: 7246 beaver skins, 178½ otter [half-otter?] skins, 675 otter skins, 48 mink skins, 36 wild-cat skins, 33 mink, 34 rat skins. Many logs of oak and nut-wood. Herewith be ye High Mighty Sirs, commended to the Almighty's grace, In Amsterdam, November 5, Anno 1626.

Your High Might.'s Obedient,
P. Schagen

Questions

1. What can you tell about the economic bases of New Netherland from this brief report?
2. Are furs a "renewable resource"? Do these numbers indicate depletion?
3. The Dutch were good at picking sites for colonization. Why did New Amsterdam survive and thrive?

2-3   A True Relation of Virginia (1608)

John Smith

Governor John Smith (1580–1631) is white America's first authentic hero (see text pp. 48–49). A soldier of fortune in Europe, he arrived in Jamestown in 1607 as one of its seven councillors. Over the next two and a half years he almost single-handedly saved the colony from starvation, served as its virtual dictator, explored and mapped the area, and was dramatically rescued from a death sentence by Pocahontas, the daughter of the Indian chief Powhatan. Smith wrote an account of events in the colony; the "True Relation" brought news of Virginia's early trials to England.

The English built a military fort at Jamestown; Smith described the log walls as "palisadoed." *Aqua vitae* ("water of life") is strong liquor—considered essential for good health.

Source: John Smith, *A True Relation of such occurrences and accidents of noate as hath happened in Virginia since the first planting of that Collony, which is now resident in the South part thereof, till the last returne from thence* (London, 1608), in Merrill Jensen, ed., *English Colonial Documents: American Colonial Documents to 1776* (New York: Oxford University Press, 1964), 132–136. Reprinted by permission of Methuen Books, London.

Kind Sir, commendations remembered, etc. You shall understand that after many crosses in the downs by tempests, we arrived safely upon the south-west part of the great Canaries. Within four or five days after, we set sail for Dominica the 26 of April. The first land we made, we fell with Cape Henry, the very mouth of the Bay of Chesapeake, which at that present we little expected, having by a cruel storm been put to the northward.

Anchoring in this bay, twenty or thirty went ashore with the captain, and in coming aboard [on land], they were assaulted with certain Indians, which charged them within pistol shot, in which conflict Captain Archer and Matthew Morton were shot, whereupon Captain Newport seconding them, made a shot at them, which the Indians little respected, but having spent their arrows retired without harm. And in that place was the box opened wherein the Council for Virginia was nominated, and arriving at the place [Jamestown] where we are now seated, the Council was sworn and the President elected, which for that year was Master Edmund Maria Wingfield, where was made choice for our situation, a very fit place for the erecting of a great city, about which some contention passed betwixt Captain Wingfield and Captain Gosnold. Notwithstanding, all our provision was brought ashore, and with as much speed as might be we went about our fortification.

[On 22 May, Captain Newport, Smith, and several others set forth to explore the country up the James River. They returned on 27 May.] . . . the first we heard was that 400 Indians the day before [26 May] had assaulted the fort and surprised it. Had not God (beyond all their expectations) by means of the ships (at whom they shot with their ordnances and muskets) caused them to retire, they had entered the fort with our own men, which were then busied in setting corn, their arms being then in dry fats and few ready but certain gentlemen of their own, in which conflict most of the Council was hurt, a boy slain in the pinnace, and thirteen or fourteen more hurt.

With all speed we palisadoed our fort; each other day for six or seven days we had alarms by ambuscadoes, and four or five cruelly wounded by being abroad. The Indians' loss we know not, but as they report three were slain and divers hurt. . . .

The day before the ship's departure the king of Pamaunke [*i.e.* Opechancanough] sent the Indian that had met us before in our discovery, to assure us peace, our fort being then palisadoed round, and all our men in good health and comfort, albeit that through some discontented humours it did not so long continue. For the President and Captain Gosnold, with the rest of the Council, being for the most part discontented with one another, in so much that things were neither carried with that discretion nor any business effected in such good sort as wisdom would, nor our own good and safety required, whereby, and through the hard dealing of our President, the rest of the Council being diversely affected through his audacious command; and for Captain Martin, albeit very honest and wishing the best good, yet so sick and weak, and myself so disgraced through others' malice, through which disorder God (being angry with us) plagued us with such famine and sickness that the living were scarce able to bury the dead; our want of sufficient and good victuals, with continual watching four or five each night at three bulwarks, being the chief cause. Only of sturgeon we had great store, whereon our men would so greedily surfeit as it cost many their lives; the sack, *aqua vitae,* and other preservatives for our health being kept only in the President's hands, for his own diet, and his few associates.

Shortly after Captain Gosnold fell sick, and within three weeks died. Captain Ratcliffe being then also very sick and weak, and myself having also tasted of the extremity thereof, but by God's assistance being well recovered. Kendall about this time, for divers reasons, deposed from being of the Council, and shortly after it pleased God in our extremity to move the Indians to bring us corn ere it was half ripe, to refresh us, when we rather expected when they would destroy us.

About the tenth of September there was about 46 of our men dead, at which time Captain Wingfield having ordered the affairs in such sort that he was generally hated of all, in which respect with one consent he was deposed from his presidency, and Captain Ratcliffe according to his course was elected.

Our provision being now within twenty days spent, the Indians brought us great store both of corn and bread ready made, and also there came such abundance of fowls into the rivers as greatly refreshed our weak estates, whereupon many of our weak men were presently able to go abroad.

As yet we had no houses to cover us, our tents were rotten, and our cabins worse than nought. Our best commodity was iron, which we made into little chisels.

The President's and Captain Martin's sickness constrained me to be cape merchant and yet to spare no pains in making houses for the company, who notwithstanding our misery, little ceased their malice, grudging, and muttering.

As at this time were most of our chiefest men either sick or discontented, the rest being in such despair as they would rather starve and rot with idleness than be persuaded to do anything for their own relief without constraint. Our victuals being now within eighteen days spent, and the Indian trade decreasing, I was sent to the mouth of the river to Kegquouhtan, an Indian town, to trade for corn, and try the river for fish, but our fishing we could not effect by reason of the stormy weather. The Indians, thinking us near famished, with careless kindness offered us little pieces of bread and small handfuls of beans or wheat for a hatchet or a piece of copper. In like manner I entertained their kindness and in like scorn offered them like commodities, but the children, or any that showed ex-

traordinary kindness, I liberally contented with free gift of such trifles as well contented them. . . .

[In January 1608], by a mischance our fort was burned and the most of our apparel, lodging, and private provision. Many of our old men [became] diseased, and [many] of our new for want of lodging perished. . . .

[O]ur men being all or the most part well recovered, and we not willing to trifle away more time than necessity enforced us unto, we thought good for the better content of the adventurers, in some reasonable sort to freight home Master Nelson [of the ship *Phenix*, which had arrived on 20 April] with cedar wood. About which, our men going with willing minds, [it] was in very good time effected and the ship sent for England [on 2 June 1608]. We now remaining being in good health, all our men well contented, free from mutinies, in love one with another, and as we hope, in a continual peace with the Indians. Where we doubt not but by God's gracious assistance, and the adventurers' willing minds and speedy furtherance to so honourable an action, in after times to see our nation to enjoy a country not only exceeding pleasant for habitation, but also very profitable for commerce in general; no doubt pleasing to Almighty God, honourable to our gracious sovereign, and commodious generally to the whole kingdom.

Questions

1. Does the early experience at Jamestown support the arguments for colonization that had been offered earlier by Richard Hakluyt (see Document 1-10)?
2. Was there any discernible economic base in Smith's Virginia? Explain.
3. What does Smith tell us about Indian-white relations in the first year of the Jamestown colony?
4. Why did Smith feel that the settlers would "rather starve and rot with idleness than be persuaded to do anything for their own relief"?

2-4   Checklist for Virginia-Bound Colonists (1624)

John Smith

When John Smith sat down to write his *Generall Historie* in 1624, he had already led Virginians through their "starving times" and the Indian massacre of 1622 (see text p. 50). He also had helped the Virginians overcome their reluctance to work. But it was from London that he kept a keen eye on the colonization of the North Atlantic coastline, including the settlement of New England. Although there is no evidence that John Smith met John Winthrop, the leader of the Puritan exodus to Massachusetts, Winthrop probably was familiar with Smith's *Generall Historie*.

Source: Captain John Smith, *The Generall Historie* (1624), edited by Edward Arber and reprinted in his *Travels and Works of Captain John Smith* (Edinburgh: J. Grant, 1910), book 4.

A particular of such necessaries as either private families, or single persons, shall have cause to provide to go to Virginia, whereby greater numbers may in part conceive the better how to provide for themselves.

Apparel

A Monmouth cap.	1s.	10d.
3 falling bands [collars].	1s.	3d.
3 shirts.	7s.	6d.
1 waistcoat.	2s.	2d.
1 suit of canvas.	7s.	6d.
1 suit of frieze [coarse wool].	10s.	
1 suit of cloth.	15s.	
3 pair of Irish stockings.	4s.	
4 pair of shoes.	8s.	8d.
1 pair of garters.		10d.
1 dozen of points [for lacing clothes].		3d.
1 pair of canvas sheets.	8s.	
7 ells of canvas to make a bed and bolster, to be filled in Virginia, serving for two men.	8s.	
5 ells of coarse canvas to make a bed at sea for two men.	5s.	
1 coarse rug at sea for two men.	6s.	

Victual for a whole year for a man, and so after the rate for more.

8 bushels of meal.	2£.	
2 bushels of peas.	6s.	
2 bushels of oatmeal.	9s.	
1 gallon of aqua vitae.	2s.	6d.
1 gallon of oil.	3s.	6d.
2 gallons of vinegar.	2s.	
	3£.	3s.

Arms for a man; but if half your men be armed it is well, so all have swords and pieces.

1 armor complete, light.		17s.	
1 long piece five feet and a half, near musket bore.	1£.	2s.	
1 sword.		5s.	
1 belt.		1s.	
1 bandolier.		1s.	6d.
20 pound[s] of powder.		18s.	
60 pound[s] of shot or lead, pistol and goose shot.		5s.	
	3£.	9s.	6d.

Tools for a family of six persons, and so after the rate for more.

5 broad hoes at 2s. apiece.	10s.	
5 narrow hoes at 16d. apiece.	6s.	8d.
2 broad axes at 3s. 8d. apiece.	7s.	4d.
5 felling axes at 18d. apiece.	7s.	6d.
2 steel handsaws at 16d. apiece.	2s.	8d.
2 two-handsaws at 5s. apiece.	10s.	
1 whipsaw, set and filed; with box, file and wrest [screw key].	10s.	
2 hammers [at] 12d. apiece.	2s.	
3 shovels at 18d. apiece.	4s.	6d.
2 spades at 18d. apiece.	3s.	
2 augers at 6d. apiece.	1s.	
6 chisels at 6d apiece.	3s.	
2 percers stocked [at] 4d apiece.		8d.
3 gimlets at 2d. apiece.		6d.
2 hatchets at 21d. apiece.	3s.	6d.
2 froes to cleave pale [make staves or shingles] [at] 18d. each.	3s.	
2 hand bills [at] 20d apiece.	3s.	4d.
1 grindstone.	4s.	
nails of all sorts to the value of	2£.	
2 pickaxes.	3s.	
	6£.	2s. 8d.

Household implements for a family and six persons, and so for more or less after the rate.

1 iron pot.	7s.	
1 kettle.	6s.	
1 large frying pan.	2s.	6d.
1 gridiron.	1s.	6d.
2 skillets.	5s.	
1 spit.	2s.	
platters, dishes, spoons of wood.	4s.	
	1£.	8s.

For sugar, spice, and fruit, and at sea for six men. 12s.6d.

So the full charge after this rate for each person, will amount to about the sum of 12£.10s.10d.

The passage of each man is 6£.

The fraught of these provisions for a man, will be about half a ton, which is 1£.10s.

So the whole charge will amount to about 20£.

Now if the number be great; [not only] nets, hooks, and lines, but cheese, bacon, kine and goats must be added.

And this is the usual proportion the Virginia Company doe[s] bestow upon their tenants they send.

Questions

1. Can you tell from this list of necessary items what kind of colony Smith hoped Virginia would become?
2. What kind of life-style do you imagine early Virginians had?
3. What is missing from this list that colonists might obtain from Virginia's environment?

Questions for Further Thought

1. Based on your reading of these four documents (2-1 through 2-4), which of the three New World colonies—Spanish, Dutch, and English—would seem to have the best prospects for long-term prosperity? Why?
2. Do you see any significant differences among the Spanish and English colonies in their attitudes toward the native inhabitants?
3. Judging from these documents, what would you characterize as the *purpose* of colonies, both in the eyes of the colonists and in those of colonial promoters back in Europe?

The Chesapeake Experience

Seventeenth-century Virginia was not a happy place for English settlers or native Americans. The colony that would produce the revolutionary leadership of Patrick Henry, George Washington, and Thomas Jefferson had extremely troubled beginnings. The colony almost did not make it. People died at an astonishing rate: 80 percent in the the first generation of settlement and 50 percent in the first half century. England poured thousands of mostly male indentured servants into Virginia to raise the tobacco crop. Many died, few married, and, increasingly, most were unable to obtain land of their own after completing a term of servitude (Document 2-5).

Beginning around the mid-seventeenth century, a wave of affluent Englishmen arrived in Virginia, buying up land, securing political power, and supporting the Green Spring faction of Governor William Berkeley (see text pp. 54–56). By the 1670s this elite leadership group was squeezing out newcomers, one of whom, Nathaniel Bacon, took advantage of hard economic times and recurring Indian attacks to mount a revolt against Berkeley (Document 2-6). Bacon's Rebellion of 1676 was the most significant event in Virginia's formative era; culminating the instability of the early seventeenth century, it rocked the colony with the largest civil uprising to occur in British America before the Revolution. In Virginia, Bacon's Rebellion led to the development of aristocratic rule, a more representative (for whites) government, a flourishing gentry culture, and African slavery. The Old South—and indeed America itself—was being born.

2-5   Notes on Indentured Servitude in Virginia (1640)

The plantation system of agriculture, in which extensive land is worked by groups of (usually forced) laborers to produce a lucrative crop for sale to a (frequently remote) market, did not—indeed, *does* not—need slavery *per se* to operate. In seventeenth-century Virginia, for instance, the original plantation work force consisted largely of white indentured servants, who worked a term of years for a master in exchange for their passage and a chance to pursue their happiness in a country less crowded, and with more accessible land, than was afforded by the England of the enclosure era (see Document 1-8). Life as a servant was not all that easy, though; one revolted ship's captain refused to transport servants to Virginia, charging that they "were sold heere upp and downe like horses." Resistance was punished severely, as the following documents show.

These documents are not original council minutes, as the source citation suggests. The original minute books of the Virginia Council and General Court were destroyed by fire in April 1865 during the evacuation of Richmond. Conway Robinson, a legal reporter, made notes from the originals, and those notes remain among our more important sources of information on seventeenth-century Virginia.

Source: H. R. McIlwaine, ed., *Minutes of the Council and General Court of Colonial Virginia, 1622–1632, 1670–1676* (Richmond: Virginia State Library, 1924), 465–467.

11TH OF DEC., 1640.

Whereas William Huddleston servant untol Mr *Canhow* [or *Cantrow*?] hath complained to the board against his master for want of all manner of apparel, *the court hath therefore ordered* that the said Mr *Canhow* [or *Cantrow*?] shall before *christmas* next provide and allow unto the said Huddleston such sufficient apparel of linen and woollen as shall be thought fit by Captain *John West* Esqr or otherwise that the said Captain *West* shall have power to dispose of the said servant until the said *Canhow* [or *Cantrow*?] do perform this order.

7TH OF OCT., 1640.

Whereas Thos Pursell servant unto *Robt Brassure* for the term of four years hath petitioned to the board for his freedom, it being denied unto him by the said *Brassure* in regard the said *Pursell* has absented himself from his said service for the space of three months or there-about *the Court hath therefore ordered* that the said *Pursell* shall be discharged from his said master but shall loose his right in apparel and corn due unto him at the Expiration of his time in respect of his absence from his service as aforesaid & that the said *Brassure* shall Deliver unto the said *Pursell* such apparel beding and what other goods do already belong unto him and are remaining in the custody of the said *Brassure*

7TH OF OCT., 1640.

Whereas it appeareth to the Court that *Roger Parke* being bound to serve Capt *Corell* for the space of three Quarters of a year and Thos Loving Being agent for the said Capt *Corell* the said *Parke* was assigned to the said *Loving* to serve the said time which the said *Parke* having not performed *the Court hath ordered* that the said *Parke* shall forthwith put in security for the payment of five pound*s* sterling within twenty days after this order unto the said *Loving* in consideration of his said service being not performed as aforesaid otherwise Execution &c

JUNE 4, 1640.

Whereas upon Information to this Board of two servants that are run away from *Maryland*, and now at the House of *George Minesye* Esqr one of which said servants doth belong unto Mr *Snow* as he pretendeth, and the other to the governour of the aforesaid *Maryland* as is informed *the court hath therefore ordered* that the said servant belonging to the said *Snow* shall be delivered unto him if upon due prooff he make his right appear and the other servant to be returned with all speed unto the said Governour.

JUNE 4, 1640.

Upon the petition of *Hugh Gwyn* gent wherein he complained to this board of three of his servants that are run away to *Maryland* to his much loss and prejudice and wherein he hath humbly requested the board that he may have liberty to make the sale or benifit of the said servants in the said *Maryland* which the Court taking into Consideration and weighing the dangerous consequences of such pernicious precident *do order* that a letter be written unto the said Governour to the intent the said servants may be returned hither to receive such exemplary and condign punishment as the nature of their offence shall justly deserve and then be to be returned to their said master

9TH OF JULY, 1640.

Whereas Hugh Gwyn hath by order from this Board Brought back from *Maryland* three servants formerly run away from the said *Gwyn, the court doth therefore order* that the said three servants shall receive the punishment of whipping and to have thirty stripes apiece one called *Victor,* a *dutchman,* the other a *Scotchman* called *James Gregory,* shall first serve out their times with their master according to their Indentures, and one whole year apiece after the time of their service is Expired. By their said Indentures in recompense of his Loss sustained by their absence and after that service to their said master is Expired to serve the colony for three whole years apiece, and that the third being a negro named *John Punch* shall serve his said master or his assigns for the time of his natural Life here or elsewhere.

JULY 22, 1640.

Whereas complaint has been made to this Board by Capt *Wm Pierce* Esqr that six of his servants and a negro of Mr *Reginolds* has plotted to run away unto the *Dutch* plantation from their said masters and did assay to put the same in Execution upon *Saturday* night being the 18th day *July* 1640 as appeared to the Board by the Examinations of *Andrew Noxe, Richd Hill, Richd Cookeson* and *John Williams* and likewise by the confession of *Christopher Miller, Peter Wilcocke,* and *Emanuel* the foresaid Negro who had at the fore said time, taken the skiff of the said Capt *Wm Pierce* their master, and corn powder and shot and guns, to accomplish their said purposes, which said persons sailed down in the said skiff to *Elizabeth* river where they were taken and brought back again, the Court taking the same into consideration, as a dangerous precident for the future time (if unpunished) did order that *Christopher Miller* a *dutchman* (a prince agent in the business) should receive the punishment of whipping and to have thirty stripes, and to be burnt in the cheek with the letter R and to work with a shakle on his legg for one whole year, and longer if said master shall see cause and after his full time of service is Expired with his said master to serve the colony for seven whole years, and the said *Peter Wilcocke* to receive thirty stripes and to be Burnt in

the cheek with the letter R and, after his term of service is Expired with his said master to serve the colony for three years and the said *Richd Cookson* after his full time expired with his master to serve the colony for two years and a half, and the said *Richd Hill* to remain upon his good behaviour until the next offence and the said *Andrew Noxe* to receive thirty stripes, and the said *John Williams* a *dutchman* and a Chirugeon after his full time of service is Expired with his master to serve the colony for seven years, and *Emanuel* the Negro to receive thirty stripes and to be burnt in the cheek with the letter R. and to work in shakle one year or more as his master shall see cause, and all those who are condemned to serve the colony after their times are expired with their masters, then their said masters are required hereby to present to this board their said servants so condemned to the colony

13TH OF OCT., 1640.

The Court hath ordered that *Wm Wootton* and *John Bradye* as principall actors and contrivers in a most dangerous conspiracy by attempting to run out of the country and Inticing divers others to be actors in the said conspiracy to be whipt from the gallows to the Court door and that the said *Bradye* shall be Branded with an Iron in the shoulder, and *Wotton* in the forehead each of them to serve the Colony seven years, the service due from the said *Wotton* to the said Mr *Sanderson* being first performed, each of them to work in Irons during the time of the said censure for the rest of these that are freemen *(viz) John Tomkinson* and *Richr West* for consenting and concealing the said plott that they shall be whipt and serve the colony two years and those that are servants *(viz) John Winchester, Wm Drummer Robt Rouse* and *Robt Mosely* to be whipt only as also *Margarett Beard,* and that the masters of the said servants shall pay the fees due from the servants to the sheriffs and the servants shall make good the same, at the Expiration of their time by a years service apiece to their said masters and that none of them shall be released from their Irons without order from this Board

OCT. 17, 1640.

Whereas we are daily given to understand of divers servants that run away from their masters whereby much loss and prejudice doth ensue to the masters of such servants, the court therefore conceiving it to be the most necessary and speedy course to apprehend the said servants *doth order* that upon complaint thereof made unto the sheriffs of the counties where any such servant or servants doth run away that the sheriff thereof or his deputies shall hereby have power to hire boat and hands to pursue the said runaways and that the charge thereof shall be borne and defrayed by the said county

Questions

1. How seriously did the court take the issue of runaway servants, and why?
2. Do you see evidence of emerging discrimination in the treatment handed out by the court to white and black servants?
3. On the other hand, do you see evidence of racial divisions among the white servant population?

2-6   Manifesto (1676)

Nathaniel Bacon

Who was Nathaniel Bacon (1647–1676)? An early twentieth-century historiography, associated with the patrician Virginian Thomas Jefferson Wertenabaker, depicted him as a popular democratic leader leading a revolt of the have-nots against the privileged few. The historian Wilcomb Washburn later dismissed him as an Indian killer, whereas Edmund S. Morgan sees Bacon's Rebellion as a war of plunder. Evidence for all these views can be found in Bacon's words. This troubled young fop who was exiled from England by his own father may not deserve a heroic reputation, but his "Manifesto" tells us what was wrong in Governor Berkeley's Virginia (see text pp. 53–56).

Source: Nathaniel Bacon, "Manifesto Concerning the Troubles in Virginia." *The Virginia Magazine of History and Biography* (1894), 1: 56–61.

If virtue be a sin, if piety be guilt, all the principles of morality, goodness and justice be perverted, we must confess that those who are now called rebels may be in danger of those high imputations. Those loud and several bulls would affright innocents and render the defence of our brethren and the inquiry into our sad and heavy oppressions, treason. But if there be, as sure there is, a just God to appeal to; if religion and justice be a sanctuary here; if to plead the cause of the oppressed; if sincerely to aim at his Majesty's honour and the public good without any reservation or by interest; if to stand in the gap after so much blood of our dear brethren bought and sold; if after the loss of a great part of his Majesty's colony deserted and dispeopled, freely with our lives and estates to endeavour to save the remainders be treason; God Almighty judge and let guilty die. But since we cannot in our hearts find one single spot of rebellion or treason, or that we have in any manner aimed at subverting the settled government or attempting of the person of any either magistrate or private man, notwithstanding the several reproaches and threats of some who for sinister ends were disaffected to us and censured our innocent and honest designs, and since all people in all places where we have yet been can attest our civil, quiet, peaceable behaviour far different from that of rebellion and tumultuous persons, let truth be bold and all the world know the real foundations of pretended guilt. We appeal to the country itself what and of what nature

their oppressions have been, or by what cabal and mystery the designs of many of those whom we call great men have been transacted and carried on; but let us trace these men in authority and favour to whose hands the dispensation of the country's wealth has been committed. Let us observe the sudden rise of their estates composed with the quality in which they first entered this country, or the reputation they have held here amongst wise and discerning men. And let us see whether their extractions and education have not been vile, and by what pretence of learning and virtue they could so soon [come] into employments of so great trust and consequence. Let us consider their sudden advancement and let us also consider whether any public work for our safety and defence or for the advancement and propagation of trade, liberal arts, or sciences is here extant in any way adequate to our vast charge. Now let us compare these things together and see what sponges have sucked up the public treasure, and whether it has not been privately contrived away by unworthy favourites and juggling parasites whose tottering fortunes have been repaired and supported at the public charge. Now if it be so, judge what greater guilt can be than to offer to pry into these and to unriddle the mysterious wiles of a powerful cabal; let all people judge what can be of more dangerous import than to suspect the so long safe proceedings of some of our grandees, and whether people may with safety open their eyes in so nice a concern.

Another main article of our guilt is our open and manifest aversion of all, not only the foreign but the protected and darling Indians. This, we are informed, is rebellion of a deep dye for that both the governor and council are by Colonel Cole's assertion bound to defend the queen and the Appamatocks with their blood. Now, whereas we do declare and can prove that they have been for these many years enemies to the king and country, robbers and thieves and invaders of his Majesty's right and our interest and estates, but yet have by persons in authority been defended and protected even against his Majesty's loyal subjects, and that in so high a nature that even the complaints and oaths of his Majesty's most loyal subjects in a lawful manner proffered by them against those barbarous outlaws, have been by the right honourable governor rejected and the delinquents from his presence dismissed, not only with pardon and indemnity, but with all encouragement and favour; their firearms so destructful to us and by our laws prohibited, commanded to be restored them, and open declaration before witness made that they must have ammunition, although directly contrary to our law. Now what greater guilt can be than to oppose and endeavour the destruction of these honest, quiet neighbours of ours? . . .

THE DECLARATION OF THE PEOPLE

For having upon specious pretences of public works, raised unjust taxes upon the commonalty for the advancement of private favourites and other sinister ends, but no visible effects in any measure adequate.

For not having during the long time of his government in any measure advanced his hopeful colony, either by fortification, towns or trade.

For having abused and rendered contemptible the majesty of justice, of advancing to places of judicature scandalous and ignorant favourites.

For having wronged his Majesty's prerogative and interest by assuming the monopoly of the beaver trade.

By having in that unjust gain bartered and sold his Majesty's country and the lives of his loyal subjects to the barbarous heathen.

For having protected, favoured and emboldened the Indians against his Majesty's most loyal subjects, never contriving, requiring, or appointing any due or proper means of satisfaction for their many invasions, murders, and robberies committed upon us.

For having, when the army of the English was just upon the track of the Indians, which now in all places burn, spoil, and murder, and when we might with ease have destroyed them who then were in open hostility, for having expressly countermanded and sent back our army by passing his word for the peaceable demeanour of the said Indians, who immediately prosecuted their evil intentions, committing horrid murders and robberies in all places, being protected by the said engagement and word passed of him, the said Sir William Berkeley, having ruined and made desolate a great part of his Majesty's country, have now drawn themselves into such obscure and remote places and are by their successes so emboldened and confirmed, and by their confederacy so strengthened that the cries of blood are in all places, and the terror and consternation of the people so great, that they are now become not only a difficult, but a very formidable enemy who might with ease have been destroyed, etc. When upon the loud outcries of blood, the Assembly had with all care raised and framed an army for the prevention of future mischiefs and safeguard of his Majesty's colony.

For having with only the privacy of some few favourites, without acquainting the people, only by the alteration of a figure, forged a commission by we know not what hand, not only without but against the consent of the people, for raising and effecting of civil wars and distractions, which being happily and without bloodshed prevented.

For having the second time attempted the same thereby calling down our forces from the defence of the frontiers, and most weak exposed places, for the prevention of civil mischief and ruin amongst ourselves, whilst the barbarous enemy in all places did invade, murder, and spoil us, his Majesty's most faithful subjects.

Of these, the aforesaid articles, we accuse Sir William Berkeley, as guilty of each and every one of the same, and as one who has traitorously attempted, violated and injured his Majesty's interest here, by the loss of a great part of his colony, and many of his faithful and loyal subjects by him betrayed, and in a barbarous and shameful manner exposed to the incursions and murders of the heathen.

And we further declare these, the ensuing persons in this list, to have been his wicked, and pernicious counsellors, aiders and assisters against the commonalty in these our cruel commotions:

Sir Henry Chicherly, Knt.	Jos. Bridger
Col. Charles Wormley	Wm. Clabourne
Phil. Dalowell	Thos. Hawkins, Jr.
Robert Beverly	William Sherwood
Robert Lee	Jos. Page, Clerk
Thos. Ballard	Jo. Cliffe, ,,
William Cole	Hubberd Farrell
Richard Whitacre	John West
Nicholas Spencer	Thos. Reade
Mathew Kemp	

And we do further demand, that the said Sir William Berkeley, with all the persons in this list, be forthwith delivered up, or surrender themselves, within four days after the notice hereof, or otherwise we declare as followeth: that in whatsoever house, place, or ship any of the said persons shall reside, be hid, or protected, we do declare that the owners, masters, or inhabitants of the said places, to be confederates and traitors to the people, and the estates of them, as also of all the aforesaid persons, to be confiscated. This we, the commons of Virginia, do declare desiring a prime union amongst ourselves, that we may jointly, and with one accord defend ourselves against the common enemy. And let not the faults of the guilty be the reproach of the innocent, or the faults or crimes of the oppressors divide and separate us, who have suffered by their oppressions.

These are therefore in his Majesty's name, to command you forthwith to seize the persons above mentioned as traitors to the king and country, and them to bring to Middle Plantation, and there to secure them, till further order, and in case of opposition, if you want any other assistance, you are forthwith to demand it in the name of the people of all the counties of Virginia.

[signed]   NATH BACON, Gen'l.
                    By the Consent of the People.

Questions

1. Bacon's Rebellion was the first serious tax revolt in American history. What evidence can you find to support this statement in Bacon's "Manifesto"?
2. Did Indian assaults trigger the rebellion? Were the native Americans pawns in a larger dispute between Bacon and Berkeley? Explain why or why not.
3. Can you find evidence of "democracy" in Bacon's "Manifesto" and declaration? Was Bacon a democrat?

Questions for Further Thought

1. Having led the forces of "the people" against "special privilege," Nathaniel Bacon is sometimes presented as the first "populist" politician in America. Does Bacon's "Manifesto" bear any relationship to the grievances of the servants of Document 2-5?
2. Chesapeake society, one historian asserts, was "frighteningly turbulent, wracked by ugly tensions." On this evidence, does it look so to you?
3. Bacon is also sometimes characterized as the first racial demagogue in American history. Do you agree? Do you think such an appeal would work with the servants described in Document 2-5?

Puritan New England

If Virginia was founded primarily as a capitalistic, money-making venture, New England was launched primarily to serve religious purposes. Other kinds of colonies would sooner or later appear in the region, but the stamp of Puritanism came first. The Puritans, or non-Separatists (Puritans remained members of the Church of England), came to America to perfect the Protestant Reformation, a task they felt had been thwarted at home by the leaders of the Anglican Church. Most of their Calvinist theology had been worked out earlier in England. Puritans believed in "predestination"; only a few—the elect—could expect God's redemption on Judgment Day. While Puritans thus did not believe that one could *achieve* salvation, they did maintain that God's grace was displayed in the life of an individual through his actions (works) and the intensity of his belief (faith).

In many ways, then, **Puritans** looked both forward and backward. On the one hand, they believed, like **their European** predecessors, that all human institutions—the church, the state, the family—were ordained of God to keep order among the people and to keep them strong in the faith. Such obedience to the community's leaders was especially important because the Puritans saw themselves as fulfilling a great historical mission (Document 2-7). On the other hand, since they believed salvation came not from the church but directly from God to the individual, the Puritan rulers and clergy were confronted from the beginning of their colony by dissidents who accused the leaders of being guilty of the same corruption and false doctrines that they had sought to leave behind in England (Document 2-8).

In the course of years the Massachusetts Bay colony, and the other New England colonies clustering around it, grew and prospered, thanks to massive in-migration in the 1630s, high birth rates and low mortality rates, and a hardworking and enterprising population. But the religious intensity of the founding generation faded over time, and prosperity introduced more of the temptations of the flesh to colonial life. Ministers increasingly felt themselves obliged to exhort their congregants to remember their heritage and restore their ancestors' sense of mission—a style of preaching that came to be known as the "jeremiad" (Document 2-9) and that would influence such later Americans as Frederick Douglass (Document 12-9) and Abraham Lincoln (Document 14-11).

2-7 A Modell of Christian Charity (1630)

John Winthrop

John Winthrop (1588–1649) was the son of a prosperous member of the English gentry. Educated at Cambridge, as a young man he became a convert to Puritanism. In the 1620s economic depression shrank his farm income, and he moved to London to take a minor position in the court system. While there, he became increasingly distressed at what he viewed as the flagrant corruption and immorality pervading both the court of King Charles I and the Church of England under Archbishop William Laud, and he grew fearful of Charles's moves against leading Puritans and the Parliament. He joined with a small group of Puritans proposing to set up a commonwealth well away from England and its dangers and, after deciding to join the exodus himself, was elected governor. In 1630 he sailed with the first group of settlers on the ship *Arbella*. While en route, he delivered the following sermon to his fellow passengers, warning them that unlike other colonists, they were not to pursue private gain but to be an example to the world of what a truly godly society should be—in the terms of scripture, a "City upon a Hill" (Matthew 5:14).

Source: John Winthrop, "A Modell of Christian Charity," in Perry Miller and Thomas H. Johnson, eds., *The Puritans,* rev. ed. (New York: Harper and Row, 1963), 1: 195–199.

Written
On Boarde the Arrabella,
On the Attlantick Ocean.
By the Honorable John Winthrop Esquire.
In His passage, (with the great Company of Religious people, of which Christian Tribes he was the Brave Leader and famous Governor;) from the Island of Great Brittaine, to New-England in the North America.
Anno 1630.

CHRISTIAN CHARITIE

A Modell Hereof

GOD ALMIGHTIE in his most holy and wise providence hath soe disposed of the Condicion of mankinde, as in all times some must be rich some poore, some highe and eminent in power and dignitie; others meane and in subieccion.

The Reason Hereof

1. Reas: *First,* to hold conformity with the rest of his workes, being delighted to shewe forthe the glory of his wisdome in the variety and differance of the Creatures and the glory of his power, in ordering all these differences for the preservacion and good of the whole, and the glory of his greatnes that as it is the glory of princes to haue many officers, soe this great King will haue many Stewards counting himselfe more honoured in dispenceing his guifts to man by man, then if hee did it by his owne immediate hand.

2. Reas: *Secondly,* That he might haue the more occasion to manifest the worke of his Spirit: first, vpon the wicked in moderateing and restraineing them: soe that the riche and mighty should not eate vpp the poore, nor the poore, and dispised rise vpp against their superiours, and shake off theire yoake; 2ly in the regenerate in exerciseing his graces in them, as in the greate ones, theire loue mercy, gentlenes, temperance etc., in the poore and inferiour sorte, theire faithe patience, obedience etc:

3. Reas: Thirdly, That every man might haue need of other, and from hence they might be all knitt more nearly together in the Bond of brotherly affeccion: from hence it appeares plainely that noe man is made more honourable then another or more wealthy etc., out of any perticuler and singuler respect to himselfe but for the glory of his Creator and the Common good of the Creature, Man; Therefore God still reserues the propperty of these guifts to himselfe as Ezek: 16. 17. he there calls wealthe his gold and his silver etc. Prov: 3. 9. he claimes theire seruice as his due honour the Lord with thy riches etc. All men being thus (by divine providence) rancked into two sortes, riche and poore; vnder the first, are comprehended all such as are able to liue comfortably by theire owne meanes duely improued; and all others are poore according to the former distribution. There are two rules whereby wee are to walke one towards another: JUSTICE and MERCY. These are allwayes distinguished in theire Act and in theire obiect, yet may they both concurre in the same Subiect in eache respect; as sometimes there may be an occasion of shewing mercy to a rich man, in some sudden danger of distresse, and allsoe doeing of meere Justice to a poor man in regard of some perticuler contract etc. There is likewise a double Lawe by which wee are regulated in our conversacion one towardes another: in both the former respects, the lawe of nature and the lawe of grace, or the morrall lawe or the lawe of the gospell, to omitt the rule of Justice as not propperly belonging to this purpose otherwise then it may fall into consideracion in some perticuler Cases: By the first of these lawes man as he was enabled soe withall [is] commaunded to loue his neighbour as himselfe vpon this ground stands all the precepts of the morrall lawe, which concernes our dealings with men. To apply this to the works of mercy this lawe requires two things first that every man afford his help to another in every want or distresse Secondly, That hee performe this out of the same af-

feccion, which makes him carefull of his owne good according to that of our Saviour Math: [7. 12.] Whatsoever ye would that men should doe to you. This was practised by Abraham and Lott in entertaineing the Angells and the old man of Gibea.

The Lawe of Grace or the Gospell hath some differance from the former as in these respectes first the lawe of nature was giuen to man in the estate of innocency; this of the gospell in the estate of regeneracy: 2ly, the former propounds one man to another, as the same fleshe and Image of god, this as a brother in Christ allsoe, and in the Communion of the same spirit and soe teacheth vs to put a difference betweene Christians and others. Doe good to all especially to the household of faith; vpon this ground the Israelites were to putt a difference betweene the brethren of such as were strangers though not of the Canaanites. 3ly. The Lawe of nature could giue noe rules for dealeing with enemies for all are to be considered as freinds in the estate of innocency, but the Gospell commaunds loue to an enemy. proofe[:] If thine Enemie hunger feede him; Loue your Enemies doe good to them that hate you Math: 5. 44.

This Lawe of the Gospell propoundes likewise a difference of seasons and occasions there is a time when a christian must sell all and giue to the poore as they did in the Apostles times. There is a tyme allsoe when a christian (though they giue not all yet) must giue beyond theire ability, as they of Macedonia. Cor: 2. 6. likewise community of perills calls for extraordinary liberallity and soe doth Community in some speciall seruice for the Churche. Lastly, when there is noe other meanes whereby our Christian brother may be releiued in this distresse, wee must help him beyond our ability, rather then tempt God, in putting him vpon help by miraculous or extraordinary meanes. . . .

1. For the persons, wee are a Company professing our selues fellow members of Christ, In which respect onely though wee were absent from eache other many miles, and had our imploymentes as farre distant, yet wee ought to account our selues knitt together by this bond of loue, and liue in the exercise of it, if wee would haue comforte of our being in Christ, this was notoroius in the practise of the Christians in former times, as is testified of the Waldenses[1] from the mouth of one of the adversaries Aeneas Syluius, mutuo [solent amare] penè antequam norint, they vse to loue any of theire own religion even before they were acquainted with them.

2ly. for the worke wee haue in hand, it is by a mutuall consent through a speciall overruleing providence, and a more then an ordinary approbation of the Churches of Christ to seeke out a place of Cohabitation and Consorte-

---

[1] *Waldenses*: A heretical sect of Christians, dating from the twelfth century but extending into the Renaissance, and centered in northern Italy; Protestants of Winthrop's time looked to the Waldenses as precursors of their own challenge to Rome. *Aeneas Sylvius* (1405–1464; later Pope Pius II) was among their great adversaries. The Latin phrase is followed by Winthrop's own translation.

shipp vnder a due forme of Government both ciuill and ecclesiasticall. In such cases as this the care of the publique must oversway all private respects, by which not onely conscience, but meare Ciuill pollicy doth binde vs; for it is a true rule that perticuler estates cannott subsist in the ruine of the publique.

3ly. The end is to improue our liues to doe more seruice to the Lord the comforte and encrease of the body of christe whereof wee are members that our selues and posterity may be the better preserued from the Common corrupcions of this euill world to serue the Lord and worke out our Salvacion vnder the power and purity of his holy Ordinances.

4ly for the meanes whereby this must bee effected, they are 2fold, a Conformity with the worke and end wee aime at, these wee see are extraordinary, therefore wee must not content our selues with vsuall ordinary meanes whatsoever wee did or ought to haue done when wee liued in England, the same must wee doe and more allsoe where wee goe: That which the most in theire Churches maineteine as a truthe in profession onely, wee must bring into familiar and constant practice, as in this duty of loue wee must loue brotherly without dissimulation, wee must loue one another with a pure hearte feruently wee must beare one anothers burthens, wee must not looke onely on our owne things, but allsoe on the things of our brethren, neither must wee think that the lord will beare with such faileings at our hands as hee dothe from those among whome wee haue liued. . . .

Thus stands the cause betweene God and vs, wee are entered into Covenant with him for this worke, wee haue taken out a Commission, the Lord hath giuen vs leaue to drawe our owne Articles wee haue professed to enterprise these Accions vpon these and these ends, wee haue herevpon besought him of favour and blessing: Now if the Lord shall please to heare vs, and bring vs in peace to the place wee desire, then hath hee ratified this Covenant and sealed our Commission, [and] will expect a strickt performance of the Articles contained in it, but if wee shall neglect the observacion of these Articles which are the ends wee haue propounded, and dissembling with our God, shall fall to embrace this present world and prosecute our carnall intencions seekeing great things for our selues and our posterity, the Lord will surely breake out in wrathe against vs be revenged of such a periured people and make vs knowe the price of the breache of such a Covenant.

Now the onely way to avoyde this shipwracke and to provide for our posterity is to followe the Counsell of Micah,[2] to doe Justly, to loue mercy, to walke humbly with our God, for this end, wee must be knitt together in this worke as one man, wee must entertaine each other in brotherly Affeccion, wee must be willing to abridge our selues of our superfluities, for the supply of others necessities, wee must vphold a familiar Commerce together in all meekenes, gentlenes, patience and liberallity, wee must delight in eache other, make others Condicions our owne reioyce together, mourne together, labour, and suffer together, allwayes haueing before our eyes our Commission and Community in the worke, our Community as members of the same body, soe shall wee keepe the vnitie of the spirit in the bond of peace, the Lord will be our God and delight to dwell among vs, as his owne people and will commaund a blessing vpon vs in all our wayes, soe that wee shall see much more of his wisdome power goodnes and truthe then formerly wee haue beene acquainted with, wee shall finde that the God of Israell is among vs, when tenn of vs shall be able to resist a thousand of our enemies, when hee shall make vs a prayse and glory, that men shall say of succeeding plantacions: the lord make it like that of New England: for wee must Consider that wee shall be as a Citty vpon a Hill, the eies of all people are vppon vs; soe that if wee shall deale falsely with our god in this worke wee haue vndertaken and soe cause him to withdrawe his present help from vs, wee shall be made a story and a byword through the world, wee shall open the mouthes of enemies to speake euill of the wayes of god and all professours for Gods sake; wee shall shame the faces of many of gods worthy seruants, and cause theire prayers to be turned into Cursses vpon vs till wee be consumed out of the good land whether wee are goeing: And to shutt vpp this discourse with that exhortacion of Moses that faithfull seruant of the Lord in his last farewell to Irsaell Duet. 30. Beloued there is now sett before vs life, and good, deathe and euill in that wee are Commaunded this day to loue the Lord our God, and to loue one another to walke in his wayes and to keepe his Commaundements and his Ordinance, and his lawes, and the Articles of our Covenant with him that wee may liue and be multiplyed, and that the Lord our God may blesse vs in the land whether wee goe to possesse it: But if our heartes shall turne away soe that wee will not obey, but shall be seduced and worshipp . . . other Gods our pleasures, and proffitts, and serue them; it is propounded vnto vs this day, wee shall surely perishe out of the good Land whether wee passe over this vast Sea to possesse it;

> Therefore lett vs choose life,
>   that wee, and our Seede,
>   may liue; by obeyeing his
>   voyce, and cleaueing to him,
>   for hee is our life, and
>   our prosperity.

---

[2]*Micah:* One of the minor Old Testament prophets. The "Counsell" Winthrop quotes appears in Micah 6:8.

Questions

1. How do Winthrop's religious views shape his vision of the proper social order for the new colony?
2. Describe the covenant entered into by the colonists aboard the *Arbella*. What obligations do the colonists have to God? What dangers does Winthrop warn his shipmates to watch out for?
3. What does Winthrop mean when he says, "wee shall be as a Citty upon a Hill, the eies of all people are uppon us"? Who, in particular, might be watching for the success or failure of the colony, and why?

2-8   Transcript of the Examination of Anne Hutchinson (1637)

Anne Hutchinson (1591–1643) brought on the first major internal crisis in the Puritan settlement at Massachusetts Bay. A follower of the brilliant Puritan divine John Cotton, she and her husband followed him to New England in 1634. Herself possessed of a keen theological mind, she took the Puritan stress on God's grace as the only source of salvation and extended it to argue that grace came to women and men through the direct revelation of the Holy Spirit. She thus denied that the authority of either church or state could "prepare" one for salvation. She also denied that a virtuous life was necessarily a sign of God's grace, and accused those who preached otherwise of claiming that one could earn salvation through good deeds—a "covenant of works." Her doctrines, expounded in weekly meetings at her home, attracted many adherents in Boston but threatened to split the colony. Her opponents, including Winthrop, finally placed her on trial for heresy; despite a brilliant defense, she was expelled from the colony. Nonetheless, in many ways she had the better of the argument. By drawing out the antiauthoritarian implications of the Puritans' own doctrine, she showed how difficult it was to justify traditional authority—of church, of state, of male patriarchs—to the European settlers of New England and the New World.

Source: Thomas Hutchinson, *History of the Colony and Province of Massachusetts Bay* (Boston, 1767).

NOVEMBER 1637.

The Examination of Mrs. Ann[e] Hutchinson at the court at Newtown.

Mr. Winthrop, governor. Mrs. Hutchinson, you are called here as one of those that have troubled the peace of the commonwealth and the churches here; you are known to be a woman that hath had a great share in the promoting and divulging of those opinions that are causes of this trouble, and to be nearly joined not only in affinity and affection with some of those the court had taken notice of and passed censure upon, but you have spoken divers things as we have been informed very prejudicial to the honour of the churches and ministers thereof, and you have maintained a meeting and an assembly in your house that hath been con-demned by the general assembly as a thing not tolerable nor comely in the sight of God nor fitting for your sex, and notwithstanding that was cried down you have continued the same, therefore we have thought good to send for you to understand how things are, that if you be in an erroneous way we may reduce you that so you may become a profitable member here among us, otherwise if you be obstinate in your course that then the court may take such course that you may trouble us no further, therefore I would intreat you to express whether you do not hold and assent in practice to those opinions and factions that have been handled in court already, that is to say, whether you do not justify Mr. Wheelwright's sermon and the petition. . . .

Mrs. H. . . . I shall not equivocate, there is a meeting of men and women, and there is a meeting only for women. . . .

Mr. Endicot. Who teaches in the men's meetings, none but men? Do not women sometimes?

Mrs. H. Never as I heard, not one. . . .

Deputy Gov. Now it appears by this woman's meeting that Mrs. Hutchinson hath so forestalled the minds of many by their resort to her meeting that now she hath a potent party in the country. Now if all these things have endangered us as from that foundation, and if she in particular hath disparaged all our ministers in the land that they have preached a covenant of works, . . . why this is not to be suffered. And therefore being driven to the foundation, and it being found that Mrs. Hutchinson is she that hath depraved all the ministers and hath been the cause of what is fallen out, why we must take away the foundation and the building will fall.

Mrs. H. I pray Sir prove it that I said they preached nothing but a covenant of works.

Deputy Gov. Nothing but a covenant of works, why a Jesuit may preach truth sometimes.

Mrs. H. Did I ever say they preached a covenant of works then?

Deputy Gov. If they do not preach a covenant of grace clearly, then they preach a covenant of works.

Mrs. H. No Sir, one may preach a covenant of grace more clearly than another, so I said.

Deputy Gov. We are not upon that now but upon position.

Mrs. H. Prove this then Sir that you say I said.

Deputy Gov. When they do preach a covenant of works do they preach truth?

Mrs. H. Yes Sir, but when they preach a covenant of works for salvation, that is not truth.

Deputy Gov. I do but ask you this, when the ministers do preach a covenant of works do they preach a way of salvation?

Mrs. H. I did not come hither to answer to questions of that sort.

Deputy Gov. Because you will deny the thing.

Mrs. H. Ey [Aye], but that is to be proved first.

Deputy Gov. I will make it plain that you did say that the ministers did preach a covenant of works.

Mrs. H. I deny that. . . . Now if you do condemn me for speaking what in my conscience I know to be truth I must commit myself unto the Lord.

Mr. Nowell. How do you know that that was the spirit?

Mrs. H. How did Abraham know that it was God that bid him offer his son, being a breach of the sixth commandment [Thou shalt not kill]?

Deputy Gov. By an immediate voice.

Mrs. H. So to me by an immediate revelation.

Deputy Gov. How! an immediate revelation.

Mrs. H. By the voice of his own spirit to my soul. . . .

Gov. The court hath already declared themselves satisfied concerning the things you hear, and concerning the troublesomeness of her spirit and the danger of her course amongst us, which is not to be suffered. Therefore if it be the mind of the court that Mrs. Hutchinson for these things that appear before us is unfit for our society, and if it be the mind of the court that she shall be banished out of our liberties and imprisoned till she be sent away, let them hold up their hands.

All but three. . . .

Mrs. Hutchinson, the sentence of the court you hear is that you are banished from out of our jurisdiction as being a woman not fit for our society, and are to be imprisoned till the court shall send you away.

Mrs. H. I desire to know wherefore I am banished?

Gov. Say no more, the court knows wherefore and is satisfied.

Questions

1. Why was Hutchinson's "immediate revelation" subversive?
2. Was this court stacked? Was there any way Hutchinson could have won?
3. Can you find evidence of sexism in this document?

2-9   Errand into the Wilderness (1670)

Samuel Danforth

Samuel Danforth (1626–1674) came to America with his father in 1634, graduated from Harvard College in 1643, and served as assistant to John Eliot at Roxbury from 1650 on. In 1670 he was invited to preach the prestigious "Election Sermon," which opened the annual session of the Massachusetts General Court, when deputies (representatives) elected the governor and other high officials of the colony. It was a golden opportunity for a minister to preach not only to the movers and shakers of the colony, but (since election sermons were frequently printed) to all the people as well. Like many others of the second generation of Puritan preachers, Danforth approached his task with concern for what he saw as the failure of New Englanders to remember their obligation to be "as a City upon a Hill" impressing the world with their godliness and virtue. He believed that the faithful were now simply going through the motions and that too many had given in to the temptations of sensual pleasures and wealth. Lacking the ideals of their forebears, New Englanders were now suffering the wrath of God and needed to rededicate themselves to their mission. This form of sermon, akin to the warnings of the prophet Jeremiah, became known as the "jeremiad."

Source: Samuel Danforth, "Errand into the Wilderness," in A. William Plumstead, ed., *The Wall and the Garden: Selected Massachusetts Election Sermons, 1670–1775* (Minneapolis: University of Minnesota Press, 1968), 54–77. (*Note:* Footnotes, except those ending with "*Ed.,*" are from the University of Minnesota edition.)

A BRIEF RECOGNITION OF NEW ENGLAND'S ERRAND INTO THE WILDERNESS.

"What went ye out into the wilderness to see? A reed shaken with the wind?

But what went ye out for to see? A man clothed in soft raiment? Behold, they that wear soft clothing are in kings' houses. But what went ye out for to see? A prophet? Yea, I say unto you, and more than a prophet" (Matt. 11. 7–9).

These words are our Savior's proem to his illustrious encomium of John the Baptist. John began his ministry not in Jerusalem nor in any famous city of Judea, but in the wilderness, i.e., in a woody, retired, and solitary place, thereby withdrawing himself from the envy and preposterous zeal of such as were addicted to their old traditions and also taking the people aside from the noise and tumult of their secular occasions and businesses, which might have obstructed their ready and cheerful attendance unto his doctrine. The ministry of John at first was entertained by all sorts with singular affection: There "went out to him Jerusalem, and all Judea, and all the region round about Jordan" (Matt. 3. 5); but after awhile the people's fervor abated, and John being kept under restraint divers months, his authority and esteem began to decay and languish (John 5. 35). Wherefore our Savior, taking occasion from John's messengers coming to him, after their departure gives an excellent elogy and commendation of John to the intent that he might ratify and confirm his doctrine and administration and revive his authority and estimation in the hearts and consciences of the people. . . .

Doctrine. *Such as have sometime left their pleasant cities and habitations to enjoy the pure worship of God in a wilderness are apt in time to abate and cool in their affection thereunto; but then the Lord calls upon them seriously and thoroughly to examine themselves, what it was that drew them into the wilderness, and to consider that it was not the expectation of ludicrous levity nor of courtly pomp and delicacy, but of the free and clear dispensation of the Gospel and kingdom of God.* . . .

The prophet Jeremiah, that he might reduce the people from their backslidings, cries in the ears of Jerusalem with earnestness and boldness, declaring unto them that the Lord remembered how well they stood affected towards him when he first chose them to be his people and espoused them to himself; how they followed him in the wilderness and kept close to him in their long and wearisome passage through the uncultured desert; how they were then consecrated to God and set apart for his worship and service, as the first fruits are wont to be sequestered and devoted to God; and thereupon expostulates with them for their forsaking the Lord, and following after their idols. . . .

Use 1. Of solemn and serious enquiry to us all in this general assembly is whether we have not in a great measure forgotten our errand into the wilderness. You have solemnly professed before God, angels, and men that the cause of your leaving your country, kindred, and fathers' houses and transporting yourselves with your wives, little ones, and substance over the vast ocean into this waste and howling wilderness, was your liberty to walk in the faith of the Gospel with all good conscience according to the order of the Gospel, and your enjoyment of the pure worship of God according to his institution without human mixtures and impositions. Now let us sadly consider whether our ancient and primitive affections to the Lord Jesus, his glorious Gospel, his pure and spiritual worship, and the order of his house, remain, abide, and continue firm, constant, entire, and inviolate. Our Savior's reiteration of this question, "What went ye out into the wilderness to see?" is no idle repetition but a sad conviction of our dullness and backwardness to this great duty and a clear demonstration of the weight and necessity thereof. It may be a grief to us to be put upon such an inquisition, as it is said of Peter, "Peter was grieved because he said unto him the third time, Lovest thou me?" (John 21. 17); but the Lord knoweth that a strict and rigid examination of our hearts in this point is no more than necessary. Wherefore let us call to remembrance the former days and consider whether "it was not then better with us than it is now" [Hos. 2. 7].

In our first and best times the kingdom of heaven brake in upon us with a holy violence and every man pressed into it. What mighty efficacy and power had the clear and faithful dispensation of the Gospel upon your hearts? How affectionately and zealously did you entertain the kingdom of God? How careful were you, even all sorts, young and old, high and low, to take hold of the opportunities of your spiritual good and edification, ordering your secular affairs (which were wreathed and twisted together with great variety) so as not to interfere with your general calling, but that you might attend upon the Lord without distraction? How diligent and faithful in preparing your hearts for the reception of the Word, "laying apart all filthiness and superfluity of naughtiness," that you might "receive with meekness the ingraffed word, which is able to save your souls" [Jas. 1. 21], "and purging out all malice, guile, hypocrisies, envies, and all evil speakings, and as newborn babes, desiring the sincere milk of the Word, that ye might grow thereby" [I Pet. 2. 1, 2]? How attentive in hearing the everlasting Gospel, "watching daily at the gates of wisdom, and waiting at the posts of her doors, that ye might find eternal life, and obtain favor of the Lord" [Prov. 8. 34, 35]? Gleaning day by day in the field of God's ordinances, even among the sheaves, and gathering up handfuls, which the Lord let fall of purpose for you, and at night going home and beating out what you had gleaned, by mediation, repetition, conference, and therewith feeding yourselves and your families. How painful were you in recollecting, repeating, and discoursing of what you heard, whetting the Word of God upon the hearts of your children, servants, and neighbors? How fervent in prayer to almighty God for his divine blessing upon the seed sown, that it might take root and fructify? O what a reverent esteem had you in those days of Christ's faithful ambassadors that declared unto you the word of reconciliation! "How beautiful" were "the feet of them that preached the Gospel of peace, and brought the glad tidings of salvation!" [Rom. 10. 15]. You "esteemed them highly in love for their work's sake" [I Thess. 5. 13]. Their persons, names, and comforts were precious in your eyes; you counted yourselves blessed in the enjoyment of a pious, learned, and orthodox ministry; and though you ate the bread of adversity and drank the water of affliction, yet you rejoiced in this, that your eyes saw your teachers, they were not removed into corners, and your ears heard a word behind you saying, "This is the way, walk ye in it," when you turned to the right hand and when you turned to the left (Isa. 30. 20, 21). What earnest and ardent desires had you in those days after communion with Christ in the holy sacraments? With desire you desired to partake of the seals of the covenant. You thought your evidences for heaven not sure nor authentic unless the broad seals of the kingdom were annexed. What solicitude was there in those days to "seek the Lord after the right order" [I Chron. 15. 13]? What searching of the holy Scriptures, what collations among your leaders, both in their private meetings

and public councils and synods, to find out the order which Christ hath constituted and established in his house? What fervent zeal was there then against sectaries and heretics and all manner of heterodoxies? "You could not bear them that were evil" [Rev. 2. 2] but tried them that pretended to new light and revelations, and found them liars. What pious care was there of sister churches, that those that wanted breasts might be supplied and that those that wanted peace, their dissensions might be healed? What readiness was there in those days to call for the help of neighbor elders and brethren in case of any difference or division that could not be healed at home? What reverence was there then of the sentence of a council as being decisive and issuing the controversy, according to that ancient proverbial saying, "They shall surely ask counsel at Abel: and so they ended the matter" (II Sam. 20. 18)? What holy endeavors were there in those days to propagate religion to your children and posterity, training them up in the nurture and admonition of the Lord, keeping them under the awe of government, restraining their enormities and extravagancies, charging them to know the God of their fathers and serve him with a perfect heart and willing mind, and publicly asserting and maintaining their interest in the Lord and in his holy covenant and zealously opposing those that denied the same? . . .

But who is there left among you that saw these churches in their first glory and how do you see them now? Are they not in your eyes in comparison thereof as nothing? "How is the gold become dim! how is the most fine gold changed!" [Lam. 4. 1]. Is not the temper, complexion, and countenance of the churches strangely altered? Doth not a careless, remiss, flat, dry, cold, dead frame of spirit grow in upon us secretly, strongly, prodigiously? They that have ordinances are as though they had none; and they that hear the Word as though they heard it not; and they that pray as though they prayed not; and they that receive sacraments as though they received them not; and they that are exercised in the holy things using them by the by as matters of custom and ceremony, so as not to hinder their eager prosecution of other things which their hearts are set upon. Yea and in some particular congregations amongst us is there not instead of a sweet smell, a stink; and instead of a girdle, a rent; and instead of a stomacher,[1] a girding with sackcloth; and burning instead of beauty?[2]

---

[1]*Stomacher*: A kind of waistcoat worn by men (usually, in the sixteenth and seventeenth centuries, of fur or lamb's skin) to protect the chest against the cold. The word also designated a medicated cloth applied to the chest (*NED*, IX, 1006).

[2]The "stink" and "rent" in "some particular congregations" is probably an allusion to the secession of a minority of the First Church congregation over appointment of John Davenport as its minister. After bitterness and subterfuge in Davenport's release from New Haven and his invitation to Boston, a group broke from the First Church and formed the Third or Old South Church at Charlestown on May 12, 1669. Danforth knew of this "rent" at first hand, for Davenport had written a letter to the church at Roxbury to dispel "reports that may be bruited" and to ask for advice. For a brief account of this

Yea "the vineyard is all overgrown with thorns, and nettles cover the face thereof, and the stone wall thereof is broken down" (Prov. 24. 31). Yea and that which is the most sad and certain sign of calamity approaching: "Iniquity aboundeth, and the love of many waxeth cold" (Matt. 24. 12). Pride, contention, worldliness, covetousness, luxury, drunkenness, and uncleanness break in like a flood upon us and good men grow cold in their love to God and to one another. . . .

What then is the cause of our coolings, faintings, and languishings? The grand and principal cause is our unbelief. We believe not the grace and power of God in Christ. Where is that lively exercise of faith which ought to be in our attendance upon the Lord in his holy ordinances? . . .

But though unbelief be the principal yet it is not the sole cause of our decays and languishings; inordinate worldly cares, predominant lusts, and malignant passions and distempers stifle and choke the Word and quench our affections to the kingdom of God (Luke 8. 14). The manna was gathered early in the morning; when the sun waxed hot, it melted (Exod. 16. 21). It was a fearful judgment on Dathan and Abiram that the earth opened its mouth and swallowed them up. How many professors of religion are swallowed up alive by earthly affections? Such as escape the lime pit of Pharisaical hypocrisy fall into the coal pit of Sadducean atheism and epicurism. Pharisaism and Sadduceism do almost divide the professing world between them. Some split upon the rock of affected ostentation of singular piety and holiness and others are drawn into the whirlpool and perish in the gulf of sensuality and luxury. . . .[3]

Use II. Of exhortation, to excite and stir us all up to attend and prosecute our errand into the wilderness. To what purpose came we into this place and what expectation drew us hither? Surely not the expectation of ludicrous levity. We came not hither to see "a reed shaken with the wind." Then let not us be reeds—light, empty, vain, hollow-hearted professors, shaken with every wind of temptation—but solid, serious, and sober Christians, constant and steadfast in the profession and practice of the truth, "trees of righteousness, the planting of the Lord, that he may be glorified" [Isa. 61. 3], holding fast the profession of our faith without wavering.

"Alas there is such variety and diversity of opinions and judgments that we know not what to believe."

Were there not as various and different opinions touching the person of Christ even in the days of his flesh? Some said that he was John the Baptist, some Elias, others Jeremias, or one of the old prophets. Some said he was a gluttonous man and a wine-bibber, a friend of publicans and sinners; others said he was a Samaritan and had a devil; yet the disciples knew what to believe. "Whom say ye that I am? Thou art Christ, the Son of the living God" (Matt. 16. 15, 16). The various heterodox opinions of the people serve as a foil or tinctured leaf to set off the luster and beauty of the orthodox and apostolical faith. This is truly commendable, when in such variety and diversity of apprehensions you are not biased by any sinister respects, but discern, embrace, and profess the truth as it is in Christ Jesus.

But to what purpose came we into the wilderness and what expectation drew us hither? Not the expectation of courtly pomp and delicacy. We came not hither to see men clothed like courtiers. The affectation of courtly pomp and gallantry is very unsuitable in a wilderness. Gorgeous attire is comely in princes' courts if it exceed not the limits of Christian sobriety; but excess in kings' houses escapes not divine vengeance. "I will punish the princes, and the kings' children, and all such as are clothed with strange apparel" (Zeph. 1. 8). The pride and haughtiness of the ladies of Zion in their superfluous ornaments and stately gestures brought wrath upon themselves, upon their husbands, and upon their children, yea and upon the whole land (Isa. 3. 16–26). How much more intolerable and abominable is excess of this kind in a wilderness, where we are so far removed from the riches and honors of princes' courts?

To what purpose then came we into the wilderness and what expectation drew us hither? Was it not the expectation of the pure and faithful dispensation of the Gospel and kingdom of God? The times were such that we could not enjoy it in our own land, and therefore having obtained liberty and a gracious patent from our Sovereign, we left our country, kindred, and fathers' houses, and came into these wild woods and deserts where the Lord hath planted us and made us "dwell in a place of our own, that we might move no more, and that the children of wickedness might not afflict us any more" (II Sam. 7. 10). What is it that distinguisheth New England from other colonies and plantations in America? Not our transportation over the Atlantic Ocean, but the ministry of God's faithful prophets and the fruition of his holy ordinances. Did not the Lord bring "the Philistines from Caphtor, and the Assyrians from Kir" as well as "Israel from the land of Egypt" (Amos 9. 7)? But "by a prophet the Lord brought Israel out of Egypt, and by a prophet was he preserved" (Hos. 12. 13). What, is the price and esteem of God's prophets and their faithful dispensations now fallen in our hearts?

The hardships, difficulties, and sufferings which you have exposed yourselves unto that you might dwell in the

---

dispute, see the "Biographical Sketch," *Letters of John Davenport,* ed. Isabel M. Calder (New Haven, 1937), 10–12, and the letters on 280ff. See also Perry Miller, *The New England Mind: From Colony to Province* (Cambridge, 1953), 106–108.

[3]*Dathan and Abiram:* Leaders of a rebellion against the authority of Moses when the Israelites were wandering through the wilderness following the Exodus from Egypt. God punished the two men by causing the earth to open up beneath them and swallow them alive. The story appears in chapter 16 of Numbers. The *Pharisees* and the *Sadducees* were Jewish sects of the time of Jesus; both sects were condemned in the Gospels for their alleged legalism and hypocrisy (the Pharisees) and their Greek-influenced epicurism (the Sadducees), although modern scholars would question the validity of the attacks. [*Ed.*]

house of the Lord and leave your little ones under the shadow of the wings of the God of Israel, have not been few nor small. And shall we now withdraw ourselves and our little ones from under those healing wings and lose that full reward which the Lord hath in his heart and hand to bestow upon us? Did we not with Mary choose this for our part, "to sit at Christ's feet, and hear his word" [Luke 10. 39]? And do we now repent of our choice and prefer the honors, pleasures, and profits of the world before it? "You did run well; who doth hinder you that you should not obey the truth?" (Gal. 5. 7).

Hath the Lord been wanting to us or failed our expectation? "O my people, what have I done unto thee? and wherein have I wearied thee? testify against me" (Mic. 6. 3). "What iniquity have your fathers found in me, that they are gone far from me? O generation, see ye the word of the Lord. Have I been a wilderness unto Israel? a land of darkness?" (Jer. 2. 5, and ver. 31). May not the Lord say unto us, as Pharaoh did to Hadad: "What hast thou lacked with me, that, behold, thou seekest to go to thine own country?" (I Kings 11. 22). Nay, "what could have been done more" than what the Lord hath done for us (Isa. 5. 4)?

How sadly hath the Lord testified against us because of our loss of our first love and our remissness and negligence in his work? Why hath the Lord smitten us with blasting and mildew now seven years together, superadding sometimes severe drought, sometimes great tempests, floods, and sweeping rains that leave no food behind them? Is it not because the Lord's house lyeth waste, temple-work in our hearts, families, churches is shamefully neglected? What should I make mention of signs in the heavens and in the earth—blazing stars, earthquakes, dreadful thunders and lightnings, fearful burnings? What meaneth the heat of his great anger in calling home so many of his ambassadors? In plucking such burning and shining lights out of the candlesticks; the principal stakes out of our hedges; the cornerstones out of our walls? In removing such faithful shepherds from their flocks and breaking down our defensed cities, iron pillars, and brazen walls? Seemeth it a small thing unto us that so many of God's prophets (whose ministry we came into the wilderness to enjoy) are taken from us in so short a time? Is it not a sign that God is making a way for his wrath when he removes his chosen out of the gap? Doth he not threaten us with a famine of the Word, the scattering of the flock, the breaking of the candlesticks, and the turning of the songs of the temple into howlings?

It is high time for us to "remember whence we are fallen, and repent, and do our first works" [Rev. 2. 5].

Wherefore let us "lift up the hands that hang down, and strengthen the feeble knees; And make straight paths for our feet, lest that which is lame be turned out of the way; but let it rather be healed" (Heb. 12. 12, 13). Labor we to redress our faintings and swervings and address ourselves to the work of the Lord. Let us arise and build and the Lord will be with us and from this day will he bless us.

"Alas, we are feeble and impotent; our hands are withered and our strength dried up."

Remember the man that had a withered hand; Christ saith unto him, "Stretch forth thy hand. And he stretched it forth; and it was restored whole, like as the other" (Matt. 12. 13). How could he stretch forth his hand when it was withered, the blood and spirits dried up and the nerves and sinews shrunk up? The almighty power of Christ accompanying his command enabled the man to stretch forth his withered hand and in stretching it forth, restored it whole like as the other. Where the sovereignty of Christ's command takes place in the conscience there is effectual grace accompanying it to the healing of our spiritual feebleness and impotency and the enabling of us to perform the duty incumbent on us. Though we have no might, no strength, yet at Christ's command, make an essay. Where the word of a king is, there is power. . . .

"But we have many adversaries and they have their subtle machinations and contrivances, and how soon we may be surprised we know not."

Our diligent attention to the ministry of the Gospel is a special means to check and restrain the rage and fury of adversaries. The people's assiduity in attendance upon Christ's ministry was the great obstacle that hindered the execution of the bloody counsels of the Pharisees. "He taught daily in the temple. But the chief priests and the scribes and the chief of the people sought to destroy him. And could not find what they might do: for all the people were very attentive to hear him" (Luke 19. 47, 48). If the people cleave to the Lord, to his prophets, and to his ordinances, it will strike such a fear into the hearts of enemies that they will be at their wits' ends and not know what to do. However, in this way we have the promise of divine protection and preservation. "Because thou hast kept the word of my patience, I also will keep thee from the hour of temptation, which shall come upon all the world, to try them that dwell upon the earth" (Rev. 3. 10). Let us with Mary choose this for our portion, "to sit at Christ's feet, and hear his word"; and whosoever complain against us, the Lord Jesus will plead for us as he did for her and say: "They have chosen that good part, which shall not be taken away from them" (Luke 10. 42). Amen.

Questions

1. What do we learn from Danforth's jeremiad about the relationship between church and state in Puritan New England? How does Danforth believe that this had changed?
2. According to Danforth, how had the colonists strayed from their "errand"?
3. Based on your knowledge of colonial New England, how do you think the colonists received Danforth's jeremiad? Who, outside New England, might have been paying attention, and why?

Questions for Further Thought

1. Historians argue that the Puritans left a lasting mark on American culture, one that persists to the present day. From your reading of Documents 2-6 through 2-8, what particulars of the Puritan legacy can you identify?
2. Based on your knowledge of other colonial experiments in the Americas, was Puritan New England unique in its emphasis on religion as the guiding force in building a society?
3. How can we explain the changing place of religion in seventeenth-century New England? What larger historical events forced change in the way the Massachusetts Bay colony was governed?

The Indians' New World

Even before they began their trek across the Atlantic, European settlers conceived of the New World as a wilderness largely devoid of inhabitants. They were wrong, of course; but the indigenous inhabitants of the Chesapeake and New England colonies made much less intensive use of the land than did Europeans, a fact attributed by such European leaders as John Winthrop to their want of "civilization" (Document 2-10). Having marginalized the natives in their minds, the settlers proceeded to marginalize the Indians in fact, swamping the land with ever-growing numbers of people. Natives occasionally fought back, most fiercely in the cases of Opecananough's war on the Virginia colony in 1622 and Metacom's war on the New Englanders in 1675–1676; but such resistance invariably ended in failure and brutal suppression by the Europeans.

Most native peoples lived initially beyond direct contact with Europeans, but few escaped the consequences of their arrival. European diseases devastated Indian peoples and forced many to abandon their traditional communities and join other tribes. As Indians entered into the fur trade with Europeans, game became depleted and warfare between tribes became more common, fundamentally altering the Indian way of life. Finally, as Europeans penetrated into the interior, those natives who did not flee westward found themselves living among strangers in a land no longer their own, one in which they increasingly were forced to follow alien rules (Document 2-11). For native Americans, it was as if the world in which they had grown up had been bewitched.

2-10   But What Warrant Have We to Take That Land? (1629)

John Winthrop

As John Winthrop wrestled with the question of whether or not to join the proposed colony of Massachusetts Bay, he committed his thoughts to paper, circulating them among his associates. These statements, which exist in several versions, are remarkable expositions of both the motives impelling Puritans to leave their homeland and the purposes to which they wished to put what they termed the American "wilderness." One objection to their scheme concerned their right to invade a land already occupied by others. Winthrop's response to this objection sets forth, with standard Puritan logic, the dominant view of the English toward the native inhabitants.

Source: From John Winthrop, *General Considerations for the Plantation in New England, with an Answer to Several Objections,* in *Winthrop Papers* (Boston: Massachusetts Historical Society, 1931), 2: 120.

Obj. 5. But what warrant have we to take that land, which is and hath been of long tyme possessed of others the sons of Adam?

Ans. That which is common to all is proper to none. This savage people ruleth over many lands without title or property; for they inclose no ground, neither have they cattell to maintayne it, but remove their dwellings as they have occasion, or as they can prevail against their neighbours. And why may not christians have liberty to go and dwell amongst them in their waste lands and woods (leaving them such places as they have manured for their corne) as lawfully as Abraham did among the Sodomites? For God hath given to the sons of men a twofould right to the earth; there is a naturall right and a civil right. The first right was naturall when men held the earth in common, every man sowing and feeding where he pleased: Then, as men and cattell increased, they appropriated some parcells of ground by enclosing and peculiar manurance, and this in tyme got them a civil right. Such was the right which Ephron the Hittite had to the field of Machpelah, wherein Abraham could not bury a dead corpse without leave, though for the out parts of the countrey which lay common, he dwelt upon them and tooke the fruite of them at his pleasure. This appears also in Jacob and his sons, who fedd their flocks as bouldly in the Canaanites land, for he is said to be lord of the country; and at Dotham and all other places men accounted nothing their owne, but that which they had appropriated by their own industry, as appears plainly by Abimelech's servants, who in their own countrey did often contend with Isaac's servants about wells which they had digged; but never about the lands which they occupied. So likewise betweene Jacob and Laban; he would not take a kidd of Laban's without speciall contract; but he makes no bargaine with him for the land where he fedd. And it is probable that if the countrey had not been as free for Jacob as for Laban, that covetuous wretch would have made his advantage of him, and have upbraided Jacob with it as he did with the rest. 2dly, There is more than enough for them and us. 3dly, God hath consumed the natives with a miraculous plague, whereby the greater part of the country is left voide of inhabitants. 4thly, We shall come in with good leave of the natives.

Questions

1. By what right does Winthrop believe the English settlers are entitled to the Indians' lands? What authority does Winthrop invoke?
2. What attitudes toward the native Americans does Winthrop exhibit? Do you think that these attitudes were typical of all English settlers?
3. Winthrop (a lawyer) argues that there are two different rights to the use of land: a "natural" right and a "civil" right. What does he mean by this, and how does it affect his response to the question in the title of this document?

2-11   Strangers in Their Own Land: The Catawbas Confront the English (1754–1755)

Sometimes, as in Metacom's war, the native inhabitants struck back at the English invaders. At other times, though, with their cultures and communities shattered by both disease and the corruption frequently flowing from trade with the Europeans, the North American Indians found themselves having to live among Europeans who increasingly turned the land to European purposes and remade it in a European image. One such Indian nation was the Catawba, actually a combination of dispossessed native groups, who by the early eighteenth century had formed settlements in the valley of the Catawba River near present-day Charlotte, North Carolina. Below appears a brief description of their plight written by Edmond Atkin, a South Carolina merchant and government official who reported on the frontier situation at the beginning of the French and Indian War. There follows an account of a 1754 meeting between the headmen of the Catawbas and representatives of the colony of North Carolina, held at the home of Matthew Tool, a backcountry Indian trader. While these documents were created long after the close of the seventeenth century, they reveal the sorts of petty tensions and mutual incomprehensions characteristic of the relationship between whites and Indians, and show how, even for native Americans who escaped war and extermination, the Indians' New World was one that left them aliens in their own land.

Sources: Wilbur R. Jacobs, ed., *Indians of the Southern Colonial Frontier: The Edmond Atkin Report and Plan of 1755* (Columbia: University of South Carolina Press, 1955), 46–47; William L. Saunders, ed., *The Colonial Records of North Carolina* (Raleigh, S.C.: Josephus Daniels, Printer to the State, 1887), 5: 141–144c.

(a) From *The Edmond Atkin Report and Plan of 1755*

. . . The Catawbas are situated about Two hundred and ten Miles N.N.W. from Charles Town on the Wateree River (near its head), which falls into the River Santee. That was some Years ago a very fit post for them, to cover the So. Carolina Settlements on that side. But of late Years abundance of People, besides the new Comers from Europe, have been induced by the extraordinary goodness of the Land and the Kindness of the Climate in those parts, to remove from the back settlements of the Northern Colonies, and settle thereabout; insomuch that those Indians are now in a fair way to be surrounded by White People. The Government of So. Carolina hath indeed restrained the making surveys of Land within 30 Miles of them. But the surveyors of No. Carolina, imagining them to be within the bounds of that Province, have lately run lines by Chain thro' their very Towns, which must make them uneasy; and will certainly end in determining them at least to remove. For on account of the difference of manners and way of life, as well as the Damage done by stocks of [livestock] Creatures to their Crops of Provision on the Ground, and the unkind Treatment of our common People, besides the making Deer scarce when they interfere, Indians generally chuse to withdraw, as white People draw near to them. . . .

(b) From *The Colonial Records of North Carolina*

[FROM MSS. RECORDS IN OFFICE OF SECRETARY OF STATE.]

NORTH CAROLINA—ROWAN & ANSON COUNTYS

At a Treaty held on Thursday the Twenty Ninth day of August one Thousand Seven Hundred and Fifty four at the house of Mr. Matthew Tool, Between Alexander Osburn & James Carter Esquire Commissioners, and the Cataba Indians—

Present

King Hagler and sundry of his headmen and Wariors

James Carter
&
Alexander Osburn
} Esquires Commissioners &c.

The Commission which was sent by his Honor the President to the above Commissioners, being Read in the presence of King Hagler and sundry of his headmen and Wariors, after which it was Interpreted by Mr. Matthew Tool, Together with the Letter which was also sent by his Honor to Captain McClenachan Andrew Perkins Esquire and Others, as Concerning said Indians

After Each sentence was Distinctly Interpreted by Mr. Tool, who was Sworn for that purpose the King made the following Speech—

BROTHERS AND WARIORS

I am Exceeding glad to meet you here this day, and to have the oppertunity of haveing a talk one with an Other in a Brotherly and Loveing manner, and to Brighten, and Strengthen, that Chain of Friendship which has so long remained between us and the people of those three Provinces, and I am Very Sorry to hear those Complaints that are Laid to our People's Charge, But now will Open our Ears to here those Grievances & Complaints that shall be made by you against our Young men and Others, and we do Heartily Thank our Good Brother the President of North Carolina for his good Talk in his Letter to us, and also for his appointing You to meet us here, to have this Discourse.

Then William Morrison Appeared, to support the Complaint that was by him Made to the Officers at a late Court martial held in Rowan County, Concerning the Indians Insults to him at his own house, some time before, when they Came to him at his mill and Attempted to Frow a pail of water into his Meal Trough, and when he would prevent them they made many attempts to striek him with their guns over his head

To which some of the Indians said what they Intended to do with the water was only to put a handful or Two of the meal into it to make a kind of a Drink which is their way and Custom.

The King also Said that it was well that one of them had killed him, for said he had they killed You or anybody Else we would surely have killed him for they would not let him Live above the ground, but would put him under the ground, as Lately we have Done to one of our Young Fellows who got Drunk and in his Liquor met with a little girl on his way below the Waxhaw Settlement and kill'd her we were Imediately aprized of it by one our own People, and we soon Discovered who, it was that Commited the fact whereupon we Directly Caused an Other young man the fellows own Cousin to kill him, which he readily did in the presence of some of our Brothers, the white people in Order to shew our Willingness to punish such offenders.

Then Came James Armstrong William Young and William McNight who Laid sundry things to the Indians Charge, (to wit) Concerning their taking Bread meat meal and Cloaths and also for attempting to Take away a child, and attempting to stab men and women if opposed by them from Committing those Crimes, To which the King & some of the Headmen, Answered

Brothers as You are Wariors Yourselves, You well know that we oftentimes goe to War against our Enemies and Many Times we are Either makeing our Escape from our Enemies or in pursuit of them, which prevents us from hunting for meat to Eat when we are in Danger, least our Enemy should Discover us; and as this is our Case many times we are forced to go to Your houses when Hungry, and no sooner we do appear but your Dogs bark and as soon as You Discover Our Comeing You Imediately hide Your Bread Meal and Meat or any Other thing that is fit to Eat about your houses, and we being sensible that this is the Case, it is True we serch, and if we finde any Eatables in the house we Take some, and Especially from those who behave so Churlish and ungreatfull to us, as they are very well assured, of our great need many times for the Reasons we now give, If we ask a little Victuals you Refuse us & then we Owne we Take a Loaf of bread a little meal or meat to Eat, and then You Complain and say those are Transgressions, it is True there are many in those Settlements that are very kind and Curtious to us when or as often as we come they give us Bread and milk meat or Butter very freely if they have any ready and never Do refuse whether we do ask or no, and if it should happen that they have nothing we goe away Contented with them, for we well know that if they had any thing ready we would have it freely &c not Refused by them. One of the Captains named James Bullin Owned that not Long agoe he and his men were in pursuit of the Enemy and then on their Track he Came to James Armstrong's house, the above Complainant, who gave him a small cake of Bread, and being very hungry he asked more for himself and his men, and being Told by sd Armstrong that there was no more ready in the house One of the Indians Lifted up a bag that lay in the house Under which they Discovered Some Bread which they had Suspected was hid from them, and taking some of it the woman struck one of them Over the head, which is the Cause of our Taking, Those things without law that we would not do to those who are kind to us in our necessity when we apply to them

KING—You I Remember Brothers accuse our People with attempting To take away a Child from one of Your People, but I hope you will not harbour this Thought of us so as to Imagine it was done in Earnest, for I am Informed it was Only done by way of a joke by one of our wild Young men in Order to Surprize the People, that were the parents of the Child, to have a Laugh at the Joke

But as to their Takeing other things such as knives Cloaths or Such Things we own it is not right to do but there are some of our young fellows will do those tricks altho' by us they are oftentimes Cautioned from such ill Doings altho' to no purpose for we Cannot be present at all times to Look after them, and when they goe to war or hunting Among the Inhabitants we generally warn them from being any ways offencive to any white person upon any Consideration whatever,

KING—Brothers here is One thing You Yourselves are to Blame very much in, That is You Rot Your grain in Tubs, out of which you take and make Strong Spirits You sell it to our young men and give it them, many times; they get very Drunk with it this is the Very Cause that they oftentimes Commit those Crimes that is offencive to You and us and all thro' the Effect of that Drink it is also very bad for our people, for it Rots their guts and Causes our men to get very sick and many of our people has Lately Died by the Effects of that strong Drink, and I heartily wish You would do something to prevent Your People from Dareing to Sell or give them any of that Strong Drink, upon any Consideration whatever for that will be a great means of our being free from being accused of those Crimes that is Committed by our young men and will prevent many of the abuses that is done by them thro' the Effects of that Strong Drink

COMMISSIONERS—King Hagler and Brethren here is one thing more that is Laid to your peoples Charge by many of the white people, that is your Comeing into our woods and among our plantations and Steale our horses mares and Young Creaturs from us and Takes them away and sell them to others under a pretence of their being your property if such Things as these were Done by any of our people against one an other, our Laws and Customs are to put them to Death, or any offender when Discovered or Catch'd in any such heinous fact, or for smaller facts they are punished according to the Nature of the Crime; but when your people do any of these things we have no remedy but are obliged to apply our selves to you, that the Offenders may be punished according to the Nature of the Crime and according to your manner and Customs, and if these Offences are by you permitted to be done it will be a great means to Breake that strong Chain of Friendship that has been so Long made Between as: it will also be a means to rise discentions among you and us and make us act and be hard towards one an other as tho' we were Entire Enemies to one an other, if this should be our Case the Great king your Father and ours would be much Displeased with you and us, as he looks upon us as his own Children and so doth the president who he sent here in his stead as a guardian over us and you, but on the other hand whilst we behave well to Each Other it will Cause them to Rejoice and they will be ready and willing to protect us from the Impositions of Insults of any other nations or that would attempt to take our properties from us or you

COMMISSIONERS—You Remember in the Letter the President wrote to you by Captain McClenachan and the other Gentlemen he told you that he had understood that Mr. Glen the Governor of South Carolina Incouraged you to Drive, all the white people from the Land within thirty miles of Your Nation, if he has told you so you Cannot Expect that this man Loves you or the white people, Because he well knows that the great king your Father & ours gave those Lands to his Children and also he gave it into the Care of the President of North Carolina to Divide according to his Discretion among his people and not to the Governor of South Carolina and it is his desire and pleasure to do Justice Between you and us, for he Looks upon you and us as his own people and would rejoice to here of our Unity and Friendship to Each Other for whilst we behave

thus to Each Other and stand by Each other we need not fear any oppressors that should attempt or Come to Dismay us.

KING—Brothers and Warriors You Talk very well, and as to your talk about our people takeing your Horses and Mares, it is very True there are a great many of our Creatures that Runs amongst the white peoples and there are also many stole from us by these people for it is not Long ago since we caught a white man with some of our Horses and sent him to Justice, but was not punished as Represented to us while agoe

COMMISSIONERS—Who was that Justice you Carried him before

INDIANS—Before Mr. McGirt in South Carolina below the Waxhaw settlement.

COMMISSIONERS—This offence was not in our power to punish for we have no authority in an other Government so that we are Excusable in this Case.

KING—As to our Liveing on those Lands we Expect to live on those Lands we now possess During our Time here for when the Great man above made us he also made this Island he also made our forefathers and of this Colour and Hue (Showing his hands & Breast) he also fixed our forefathers and us here and to Inherit this Land and Ever since we Lived after our manner and fashion we in those Days, had no Instruments To support our living but Bows which we Compleated with stones, knives we had none, and as it was our Custom in those days to Cut our hair, which we Did by Burning it of our heads and Bodies with Coals of Fire, our Axes we made of stone we bled our selves with fish Teeth our Cloathing were Skins and Furr, instead of which we Enjoy those Cloaths which we got from the white people and Ever since they first Came among us we have Enjoyed all those things that we were then destitute of for which we thank the white people, and to this Day we have Lived in a Brotherly Love & peace with them and more Especially with these Three Governments and it is our Earnest Desire that Love and Friendship which has so Long remain'd should Ever Continue.

KING—Our Brother the Governor of Virginia sent for us not Long agoe, we gladly answered his Call, and he Entertained us and shook hands with us very kindly, and had he Indulged us we would have Gone with the white people to war against their Enemies the French, but arms and ammunition being not sufficient to supply the white people who were then going out, we were forced to Return Back to our Nation again untill further Instructions from him

We understand that our Brothers and the french has had a battle and that several of our friends were kill'd I am heartily sorry for it

We Never had the pleasure of seeing our Good Brother the President of North Carolina as yet, but this Let our Brother know that we want to be brothers and Friends with him & all his people, and with the great king over the water, and all his Children, and to Confirm the same I shall as soon as get home I will Call all our nation Together and charge the young men and Wariors Not to Misbehave on any Consideration whatever to the white people and as we do Expect an Everlasting Friendship between you and us, we Expect your kinds to us for ever as you may depend upon our Friendship and kindness to you.

And Tell our Brother the President of North Carolina that if this war Continues between the white people and the french that I and my people are ready and Willing to Obey his Orders in giveing all possible assistance in my power to him when called by him or the Governor of Virginia and as a pledge of the same Take our Brother this letter as a token of Everlasting Friendship and return him Thanks for our good Talk this, Day with Each other.

Then they shook Hands all round.   KING HAGLER

A True Coppy as to me Delivered by Mr. Matthew Toole Interpreter at the above Treaty.

JOHN DUNN

Questions

1. Identify the main points of conflict between the white settlers of North Carolina and the Catawbas. How does King Hagler respond to the white charges?
2. In what ways does King Hagler believe that the white settlers are to blame for the conduct of some of the Indians?
3. Is this conflict an example of cultural miscommunication, or is one of the parties at fault?

Questions for Further Thought

1. From your reading of Documents 2-9 and 2-10, how did the European settlers define "property"? How does this compare with the way the native Americans understood ownership of the land?
2. Was there anything that the Indians could have done to live in peace with the white settlers? Or, was the cultural divide too great for finding common ground?
3. Based on the readings, draw up a list of white cultural attitudes toward the native Americans. How might native Americans have seen the white settlers?

CHAPTER 3

The British Empire in America, 1660–1750

★   ★   ★

The Politics of Empire, 1660–1713

By 1660 England had established a series of colonies in America but did not have a system in place for controlling them. Over the next quarter-century, the Stuarts would tighten their control economically and politically. A generous and extravagant man, Charles II rewarded his supporters with millions of acres of land by creating proprietorships in New York, New Jersey, the Carolinas, and Pennsylvania. For example, eight noble supporters of King Charles were granted an extensive tract of land between Virginia and Spanish Florida that they named Carolina after the Latin form (*Carolus*) of the king's name (Document 3-1). Except for the requirement that the colonies conform broadly to the laws of England, the proprietors could do as they pleased with their vast domains.

Although the king doled out land liberally to pay his political and financial debts, he kept tight control over colonial trade, which was an important source of royal revenue. Following a pattern established by the Navigation Act of 1651, Charles II and several English governments enacted a series of measures designed to confer on England the full benefit of colonial trade while excluding the Dutch (Document 3-2).

The new mercantilism constituted a successful trade policy but was resented as an intrusion into the colonies' internal affairs. The Stuart monarchs then went a step further to establish political control. With the accession to the throne of James II in 1685, the charters of Rhode Island and Connecticut were revoked; the two colonies were merged with the Massachusetts Bay and Plymouth colonies to form a new royal province, the Dominion of New England. Two years later New York and New Jersey were added, creating a political unit that extended from Maine to the Hudson River. The dominion represented a new kind of authoritarian administration that attacked local institutions by abolishing legislative assemblies and town meetings, levying arbitrary taxes, and challenging land titles under the original charters. The Glorious Revolution of 1688 in England triggered a series of insurrections in the colonies (Document 3-3). Local differences, including ethnic rivalry in New York and Protestant-Catholic conflict in Maryland, influenced the causes and outcomes. But everywhere the rebellions marked a turning point in the history of the colonies. They ended authoritarian rule and brought both a new era of political stability and an imperial presence limited mainly to the supervision of colonial trade.

3-1   The Fundamental Constitutions of Carolina (1669)

The colony of Carolina was, like most of the colonies, essentially a real-estate development, in this case the project of eight well-connected English noblemen (the "Lords Proprietors"). The leading role in the enterprise was assumed by Anthony Ashley Cooper (later Lord Shaftesbury), a prominent English politician, who set out to devise a plan of government for the colony in collaboration with his personal secretary, the philosopher John Locke. Taking full advantage of the broad latitude granted to the proprietors in their charter, Cooper and Locke sought to impose their own, very personal visions upon the as-yet-unformed colony. The resulting document, the "Fundamental Constitutions of Carolina," has been viewed as both a joke and a puzzle ever since—a strange mixture of medieval fantasy, utopian dream, and shrewd land promotion. Even its framers admitted that it was too elaborate for immediate adoption, and the actual settlers of Carolina gave it short shrift. Nonetheless, some of the provisions were quite liberal for the time, and others were expressions of an attitude common among other English colonizers, including John Winthrop (see Document 2-6): that the "New World" was an empty stage upon which they could create a new, and better, society.

Source: The Fundamental Constitutions of Carolina (London, 1682; original in Huntington Library), 1–6, 10–11, 14, 16, 18–20.

OUR SOVERAIGN LORD THE KING having out of His Royal Grace and Bounty, granted unto us the Province of *Carolina,* with all the Royalties, Proprieties, Jurisdictions, and Priviledges of a *County Palatine,* as large and ample as the County Palatine of *Durham,* with other great Priviledges; for the better settlement of the Government of the said place, and establishing the Interest of the *Lords Proprietors* with Equality, and without Confusion, and that the Government of this Province may be made most agreeable to the *Monarchy* under which we live, and of which this Province is a part; and that we may avoid erecting a numerous *Democracy,* we the *Lords and Proprietors* of the Province aforesaid, have agreed to this following Form of *Government,* to be perpetually established amongst us, unto which we do Oblige our selves, our Heirs, Assignes and Successors, in the most binding ways that can be devised.

The *eldest* of the *Lords Proprietors* shall be *Pallatine,* and upon the decease of the *Pallatine,* the eldest of those who were *Proprietors* the first of *March,* One thou-

sand six hundred sixty and Nine, shall succeed him. And when none of them are living, he that hath been longest a *Proprietor* shall succeed; but after the Year One thousand seven hundred, the eldest man of the *Lords Proprietors* shall always be *Pallatine.*

There shall be *seven* other *chief offices* erected, *viz.* The *Admirals, Chamberlains, Chancellors, Constables, Chief Justices, High Stewards,* and *Treasurers;* which places shall be enjoyed by none but the *Lords Proprietors;* to be assigned at first by Lott, and upon the Vacancy of any one of the *Seven* great *Offices* by death or otherwise, the eldest of those who were *Proprietors* the first of *March* One thousand six hundred sixty and Nine, shall have his choyce; and when none of them are living, he that hath been longesh a *Proprietor* shall have his choyce: But after the Year One thousand seven hundred, if none of those that were *Proprietors* in the Year One thousand six hundred sixty and Nine, are then living, the eldest man of the then *Lords Proprietors* shall have his choyce.

The whole Province shall be *divided* into *Counties;* each *County* shall consist of eight *Signiories,* eight *Bar-*

onies, and four *Precincts;* each *Precinct* shall consist of six *Colonies.*

Each *Signiory, Barony,* and *Colony,* shall consist of twelve thousand Acres, the eight *Signiories* being the Share of the eight *Proprietors,* and the eight *Baronies* of the *Nobility,* both which Shares being each of them one fifth part of the whole, are to be perpetually annexed, the one to the *Proprietors,* the other to the hereditary *Nobility,* leaving the *Colonies,* being three Fifths, amongst the People; that so in Setting out, and Planting the Lands, the *Ballance* of the *Government* may be preserved. . . .

There shall be just as many *Landgraves* as there are *Counties,* and twice as many *Cassiques,* and no more.[1] These shall be the hereditary *Nobility* of the Province, and by right of their *Dignity* be Members of *Parliament.* Each *Landgrave* shall have four *Baronies,* and each *Cassique* two *Baronies, hereditarily* and *unalterably* annexed to, and settled upon the said *Dignity.* . . .

In every *Signiory, Barony,* and *Mannor,* the respective Lord shall have power in his own Name to hold *Court-Leet* there for Trying of all Causes both Civil and Criminal; but where it shall concern any Person being no *Inhabitant, Vassal,* or *Leet-man* of the said *Signiory, Barony,* or *Mannor,* he upon paying down of forty Shillings to the *Lords Proprietors* use, shall have an *Appeal* from the *Signiory* or *Barony* Court, to the *County Court,* and from the *Mannor Court* to the *Precinct Court.* . . .[2]

In every *Signiory, Barony,* and *Mannor,* all the *Leet-men* shall be under the Jurisdiction of the respective Lords of the said *Signiory, Barony,* or *Mannor,* without Appeal from him. Nor shall any *Leet-man* or *Leet-woman* have liberty to go off from the Land of their particular Lord, and live any where else, without License obtained from their said Lord, under Hand and Seal.

All the Children of *Leet-men* shall be *Leet-men,* and so to all Generations

No Man shall be capable of having a *Court-Leet* or *Leet-Men,* out a *Proprietor, Landgrave, Cassique,* or *Lord of a Mannor.*

Whoever shall voluntarily Enter himself a *Leet-man* in the Registry of the County Court, shall be a *Leet-man.*

Whoever is Lord of *Leet-men,* shall upon the *Marriage* of a *Leet-man* or *Leet-woman* of his, give them ten Acres of Land for their Lives, they paying to him therefore not more than one eighth part of all the yearly Produce and Growth of the said ten Acres. . . .

The *Grand Council* shall consist of the *Palantine* and seven *Proprietors,* and the forty two *Councellors* of the several *Proprietors Courts,* who shall have power to Determine any Controversies that may arise between any of the *Proprietors Courts,* about their respective *Jurisdictions,* or between the Members of the same Court, about their *Mannor* and *Methods of Proceeding:* To make *Peace* and *War, Leagues, Treaties,* &c. with any of the neighbour *Indians:* To issue out their general Orders to the *Constable's* and *Admiral's Courts,* for the Raising, Disposing, or Disbanding the *Forces* by Land or by Sea.

The *Grand Council* shall prepare all Matters to be proposed in *Parliament.* Nor shall any Matter whatsoever be proposed in *Parliament,* except as in §. 66, but what hath first passed the *Grand Council,* which after having been read three several dayes in the *Grand Council,* and there carried by majority of Votes, shall be proposed to the *Parliament;* and in such Proposal, it shall not be necessary to have the consent of the *Palatine's Court:* which Law so proposed by the *Grand Council,* having been read three several dayes in *Parliament,* shall by majority of Votes be there passed or rejected. . . .

It shall be a base and vile thing to *Plead* for *Money* or *Reward;* nor shall any one (except he be a near Kinsman, not farther off than Cousin german to the Party concerned) be permitted to *Plead* another Man's Cause, till before the *Judge* in open Court he hath taken an Oath, that he doth not *Plead* for *Money* or *Reward,* nor hath nor will receive, nor directly nor indirectly Bargained with the Party whose Cause he is going to *Plead,* for *Money* or any other *Reward* for *Pleading* his Cause.

There shall be a *Parliament,* consisting of the *Proprietors* or their *Deputies,* and *Landgraves* and *Cassiques,* and one *Freeholder* out of every *Precinct,* to be chosen by the *Freeholders* of the said *Precinct* respectively. They shall Sit together in one Room, and have every Member one Vote.

No Man shall be chosen a *Member* of *Parliament,* who hath less than five hundred Acres of Freehold within the *Precinct* for which he is chosen; nor shall any have a Vote in chusing the said *Member* that hath less than fifty Acres of Freehold within the said *Precinct.* . . .

Since multiplicity of *Comments* as well as of *Laws,* have great inconveniencies, and serve only to obscure and perplex. All manner of *Comments* and *Expositions* on any part of these FUNDAMENTAL CONSTITUTIONS, or any part of the *Common,* or *Statute Law* of Carolina, are absolutely *Prohibited.* . . .

No Man shall be permitted to be a *Freeman* of Carolina, or to have any Estate or Habitation within it, that doth not acknowledge a GOD, and that GOD is publickly and solemnly to be *Worshipped,* and that there is a future Being after this Life, of *Happiness* or *Misery.*

As the Country comes to be sufficiently Planted and Distributed into fit Divisions, it shall belong to the *Parlia-*

---

[1]*Landgraves* and *caciques:* Under the terms of King Charles II's grant, the Lords Proprietors of Carolina were not given right to grant titles of nobility such as were available in England. Therefore, Shaftesbury and Locke borrowed titles from elsewhere: "landgraves" (a German noble title) were to constitute the greater nobility, and "caciques" (an Arawak term for "chieftain") the lesser nobility.

[2]*Court-leet:* A "court-leet" was a manorial court; the Fundamental Constitutions allowed the nobility to dispense justice in their own domains. *Leet-men* and *leet-women* were inhabitants of the territory ruled by a nobleman; they were attached to the estate as serfs were, and their progeny inherited their status.

ment to take care for the building of *Churches,* and the publick Maintenance of *Divines,* to be employed in the Exercise of *Religion,* according to the *Church of England,* which being the *Religion* of the Government of *England,* it alone shall be allowed to receive publick *Maintenance* by Grant of *Parliament.*

But since the *Natives* of that place, who will be concerned in our *Plantation,* are utterly Strangers to *Christianity,* whose Idolatry, Ignorance, or Mistake, gives us no right to expel, or use them ill; and those who remove from other parts to Plant there, will unavoidably be of different Opinions concerning Matters of *Religion,* the *Liberty* whereof they will expect to have allowed them, and it will not be reasonable for us on this account to keep them out; that *Civil Peace* may be maintained amidst the diversity of Opinions, and our *Agreement* and *Compact* with all Men may be duly and faithfully observed, the violation whereof upon what pretence soever, cannot be without great offence to *Almighty God,* and great scandal to the true *Religion* which we profess; and also that *Jews, Heathens,* and other *Dissenters* from the purity of *Christian Religion,* may not be feared and kept at a distance from it, but by having an opportunity of acquainting themselves with the truth and reasonableness of its *Doctrines,* and the peaceableness and inoffensiveness of its *Professors,* may be *good usage* and *perswation,* and all those convincing Methods of *gentleness* and *meekness,* suitable to the Rules and Design of the *Gospel,* be won over to embrace, and unfeignedly receive the *Truth;* Therefore any Seven, or more Persons agreeing in any *Religion,* shall Constitute a *Church* or *Profession,* to which they shall give some Name, to distinguish it from others.

The *Terms* of *Admittance* and *Communion* with any *Church* or *Profession* shall be written in a Book, and therein be Subscribed by all the Members of the said *Church* or *Profession;* which Book shall be kept by the publick *Register* of the *Precinct* where they reside.

The *Time* of every ones *Subscription* and *Admittance,* shall be Dated in the said Book or *religious Record.*

In the *Terms* of *Communion* of every *Church* or *Profession,* these following shall be three, without which no *Agreement* or *Assembly* of Men, upon pretence of *Religion,* shall be accounted a *Church* or *Profession,* within these Rules:

I. *That there is a GOD.*

II. *That GOD is publickly to be Worshipped.*

III. *That it is lawful, and the Duty of every Man, being thereunto called by those that Govern, to bear Witness to Truth; and that every Church or Profession shall in their Terms of Communion set down the external Way whereby*

they witness a Truth as in the presence of GOD, *whether it be by laying Hands on, or kissing the Bible, as in the* Church of England, *or by holding up the Hand, or any other sensible way.*

No Person above seventeen Years of Age, shall have any benefit or protection of the Law, or be capable of any place of Profits or Honour, who is not a *Member* of some *Church* or *Profession,* having his Name Recorded in some one, and but one *religious Record* at once.

No Person of any other *Church* or *Profession* shall disturb or molest any *religious Assembly.*

No Person whatsoever shall speak any thing in their *religious Assembly,* irreverently or seditiously of the *Government* or *Governours,* or *State-Matters.*

Any Person Subscribing the *Terms of Communion* in the Record of the said *Church or Profession* before the *Precinct Register,* and any five *Members* of the said *Church* or *Profession,* shall be thereby made a Member of the said *Church* or *Profession.*

Any *Person* striking out his own Name out of any *religious Record,* or his Name being struck out by any Officer thereunto authorized by each *Church* or *Profession* respectively, shall cease to be a *Member* of that *Church* or *Profession.*

No man shall use any *reproachful, reviling,* or *abusive Language,* against the *Religion* of any *Church* or *Profession,* that being the certain way of disturbing the *Peace,* and of hindring the *Conversion* of any to the *Truth,* by engaging them in Quarrels and Animosities, to the hatred of the *Professors* and that *Profession,* which otherwise they might be brought to assent to.

Since *Charity* obliges us to wish well to the *Souls* of all Men, and *Religion* ought to alter nothing in any Man's Civil Estate or Right, it shall be lawful for *Slaves* as well as others, to Enter themselves, and be of what *Church* or *Profession* any of them shall think best, and thereof be as fully *Members* as any *Freeman.* But yet no *Slave* shall hereby be exempted from that *Civil Dominion* his Master hath over him, but be in all other things in the same State and Condition he was in before.

Assemblies upon what pretence soever of *Religion,* not observing and performing the abovesaid Rules, shall not be esteemed as *Churches,* but unlawful *Meetings,* and be punished as other *Riots.*

No Person whatsoever shall *disturb, molest* or *persecute* another for his speculative Opinions in *Religion,* or his Way of *Worship.*

Every *Freeman* of *Carolina* shall have absolute Power and Authority over his *Negro Slaves,* of what Opinion or Religion soever. . . .

Questions

1. How could the Fundamental Constitutions allow for members of "a Parliament . . . to be chosen by the Freeholders" and still "avoid erecting a numerous Democracy"? What kind of government, by what kind of people, did the founders of Carolina have in mind for their colony?

2. What religious liberties does the Fundamental Constitutions guarantee Carolina's settlers? How does Carolina's position on religion compare with those of the other British American colonies?

3. What rights did Negro slaves have under the Fundamental Constitutions? Do you think the Fundamental Constitutions were in any way a reaction against developments in the Chesapeake and New England colonies? Why or why not?

3-2 The Navigation Act of 1660

The Acts of Trade and Navigation (see Table 3.2, text pp. 74–75) were designed to further the mercantilist aims of the British empire. The first was enacted by Parliament in 1651. The Act of 1660 strengthened the original act's intent of blocking Holland from all trade with England and its colonies. But it also made more specific the provisions requiring the colonies to produce raw products only and ship them directly to England in English or colonial ships.

Source: D. Pickering, ed., *Statutes at Large* (1762–1807), 7: 452–454, 459–460.

For the increase of shipping and encouragement of the navigation of this nation wherein, under the good providence and protection of God, the wealth, safety, and strength of this kingdom is so much concerned; . . . (2) be it enacted . . . from thence forward, no goods or commodities whatsoever shall be imported into or exported out of any lands, islands, plantations, or territories to his Majesty belonging or in his possession . . . in Asia, Africa, or America, in any other ship or ships, vessel or vessels whatsoever, but in such ships or vessels as do . . . belong only to the people of England or Ireland, dominion of Wales . . . or are of the build of and belonging to any the said lands, islands, plantations, or territories, as the proprietors and right owner thereof, and whereof the master and three fourths of the mariners at least are English. . . .

III. And it is further enacted . . . that no goods or commodities whatsoever, of the growth, production or manufacture of Africa, Asia, or America, or of any part thereof . . . be imported into England, Ireland, or Wales . . . in any other ship or ships vessel or vessels whatsoever, but in such as do . . . belong only to the people of England or Ireland, dominion of Wales . . . or of the lands, islands, plantations or territories in Asia, Africa, or America, to his Majesty belonging. . . .

XVIII. And it is further enacted . . . that . . . no sugars, tobacco, cotton-wool, indigoes, ginger, fustic, or other dyeing wood, of the growth, production, or manufacture of any English plantations in America, Asia, or Africa, shall be . . . transported from any of the said English plantations to any land . . . other than to such other English plantations as do belong to his Majesty. . . .

XIX. And be it further enacted . . . that for every ship or vessel which . . . shall set sail out of or from England, Ireland, Wales . . . for any English plantation in America, Asia, or Africa, sufficient bond shall be given with one surety . . . that the same commodities shall be by the said ship brought to some port . . . and shall there unload. . . .

Questions

1. What was the stated purpose of the Navigation Act of 1660?
2. What limits did the act place on colonial trade?
3. How did the act define an "English" ship?

3-3   The Glorious Revolution in Massachusetts (1689)

Thomas Danforth

When the Protestants William and Mary replaced James II as England's monarchs (see text pp. 76–77), New Englanders rebelled against Governor Edmund Andros, an unpopular governor who had been appointed by James II. The author of the following account, Thomas Danforth, had been a leading participant in the uprising. Although he seems to have been apprehensive about prosecution, none of the participants were punished. Danforth's correspondent, Increase Mather, had been sent to London to plead with James II for restoration of the colony's charter; he stayed on to negotiate a new charter with William and Mary.

Source: Thomas Danforth to the Rev. Increase Mather, 30 July 1689, in Thomas Hutchinson, *A Collection of Original Papers Relative to the History of the Colony of Massachusetts-Bay* (Boston, 1769), 567–571.

It is now fourteen weeks since the revolution of the government here. Future consequences we are ignorant of, yet we know that, at present, we are eased of those great oppressions that we groaned under, by the exercise of an arbitrary and illegal commission.

The business [i.e., the seizure of Governor Andros] was acted by the soldiers that came armed into Boston from all parts, being greatly animated by the Prince's [William of Orange] declarations, which about that time came into the country, and heightened by the oppressions of the governor, judges, and the most wicked extortion of their debauched officers. The ancient magistrates and elders, although they had strenuously advised to further waiting for orders from England, were compelled to assist with their presence and counsels for the prevention of bloodshed, which had most certainly been the result if prudent counsel had not been given to both parties. . . .

I am deeply sensible that we have a wolf by the ears. I do therefore earnestly entreat of you to procure the best advice you can in this matter that, if possible, the good intents of the people and their loyalty to the Crown of England may not turn to their prejudice. The example of England, the declarations put forth by the Prince of Orange, now our King, the alteration of the government in England making the arbitrary commission of Sir Edmund [Andros] null and void in the law; these considerations, in conjunction with the great oppressions the people lay under, were so far prevalent in the minds of all, that although some could not advise to the enterprise, yet are hopeful that we shall not be greatly blamed, but shall have a pardon granted for any error the law will charge us with in this matter.

We do crave that the circumstances of our case and condition in all respects may be considered. Nature has taught us self-preservation. God commands it as being the rule of charity toward our neighbor. Our great remoteness from England denies us the opportunity of direction for the regulation of ourselves in all emergencies, nor have we means to know the laws and customs of our nation. These things are our great disadvantage. We have always endeavored to prove ourselves loyal to the Crown of England. And we have also labored to attend the directions of our charter, under which were laid by our fathers the foundation of this His Majesty's colony; and we are not without hopes but that we shall receive from Their Royal Majesties the confirmation of our charter, with such addition of privileges as may advance the revenue of the Crown, and be an encouragement to Their Majesties' subjects here.

Questions

1. What justification does Danforth give for the rebellion?
2. What problems does Danforth fear may result from the rebellion?
3. What does Danforth hope the rebellion will achieve?

Questions for Further Thought

1. Following the founding of the Massachusetts Bay colony, political and social up-heaval in England had a profound effect on the development of the American colonies. How is this reflected in the Fundamental Constitutions of Carolina, the Navigation Acts, and the Glorious Revolution in Massachusetts (Documents 3-1 through 3-3)?
2. Why did the Restoration monarchs attempt to establish tighter British control over the American colonies? Why had the Crown not attempted this sooner, and how did the Glorious Revolution affect England's colonial policy?
3. In the seventeenth century, settlers throughout the North American British colonies developed the habit of self-government. Based on your reading of Documents 3-1 through 3-3 and your general knowledge of the period, describe the social, economic, and political relationships between England and the colonies. Why, by the late seventeenth century, might the colonists and the Crown have come to view the status of the colonies within the British empire differently?

The Imperial Slave Economy

The creation of a new agricultural system in America profoundly affected the history of four continents. Lands seized from Indians in North America and South America were used to raise sugar, tobacco, and other staples. These lands were worked by millions of slaves from Africa and triggered a commercial revolution in Europe. The impact on western Africa and parts of eastern Africa was tragic, as ten to twelve million people were transplanted, draining Africa of its population and lowering its standard of living. The spiritual and cultural costs may have been higher, disrupting lives, encouraging tribal violence in a struggle for control over the slave trade, and transforming African political structures.

Although there were a few Africans in Virginia as early as 1619, they were not fully defined as slaves until, beginning in the 1660s, new statutes gradually began to designate them as chattel bound for life. Blackness was becoming a mark of inferiority. In the Chesapeake, as in the West Indies and later the Carolinas, the English built an economy based on slave labor (Documents 3-5 and 3-6).

Slavery was a brutal experience, from the initial capture in Africa, to the Middle Passage (Document 3-4), to a degrading life of labor in America. Sugar growing in the West Indies was the worst killer; the loss of life from disease and oppressive labor was staggering. The Chesapeake was less deadly to slaves. The cultivation of tobacco was less physically demanding and only modestly profitable, so planters had neither the need to constantly replace their labor force nor the resources to do so. In South Carolina, however, the death rate was high and the reproduction rate was low, so planters imported large numbers of Africans. Throughout the southern colonies, the growers of staple export crops turned slavery into a central feature of their economic and social systems.

3-4   A Journal of a Voyage Made in the *Hannibal* (1693–1694)

Thomas Phillips

England was a relative latecomer to the transatlantic trade in African slaves. It was only after the restoration of the Stuarts to the throne of England in 1660 that a powerful joint-stock company, known after 1672 as the Royal African Company, could emerge. The Royal African Company, which had a monopoly until 1698, established a network of trading stations along the African coast. In 1693, one Thomas Phillips entered the service of the company and undertook a slave-trading voyage as commander of the ship *Hannibal*. Phillips went first to Guinea, where he collected his cargo at the trading station of Whidaw (or Whydah), then set sail for Barbados. He completed the four-thousand-mile journey in November 1693 with 372 of his original cargo of 700 men and women still alive. Phillips's account of his journey, which follows, is remarkably vivid in its descriptions of both the business of slave-trading and the horrors of the Middle Passage.

Source: Thomas Phillips, "A Journal of a Voyage Made in the *Hannibal* of London, Ann. 1693–1694, from England, to Cape Monseradoe, in Africa . . ." in Elizabeth Donnan, ed., *Documents Illustrative of the History of the Slave Trade to America* (Washington: The Carnegie Institution of Washington, 1930–1935), 1: 398–403, 406–410. (*Note:* Footnotes, except those ending with "*Ed.*," are from the Carnegie Institution edition.)

. . . *May the 21st.* This morning I went ashore at Whidaw, accompany'd by my doctor and purser, Mr. Clay, the present Capt. of the *East-India Merchant,* his doctor and purser, and about a dozen of our seamen for our guard, arm'd, in order here to reside till we could purchase 1300 negro slaves, which was the number we both wanted, to compleat 700 for the *Hannibal,* and 650 for the *East-India Merchant,* according to our agreement in our charter-parties with the royal African company; in procuring which quantity of slaves we spent about nine weeks. . . .

Our factory [at Whydah] lies about three miles from the sea-side, where we were carry'd in hamocks, which the factor Mr. Joseph Peirson, sent to attend our landing, with several arm'd blacks that belong'd to him for our guard; we were soon truss'd in a bag, toss'd upon negroes heads, and convey'd to our factory. . . .

Our factory built by Capt. Wilburne, Sir John Wilburne's brother, stands low near the marshes, which renders it a very unhealthy place to live in; the white men the African company send there, seldom returning to tell their tale: 'tis compass'd round with a mud-wall, about six foot high, and on the south-side is the gate; within is a large yard, a mud thatch'd house, where the factor lives, with the white men; also a store-house, a trunk for slaves, and a place where they bury their dead white men, call'd, very improperly, the hog-yard; there is also a good forge, and some other small houses. . . . And here I must observe that the rainy season begins about the middle of May, and ends the beginning of August, in which space it was my misfortune to be there, which created sicknesses among my negroes aboard, it being noted for the most malignant season by the blacks themselves, who while the rain lasts will hardly be prevail'd upon to stir out of their huts. . . .

According to promise we attended his majesty with samples of our goods, and made our agreement about the prices, tho' not without much difficulty; he and his cappasheirs[1] exacted very high, but at length we concluded as per the latter end; then we had warehouses, a kitchen, and lodgings assign'd us, but none of our rooms had doors till we made them, and put on locks and keys; next day we paid our customs to the king and cappasheirs, as will appear hereafter; then the bell was order'd to go about to give notice to all people to bring their slaves to the trunk to sell us: this bell is a hollow piece of iron in shape of a sugar loaf, the cavity of which could contain about 50 lb. of

---

[1]*Cappasheir:* A nobleman. [*Ed.*]

cowries.[2] This a man carry'd about and beat with a stick, which made a small dead sound. . . .

When we were at the trunk, the king's slaves, if he had any, were the first offer'd to sale, which the cappasheirs would be very urgent with us to buy, and would in a manner force us to it ere they would shew us any other, saying they were the Reys Cosa,[3] and we must not refuse them, tho' as I observ'd they were generally the worst slaves in the trunk, and we paid more for them than any others, which we could not remedy, it being one of his majesty's prerogatives: then the cappasheirs each brought out his slaves according to his degree and quality, the greatest first, etc. and our surgeon examin'd them well in all kinds, to see that they were sound wind and limb, making them jump, stretch out their arms swiftly, looking in their mouths to judge of their age; for the cappasheirs are so cunning, that they shave them all close before we see them, so that let them be never so old we can see no grey hairs in their heads or beards; and then having liquor'd them well and sleek with palm oil, 'tis no easy matter to know an old one from a middle-age one, but by the teeths decay; but our greatest care of all is to buy none that are pox'd, lest they should infect the rest aboard. . . .

When we had selected from the rest such as we liked, we agreed in what goods to pay for them, the prices being already stated before the king, how much of each sort of merchandize we were to give for a man, woman, and child, which gave us much ease, and saved abundance of disputes and wranglings, and gave the owner a note, signifying our agreement of the sorts of goods; upon delivery of which the next day he receiv'd them; then we mark'd the slaves we had bought in the breast, or shoulder, with a hot iron, having the letter of the ship's name on it, the place being before anointed with a little palm oil, which caus'd but little pain, the mark being usually well in four or five days, appearing very plain and white after. . . .

When our slaves were come to the seaside, our canoes were ready to carry them off to the longboat, if the sea permitted, and she convey'd them aboard ship, where the men were all put in irons, two and two shackled together, to prevent their mutiny, or swimming ashore.

The negroes are so wilful and loth to leave their own country, that they have often leap'd out of the canoes, boat and ship, into the sea, and kept under water till they were drowned, to avoid being taken up and saved by our boats, which pursued them; they having a more dreadful apprehension of Barbadoes than we can have of hell, tho' in re-

ality they live much better there than in their own country; but home is home, etc: we have likewise seen divers of them eaten by the sharks, of which a prodigious number kept about the ships in this place, and I have been told will follow her hence to Bardadoes, for the dead negroes that are thrown over-board in the passage. I am certain in our voyage there we did not want the sight of some every day, but that they were the same I can't affirm.

We had about 12 negroes did wilfully drown themselves, and others starv'd themselves to death; for 'tis their belief that when they did they return home to their own country and friends again.

I have been inform'd that some commanders have cut off the legs and arms of the most wilful, to terrify the rest, for they believe if they lose a member, they cannot return home again: I was advis'd by some of my officers to do the same, but I could not be perswaded to entertain the least thought of it, much less put in practice such barbarity and cruelty to poor creatures, who, excepting their want of christianity and true religion (their misfortune more than fault) are as much the works of God's hands, and no doubt as dear to him as ourselves; nor can I imagine why they should be despis'd for their colour, being what they cannot help, and the effect of the climate it has pleas'd God to appoint them. I can't think there is any intrinsick value in one colour more than another, not that white is better than black, only we think so because we are so, and are prone to judge favorable in our own case, as well as the blacks, who in odium of the colour, say, the devil is white, and so paint him. . . .

. . . When our slaves are aboard we shackle the men two and two, while we lie in port, and in sight of their own country, for 'tis then they attempt to make their escape, and mutiny; to prevent which we always keep centinels upon the hatchways, and have a chest full of small arms, ready loaden and prim'd, constantly lying at hand upon the quarter-deck, together with some granada shells; and two of our quarter-deck guns, pointing on the deck thence, and two more out of the steerage, the door of which is always kept shut, and well barr'd; they are fed twice a day, at 10 in the morning, and 4 in the evening, which is the time they are aptest to mutiny, being all upon deck; therefore all that time, what of our men are not employ'd in distributing their victuals to them, and settling them, stand to their arms; and some with lighted matches at the great guns that yaun upon them, loaden with partridge, till they have done and gone down to their kennels between decks: Their chief diet is call'd dabbadabb, being Indian corn ground as small as oat-meal, in iron mills, which we carry for that purpose; and after mix'd with water, and boil'd well in a large copper furnace, till 'tis as thick as a pudding, about a peckful of which in vessels, call'd crews, is allow'd to 10 men, with a little salt, malagetta, and palm oil, to relish; they are divided into messes of ten each, for the easier and better order in serving them: Three days a week they have horse-beans boil'd for their dinner and supper, great quantities of

---

[2]*Cowrie:* A seashell commonly used as money on the African coast. [*Ed.*]

[3]*Reys Cosa,* or slaves of the king. Phillips, engaged in the English trade, Barbot, in the French trade, and Bosman, in the Dutch, all traded on the coast at the end of the seventeenth century and all have left somewhat detailed descriptions of the processes of trade which make possible a comparison of their trade and their dealings with the natives.

which the African company do send aboard us for that purpose; these beans the negroes extremely love and desire, beating their breast, eating them, and crying Pram! Pram! which is Very good! they are indeed the best diet for them, having a binding quality, and consequently good to prevent the flux, which is the inveterate distemper that most affects them, and ruins our voyages by their mortality: The men are all fed upon the main deck and forecastle, that we may have them all under command of our arms from the quarterdeck, in case of any disturbance; the women eat upon the quarterdeck with us, and the boys and girls upon the poop; after they are once divided into messes, and appointed their places, they will readily run there in good order of themselves afterwards; when they have eaten their victuals clean up, (which we force them to for to thrive the better) they are order'd down between decks, and every one as he passes has a pint of water to drink after his meat, which is serv'd them by the cooper out of a large tub, fill'd before-hand ready for them. . . .

When we come to sea we let them all out of irons, they never attempting then to rebel, considering that should they kill or master us, they could not tell how to manage the ship, or must trust us, who would carry them where we pleas'd; therefore the only danger is while we are in sight of their own country, which they are loth to part with; but once out of sight out of mind: I never heard that they mutiny'd in any ships of consequence, that had a good number of men, and the least care; but in small tools where they had but few men, and those negligent or drunk, then they surpriz'd and butcher'd them, cut the cables, and let the vessel drive ashore, and every one shift for himself. However, we have some 30 or 40 gold coast negroes, which we buy, and are procur'd us there by our factors, to make guardians and overseers of the Whidaw negroes, and sleep among them to keep them from quarrelling; and in order, as well as to give us notice, if they can discover any caballing or plotting among them, which trust they will discharge with great diligence: they also take care to make the negroes scrape the decks where they lodge every morning very clean, to eschew any distempers that may engender from filth and nastiness; when we constitute a guardian, we give him a cat of nine tails as a badge of his office, which he is not a little proud of, and will exercise with great authority. We often at sea in the evenings would let the slaves come up into the sun to air themselves, and make them jump and dance for an hour or two to our bag-pipes, harp, and fiddle, by which exercise to preserve them in health; but notwithstanding all our endeavour, 'twas my hard fortune to have great sickness and mortality among them. . . .

Having completed all my business ashore in fourteen days that I lay here, yesterday in the afternoon I came off with a resolution to go to sea. Accordingly about six in the evening we got up our anchors, and set sail for Barbadoes, being forc'd to leave the *East-India merchant* behind, who could not get ready to sail in nine or ten days; which time I

could not afford to stay, in respect to the mortality of my negroes, of which two or three died every day, also the small quantity of provisions I had to serve for my passage to Barbadoes. . . .[4]

We spent in our passage from St. Thomas to Barbadoes two months eleven days, from the 25th of August to the 4th of November following: in which time there happen'd much sickness and mortality among my poor men and negroes, that of the first we buried 14, and of the last 320, which was a great detriment to our voyage, the royal African company losing ten pounds by every slave that died, and the owners of the ship ten pounds ten shillings, being the freight agreed on to be paid them by the charter-party for every negroe deliver'd alive ashore to the African company's agents at Barbadoes; whereby the loss in all amounted to near 6560 pounds sterling. The distemper which my men as well as the blacks mostly die of, was the white flux, which was so violent and inveterate, that no medicine would in the least check it; so that when any of our men were seiz'd with it, we esteem'd him a dead man, as he generally proved. I cannot imagine what should cause it in them so suddenly, they being free from it till about a week after we left the island of St. Thomas. And next to the malignity of the climate, I can attribute it to nothing else but the unpurg'd black sugar, and raw unwholesome rum they bought there, of which they drank in punch to great excess, and which it was not in my power to hinder, having chastis'd several of them, and flung overboard what rum and sugar I could find. . . .

The negroes are so incident to the small-pox, that few ships that carry them escape without it, and sometimes it makes vast havock and destruction among them: but tho' we had 100 at a time sick of it, and that it went thro' the ship, yet we lost not above a dozen by it. All the assistance we gave the diseased was only as much water as they desr'd to drink, and some palm-oil to anoint their sores, and they would generally recover without any other helps but what kind nature gave them.

One thing is very surprizing in this distemper among the blacks, that tho' it immediately infects those of their own colour, yet it will never seize a white man; for I had several white men and boys aboard that had never had that distemper, and were constantly among the blacks that were sick of it, yet none of them in the least catch'd it, tho' it be the very same malady in its effects, as well as symptoms, among the blacks, as among us in England, beginning with the pain in the head, back, shivering, vomiting, fever, etc. But what the small-pox spar'd, the flux swept off, to our

---

[4]Here follows a table giving daily observations of wind, weather, and the course of the vessel. Phillips reckoned it 4075 miles to Barbados. Early in the voyage, fearing that his provisions would become exhausted, he limited the men to "short allowance of provisions, and to two quarts of water per man per day, boiling our provisions in salt water." It is difficult to see why Phillips failed to provide ample provisions unless he found it impossible to barter the goods he carried for food. He makes no mention of such difficulty save at Santiago.

great regret, after all our pains and care to give them their messes in due order and season, keeping their lodgings as clean and sweet as possible, and enduring so much misery and stench so long among a parcel of creatures nastier than swine; and after all our expectations to be defeated by their mortality. No gold-finders can endure so much noisome slavery as they do who carry negroes; for those have some respite and satisfaction, but we endure twice the misery; and yet by their mortality our voyages are ruin'd, and we pine and fret our selves to death, to think that we should undergo so much misery, and take so much pains to so little purpose.

I deliver'd alive at Barbadoes to the company's factors 372, which being sold, came out at about nineteen pounds per head one with another. . . .

Questions

1. What European attitudes toward black Africans does Thomas Phillips reflect? How might Africans have perceived the Europeans?

2. In what ways do Phillips's religious views affect his decisions aboard the *Hannibal?*

3. Describe the Middle Passage. How did the white slave traders exploit to their advantage the tribal differences among the Africans?

3-5 Slavery and Prejudice: An Act for the Better Order and Government of Negroes and Slaves, South Carolina (1712)

Until the early 1700s most legislation involving African Americans was concerned with the personal status of slaves and was motivated primarily by racial prejudice. Subsequently, another element came into play: fear of their growing numbers. The presence of a servile but potentially rebellious population made it seem necessary to adopt measures of control (see text pp. 94–95). The act passed by South Carolina served as a model for slave codes in the colonial South and later in the southern states.

Source: Thomas Cooper and David J. McCord, eds., *Statutes at Large of South Carolina* (1836–1841), 7: 352–357.

WHEREAS, the plantations and estates of this Province cannot be well and sufficiently managed and brought into use, without the labor and service of negroes and other slaves [i.e., Indians]; and forasmuch as the said negroes and other slaves brought unto the people of this Province for that purpose, are of barbarous, wild, savage natures, and such as renders them wholly unqualified to be governed by the laws, customs, and practices of this Province; but that it is absolutely necessary, that such other constitutions, laws and orders, should in this Province be made and enacted, for the good regulating and ordering of them, as may restrain the disorders, rapines and inhumanity, to which they are naturally prone and inclined, and may also tend to the safety and security of the people of this Province and their estates; to which purpose, . . .

II. . . . That no master, mistress, overseer, or other person whatsoever . . . shall give their negroes and other slaves leave . . . to go out of their plantations, except such negro or other slave as usually wait upon them at home or abroad, or wearing a livery; and every other negro or slave that shall be taken hereafter out of his master's plantation, without a ticket, or leave in writing, from his master or mistress, or some other person by his or her appointment, or some white person in the company of such slave, to give an account of his business, shall be whipped; and every person who shall not (when in his power) apprehend every negro or other slave which he shall see out of his master's plantation, without leave as aforesaid, and after apprehended, shall neglect to punish him by moderate whipping, shall forfeit twenty shillings. . . . And for the better security of all such persons that shall endeavor to take any runaway, or shall examine any slave for his ticket, passing to and from his master's plantation, it is hereby declared lawful for any white person to beat, maim or assault, and if such negro or slave cannot otherwise be taken, to kill him, who shall refuse to shew his ticket, or, by running away or resistance, shall endeavor to avoid being apprehended or taken.

III. And be it further enacted by the authority aforesaid, That every master, mistress or overseer of a family in this Province, shall cause all his negro houses to be searched diligently and effectually, once every fourteen days, for fugitive and runaway slaves, guns, swords, clubs, and any other mischievous weapons, and finding any, to take them away, and cause them to be secured. . . .

VI. And be it further enacted . . . That every master or head of any family, shall keep all his guns and other arms, when out of use, in the most private and least frequented room in the house, upon the penalty of being convicted of neglect therein, to forfeit three pounds.

IX. And be it further enacted by the authority aforesaid, That upon complaint made to any justice of the peace, of any heinous or grievous crime, committed by any slave or slaves, as murder, burglary, robbery, burning of houses, or any lesser crimes, as killing or stealing any meat or other cattle, maiming one the other, stealing of fowls, provisions, or such like trespasses or injuries, the said justice shall issue out his warrant for apprehending the offender or offenders, . . . he shall commit him or them to prison, or immediately proceed to tryal of the said slave or slaves . . . [and if] they shall find such negro or other slave or slaves guilty thereof, they shall give sentence of death, if the crime by law deserve the same. . . .

X. And in regard great mischiefs daily happen by petty larcenies committed by negroes and slaves of this Province,

Be it further enacted by the authority aforesaid, That if any negro or other slave shall hereafter steal or destroy any goods, chattels, or provisions whatsoever, of any other person than his master or mistress . . . [if] adjudged [guilty is] to be publicly and severely whipped, not exceeding forty lashes; and if such negro or other slave punished as aforesaid, be afterwards, by two justices of the peace, found guilty of the like crimes, he or they, for such his or their second offence, shall either have one of his ears cut off, or be branded in the forehead with a hot iron, that the mark thereof may remain; and if after such punishment, such negro or slave for his third offence, shall have his nose slit; and if such negro or other slave, after the third time as aforesaid, be accused of petty larceny, or of any of the offences before mentioned, such negro or other slave shall be tried in such manner as those accused of murder, burglary, etc. are before by this Act provided for to be tried, and in case they shall be found guilty a fourth time of any the offences before mentioned, then such negro or other slave shall be adjudged to suffer death, or other punishment, as the said justices shall think fitting. . .

XII. And It is Further enacted by the authority aforesaid, That if any negroes or other slaves shall make mutiny or insurrection . . . the offenders shall be tried by two justices of the peace and three freeholders . . . who are hereby empowered and required to . . . inflict death, or any other punishment, upon the offenders . . . if the Governor and council of this Province shall think fitting . . . that only one or more of the said criminals should suffer death as exemplary, and the rest to be returned to the owners. . . .

Questions

1. What is the assumption of this act concerning the cultural level of the slave population?
2. What are the responsibilities and duties of slave owners in regard to governing their slaves?
3. What does the willingness of white South Carolinians to carry out sentences of death or mutilation on slaves, who represented a capital investment, imply about race relations at that time?

3-6   Conflicts between Masters and Slaves: Maryland in the Mid-Seventeenth Century

Almost from the beginning of Maryland and Virginia's slave history, as the first legislation defined the lifelong condition of slavery, colonists imposed harsher punishments against laborers of African descent than against white servants. Masters could, for example, whip a naked slave without breaking the law, and there were no laws requiring that food and clothing be provided to slaves. But there were limits to punishment and daily mistreatment of slaves, as the following case outlines. In the end, however, the case was referred to a higher court, where testimony was given that the slave, Tony, was a rogue and persistent runaway. At that point the court acquitted Overzee for cruelty against the slave.

Source: "Att a Provincial Court Held att St. Clement's Manor December 2, 1658," Provincial Court Proceedings, *Archives of Maryland* (Baltimore: Maryland Historical Society, 1941), 41: 190–191.

Att a Provincial Court Held att St. Clement's Manor December 2, 1658

Attorney General v. [Symon] Overzee

Mr. William Barton informes the court against Mr. Symon Overzee, for that the said Overzee correcting his negro servant the said negro dyed under his said correction.

The examination of Hannah Littleworth aged 27 yeares or thereabouts taken the 27th of November 1658, before Philip Calvert, Esq.

This Examinant sayth that sometime (as shee conseives) in September was two yeares, Mr. Overzee commanded a negro (commonly called Tony) formerly chayned up for some misdemeanors by the command of Mr. Overzee (Mr. Overzee being then abroad) to be lett loose, and ordered him to goe to worke, but instead of goeing to worke the said negro layd himselfe downe and would not stirre. Whereupon Mr. Overzee beate him with some peare tree wands or tweiggs to the bigness of man's finger att the biggest end, which hee held in his hand, and upon the stubberness of the negro caused his dublett to be taken of, and whip'd him upon his bare back, and the negro still remayned in his stubberness, and feyned himselfe in fitts, as hee used att former times to doe. Whereuppon Mr. Overzee commanded this examinant to heate a fyre shovel, and to bring him some lard, which shee did and sayth that the said fyre shovel was hott enough to melt the lard, but not soe hot as to blister anyone, and that it did not blister the negro, on whom Mr. Overzee powr'd it. Immediately thereuppon the negro rose up, and Mr. Overzee commanded him to be tyed to a Ladder standing on the foreside of the dwelling howse, which was accordingly done by an Indian slve, who tyed him by the wrist, with a piece of dryed hide, and (as she remembers but cannot justly say) that hee did stand uppong the grownd. And still the negro remayned mute or stubborne, and made noe signs of conforming himselfe to his masters will or command. And about a quarter of an howre after, or less, Mr. Overzee and Mrs. Overzee went from home, and [she] doth not know of any order Mr. Overzee gave concerning the said negro. And that while Mr. Overzee beate the negro and powred the lard on him, there was nobody by, save only Mr. Mathew Stone, and Mrs. Overzee now deceased. And that from the time of Mr. Overzee and his wife going from hime, till the negro was dead, there was nobody about the howse but only the said Mr. Mathew Stone, William hewes, and this examinant, and a negro woman in the quartering house, who never stir'd out. And that after Mr. Overzee was gone, upon the relation of Mr. Mathew Stone, in the presence of William Hewes that the negro was dying, this examinant desyred Mr. Mathew Stone to cut the negro downe, and hee refused to doe it, William Hewes allso bidding him let him alone and within lesse then halfe a howre after the negro dyed, the wind comming up att northwest soone after hee was soe tyed, and hee was tyed up betweene three and fowre o'clock in the afternoone, and dyed about six or seaven. . . .

William Hewes sworne in upon court sayth that hee was present, att the time when Mr. Overzee beate the negro, and saw him allso powre lard upon him, and that as hee conceaves and remembers, he saw noe blood drawne of the negro, and this deponent being willing to help the negro from the grownd, Mr. Overzee haveing his knife in his hand, cutting the twigs, threatened him to runne his knife in him (or words to that effect) if he molested him, and that the negro (as he think, but cannot justly say) stood uppon the grownd, and sayth further that the negro did commonly use to runne away, and absent himselfe from his Mr. Overzees service. . . .

Questions

1. What was Symon Overzee tried for? What were the excuses he gave, according to the witnesses?
2. Do the witnesses offer unambiguous testimony, or did you develop doubts about their memories of details?
3. What is the tone of the testimony given? What might Tony have offered as a defense of his behavior?

3-7   An Early Slave Narrative: Ayubah Suleiman Diallo, or "Job" (1734)

Slave narratives before 1750 are rare. One that has survived is that of Ayubah Suleiman Diallo, a priest and merchant of the Senegal region of West Africa. Diallo was captured in 1730 and transported across the Atlantic in a slave ship; he was a slave on a Maryland plantation for two years before coming to the attention of Thomas Bluett, an English gentleman, and others, including James Oglethorpe, the philanthropist who played a leading role in the founding of Georgia (see text pp. 101–103). These men took a personal interest in Diallo, with Oglethorpe putting up bond to allow him to leave for England and gentlemen there raising his purchase price and his transportation home to Africa. Clearly Diallo, or "Job" as he was known to his English friends, was a most unusual slave; furthermore, while a learned man, he relied on Bluett to render his story into English. Nonetheless, his story remains an important early look at how the Atlantic slave system dealt with one caught up in its workings.

Source: Thomas Bluett, *Some Memoirs of the Life of Job, the Son of Solomon the High Priest of Boonda in Africa; Who was a slave about two years in Maryland . . .* (London: Printed for Richard Ford, at the Angel in the Poultry, over against the Compter, 1734), 12–24, 54–53.

SECT. I.

An Account of the Family of JOB; *his Education; and the more remarkable Circumstances of his Life, before he was taken Captive.*

JOB's Countrymen, like the Eastern People and some others, use to design themselves by the Names of their Ancestors, and in their Appellations mention their Progenitors several Degrees backward; tho' they also have Sirnames for distinguishing their particular Families, much after the same Manner as in *England.* JOB's Name, in his own Country, is HYUBA, BOON SALUMENA, BOON HIBRAHEMA; *i.e.* JOB, the Son of *Solomon,* the Son of *Abraham.* The Sirname of his Family is *Jallo.*

JOB, who is now about 31 or 32 Years of age, was born at a Town called *Boonda* in the County of *Galumbo* (in our Maps *Catumbo*) in the Kingdom of *Futa* in *Africa;* which lies on both Sides the River *Senegal,* and on the south Side reaches as far as, the River *Gambia.* These two Rivers, JOB assured me, run pretty near parallel to one another, and never meet, contrary to the Position they have in most of our Maps. The Eastern Boundary of the Kingdom of *Futa* or *Senega* is the great Lake, called in our Maps *Lacus Guarde.* The Extent of it, towards the North, is not so certain. The chief City or Town of it is *Tombut;* over against which, on the other side of the River, is *Boonda,* the Place of JOB's Nativity.

About fifty Years ago *Hibrahim,* the Grandfather of JOB, founded the Town of *Boonda,* in the Reign of *Bubaker,* then King of *Futa,* and was, by his Permission, sole Lord Proprietor and Governor of it, and at the same Time High Priest, or *Alpha;* so that he had a Power to make what Laws and Regulations he thought proper for the Increase and good Government of his new City. Among other Institutions, one was, that no Person who flies thither for Protection shall be made a Slave. This Privilege is in force there to this Day, and is extended to all in general, that can read and know God, as they express it; and it has contributed much to the Peopling of the Place, which is now very large and flourishing. Some time after the Settlement of this Town *Hibrahim* died; and, as the Priesthood is hereditary there, *Salumen* his Son, the Father of JOB, became High Priest. About the same Time *Bubaker* the King dying, his Brother *Gelazi,* who was next Heir, succeeded him. *Gelazi* had a Son, named *Sambo,* whom he put under the Care of Salumen, JOB's Father, to learn the *Koran* and *Arabick* Language. JOB was at this Time also with his Father, was Companion to *Sambo,* and studied along with him. *Sambo,* upon the Death of *Gelazi,* was made King of *Futa,* and reigns there at present. When JOB was fifteen Years old, he assisted his Father as *Emaum,* or Sub-priest. About this Age he married the Daughter of the Alpha of *Tombut,* who was then only eleven Years old. By her he had a Son (when she was thirteen Years old) called *Abdolah;* and after that two more Sons, called *Hibrahim* and *Sambo.* About two Years before his Captivity he married a second Wife, Daughter of the Alpha of *Tomga;* by whom he has a Daughter named *Fatima,* after the Daughter of their Prophet *Mahommed.* Both these Wives, with their Children, were alive when he came from Home.

SECT. II.

Of the Manner of his being taken Captive; and what followed upon it, till his Return.

IN *February,* 1730. JOB's Father hearing of an *English* Ship at *Gambia* River, sent him, with two Servants to attend him, to sell two Negroes and to buy Paper, and some other Necessaries; but desired him not to venture over the River, because the Country of the *Mandingoes,* who are Enemies to the People of *Futa,* lies on the other side. JOB not agreeing with Captain *Pike* (who commanded the Ship, lying then at *Gambia,* in the Service of Captain *Henry Hunt,* Brother to Mr. *William Hunt,* Merchant, in *Little Tower-Street, London*) sent back the two Servants to acquaint his Father with it, and to let him know that he intended to go farther. Accordingly, having agreed with another Man, named *Loumein Yoas,* who understood the *Mandingoe* Language, to go with him as his Interpreter, he crossed the River *Gambia,* and disposed of his Negroes for some Cows. As he was returning Home, he stopp'd for some Refreshment at the House of an old Acquaintance; and the Weather being hot, he hung up his Arms in the House, while he refresh'd himself. Those Arms were very valuable; consisting of a Gold-hilted Sword, a Gold Knife, which they wear by their Side, and a rich Quiver of Arrows, which King *Sambo* had made him a Present of. It happened that a Company of the *Mandingoes,* who live upon Plunder, passing by at that Time, and observing him unarmed, rush'd in, to the Number of seven or eight at once, at a back Door, and pinioned JOB, before he could get to his Arms, together with his Interpreter, who is a Slave in *Maryland* still. They then shaved their Heads and Beards, which JOB and his Man resented as the highest Indignity; tho' the *Mandingoes* meant no more by it, than to make them appear like Slaves taken in War. On the 27th of *February,* 1730. they carried them to Captain *Pike* at *Gambia,* who purchased them; and on the first of *March* they were put on Board. Soon after JOB found means to acquaint Captain *Pike* that he was the same Person that came to trade with him a few Days before, and after what Manner he had been taken. Upon this Captain *Pike* gave him leave to redeem himself and his Man; and JOB sent to an Acquaintance of his Father's, near *Gambia,* who promised to send to JOB's Father, to inform him of what had happened, that he might take some Course to have him set at Liberty. But it being a Fortnight's journey between that Friend's House and his Father's, and the Ship failing in about a Week after, JOB was brought with the rest of the Slaves to *Annapolis* in *Maryland,* and delivered to Mr. *Vachell Denton,* Factor to Mr. *Hunt,* before mentioned. JOB heard since, by Vessels that came from *Gambia,* that his Father sent down several Slaves, a little after Captain *Pike* failed, in order to procure his Redemption; and that *Sambo,* King of *Futa,* had made War upon the *Mandingoes,* and cut off great Numbers of them, upon account of the Injury they had done to his Schoolfellow.

Mr. *Vachell Denton* sold JOB to one Mr. *Tolsey* in *Kent* Island in *Maryland,* who put him to work in making Tobacco; but he was soon convinced that JOB had never been used to such Labour. He every Day shewed more and more Uneasiness under this Exercise, and at last grew sick, being no way able to bear it; so that his Master was obliged to find easier Work for him, and therefore put him to tend the Cattle. JOB would often leave the Cattle, and withdraw into the Woods to pray; but a white Boy frequently watched him, and whilst he was at his Devotion would mock him, and throw Dirt in his Face. This very much disturbed JOB, and added to his other Misfortunes; all which were increased by his Ignorance of the *English* Language, which prevented his complaining, or telling his Case to any Person about him. Grown in some measure desperate, by reason of his present Hardships, he resolved to travel at a Venture; thinking he might possibly be taken up by some Master, who would use him better, or otherwise meet with some lucky Accident, to divert or abate his Grief. Accordingly, he travelled thro' the Woods, till he came to the County of *Kent,* upon *Delaware Bay,* now esteemed Part of *Pensilvania;* altho' it is properly a Part of *Maryland,* and belongs to my Lord *Baltimore.* There is a Law in force, throughout the Colonies of *Virginia, Maryland, Pensilvania,* &c. as far as *Boston* in *New England,* viz. That any Negroe, or white Servant who is not known in the County, or has no Pass, may be secured by any Person, and kept in the common Goal, till the Master of such Servant shall fetch him. Therefore JOB being able to give no Account of himself, was put in Prison there.

This happened about the Beginning of *June,* 1731. when I, who was attending the Courts there, and had heard of JOB, went with several Gentlemen to the Goaler's House, being a Tavern, and desired to see him. He was brought into the Tavern to us, but could not speak one Word of *English.* Upon our Talking and making Signs to him, he wrote a Line or two before us, and when he read it, pronounced the Words *Allah* and *Mahommed;* by which, and his refusing a Glass of Wine we offered him, we perceived he was a *Mahometan,* but could not imagine of what Country he was, or how he got thither; for by his affable Carriage, and the easy Composure of his Countenance, we could perceive he was no common Slave.

When JOB had been some time confined, an old Negroe Man, who lived in that Neighbourhood, and could speak the *Jalloff* Language, which JOB also understood, went to him, and conversed with him. By this Negroe the Keeper was informed to whom JOB belonged, and what was the Cause of his leaving his Master. The Keeper thereupon wrote to his Master, who soon after fetch'd him home, and was much kinder to him than before; allowing him a Place to pray in, and some other Conveniencies, in order to make his Slavery as easy as possible. Yet Slavery and Confinement was by no means agreeable to JOB, who had never been used to it; he therefore wrote a Letter in *Arabick* to his Father, acquainting him with his Misfortunes, hoping he might yet find Means to redeem him. This Letter he sent to Mr. *Vachell Denton,* desiring it might be sent to *Africa* by Captain *Pike;* but he being gone to *England,* Mr. *Denton* sent the Letter inclosed to Mr. *Hunt,* in order to be sent to *Africa* by Captain *Pike* from *England;* but Captain *Pike* had sailed for *Africa* before the Letter came to Mr. *Hunt,* who therefore kept it in his own Hands, till he should have a proper Opportunity of sending it. It happened that this Letter was seen by *James Oglethorpe,* Esq; who, according to his usual Goodness and Generosity, took Compassion on JOB, and gave his Bond to Mr. *Hunt* for the Payment of a certain Sum, upon the Delivery of JOB here in *England.* Mr. *Hunt* upon this sent to Mr. *Denton,* who purchas'd him again of his Master for the same Money which Mr. *Denton* had formerly received for him; his Master being very willing to part with him, as finding him no ways fit for his Business. . . .

CONCLUSION;

Containing Some REFLECTIONS upon the whole.

One can't but take Notice of a very remarkable Series of Providence, from the Beginning of JOB's Captivity, till his Return to his own Country. When we reflect upon the Occasion and Manner of his being taken at first, and the Variety of Incidents during his Slavery, which, from slight and unlikely Beginnings, gradually brought about his Redemption, together with the singular Kindness he met with in this Country after he was ransomed, and the valuable Presents which he carried over with him; I say, when all these Things are duly considered, if we believe that the wise Providence of the great Author of Nature governs the World, 'tis natural for us to conclude that this Process, in the divine Oeconomy of Things, is not for nought, but that there is some important End to be served by it.

Our own imperfect Observations have discovered to us innumerable Instances of Design and Contrivance in the natural World; and tho' we cannot assign the immediate Causes and Ends of all the Phenomena of Nature, yet we know enough of them to convince us that the same uniform Design, the same wife and beautiful Order is carried on and maintained throughout the whole. And as there is a manifest Analogy between the Methods of Government in the natural and moral Worlds, so that they seem to be but as different Acts of the same grand Drama; and since the Providence of God is no less certain than his Existence, Chance being as unable to govern a World as to make one; we may safely, and on good Grounds infer, that the various Occurrences in human Life, however inconsiderable or perplex'd they may appear to us, are neither beneath the Care, nor inextricable to the Wisdom of him who rules the Universe: No; they have all their proper Places in the great Scheme; and all conspire in a regular Gradation, to bring about their several Ends, in Subserviency to the whole.

'Tis true, neither the Extent of our Lives nor Capacities will permit us to view any very great Part of the Works of God; and what we do see, we are too apt to put a wrong Construction upon, being unacquainted in a great measure with the secret Springs of Nature, and altogether unable to take in the vast Projects of infinite Wisdom: But the particular Scenes that we are sometime presented with, appear so full of deep Design, and are executed with such divine Art, that they cannot but strike the sober Part of Mankind with Impressions of the highest Wonder, and loudly call for the Attention of a reasonable Being.

History, and our own Experience, furnish us with several amazing Instances of the Conduct of Providence, as well as Nature; which, tho' they cannot be fully or equally accounted for by us, yet may be improved by a well-disposed Mind to very good Purposes; as they serve to increase the high Veneration which we all ought to have for the supreme Lord and Governor of the World, and naturally suggest to us our Dependance upon him; as they tend to confirm our Belief of a Providence, and encourage us to trust our selves intirely in the Hands of our Maker, which is the great Support of every good Man amidst the Calamities of this present Life. In short, as it is very happy for us that the Direction of all Events belongs to God; so we ought to take all Opportunities to excite and strengthen in our selves, and others, a due Sense of his Government, a becoming Regard to his Works, and just Sentiments of the Relation which we bear to him.

With some such Reflections as these JOB used to comfort himself in his Captivity; and upon proper Occasions, in Conversation, would speak very justly and devoutly of the Care of God over his Creatures, and particularly of the remarkable Changes of his own Circumstances; all which he piously ascribed to an unseen Hand. He frequently compared himself to *Joseph;* and when he was informed that the King of *Futa* had killed a great many of the *Mandingoes* upon his Account, he said, with a good deal of Concern, if he had been there he would have prevented it; for it was not the *Mandingoes,* but God, who brought him into a strange Land.

It would be Presumption in us to affirm positively what God is about to do at any Time; but may we not be allowed humbly to hope that one End of JOB's Captivity, and happy Deliverance, was the Benefit and Improvement of himself and his People? His Knowledge is now extended to a Degree which he could never have arrived at in his own Country; and the Instruments which he carried over, are well adjusted to the Exigencies of his Countrymen. Who can tell, but that thro' him a whole Nation may be made happy? The Figure which he makes in those Parts, as Presumptive High-priest, and the Interest which he has with the King of the Country, considering the singular Obligations he is under to the *English,* may possibly, in good time, be of considerable Service to us also; and we have reason to hope this, from the repeated Assurances we had from JOB, that he would, upon all Occasions, use his best Endeavours to promote the *English* Trade before any other. But whatever be the Consequences, we cannot but please our selves with the Thoughts of having acted so good and generous a Part to a distressed Stranger. And as this gives me occasion to recommend Hospitality, I cannot conclude, without saying something in favour of it.

Among the various Branches of Friendship and Beneficence, there is none of a more noble and disinterested Nature, or that tends more directly to the Union, and consequently the Subsistence of the human Species, than that of Hospitality and Kindness to Strangers. In many Instances of private Friendship, we are apt to be guided by our own private Interest; and very often the Exchange of good Offices among Friends, is little better than mere Barter, where an Equivalent is expected on both Sides. In most Acts of Charity and Compassion too, we may be, and very often are wrought upon by the undue Influence of some selfish View, and thereby we destroy in good measure the Merit of them: But in shewing Pity to Strangers, as such, and kindly relieving them in their Distress, there is not such Danger of being influenced by private Regards; nor is it likely that we are so. Here we act for God's sake, and for the sake of human Nature; and we seem to have no Inducement superior to the Will of Heaven, and the Pleasure that results from the Consciousness of a generous Respect for our common Humanity.

There is something singularly sublime, and even God-like, in this benevolent Disposition towards Strangers. The common Parent of the Universe pours out his Blessings daily upon all Mankind, in all Places of the Earth; the Just and the Unjust, the Rich and the Poor, all the Classes, all the Families of human Creatures, subsist by his Bounty, and have their Share of his universal Favours. The good hospitable Man, in his low Sphere, imitates his Maker, and deals about him to his Fellow Mortals with great Chearfulness. He considers his Species in one complex View, and wishes that his Abilities were as extensive as his Inclinations. He does not confine his Benevolence to his Relations, or any particular Party of Men; his Affections are too warm, too general to be thus circumscribed; they must range round the whole Globe, and exert themselves in all Places, where an Opportunity offers.

Such a happy Temper of Mind appeared eminently in those worthy Gentlemen that promoted and encouraged a Subscription for the Relief of JOB; and we hope there are many such Instances of Hospitality among us, which is one very honourable Part of the Character of the *English*.

Questions

1. What does this narrative tell us about the process of enslavement?
2. Some historians have seen the Middle Passage as producing a sharp break between the former lives of slaves and their new life in the New World. On the evidence of this narrative, how traumatic was the break between Africa and Maryland?
3. At the end of this narrative, Diallo's English transcriber suggests that a moral lesson is to be learned from this story. Is it the moral lesson that comes to *your* mind? How might the transcriber's own understanding of the world affect the character of this narrative?

3-8   Early Protests against Slavery: The Mennonites (1688)

The spread of slavery in the English New World pricked few consciences at the time. Slavery had been an ancient institution, supported by what Europeans regarded as ample biblical and natural precedent. Furthermore, Europeans generally were of the belief that certain peoples were "natural" slaves, especially if they were clearly "heathen" and non-European, and if (like most Africans caught up in the trade) they had already been enslaved by others. Thus slavery took root in all the seventeenth-century colonies of English (later British) North America, from Puritan Massachusetts to rice-planting South Carolina. Even in William Penn's Pennsylvania a harsh slave code was enacted, and Quakers (including Penn himself) owned and traded in slaves.

Nonetheless, the institution rested uneasily on the Quaker conscience. Much as Anne Hutchinson did (Document 2-8), Quakers rejected earthly religious authority in favor of the "inner light" of personal religious experience. Insistent that believers had to be free to follow the promptings of the spirit, Quakers found all restrictions on spiritual freedom troubling. Inevitably, this led some to question slavery itself as they came to view the institution both as a stumbling block to salvation for the slave and as a sin for the master. One such group of Quakers was a community of former Mennonites who had migrated to Pennsylvania shortly after its founding and had settled in Germantown (now part of Philadelphia). In February 1688 they penned this petition of protest and forwarded it to the "Monthly," "Quarterly," and "Yearly" Meetings of the Society of Friends. The Yearly Meeting tabled it, and it was quickly forgotten even by antislavery Quakers until it was rediscovered in the nineteenth century. Still, it was a harbinger of things to come.

Source: Peter G. Mode, ed., *Source Book and Bibliographical Guide for American Church History* (Boston: J. S. Canner and Co., 1964), 552–553.

This is to the monthly meeting held at Richard Worrell's:

These are the reasons why we are against the traffic of men-body, as followeth: Is there any that would be done or handled in this manner? viz., to be sold or made a slave for all the time of his life? How fearful and faint-hearted are many at sea, when they see a strange vessel, being afraid it should be a Turk, and they should be taken, and sold for slaves into Turkey. Now, what is *this* better done, than Turks do? Yea, rather it is worse for them, which say they are Christians; for we hear that the most part of such negers are brought hither against their will and consent, and that many of them are stolen. Now, though they are black, we cannot conceive there is more liberty to have them slaves, as it is to have other white ones. There is a saying, that we should do to all men like as we will be done ourselves; making no difference of what generation, descent, or colour they are. And those who steal or rob men, and those who buy or purchase them, are they not all alike? Here is liberty of conscience, which is right and reasonable; here ought to be likewise liberty of the body, except of evil-doers, which is another case. But to bring men hither, or to rob and sell them against their will, we stand against. In Europe there are many oppressed for conscience-sake; and here there are those oppressed which are

of a black colour. . . . Ah! do consider well this thing, you who do it, if you would be done at this manner—and if it is done according to Christianity! You surpass Holland and Germany in this thing. This makes an ill report in all those countries of Europe, where they hear of [it], that the Quakers do here handel men as they handel there the cattle. And for that reason some have no mind or inclination to come hither. And who shall maintain this your cause, or plead for it? Truly, we cannot do so, except you shall inform us better hereof, viz.: that Christians have liberty to practice these things. Pray, what thing in the world can be done worse towards us, than if men should rob or steal us away and sell us for slaves to strange countries; separating husbands from their wives and children. Being now this is not done in the manner we would be done at; therefore, we contradict, and are against this traffic of men-body. . . .

If once these slaves (which they say are so wicked and stubborn men) should join themselves—fight for their freedom, and handel their masters and mistresses, as they did handel them before; will these masters and mistresses take the sword at hand and war against these poor slaves, like, as we are able to believe, some will not refuse to do? Or, have these poor negers not as much right to fight for their freedom, as you have to keep them slaves? . . .

Questions

1. Compare the reference to the "Turks" in this document to that in Benjamin Franklin's essay "On the Slave Trade" (Document 6-14). What purpose does it serve?

2. The petitioners recognize that they have to answer proslavery counterarguments if they are to carry the day. What arguments do they anticipate here?

3. Do you see any similarities between this document and John Winthrop's *Arbella* sermon (Document 2-7)?

Questions for Further Thought

1. Why did the English begin importing slaves into Virginia in 1619? By the end of the seventeenth century, why had race-based chattel slavery become the labor system of choice, especially in the southern colonies and West Indies?

2. What other types of unfree labor existed in the British North American colonies? Compare and contrast these with chattel slavery.
3. Why do you think the Mennonite protesters of Document 3-8 were so isolated? In what way do you see them as representatives of an *American* tradition?

The New Politics of Empire, 1714–1750

Before 1689 the English government ruled most colonies with authoritarian statutes and in accordance with authoritarian principles. After the Glorious Revolution and Queen Anne's War, however, colonial assemblies gained greater autonomy from governors and royal placemen. In addition, there was a growing colonial interest in defining political liberties, some of which were perceived by colonists as different from the deference and patronage of "the English system" of rule (Document 3-10). In everyday business and trade, colonists began to challenge the core of mercantilist tenets; as Document 3-9 shows, the impending Molasses Act of 1733 gave rise to concern about continuing colonial prosperity. The colonies had reached a high level of maturity and independence that they sought to protect as the eighteenth century progressed.

3-9   The Necessity of the West Indies Trade (1732)

Captain Fayrer Hall

When news reached the colonies that Parliament was considering passing what would later be known as the Molasses Act (see text p. 103), few colonists favored its provisions. Even in England international traders and captains familiar with the profitable commerce in the West Indies raised their voices against the new restrictions on colonial transport of Caribbean commodities. One of the many protests heard in a long Parliamentary investigation about the effects of new mercantile regulations was delivered in a speech by Captain Fayrer Hall in 1732.

Source: The New York Gazette, 17–31 July, 1732.

Capt. Fayrer Hall's Evidence before a Committee of the whole House of Commons, in relation to the Trade carried on between our Plantations and the Foreign Colonies. . . .

Capt. Fayrer Hall, you will acquaint the Committee whether you know the Trade between the West-Indies and Northern Colonies?

I have lived in and traded for twenty Years past to the West-Indies, and the Northern Colonies. . . .

What Quantities of Lumber do the French take off [from the northern colonies]?

Martineco, Gardaloupa, Grand-terre, Marigalant & Granada, these Islands all together, I believe, may take off as much, or more than [the British-owned islands] do. . . .

Is there a sufficient Quantity of Molasses made at our [British] Sugar Islands to supply the Northern Colonies?

No, they have a Demand for a much greater Quantity than they can make, for they take all that is made at our own [British] islands, and, if I am rightly informed, as much or more from the foreign Settlements; ever since I remember our People have taken Molasses from [Dutch] Suranam, I believe near as much as they did from all our [British] Islands; and the Demand is so much increased, that the Northern People could use and vend more, if they knew where to get more, even nothwithstanding what they have from the French. . . .

Have our [British] Sugar Islands a demand for all their [northern colonial] Lumber & Horses?

It is impossible; I have known many losing Voyages [from the northern colonies] by sending of Lumber and Horses, and they the [British] Islanders have sent [the unsold portions of the goods] to other Islands. The Northern Colonies are capable of selling and sending a thousand

Times as much [as the British islands can buy]; the District of Land is larger than all Europe.

Supposing they were confined only to sell their Lumber and Horses to our [British] Islands?

It would destroy the Employment of three hundred sail of Ships and Vessels; we have three sail to one of any other Nation's. It is not long ago that the Dutch . . . had ten to our one, but the Act of Navigation put an end to that; we are now what the Dutch were at that Time, we have three sail to one, we are the Carriers as they used to be; but if this [Molasses] Act passes, the French will have the far greater Number of Ships, as we have now. There is no more Difficulty in going to Mississippi, than to our Northern Colonies, and the Passage there will be gained in a quarter of the time; now if we were to suppose that the Passage from Mississippi or Mobile, were to be near twice as long from thence to Martineco, as from Boston to Martineco, the French would be, in all Respects, in a much better Case. And there is no other Reason that they are not supplied from their own [French] Settlements [on the Mississippi River] than that we have got the [business from them first], and at present sell cheaper [goods from the northern colonies]; that is the only Reason the french have not [diverted their trade]. . . .

How is the Ballance [of Payments] in regard to the Northern Colonies? Do they take more Goods [from English merchants] than they send us [from the colonies]?

Yes, they have no other way of paying [English merchants] but by the Remittance of Money which they have from the Dutch & French [trade in the West Indies]. . . .

Supposing the Northern Colonies are not suffered to take their Molasses, will not that put a Stop to the Trade of their Lumber and Horses?

Yes. . . . We receive Money from [the French] now, and we never got so much from any of our own [British] Islands; besides, they produce more Sugar, Rum, and Molasses lately, then they used to do, and Barbados is not so good, it is almost worn out . . . the French have the Advantage of us in their having better Ground, as well as better Management.

Questions

1. What goods did the northern colonists send to the Caribbean, and what did they get in return that was essential for their trade with England? Why would the Molasses Act upset that set of relationships?
2. Why did English authorities fear the trade of northern colonists with foreign islands?
3. What was the significance of the lower Mississippi River trade?

3-10   Governor Alexander Spotswood Tangles with the Virginia Burgesses (1712–1714)

Prior to Bacon's Rebellion (Document 2-6), the colony of Virginia had been dominated by a small, corrupt faction. In the following years, though, the ruling elite in Virginia became broader and less divided. Moreover, the replacement of white servants by African slaves as the plantation work force, coupled with the expanding territory of the colony, offered increasing numbers of small planters the opportunity to achieve some economic independence and to participate in public life, at least as voters. The elite of both the council and the House of Burgesses cultivated these voters, who generally saw their interests—in keeping taxes low, slaves under control, and the power of the mother country at arm's length—coinciding with those of the gentry. The political leadership of the colony, in turn, jealously defended and expanded their prerogatives, and those of their constituents, against the royal governors sent from London. One of those governors, Alexander Spotswood (1676–1740)—a military officer used to being obeyed, not challenged—was to learn his true place the hard way.

Source: R. A. Brock, ed., *The Official Letters of Alexander Spotswood* (Richmond: Virginia Historical Society, 1885), 2: 1–2, 124, 154–155; H. R. McIlwaine, ed., *Executive Journals of the Council of Colonial Virginia* (Richmond: Virginia State Library, 1928), 3: 392.

(a) Letters of Governor Spotswood

To ye Council of Trade, Virginia, October 15, 1712

MY LORDS:

. . . The Indians continue their Incursions in North Carolina, and the Death of Colo. Hyde, their Gov'r, w'ch happened the beginning of last Month, increases the misery of that province, so much weakened already by their own divisions, that no measures projected by those in the Governm't for curbing the Heathen can be prosecuted.

This Unhappy State of her Maj't's Subjects in my Neighbourhood is ye more Affecting to me because I have very little hopes of being enabled to relieve them by our Assembly, which I have called to meet next Week; for the Mob of this Country, having tryed their Strength in the late Election and finding themselves able to carry whom they please, have generally chosen representatives of their own Class, who as their principal Recommendation have declared their resolution to raise no Tax on the people, let the occasion be what it will. This is owing to a defect in the Constitution, which allows to every one, tho' but just out of the Condition of a Serv't, and that can but purchase half an acre of Land, an equal Vote with the Man of the best Estate in the Country.

The Militia of this Colony is perfectly useless without Arms or amunition, and by an unaccountable infatuation, no arguments I have used can prevail on these people to make their Militia more Serviceable, or to fall into any other measures for the Defence of their Country. The fear of Enemys by Sea, (except that of pyrates,) are now happily removed by the peace, (which if on no other acc't than that alone,) ought to be received here as the greatest and most valuable blessing; but the Insurrections of our own Negroes, or the Invasions of the Indians, are no less to be dreaded, while the people are so stupidly averse to the only means they have left to protect themselves Against either of these Events. I shall, for my own part, take all the care I am capable of (under these disadvantages) for the safety of her Ma'tie's Subjects, and still endeav'r to testify to yo'r Lord'ps, that I am, with due respect.

To Mr. Secretary James Stonhope, July 15, 1715
[Secretary of State]

. . . I cannot forbear regretting y't I must always have to do w'th ye Representatives of ye Vulgar People, and mostly with such members as are of their Stamp and Understanding, for so long as half an Acre of Land, (which is of small value in this Country,) qualifys a man to be an Elector, the meaner sort of People will ever carry ye Elections, and the humour generally runs to choose such men as are their most familiar Companions, who very eagerly seek to be Burgesses merely for the lucre of the Salary, and who, for fear of not being chosen again, dare in Assembly do nothing that may be disrelished out of the House by ye Common People. Hence it often happens y't what appears prudent and feasible to his Maj's Governors and Council here will not pass with the Ho. of Burgesses, upon whom they must depend for the means of putting their designs in Execution, the common Topick of Poverty, (w'ch in this Colony is in some measure true,) and the fond hopes y't Dangers, yet a Distance, may vanish of themselves, are excuses sufficient w'th many to save Expence. However, as my general Success hitherto with this sort of Assemblys is not to be Complain'd of, and as I have brought them, in some particulars, to place greater Trust in me than ever they did in any Governor before, and Seeing their Confidence in Me has encreased with their Knowledge of me, I have great hopes to lead even this new Assembly into measures that may be for the hon'r and safety of these parts of his Maj't's Dominions. . . .

To the Lords Commissioners of Trade, May 23, 1716

. . . The behaviour of this Gentleman [Philip Ludwell, Jr.: Auditor] in constantly opposing whatever I have offered for ye due collecting the Quitt rents and regulating the Acc'ts; his stirring up ye humours of the people before the last election of Burgesses; tampering with the most mutinous of that house, and betraying to them the measures resolved on in Council for his Maj't's Service, would have made me likewise suspend him from ye Council, but I find by the late Instructions I have received from his Maj'tie that Power is taken from ye Govern'r and transferred upon the majority of that Board, and while there are no less than seven of his Relations there, it is impossible to get a Majority to consent to the Suspension of him or any other of that kindred. Your Lo'ps no doubt had reason offered for inserting in these Instructions such a Restriction upon the Govern'r as never was contained in any former Instruction, but I beg your Lo'ps to consider how consistent it is with His Maj't's Interest, as ye Case stands here, and how the Restriction agrees with the latter part of the Instruction, since, if a Govern'r cannot suspend a Councillor without the Consent of the Major part of that body, how can he help entering his Reasons on ye Council books, or prevail with them implicitly to joyn with him to degrade one of their own body without their knowing ye Reasons for ye Same, notwithstanding he may have never so just a Cause for keeping them Secret, and I cannot, but with the greatest Submission to y'r Lo'ps' Judgment, think it more advisable that a Gov'r should be entirely restrained from suspending any of the Council than that he should be obliged to seek the Concurrence of a Majority which he is never like to obtain while the Council are so constituted, and thereby expose his Majesty's Authority to the Contempt of those he intended to displace. . . .

(b) Executive Journals of the Council of Colonial Virginia

December the 17th 1714
Present
As before

The Governor this day laying before the Council a letter from the Right Honorable the Lords Commissioners for Trade dated the 23d of April 1713 directing him to advise with the Council & to recommend to the Generall Assembly to pass a law for qualifying the Electors & the persons Elected Burgesses to serve in the Generall Assembly of this Colony in a more just & equal manner than the Laws now in force do direct; and the Governor thereupon desiring the advice of the Council whether he shall now recommend that matter to the House of Burgesses The Council declare that they cannot advise the Governor to move for any alteration in the present method of Electing of Burgesses, some being of opinion that this is not a proper time, & others that the present manner of electing of Burgesses & the qualifications of the Elected is sufficiently provided for by the Laws now in force, & suitable to the circumstances of the Country.

Questions

1. What, specifically, is Governor Spotswood asking the Council of Trade to do? What is the reason for his complaint?

2. From your reading of Governor Spotswood's letter, why did Britain's royal governors have such a difficult time carrying out imperial policy in the colonies?

3. Spotswood notes, with obvious disdain, the influence of "ye Vulgar People" and "ye Common People." Was Virginia becoming more democratic? Explain your answer.

Questions for Further Thought

1. By the early eighteenth century, what social, economic, and political developments in colonial American society might have led some colonists to question their place in the British Empire? In what ways might the colonial view of the empire have become different from that of the royal authorities in Britain? Why?

2. Based on your reading of Documents 3-9 and 3-10, what means did the Crown have to enforce royal authority in the colonies?

3. Judging from these documents, why, from the Glorious Revolution to the mid-eighteenth century, did British authorities more often than not let colonial affairs drift? Why might it have been in their interests to do so?

CHAPTER 4

Growth, Diversity, and Crisis: Colonial Society, 1720–1765

★   ★   ★

Freehold Society in New England

After 1720 the population and economies of the mainland British colonies grew dramatically, and those colonies developed distinctively American characteristics. In New England that distinctiveness was characterized by the existence of communities of independent property owners. In Great Britain, 75 percent of the land was owned by the gentry and nobility; in New England 70 percent was owned by freeholding families. Strategies for maintaining this system varied (Document 4-1).

Although the pattern of land ownership was distinctive, the place of women in rural New England was similar to that in Britain. Women were socialized to accept a subordinate role; their marriage portions were smaller than those of their brothers and they received no land. Women also had few property rights. Although a woman had the right to use a third of the family estate after her husband died, legally it belonged to her children. A woman was expected to be deferential toward her father and then her husband and to work hard to help them. Her work usually included a broad spectrum of household tasks, as well as the bearing and raising of children (Document 4-2).

The stability of the system depended on parents' ability to provide land for their children, but its very success created a crisis. A population of 100,000 in 1700 had grown to 400,000 by 1750, and even though the average birth rate of five to seven children declined to four after 1750, many parents could no longer provide land for their children. Farm communities responded to this crisis in ways that preserved a freehold society: many towns created new communities in frontier areas, and the people who remained increased productivity by introducing new crops and helping one another.

4-1   A New Hampshire Will (1763)

Nicholas Dudley

This document is illustrative of the New England system of inheritance (see text pp. 109–110). The colonial woman's most important legal right was her dower right: under common law a man had to leave his wife at least a life interest in one-third of his real estate, which after her death or remarriage would go to his heirs. At the same time the husband's will was intended to perpetuate the pattern of independent property holding.

Source: The Will of Nicholas Dudley, 1763, in Dean Dudley, *The History of the Dudley Family* (Montrose, Mass., 1894), 1: 242–247.

I Nicholas Dudley give and bequeath to my well-beloved wife Elizabeth Dudley the use and improvement of all my lands in Brentwood called my home place, with the buildings thereon, and also the use and improvement of all my stock of cattle, sheep, swine, and horses, and my quarter part of Deer Hill saw mill, so long as she remains my widow. . . .

I give and bequeath to my son Nicholas Dudley all my right in Deer Hill mill pond during his natural life, and also the improvements of the same to Abigail Dudley, his wife, if she should survive him, so long as she remains his widow. And then the said right in the said mill pond I give, devise, and bequeath to my grandson Nicholas Dudley, son of Trueworthy Dudley, deceased, to be at his disposal forever.

I give to my son John Dudley twenty shillings . . . he having received his portion of my estate.

I give to my son Byley Dudley twenty shillings . . . he having received his portion of my estate.

I give to my son Joseph Dudley and to his four sons . . . all my land in the parish of Epping, called my common right, excepting the fifty acres I sold to Nicholas Gilman.

I give, devise, and bequeath to my daughters Sarah Robinson and Betty Hill, and to my grandson John Dudley, son of Trueworthy Dudley, deceased, their heirs and assigns, forever, after the decease or second marriage of my wife aforesaid all my lands in Brentwood, called my home place, except the mill pond aforesaid, with the buildings thereon, my stock of cattle, sheep, swine, and horses, excepting one cow and also all my out-door moveables after the decease or second marriage of my wife aforesaid. . . .

Questions

1. What actions did Nicholas Dudley take to protect the livelihood of his widow? Why do you think he took those actions?
2. Does he treat his male heirs equally? If your answer is no, why do you think he treats them differently?
3. Does he treat his daughters as beneficiaries?

4-2   The Obligations of a Wife (1712)

Benjamin Wadsworth

This selection comes from a Puritan marriage manual in which the author is attempting to define the duties and obligations of each member of the family, particularly the husband and the wife. It is a good example of what was expected of a deferential wife (see text pp. 108–109).

Source: Benjamin Wadsworth, *The Well-Ordered Family, or Relative Duties* (Boston, 1712), 22–47.

Wives are part of the House and Family, and ought to be under the Husband's Government: they should Obey their own Husbands. Though the Husband is to rule his Family and his Wife yet his Government of his Wife should not be with rigour, haughtiness, harshness, severity; but with the greatest love, gentleness, kindness, tenderness that may be. Though he governs her, he must not treat her as a Servant, but as his own flesh: he must love her as himself. He should make his government of her, as easie and gentle as possible; and strive more to be lov'd than fear'd; though neither is to be excluded. On the other hand, Wives ought readily and cheerfully to obey their Husbands. Wives submit your selves to your own Husbands, be in subjection to them.

Those Husbands are much to blame, who dont carry it [behave] lovingly and kindly to their Wives. O man, if thy Wife be not so young, beautiful, healthy, well temper'd and qualify'd as thou couldst wish; if she brought not so much Estate to thee, or cannot do so much for thee, as some other women brought to or have done for their Husbands; nay, if she does not carry it so well to thee as she should yet she is thy Wife, and the Great God Commands thee to love her, not to be bitter, but kind to her. What can be more plain and express than that? Let every one of you in particular, so love his Wife even as himself. . . . Those Wives are much to blame who dont carry it lovingly and obediently to their own Husbands. O Woman, if thy Husband be not so young, beautiful, healthy, so well temper'd and qualified as thee couldst wish; if he has not such abilities, riches, honours, as some others have; if he does not carry it so well as he should; yet he's thy Husband, and the Great God Commands thee to love, honour and obey him. Yea, though possibly thou hast greater abilities of mind than he has, wast of some high birth, and he of a more mean Extract, or didst bring more Estate at Marriage than he did; yet since he is thy Husband, God has made him thy Head, and set him above thee, and made it thy duty to love and reverence him. . . .

Questions

1. How is a husband expected to behave toward his wife?
2. How is a wife expected to behave toward her husband?
3. Does higher birth, intelligence, or estate alter a wife's obligation to her husband? Why or why not?

Questions for Further Thought

1. What do Nicholas Dudley's will (Document 4-1) and the selection from the Puritan marriage manual (Document 4-2) tell us about the structure of the colonial New England family?
2. What obligations and responsibilities do the different family members have to each other (be sure to consider gender and age)? How does the colonial New England family compare with the American family of today?
3. Based on the readings and your general knowledge of the period, how and in what circumstances was property transferred from father to son? At what point in his life did a father usually pass his property on to his son? How might a son force his father's hand and obtain his inheritance early?

The Mid-Atlantic: Toward a New Society, 1720–1765

Unlike New England, the middle colonies of New York, New Jersey, and Pennsylvania had a mixture of peoples with diverse religious and ethnic backgrounds. Quakers were the dominant group in Pennsylvania and also were highly influential in New Jersey. In the eighteenth century they were followed by three waves of Germans and large numbers of Scots-Irish (Document 4-5). Land was available for the Pennsylvania newcomers. In contrast, the more recent German and Irish immigrants to New York found a scarcity of freehold land and instead were forced to become tenants on large estates

(Document 4-4). Landholding in New York was dominated by the long-established Dutch patronships in the Hudson River Valley, and by a few families holding large tracts that had been granted them by the first English governors.

The middle colonies prospered because of a growing demand for wheat in western Europe; however, by mid-century this prosperity had turned a system offering early equality into one with increasing social divisions. Tensions continued and could sometimes be traumatic, but many ethnic and religious groups developed self-governing churches and created an increasingly open and competitive political system. This religious, ethnic, and political pluralism was a distinctively American phenomenon (Document 4-3).

4-3   A Description of Philadelphia (1748)

Peter Kalm

Probably the most striking features of the British middle colonies of North America were their prosperity, diverse ethnic makeup, and multiplicity of religious forms. The following selection consists of the observations of Peter Kalm, a Swedish naturalist who toured the colonies from 1748 to 1751. During his visit to Philadelphia in 1748 Kalm noted the town's prosperity and its religious and ethnic diversity.

Source: Peter Kalm, *Travels in North America*, trans. John Reinhold Forester (London, 1770), 1: 36–43, 58–60.

The town is now quite filled with inhabitants, which in regard to their country, religion, and trade, are very different from each other. You meet with excellent masters in all trades, and many things are made here full as well as in England. Yet no manufactures, especially for making fine cloth, are established. Perhaps the reason is, that it can be got with so little difficulty from England, and that the breed of sheep which is brought over, degenerates in process of time, and affords but a coarse wool.

Here is great plenty of provisions, and their prices are very moderate. There are no examples of an extraordinary dearth. Every one who acknowledges God to be the Creator, preserver, and ruler of all things, and teaches or undertakes nothing against the state, or against the common peace, is at liberty to settle, stay, and carry on his trade here, be his religious principles ever so strange. No one is here molested on account of the erroneous principles of the doctrine which he follows, if he does not exceed the above-mentioned bounds. And he is so well secured by the laws in his person and property, and enjoys such liberties, that a citizen of Philadelphia may in a manner be said to live in his house like a king.

On a careful consideration of what I have already said, it will be easy to conceive how this city should rise so suddenly from nothing, into such grandeur and perfection, without supposing any powerful monarch's contributing to it, either by punishing the wicked, or by giving great supplies in money. And yet its fine appearance, good regulations, agreeable situation, natural advantages, trade, riches and power, are by no means inferior to those of any, even of the most ancient towns in Europe. It has not been necessary to force people to come and settle here; on the contrary, foreigners of different languages have left their country, houses, property, and relations, and ventured over wide and stormy seas, in order to come hither. Other countries, which have been peopled for a long space of time, complain of the small number of their inhabitants. But Pennsylvania, which was no better than a desert in the year 1681, and hardly contained five hundred people, now vies with several kingdoms in Europe in number of inhabitants. It has received numbers of people, which other countries, to their infinite loss, have either neglected or expelled.

Questions

1. What factors does Kalm believe were the most significant in accounting for Philadelphia's rapid rise to prominence?
2. What is Kalm's perception of the religious environment in Philadelphia?
3. In Kalm's view, has the immigration to Philadelphia of people neglected in or expelled from other colonies and countries had a positive effect? Why or why not?

4-4   Class Structure in New York (1765)

Cadwallader Colden

Cadwallader Colden, lieutenant governor of New York from 1761 to 1776, lived in America for fifty-six years. Merchant, writer, scientist, philosopher, and politician, he was a perceptive observer of colonial life. Colden's attitudes can be discerned in this description of the class structure in New York. Unlike observers such as Crèvecoeur (see text p. 280), Colden did not view America as a classless society.

Source: Cadwallader Colden, "State of the Province of New York" (1765), in *Collections of the New-York Historical Society* (1878), 10: 68–69.

The people of New York are properly Distinguished into different Ranks.

1. The Proprietors of the large Tracts of Land, who include within their claims from 100,000 acres to above one Million of acres under one Grant. Some of these remain in one single Family. Others are, by Devises and Purchases claim'd in common by considerable numbers of Persons.

2. The Gentlemen of the Law make the second class in which properly are included both the Bench and the Bar. Both of them act on the same Principles, and are of the most distinguished Rank in the Policy of the Province.

3. The Merchants make the third class. Many of them have rose suddenly from the lowest Rank of the People to considerable Fortunes, and chiefly by illicit Trade in the last War [French and Indian War]. They abhor every limitation of Trade and Duty on it, and therefore gladly go into every Measure whereby they hope to have Trade free.

4. In the last Rank may be placed the Farmers and Mechanics. Tho' the Farmers hold their Lands in fee simple, they are as to condition of Life in no way superior to the common Farmers in England; and the Mechanics such only as are necessary in Domestic Life. This last Rank comprehends the bulk of the People, and in them consists the strength of the Province. They are the most useful and the most Morall, but allwise made the Dupes of the former; and often are ignorantly made their Tools for the worst purposes.

Questions

1. What factors determined the distinctions of rank in Colden's New York?
2. According to Colden, which rank is the most "useful" to the province? Why?
3. For which rank does Colden have the least regard? Why?

4-5   Letter from a Scots-Irish Immigrant (1767)

Job Johnson

In the eighteenth century the character of colonial immigration shifted. As New England became increasingly crowded, and as slave plantations came to dominate the southern colonies, the relatively open middle colonies became the destination of choice for European newcomers to America. Furthermore, a large proportion of the new migrants were non-English. Germans fled from increased crowding and religious persecution, but the greatest immigrant stream now came from the "Celtic fringe" of the British Isles, especially the Presbyterian inhabitants of Scotland and Ulster (Northern Ireland). The latter group, the Scots-Irish, had been recruited to colonize Ulster in the seventeenth century. By the eighteenth century, however, that land was overpopulated, English landlords were raising rents, taxes were rising, and Ulster manufactures were being shut out of English markets. Accordingly, the Scots-Irish began a massive exodus to the New World. Settling at first in Pennsylvania, they soon came to dominate that colony's western frontier and from there spread southward into the backcountry of the southern colonies.

The letter excerpted below was written by Job Johnson, an Ulster immigrant, who arrived in the 1760s and settled near the Susquehanna River to the west of Philadelphia.

Source: Alun C. Davies, "'As Good a Country as Any Man Needs to Dwell In': Letters from a Scotch-Irish Immigrant in Pennsylvania, 1766, 1767, and 1784," *Pennsylvania History* 50 (October 1983): 318–321.

Oxford Township, November 27th 1767.
My Very dear Brethern,
Not being willing to neglect any opportunity that I have in my power to writ unto you, I have thought proper to address myself to you all in a few lines hopeing that they may find you all in good Health, as thanks be to God they Leave Me. . . . I wrote seven letters home last year . . . but I do not know whether or not you have Got them, and I have Got No answer therefore I have nothing further to writ; only knowing that it is common [   ] at home to expect something Concerning this Country its property and Quality, therefore this is Really my Judgement of it, that it is as Good as Country as any Man needs to Dwell in; and it is Much better than I expected it to be in every way I assure you, and I really likes it so well and it is so pleasant to me that it would be a good Estate in Ireland that would Make Me Stay there, and indeed many times when I have been by myself and think of the Lord's Good Dealings unto Me, I cannot but admire him for his Mercies that ever he turned My face hitherward; and Give Me strength and Confidence in himself and boldness by faith, to oppose all Gainsayers, though never so strong, although I cannot say that then, it seemed so Clear for Me to leave the land of My Nativity. Yet Now to Me it is a Certainty that My Removal was right and in what I Did I had peace, and in all My exercises by sea and Land, I never felt the Least in Me, as to Desire I had not come forward, but rather rejoiced

(Turn over) in the Midst of them all. My Brother was not so clear in these things untill he had Been a year in the Country, Which indeed is Mostly the Case, with all the first year after they Come here: but Blessed be God all is well to our content. And if one heard every objection that lay in the way of Coming here, it would be work enough. But My resolutions were, and my sayings to several opposers, that I would come, if God hindered me not no Man should. And I do not know one that has come here that Desires to be in Ireland again, for to Live there and I have often wondered at our Countryfolk that was hard of belief in regard of what was said of their Country, and would rather live in Slavery, and work all the year round, and not be threepence the better at the years end than stir out of the Chimney Corner and transport themselves to a place where with the like pains, in two or three years, they might know better things. The only encouragement that I had to Come away was because Many Go to America worth nothing yet some of them servants and to hear or see them Come back again, in two or three years worth more than they would have been by staying at home while they lived and yet they would Not Content themselves at home, but went back again which was sufficient to Convince any one that the Country was Good. But there are Many in Ireland that Desire to hear ill of this place, because they would keep their friends there with them, in Bondage and Slavery, rather than let them come here, and they think we never writ enough of the Bad properties of this Country and the Vermin in it. Now this I must say in report that there are Bears, Wolves & Foxes, Rattles snakes, and several other such creatures, but Not in this part as ever I seen, as I have Travelled Many Miles to & fro. But I suppose the fear of those Creatures in Ireland is far worse to Some there, than the hurt of them is here. But I believe that this Province of Pennsylvania by all I have see and heard of it, is a Good a one as any in America. I have seen in all places I have travelled, Orchards Laden with fruit to admiration, their very Limbs torn to pieces with the weight, and Most Delicious to the Taste I have seen a Barrel of Curious Cyder from an apple tree; and peaches in Great plenty. I could Not but at first smile at the Conceit of them, they are a very Delicate fruit, and hang almost like our onions that are tied on a rope. . . . And indeed this is a Brave Country, although no place will please all. And some may be ready to say I writ of Conveniences; but not of Inconveniences; My answer to those I honestly Declare there is some barren Land; as, I suppose there is in Most places of the World; and Land in this part is very high, selling Commonly at six and seven pounds per acre. Neither will such land Produce Corn without something to buy them. Not Bread will not be got with Idleness else it would be a Brave Country indeed, and I Question not, but all them would give it a Good word. For my part I never would had the Least thought of returning home only through regard of seeing you all again. . . .

Questions

1. According to Job Johnson, what are the attractions of Pennsylvania? What did Pennsylvania have to offer the Scots-Irish immigrant that was worth his breaking his ties to the land of his birth?
2. What special concerns does Johnson feel the need to address? What rumors about America does he attempt to dispel?
3. How do you think Johnson's letter was received back home in Ulster?

Questions for Further Thought

1. The remarks about society in the middle colonies expressed in these documents (4–3, 4–4, and 4–5) were all made by observers born outside America. How might the different backgrounds of Peter Kalm, Cadwallader Colden, and Job Johnson have colored their views?
2. Compare and contrast society in the middle colonies with that of New England and the South. In what ways are the regional blocks of colonies different, and how can we account for this? What made the middle colonies unique, and why?
3. On the other hand, in what ways were all the British American colonies similar? From your readings, is it possible to establish a common ground that united colonists from South Carolina to Massachusetts?

The Enlightenment and the Great Awakening, 1740–1765

As the societies of British North America were transformed from relatively simple frontier communities to complex but distinctive extensions of Europe, they began to participate in the religious and intellectual movements of the larger European world. Two powerful continental movements in particular transformed the cultural and intellectual life of the colonies. The Enlightenment emphasized the power of human reason and had its roots in the scientific revolution of the seventeenth century. If any single individual epitomized the American Enlightenment, it was Benjamin Franklin (Document 4-6); if any single place was its center, it was Franklin's Philadelphia.

The second movement was more spiritual in nature. As some Americans were abandoning, or at least revising, an older religious world view, many more were embracing a new one. Pietism, which came to America from Europe with German immigrants in the 1720s, led to religious revivals throughout the colonies. Little concerned with formal theology, it emphasized moral behavior and a mystical union with God. Charismatic preachers such as Theodore Jacob Freylinghuysen, William and Gilbert Tennant, and Jonathan Edwards played key roles in the revivals. From 1739–1741, the powerful British evangelist George Whitefield preached to huge audiences throughout the colonies, knitting local revivals together into a single movement subsequently known as the Great Awakening.

The Great Awakening was a social upheaval that created controversy and divided churches, leading to the creation of new congregations. It also inspired its adherents to question the need for religious taxes, the idea of an established church, the authority of ministers, and the morality of economic competition (Documents 4-7 and 4-8).

4-6   On Education during the American Enlightenment (1749)

Benjamin Franklin

Benjamin Franklin was one of colonial America's outstanding examples of the influence of Enlightenment ideas (see text pp. 122–123). In the document that follows, Franklin proposes methods for the education of colonial youth that departed dramatically from the founding generations' more modest attention to training in the "domestic arts" or a trade. Franklin's proposal resulted in the creation of an academy in Philadelphia in 1751.

Source: Benjamin Franklin, *Proposals Relating to the Education of Youth in Pensilvania, Philadelphia* (1749; facsimile reprint, edited by William Pepper, Philadelphia: University of Pennsylvania, 1931).

"Proposals Relating to the Education of Youth in Pensilvania, Philadelphia," 1749.

It has long been regretted as a Misfortune to the Youth of this Province, that we have no Academy, in which they might receive the Accomplishments of a regular Education . . . the Sentiments and Advice of Men of Learning, Understanding, and Experience. . . .

The good Education of Youth has been esteemed by wise Men in all Ages, as the surest Foundation of the Happiness both of private Families and of Commonwealths. Almost all Governments have therefore made it a principal Object of their Attention, to establish and endow with proper Revenues, such Seminaries of Learning, as might supply the succeeding Age with Men qualified to serve the Publick with Honour to themselves, and to their Country. . . .

It is propos'd

That some Persons of Leisure and publick Spirit apply for a Charter, by which they may be incorporated, with Power to erect an Academy for the Education of Youth, to govern the same, provide Masters, make Rules, receive Do-

nations, purchase Lands, etc., and to add to their Number, from Time to Time such other Persons as they shall judge suitable.

That the Members of the Corporation make it their Pleasure and in some Degree their Business, to visit the Academy often, . . . advance the Usefulness and Reputation of the Design; that they look on the Students as in some Sort their Children, treat them with Familiarity and Affection. . . .

That a House be provided for the Academy, if not in the Town, not many Miles from it . . . having a Garden, Orchard, Meadow, and a Field or two.

That the House be furnished with a Library . . . with Maps of all Countries, Globes, some mathematical Instruments, an Apparatus for experiments in Natural Philosophy, and for Mechanics; Prints, of all Kinds, Prospects, Buildings, Machines, etc.

That the Rector be a Man of good Understanding, good Morals, diligent and patient, learn'd in the Languages and Sciences, and a correct Speaker and Writer of the English Tongue; to have such Tutors under him as shall be necessary. . . .

As to their Studies, it would be well if they could be taught every Thing that is useful, and every Thing that is ornamental: But Art is long, and their Time is short. It is therefore propos'd that they learn those Things that are likely to be most useful and most ornamental. . . . All should be taught to write a fair Hand, and swift . . . Drawing . . . Arithmetick, Accounts . . . Geometry and Astronomy.

The English Language might be taught by Grammar; in which some of our best Writers, as Tillotson, Addison, Pope, Algernoon Sidney, Cato's Letters, etc. should be Classicks. . . .

Antient Customs, religious and civil . . . Morality, be descanting and making continual Observations on the Causes of the Rise or Fall of any Man's Character, Fortune, Power etc. . . . the Advantages of Temperance, Order, Frugality, Industry, Perseverance etc. . . .

While they are reading Natural History, might not a little Gardening, Planting, Grafting, inoculating, etc., be taught and practised; and now and then Excursions made to the neighbouring Plantations of the best Farmers. . . . The History of Commerce, of the Invention of Arts, Rise of Manufactures, Progress of Trade, Change of its Seats . . . will be useful to all. And this, with the Accounts in other History of . . . Engines and Machines used in War, will naturally introduce a Desire to be instructed in Mechanicks, and to be inform'd of the Principles of that Art by which weak Men perform such Wonders, Labour is sav'd, Manufactures expedited, etc. . . .

With the whole should be constantly inculcated and cultivated, that Benignity of Mind, which shows itself in . . . Good Breeding; highly useful to the Possessor, and most agreeable to all. . . .

Questions

1. According to Franklin, why should young colonial men attend school when there are many practical reasons not to?
2. What are the things young Pennsylvanians should be learning?
3. How does Franklin reconcile public service, the benefits of classical learning, and the necessity of practical training for young people in the colony?

4-7 An Evangelical Preacher's Trials (1760s)

The Reverend James Ireland

Of all the preachers who introduced the evangelical gospel into the southern colonies, James Ireland (1748–1806) has left perhaps the fullest account of his conversion, labors, and trials. Born in Edinburgh, he was raised as a Presbyterian and educated as a lawyer, but he came to Virginia as a young man to serve as a schoolmaster. At first Ireland cut a fine figure in local gentry society, joining the Masonic order and becoming well known for his dancing skill. However, on encountering the Baptists and their message, he underwent an emotional conversion and abandoned his former way of life. The sharpness of the break is shown in the confrontation that opens this document.

After becoming a Baptist minister, Ireland preached extensively throughout the Virginia Piedmont, stirring opposition from both the clergy of the established Church of England and the local gentry. In 1769 the latter briefly jailed him at Culpeper Court House, a place where he had engaged in an earlier controversy with the local parson. The persecution he suffered from "the politest part of the people," though, he contrasted with the piety, tolerance, and religious diversity of the newer settlements of the Shenandoah Valley. Predominantly composed of Scots-Irish and Germans moving southwestward from Pennsylvania, these backcountry settlers were introducing a new sensibility into the southern colonies, and a new source of social division as well.

Source: The Life of the Rev. James Ireland (Winchester, Va.: J. Foster, 1819), 82–86, 130–135, 157–160, 181–185.

It comes now into my way to make some remarks about a man whom I referred to some pages back, and from whom I expected to receive some information relative to my parents and relations. Although a friendship existed between his father's family and my father's family, yet he never was an associate and companion of mine, by reason of the disparity of years between us; yet upon the remembrance of past family acquaintance from the instant of seeing each other, we conceived and preserved a singular affection for each other. He was a member of that fraternity [Freemasonry] to which I hinted before, I had joined; and was very instrumental in persuading me thereunto; he at the same time possessing the highest place in that society. The news of my awakening impressions, had diffused itself through every part of the settlement and its vicinity. It became the topic in all companies that "James Ireland was going to be mighty good now, for he is going to get converted." My acquaintance had not seen me for some short period, previous to my soul's distresses. There was a dance appointed to be held the Monday following, at a wealthy neighbour's house. My countryman in company with others, hearing the remarks they were making about me, and being tolerably dissipated in language at times, swore they need not believe any thing about it, for there could not be a dance in the settlement without my being there, and if they would leave it to him, he would convert me, and that to the dance, on Monday; and they would see me lead the ball that day. The deep impressions upon my soul had a very considerable influence upon my exterior appearance of body; that wild vivacity that flashed in my eyes, and natural cheerfulness that appeared in my countenance, was entirely gone; my eyes appeared solemn and heavy, my flesh began to pine away, my ruddy cheeks and countenance had vanished, and all that remained was a solemn gloomy paleness, whilst my head was often hanging down like a bulrush, under the internal pressure of my guilty state. This my friend, who had bound himself under an oath that he would convert me to the ball, had never yet seen. Determined however to prosecute his purpose, which I had also been informed of, disposed me to expect a visit from him, in which he did not deceive me. He came to my school house; being there myself, I heard the noise of a creature's feet some little distance from me, which disposed me to look about, and soon I descryed the rider to be my friend, coming to see me. Being fully persuaded he would use all the influence he was master of, to persuade me to his wishes, I was seized with a momentary panic, which disposed me to lift up my heart to the Lord, and implore him not to suffer any reasonings he could use to have the least influence upon my mind, as also that the Lord would direct some word or other, that might be for his benefit. When I viewed him riding up, I never beheld such a display of pride in any man, before or since, as I beheld in him at that juncture, arising from his deportment, attitude and jesture, he rode a lofty elegant horse, and exhibited all the affectation possible, whilst his countenance appeared to

me as bold and daring as satan himself, and with a commanding authority called upon me, if I were there to come out, which I accordingly did, with a fearful and timorous heart. But O! how quickly can God level pride to the ground, if he does but once touch the heart, as was soon manifested in him. In a few minutes did the person, who, no doubt, made sure, as he came to visit me, of making an easy conquest of me, find, that the race is not to the swift nor the battle to the strong. For no sooner did he behold my disconsolate looks, emaciated countenance and solemn aspect, than he instantly appeared, as if he was riveted to the beast he rode on; his passions were so powerfully impressed, that I conceived he would have fainted and dropped from his horse.

For some short space of time, he was past utterance, and did nothing but stare at me with wild amazement. As soon as he could articulate a little his eyes fixed upon me, and his first address was this; "In the name of the Lord, what is the matter with you?" To which I replied if he would light, from his horse, and come into the house, I would tell him. I stepped into the house before him, begging of the Lord to direct my speech unto him; his surprise and consternation still attending him, he repeated his former expression; "In the name of the Lord what is the matter with you?" I instantly took him by the hand, and with a tender heart, and tears streaming from my eyes, spoke to him as follows. "My dear friend I possess a soul that will be either happy or miserable in the world to come; and God has been pleased to give me a view of the worth of my soul, as also of the guilty and condemned state it lies in by reason of sin; and I plainly see that if my soul is not converted, regenerated and born again, I will be damned." Holding my hand fast in his, and looking at me, with all the eagerness of desire, he burst out into the following words—"O! you will not leave me nor forsake me now." To which I answered that "I would not, upon condition he would renounce his former wicked ways, as I had done, and seek God through Jesus Christ, for pardon and salvation to our poor souls." To which he replied, with streaming eyes, "from that moment forward, through the strength of the Lord Jesus Christ, he would." His convictions were formed that very instant; and from my knowledge of him, meeting often by appointment to pray together to God for the salvation of our souls, I am satisfied that his impressions never subsided until he came to a well grounded hope of an interest in the salvation of God, through the merits of the precious Redeemer. . . .

. . . At that time the Church of England Parsons were exalted in domination over all dissenters in the colony, as it was then called, of Virginia. The dissenters had to pay their proportion for the building of Churches, and sixteen thousand weight of tobacco annually for the support of those Clergymen, exclusive of building their own houses for worship, supporting their own Ministers, and being precluded the benefit of marrying the members of their own society, except they procured and paid to the Church

Parson of their Parish a full marriage fee for each couple. And this galling yoke continued on the necks of the dissenters until some time after our glorious revolution took place.

The Church Parson in Culpepper County had made it a practice, where any of those Baptist Preachers would have an appointment for preaching, to go in person to those meetings, taking some aids with him, who were as much prejudiced against that sect as he was. Being a man of rapid flow of misrepresentation and persecution, upon religious subjects, would by his dogmatical manner, appear frequently to an audience he would address, to gain his point and acquire the mastery over his opponents.

This personage attended at Capt. McClanagan's in order to detect the falsity of Mr. Pickett's doctrines before his parishioners. Being acquainted with Mr. Pickett's disposition and turn of mind, I felt very uneasy that day, when I saw the position the Parson took. The place Mr. Pickett was to preach in, was pretty capacious for the congregation; the parson had a chair brought for himself, which he placed three or four yards in front of Mr. Pickett, on which he seated himself, taking out his pen, ink and paper, to take down notes of what he conceived to be false doctrine. By the countenance of Parson Meldrum's Parishioners, they appeared to be highly elated, under an assured expectation of his baffling the new light, as they called him. I discovered it was some embarrassment to Mr. Pickett, and impeded his delivery, but I possessed a confidence that he preached the truth, and nothing but the truth, which could be supported and defended against its enemies.

As soon as Mr. Pickett had finished his discourse, the Parson called him a schismatick, a broacher of false doctrines, and that he held up damnable errors that day. Mr. Pickett answered him with a great deal of candour, and supported the doctrines he had advanced, to the satisfaction of all those who were impartial judges of doctrine. He was a man slow in argument, and when contradicted it would in a measure confuse him, which I soon observed, by some points he advanced, in which, in my judgment, he was perfectly right. The Parson at the same time, I observed, was taking notes of what the other said, which made me careful to retain it on my memory, standing close by Mr. Pickett when he spoke. The notes the Parson took, were absolutely the reverse of what Mr. Pickett delivered, and the Parson asserting them with dogmatical precision, and his parishioners exulting in the same, I could not forbear immediately interfering. . . .

Understanding he had been raised a Presbyterian, before he commenced Episcopalian, I formed the plan of entering into a discourse with him. First, upon the doctrines of religion, and secondly, upon the practice of it. This was with a view to endeavour to gain his consent that what he called damnable errors were consistant with gospel principles and practices. . . .

However, I discovered that pursuing the argument was and would be at the risque of incurring the displeasure of

both gentlemen and ladies of his society, and perhaps the greater bulk of them. They would look at me with the utmost contempt and disdain, supposing it no doubt, presumption in such a youth as I, to enter into an argument with the teacher of the county. In the course of our argument, they would repeatedly help him to scripture, in order to support his arguments, which made me observe to them that they did not treat me with common justice, that I had none that helped me, whilst they were supplying their Pastor with every help they could afford. . . .

I immediately got up and addressed one of the gentlemen who had been so officious in helping his teacher; he was a magistrate at that time, and one of those who afterwards committed me to prison. I addressed him in this manner, "Sir, as the dispute between the Parson and myself is ended, if you are disposed to argue the subject over again, I am willing to enter upon it with you." He stretched out his arm straight before him, at that instant, and declared I should not come nigher than that length. I concluded what the consequence would be, therefore made a peaceable retreat.

Mr. Pickett's next meeting was to be contiguous to Col. Easom's, in an old field under some comfortable shades. It being on the Lord's day, the Parson had to attend his parish church, so that we met with no opposition from that quarter, but we it from another; as the congregation was very large, amongst them there were abundance of negroes the patrolers were let loose upon them, being urged thereto by the enemies and opposers of religion. Never having seen such a circumstance before, I was equally struck with astonishment and surprise, to see the poor negroes flying in every direction, the patrolers seizing and whipping them, whilst others were carrying them off prisoners, in order, perhaps, to subject them to a more severe punishment. Meeting being concluded, Mr. Pickett, with myself and a number of others from our parts, that had come over to this day's meeting, took our leave of each other that evening, and returned to our respective settlements. . . .

. . . I went on that evening to Capt. Thomas McClanahan's, a worthy gentleman at whose house I had the dispute with the church parson: there I was informed that if I preached next day at Mr. Manifa's, I should be taken by squire Strother and squire Slaughter. I sat down and counted the cost, freedom or confinement, liberty or a prison; it admitted of no dispute. Having ventured all upon Christ, I determined to suffer all for him. Next morning I set off for Mr. Manifa's, at whose house I was to preach, accompanied with the capt. and his whole family. When I arrived at the place of preaching, Mr. Manifa addressed me thus, "Sir, you may expect to be taken up to day, if you preach, a certain fine (I am told) will be imposed upon you, and so much upon each individual that will attend your preaching, as well as a fine of twenty pounds on me for granting you my house to preach in. This the justices have made me acquainted with, and have advised me for my own advantage, not to suffer the meeting."

Mr. Manifa being a man under awakening impressions, told me not to flinch from my duty, if I thought it a duty, to go on. I requested him to show me the line of his land, ordered a table to be taken out and placed with its feet on each side of the line; whether it might have answered any purpose or not, I cannot tell. However I told him, that when I stood on the table I would not preach on his land no more than on anothers.

Preaching being over, and I concluding with prayer, heard a rustling noise in the woods, and before I opened my eyes to see who it was, I was seized by the collar by two men whilst standing on the table. Stepping down off the table, and beholding a number of others walking up, it produced a momentary confusion in me. The magistrates instantaneously demanded of me, what I was doing there with such a conventicle of people? I replied that I was preaching the Gospel of Christ to them. They asked who gave me authority so to do? I answered, he that was the author of the Gospel, had a right to send forth whom he had qualified to dispense it. They retorted upon me with abusive epithets, and then enquired of me if I had any authority from man to preach? I produced my credentials, but these would avail nothing, not being sactioned and commissioned by the Bishop. They told me that I must give security not to teach, preach or exhort, for twelve months and a day, or go to jail. I choose the last alternative. The magistrates then addressed their neighbours and informed them that they were open to law, but there the preacher stands on one side, and here we stand on the other; and as we believe you have been deceived by him, if you will confess it by coming over from the side where he is, to our side, we will take that act as your concession, and the law will not be put in force against you. The people were much incensed against the magistrates, and told them that they had heard nothing preached but the Gospel of Christ, and that if they had not money to pay their fines, they were willing to go to jail also. The magistrates were much mortified at seeing the ill will they had got from their neighbours, and their ignorance being by me, at the same time exposed before the congregation.

I gave security to attend court in a few days, which I accordingly did. By the complexion of the courts I saw there was no liberty for me. There were eleven magistrates sat as a quorum. They brow-beat me, mall treated me, and throwed out the most approbrious appellations against me—would admit of no defence I could make, but ordered me to hold my tongue, and let them hear no more of my vile, pernicious, abhorrible, detestable, abominable, diabolical doctrines, for they were naucious to the whole court. I found it of no consequence to defend myself any further, since imprisonment was inevitable, and they were determined to make an example of me.

I delivered up my riding horse to a friend to take care of him that night, and apply to me next day for further instructions. The sheriffs were ordered to attend me to my little limbo, with a considerable parade of people, with such vollies of oaths and abuse as if I were a being unfit to exist on the earth. A very uncomfortable night I passed, in consequence of the oaths &c. that continued through the same. Sticks and stones they were throwing during the whole night upon me. . . .

From what has been said, you cannot help taking notice of the awful darkness which overspread Virginia at that time; although in speaking of it more particularly I shall divide it into three districts of country, and touch upon the general character of the inhabitants of each, so far as I was then, and shortly afterwards, acquainted with them.

The first, from the blue ridge of mountains down towards the bay, they were considered as the politest part of the people, prior to any spread of the Gospel therein. Religion was a subject that did not concern their minds, unless it was in their opposition against those who felt the earliest impressions of it; they resigned and gave up their spiritual concerns to the guidance and direction of their spiritual guides: like *priest* like *people,* they appeared all to be in the ditch, put their trust in men, and made flesh their arm. Scarcely a persecution took place, in that quarter, but had a Priest at the head of it, and received the hearty concurrence of their parishoners.

In early stages of my ministry, I made a visit almost down to the Bay; in that course of preaching, I travelled a considerable distance, and met with exceeding few that had any desire for the conversion of their souls.

From reasons heretofore assigned in my narration, I shall not discuss the circumstances attending my journey any further than mentioning a few particulars which I shall blend together.

Opposition attended me every where; in the time of preaching, one body of the congregation would be calling out to the other to whip the fellow off the ground; half a dozen of fists would be drawn at a time, when I expected to be knocked down every minute; sailors were brought on shore from their vessels, through the influence of the people, in order to take me out into the stream, hoist me up to the yards arm and so to give me a ducking. At other places public teachers would, after sermon, introduce controversies, principally on the ordinance of baptism, which I would undertake accordingly to the mortification of those who introduced them; by which their congregations were convinced of the propriety of believing baptism by immersion.

Without any more animadversion, there was always a party in favour of the cause I had espoused; often soliciting me to visit them again: and when ever the Lord was pleased to form any opening upon their minds, it was surprising to see how docile and tractable they were to receive instruction. They were a people possessing good parts naturally; all that they wanted for religious advancement, and divine improvement, was the quickening, awakening, convincing and divine teaching of the holy spirit, attended with the heart changing and efficacious grace of God upon their souls, which was opening upon them at that period, and many of them soon manifested divine progress, in the ways of Jesus.

The prisons, in divers places, were honoured with the poor despised preachers: however their situations were much more comfortable than mine; because none were precluded from visiting them; none of those punishments inflicted on me attended them; whilst several of them at a time would be in company together, by which means, they proved a mutual comfort and establishment to each other. By comparing their situation with mine already given, the reader may easily draw inferences from the premises.

Being two hundred miles from my residence, I longed to be back among those called my own people; that being the *second* division, which lays between the Blue Ridge and Alleghany mountains. The people inhabiting these valleys, were better informed, arising from the following considerations: they were a divided people as to religious persuasions, consisting of Baptists, Presbyterians, Methodists, Quakers, Menonists, Tunkers and Churchmen, with a va-riety of others. As persecution was not a reigning principle among them, and they lived in a common state of sociability, it gave them an opportunity of being acquainted with each other's principles and practices, by which their *ideas* became more enlarged, and their *judgments* more generally informed than those of the first division.

With regard to the *third* division, who lived beyond the Alleghany mountains, in our western settlements, it would be hard for one to give a proper description of them, until time and opportunity of action, would enable such to form a correct opinion. But as kind providence had allotted, under the Blue Ridge, through all the courses and windings of this valley, (between the Ridge and Alleghany) and from the other side of the Alleghany down upon the Ohio, to be the sphere of my ministerial labours, and public services put in my power, were it necessary, I could give a full detail respecting them. When I went among them, I found them to be an uncultivated people; the farther I went back the more rude and illiterate they were: I often thought they constituted a compound of the barbarian and the indian; although I found among them, a number of respectable and well behaved people. . . .

Questions

1. Why did the Baptists and other evangelical sects pose such a threat to the established religious order in colonial Virginia? How might the threat have been social as well as religious?
2. How are Ireland's attitudes toward slaves shaped by his religious beliefs?
3. To what does Ireland attribute what he describes as the greater tolerance of peoples living in the western valleys of Virginia? How might this illuminate for you the origins of the religion clause of the First Amendment to the U.S. Constitution?

4-8   Reaction against the Great Awakening (1742)

Charles Chauncy

Though at first welcoming the Great Awakening, Old Light ministers began denouncing a movement that was, it seemed to them, unhinging reason and order. A leader of the Old Light reaction was Charles Chauncy, a Congregational minister of the First Church in Boston (see text p. 125). Chauncy's religious views, as revealed in the following excerpt from one of his sermons, were strongly influenced by the Enlightenment and in many respects resembled those of Benjamin Franklin. His attack on religious enthusiasm reflects an educated gentleman's disgust at the New Lights' attacks on the rational learning of the orthodox clergy and an intellectual conservative's suspicion of the emotional hysteria of the lower classes, the divisive effect of revivalism on churches and communities, and challenges to authority.

Source: Charles Chauncy, *Enthusiasm Describ'd and Caution'd against* (Boston, 1742), 3–7.

[The] Enthusiast is one who has a conceit of himself as a person favored with the extraordinary presence of the Deity. He mistakes the workings of his own passions for divine communications, and fancies himself immediately inspired by the Spirit of God, when all the while, he is under no other influence than that of an overheated imagination.

The cause of this enthusiasm is a bad temperament of the blood and spirits; 'tis properly a disease, a sort of madness, and there are few, perhaps none at all, but are subject to it; though none are so much in danger of it as those in whom melancholy is the prevailing ingredient in their constitution. . . .

And various are the ways in which their enthusiasm discovers itself. Sometimes, it may be seen in their countenance. A certain wildness is discernable in their look and air, especially when their imaginations are moved and fired. Sometimes, it strangely loosens their tongues and gives them such an energy, as well as fluency and volubility in speaking, as they themselves, by their utmost efforts, can't so much as imitate, when they are not under the enthusiastic influence. . . . Sometimes, it appears in their imaginary peculiar intimacy with heaven. They are, in their own opinion, the special favorites of God, have more familiar converse with Him than other good men, and receive immediate, extraordinary communications from Him. . . . And what extravagances, in this temper of mind, are they not capable of, and under the specious pretext, too, of paying obedience to the authority of God? . . . But in nothing does the enthusiasm of these persons discover itself more than in the disregard they express to the dictates of reason. They are above the force of argument. . . . And in vain will you endeavor to convince such persons of any mistakes they are fallen into. . . .

Questions

1. According to Chauncy, what are the causes of religious enthusiasm?
2. Which manifestations of that enthusiasm does Chauncy find disturbing? Why do you think they upset him?
3. As a minister, why is Chauncy so disturbed by the revivalist belief in direct contact with God?

Questions for Further Thought

1. In what ways did the ideas of the Enlightenment and the Great Awakening challenge the authority of the established social and cultural order of colonial American society?
2. Since the seventeenth century, New England's Congregational ministers had been preaching jeremiads warning their members to revitalize their faith, but in the 1730s and 1740s, many of the Old Light clergy like Boston's Charles Chauncy rejected the enthusiastic religious upsurge of the Great Awakening. Why was this so?
3. Why did Americans in the eighteenth century embrace both religion and science with equal fervor? What was it about pietistic religion and Enlightenment rationalism that Americans found so attractive, and why?

The Midcentury Challenge: War, Trade, and Social Conflict, 1750–1765

In the years 1740–1765, the British Empire in North America was redefined by three sets of events: the French and Indian War, an expansion of transatlantic trade that increased prosperity but raised colonial debt, and a great westward movement.

In the late 1740s, a shortage of land and the influx of immigrants into the middle and southern colonies brought pressure for expansion, leading to a clash between Britain and France for the interior of North America. At first the war in America went badly for the British (Document 4-9). When William Pitt the Elder became first minister in 1757, he devised a strategy that turned the conflict into a great war for empire. The turning point in North America was the British capture of Quebec in 1759; the war ended with the reduction of the French Empire in North America to a handful of islands.

As the colonial population continued to expand, serious land shortages led to conflicts over land rights, Indian policy, law and order, and political representation. For example, Connecticut fought with Pennsylvania over settlement in the Wyoming Valley. In Pennsylvania, conflicts between Scots-Irish immigrants along the frontier and the Quaker political establishment stirred violence and nearly led to civil war (Document 4-10). Such conflicts also led to frontier rebellions in North Carolina and South Carolina (Document 4-11).

4-9 Report to Governor Robert Dinwiddie of Virginia on the Defeat of General Braddock (1755)

George Washington

The French and Indian War began in the Ohio Valley in 1754 when Robert Dinwiddie, Virginia's royal governor, dispatched a force of militiamen under the command of Colonel George Washington to secure British claims. Britain then sent Sir Edward Braddock and two regiments of troops to America. In May 1755 a small force of French and Indians launched an attack and killed Braddock and half his men. The following account by Washington, the commander of the Virginia militia, describes this disastrous defeat of combined British-Virginian forces (see text p. 134). Washington's original spelling and punctuation have been preserved.

Source: In W. W. Abbot, ed., *The Papers of George Washington, vol. 1: Colonial Series, 1748–August 1755* (Charlottesville: University of Virginia Press, 1983), 339–340.

As I am favour'd with an oppertunity, I should think myself inexcusable, was I to omit givg you some acct of our late Engagemt with the French on the Monongahela the 9th Inst.

We continued our March from Fort Cumberland to Frazer's (which is within 7 Miles of Duquisne) witht meetg any extraordinary event, havg only a stragler or two picked Up by the French Indians. When we came to this place, we were attackd, (very unexpectedly) by abt 300 French and Indns; Our number's consisted of abt 1300 well armd Men, chiefly regular's, who were immediately struck with such a Panick, that nothing but confusion and disobedience of order's prevaild amongst them: The Officer's in genl behavd with incomparable bravery, for which they greatly sufferd, there being near 60 killd and woundd A large proportion out of the number we had! The Virginian behavd like Men, and died like Soldier's; for I believe out of 3 Companys that were that Day, scarce 30 were left alive: Captn Peyrouny and all his Officer's down to a Corporal, were killd; Captn Polson shard almost as hard a Fate, for only one of his Escap'd: In short the dastardly be-

haviour of the Regular Troops exposd all those who were inclin'd to do their duty, to almost certai[n] death; and at length, in despight of every effort to the contrary, broke & run as Sheep before Hounds, leavg the Artillery, Ammunition, Provisions, Baggage & in short every thing a prey to the Enemy; and when we endeavourd to rally them in hopes of regaining the ground and what we had left upon it was with as little success as if we had attempted to have stopd the wild Bears of the Mountains or rivulets with our feet, for they wd break by in spite of the every effort that could be made to prevent it.

The Genl was wounded in the Shoulder, & the Breast; of wch he died three days after; his two Aids de Camp were both wounded, but are in a fair way of Recovering; Colo Burton and Sir Jno St Clair are also wounded, and I hope will get over it; Sir Peter Halket, with many other brave Officers were killd in the Field; [I luckily escapd with a wound, tho I had four Bullets through my Coat and two Horses shot under me:] It is supposed that we had 300 or more killed in the Field; abt that number we brought of wounded; and it is conjectured (I believe with much truth) that two thirds of both receiv'd their shott from our own cowardly Regulars, who gatherd themselves into a body contrary to orders 10 or 12 deep, woud then level, Fire, & shoot down the Men before them.

I Tremble at the consequences that this defeat may have upon our back setlers, who I suppose will all leave their habitation's unless their are proper measures taken for their security.

Questions

1. To what factors does Washington attribute the shattering defeat of the Anglo-Virginian force?
2. What is Washington's assessment of the performance of the British regulars? Of the Virginia militia?
3. What consequences does Washington predict will result from this defeat?

4-10   Protests on the Frontier I: The Paxton Riots (1764)

In December 1763 a group of frontiersmen from Paxton Township, Pennsylvania, fell upon a small, peaceful group of Conestoga Indians, killing six. When the magistrates of nearby Lancaster sheltered the Native American survivors in the workhouse, a mob invaded the town, broke into the workhouse, and murdered fourteen more Indians. Soon after, two hundred of the "Paxton Boys" marched on Philadelphia in pursuit of Indian refugees there; civil war was averted only by the diplomacy of Benjamin Franklin and others, who promised a hearing for the Paxton grievances if the men would return home.

The Paxton incident brought to a focus numerous tensions resulting from frontier expansion, the increasingly multiethnic character of Pennsylvania, and continued tight control of the colony by the Penn family and the Quaker elite of Philadelphia. All of these tensions are displayed vividly in this early manifesto, circulated along the frontier and reproduced in a pamphlet written by one of their defenders. Compare with Document 2-6.

Source: Thomas Barton, "The Conduct of the Paxton-Men, Impartially Represented . . . ," in John R. Dunbar, ed., *The Paxton Papers* (The Hague: Martinus Nijhoff, 1957), 269–275. (*Note:* Footnotes are from the original document.)

For my Part, I am no Adept in Politicks, and have but seldom troubled my Head about that Science, beyond the reading of a common News-Paper.—It has long been my unhappy Lot to be a Spectator of the Distresses and Sufferings of my Fellow Subjects; my Heart has often bled for them;—and I should still have continued a secret Mourner for what I had not Power to redress, had not the unaccoutable [sic] Conduct of your City Quakers provoked me to speak my Sentiments, and unburthen myself to my Friend.—By my Principles as well as Situation in Life, you know, my dear Sir, that I have no political Ends to serve; that I have nothing to hope or fear from Party Connections; and that I can have no other View in troubling you with this Letter than to rescue the miserable Frontier People, who lately rose in Arms, from the Infamy and Odium thrown upon them, by *those* whose unfeeling Hearts have never suffered them to look beyond their own private Interest and Party.[1]

The INSURGENTS themselves hand about a Kind of *Manifesto,* which contains the following Declaration, Grievances, Complaints, &c.—viz.

---

[1] The Author of this Letter, hopes he will not be understood as approving of these People's having taken up Arms. Such violent Steps can never possibly be productive of anything, but WILD UPROAR and CONFUSION. Whatever therefore can have a Tendency to promote this; or that offers the *least Insult* to the LAWS and GOVERNMENT of this Country, he will ever think it his Duty to bear his Testimony against, and to discountenance by every Means in his Power.

"That a trifling Dispute, between a few English and French Traders upon the *Ohio,* was neglected; the profer'd Mediation and Assistance of the Indians to end the Quarrel, and the Proprietary-Offer of £. 400, for erecting a small Fortification there, together with £. 100 yearly, towards the Support of it, were contemptuously rejected, till it kindled the Flames of War, which at last spread and raged over half the Globe.—That from the Neglect of the *Legislative Part* of this Province, and the horrid Doctrines of *Non-Resistance* at that Times so strenuously maintain'd, such Calamities ensued, that near *one Hundred Miles* of as thriving a Settlement as any in Pennsylvania has been reduced to Desolation; many of the Inhabitants murdered or carried into Captivity, and the Rest often drove from their Habitations in the utmost Distress and Want.—And besides these particular Effects of this War, some of the best Blood in Christendom has been spilt in it—whole Kingdoms have been almost depopulated; and Misery and Ruin entail'd upon Millions of their Fellow Creatures.

"That even in the Midst of this Desolation and Carnage, every publick Measure was clogg'd—the King's Demands for Men and Money procrastinated—unnecessary, or at least ill-timed Disputes, about *Proprietary Instructions and Taxes,* were brought upon the Carpet, in Order to divert the Reproach and Dishonour which the Province, thro' Quakers Measures, had incurr'd, and throw the whole Blame of the War at the Proprietary Doors. And that this villainous Scheme might carry with it a better Face, the late infamous TEDYUSCUNG[2] was treated with, and employed to charge the Proprietaries with having defrauded the Indians of some Lands, and to declare that this was the Occasion of all their Uneasiness and Enmity to the *English.*—But infamous as TEDYUSCUNG was, he own'd at lastt [sic] that his Complaints were unjust; publickly renounc'd his Claim, and declared in open Treaty that he was urged to act this base Part, and that he was only the *Mouth of some Persons* in Philadelphia, whom he did not chuse to name.

"That they have always manifested, and are still upon every occasion ready to manifest their Allegiance and Loyalty to their most gracious Sovereign King GEORGE, whom they have ever esteemed as the kind and careful Father of his People.

"That tho' born to Liberty, and all the glorious Rights and Privileges of BRITISH SUBJECTS, they were denied Protection, at a Time when the Cries of Murder and Distress might have made the very Stones relent; and tho' roused to Vengeance and eager to maintain and defend their Lives and sacred Rights, their Hands were basely tied up!

"They could obtain no proper Law to collect their Strength; nor any Sanction or Encouragement to pursue the Enemies of their Country!

"That they have suffered and bled in the Cause of their Country, and have done more to protect it from the Violence of a rapacious Enemy than any others in the Province.

"That agreeable to the Command of the Prophet, they have 'fought for their Brethren, their Sons, and their Daughters, their Wives and their Houses.'—That in this Context, many of them have lost their dearest Relatives; their Houses, their Lands, their all; and from a plentifull independent People have been reduced to Misery and Want.

"That they have been treated as *Aliens* of the Common-Wealth, and denied a just and *proportionable Share in Legislation:* For that out of 36 Members which the eight Counties in the Province send to Assembly, the three Counties of *Philadelphia, Chester* and *Bucks,* where the Quakers are chiefly settled, return 26 of that Number; while the 5 remaining Counties, where these LORDLY RULERS could have no Chance of getting elected, are suffered to send but the other Ten.

"That by this iniquitous Policy, the Inhabitants of these five Frontier Counties, altho' a great Majority, have been rendered unable to act in Defense of their Lives and Properties; and therefore have lain for above eight Years at the Mercy of a cruel Savage Enemy and an unrelenting Quaker Faction: Whereas had they been justy [sic] represented in Legislation, instead of presenting PACIFICK ADDRESSES to the Assembly, telling them that 'the raising large Sums of Money, and putting them into Hands of COMMITTEES, who might apply them to Purposes inconsistent with their PEACEABLE TESTIMONY, was in its Consequences destructive of RELIGIOUS LIBERTY.' Instead of doing this, I say,—the first great Law of Nature, that of SELF-DEFENCE, would have been administred to the People upon the first Alarm of Danger, and the Hands of the HARDY and the BRAVE would have been set at Liberty, till they had taken ample Vengeance of their MURDERERS.

"That they have often, in the most suppliant Manner, laid their Grievances before the Assembly; and instead of being redress'd, have been abused, insulted, and even by some Members of that *venerable House,* deem'd as unworthy of Protection, as 'A Pack of insignificant SCOTCH-IRISH, who, if they were all *killed* could well enough be spared.[3]

"That whilst they were thus abused, and thus stript of their Birth-Rights,—ISRAEL and JOSEPH,[4] two petty Fellows, who ought to have no higher Claims than themselves, were permitted to lord it over the Land; and in Contempt of the Government, and the express Orders of the Crown, for-

---

[2]Teedyuscung: 1700?–1763. Delaware chief. After Braddock's defeat he assembled the Delawares and Shawnees in Wyoming Valley to fight the whites. He was pacified by treaties at Easton in 1756 and 1757.

[3]This unchristian and ungenerous Speech was made by N———L G———B, a Quaker, Member of Assembly for *Chester* County, and some others.

[4]Israel Pemberton and Joseph Fox. This refers to their work as leaders in The Friendly Association.

biding them to hold private Treaties with the Indians, exchange Belts of Wampum with them—make them Presents—all this they have done, and in their own Name, without so much as including the simple MENONISTS, from whom they had extorted large sums of Money to Support this Expence.——Nay, even with the most matchless Impudence, insinuated to the Indians that they were Rulers and Governors; as plainly appear'd at the late Treaty at LANCASTER, where the Principal CHEIF [sic] and SPEAKER told Mr. H———N,[5] then Governor, 'That as he understood there were two GOVERNORS in the Province, he would be glad to know which of them he was to treat with.'[6]

"That the Indians were induced to look upon ISRAEL as the *first* Man, or CHEIF [sic] SACHEM of the Province, from seeing the Haughtiness and Contempt with which he treated his Fellow Subjects, and his insolent and arrogant Behaviour to Sir W———M J———N[7] at *Easton;* and to Governor H———N, at *Lancaster:* And that this, among other Things, has been productive of manifold Evils, by weakening our Credit with Indians, frustrating the good Intention of holding Treaties with them, and encouraging them, after they return'd from us loaded with Money, Cloaths, Arms and Ammunition, to look with Contempt upon us as a pusillanimous Pack of *old Women,* divided among ourselves, without SPIRIT or RESOLUTION to call them to an Account, let them commit what Outrages they pleased upon us.——

"That they have been made Tributaries to support the immense Expence of Indian Treaties; to which they chearfully submitted, in Hopes that their dear Relations and Fellow Subjects, who have been long detained in barbarous Captivity, would have been restored; But that instead of insisting upon the Promises and Engagements made by the Indians to this End, an extensive and valuable Trade was opened with these faithless and perfidious Villains; and their poor unhappy Friends left to spend perhaps the Remainder of their days, in all the Sorrow and Miseries of Heathenism and Barbarity, and to bow their Necks to the cruel Slavery of Savages.

---

[5]James Hamilton.

[6]That you may be convinced that such was the Opinion of the *Indians,* I must observe to you, that one PATRICK AGNEW, of the Borough of *Lancaster,* White-Smith, having been duly sworn upon the HOLY EVANGELISTS, before the CHIEF BURGESS of that Town, hath deposed and said, That he, the said Deponent, being a Constable at the last Indian Treaty at Lancaster, was commanded by the *Governor,* to proclaim, that no Person should sell or give any Kind of spirituous Liquors to the Indians, on any Pretence whatever; that he proclaim'd this Order thro' the Town accordingly, and that upon his making Proclamation, and saying, *by Order of the Governor,* an Indian named TEDYUSCUNG, cry'd out 'D—n your G———r, D—n your G———r; P—m—t-n is my Governor, P—m—t-n is our Governor, he allows RUM enough;' and offer'd Violence to this Deponent; who also, upon his Oath, declares that, notwithstanding the Proclamation, the Indians were privately entertain'd at a certain Tavern in the Town.

[7]Sir William Johnson.

"That at a Time when their ungenerous and merciless Enemies, had again, without the least provocation, invaded the Province, with the very Arms and Ammunition which they received at the late Treaties; and when the Frontiers were yet reeking with the Blood of their slaughter'd Inhabitants; and the murdered Ghosts of their Friends and Relatives cry'd aloud for Vengeance, a Number of Indians (many of which were concerned in this horrid Butchery) were escorted to the *Metropolis,* and there protected, cherished, and maintained in Luxury and Idleness, whilst they, the poor Sufferers, were abandoned to Misery, and left to starve, or beg their Bread.

"That upon seeing themselves thus abused and thus neglected, and considering that the Influence of a *Quaker Faction* was the Source from whence all these Evils flow'd; and that *pretended* Scruples against War and Fighting were the Root from whence all their Calamities and heavy Sufferings sprang, and if yet permitted, might produce worse and more heavy, they were determined to bear no longer.

"That *Pennsylvania* appear'd to them to be really in a dangerous CACHEXY;[8] and that at such a Crisis they look'd upon it as their Duty to administer such Remedies (however severe they might be look'd upon by some) as might raise her drooping Head, and restore her to Health and Vigour.——And should their first Trial fail of Success, that in the Case they are determined to *double the Potion,*[9] which they hope will intirely purge off the peccant Humours, restore the Solids, and secure her hereafter from the Infection of *Quaker Non-Resistance.*"

Such is the Declaration, and such the Complaints of these People.——And indeed nine Tenths of the Inhabitants of the Back-Counties either tacitly, or openly, approve and support them—Every cool and well thinking Man, as well as Men among themselves, are sensibly concern'd that they were reduced to the Necessity of having Recourse to such Methods as might be deem'd an Insult to the Government and Laws of their King and Country.

The Names of RIOTERS, REBELS, MURDERERS, WHITE SAVAGES, &c. have been liberally and indiscriminately bestowed upon them: But all this they look upon only as the Effects of disappointed Malice, and the Resentment of a destructive FACTION, who see their *darling Power* in Danger.——The *Merciful* and the *Good* however, they trust, will rather pity than condemn them.—And they are pleased with the Thoughts that they have been able at last to lay bare the PHARASAICAL BOSOM OF QUAKERISM, by obliging the NONRESISTING QUALITY to take up Arms, and to become Proselytes to *the first great Law of Nature. . . .*

---

[8]Depraved condition of the body politic.

[9]By this Expression, I am told, these People mean, that they will renew their Application and ADDRESSES, with DOUBLE the NUMBER of Signers; and it is said, they are likely to get TEN to ONE, that they had before, to remonstrate with them.

Questions

1. What do we learn about mid-eighteenth-century Pennsylvania politics from the Paxton manifesto? What sorts of social, economic, political, and religious issues divided the colony?
2. What grievances does the author of the manifesto articulate? Where does he lay the blame for the conflict, and why?
3. Why do you think the author of the manifesto feels the need to state explicitly the loyalty of the Paxton Boys to King George?

4-11   Protests on the Frontier II: The North Carolina Regulators (1769)

While tensions were rising on the Pennsylvania frontier, other conflicts were brewing farther to the south. By the close of the French and Indian War, when the Proclamation Line of 1763 defined the extent of British jurisdiction on the frontier, thousands of new farms and villages dotted the countryside, not only in Pennsylvania but also in western Virginia and the backcountry of North and South Carolina. Many of these people had just arrived from Scotland, Ireland, Wales, and Germany, although a significant number also came from the older coastal settlements. Everywhere on this developing frontier, people struggled to define political institutions and challenged the dominant elites of the coastal regions. Sometimes this strife erupted into violent conflict between the judges, sheriffs, and tax collectors who attempted to enforce imperial laws and the frontier settlers who rejected them. In North Carolina, a so-called Regulator group arose to voice, and often act on, the concerns of backcountry settlers, and by the early 1770s its members were engaged in a virtual civil war with the Tidewater authorities. The Regulators were smashed in 1774 at the Battle of Alamance Creek, but the conflict left a legacy of bitterness that would severely complicate later Patriot efforts to gain independence from Great Britain (see Document 6-10).

Source: "To the INHABITANTS of the Province of North-Carolina," Salisbury, North Carolina, September 14, 1769, in William K. Boyd, ed., *Some Eighteenth Century Tracts Concerning North Carolina* (Raleigh, N.C.: Edwards & Broughton Company, 1927), 301–304.

"To the INHABITANTS of the Province of *North-Carolina*"

Dear Brethren,

Nothing is more common than for Persons who look upon themselves to be injured than to resent and complain. These are sounded aloud, and plain in Proportion to the Apprehension of it. Our Fearfulness too, frequently augment our real as well as apparent Dangers. Let us adjust our Complaints or Resentments to the Reality as well as the Nature of the Injury received.

Excess in any Matter breeds Contempt; whereas strict Propriety obtains the Suffrage of every Class. The Oppression of inferior Individuals must only demand Tutelage of superiors; and in civil Matters our Cries should reach the authorative Ear, when the Weight that crusheth from the higher Powers. —But when imposed by the Populace, to the Populace our complaints must extend. —When therefore the Cry of any City, Province or Nation is general, it must be generally directed to the Source from whence the Cry is caused.

The late Commotions and crying Dissatisfactions among the common People of this Province, is not unknown nor unfelt by any thinking Person. —No Person among you could be at a Loss to find out the true Cause. —I dare venture to assert you [are] all advised to the Application of the Public Money; —these you saw misapplied to the enriching of Individuals, or at least embezzled in some way without defraying the publick Expenses. Have not your Purses been pillaged by the exorbitant and unlawful Fees taken by Officers, Clerks, &c. —I need not mention the intolerable expensive Method of Recovery by Law, occasioned by the narrow Limits of the inferior Court's Jurisdiction. —Have you not been grieved to find the Power of our County Courts so curtailed, that scarce the Shadow of Power is left. This Body, however respectable, is intrusted with little more than might pertain to the Jurisdiction of a single Magistrate, or at least two or three Justices of the Peace in Conjunction. —In Consequence of this, very small Sums drags us to Superior Courts. —These must be attended with all our Evidences, altho many at the Distance of 150 Miles. Add to this a double Fee to all Officers; Hence we are made feelingly sensible, that our necessary Expenses, with the additional Costs, are equal, if not surpass the original Sum.

For what End was the Jurisdiction of the Courts reduced to such narrow Limits? Is it not to fill the Superior Houses with Business? Why has the Authority fallen upon this wonderful Expedient? Is it not evident, that this was calculated for the Emolument of Lawyers, Clerks, &c. What other Reason can be assigned for this amazing Scheme? —none Brethren, none! . . .

The Exorbitant, not to say unlawful Fees, required and assumed by Officers, —the unnecessary, not to say destructive Abridgement of a Court's Jurisdiction, —the enormous Encrease of the provincial tax unnecessary; these are Evils of which no Person can be insensible, and which I doubt not has been lamented by each of you. It must have obliged you to examine from what Quarter Relief might be found against these sad Calamities —In Vain will you search for a Remedy until you find out the Disease.

Many are accusing the Legislative Body as the Source of all those woful Calamities. —These, it must be confessed, are the instrumental Cause; they can, yea do impose some of these heavy Burdens. —But whence received they this Power? Is not their Power delegated from the Populace? The original principal Cause is our own blind stupid Conduct.

If it be queried, How doth our Conduct contribute to this? Answer presents itself—we have chosen Persons to represent us to make Laws, &c. whose former Conduct and Circumstance might have given us the highest Reason to expect they would sacrifice the true Interest of their Country to Avarice, or Ambition, or both.

I need not inform you, that a Majority of our Assembly is composed of Lawyers, Clerks, and others in Connection with them, while by our own Voice we have excluded the Planter. —Is it not evident their own private Interest is,

designed in the whole Train of our Laws? —We have not the least Reason to expect the Good of the Farmer, and consequently of the Community, will be consulted, by those who hang on Favour, or depend on the Intricacies of the Laws. —What can be expected from those who have ever discovered a Want of good Principles, and whose highest Study is the Promotion of their Wealth; and with whom the Interest of the Publick, when it comes in Competition with their private Advantages, is suffered to sink? —nothing less than the Ruin of the Publick. . . . Doth not Reason declare we might expect such cringing Vassals would readily sacrifice the Interest of the Community to the Idol Self? . . . .

But you will say, what is the Remedy against this malignant Disease?

I will venture to prescribe a sovereign one if duly applied; that is, as you have now a fit Opportunity, choose for your Respresentatives or Burgesses such Men as have given you the strongest Reason to believe they are truly honest: Such as are disinterested, publick spirited, who will not allow their private Advantage once to stand in Competition with the publick Good. . . . Let your Judgment be formed on their past Conduct; let them be such as have been unblamable in Life, independent in their Fortunes, without Expectations from others; let them be such as enjoy no Places of Benefit under the Government; such as do not depend upon Favour for their Living, nor do derive Profit or Advantage from the intricate Perplexity of the Law. In short, let them be Men whose private Interest neither doth nor can clash with the Interest or special Good of their Country.

Are you not sensible, Brethren, that we have too long groaned in Secret under the Weight of these crushing Mischiefs? How long will ye in this servile Manner subject yourselves to Slavery? Now shew yourselves to be Freemen, and for once assert your Liberty and maintain your Rights—This, this Election let us exert ourselves, and show, that we will not through Fear, Favour or Affection, bow and subject ourselves to those who, under the Mask of Friendship, have long drawn Calamities upon us. . . .

Have they not monopolized your Properties; and what is wanting but Time to draw from you the last Farthing? Who that has the Spirit of a Man could endure this? Who that has the least Spark of Love to his Country or to himself would bear the Delusion?

In a special Manner then, let us, at this Election, rose all our Powers to act like free publick spirited Men, knowing that he that betrays the Cause now betrays his Country, and must sink in the general Ruin . . . .

Salisbury, [North Carolina], September 14, 1769

Questions

1. What are the Regulators' major grievances? Do they sound anything like the grievances colonists express against imperial authorities during the Revolutionary crisis?
2. What kind of people do the Regulators oppose—what kind of character do they have, what kind of occupations do they have, and what makes them so different from the frontiersmen writing this document?
3. What do the Regulators mean when they write about a "public good"? What do they mean by "self interest"?

Questions for Further Thought

1. What do Documents 4-9, 4-10, and 4-11 tell us about the social makeup of the American backcountry in the mid-eighteenth century?
2. What tensions existed along the American frontier? Why at mid-century did they often flare into violence?
3. Frequently, pre–Revolutionary War violence in the American backcountry was sparked by conflicts between white settlers and local Indians. In many instances— as with the Paxton riots—the backcountry settlers believed that their colony's government had not acted to protect their interests. Why might the settlers have thought this? Do you think that they were correct? Why or why not?

CHAPTER 5

Toward Independence: Years of Decision, 1763–1775

★   ★   ★

The Reform Movement, 1763–1765, and *The Dynamics of Rebellion, 1765–1766*

In 1763 the British Empire, which included almost forty colonies, was magnificent in its scope and potential (see Map 5.1 on text p. 147). However, as the textbook (pp. 146–148) shows, the empire had problems. British statesmen were aware that the established mainland colonies of North America had a history of circumventing British regulation and control. With the mother country deeply in debt, it was evident that imperial reform was required and that Britain's New World colonists would have to pay more of the cost of running the empire. Document 5-1, Jared Ingersoll's report on British attitudes and the debate in Parliament over the passage of the Stamp Act, reveals what British politicians believed about the logic of taxing the colonists and about the issue of their constitutional right do so.

The other documents in this section illustrate the nature of the colonial response to the Stamp Act. As is demonstrated in the textbook (pp. 152–155), crowd actions played a crucial role in the colonists' attack on the Stamp Act. Indeed, Thomas Hutchinson's account of his confrontation with such a crowd (Document 5-2) reminds us that significant crowd actions occurred even before the Stamp Act was scheduled to take effect. Such actions, which occurred throughout the colonies in 1765, effectively blocked the implementation of the Stamp Act—for the moment.

The colonists' ultimate goal was to have Parliament repeal the new revenue laws. To achieve that end, their weapon of choice was the economic boycott (see text pp. 152–153). The agreement signed in New York (Document 5-3) describes how the boycott was organized. The resolutions of the Norfolk, Virginia, Sons of Liberty (Document 5-4) describe some of the measures that were employed to get the Stamp Act repealed. To further their cause, the colonial governments, which were notorious for quarreling with each other, held an intercolonial congress. The "Declarations" of the Stamp Act Congress (Document 5-5) enunciated the colonists' essential position on both the Stamp Act and the issue of imperial reform. The "Declarations" also clearly reflect the roots of the colonists' ideology.

5-1   Report on the Debates in Parliament (1765)

Jared Ingersoll

Jared Ingersoll, a Connecticut lawyer who was in Great Britain on business, accepted a commission from his home colony to do what he could to oppose the Stamp Act, which it appeared Parliament would soon pass. By communicating with Thomas Whately, who played a central role in the drafting of the bill, Ingersoll obtained a few minor modifications. However, he could not persuade British officials to abandon the idea of passing a Stamp Act for America.

As part of his effort to oppose the Stamp Act, Ingersoll attended the debates on the proposed legislation in Parliament. On February 11, 1765, he sent a lengthy report on those debates to Thomas Fitch, the governor of Connecticut. The sections of that letter reprinted here describe the general British attitude and the attitudes of different segments of Parliament toward the Stamp Act.

Source: New Haven Colonial Historical Society, *Papers* (1918), 9: 306–315, passim.

The principal Attention has been to the Stamp bill that has been preparing to Lay before Parliament for taxing America. The Point of the Authority of Parliament to impose such Tax I found on my Arrival here was so fully and Universally yielded, that there was not the least hopes of making any impressions that way. Indeed it has appeared since that the House would not suffer to be brought in, nor would any one Member Undertake to Offer to the House, any Petition from the Colonies that held forth the Contrary of that Doctrine. I own I advised the Agents if possible to get that point Canvassed that so the Americans might at least have the Satisfaction of having the point Decided upon a full Debate, but I found it could not be done, and here before I proceed to acquaint you with the Steps that have been taken, in this Matter, I beg leave to give you a Summary of the Arguments which are made Use of in favour of such Authority.

The House of Commons, say they, is a branch of the supreme legislature of the Nation, and which in its Nature is supposed to represent, or rather to stand in the place of, the Commons, that is, of the great body of the people, who are below the dignity of peers; that this house of Commons Consists of a certain number of Men Chosen by certain people of certain places, which Electors, by the Way, they Insist, are not a tenth part of the people, and that the Laws, rules and Methods by which their number is ascertained have arose by degrees and from various Causes and Occasions, and that this house of Commons, therefore, is now fixt and ascertained and is a part of the Supreme unlimited power of the Nation, as in every State there must be some unlimited Power and Authority; and that when it is said they represent the Commons of England, it cannot mean that they do so because those Commons choose them, for in fact by far the greater part do not, but because by their Constitution they must themselves be Commoners, and not Peers, and so the Equals, or of the same Class of Subjects, with the Commons of the Kingdom. They further urge, that the only reason why America has not been heretofore taxed in the fullest Manner, has been merely on Account of their Infancy and Inability; that there have been, however, not wanting Instances of the Exercise of this Power, in the various regulations of the American trade, the Establishment of the post Office etc., and they deny any Distinction between what is called an internal and external Tax as to the point of the Authority imposing such taxes. And as to the Charters in the few provinces where there are any, they say, in the first place, the King cannot grant any that shall exempt them from the Authority of one of the branches of the great body of Legislation, and in the second place say the King has not done, or attempted to do it. In that of Pensilvania the Authority of Parliament to impose taxes is expressly mentioned and reserved; in ours tis said, our powers are generally such as are *According to the Course of other Corporations in England* (both which Instances by way of Sample were mentioned and referred to by Mr. Grenville in the House); in short they say a Power to tax is a necessary part of every Supreme Legislative Authority, and that if they have not that Power over America, they have none, and then America is at once a Kingdom of itself.

On the other hand those who oppose the bill say, it is true the Parliament have a supreme unlimited Authority over every Part and Branch of the Kings dominions and as well over Ireland as any other place, yet we believe a British parliament will never think it prudent to tax Ireland. Tis true they say, that the Commons of England and of the british Empire are all represented in and by the house of Commons, but this representation is confessedly on all hands by Construction and Virtually only as to those who have no hand in choosing the representatives, and that the Effects of this implied Representation here and in America must be infinitely different in the Article of Taxation. Here in England the Member of Parliament is equally known to the Neighbour who elects and to him who does not; the Friendships, the Connections, the Influences are spread through the whole. If by any Mistake an act of Parliament is made that prove injurious and hard the Member of Parliament here sees with his own Eyes and is moreover very accessible to the people, not only so, but the taxes are laid equally by one Rule and fall as well on the Member himself as on the people. But as to America, from the great distance in point of Situation, from the almost total unacquaintedness, Especially in the more northern Colonies, with the Members of Parliament, and they with them, or with the particular Ability and Circumstances of one another, from the Nature of this very tax laid upon others not Equally and in Common with ourselves, but with express purpose to Ease ourselves, we think, say they, that it will be only to lay a foundation of great Jealousy and Continual Uneasiness, and that to no purpose, as we already by the Regulations upon their trade draw from the Americans all that they can spare, at least they say this Step should not take place untill or unless the Americans are allowed to send Members to Parliament; for *who of you,* said Col. Barre Nobly in his Speech in the house upon this Occasion, *who of you reasoning upon this Subject feels warmly from the Heart* (putting his hand to his own breast) *for the Americans as they would for themselves or as you would for the people of your own native Country?* and to this point Mr. Jackson produced Copies of two Acts of Parliament granting the priviledge of having Members to the County Palitine of Chester and the Bishoprick of Durham upon Petitions preferred for that purpose in the Reign of King Henry the Eighth and Charles the first, the preamble of which Statutes counts upon the Petitions from those places as setting forth that being in their general Civil Jurisdiction Exempted from the Common Law Courts etc., yet being Subject to the general authority of Parliament, were taxed in Common with the rest of the Kingdom, which taxes by reason of their having no Members in Parliament to represent their Affairs, often proved hard and injurious etc. and upon that ground they had the priviledge of sending Members granted them— and if this, say they, could be a reason in the case of Chester and Durham, how much more so in the case of America.

Thus I have given you, I think, the Substance of the Arguments on both sides of that great and important Question of the right and also of the Expediency of taxing America by Authority of Parliament. I cannot, however, Content myself without giving you a Sketch of what the aforementioned Mr. Barre said in Answer to some remarks made by Mr. Ch. Townsend in a Speech of his upon this Subject. I ought here to tell you that the Debate upon the American Stamp bill came on before the house for the first time last Wednesday, when the same was open'd by Mr. Grenville the Chanceller of the Exchequer, in a pretty lengthy Speech, and in a very able and I think in a very candid manner he opened the Nature of the Tax, Urged the Necessity of it, Endeavoured to obviate all Objections to it—and took Occasion to desire the house to give the bill a most Serious and Cool Consideration and not suffer themselves to be influenced by any resentments which might have been kindled from any thing they might have heard out of doors—alluding I suppose to the N. York and Boston Assemblys' Speeches and Votes—that this was a matter of revenue which was of all things the most interesting to the Subject etc. The Argument was taken up by several who opposed the bill (viz) by Alderman Beckford, who, and who only, seemed to deny the Authority of Parliament, by Col. Barre, Mr. Jackson, Sir William Meredith and some others. Mr. Barre, who by the way I think, and I find I am not alone in my Opinion, is one of the finest Speakers that the House can boast of, having been some time in America as an Officer in the Army, and having while there, as I had known before, contracted many Friendships with American Gentlemen, and I believe Entertained much more favourable Opinions of them than some of his profession have done, Delivered a very handsome and moving Speech upon the bill and against the same, Concluding by saying that he was very sure that Most who Should hold up their hands to the Bill must be under a Necessity of acting very much in the dark, but added, perhaps as well in the Dark as any way.

After him Mr. Charles Townsend spoke in favour of the Bill—took Notice of several things Mr. Barre had said, and concluded with the following or like Words:—And now will these Americans, Children planted by our Care, nourished up by our Indulgence untill they are grown to a Degree of Strength and Opulence, and protected by our Arms, will they grudge to contribute their mite to releive us from the heavy weight of that burden which we lie under? When he had done, Mr. Barre rose and having explained something which he had before said and which Mr Townsend had been remarking upon, he then took up the beforementioned Concluding words of Mr. Townsend, and in a most spirited and I thought an almost inimitable manner, said—

"They planted by your Care? No! your Oppressions planted em in America. They fled from your Tyranny to a then uncultivated and unhospitable Country—where they exposed themselves to almost all the hardships to which human Nature is liable, and among others to the Cruelties of a Savage foe, the most subtle and I take upon me to say the most formidable of any People upon the face of Gods Earth. And yet, actuated by Principles of true english Lyberty, they met all these hardships with pleasure, compared with those they suffered in their own Country, from the hands of those who should have been their Friends.

"They nourished up by *your* indulgence? they grew by your neglect of Em:—as soon as you began to care about Em, that Care was Excercised in sending persons to rule over Em, in one Department and another, who were perhaps the Deputies of Deputies to some Member of this house—sent to Spy out their Lyberty, to misrepresent their Actions and to prey upon Em; men whose behavior on many Occasions has caused the Blood of those Sons of Liberty to recoil within them; men promoted to the highest Seats of Justice, some, who to my knowledge were glad by going to a foreign Country to Escape being brought to the Bar of a Court of Justice in their own.

"They protected by *your* Arms? they have nobly taken up Arms in your defence, have Exerted a Valour amidst their constant and Laborious industry for the defence of a Country, whose frontier, while drench'd in blood, its interior Parts have yielded all its little Savings to your Emolument. And believe me, remember I this Day told you so, that same Spirit of freedom which actuated that people at first, will accompany them still.—But prudence forbids me to explain myself further. God knows I do not at this Time speak from motives of party Heat, what I deliver are the genuine Sentiments of my heart; however superiour to me in general knowledge and Experience the reputable body of this house may be, yet I claim to know more of America than most of you, having seen and been conversant in that Country. The People I believe are as truly Loyal as any Subjects the King has, but a people Jealous of their Lyberties and who will vindicate them, if ever they should be violated—but the Subject is too delicate and I will say no more."

These Sentiments were thrown out so intirely without premeditation, so forceably and so firmly, and the breaking off so beautifully abrupt, that the whole house sat awhile as Amazed, intently Looking and without answering a Word.

I own I felt Emotions that I never felt before and went the next Morning and thank'd Col. Barre in behalf of my Country for his noble and spirited Speech.

However, Sir after all that was said, upon a Division of the house upon the Question, there was about 250 to about 50 in favour of the Bill. . . .

The Merchants in London are alarmed at these things; they have had a meeting with the Agents and are about to petition Parliament upon the Acts that respect the trade of North America.

What the Event of these things will be I dont know. . . .

Your Most Obedient Humble Servant.

J. Ingersoll.

Questions

1. On the basis of Ingersoll's observations, how sympathetic were British politicians and the British people to the colonists' view that Parliament did not have the right to tax them?
2. Do the members of Parliament seem well informed about the situation in the mainland colonies of North America? Why or why not?
3. Do the members of Parliament believe that they rather than the colonists are acting to preserve essential British rights? Why or why not?

5-2   An Account of a Crowd Action (1765)

Thomas Hutchinson

Thomas Hutchinson, a descendant of Anne Hutchinson, was born in Boston in 1711. In 1765 he held a number of appointed political offices. In addition to serving, as he had since 1749, on the Governor's Council, Hutchinson was both the chief justice and the lieutenant governor of Massachusetts. He served as the colony's acting governor from 1769 to 1771 and then as its governor until he moved to Great Britain in 1774. He died in Britain in 1780.

Hutchinson was a leading and wealthy conservative, and many colonists saw him as a symbol of British imperial rule. These factors made him an appealing target during the Stamp Act controversy, and as the letter he wrote on August 30, 1765, indicates, Hutchinson personally experienced the fury of the Boston crowds (see text pp. 152–154). Ironically, Hutchinson had opposed the Stamp Act and had tried to convince the Grenville administration that enacting it would be a mistake.

Source: Thomas Hutchinson to Richard Jackson, August 30, 1765, *Massachusetts Archives,* 26: 146–147.

Boston, August 30, 1765

My Dear Sir

I came from my [country] house at Milton with my family the 26th in the morning. After dinner it was whispered in town there would be a mob at night and that Paxtons Hallowell, and the custom-house and admiralty officers houses would be attacked but my friends assured me the rabble were satisfied with the insult I had received and that I was become rather Popular. In the evening whilst I was at supper and my children round me somebody ran in and said the mob were coming. I directed my children to fly to a secure Place and shut up my house as I had done before intending not to quit it but my eldest daughter repented her leaving me and hastened back and protested she would not quit the house unless I did. I could not stand against this and withdrew with her to a neighbouring house where I had been but a few minutes before the hellish crew fell upon my house with the Rage of devils and in a moment with axes split down the doors and entred my son being in the great entry heard them cry damn him he is upstairs we'll have him. Some ran immediately as high as the top of the house others filled the rooms below and cellars and others Remained without the house to be employed there. Messages soon came one after another to the house where I was to inform me the mob were coming in Pursuit of me and I was obliged to retire thro yards and gardens to a house more remote where I remained until 4 o'clock by which time one of the best finished houses in the Province had nothing remaining but the bare walls and floors. Not contented with tearing off all the wainscot and hangings and splitting the doors to pieces they beat down the Partition walls and altho that alone cost them near two hours they cut down the cupola or lanthern and they began to take the slate and boards from the roof and were prevented only by the approaching daylight from a total demolition of the building. The garden fence was laid flat and all my trees etc. broke down to the ground. Such ruins were never seen in America. Besides my Plate and family Pictures houshold furniture of every kind my own my children and servants apparel they carried off about £900 sterling in money and emptied the house of every thing whatsoever except a part of the kitchen furniture not leaving a single book or paper in it and have scattered or destroyed all the manuscripts and other papers I had been collecting for 30 years together besides a great number of Publick Papers in my custody. The evening being warm I had undressed me and slipt on a thin camlet surtout over my wastcoat, the next morning the weather being changed I had not cloaths enough in my possession to defend me from the cold and was obliged to borrow from my host. Many articles of clothing and good part of my Plate have since been picked up in different quarters of the town but the Furniture in general was cut to pieces before it was thrown out of the house and most of the beds cut open and the feathers thrown out of the windows. The next evening I intended with my children to Milton but meeting two or three small Parties of the Ruffians who I suppose had concealed themselves in the country and my coachman hearing one of them say there he is, my daughters were terrified and said they should never be safe and I was forced to shelter them that night at the castle.

The encouragers of the first mob never intended matters should go this length and the people in general express the utmost detestation of this unparalleled outrage and I wish they could be convinced what infinite hazard there is of the most terrible consequences from such daemons where they are let loose in a government where there is not constant authority at hand sufficient to suppress them.

I am told the government here will make me a compensation for my own and my family's loss which I think cannot be much less than £3000 sterling. I am not sure that they will. If they should not it will be too heavy for me and I must humbly apply to his Majesty in whose service I am a sufferer but this and a much greater sum would be an insufficient compensation for the constant distress and anxiety of mind I have felt for some time past and must feel for months to come. You cannot conceive the wretched state we are in. Such is the resentment of the people against the stamp duty that there can be no dependence upon the general court to take any steps to enforce or rather advise the payment of it. On the other hand, such will be the effects of not submitting to it that all trade must cease all courts fall and all authority be at an end. Must not the ministry be extremely embarrassed. On the one hand it will be said if concessions be made the Parliament endanger the loss of their authority over the colonies on the other hand if external force should be used there seems to be danger of a total lasting alienation of affection. Is there no alternative? May the infinitely wise God direct you. I am with the greatest esteem

Sir Your most faithful humble servant

Questions

1. Considering the damage done to Hutchinson's property and the time and effort it took to inflict that damage, is Hutchinson's use of the word *mob* misleading? Why or why not?
2. Does it appear that Hutchinson was attacked both because he was a symbol of British rule and because he was a member of the Massachusetts economic elite? Why or why not?
3. Faced with the threat of crowd action, did Hutchinson display personal courage? Do you find his report of the incident believable? Why or why not?

5-3   New York Merchant Boycott Agreement (1765)

Crowd actions prevented the Stamp Act from being enforced when it was scheduled to take effect on November 1, 1765. Members of Parliament were outraged by those actions. Thus, it seemed unlikely that crowds could achieve the colonists' ultimate goal: getting the Stamp Act repealed. Realizing that economic pressure might impel British merchants to lobby for repeal, Patriots in many locations entered into formal agreements to boycott British goods. The article reprinted below, which first appeared in the *Pennsylvania Gazette* on November 7, 1765, describes an agreement entered into and signed by more than 200 of the "principal Merchants" of New York (see text p. 153).

Source: Pennsylvania Gazette, 7 November 1765.

At a general Meeting of the Merchants of the City of New-York, trading to Great-Britain, at the House of Mr. George Burns, of the said City, Innholder, to consider what was necessary to be done in the present Situation of Affairs, with respect to the STAMP ACT, and the melancholy State of the North-American Commerce, so greatly restricted by the Impositions and Duties established by the late Acts of Trade: They came to the following Resolutions, viz.

FIRST, That in all Orders they send out to Great-Britain, for Goods or Merchandize, of any Nature, Kind or Quality whatsover, usually imported from Great-Britain, they will direct their Correspondents not to ship them, unless the STAMP ACT be repealed: It is nevertheless agreed, that all such Merchants as are Owners of, and have Vessels already gone, and now cleared out for Great-Britain, shall be at Liberty to bring back in them, on their own Accounts, Crates and Casks of Earthen Ware, Grindstones, Pipes, and such other bulky Articles, as Owners usually fill up their Vessels with.

SECONDLY, It is further unanimously agreed, that all Orders already sent Home, shall be countermanded by the very first Conveyance; and the Goods and Merchandize thereby ordered, not to be sent, unless upon the Condition mentioned in the foregoing Resolution.

THIRDLY, It is further unanimously agreed, that no Merchant will vend any Goods or Merchandize sent upon Commission from Great-Britain, that shall be shipped from thence after the first Day of January next, unless upon the Condition mentioned in the first Resolution.

FOURTHLY. It is further unanimously agreed, that the foregoing Resolutions shall be binding until the same are abrogated at a general Meeting hereafter to be held for that Purpose.

In Witness whereof we have hereunto respectively subscribed our Names. [*This was subscribed by upwards of Two Hundred principal Merchants.*]

Questions

1. How clearly, if at all, do the merchants spell out the basic rights they believe they are defending?
2. Do the merchants seem as concerned about not losing money as about defending basic British constitutional rights? Why or why not?
3. To what extent do the merchants seem to be concerned about creating an effective way to enforce the boycott? Do they recommend fair and effective means for achieving this purpose? Explain.

5-4   Norfolk Sons of Liberty Pronouncement (1766)

Having instituted a boycott movement, the Patriots needed an apparatus to ensure that it would not be violated. Taking their name from the phrase used by Colonel Barré in his speech against the Stamp Act (Document 5-1), Patriots calling themselves Sons of Liberty formed committees and organizations to enforce the boycott against the Stamp Act. While doing this, the Patriots routinely emphasized their loyalty to George III and their commitment to the rule of law. The statement issued by the Norfolk, Virginia, Sons of Liberty, which is reprinted from the *Pennsylvania Journal* of April 17, 1766, describes both the philosophy and the enforcement measures typically espoused by the Sons of Liberty.

Source: Pennsylvania Gazette, 17 April 1766.

At a meeting of a considerable number of inhabitants of the town and county of Norfolk, *and others,* SONS OF LIBERTY, *at the Court House of the said county, in the colony of* Virginia, *on* Monday *the 31st of* March, 1766.

Having taken into consideration the evil tendency of that oppressive and unconstitutional act of parliament commonly called the Stamp Act, and being desirous that our sentiments should be known to posterity, and recollecting that we are a part of the colony, who first, in General Assembly, openly expressed their detestation to the said act, which is pregnant with ruin, and productive of the most pernicious consequences; and unwilling to rivet the shackles of slavery and oppression on ourselves, and millions yet unborn, have unanimously come to the following resolutions:

I. Resolved, That we acknowledge our sovereign Lord King George III to be our rightful and lawful King, and that we will at all times, to the utmost of our power and ability, support and defend his most sacred person, crown, and dignity; and will be always ready, when constitutionally called upon, to assist his Majesty with our lives and fortunes, and defend all his just rights and prerogatives.

II. Resolved, That we will by all lawful ways and means, which divine providence hath put into our hands, defend ourselves in the full enjoyment of, and preserve inviolate to posterity, those inestimable privileges of all free-born British subjects, of being taxed by none but representatives of their own choosing, and of being tried only by a jury of their own Peers; for, if we quietly submit to the execution of the said Stamp Act, all our claims to civil liberty will be lost, and we and our posterity become absolute slaves.

III. Resolved, That we will, on any future occasion, sacrifice our lives and fortunes, in concurrence with the other Sons of Liberty in the American provinces, to defend and preserve those invaluable blessings transmitted us by our ancestors.

IV. Resolved, That whoever is concerned, directly or indirectly, in using, or causing to be used, in any way or manner whatever, within this colony, unless authorized by the General Assembly thereof, those detestable papers called the Stamps, shall be deemed, to all intents and purposes, an enemy to his country, and by the Sons of Liberty treated accordingly.

V. Resolved, That a committee be appointed to present the thanks of the Sons of Liberty to Colonel Richard Bland, for his treatise entitled "An Inquiry into the Rights of the British Colonies."

VI. Resolved, That a committee be appointed, who shall make public the above resolutions, and correspond as they shall see occasion, with the associated Sons and Friends of Liberty in the other British colonies in America.

Questions

1. How clearly, if at all, do the Sons of Liberty spell out the basic rights they believe they are defending?
2. What measures do the Sons of Liberty propose to take to defend their rights?
3. At this stage of the conflict between Great Britain and the colonies, how do these colonists view their relationship to the mother country?

5-5   Declarations of the Stamp Act Congress (1765)

Boston was the scene of the first major crowd actions against the Stamp Act. Those actions and others effectively blocked the implementation of the act. Also, it was Massachusetts that suggested that each colony send delegates to a special intercolonial congress that would formulate a unified response to the detested British legislation. The colonies of Virginia, North Carolina, and Georgia could not attend because their governors refused to convene their assemblies; New Hampshire chose not to send delegates. However, twenty-seven delegates representing the other colonies met in New York on October 7, 1765. During twelve days of deliberations the members of the Stamp Act Congress prepared a petition to the king, a memorial to the House of Lords, a petition to the House of Commons, and a series of "Declarations . . . respecting the most Essential Rights and Liberties of the Colonists." The "Declarations" of the Stamp Act Congress provide the clearest statement of the pragmatic and philosophical positions of the colonists on the Stamp Act and the efforts of the British government to institute general imperial reform.

Source: Proceedings of the Congress at New-York (1766), 15–16.

The Members of this Congress, sincerely devoted, with the warmest Sentiments of Affection and Duty to his Majesty's Person and Government, inviolably attached to the present happy Establishment of the Protestant Succession, and with Minds deeply impressed by a Sense of the present and impending Misfortunes of the *British* Colonies on this Continent; having considered as maturely as Time will permit, the Circumstances of the said Colonies, esteem it our indispensable Duty, to make the following Declarations of our humble Opinion, respecting the most Essential Rights and Liberties of the Colonists, and of the Grievances under which they labour, by Reason of several late Acts of Parliament.

I. That his Majesty's Subjects in these Colonies, owe the same Allegiance to the Crown of *Great-Britain*, that is owing from his Subjects born within the Realm, and all due Subordination to that August Body the Parliament of *Great-Britain*.

II. That his Majesty's Liege Subjects in these Colonies, are entitled to all the inherent Rights and Liberties of his Natural born Subjects, within the Kingdom of *Great-Britain*.

III. That it is inseparably essential to the Freedom of a People, and the undoubted Right of *Englishmen*, that no Taxes be imposed on them, but with their own Consent, given personally, or by their Representatives.

IV. That the People of these Colonies are not, and from their local Circumstances cannot be, Represented in the House of Commons in *Great-Britain*.

V. That the only Representatives of the People of these Colonies, are Persons chosen therein by themselves, and that no Taxes ever have been, or can be Constitutionally imposed on them, but by their respective Legislature.

VI. That all Supplies to the Crown, being free Gifts of the People, it is unreasonable and inconsistent with the Principles and Spirit of the *British* Constitution, for the People of *Great-Britain*, to grant to his Majesty the Property of the Colonists.

VII. That Trial by Jury, is the inherent and invaluable Right of every *British* Subject in these Colonies.

VIII. That the late Act of Parliament, entitled, *An Act for granting and applying certain Stamp Duties, and other Duties, in the* British *Colonies and Plantations* in America, etc. by imposing Taxes on the Inhabitants of these Colonies, and the said Act, and several other Acts, by extending the Jurisdiction of the Courts of Admiralty beyond its ancient Limits, have a manifest Tendency to subvert the Rights and Liberties of the Colonists.

IX. That the Duties imposed by several late Acts of Parliament, from the peculiar Circumstances of these Colonies, will be extremely Burthensome and Grievous; and from the scarcity of Specie, the Payment of them absolutely impracticable.

X. That as the Profits of the Trade of these Colonies ultimately center in *Great-Britain*, to pay for the Manufactures which they are obliged to take from thence, they eventually contribute very largely to all Supplies granted there to the Crown.

XI. That the Restrictions imposed by several late Acts of Parliament, on the Trade of these Colonies, will render them unable to purchase the Manufactures of *Great-Britain*.

XII. That the Increase, Prosperity, and Happiness of these Colonies, depend on the full and free Enjoyment of their Rights and Liberties, and an Intercourse with *Great-Britain* mutually Affectionate and Advantageous.

XIII. That it is the Right of the *British* Subjects in these Colonies, to Petition the King, or either House of Parliament.

Lastly, That it is the indispensable Duty of these Colonies, to the best of Sovereigns, to the Mother Country, and to themselves, to endeavour by a loyal and dutiful Address to his Majesty, and humble Applications to both Houses of Parliament, to procure the Repeal of the Act for granting and applying certain Stamp Duties, of all Clauses of any other Acts of Parliament, whereby the Jurisdiction of the Admiralty is extended as aforesaid, and of the other late Acts for the Restriction of *American* Commerce.

Questions

1. Does it appear that the members of the Stamp Act Congress are determined to demonstrate that they are not rebels but loyal British subjects? Why or why not?
2. According to the Congress, what basic constitutional rights do the colonists have?
3. In what ways does the Congress emphasize pragmatic as well as philosophical arguments against British imperial reforms?
4. Considering the British ideas about the mother country's rights explained in Document 5-1, how convincing is the case the Congress makes against the Stamp Act?

Questions for Further Thought

1. What principal rights did the colonists claim they were defending in opposing the Sugar and Stamp acts?
2. To what extent do these documents suggest that on the issue of taxation the colonists were as determined to oppose the supremacy of Parliament as Parliament was to assert it?
3. Does it appear that the colonists were concerned more with evading their responsibilities as members of the British Empire than with defending basic British constitutional rights? Why or why not?
4. Would British politicians have agreed with colonists who suggested that something more than money was at stake in the British effort at imperial reform? What, if any, vital noneconomic considerations were at issue in the fight over the Sugar and Stamp acts?

The Growing Confrontation, 1767–1770

As chancellor of the exchequer, Charles Townshend was as determined as George Grenville had been to tax the colonists and rein in their representative political institutions. He hoped that the duties placed on paper, paint, glass, and tea imported into the colonies in the Townshend Act of 1767, which came to be called the Townshend duties, could be slipped quietly by the colonists (see text pp. 158–159). The duties were small, and the colonists supposedly drew a distinction between internal taxes such as the Stamp Act and external taxes such as the Townshend duties. However, as shown in the textbook and revealed in the arguments of John Dickinson (Document 5-6), the colonists did not make that a distinction. Equally important, Dickinson forcefully explored the issue of what the colonists had to do to defend their claim that they could not legally be taxed by Parliament.

To oppose the Townshend duties, colonists turned to the tactic that had won repeal of the Stamp Act: an economic boycott of British goods (see text pp. 159–160). The imposition of organized and ongoing boycotts drew women into the political process on a scale unprecedented in the colonies (see text pp. 160–161). Because of their traditional role as managers of the home, women were essential to the success of the boycott. Document 5-7, the boycott agreements entered into by a large number of Boston women in 1770, illustrates how that was done.

Believing that colonial opposition to imperial reform would wilt if more pressure were applied, the British government escalated the confrontation. An important illustration of that escalation was the placing of troops in Boston, a hotbed of opposition to the reform measures (see text pp. 161–162). The growing confrontation of the late 1760s scared many colonists, especially those who eventually joined the ranks of the Loyalists (see text pp. 163, 170–171). Peter Oliver, the author of Document 5-8, shared that fear. His judgments on the breadth and depth of the growing opposition to British policy reflect the view held by many future Loyalists and the great majority of politicians in Britain. Captain Thomas Preston's account of the "Boston Massacre" (Document 5-9) relates how the conflict, fueled by the determination of British officials and of most colonists to protect what each group saw as its basic rights, turned shockingly bloody in 1770.

5-6   Letter VII from a Farmer (1768)

John Dickinson

John Dickinson, who was born in Maryland in 1732, studied law in London and returned to Philadelphia in 1757. He began publishing attacks on British reforms in a 1765 pamphlet, *The Late Regulations Respecting the British Colonies*. In that work Dickinson argued that the Sugar and Stamp Acts would be detrimental to the British mercantile system. Writing anonymously under the pen name "A Farmer," this sophisticated lawyer won fame and popularity with a series of twelve essays attacking the Townshend duties (see text pp. 158–159). These essays appeared in the *Pennsylvania Chronicle* between December 1767 and February 1768 and were then issued in pamphlet form as *Letters from a Farmer in Pennsylvania to the Inhabitants of the British Colonies* (1768). Letter VII was first published on January 11, 1768. The essays were so popular that other authors soon could simply refer to "The Farmer" or "The Farmer's Letters" and expect readers to recognize the reference.

Source: *Pennsylvania Chronicle and Universal Advertiser,* 11 January 1768.

There are two ways of laying taxes. One is, by imposing a certain sum on particular kinds of property, to be paid by the *user* or *consumer*, or by rating the *person* at a certain sum. The other is, by imposing a certain sum on particular kinds of property, to be paid by the *seller.*

When a man pays the first sort of tax, he *knows with certainty* that he pays so much money *for a tax.* The *consideration* for which he pays it, is remote, and, it may be, does not occur to him. He is sensible too, that he is *commanded and obliged* to pay it *as a tax*; and therefore people are apt to be displeased with this sort of tax.

The other sort of tax is submitted to in a very different manner. The purchaser of an article, very seldom reflects that the seller raises his price, so as to indemnify himself for the tax *he* has paid. He knows that the prices of things are continually fluctuating, and if he thinks about the tax, he thinks at the same time, in all probability, that he *might* have paid as much, if the article he buys had not been taxed. He gets something *visible* and *agreeable* for his money; and tax and price are so confounded together, that he cannot separate, or does not chuse to take the trouble of separating them.

This mode of taxation therefore is the mode suited to arbitrary and oppressive governments. The love of liberty is so natural to the human heart, that unfeeling tyrants think themselves obliged to accommodate their schemes as much as they can to the appearance of justice and reason, and to deceive those whom they resolve to destroy, or oppress, by presenting to them a miserable picture of freedom, when the inestimable original is lost.

I shall now apply these observations to the late act of parliament. Certain duties are thereby imposed on paper and glass, etc. imported into these colonies. By the laws of *Great-Britain* we are prohibited to get these articles from any other part of the world. We cannot at present, nor for many years to come, tho' we should apply ourselves to these manufactures with the utmost industry, make enough ourselves for our own use. That paper and glass are not only convenient, but absolutely necessary for us, I imagine very few will contend. Some perhaps, who think mankind grew wicked and luxurious, as soon as they found out another way of communicating their sentiments than by speech, and another way of dwelling than in caves, may advance so whimsical an opinion. But I presume no body will take the unnecessary trouble of refuting them.

From these remarks I think it evident, that we *must* use paper and glass; that what we use *must* be *British*; and that we *must* pay the duties imposed, unless those who sell these articles, are so generous as to make us presents of the duties they pay.

Some persons may think this act of no consequence, because the duties are so *small.* A fatal error. *That* is the very circumstance most alarming to me. For I am convinced, that the authors of this law would never have obtained an act to raise so trifling a sum as it must do, had they not intended by *it* to establish a *precedent* for future use. To console ourselves with the *smallness* of the duties, is to walk deliberately into the snare that is set for us, praising the *neatness* of the workmanship. Suppose the duties imposed by the late act could be paid by these distressed colonies with the utmost ease, and that the purposes to which they are to be applied, were the most reasonable and equitable that can be conceived, the contrary of which I hope to demonstrate before these letters are concluded; yet even in such a supposed case, these colonies ought to regard the act with abhorrence. For WHO ARE A FREE PEOPLE? Not *those*, over whom government is reasonably and equitably exercised, but *those*, who live under a government *so constitutionally checked* and *controuled*, that proper provision is made against its being otherwise exercised.

The late act is founded on the destruction of this constitutional security. If the parliament have a right to lay a duty of Four Shillings and Eight-pence on a hundred weight of glass, or a ream of paper, they have a right to lay a duty of any other sum on either. They may raise the duty, as the author before quoted says has been done in some countries, till it "exceeds seventeen or eighteen times the value of the commodity." In short, if they have a right *to* levy a tax of *one penny* upon us, they have a right to levy a *million* upon us: For where does their right stop? At any given number of Pence, Shillings or Pounds? To attempt to limit their right, after granting it to exist at all, is as contrary to reason—as granting it to exist at all, is contrary to justice. If *they* have any right to tax *us*—then, whether *our own money* shall continue in *our own pockets* or not, depends no longer on *us*, but on *them*. [As Lord Cambden said,] "There is nothing which" we can call our own; or, to use the words of Mr. *Locke*—"WHAT PROPERTY HAVE WE IN THAT, WHICH ANOTHER MAY, BY RIGHT, TAKE, WHEN HE PLEASES, TO HIMSELF?"

These duties, which will inevitably be levied upon us—which are now levying upon us—are *expressly* laid FOR THE SOLE PURPOSES OF TAKING MONEY. This is the true definition of "*taxes.*" They are therefore *taxes.* This money is to be taken from *us. We* are therefore taxed. *Those* who are *taxed* without their own consent, given by themselves or their representatives, are slaves. *We are* *taxed* without our own consent, expressed by ourselves or our representatives. We are therefore—I speak it with grief—I speak it with indignation—We are SLAVES. . . .

A FARMER.

Questions

1. Would Dickinson agree with those who stated that British politicians were sincerely concerned about the needs and concerns of the colonists? Why or why not?
2. According to Dickinson, why did colonists have to refuse to pay the small Townshend duties?
3. Would you describe Dickinson's argument as an emotional appeal or a pragmatic appeal? Why?

5-7　The Boycott Agreements of Women in Boston (1770)

Women, who in accordance with the standards of the day were not permitted to vote, were traditionally excluded from participating in the hurly-burly of politics (see text pp. 160–161). However, because of their role in the management of households, unless women actively participated, the boycott against the Townshend duties would fail. While never intending that women be allowed to participate in electoral politics, the men who organized the boycott urged them to support liberty by joining the boycott. As the following reports show, women gave positive demonstrations of their ability to organize in support of the boycott.

Source: Boston Evening-Post, 12 February 1770; *Boston Gazette,* 19 February 1770, as reprinted in *Pennsylvania Gazette,* 8 March 1770.

The following Agreement has lately been come into by upwards of 300 Mistresses of Families in this Town; in which Number the Ladies of the highest Rank and Influence, that could be waited upon in so short a Time, are included.
Boston, *January* 31, 1770.

["]At a Time when our invaluable Rights and Privileges are attacked in an unconstitutional and most alarming Manner, and as we find we are reproached for not being so ready as could be desired, to lend our Assistance, we think it our Duty perfectly to concur with the true Friends of Liberty, in all the Measures they have taken to save this abused Country from Ruin and Slavery: And particularly, we join with the very respectable Body of Merchants, and other Inhabitants of this Town, who met in Faneuil-Hall the 23d of this Instant, in their Resolutions, *totally* to abstain from the Use of TEA: And as the greatest Part of the Revenue arising by Virtue of the late Acts, is produced from the Duty paid upon Tea, which Revenue is wholly expended to support the American Board of Commissioners, We the Subscribers do strictly engage, that we will *totally* abstain from the Use of that Article (Sickness excepted) not only in our respective Families; but that we will absolutely refuse it, if it should be offered to us upon any Occasion whatsoever. This Agreement we chearfully come into, as we believe the very distressed Situation of our Country requires it, and we do hereby oblige ourselves religiously to observe it, till the late Revenue Acts are repealed."

The following is a Copy of the Agreement of the young Ladies of this Town against drinking foreign TEA.
Boston, *February* 12, 1770.

["]We the Daughters of those Patriots who have, and now do appear for the public Interest, and in *that* principally for *us* their Posterity; we, as such, do with Pleasure engage with them, in denying ourselves the drinking of foreign *Tea,* in Hopes to frustrate a Plan that tends to deprive the whole Community of their *All* that is valuable in Life."
To the above Agreement 126 young Ladies have already signed. In Addition to the List of Mistresses of Families, who signed the Agreement against drinking foreign Tea, 110 have been added the Week past.

Questions

1. Do the women who made these agreements appear to be leaders of the boycott movement, or do they appear to be responding to the actions of others?
2. To what extent, if any, do the signers of the agreements spell out the basic rights they believe they are supporting?
3. Does it appear that the specifics of the agreements, including any provisions for their enforcement, will help make the tea boycott effective? Why or why not?

5-8 Origin and Progress of the American Rebellion (1780s)

Peter Oliver

Peter Oliver, who was born in Boston in 1713 and educated at Harvard, detested protests against the reform of British imperial policy. A wealthy member of the legal profession, Oliver was a part of the British system: beginning in 1756, he served as a judge of the superior court of Massachusetts. In addition, the first great Stamp Act crowd action (August 14, 1765, in Boston) was directed against the property of Andrew Oliver, his brother (see text p. 152). Once the Revolution broke out, Oliver went to Britain, fully expecting to return to Massachusetts once the "rebellion" had been put down. However, Oliver never returned; he died in Britain in 1791. He expressed his thoughts about the causes of the Revolution in his "Origin & Progress of the American Rebellion." This work, written in the early 1780s, was not published until the twentieth century.

Source: Reprinted with the permission of the Henry E. Huntington Library from Douglas Adair and John A. Schutz, eds., *Peter Oliver's Origin & Progress of the American Rebellion: A Tory View,* rev. ed. (Stanford, Calif.: Stanford University Press, 1967), 60–65 passim.

I am now come to the Year 1767, a Year fraught with Occurrences, as extraordinary as 1765, but of a different Texture. Notwithstanding the Warnings that the Colonies had repeatedly given, of their determined Resolution to throw off the Supremacy of the british Parliament, yet the then Ministry chose to make another Trial of Skill; never adverting to the ill Success of former Attempts. They might have known, that the Contest had reached so great an Height, that the Colonists would never descend one Step untill they had first ascended the last Round of the Ladder. . . . It required no great Degree of second Sight to calculate Consequences. But the Ministry confiding in their own good Intentions, and placing too much Confidence in the Gratitude of the Colonists to the parent State (which by the Way they did not possess a Spark of, neither is it to be but seldom Expected to find it inhabit any where but in the private Breast, and too seldom there; to the Disgrace of human Nature), they procured a new Act to be passed, laying Duties upon *Tea, Glass, Paper, and Painters Colours.* This Act was not more unreasonable than many other Acts which had been submitted to for many Years past, and which, even at this Time, they made no Objection to. But the Colonists had succeeded in their first Experiment of Opposition, and their new Allies in Parliament increased their Importance.

As to the *Glass* in particular, the Duty was so trifling, that it would not have enhanced the Price of it to the Purchaser; for there were so many Sellers who aimed at a Market for their Commodities, and the Merchants had so great a Profit upon their Goods, that they could render the Duty of little or no Importance in their Sales; and this was actually the Case. For the Glass, during the Continuance of the Act, was sold at the same Price which it commanded before the Commencement of the Act. The true Reason of Opposition was this. The Inhabitants of the Colonies were a Race of Smugglers. . . .

The Smugglers then, who were the prevailing Part of the Traders in the Capitals of the several Provinces, found it necessary for their Interest, to unite in defeating the Operation of the Act; and *Boston* appeared in the Front of the Battle. Accordingly they beat to Arms, and manœuvred in a new invented Mode. They entred into nonimportation

Agreements. A Subscription Paper was handed about, enumerating a great Variety of Articles not to be imported from *England*, which they supposed would muster the Manufacturers in *England* into a national Mob to support their Interests. Among the various prohibited Articles, were *Silks, Velvets, clocks, Watches, Coaches and Chariots*; and it was highly diverting, to see the names and marks, to the Subscription, of Porters and Washing Women. But every mean and dirty Art was used to compass all their bad Designs. One of those who handed about a Subscription Paper being asked, whether it could be imagined that such Tricks would effectuate their Purposes? He replyed "Yes! It would do to scare them in England:" and perhaps there never was a Nation so easy to be affrighted: witness the preceding Repeal of the Stamp Act.

In order to effectuate their Purposes to have this Act repealed also, they formed many Plans of Operation. Associations were convened to prevent the Importation of Goods from *Great Britain*, and to oblige all those who had already sent for them, to reship them after their arrival. This was such an Attack upon the mercantile Interest, that it was necessary to use private evasive Arts to decieve the Vulgar. Accordingly, when the Goods arrived, they were to be in Warehouses, which were to be guarded by a publick Key, at the same Time the Owners of the Stores and Goods had a Key of their Own. This amused the Rabble, whom the Merchants had set to mobbing; and such were the blessed Effects of some of those Merchants Villainy, that Bales and Trunks were disgorged of their Contents and refilled with Shavings, Brickbats, Legs of Bacon and other Things, and shipped for *England*; where some of them were opened on the King's Wharves or Quays, and the Fraud discovered. Many of those Merchants also continued to import the prohibited Goods, in Disguise; of which a bold Printer of *Boston* detected them in his publick Papers; for which they, out of Revenge, in 1768, attempted to murder him; but narrowly escaping with his Life he fled to *England*, as the civil Power of the Country was not sufficient to protect any one who was obnoxious to the Leaders of the Faction. . . .

Mr. [James] *Otis's* black Regiment, the dissenting Clergy, were also set to Work, to preach up Manufactures instead of Gospel. They preached about it and about it; untill the Women and Children, both within Doors and without, set their Spinning Wheels a whirling in Defiance of *Great Britain*. The female Spinners kept on spinning for 6 Days of the Week; and on the seventh, the Parsons took their Turns and spun out their Prayers and Sermons to a long Thread of Politicks, and to much better Profit than the other Spinners; for they generally cloathed the Parson and his Family with the Produce of their Labor. This was a new Species of Enthusiasm, and might be justly termed, the Enthusiasm of the Spinning Wheel.

An *American* is an adept in the Arts of Shrewdness. In these he is *generally* an Overmatch for a *Briton*, although he may sometimes fail in the Execution. As an Instance of each, take the following Anecdote of a Deacon of one [of]

the dissenting Congregations in *Boston*, who imported large Quantities of Woolens from *England*. *Hogarth* drew his Line of Beauty for the Leg of a Chair; so this Person had sat so long in a Deacon's Seat, that the Muscles of his Face were so contracted into the Line of Sanctity, that he passed himself upon the World as a Man of great Reputation for Honesty. He was also a great Stickler for the Manufactures of *America*; and in the Heighth of his pious Zeal for the good old Cause, wrote to his Correspondent in *London* about american Grievances; and informed him, that unless they were redressed, they not only could, but they would redress them their selves by making Cloths from their own Produce. As a Proof that they could do it, he sent Patterns of fine broad Cloths, which he said were manufactured in *America*. His Correspondent was surprized on seeing the Patterns, and shewed them to the Manufacturer of whom he had bought them. He also was surprized; but, on examination, told the Merchant that those were the very Cloths he had sold him to ship to *America*—such are the blessed Effects of Cant and Hypocrisy. . . .

All this Struggle and Uproar arose from the selfish Designs of the Merchants. They disguised their Private Views by mouthing it for Liberty. The Magick of this Sound echoed through the interior Parts of the Country, and the deluded Vulgar were charmed with it—like the poor harmless *Squirrel* that runs into the Mouth of the *Rattlesnake*, the Fascination in the Word *Liberty* threw the People into the harpy Claws of their Destroyers; and for what? But to gratifie the artfull Smugglers in carrying on their contraband Tea Trade with the Dutch, to make their deluded Consumers purchase at their Prices who were the Venders; for the act of Parliament had reduced the Duties upon it from 12 d p [Pence per] Pound to three Pence, with a View to prevent Smugling; which would effectually have prevented it, had the Act been in Force a few Years, and would have broke up the Nests of those worse than Highway Men; who, for many Years, had kept the Province in a Ferment, and created Uneasiness in the parent State.

As for the People in general, they were like the Mobility of all Countries, perfect Machines, wound up by any Hand who might first take the Winch; they were like the poor Negro Boy, who, in the Time of the late Stamp Act, was bid by his Master, in the Evening, to fetch something from his Barn; but did not move at the command. His Master spoke to him with Severity, and asked him why he did not go as he was bid? The poor Wretch replied, with Tears in his Eyes, "me fraid Massah Tamp Act he catch me." Thus the common People had had that Act, and all the Acts of Parliament since, dressed up by their seditious Leaders, either with raw Head and bloody Bones, or with Horns, Tails, and cloven Feet, which were sufficient to affright their weak Followers. And as for Men of Sense, who could see through the Delusion, it would have been imprudent for them to have interposed; for the Government was in the Hands of the Mob, both in Form and Substance, and it was in vain to combat a Whirlwind or a Hurricane.

Questions

1. What, if any, significance can you discern in the fact that Oliver referred to his study as the "Origin & Progress of the American Rebellion" rather than the "Origin & Progress of the American Revolution"?
2. Judging from this excerpt, is it accurate to say that Oliver was a philosophical conservative? Why or why not?
3. On the basis of this excerpt, is it accurate to say that Oliver respected ordinary people? Why or why not?

5-9   An Account of the Boston Massacre (1770)

Captain Thomas Preston

When the British escalated the growing confrontation by placing troops in Boston as a kind of police force to enforce imperial reform measures (see text pp. 161–162), many colonists considered this another step on the road to political slavery. Bostonians' horror at being "occupied" by a standing army in peacetime was only part of the problem. Because off-duty soldiers were allowed to take civilian employment, they competed, often successfully, for jobs that were essential to many in Boston's lower classes. Tensions mounted, and many claimed that Boston would face more dramatic events. The infamous "Boston Massacre" of March 5, 1770, proved them right. The following description of the event was written by Captain Thomas Preston, who was in command of the British troops directly involved in the massacre. Preston was tried for murder and acquitted.

Source: "Historical Chronicle," *Gentlemen's Magazine* 40 (April 1770), 189.

Saturday, 28 April, 1770. The Representation of the Affairs at Boston ["the Massacre," March 5] by the Town Committee, having been inserted in the beginning of the Magazine, the case of Capt. Preston here epitomized, will serve to show the other side of the question.

It is a matter of too great notoriety to need proofs, that the arrival of his majesty's troops in Boston was extremely obnoxious to its inhabitants. They have ever used all means in their power to weaken the regiments, and to bring them into contempt, by promoting desertions, and by grossly and falsely propagating untruths concerning them. On the arrival of the 64th and 65th, their ardour seemingly began to abate; it being too expensive to buy off so many. But the same spirit revived immediately on its being known that those regiments were ordered for Halifax. After their embarkation, one of their justices, from the seat of justice, declared, "that the soldiers must now take care of themselves, nor trust too much to their arms, for they were but a handful." This was an alarming circumstance to the soldiery, since which several disputes have happened between the towns-people and the soldiers of both regiments. In general such disputes have been kept too secret from the officers. On the 2d instant, two of the 29th going through one Gray's Rope Walk,[1] the rope-makers insultingly asked them if they would empty a vault. This unfortunately had the desired effect by provoking the soldiers, and from words they went to blows. Both parties suffered in this affray, and finally, the soldiers retired to their quarters. The insolence, as well as utter hatred of the inhabitants to the troops increased daily; insomuch, that Monday and Tuesday, the 5th and 6th instant, were privately agreed on for a general engagement; in consequence of which, several of the militia came from the country, armed, to join their friends, menacing to destroy any who should oppose them. This plan has since been discovered.

On Monday night about eight o'clock, two soldiers were attacked and beat. About nine some of the guard informed me, the town inhabitants were assembling to attack the troops, and that the bells were ringing as a signal,

---

[1]*Rope walk:* A long, narrow building used for the twisting of rope, especially for ships. Rope walks were common in port cities such as Boston.

and not for fire, and the Beacon intended to be fired to bring in the distant people of the country. Being captain of the day, I repaired immediately to the main guard. In my way, I saw the people in great commotion. In a few minutes about 100 people passed and went toward the custom-house, where the King's money is lodged. They immediately surrounded the sentinel posted there, and with clubs and other weapons threatened to execute their vengeance on him. A Townsman assured me he heard the mob declare they would murder him. I fearing their plundering the King's chest, immediately sent a non-commissioned officer and 12 men to protect both the sentinel and the King's money, and very soon followed myself, to prevent disorder. The troops rushed thro' the people, and, by charging their bayonets in half circle, kept them at a distance. So far was I from intending death, that the troops went to the spot where the unhappy affair took place, without loading their pieces.

The mob still increased, and were more outrageous, striking bludgeons one against another, and calling out, "Come on, you Rascals, you bloody backs, you lobster scoundrels; fire if you dare; G—d damn you, fire and be damned; we know you dare not;" and much more such language was used. They advanced to the points of the bayo-

nets, stuck some of them, and even the muzzles of the pieces, and seemed to be endeavouring to close with the soldiers. Some well-behaved persons asked me if their guns were charged? I replied, yes. If I intended to order the men to fire? I answered no. While I was speaking, a soldier having received a severe blow with a stick, instantly fired. On reprimanding him, I was struck with a club on my arm, so violent a blow, that had it fallen on my head, probably it would have destroyed me. A general attack was then made on the men by heaving clubs, and snow balls, by which all our lives were in imminent danger; some persons from behind called out, "Damn your bloods, why don't you fire?" Instantly three or four of the soldiers fired, one after another, and directly after, three more in the same confusion and hurry.

The mob then ran away, except three unhappy men who instantly expired. . . . The whole of this melancholy affair was transacted in almost 20 minutes. . . .

On examination before the justices they have sworn, that I used the word fire, and so bitter and inveterate are the malcontents against the officers and troops, that I am, though perfectly innocent, under most unhappy circumstances, having nothing in reason to expect but the loss of life in a very ignominious manner, without the interposition of his majesty's royal goodness.

Questions

1. According to Captain Preston, did the Bostonians have legitimate reasons for being unhappy about the fact that British troops were stationed in their city?
2. Judging from Preston's account, does the term *Boston Massacre* seem accurate? Why or why not?
3. Since Preston would naturally be inclined to present his actions and the actions of his men in the best light, how believable is his account of what happened?

Questions for Further Thought

1. Considering the fact that the British government was eager to raise significant sums by taxing the colonists, why were the Townshend duties so small?
2. Compare the boycott agreement entered into in New York against the Stamp Act (Document 5-3) with the agreements by Boston women in 1770 to oppose the Townshend duties (Document 5-7). Do the differences reflect the experience that the colonists had gained between 1765 and 1770 or the fact that the New York document was produced by men and the Boston agreements were produced by women?
3. According to Peter Oliver (Document 5-8), why was there a dangerous and growing confrontation between the colonies and Britain? Is his view of the situation convincing? Why or why not?
4. On the basis of these documents, do you think British politicians or the colonists were more to blame for the confrontations of 1767–1770? Or were both groups equally to blame? (Is *blame* the wrong word? Should one instead try to assess *responsibility*?)

The Road to Rebellion, 1771–1775

At the time of the Boston Massacre, the colonists did not know that the British government, beset by troubles at home, was again ready to succumb to an economic boycott (see text p. 162). Ironically, Parliament debated repeal on the very day of the Massacre and formally rescinded all the Townshend duties except that on tea in April 1770. In response to the Massacre itself, the British pulled their troops out of Boston proper. As the relatively quiet period that developed after the traumatic events of 1770 revealed, the British government seemed willing, at least temporarily, to stop escalating the confrontation with the colonists. But when Parliament passed the Tea Act of 1773 (see text pp. 164–165), it raised a new threat of economic monopoly. Colonists looked again to the tactics they had used against the Stamp Act; they also tried newer techniques, such as the threat of tar and feathering. Once again Boston became the scene of vigorous action. Document 5-10, a participant's account of the Boston Tea Party of 1773, illustrates the degree of organization and the effectiveness of that crowd operation. Not surprisingly, the Patriots turned again to an economic boycott. The agreement was signed by fifty-one women of Edenton, North Carolina (Document 5-11); and the illustration on text p. 170 demonstrates their commitment to the Patriot cause.

When news of the Boston Tea Party reached Parliament, the members expressed outrage over the destruction of private property. Determined to punish Boston—which had become known as "the Metropolis of Sedition"—the British government passed the infamous Coercive Acts (see text pp. 165, 168). As they had done in response to the Stamp Act, the colonists called an intercolonial congress (see text pp. 168–169). This Continental Congress, which opened in Philadelphia on September 5, 1774, deliberated until late October. As the textbook authors note, "men of 'loyal principles'" at the Continental Congress supported a plan to create a new structure of empire (see text p. 168). That plan (Document 5-12) was not adopted, and the Continental Congress became a milestone in the ongoing and organized opposition to Britain's renewed efforts to exert control over the colonies. The Congress's Plan of Association (Document 5-13) shows the detailed program advanced by the Congress to counter the Coercive Acts and the British imperial reform effort.

5-10   An Account of the Boston Tea Party of 1773

George Robert Twelve Hewes   Boston was the site of many crowd actions that marked the growing confrontation and the march toward the War of Independence. On the night of December 16, 1773, Bostonians staged the Boston Tea Party to show their opposition to the Tea Act of 1773. George Robert Twelve Hewes, the Boston shoemaker whose life story is given in the textbook (see "American Lives," text pp. 166–167), was one of the participants. Late in his long life, Hewes provided the following description of what occurred in Boston's harbor that December night in 1773.

Source: James Hawkes, *A Retrospect of the Boston Tea-Party, with a Memoir of George R. T. Hewes, a Survivor of the Little Band of Patriots Who Drowned the Tea in Boston Harbour in 1773* (1834), 37–41.

The tea destroyed was contained in three ships, laying near each other, at what was called at that time Griffin's wharf, and were surrounded by armed ships of war; the commanders of which had publicly declared, that if the rebels, as they were pleased to style the Bostonians, should not withdraw their opposition to the landing of the tea before a certain day, the 17th day of December, 1773, they should on that day force it on shore, under the cover of their cannon's mouth. On the day preceding the seventeenth, there was a meeting of the citizens of the county of Suffolk, convened at one of the churches in Boston, for the purpose of consulting on what measures might be considered expedient to prevent the landing of the tea, or secure the people from the collection of the duty. At that meeting a committee was appointed to wait on Governor Hutchinson, and request him to inform them whether he would take any measures to satisfy the people on the object of the meeting. To the first application of this committee, the governor told them he would give them a definite answer by five o'clock in the afternoon. At the hour appointed, the committee again repaired to the governor's house, and on inquiry found he had gone to his country seat at Milton, a distance of about six miles. When the committee returned and informed the meeting of the absence of the governor, there was a confused murmur among the members, and the meeting was immediately dissolved, many of them crying out, Let every man do his duty, and be true to his country; and there was a general huzza for Griffin's wharf. It was now evening, and I immediately dressed myself in the costume of an Indian, equipped with a small hatchet, which I and my associates denominated the tomahawk, with which, and a club, after having painted my face and hands with coal dust in the shop of a blacksmith, I repaired to Griffin's wharf, where the ships lay that contained the tea. When I first appeared in the street, after being thus disguised, I fell in with many who were dressed, equipped and painted as I as, and who fell in with me, and marched in order to the place of our destination. When we arrived at the wharf, there were three of our number who assumed the authority to direct our operations, to which we readily submitted. They divided us into three parties, for the purpose of boarding the three ships which contained the tea at the same time. The name of him who commanded the division to which I was assigned, was Leonard Pitt. The names of the other commanders I never knew. We were immediately ordered by the respective commanders to board all the ships at the same time, which we promptly obeyed. The commander of the division to which I belonged, as soon as we were on board the ship, appointed me boatswain, and ordered me to go to the captain and demand of him the keys to the hatches and a dozen candles. I made the demand accordingly, and the captain promptly replied, and delivered the articles; but requested me at the same time to do no damage to the ship or rigging. We then were ordered by our commander to open the hatches, and take out all the chests of tea and throw them overboard, and we immediately proceeded to execute his orders; first cutting and splitting the chests with our tomahawks, so as thoroughly to expose them to the effects of the water. In about three hours from the time we went on board, we had thus broken and thrown overboard every tea chest to be found in the ship; while those in the other ships were disposing of the tea in the same way, at the same time. We were surrounded by British armed ships, but no attempt was made to resist us. We then quietly retired to our several places of residence, without having any conversation with each other, or taking any measures to discover who were our associates; nor do I recollect of our having had the knowledge of the name of a single individual concerned in the affair, except that of Leonard Pitt, the commander of my division, who I have mentioned. There appeared to be an understanding that each individual should volunteer his services, keep his own secret, and risk the consequences for himself. No disorder took place during the transaction, and it was observed at that time, that the stillest night ensued that Boston had enjoyed for many months.

During the time we were throwing the tea overboard, there were several attempts made by some of the citizens of Boston and its vicinity, to carry off small quantities of it for their family use. To effect that object, they would watch their opportunity to snatch up a handful from the deck, where it became plentifully scattered, and put it into their pockets. One Captain O'Conner, whom I well knew, came on board for that purpose, and when he supposed he was not noticed, filled his pockets, and also the lining of his coat. But I had detected him, and gave information to the captain of what he was doing. We were ordered to take him into custody, and just as he was stepping from the vessel, I seized him by the skirt of his coat, and in attempting to pull him back, I tore it off; but springing forward, by a rapid effort, he made his escape. He had however to run the gauntlet through the crowd upon the wharf; each one, as he passed, giving him a kick or a stroke.

The next day we nailed the skirt of his coat, which I had pulled off, to the whipping post in Charlestown, the place of his residence, with a label upon it, commemorative of the occasion which had thus subjected the proprietor to the popular indignation.

Another attempt was made to save a little tea from the ruins of the cargo, by a tall aged man, who wore a large cocked hat and white wig, which was fashionable at that time. He had slightly slipped a little into his pocket, but being detected, they seized him, and taking his hat and wig from his head, threw them, together with the tea, of which they had emptied his pockets, into the water. In consideration of his advanced age, he was permitted to escape, with now and then a slight kick.

The next morning, after we had cleared the ships of the tea, it was discovered that very considerable quantities of it was floating upon the surface of the water; and to prevent the possibility of any of its being saved for use, a number of small boats were manned by sailors and citizens, who rowed them into those parts of the harbour wherever the tea was visible, and by beating it with oars and paddles, so thoroughly drenched it, as to render its entire destruction inevitable.

Questions

1. How thorough was the planning for the Boston Tea Party?
2. Were the participants eager to have their names known? Why or why not?
3. What, if any, specific rights does Hewes claim that he was trying to support by participating in the Boston Tea Party?

5-11   The Edenton, North Carolina, Boycott Agreement (1774)

When colonists decided to attack the Tea Act of 1773 by boycotting British goods, they were using a tried and heretofore effective means of countering British legislation. Therefore, it was logical for the convention called in New Bern, North Carolina, in August 1774 to protest the Port of Boston Act to call for nonimportation of any British East India Company goods, British manufactures, slaves, and tea, and for a ban on all consumption of tea in the province. Furthermore, as Document 5-5 shows, women had signed such agreements before, at least in Boston in 1770. But the agreement that the women of Edenton, North Carolina, signed on October 25, 1774, shortly after the adjournment of the New Bern convention struck contemporaries as particularly unusual. Indeed, the women's action was judged so extraordinary that a British print reproduced in the textbook (p. 170) was issued to ridicule it.

Source: Peter Force, ed., *American Archives,* 4th ser. (1837), 1: 891–892.

ASSOCIATION SIGNED BY LADIES OF EDENTON, NORTH CAROLINA, OCTOBER 25, 1774
As we cannot be indifferent on any occasion that appears to affect the peace and happiness of our country; and as it has been thought necessary for the publick good to enter into several particular Resolves by a meeting of Members of Deputies from the whole Province, it is a duty that we owe not only to our near and dear relations and connexions, but to ourselves, who are essentially interested in their welfare, to do every thing as far as lies in our power to testify our sincere adherence to the same; and we do therefore accordingly subscribe this paper as a witness of our fixed intention and solemn determination to do so.
Signed by fifty-one Ladies

Questions

1. Do the women who entered into this agreement appear to be leaders of the boycott movement, or do they appear to be responding to the actions of others?
2. To what extent, if any, do the signers of the agreement clearly spell out the basic rights they believed they were supporting?
3. Does it appear that the specifics of the agreement, including any provisions for its enforcement, would help make the boycott effective?
4. If you compare this document with the agreements signed by Boston women in 1770 (Document 5-7), would you say that what the Edenton women did was much more radical than what the Boston women had done? Why or why not?

5-12   Plan of Union (1774)

Joseph Galloway

Despite the British reform efforts that produced such conflict and hostility between colonists and the British government, Americans moved toward independence reluctantly and cautiously (see text pp. 168–170). Indeed, as the authors of the textbook note, support for the Patriot cause was far from unanimous. Joseph Galloway of Pennsylvania took a leading role among those members of the Continental Congress who, as the textbook authors note, considered themselves "men of 'loyal principles'"(text p. 168). Galloway offered the following plan in the hope that it would allow America and Britain to end the growing confrontation. But the Continental Congress rejected Galloway's plan. When the colonists declared their independence, Galloway cast his lot with Great Britain, moved to England in 1778, and lived out his life as an exile from his native land.

Source: W. C. Ford, ed., *Journals of the Continental Congress, 1774–1789* (Washington, D.C.: U.S. Government Printing Office, 1904), 1: 49–51.

[28 September, 1774]

Resolution submitted by Joseph Galloway:

Resolved, That the Congress will apply to his Majesty for a redress of grievances under which his faithful subjects in America labour; and assure him, that the Colonies hold in abhorrence the idea of being considered independent communities on the British government, and most ardently desire the establishment of a Political Union, not only among themselves, but with the Mother State, upon those principles of safety and freedom which are essential in the constitution of all free governments, and particularly that of the British Legislature; and as the Colonies from their local circumstances, cannot be represented in the Parliament of Great-Britain, they will humbly propose to his Majesty and his two Houses of Parliament, the following plan, under which the strength of the whole Empire may be drawn together on any emergency, the interest of both countries advanced, and the rights and liberties of America secured.

A Plan of a proposed Union between Great Britain and the Colonies.

That a British and American legislature, for regulating the administration of the general affairs of America, be proposed and established in America, including all the said colonies; within, and under which government, each colony shall retain its present constitution, and powers of regulating and governing its own internal police, in all cases what[so]ever.

That the said government be administered by a President General, to be appointed by the King, and a grand Council, to be chosen by the Representatives of the people of the several colonies, in their respective assemblies, once in every three years.

That the several assemblies shall choose members for the grand council. . . .

Who shall meet at the city of   for the first time, being called by the President-General, as soon as conveniently may be after his appointment.

That there shall be a new election of members for the Grand Council every three years; and on the death, removal or resignation of any member, his place shall be supplied by a new choice, at the next sitting of Assembly of the Colony he represented.

That the Grand Council shall meet once in every year, if they shall think it necessary, and oftener, if occasions shall require, at such time and place as they shall adjourn to, at the last preceding meeting, or as they shall be called to meet at, by the President-General, on any emergency.

That the grand Council shall have power to choose their Speaker, and shall hold and exercise all the like rights, liberties and privileges, as are held and exercised by and in the House of Commons of Great-Britain.

That the President-General shall hold his office during the pleasure of the King, and his assent shall be requisite to all acts of the Grand Council, and it shall be his office and duty to cause them to be carried into execution.

That the President-General, by and with the advice and consent of the Grand-Council, hold and exercise all the legislative rights, powers, and authorities, necessary for regulating and administering all the general police and affairs of the colonies, in which Great-Britain and the colonies, or any of them, the colonies in general, or more than one colony, are in any manner concerned, as well civil and criminal as commercial.

That the said President-General and the Grand Council, be an inferior and distinct branch of the British legislature, united and incorporated with it, for the aforesaid general purposes; and that any of the said general regulations may originate and be formed and digested, either in the Parliament of Great Britain, or in the said Grand Council, and being prepared, transmitted to the other for their approbation or dissent; and that the assent of both shall be requisite to the validity of all such general acts or statutes.

That in time of war, all bills for granting aid to the crown, prepared by the Grand Council, and approved by the President General, shall be valid and passed into a law, without the assent of the British Parliament.

Questions

1. As the authors of the textbook indicate, the colonists had staunchly resisted British efforts to tax them without their consent. Under Galloway's plan, would Parliament be able to tax the colonies? Why or why not?

2. As the authors of the textbook indicate, Benjamin Franklin and Thomas Hutchinson had sharply differing views about the issue of sovereignty and the British empire (text p. 163). Considering the basic features of the Galloway plan, does it seem closer to the view of Franklin or to Hutchinson's views? Why?

3. If the Continental Congress had been willing to support Galloway's plan, do you believe the British government would have been willing to endorse and implement the plan? Why or why not? (*Hint*: In addition to considering the material in the text, it might be helpful to review Document 5-1.)

5-13   The Continental Congress Creates the Association (1774)

As described in the textbook (pp. 168–169), the harsh British response to the Boston Tea Party spurred the colonists to create a Continental Congress to coordinate opposition to British imperial reform measures, especially the Coercive Acts. The Congress began deliberations in Philadelphia on September 5, 1774, and adjourned on October 26, 1774. As part of its general effort to defend colonial rights, the Congress created a Plan of Association. The Association, as it was called, outlined actions that the Congress and the people would take to try to force Britain into rescinding the measures that the colonists believed threatened their basic rights. The Association was passed on October 18; the formal copy was signed two days later.

Source: W. C. Ford, ed., *Journals of the Continental Congress, 1774–1789* (1904), 1: 75–80.

We, his majesty's most loyal subjects, the delegates of the several colonies of New-Hampshire, Massachusetts-Bay, Rhode-Island, Connecticut, New-York, New-Jersey, Pennsylvania, the three lower counties of New-Castle, Kent and Sussex, on Delaware, Maryland, Virginia, North-Carolina, and South-Carolina, deputed to represent them in a continental Congress, held in the city of Philadelphia, on the 5th day of September, 1774, avowing our allegiance to his majesty, our affection and regard for our fellow-subjects in Great-Britain and elsewhere, affected with the deepest anxiety, and most alarming apprehensions, at those grievances and distresses, with which his Majesty's American subjects are oppressed; and having taken under our most serious deliberation, the state of the whole continent, find, that the present unhappy situation of our affairs is occasioned by a ruinous system of colony administration, adopted by the British ministry about the year 1763, evidently calculated for inslaving these colonies, and, with them, the British empire. In prosecution of which system, various acts of parliament have been passed, for raising a revenue in America, for depriving the American subjects, in many instances, of the constitutional trial by jury, exposing their lives to danger, by directing a new and illegal trial beyond the seas, for crimes alleged to have been committed in America: and in prosecution of the same system, several late, cruel, and oppressive acts have been passed, respecting the town of Boston and the Massachusetts-Bay, and also an act for extending the province of Quebec, so as to border on the western frontiers of these colonies, establishing an arbitrary government therein, and discouraging the settlement of British subjects in that wide extended country; thus, by the influence of civil principles and ancient prejudices, to dispose the inhabitants to act with hostility against the free Protestant colonies, whenever a wicked ministry shall chuse so to direct them.

To obtain redress of these grievances, which threaten destruction to the lives, liberty, and property of his majesty's subjects, in North America, we are of opinion, that a non-importation, non-consumption, and non-exportation agreement, faithfully adhered to, will prove the most speedy, effectual, and peaceable measure: and, therefore, we do, for ourselves, and the inhabitants of the several colonies, whom we represent, firmly agree and associate, under the sacred ties of virtue, honour and love of our country, as follows:

1. That from and after the first day of December next, we will not import, into British America, from Great-Britain or Ireland, any goods, wares, or merchandise whatsoever, or from any other place, any such goods, wares, or merchandise, as shall have been exported from Great-Britain or Ireland; nor will we, after that day, import any East-India tea from any part of the world; nor any molasses, syrups, paneles, coffee, or pimento, from the British plantations or from Dominica; nor wines from Madeira, or the Western Islands; nor foreign indigo.

2. We will neither import nor purchase, any slave imported after the first day of December next; after which time, we will wholly discontinue the slave trade, and will neither be concerned in it ourselves, nor will we hire our vessels, nor sell our commodities or manufactures to those who are concerned in it.

3. As a non-consumption agreement, strictly adhered to, will be an effectual security for the observation of the non-importation, we, as above, solemnly agree and associate, that, from this day, we will not purchase or use any tea, imported on account of the East-India company, or any on which a duty hath been or shall be paid; and from and after the first day of March next, we will not purchase or use any East-India tea whatever; nor will we, nor shall any person for or under us, purchase or use any of those goods, wares, or merchandise, we have agreed not to import, which we shall know, or have cause to suspect, were imported after the first day of December, except such as come under the rules and directions of the tenth article hereafter mentioned.

4. The earnest desire we have, not to injure our fellow-subjects in Great-Britain, Ireland, or the West-Indies, induces us to suspend a non-exportation, until the tenth day of September, 1775; at which time, if the said acts and parts of acts of the British parliament herein after mentioned are not repealed, we will not, directly or indirectly, export any merchandise or commodity whatsoever to Great-Britain, Ireland, or the West-Indies, except rice to Europe.

5. Such as are merchants, and use the British and Irish trade, will give orders, as soon as possible, to their factors, agents and correspondents, in Great-Britain and Ireland, not to ship any goods to them, on any pretence whatsoever, as they cannot be received in America; and if any merchant, residing in Great-Britain or Ireland, shall directly or indirectly ship any goods, wares or merchandise, for America, in order to break the said non-importation agreement, or in any manner contravene the same, on such unworthy conduct being well attested, it ought to be made public; and on the same being so done, we will not, from thenceforth, have any commercial connexion with such merchant.

6. That such as are owners of vessels will give positive orders to their captains, or masters, not to receive on board their vessels any goods prohibited by the said non-importation agreement, on pain of immediate dismission from their service.

7. We will use our utmost endeavours to improve the breed of sheep, and increase their number to the greatest extent; and to that end, we will kill them as seldom as may be, especially those of the most profitable kind; nor will we export any to the West-Indies or elsewhere; and those of us, who are or may become overstocked with, or can conveniently spare any sheep, will dispose of them to our neighbours, especially to the poorer sort, on moderate terms.

8. We will, in our several stations, encourage frugality, economy, and industry, and promote agriculture, arts and the manufactures of this country, especially that of wool; and will discountenance and discourage every species of extravagance and dissipation, especially all horse-racing, and all kinds of gaming, cock-fighting, exhibitions of shews, plays, and other expensive diversions and entertainments; and on the death of any relation or friend, none of us, or any of our families, will go into any further mourning-dress, than a black crape or ribbon on the arm or hat, for gentlemen, and a black ribbon and necklace for ladies, and we will discontinue the giving of gloves and scarves at funerals.

9. Such as are venders of goods or merchandise will not take advantage of the scarcity of goods, that may be occasioned by this association, but will sell the same at the rates we have been respectively accustomed to do, for twelve months last past.—And if any vender of goods or merchandise shall sell any such goods on higher terms, or shall, in any manner, or by any device whatsoever violate or depart from this agreement, no person ought, nor will any of us deal with any such person, or his or her factor or agent, at any time thereafter, for any commodity whatever.

10. In case any merchant, trader, or other person, shall import any goods or merchandise, after the first day of December, and before the first day of February next, the same ought forthwith, at the election of the owner, to be either re-shipped or delivered up to the committee of the county or town, wherein they shall be imported, to be stored at the risque of the importer, until the non-importation agree-

ment shall cease, or be sold under the direction of the committee aforesaid; and in the last-mentioned case, the owner or owners of such goods shall be reimbursed out of the sales, the first cost and charges, the profit, if any, to be applied towards relieving and employing such poor inhabitants of the town of Boston, as are immediate sufferers by the Boston port-bill; and a particular account of all goods so returned, stored, or sold, to be inserted in the public papers; and if any goods or merchandises shall be imported after the said first day of February, the same ought forthwith to be sent back again, without breaking any of the packages thereof.

11. That a committee be chosen in every county, city, and town, by those who are qualified to vote for representatives in the legislature, whose business it shall be attentively to observe the conduct of all persons touching this association; and when it shall be made to appear, to the satisfaction of a majority of any such committee, that any person within the limits of their appointment has violated this association, that such majority do forthwith cause the truth of the case to be published in the gazette; to the end, that all such foes to the rights of British-America may be publicly known, and universally contemned as the enemies of American liberty; and thenceforth we respectively will break off all dealings with him or her.

12. That the committee of correspondence, in the respective colonies, do frequently inspect the entries of their custom-houses, and inform each other, from time to time, of the true state thereof, and of every other material circumstance that may occur relative to this association.

13. That all manufactures of this country be sold at reasonable prices, so that no undue advantage be taken of a future scarcity of goods.

14. And we do further agree and resolve, that we will have no trade, commerce, dealings or intercourse whatsoever, with any colony or province, in North-America, which shall not accede to, or which shall hereafter violate this association, but will hold them as unworthy of the rights of freemen, and as inimical to the liberties of their country.

And we do solemnly bind ourselves and our constituents, under the ties aforesaid, to adhere to this association, until such parts of the several acts of parliament passed since the close of the last war, as impose or continue duties on tea, wine, molasses, syrups, paneles, coffee, sugar, pimento, indigo, foreign paper, glass, and painters' colours, imported into America, and extend the powers of the admiralty courts beyond their ancient limits, deprive the American subject of trial by jury, authorize the judge's certificate to indemnify the prosecutor from damages, that he might otherwise be liable to from a trial by his peers, require oppressive security from a claimant of ships or goods seized, before he shall be allowed to defend his property, are repealed.—And until that part of the act of the 12 G. 3. ch. 24, entitled "An act for the better securing his majesty's dock-yards, magazines, ships, ammunition, and stores," by which any persons charged with committing any of the offences therein described, in America, may be tried in any shire or county within the realm, is repealed—and until the four acts, passed the last session of parliament, viz. that for stopping the port and blocking up the harbour of Boston—that for altering the charter and government of the Massachusetts-Bay—and that which is entitled "An act for the better administration of justice, &c."—and that "for extending the limits of Quebec, &c." are repealed. And we recommend it to the provincial conventions, and to the committees in the respective colonies, to establish such farther regulations as they may think proper, for carrying into execution this association.

The foregoing association being determined upon by the Congress, was ordered to be subscribed by the several members thereof; and thereupon, we have hereunto set our respective names accordingly.

IN CONGRESS, PHILADELPHIA, *October 20, 1774*

Questions

1. What essential tool did the Congress hope to use to get Britain to rescind its imperial reforms? Does it appear that the Congress was well versed in the use of that tool?

2. How fully and forcefully, if at all, does the Association state what the Congress considered to be the essential basic rights of the colonists?

3. What measures did the Congress propose to ensure that its dictates were followed? Would you expect those measures to be effective? Why or why not?

4. Judging from the Association, what kind of imperial policies did the Continental Congress want the British government to follow? What would the British government have to do to restore harmony?

5. What insights does the document give you into the principal economic activities of the American colonies at that time?

Questions for Further Thought

1. On the basis of these documents, what basic political rights did the Patriots believe they were supporting?

2. In what ways are the statements about basic rights in these documents similar or dissimilar to those advanced in Documents 5-3 through 5-5?

3. Did the colonists who opposed British imperial policies seem more concerned about basic political rights or about avoiding taxes?

4. Considering the positions taken and the arguments advanced by the Patriots in the period after the Boston Massacre, what would the British government have had to do to restore harmony and stop the process that led to war in April 1775?

CHAPTER **6**

War and Revolution, 1775–1783

★   ★   ★

Toward Independence, 1775–1776

Many troubles beset the American colonists when they went to war against Great Britain, the greatest imperial power in the world. One problem was that the movement toward war and the opening of hostilities produced a sharpening of the social divisions among Americans. The coming of war brought with it the possibility that artisans and people even lower on the socioeconomic ladder would gain more power. As Gouverneur Morris's observations (Document 6-1) show, some upper-class Patriots were bothered that less politically influential lower-class Patriots would use the Revolutionary War to increase their power.

The Revolution's opponents exploited the contradictions between Revolutionary appeals to "liberty" and Revolutionary leaders' own continuing devotion to race inequality. Lord Dunmore, the last royal governor of Virginia, sought to strike at the slave system on which rested the power of that colony's revolutionaries (Document 6-2), while the London Tory Samuel Johnson openly derided the contradictions of the Patriots' claims (Document 6-3). Thomas Jefferson himself was forced to wrestle with the contradiction between American aspirations to liberty and American slavery (Document 6-4).

It was also difficult to declare independence because the colonists had consistently stated that they loved the British monarchy and that George III was a noble monarch. Thus, Patriots believed that their fight was with Parliament, not with the king. With the publication of Thomas Paine's stunningly popular *Common Sense*, those issues were addressed directly and forcefully. As British efforts to suppress the "rebellion" took on the characteristics of a foreign invasion, attacks on King George III became the order of the day; even conservative Americans began to see separation from the only sovereign they had ever known as the only way to preserve social order (Document 6-5). When the Continental Congress finally declared independence on July 2, 1776, and then explained its reasons for doing so in the Declaration of Independence approved two days later, it simply crystallized the thinking of large numbers of its constituents.

6-1   The Poor Reptiles (1774)

Gouverneur Morris

Gouverneur Morris, who came from an established and wealthy New York family, was not a leading revolutionary Patriot in 1774. He had been graduated from King's College at the age of sixteen in 1768; six years later he was on the verge of starting his career as one of the leaders of the Revolution. Morris's service culminated in his appointment as a delegate to the U.S. Constitutional Convention. In a letter he wrote to Thomas Penn on May 20, 1774, Morris offered his judgment on how the movement toward independence might transform America's political society. In doing so, he illustrates that social divisions were sharpened during the era of the War of Independence.

Source: Peter Force, ed., *American Archives,* 4th ser. (1837) 1: 342–343.

DEAR SIR:

You have heard, and you will hear a great deal about politics, and in the heap of chaff you may find some grains of good sense. Believe me, sir, freedom and religion are only watchwords. We have appointed a committee, or rather we have nominated one. Let me give you the history of it. It is needless to premise that the lower orders of mankind are more easily led by specious appearances than those of a more exalted station. This, and many similar propositions, you know better than your humble servant.

The troubles in America during Grenville's administration put our gentry upon this finesse. They stimulated some daring coxcombs to rouse the mob into an attack upon the bounds of order and decency. These fellows became the Jack Cades of the day, the leaders in all the riots, the bell-wethers of the flock. The reason of the manœuvre in those who wished to keep fair with the government, and at the same time to receive the incense of popular applause, you will readily perceive. On the whole, the shepherds were not much to blame in a politic point of view. The bell-wethers jingled merrily and roared out liberty and property, and religion, and a multitude of cant terms which everyone thought he understood, and was egregiously mistaken. For you must know the shepherds kept the dictionary of the day, and like the mysteries of the ancient mythology, it was not for profane eyes or ears. This answered many purposes; the simple flock put themselves entirely under the protection of these most excellent shepherds. By and by, behold a great metamorphosis without the help of Ovid or his divinities, but entirely effectuated by two modern Genii, the god of Ambition and the goddess of Faction. The first of these prompted the shepherds to shear some of their flock, and then in conjunction with the other, converted the bell-wethers into shepherds. That we have been in hot water with the British Parliament ever since everybody knows. Consequently these new shepherds had their hands full of employment. The old ones kept themselves least in sight, and a want of confidence in each other was not the least evil which followed. The port of Boston has been shut up. These sheep, simple as they are, cannot be gulled as heretofore. In short, there is no ruling them, and now, to leave the metaphor, the heads of the mobility grow dangerous to the gentry, and how to keep them down is the question. While they correspond with the other colonies, call and dismiss popular assemblies, make resolves to bind the consciences of the rest of mankind, bully poor printers, and exert with full force all their other tribunitial powers, it is impossible to curb them.

But art sometimes goes farther than force, and therefore, to trick them handsomely a committee of patricians was to be nominated, and into their hands was to be committed the majesty of the people, and the highest trust was to be reposed in them by a mandate that they should take care, that the republic should not suffer injury. The tribunes, through the want of good legerdemain in the senatorial order, perceived the finesse; and yesterday I was present at a grand division of the city, and there I beheld my fellow-citizens very accurately counting all their chickens, not only before any of them were hatched, but before above one half of the eggs were laid. In short, they fairly contended about the future forms of our government, whether it should be founded upon aristocratic or democratic principles.

I stood in the balcony, and on my right hand were ranged all the people of property, with some few poor dependents, and on the other all the tradesmen, etc., who thought it worth their while to leave daily labour for the good of the country. The spirit of the English constitution has yet a little influence left, and but a little. The remains of it, however, will give the wealthy people a superiority this time, but would they secure it they must banish all schoolmasters and confine all knowledge to themselves. This cannot be. The mob begin to think and to reason. Poor reptiles! It is with them a vernal morning; they are struggling to cast off their winter's slough, they bask in the sunshine, and ere noon they will bite, depend upon it. The gentry begin to fear this. Their committee will be appointed, they will deceive the people and again forfeit a share of their confidence. And if these instances of what with one side is policy, with the other perfidy, shall continue to increase and become more frequent, farewell aristocracy. I see, and I see it with fear and trembling, that if the disputes with Great Britain continue, we shall be under the worst of all possible dominions; we shall be under the domination of a riotous mob.

It is the interest of all men, therefore, to seek for reunion with the parent state. . . .

Questions

1. What vital change in the American political system does Morris think is occurring?
2. Does he approve of that change? Why or why not?
3. When Morris talks of the "bell-wethers of the flock," he is talking about the leaders (the bellwethers) of sheep (the flock). What does this image tell you about his view of the average person?
4. In what ways, if any, do Morris's judgments remind you of the Loyalist Peter Oliver's pronouncements (Document 5-8)?

6-2 A Proclamation (1775)

Lord Dunmore

John Murray, earl of Dunmore (1732–1809) and the last royal governor of Virginia, was a beleaguered man in 1775. Lacking a standing army to enforce the king's will, he had effectively lost control of the colony to the Patriot gentry. Nonetheless, he thought he could recover by striking at the colonists' Achilles' heel: slavery. Thanks to a 1772 English court ruling, rumors abounded among Virginia slaves that they would be free if they got to English soil. Shortly after the Battles of Lexington and Concord, a group of slaves had offered Dunmore their services in exchange for their freedom. In November, after a unit of Dunmore's troops that included slaves had defeated the colonial militia, Dunmore issued this famous proclamation. Dunmore's promise was effective in attracting increasing numbers of runaway slaves to the Tory cause, and by December 1775 some three hundred African Americans were members of "Lord Dunmore's Ethiopian Regiment," wearing uniforms inscribed with the slogan "Liberty to Slaves." Shortly afterward, though, Dunmore was forced to abandon the mainland, and over the winter his waterborne troops were decimated by disease. But the episode sufficed to frighten Virginia slaveholders, including Thomas Jefferson (see Document 6-4).

Source: American Antiquarian Society, *Early American Imprints*, 1st ser., no. 14592.

By his Excellency the Right Honourable JOHN Earl of Dunmore, his Majesty's Lieutenant and Governour-General of the Colony and Dominion of Virginia, and Vice-Admiral of the same:

A PROCLAMATION.

As I have ever entertained Hopes that an Accommodation might have taken Place between *Great Britain* and this Colony, without being compelled, by my Duty, to this most disagreeable, but now absolutely necessary Step, rendered so by a Body of armed Men, unlawfully assembled, firing on his Majesty's Tenders, and the Formation of an Army, and that Army now on their March to attack his Majesty's Troops, and destroy the well-disposed Subjects of this Colony: To defeat such treasonable Purposes, and that all such Traitors, and their Abetters, may be brought to Justice, and that the Peace and good Order of this Colony may be again restored, which the ordinary Course of the civil Law is unable to effect, I have thought fit to issue this my Proclamation, hereby declaring, that until the aforesaid good Purposes can be obtained, I do, in Virtue of the Power and Authority to me given, by his Majesty, determine to execute martial Law, and cause the same to be executed throughout this Colony; and to the End that Peace and good Order may the sooner be restored, I do require every Person capable of bearing Arms to resort to his Majesty's STANDARD, or be looked upon as Traitors to his Majesty's Crown and Government, and thereby become liable to the Penalty the Law inflicts upon such Offences, such as Forfeiture of Life, Confiscation of Lands, &c. &c. And I do hereby farther declare all indented Servants, Negroes, or others (appertaining to Rebels) free, that are able and willing to bear Arms, they joining his Majesty's Troops, as soon as may be, for the more speedily reducing this Colony to a proper Sense of their Duty, to his Majesty's Crown and Dignity. I do farther order, and require, all his Majesty's liege Subjects to retain their Quitrents, or any other Taxes due, or that may become due, in their own Custody, till such Time as Peace may be again restored to this at present most unhappy Country, or demanded of them for their former salutary Purposes, by Officers properly authorised to receive the same.

GIVEN under my Hand, on Board the Ship William, *off* Norfolk, *the 7th of* November, *in the 16th Year of his Majesty's Reign.*

DUNMORE.

GOD SAVE THE KING.

Questions

1. How does Lord Dunmore instruct the Crown's loyal subjects to behave? What does he request that they do?
2. Do you think that Lord Dunmore's move to free the slaves of the "Rebels" convinced many of Virginia's rebellious gentry to switch sides and support the Crown? How do you think that Virginia's gentry reacted to Dunmore's edict on the status of their slaves?
3. Looking at this document, do you see any reason why a slave might find Dunmore's offer suspect?

6-3   On Liberty and Slavery (1775)

Samuel Johnson

At the time of its first meeting in September and October of 1774, the First Continental Congress issued a number of declarations setting forth the position of the colonists against the mother country, declarations that circulated widely in Britain and stirred considerable sympathy for the American cause. In an effort to respond, the government of Lord North recruited the eminent man of letters (and doughty Tory) Samuel Johnson to make its case. Dr. Johnson's product, the pamphlet *Taxation No Tyranny*, had to be toned down by the government before it was issued. Even then, Johnson's derisive tone and blunt conservatism guaranteed his pamphlet a hostile reception. Johnson had a keen eye for the contradictions built into the American case, especially regarding the colonies' claims of a legal right to disobey the government. He also found much merriment in their warnings that the mother country sought to impose "slavery" on a free land, as the following excerpts show.

Source: Donald J. Greene, ed., *Political Writings, The Yale Edition of the Works of Samuel Johnson* (New Haven, Conn.: Yale University Press, 1977), 411–412, 428–429, 436–437, 441–443, 448–451, 453–454. (*Note:* Footnotes are from the Yale University Press edition.)

TAXATION NO TYRANNY;
AN ANSWER TO THE RESOLUTIONS AND ADDRESS OF THE AMERICAN CONGRESS

In all the parts of human knowledge, whether terminating in science merely speculative, or operating upon life private or civil, are admitted some fundamental principles, or common axioms, which being generally received are little doubted, and being little doubted have been rarely proved. . . .

Of this kind is the position that "the supreme power of every community has the right of requiring from all its subjects such contributions as are necessary to the public safety or public prosperity,"[1] which was considered by all mankind as comprising the primary and essential condition of all political society, till it became disputed by those zealots of anarchy, who have denied to the Parliament of Britain the right of taxing the American colonies. . . .

But hear, ye sons and daughters of liberty, the sounds which the winds are wafting from the western continent. The Americans are telling one another, what, if we may judge from their noisy triumph, they have but lately discovered, and what yet is a very important truth. "That they are entitled to life, liberty, and property, and that they have never ceded to any sovereign power whatever a right to dispose of either without their consent."

While this resolution stands alone, the Americans are free from singularity of opinion; their wit has not yet betrayed them to heresy. While they speak as the naked sons of Nature, they claim but what is claimed by other men, and have withheld nothing but what all withhold. They are here upon firm ground, behind entrenchments which never can be forced.

Humanity is very uniform. The Americans have this resemblance to Europeans, that they do not always know when they are well. They soon quit the fortress that could neither have been mined by sophistry, nor battered by declamation. Their next resolution declares, that "their ancestors, who first settled the colonies, were, at the time of their emigration from the mother-country, entitled to all the rights, liberties, and immunities of free and natural-born subjects within the realm of England."

This likewise is true; but when this is granted, their boast of original rights is at an end; they are no longer in a state of nature. These lords of themselves, these kings of *Me*, these demigods of independence, sink down to colonists, governed by a charter. If their ancestors were subjects, they acknowledged a sovereign; if they had a right to English privileges, they were accountable to English laws, and what must grieve the lover of liberty to discover, had ceded to the King and Parliament, whether the right or not, at least the power, of disposing, "without their consent, of their lives, liberties, and properties." It therefore is required of them to prove, that the Parliament ever ceded to them a dispensation from that obedience, which they owe as natural-born subjects, or any degree of independence or immunity not enjoyed by other Englishmen.

They say, that by such emigration they by no means forfeited, surrendered, or lost any of those rights; but that "they were, and their descendents now are, entitled to the exercise and enjoyment of all such of them as their local and other circumstances enable them to exercise and enjoy."

That they who form a settlement by a lawful charter, having committed no crime, forfeit no privileges, will be readily confessed; but what they do not forfeit by any judicial sentence, they may lose by natural effects. As man can be but in one place at once, he cannot have the advantages of multiplied residence. He that will enjoy the brightness of sunshine, must quit the coolness of the shade. He who goes voluntarily to America, cannot complain of losing what he leaves in Europe. . . .

It must always be remembered that they are represented by the same virtual representation as the greater part of Englishmen; and that if by change of place they have less share in the legislature than is proportionate to their opulence, they by their removal gained that opulence, and had originally and have now their choice of a vote at home, or riches at a distance. . . .

The friends of the Americans indeed ask for them what they do not ask for themselves. This inestimable right of representation they have never solicited. They mean not to exchange solid money for such airy honour. They say, and say willingly, that they cannot conveniently be represented; because their inference is, that they cannot be taxed. They are too remote to share the general govern-

---

[1] If this is a quotation, its source has not been traced. But it may be SJ's own formulation (of a position common enough in earlier works on government). . . . The *Monthly Review* (Mar 1775, p. 253), which devotes considerable space to examining the proposition, seems to treat the phraseology as SJ's own; so does Sir John Hawkins (*Life*, ed. B. H. Davis, 1961, p. 218).

ment, and therefore claim the privilege of governing themselves. . . .

One mode of persuasion their ingenuity has suggested, which it may perhaps be less easy to resist. That we may not look with indifference on the American contest, or imagine that the struggle is for a claim, which, however decided, is of small importance and remote consequence, the Philadelphian Congress has taken care to inform us, that they are resisting the demands of Parliament, as well for our sakes as their own.

Their keenness of perspicacity has enabled them to pursue consequences to a great distance; to see through clouds impervious to the dimness of European sight; and to find, I know not how, that when they are taxed, we shall be enslaved.

That slavery is a miserable state we have been often told, and doubtless many a Briton will tremble to find it so near as in America; but how it will be brought hither, the Congress must inform us. The question might distress a common understanding; but the statesmen of the other hemisphere can easily resolve it. Our ministers, they say, are our enemies, and "if they should carry the point of taxation, may with the same army enslave us. It may be said, we will not pay them; but remember," say the western sages, "the taxes from America, and we may add the men, and particularly the Roman Catholics of this vast continent will then be in the power of your enemies. Nor have you any reason to expect, that after making slaves of us, many of us will refuse to assist in reducing you to the same abject state."

Thus formidable are their menaces; but suspecting that they have not much the sound of probability, the Congress proceeds: "Do not treat this as chimerical. Know that in less than half a century the quit-rents reserved to the crown from the numberless grants of this vast continent will pour large streams of wealth into the royal coffers. If to this be added the power of taxing America at pleasure, the crown will possess more treasure than may be necessary to purchase *the remains* of liberty in your island."

All this is very dreadful; but amidst the terror that shakes my frame, I cannot forbear to wish that some sluice were opened for these floods of treasure. I should gladly see America return half of what England has expended in her defence; and of the "stream" that will "flow so largely in less than half a century," I hope a small rill at least may be found to quench the thirst of the present generation, which seems to think itself in more danger of wanting money than of losing liberty.

It is difficult to judge with what intention such airy bursts of malevolence are vented: if such writers hope to deceive, let us rather repel them with scorn, than refute them by disputation.

In this last terrifick paragraph are two positions that, if our fears do not overpower our reflection, may enable us to support life a little longer. We are told by these croakers of calamity, not only that our present ministers design to

enslave us, but that the same malignity of purpose is to descend through all their successors, and that the wealth to be poured into England by the Pactolus[2] of America will, whenever it comes, be employed to purchase "the remains of liberty."[3] . . .

It has been of late a very general practice to talk of slavery among those who are setting at defiance every power that keeps the world in order. If the learned author of the *Reflections on Learning* has rightly observed, that no man ever could give law to language, it will be vain to prohibit the use of the word "slavery"; but I could wish it more discreetly uttered; it is driven at one time too hard into our ears by the loud hurricane of Pennsylvanian eloquence, and at another glides too cold into our hearts by the soft conveyance of a female patriot bewailing the miseries of her "friends and fellow-citizens."[4]

Such has been the progress of sedition, that those who a few years ago disputed only our right of laying taxes, now question the validity of every act of legislation. They consider themselves as emancipated from obedience, and as being no longer the subjects of the British Crown. They leave us no choice but of yielding or conquering, of resigning our dominion, or maintaining it by force.

From force many endeavours have been used, either to dissuade, or to deter us. Sometimes the merit of the Americans is exalted, and sometimes their sufferings are aggravated. We are told of their contributions to the last war, a war incited by their outcries, and continued for their protection, a war by which none but themselves were gainers. All that they can boast is, that they did something for themselves, and did not wholly stand inactive, while the sons of Britain were fighting in their cause.

If we cannot admire, we are called to pity them; to pity those that shew no regard to their mother country; have obeyed no law which they could violate; have imparted no good which they could withold; have entered into associations of fraud to rob their creditors; and into combinations to distress all who depended on their commerce. We are reproached with the cruelty of shutting one port, where every port is shut against us. We are censured as tyrannical for hindering those from fishing, who have condemned our merchants to bankruptcy and our manufacturers to hunger.

Others persuade us to give them more liberty, to take off restraints, and relax authority; and tell us what happy consequences will arise from forbearance: How their affections will be conciliated, and into what diffusions of benef-

---

[2]The river in which Midas bathed, and which thus became gold-bearing.

[3]Quoted from *Votes and Proceedings*, p. 40.

[4]Catharine Sawbridge Macaulay, *An Address to the People of England, Scotland and Ireland, on the Present Important Crisis of Affairs* (1775), p. 5: "It can be no secret to you, my friends and fellow-citizens. . . ." She continues to use the phrase *ad nauseam*. Mrs. Macaulay's pamphlet was in part a direct attack on SJ's *The Patriot*.

icence their gratitude will luxuriate. They will love their friends, they will reverence their protectors. They will throw themselves into our arms, and lay their property at our feet. They will buy from no other what we can sell them; they will sell to no other what we wish to buy.

That any obligations should overpower their attention to profit, we have known them long enough not to expect. It is not to be expected from a more liberal people. With what kindness they repay benefits, they are now shewing us, who, as soon as we have delivered them from France, are defying and proscribing us.

But if we will permit them to tax themselves, they will give us more than we require. If we proclaim them independent, they will during pleasure pay us a subsidy. The contest is not now for money, but for power. The question is not how much we shall collect, but by what authority the collection shall be made. . . .

The Dean of Gloucester has proposed, and seems to propose it seriously, that we should at once release our claims, declare them masters of themselves, and whistle them down the wind. His opinion is, that our gain from them will be the same, and our expence less. What they can have most cheaply from Britain, they will still buy, what they can sell to us at the highest price they will still sell.

It is, however, a little hard, that having so lately fought and conquered for their safety, we should govern them no longer. By letting them loose before the war, how many millions might have been saved. One wild proposal is best answered by another. Let us restore to the French what we have taken from them. We shall see our colonists at our feet, when they have an enemy so near them. Let us give the Indians arms, and teach them discipline, and encourage them now and then to plunder a plantation. Security and leisure are the parents of sedition.

While these different opinions are agitated, it seems to be determined by the legislature, that force shall be tried. Men of the pen have seldom any great skill in conquering kingdoms but they have strong inclination to give advice. I cannot forbear to wish, that this commotion may end without bloodshed, and that the rebels may be subdued by terrour rather than by violence; and therefore recommend such a force as may take away, not only the power, but the hope of resistance, and by conquering without a battle, save many from the sword.

If their obstinacy continues without actual hostilities, it may perhaps be mollified by turning out the soldiers to free quarters, forbidding any personal cruelty or hurt. It has been proposed, that the slaves should be set free, an act which surely the lovers of liberty cannot but commend. If they are furnished with fire arms for defence, and utensils for husbandry, and settled in some simple form of government within the country, they may be more grateful and honest than their masters. . . .

Since the Americans have made it necessary to subdue them, may they be subdued with the least injury possible to their persons and their possessions. When they are reduced to obedience, may that obedience be secured by stricter laws and stronger obligations.

Nothing can be more noxious to society than that erroneous clemency, which, when a rebellion is suppressed, exacts no forfeiture and establishes no securities, but leaves the rebels in their former state. Who would not try the experiment which promises advantage without expence? If rebels once obtain a victory, their wishes are accomplished; if they are defeated, they suffer little, perhaps less than their conquerors; however often they play the game, the chance is always in their favour. In the mean time, they are growing rich by victualing the troops that we have sent against them, and perhaps gain more by the residence of the army than they lose by the obstruction of their port.[5]

Their charters being now, I suppose, legally forfeited, may be modelled as shall appear most commodious to the mother-country. Thus the privileges, which are found by experience liable to misuse, will be taken away, and those who now bellow as patriots, bluster as soldiers, and domineer as legislators, will sink into sober merchants and silent planters, peaceably diligent, and securely rich.

But there is one writer, and perhaps many who do not write, to whom the contraction of these pernicious privileges appears very dangerous, and who startle at the thoughts of "England free and America in chains."[6] Children fly from their own shadow, and rhetoricians are frighted by their own voices. "Chains" is undoubtedly a dreadful word; but perhaps the masters of civil wisdom may discover some gradations between chains and anarchy. Chains need not be put upon those who will be restrained without them. This contest may end in the softer phrase of English superiority and American obedience.

We are told, that the subjection of Americans may tend to the diminution of our own liberties: an event, which none but very perspicacious politicians are able to foresee. If slavery be thus fatally contagious, how is it that we hear the loudest yelps for liberty among the drivers of negroes?[7] . . .

---

[5] In May 1774 General Gage, the new Governor of Massachusetts, arrived in Boston with four regiments, to enforce the Boston Port Act.

[6] Perhaps a reference to the opening of the Continental Congress's Address to the People of Great Britain (in *Votes and Proceedings*): "When a nation, led to greatness by the hand of Liberty, and possessed by all the glory that heroism, munificence, and humanity can bestow, descends to the ungrateful task of forging chains for her Friends and Children, and instead of giving support to Freedom, turns advocate for Slavery and Oppression. . . ." The author may have been John Jay (cf. Edmund Cody Burnett, *The Continental Congress*, 1941, p. 52).

[7] Southern slave-owners, notably Patrick Henry and Thomas Jefferson, were among the most voluble propagandists for American "freedom." It may be to this memorable comment that SJ referred four years later in his "Life of Milton": "It has been observed that they who most loudly clamour for liberty do not most liberally grant it" (*Lives*, 1.157, par. 170).

Questions

1. On what grounds does Johnson make the British case against the American position on independence? Where does he believe that the American Patriots exhibit faulty reasoning? What is his overall argument?
2. In Johnson's view, taxes and money are not the real issues at stake. What does he believe that the colonists really want? How negotiable is the Crown's position?
3. British and Americans alike use words like *freedom, liberty,* and *slavery* to define their positions. In the excerpt from Johnson's pamphlet, is it fair to say that to the British and Americans, these words meant very different things to each side? Explain.

6-4 Condemning the King on the Issue of Slavery (1776)

Thomas Jefferson

As the full text of the Declaration of Independence reveals (see text pp. D1–D2), Thomas Jefferson, the principal author, prepared a lengthy and varied bill of indictment against George III. However, not all the charges Jefferson drew up gained the approval of the Continental Congress. Indeed, the Congress totally expunged from its records what would have been the longest section in Jefferson's list of charges against the king. Congress took that extraordinary action because the Georgia and South Carolina delegations had said that they would not sign the Declaration unless that section was eliminated. The "missing" section is reprinted here.

Source: Julian P. Boyd, ed., *The Papers of Thomas Jefferson,* 1: 426. Copyright © 1950 by Princeton University Press. Reprinted by permission of Princeton University Press.

He [the king] has waged cruel war against human nature itself, violating it's most sacred rights of life & liberty in the persons of a distant people who never offended him, captivating & carrying them into slavery in another hemisphere, or to incur miserable death in their transportation thither. this piratical warfare, the opprobrium of *infidel* powers, is the warfare of the CHRISTIAN king of Great Britain. determined to keep open a market where MEN should be bought & sold, he has prostituted his negative for suppressing every legislative attempt to prohibit or to restrain this execrable commerce: and that this assemblage of horrors might want no fact of distinguished die, he is now exciting those very people to rise in arms among us, and to purchase that liberty of which *he* has deprived them, by murdering the people upon whom *he* also obtruded them; thus paying off former crimes committed against the *liberties* of one people, with crimes which he urges them to commit against the *lives* of another.

Questions

1. Comparing this section with the pronouncement in the Declaration of Independence that "all men are created equal" (see text p. D-1), is it accurate to say that as Jefferson uses it, the term *men* stands for both men and women?
2. Is Jefferson saying that slavery is wrong or just that the slave trade is wrong? Why or why not?
3. Must the colonists share the blame for allowing the evils Jefferson denounces? Why or why not?

6-5   Two Local Declarations of Independence (1776)

Well before the drafting of the document we call *the* Declaration of Independence, state and local governments and citizens' groups were calling for separate nationhood. The arguments offered by these bodies in favor of independence varied according to their circumstances: some arguments were more elaborate than others; some were more reluctant in their conclusions than others. The two statements below are roughly representative of what the articulate citizenry of the colonies were telling their representatives in the Continental Congress, well before the Congress was ready to make the leap to independence. Note especially how the Buckingham freeholders retrace the steps that led them to their final position.

Source: Peter Force, *American Archives,* 4th ser. (Washington, D.C.: M. St. Clair Clarke and Peter Force, 1846), 6: 614-615, 1205-1209.

(a) Address and Instructions of the Freeholders (Buckingham County, Virginia, 1776)

To CHARLES PATTERSON *and* JOHN CABELL, *Gentlemen Delegates for the County of Buckingham, now in General Convention:*
The Address and Instructions of the Freeholders of the said County.

As you were elected and deputed by us to fill the most difficult and important places that the Representatives of this County were ever appointed to act in, we cannot, in justice to ourselves and posterity, forbear to give some instructions concerning the discharge of your great trust. In this we have the example of many; but would not tie you down in a manner too strict and positive. Though a general confidence in your honesty and wisdom may be required; yet, in some great and leading questions, it may not be unnecessary to take the sense of your constituents: we give you ours in the plainest, easiest, and best method it can be collected. If it does not agree with the general opinion, we trust, at least, it will be pardonable. Actuated by a warm and sincere regard for the interests and rights of mankind, and a deep sense of our present situation, we wish to think and proceed aright in affairs of such great consequence; and are willing, therefore, to submit our opinions to the candid judgment of the publick.

The unhappy dispute between *Great Britain* and these United Colonies seems now arrived to a crisis, from whence events ought to take place which, at the beginning, we believe, were in contemplation of but few, and even by them viewed at a much greater distance. When dissensions first arose, we felt our hearts warmly attached to the King of *Great Britain* and the Royal family; but now the case is much altered. At that time we wished to look upon the Ministry and Parliament as the only fountains from which the bitter waters flowed, and considered the King as deceived and misguided by his counsellors; and were therefore led to think that he might, in a proper time, open his eyes, and become a mediator between his contending subjects. The measures, however, still pursued against *America* leave no room to expect such an interposition from motives of goodness and affection, or with concessions, which may be justly required. Our enemies denounce our ruin, from the whole tenour of their conduct; and the King's speeches, and addresses, resolutions, and acts of the Parliament, are evidently concerted to carry their great favourite point. Prospects of a reconciliation have opened themselves to some; but they, we fear, were only the ignorant, credulous, and unwary; and even to them they must, ere this, have closed with more threatening appearances. The gracious receipt of a Continental petition, and the bare mention of Commissioners, have been severally construed good marks of reconcilement and peace, by those who too fondly hoped what was generally desired. . . .

When the *British* Parliament assumed an absolute power over us, and attempted to exercise that power, an opposition was formed in the United Colonies, the most pacifick which could be adopted, with any probability of success, in the last resort, should our enemies persist in their measures, and endeavour to drive us into submission by force. This opposition became a great offence in their eyes: our petitions were treated with contempt, our actions termed rebellious, and arms used to subdue us. As the Colonies seemed determined, from the first, to maintain their rights, and the rights of a free people, they were obliged to repel force by force; and, for the effectual purpose thereof, as occasions required, to take into their own hands the Legislative, Executive, and Judicial powers of Government. This was a necessary consequence, and no settled and permanent opposition could be made without it. They violated the faith of Charters, the principles of the Constitution, and attempted to destroy our legal as well as natural rights. We could do nothing without forming at least a temporary Government of our own, by laying aside that part, and dispensing with those forms, of the old Constitution, which were incompatible with our safety or success. They have broken through positive laws, and express acts of Assembly, as well as the ties which unite man to man in general affection; by which means they have become felons and enemies under those laws. In the struggle, the lives of hundreds have been destroyed; flourishing towns burnt down and demolished; property seized and taken, secretly and openly; thousands reduced from easy and affluent circumstances to poverty and distress; and all the horrors of an expensive and dreadful war experienced. We have opposed with arms, and persevered in our measures, with a resolution to maintain our rights, and regarded no law heretofore made but as it was found consistent with such a laudable design. Both sides grew every day more and more incensed, from circumstances which always arise in such contests; and that general confidence, so necessary to the support of every kind of Government, seems entirely annihilated, without a prospect of reunion of affections sufficient to restore it; it becomes daily more out of their power and farther from their inclinations to put us on the footing we stood at the close of the last war, or repair the great damages we have sustained; which, if they should ever confess their errors, and desire to close with us on the terms we have hitherto offered, they must, in justice and reason, agree ought to be done.

Besides, the welfare of ourselves and future generations obliges us to turn matters over in every point of view, and consider what has been the issue of contests most similar to our own. As virtue or publick spirit cannot be thoroughly lost in any country, but must survive in the breasts of many individuals, so it would be too sanguine to imagine that any country is without some men of ambitious and selfish views, who, taking the advantage of favourable opportunities and an unsettled state, turn the scale too much to their own side, and destroy the liberty or fix the chains of their country. This evil we find generally arises in or after civil broils, when the people have no established Government, or are led, from a sense of danger or unlimited confidence, to give themselves up blindly to their leaders. This misfortune, we hope, will never happen among us; nor do we believe that, at this time, there is any influence or inclination to effect or desire it. However, it is better to prevent evils than have them to remedy; and no precaution can be too great for the attainment of every valuable end to mankind. When things are fixed in a point beyond the present, many advantages may probably accrue; we, therefore, your constituents, recommend and instruct you, as far as your voices will contribute, to cause a total and final separation from *Great Britain* to take place as soon as possible; or, as we conceive this great point will not come within your immediate province, that, as far as in your power, you cause such instructions to be given to the Delegates from this Colony to the Continental Congress; that you weigh well the importance of the matter, and endeavour to lodge power in the hands of those whose honesty, wisdom, and love for their country, will direct them to use it for the publick good; that, as far as you conceive are ad-

mitted, you cause a free and happy Constitution to be established, with a renunciation of the old, or so much thereof as has been found inconvenient and oppressive; and that you endeavour to fix a publick jealousy in this Constitution, as an essential principle of its support.

In the present unsettled state of affairs, when the Government erected among us is confessed on all hands to be only temporary, for the immediate purpose of opposing the arbitrary strides of *Great Britain*, and effecting a reconciliation with the mother country; when the contest is between subject and subject, with the established power of peace and war at the head of our enemies, and our professions and actions tend only to bring about a reconciliation, we have not the least room to believe that any foreign nation will espouse our cause in an open and an avowed manner; but when we lay aside these considerations, and bid the last adieu, some foreign power may, for their own interest, lend an assisting hand, settle a trade, and enable us to discharge the great burdens of the war, which otherwise may become intolerable. . . .

Here, again, we would direct you, as far as relates to your Province, to beware of any other than commercial alliances with foreigners; and to keep their armies off your shores, if possible. We ask for a full representation; free and frequent elections; and that no standing armies whatever should be kept up in time of peace. We trust you will use your utmost care and circumspection at this trying crisis, that, as *America* is the last of the world which has contended for her liberty, so she may be the most free and happy. She has many advantages which others in nearly her circumstances have not known, arising from her situation and strength, and the experience of all before to profit by. View well the defects in other Governments, and consider the visible causes which reduced them from freedom to slavery, or raised them from slavery to liberty; and learn by these examples. It was by a Revolution, and the choice of the people, that the present Royal family was seated on the Throne of *Great Britain*; and we conceive the Supreme Being hath left it in our power to choose what Government we please for our civil and religious happiness; and when that becomes defective, or deviates from the end of its institution, and cannot be corrected, that the people may form themselves into another, avoiding the defects of the former. This we would now wish to have effected, as soon as the general consent approves, and the wisdom of our councils will admit; that we may, as far as possible, keep up our primary object, and not lose ourselves in hankering after a reconciliation with *Great Britain*.

Good Government alone, and the prosperity of mankind, can be in the Divine intention; we pray, therefore, that, under the superintending providence of the Ruler of the Universe, a Government may be established in *America*, the most free, happy, and permanent, that human wisdom can contrive, and the perfection of man maintain.

Published by order of the Committee:

ROLFE ELDRIDGE, *Clerk.*

(b) Address of the General Committee of Mechanicks in Union (New York, 1776)

To the Honourable the Representatives of the Province of NEW-YORK, *in Provincial Congress convened.*

The humble Address of the General Committee of Mechanicks in union, of the City and County of NEW-YORK, *in behalf of themselves and their constituents:*

GENTLEMEN: We, as a part of your constituents, and devoted friends to our bleeding country, beg leave, in a dutiful manner, at this time to approach unto you, our Representatives, and request your kind attention to this our humble address.

When we cast a glance upon our beloved continent, where fair freedom, civil and religious, we have long enjoyed, whose fruitful fields have made the world glad, and whose trade has filled with plenty of all things, sorrow fills our hearts to behold her now struggling under the heavy load of oppression, tyranny, and death. But when we extend our sight a little farther, and view the iron hand that is lifted up against us, behold it is our King; he who, by his oath and station, is bound to support and defend us in the quiet enjoyment of all our glorious rights as freemen, and whose dominions have been supported and made rich by our commerce. Shall we any longer sit silent, and contentedly continue the subjects of such a Prince, who is deaf to our petitions for interposing his Royal authority in our behalf, and for redressing our grievances, but, on the contrary, seems to take pleasure in our destruction? When we see that one whole year is not enough to satisfy the rage of a cruel Ministry, in burning our towns, seizing our vessels, and murdering our precious sons of liberty; making weeping widows for the loss of those who were dearer to them than life, and helpless orphans to bemoan the death of an affectionate father; but who are still carrying on the same bloody pursuit; and for no other reason than this, that we will not become their slaves, and be taxed by them without our consent,—therefore, as we would rather choose to separate from, than to continue any longer in connection with such oppressors, We, the Committee of Mechanicks in union, do, for ourselves and our constituents, hereby publickly declare that, should you, gentlemen of our honourable Provincial Congress, think proper to instruct our mode honourable Delegates in Continental Congress to use their utmost endeavours in that august assembly to cause these United Colonies to become independent of *Great Britain,* it would give us the highest satisfaction; and we hereby sincerely promise to endeavour to support the same with our lives and fortunes.

Signed by order of the Committee:

LEWIS THIBOU, *Chairman.*

Mechanick-Hall, New-York, May 29, 1776.

Questions

1. Unlike the Norfolk, Virginia, Sons of Liberty (see Document 5-4), the citizens of Buckingham County, Virginia, and the Mechanicks of New York do not legitimize their protest by declaring their loyalty to the British king. What do these colonists indicate that the king had done by the summer of 1776 to lose their allegiance?

2. For the colonists, how significant do you think that this loss of respect for the king was in making their final decision to declare independence?

3. The citizens of Buckingham County, Virginia, present a compelling narrative of their road to rebellion. Based on your knowledge of the period, is the chain of events that they present accurate? Are the grievances listed by the Mechanicks of New York believable? Do you agree that the king and Parliament left the colonists no choice but to demand "a total and final separation from *Great Britain*"?

Questions for Further Thought

1. Imagine yourself a citizen of Buckingham County, Virginia, or a Mechanick in New York. How would you respond to Gouverneur Morris's characterization of common people as "sheep" and "Poor Reptiles" (Document 6-1)?

2. Taking into account Thomas Jefferson's denunciation of slavery (Document 5-4) and the American emphasis on liberty and freedom (Document 5-5), why didn't the colonial governments move to end slavery as part of their campaign for independence from Britain? What was it about the institution of slavery and its place in colonial society that silenced slavery's critics?

3. From your reading of the documents, is it possible to define a coherent colonial position common to all the authors? Were all the colonists willing to risk war for the same reasons? Do you think that Morris, Jefferson, and the Mechanicks of New York had different expectations for the outcome of the conflict?

4. Was the Revolution inevitable? Do you think that the possibility of a settlement short of war existed? If so, what might it have been?

The Perils of War and Finance, 1776–1778, and *The Path to Victory, 1778–1783*

Despite some heroic achievements, the rebel forces fared poorly in the military conflict in 1775–1776. Thomas Paine's famous commentary on the "times that try men's souls" (Document 6-6) illustrates some of the many difficulties the Patriots faced. Documents 6-7 and 6-8 demonstrate how the Revolutionary effort attracted a broad range of participants, including those from the less powerful segments of society, such as women. Despite the efforts of Lord Dunmore (Document 6-2), and the response of many slaves to British offers of freedom for support of the Loyalist cause, even African Americans fought to win independence for America. Winning independence proved to be a long and difficult task. As a group, Documents 6-7 through 6-10 illustrate the nature of the military conflict that ranged broadly across and even beyond the area of settlement. They reveal that the fighting could be especially vicious when Patriots opposed Loyalists or native Americans. In a very real sense the American War for Independence was a civil war, and in the end the losers included not only the British, but many colonists and native Americans as well.

An end finally came, however, thanks in large part to the success of American diplomats, notably Benjamin Franklin, in expanding the scope of the conflict by concluding an alliance with the French in 1778. Beset on the high seas by the French and later by the Spanish, and defeated in their efforts to subdue the northern colonies at Saratoga in 1777, British forces devised a "southern strategy" of occupying the wealthy southern colonies while taking advantage of backcountry-Tidewater divisions to recruit loyalist supporters (see Documents 4-11 and 6-10). Southern Patriot militia, however, devised a "partisan war" that effectively neutralized the occupation forces of Lord Cornwallis. In 1781 a coordinated American-French operation finally trapped Cornwallis on the peninsula between the York and James Rivers in Virginia; with his surrender, independence was assured.

6-6   The American Crisis, Number I (December 1776)

Thomas Paine

Thomas Paine's literary contributions to the cause of American independence did not end with the publication of the many editions of *Common Sense.* In the bleak days of December 1776 Paine, who was then serving in the army, published an essay in the *Pennsylvania Journal* (December 19, 1776) that echoed the sense of travail that permeated rebel thought. This was the first essay in a series Paine called "The American Crisis"; he wrote a dozen more essays in the series by April 19, 1783. On December 9, 1783, he published what an editor of his papers called "A Supernumerary Crisis." In that work Paine discussed the question of American trade with the British. The essays that form what is commonly referred to as "The Crisis" reveal Paine's ability to put words together in powerful and memorable ways. That is especially true of the first installment of "The American Crisis," sections of which are reprinted here.

Source: Pennsylvania Journal, 19 December 1776.

THESE are the times that try men's souls. The summer soldier and the sunshine patriot will, in this crisis, shrink from the service of their country; but he that stands it *now*, deserves the love and thanks of man and woman. Tyranny, like hell, is not easily conquered; yet we have this consolation with us, that the harder the conflict, the more glorious the triumph. What we obtain too cheap, we esteem too lightly: it is dearness only that gives every thing its value. Heaven knows how to put a proper price upon its goods; and it would be strange indeed if so celestial an article as FREEDOM should not be highly rated. Britain, with an army to enforce her tyranny, has declared that she has a right (*not only to* TAX) but "to BIND *us in* ALL CASES WHATSOEVER," and if being *bound in that manner,* is not slavery, then is there not such a thing as slavery upon earth. Even the expression is impious; for so unlimited a power can belong only to God. . . .

I have as little superstition in me as any man living, but my secret opinion has ever been, and still is, that God Almighty will not give up a people to military destruction, or leave them unsupportedly to perish, who have so earnestly and so repeatedly sought to avoid the calamities of war, by every decent method which wisdom could invent. Neither have I so much of the infidel in me, as to suppose that He has relinquished the government of the world, and given us up to the care of devils; and as I do not, I cannot see on what grounds the king of Britain can look up to heaven for help against us: a common murderer, a highwayman, or a house-breaker, has as good a pretence as he.

'Tis surprising to see how rapidly a panic will sometimes run through a country. All nations and ages have been subject to them: Britain has trembled like an ague at the report of a French fleet of flat bottomed boats; and in the fourteenth [fifteenth] century the whole English army, after ravaging the kingdom of France, was driven back like men petrified with fear; and this brave exploit was performed by a few broken forces collected and headed by a woman, Joan of Arc. Would that heaven might inspire some Jersey maid to spirit up her countrymen, and save her fair fellow sufferers from ravage and ravishment! Yet panics, in some cases, have their uses; they produce as much good as hurt. Their duration is always short; the mind soon grows through them, and acquires a firmer habit than before. But their peculiar advantage is, that they are the touchstones of sincerity and hypocrisy, and bring things and men to light, which might otherwise have lain forever undiscovered. In fact, they have the same effect on secret traitors, which an imaginary apparition would have upon a private murderer. They sift out the hidden thoughts of man, and hold them up in public to the world. . . .

I shall conclude this paper with some miscellaneous remarks on the state of our affairs; and shall begin with asking the following question, Why is it that the enemy have left the New-England provinces, and made these middle ones the seat of war? The answer is easy: New-England is not infested with tories, and we are. I have been tender in raising the cry against these men, and used numberless arguments to show them their danger, but it will not do to sacrifice a world either to their folly or their baseness. The period is now arrived, in which either they or we must change our sentiments, or one or both must fall. And what is a tory? Good God! what is he? I should not be afraid to go with a hundred whigs against a thousand tories, were they to attempt to get into arms. Every tory is a coward; for servile, slavish, self-interested fear is the foundation of toryism; and a man under such influence, though he may be cruel, never can be brave.

But, before the line of irrecoverable separation be drawn between us, let us reason the matter together: Your conduct is an invitation to the enemy, yet not one in a thousand of you has heart enough to join him. Howe is as much deceived by you as the American cause is injured by you. He expects you will all take up arms, and flock to his standard, with muskets on your shoulders. Your opinions are of no use to him, unless you support him personally, for 'tis soldiers, and not tories, that he wants.

I once felt all that kind of anger, which a man ought to feel, against the mean principles that are held by the tories: a noted one, who kept a tavern at Amboy, was standing at his door, with as pretty a child in his hand, about eight or nine years old, as I ever saw, and after speaking his mind as freely as he thought was prudent, finished with this unfatherly expression, *"Well! give me peace in my day."* Not a man lives on the continent but fully believes that a separation must some time or other finally take place, and a generous parent should have said, *"If there must be trouble, let it be in my day, that my child may have peace;"* and this single reflection, well applied, is sufficient to awaken every man to duty. Not a place upon earth might be so happy as America. Her situation is remote from all the wrangling world, and she has nothing to do but to trade with them. A man can distinguish himself between temper and principle, and I am as confident, as I am that Good governs the world, that America will never be happy till she gets clear of foreign dominion. Wars, without ceasing, will break out till that period arrives, and the continent must in the end be conqueror; for though the flame of liberty may sometimes cease to shine, the coal can never expire.

Quitting this class of men, I turn with the warm ardor of a friend to those who have nobly stood, and are yet determined to stand the matter out: I call not upon a few, but upon all: not on *this* state or *that* state, but on *every* state: up and help us; lay your shoulders to the wheel; better have too much force than too little, when so great an object is at stake. Let it be told to the future world, that in the depth of winter, when nothing but hope and virtue could survive, that the city and the country, alarmed at one common danger, came forth to meet and to repulse it. Say not that thousands are gone, turn out your tens of thousands; throw not the burden of the day upon Providence, but *"show your faith by your works,"* that God may bless you. It matters not where you live, or what rank of life you hold, the evil or the blessing will reach you all. The far and the near, the home counties and the back, the rich and the poor, will suffer or rejoice alike. The heart that feels not now, is dead: the blood of his children will curse his cowardice, who shrinks back at a time when a little might have saved the whole, and made *them* happy. I love the man that can smile in trouble, that can gather strength from distress, and grow brave by reflection. 'Tis the business of little minds to shrink; but he whose heart is firm, and whose conscience approves his conduct, will pursue his principles unto death. . . .

I thank God, that I fear not. I see no real cause for fear. I know our situation well, and can see the way out of it. While our army was collected, Howe dared not risk a battle; and it is no credit to him that he decamped from the White Plains, and waited a mean opportunity to ravage the defenceless Jerseys; but it is great credit to us, that, with a handful of men, we sustained an orderly retreat for near an hundred miles, brought off our ammunition, all our field pieces, the greatest part of our stores, and had four rivers to pass. None can say that our retreat was precipitate, for we were near three weeks in performing it, that the country might have time to come in. Twice we marched back to meet the enemy, and remained out till dark. The sign of fear was not seen in our camp, and had not some of the cowardly and disaffected inhabitants spread false alarms through the country, the Jerseys had never been ravaged. Once more we are again collected and collecting; our new army at both ends of the continent is recruiting fast, and we shall be able to open the next campaign with sixty thousand men, well armed and clothed. This is our situation, and who will may know it. By perseverance and fortitude we have the prospect of a glorious issue; by cowardice and submission, the sad choice of a variety of evils—a ravaged country—a depopulated city—habitations without safety, and slavery without hope—our homes turned into barracks and bawdy-houses for Hessians, and a future race to provide for, whose fathers we shall doubt of. Look on this picture and weep over it! and if there yet remains one thoughtless wretch who believes it not, let him suffer it unlamented.

COMMON SENSE.

Questions

1. According to Paine, what problems did the Patriots face?
2. In what ways does Paine suggest that the war is an *internal* struggle as well as one against an external enemy?
3. In December 1776 the Patriot cause looked "objectively" hopeless. What hope did Paine hold out?

6-7   An Account of Life with the Army (1780–1783)

Sarah Osborn

In colonial America women had been almost totally excluded from a role in public politics. However, as Documents 5-7 and 5-11 demonstrate, women were drawn into some of the political conflicts that marked the movement toward independence. Also, as the textbook emphasizes (pp. 160–161, 169–170, 201–202), during the war women actively participated in the Patriots' efforts at a number of levels. Sarah Osborn was one of the women who traveled with the army (see text p. 187). We know about her activities because in 1832 Congress passed what the historian John C. Dann describes as the first comprehensive pension act for veterans and the widows of veterans of the

American Revolution. Under that and subsequent legislation, the applicant had to provide a statement to prove his or her right to a pension. Osborn prepared her account in 1837. It was given in the legal deposition form, which is why Osborn is referred to as "deponent." Osborn was eighty-one in 1837, but her powerful memory had not dimmed; her account, as far as it can be verified, is accurate. The section reprinted here describes her activities as the spouse of Aaron Osborn, a soldier she married in January 1780. Professor Dann, whose work with the pension records led him to edit the insightful collection of accounts entitled *The Revolution Remembered* (Chicago: University of Chicago Press, 1980), notes that Sarah Osborn's deposition may be the only extant autobiographical account of a woman who traveled with the army (*The Revolution Remembered*, 240).

Source: Sarah Osborn's application for a pension, Record Group 15 of the Records of the Veterans Administration, National Archives, in John C. Dann, ed., *The Revolution Remembered: Eyewitness Accounts of the War for Independence* (Chicago: University of Chicago Press, 1980), 242–250 passim.

After deponent had married said [Aaron] Osborn, he informed her that he was returned during the war, and that he desired deponent to go with him. Deponent declined until she was informed by Captain Gregg that her husband should be put on the commissary guard, and that she should have the means of conveyance either in a wagon or on horseback. That deponent then in the same winter season in sleighs accompanied her husband and the forces under command of Captain Gregg on the east side of the Hudson river to Fishkill, then crossed the river and went down to West Point. There remained till the river opened in the spring, when they returned to Albany. Captain Gregg's company was along, and she thinks Captain Parsons, Lieutenant Forman, and Colonel Van Schaick, but is not positive.

Deponent, accompanied by her said husband and the same forces, returned during the same season to West Point. Deponent recollects no other females in company but the wife of Lieutenant Forman and of Sergeant Lamberson. . . .

Deponent further says that she and her husband remained at West Point till the departure of the army for the South, a term of perhaps one year and a half, but she cannot be positive as to the length of time. While at West Point, deponent lived at Lieutenant Foot's, who kept a boardinghouse. Deponent was employed in washing and sewing for the soldiers. Her said husband was employed about the camp. . . .

When the army were about to leave West Point and go south, they crossed over the river to Robinson's Farms and remained there for a length of time to induce the belief, as deponent understood, that they were going to take up quarters there, whereas they recrossed the river in the nighttime into the Jerseys and traveled all night in a direct course for Philadelphia. Deponent was part of the time on horseback and part of the time in a wagon. Deponent's

said husband was still serving as one of the commissary's guard. . . . They continued their march to Philadelphia, deponent on horseback through the streets, and arrived at a place towards the Schuylkill where the British had burnt some houses, where they encamped for the afternoon and night. Being out of bread, deponent was employed in baking the afternoon and evening. Deponent recollects no females but Sergeant Lamberson's and Lieutenant Forman's wives and a colored woman by the name of Letta. The Quaker ladies who came round urged deponent to stay, but her said husband said, "No, he could not leave her behind." Accordingly, next day they continued their march from day to day till they arrived at Baltimore, where deponent and her said husband and the forces under command of General Clinton, Captain Gregg, and several other officers, all of whom she does not recollect, embarked on board a vessel and sailed down the Chesapeake. . . .They continued sail until they had got up the St. James River as far as the tide would carry them, about twelve miles from the mouth, and then landed, and the tide being spent, they had a fine time catching sea lobsters, which they ate.

They, however, marched immediately for a place called Williamsburg, as she thinks, deponent alternately on horseback and on foot. There arrived, they remained two days till the army all came in by land and then marched for Yorktown, or Little York as it was then called. The York troops were posted at the right, the Connecticut troops next, and the French to the left. In about one day or less than a day, they reached the place of encampment about one mile from Yorktown. Deponent was on foot and the other females above named and her said husband still on the commissary's guard. . . . Deponent took her stand just back of the American tents, say about a mile from the town, and busied herself washing, mending, and cooking for the soldiers, in which she was assisted by the other females; some men washed their own clothing. She heard the roar of the artillery for a number of days, and the last night the Americans threw up entrenchments, it was a misty, foggy night, rather wet but not rainy. Every soldier threw up for himself, as she understood, and she afterwards saw and went into the entrenchments. Deponent's said husband was there throwing up entrenchments, and deponent cooked and carried in beef, and bread, and coffee (in a gallon pot) to the soldiers in the entrenchment.

On one occasion when deponent was thus employed carrying in provisions, she met General Washington, who asked her if she "was not afraid of the cannonballs?"

She replied, "No, the bullets would not cheat the gallows," that "It would not do for the men to fight and starve too."

They dug entrenchments nearer and nearer to Yorktown every night or two till the last. While digging that, the enemy fired very heavy till about nine o'clock next morning, then stopped, and the drums from the enemy beat excessively. Deponent was a little way off in Colonel Van Schaick's or the officers' marquee and a number of officers were present, among whom was Captain Gregg, who, on account of infirmities, did not go out much to do duty.

The drums continued beating, and all at once the officers hurrahed and swung their hats, and deponent asked them, "What is the matter now?"

One of them replied, "Are not you soldier enough to know what it means?"

Deponent replied, "No."

They then replied, "The British have surrendered."

Deponent, having provisions ready, carried the same down to the entrenchments that morning, and four of the soldiers whom she was in the habit of cooking for ate their breakfasts.

Deponent stood on one side of the road and the American officers upon the other side when the British officers came out of the town and rode up to the American officers and delivered up [their swords, which the deponent] thinks were returned again, and the British officers rode right on before the army, who marched out beating and playing a melancholy tune, their drums covered with black handkerchiefs and their fifes with black ribbands tied around them, into an old field and there grounded their arms and then returned into town again to await their destiny. Deponent recollects seeing a great many American officers, some on horseback and some on foot, but cannot call them all by name. Washington, Lafayette, And Clinton were among the number. The British general at the head of the army was a large, portly man, full face, and the tears rolled down his cheeks as he passed along. She does not recollect his name, but it was not Cornwallis. She saw the latter afterwards and noticed his being a man of diminutive appearance and having cross eyes. . . .

After two or three days, deponent and her husband, Captain Gregg, and others who were sick or complaining embarked on board a vessel from Yorktown, not the same

they came down in, and set sail up the Chesapeake Bay and continued to the Head of Elk, where they landed. The main body of the army remained behind but came on soon afterwards. Deponent and her husband proceeded with the commissary's teams from the Head of Elk, leaving Philadelphia to the right, and continued day after day till they arrived at Pompton Plains in New Jersey. Deponent does not recollect the county. They were joined by the main body of the army under General Clinton's command, and they set down for winter quarters. Deponent and her husband lived a part of the time in a tent made of logs but covered with cloth, and a part of the time at a Mr. Manuel's near Pompton Meetinghouse. She busied herself during the winter in cooking and sewing as usual. Her said husband was on duty among the rest of the army and held the station of corporal from the time he left West Point.

In the opening of spring, they marched to West Point and remained there during the summer, her said husband still with her. In the fall they came up a little back of Newburgh to a place called New Windsor and put up huts on Ellis's lands and again sat down for winter quarters, her said husband still along and on duty. The York troops and Connecticut troops were there. In the following spring or autumn they were all discharged. Deponent and her said husband remained in New Windsor in a log house built by the army until the spring following. Some of the soldiers boarded at their house and worked round among the farmers, as did her said husband also.

Deponent and her said husband spent certainly more than three years in the service, for she recollects a part of one winter at West Point and the whole of another winter there, another winter at Pompton Plains, and another at New Windsor. And her husband was the whole time under the command of Captain Gregg as an enlisted soldier holding the station of corporal to the best of her knowledge.

In the winter before the army were disbanded at New Windsor, on the twentieth of February, deponent had a child by the name of Phebe Osborn, of whom the said Aaron Osborn was the father. A year and five months afterwards, on the ninth day of August at the same place, she had another child by the name of Aaron Osborn, Jr., of whom the said husband was the father. . . .

About three months after the birth of her last child, Aaron Osborn, Jr., she last saw her said husband, who then left her at New Windsor and never returned. He had been absent at intervals before this from deponent, and at one time deponent understood he was married again to a girl by the name of Polly Sloat above Newburgh about fifteen or sixteen miles. Deponent got a horse and rode up to inquire into the truth of the story. She arrived at the girl's father's and there found her said husband, and Polly Sloat, and her parents. Deponent was kindly treated by the inmates of the house but ascertained for a truth that her husband was married to said girl. After remaining overnight, deponent determined to return home and abandon her said husband forever, as she found he had conducted in such a way as to leave no hope of reclaiming him. About two weeks afterwards, her said husband came to see deponent in New Windsor and offered to take deponent and her children to the northward, but deponent declined going, under a firm belief that he would conduct no better, and her said husband the same night absconded with two others, crossed the river at Newburgh, and she never saw him afterwards. This was about a year and a half after his discharge. . . .

After deponent was thus left by Osborn, she removed from New Windsor to Blooming Grove, Orange County, New York, about fifty years ago, where she had been born and brought up, and, having married Mr. [John] Benjamin . . . she continued to reside there perhaps thirty-five years, when she and her husband Benjamin removed to Pleasant Mount, Wayne County, Pennsylvania, and there she has resided to this day. Her said husband, John Benjamin, died there ten years ago last April, from which time she has continued to be and is now a widow.

Questions

1. What motivated Sarah Osborn to serve in what was at least a quasi-military capacity?
2. Does it appear that the officers and men understood the value of Osborn's support of the war effort? Why or why not?
3. Does her account strike you as believable? Why or why not?

6-8 An Account of His War Service (1775–1777)

Jacob Francis

The evidence suggests that for the reasons illustrated in Document 6-2, African Americans were more likely to join the British than join the rebels. However, African Americans fought on both sides in the Revolution. As in the case of Sarah Osborn, we know about the actions of the African American Jacob Francis because he applied for a federal pension. Francis was born to a slave woman in New Jersey in 1754 but apparently was treated as an indentured servant rather than a slave. That interpretation is supported by the fact that he gained his freedom in January 1775, when he turned twenty-one. At that time twenty-one was the standard age at which men who had been bound to service as youngsters achieved their freedom. Francis completed a number of tours of duty and fought in several engagements. The sections of his 1836 deposition reprinted here recount his service in the war in the North in 1776.

Source: Jacob Francis's application for a pension, Record Group 15 of the Records of the Veterans Administration, National Archives, in John C. Dann, ed., *The Revolution Remembered: Eyewitness Accounts of the War for Independence* (Chicago: University of Chicago Press, 1980), 391–396 passim.

[I arrived in Salem, Massachusetts, about November 1769.] I lived and served in Salem until my time was out, which was in January 1775. I lived in Salem and worked for different persons till the fall of 1775. In the spring of that year the war had commenced, and the battles of Bunker Hill and Lexington had taken place. About the last of October, I enlisted as a soldier in the United States service for one year. I was told they were enlisting men to serve one year from the first of January, 1776, but I should receive pay from the time I enlisted, and I enlisted and entered the service about the last of October and received two months' pay for my service up to 1 January 1776. I enlisted at Cambridge . . . in Col. Paul Dudley Sergeant's regiment. . . . At the time I was enlisted, the British army lay in Boston. After that, I remained with the regiment at Cambridge and in the neighborhood of Boston until the British were driven out of Boston. . . .

In 1776, after the British left Boston, the army, with our regiment and myself along with them, marched by way of Roxbury (that way we could go by land) over a causeway into Boston and lay over two or three days, then were ordered out to Bunker Hill. We marched out and encamped there and lay there some time. Then our regiment was ordered to an island at that time called Castle William. . . . Then we left the island and was ordered to New York from the island. . . . [At] a place called Hell Gate, on the north side of the East River, . . . we threw up breastworks, and the British threw up breastworks on Long Island on the opposite side of the East River and used to fire across. We lay there some time.

While we lay there, the Battle of Long Island took place. There was a number of men detailed from our regiment, so many from each company, to go over and join the American army, perhaps two hundred men. I was one. We crossed the river at Hell Gate and marched on to the island in the direction we was ordered, but did not get to join the army till the battle had commenced and our army was on the retreat. We had to cross a creek to get to our army, who had engaged the enemy on the other side, but before we got to that creek our army was repulsed and retreating, and many of them were driven into the creek and some drowned. The British came in sight, and the balls flew round us, and our officers, finding we could do no good, ordered us to retreat, which we did under the fire of the enemy. We retreated back to Hell Gate and recrossed to our fortifications. Soon after that, we had orders to leave that place and marched to Westchester by way of Kingsbridge. We lay there some time, and every night we had a guard stationed out two or three miles from where the regiment lay at a place called Morrisania. I mounted guard there every time it came to my turn. There was an island near there. The tide made up round it. The British had a station on the island, and a British ship lay there. In an attack on the island one night, Colonel Jackson was wounded. After some time, we were ordered to march to the White Plains. We marched there and there joined General Washington's army.

We lay some time at the White Plains. While we lay there, the British landed and attacked some of our troops and had a brush there. Our regiment and I with them marched by General Washington's orders toward a hill where the engagement was, but the British got possession of the hill, and we retreated back to the camp. The British established a garrison on that hill. I stood sentinel that night in a thicket between the American camp and the hill, so near the British lines that I could hear the Hessians in the garrison, which was between one-quarter and one-half mile from me. The British lay there awhile and then left that place, and our regiments marched after them about three or four miles farther east. Then we received orders and marched to Peekskill on the North River. We halted a day and night a little distance from the river and there crossed at Peekskill to the west side of the river. From thence we marched on, and I do not recollect the names of places we passed through till we got to Morristown, New Jersey. We lay there one night, then marched down near to Baskingridge and lay there the next night. That night General Lee was taken in or about Bask-

ingridge. I heard the guns firing. The next morning we continued our march across Jersey to the Delaware and crossed over to Easton. From thence we marched down the Pennsylvania side into Bucks County.

It was then cold weather, and we were billeted about in houses. Our company lay off from the river a few miles below Coryell's Ferry and above Howell's Ferry. We lay there a week or two; then we received orders to march and, Christmas night, crossed the river and marched down to Trenton early in the morning. . . . We marched down the street from the River Road into the town to the corner where it crosses the street running up towards the Scotch Road and turned up that street. General Washington was at the head of that street coming down towards us and some of the Hessians between us and them. We had the fight. . . . After about half an hour the firing ceased, and some officers, among whom I recollect was General Lord Stirling, rode up to Colonel Sergeant and conversed with him. Then we were ordered to follow them, and with these officers and Colonel Sergeant at our head, we marched down through the town toward Assanpink and up the Assanpink on the north side of it and to the east of the town, where we were formed in line and in view of the Hessians, who were paraded on the south side of the Assanpink and grounded their arms and left them there and marched down to the old ferry below the Assanpink, between Trenton and Lamberton.

Soon after that, a number of men from our regiment were detailed to go down and ferry the Hessians across to Pennsylvania. I went as one, and about noon it began to rain and rained very hard. We were engaged all the afternoon ferrying them across till it was quite dark, when we quit. I slept that night in an old millhouse above the ferry on Pennsylvania side. The next morning I joined my regiment where I had left them the day before up the Assanpink, east of Trenton. We lay there a day or two, and then the time of the year's men was out, and our regiment received part of their pay and were permitted to return home. I did not get a discharge. At that time I had seven and a half months' pay due to me, and I believe others had the same. I received three months' pay, and all the rest of the regiment received the same, and we were ordered after a certain time to come to Peekskill on the North River, and then we should receive our pay and get our discharges. I was with the regiment and in service from the time of enlistment till that time about fourteen months and never left it until I had received the three months' pay and had permission to return to the place of my nativity in Amwell, about fifteen miles from Trenton. I immediately returned to Amwell and found my mother living, but in ill health. I remained with her, and when the time came to go to Peekskill for my pay and discharge, I gave up going and never received either my pay or a discharge in writing. That pay, four and one-half months at forty shillings a month (nine pounds proclamation money equal to twenty-four dollars), is yet due to me from the United States.

Questions

1. On the basis of his account, what do you believe motivated Francis to serve in the military?
2. Does his account strike you as believable? Why or why not?
3. Does Francis's account support or challenge the views of Peter Oliver (Document 5-8) about the ordinary people of America? Why or why not?

6-9   An Account of War on the Frontier (1777–1782)

John Struthers

As the textbook authors indicate (pp. 184–186), the long-running battle between British colonists and native Americans for control of the land carried over into the War of Independence. John Struthers, who was born in Maryland in 1759 and moved to Pennsylvania in 1775, was one of the many frontier colonists who became involved in that ongoing conflict. In 1841 Struthers, as many others had, applied for a federal pension for his service (see Documents 6-7 and 6-8). However, as was the case with most of those who asked for pensions on the basis of service on the frontier, his request was denied. The sections of his application reprinted here reveal the nature of the conflict between native Americans and colonists.

Source: John Struthers's application for a pension, Record Group 15 of the Records of the Veterans Administration, National Archives, in John C. Dann, ed., *The Revolution Remembered: Eyewitness Accounts of the War for Independence* (Chicago: University of Chicago Press, 1980), 253–258 passim.

The summer of 1777 was a season of great alarm, and the whole settlement from Fort Pitt to Kentucky was broken up. A number of families assembled at the house of my father in order to erect a fort, but, hearing that families had collected at Hoagland's and Beelor's, eight or ten miles nearer to the Ohio, for the same purpose, they only repaired the cabins as well as they could to resist an attack and remained in them during the summer. The others went on and built forts.

It was early resolved to raise a small company of volunteers to act as spies and wood rangers. Capt. James Scott, a brave and experienced officer, offered his services and appointed a place of rendezvous, and in a few days had upwards of twenty, of whom I was one, enrolled and ready to march with as much provision as we could conveniently carry. We started about the first of May, as nearly as I can now state, and I state it accordingly to be on that day. The country traversed was from a few miles below Fort Pitt, down the Ohio, crossing Raccoon Creek, Traver's and Tomlinson's Runs, Cross Creek, King's and Heoman's creeks, near their junction with the Ohio, passing on our way down Reardon's and Holliday's stations, where we occasionally drew provisions. From Holliday's

Cove, we traversed the country backward and forward, carefully watching the Indian warpaths until we arrived at some one of the forts or stations on the headwaters of some of the streams above mentioned, in the vicinity of which most of our company resided, where we remained a day or two to get washing and mending done and a recruit of provisions, and at every station would spend an hour or two in the exercise of the tomahawk and rifle, not only for our own improvement in the use of these weapons of warfare but also to alarm the savages if they should be lurking in the neighborhood.

In the latter part of the season, the alarm was still kept up and increased by the attack (as was reported at the time) of two or three hundred Indians on Wheeling Fort, and in this stage of alarm many others volunteered to protect the frontier, and so effectually was the country scoured from Holliday's Cove to Fort Pitt, that, though we had no triumphs in battle to record nor defeats to lament, yet not an individual was massacred by the savages in that region during this year.

In the spring of 1778 the Indians broke out earlier than usual and committed several murders on Ten Mile Creek, which was then considered an interior settlement and, although not within the range of my excursions the preceding year, was within ten or twelve miles of my father's dwelling. I believe it was in March, and the whole settlement, from Wheeling upwards, was broken up and retired into forts, of which there was now perhaps too many, as from the paucity of males in each they could spare none to act as spies or wood rangers and scarce enough to defend the forts if they should be attacked. On my return from an ineffectual scout in pursuit of the savages who had committed these barbarities, though we passed two men whom they had murdered and scalped and who were not yet cold, yet they escaped punishment. On my return from this scout, which lasted but three or four days, a request was sent me from Hoagland's Fort to turn out with as many volunteers as I could collect. I did so and, referring to my previous acquaintance with the woods and Indian warpaths, was (though among the youngest) elected to head about fifteen or sixteen active and brave men and continued during the greater part of the season, that is, from March to November with short intervals to obtain ammunition, clothing, etc., on the same route as in the preceding year but not quite so extensive. The result, however, was that no Indian depredations were committed in that settlement during the whole season. . . .

In March 1779 I entered a volunteer in Capt. David Vance's company of mounted men, in General McIntosh's campaign to Fort Laurens on Tuscarawas. . . . I returned home in April and spent the remainder of the Indian season on the same route and in the same manner as during the two preceding summers. And during this season, according to the best of my knowledge and belief, I served at least six months.

Early in the spring of 1780 intelligence was received, I do not remember how, that a large body of Indians were on their march to devastate the whole country from Wheeling to Fort Pitt. This news was either not believed or at least not heeded until a party of them, crossing below Wheeling, had penetrated nearly halfway from the Ohio to Catfish Camp, now the seat of justice for Washington County, Pennsylvania. They had taken a number of prisoners but, becoming alarmed, speedily retraced their steps to the Ohio and murdered all their male prisoners on the way. The main body of those who were expected to have ravaged Raccoon Settlement, it was supposed, never crossed the Ohio, but sent two of their warriors to reconnoiter, who, approaching Dillow's Fort late in the evening, spied two boys at play and tomahawked and scalped them within two hundred yards of the fort and escaped. And it was supposed that their report was rather unfavorable, and that they immediately commenced their retrograde march, as no other mischief was done by them this season. Colonel Broadhead commanded at Fort Pitt, and this was the summer of his campaigns to the Muncee towns up the Allegheny River and to Coshocton at the forks of Muskingum, at which two places he was supposed to have destroyed five hundred acres of corn. . . .

Early in the year 1781 the Indians made an incursion into the upper settlements of Buffalo Creek and, notwithstanding the vigilance and bravery of Col. David Williamson and his party, cruelly murdered several persons in his immediate neighborhood and took others prisoners. This caused a general alarm through all the settlements, and the people crowded into the forts, but still their great dependence for safety was on the volunteer spies and wood rangers; so I spent from April till November, at least five months, in scouting the frontier and watching the Indian crossing places and warpaths.

In the fall of this year too was the first expedition of Colonel Williamson to the Moravian Towns on the Tuscarawas, in which I (at the risk of my popularity as a soldier) declined taking a part. In the latter part of February 1782, the Indians invaded the settlement of Raccoon and murdered the family of a Mr. Wallace and took John Carpenter prisoner and took his two horses. He, however, soon made his escape and brought his horses with him.

In March, another expedition under Colonel Williamson started to the Moravian Towns and destroyed them with the inhabitants, amounting to nearly a hundred of all ages and sexes. In this, also, I refused to be concerned. These occurrences were considered by the settlers as harbingers of great distress and suffering during the summer. Yet such was the vigilance of the settlers and spies that no other mischief was done, save in one instance, and they paid dearly for their temerity. Six Indians had crawled up ten or twelve miles into the settlement and captured an old lone man of the name of William Jackson and plundered his cabin and retreated; but, so instant was the pursuit, they were overtaken at the river before they had time to embark, and a skirmish ensued wherein five Indians were killed and the other wounded in the abdomen. . . . This was the only skirmish that I recollect took place in that region during the Revolutionary War.

In the spring of this year I was elected to the command of a militia company, and my attention to the duties of that office caused necessarily a relaxation of my excursions on the frontiers; yet I spent at least two months in that service during the season, which, added to the services heretofore listed, will amount to two years and seven months. Although from the lapse of so many years and the absence of other data than memory it is impossible to specify correctly the weeks and months spent as a volunteer on the frontier during the Revolutionary War, yet I believe the statement several months less than the services really performed. I am the more confirmed in this opinion by this, that in frequent conversations with several young men, my neighbors, who had listed for three years and returned at the close of the war, it was admitted by all that I and my companions had actually served longer and endured more fatigue and hardship than they had. These conversations it is probable would not now be thought of, but that they were sometimes carried on with a considerable degree of acrimony, the regulars affecting to consider the volunteers as an inferior class, and these retorting on those as a worthless set, not daring to set heads outside the gates but under the protection of volunteers and so on.

The regular soldier performs only during the summer and then retires to winter quarters, receiving pay and clothing and rations for the whole year. The volunteers, to whom I belonged, performed at least an equal amount of service and retired home during the winter, not receiving either pay or rations and not even clothing for any part of the time, with the trifling exception of a little flour obtained now and then at the posts, or stations, and furnishing their own ammunition. Justice therefore requires that

these volunteers, on applying for pensions, should have their time calculated in the same rule as the regulars. The few regulars stationed along the Ohio, from Pitt to Wheeling, and I here speak of them only, the only reliance placed on them was to defend the forts should they be attacked. Indeed, it was admitted by everyone at the time that the only security of the people along the river and adjacent settlements was the vigilance of the volunteers in watching their crossing places and warpaths and ferreting them out of their lurking places near the stations, and that by their means, principally, was the settlement saved from savage vengeances.

Questions

1. On the basis of his account, what do you believe motivated Struthers to serve in the military?
2. Does his account strike you as believable? Why or why not?
3. Does Struthers's account support or challenge the views of Peter Oliver (Document 5-8) about the ordinary people of America? Why or why not?
4. To what extent does Struthers's account explain why the fighting between Americans on the frontier and native Americans was so vicious?

6-10   Civil War in the Southern Backcountry (1781)

The Revolutionary War was by no means simply a war fought by "Americans" against foreign invaders. It also exposed and exacerbated serious divisions among the Americans themselves, adding the dimension of civil war to the conflict. Nowhere was this more true than in the backcountry of North Carolina; there, bitterness over the outcome of the Regulator crisis (see text pp. 139–141), and a diverse population including Scottish Highlanders, Scots-Irish, and German Moravians as well as English, made it difficult for the eastern-based Revolutionary leadership to mobilize full support. What resulted was a crazy quilt of shifting allegiances. Tory guerrilla leaders such as David Fanning committed numerous atrocities, answered in kind by Whigs. The following letters, from the Revolutionary general Herndon Ramsay to Governor Thomas Burke, from Major James H. Craig (British commander at Wilmington) to Governor Abner Nash, and from Burke to Craig, illustrate the brutality to which the conflict had descended by 1781.

Source: Walter Clark, ed., *The State Records of North Carolina*, 26 vols. (Goldsboro, N.C.: Nash Brothers, 1886–1907), 22: 550–551, 1023–1025, 1026–1029.

(a) Gen. Ramsey and Others to Gov. Burke

CAMP at MCFALL'S MILL, RAFT SWAMP,
22nd of July, 1781.

Sir:—On Tuesday last we were captured at Chatham Court House by a party under the Command of Col. David Fanning, which party we found consisted of persons who complained of the greatest cruelties, either to their persons or

property. Some had been unlawfully Drafted, Others had been whipped and ill-treated, without tryal; Others had their houses burned, and all their property plundered, and Barbarous and cruel Murders had been committed in their Neighborhoods. The Officers they complain of are Maj. Neal, Capt. Robertson, of Bladen, Capt. Crump, Col. Wade and Phil Alston, the latter a day or two ago a few miles in our rear took a man on the road and put him to instant Death, which has much incensed the Highlanders in this part of the County. A Scotch Gentleman the same day was taken at one MacAfee's Mill and ill treated. He is said to be a peaceable and inoffensive man, in name we do not know. He lives in the Raft Swamp. Should be happy if he could be liberated. Notwithstanding the Cruel treatment these people have received, We have been treated with the greatest Civility and with the utmost respect and politeness by our Commanding Officer, Col. Fanning, to whom we are under the greatest Obligations, and we beg leave to inform your Excellency that unless an immediate stop is put to such inhuman practices we plainly discover the whole country will be deluged in Blood, and the innocent will suffer for the guilty. We well know your abhorrence of such inhuman conduct, and your steady intention to prevent it. All we mean is information. We expect to be delivered to Major Craig at Wilmington in two or three days, entirely destitute of Money or Cloathes. How long we shall remain so, God only Knows. All we have to ask is that the perpetrators of such horrid Deeds may be brought to tryall, that prisoners may be well treated in future, and we are

Your Excellency's most obedient Servts.,
GEN'L HERNDON RAMSEY,
JOSEPH HINE,
MATT. RAMSEY,
W. KINCHIN,
JOHN BIRDSONG,
JAMES WILLIAMS,
MATTHEW JONES,
THOS. SURLOCK,
JAMES HERNDON,
M. GREGORY.

P. S. Simon Terril is paroled to carry this Letter and return to Wilmington.

(b) Major Craig of British Troops to Governor Nash

WILMINGTON, 20th June, 1781.

SIR:

I cannot let pass this opportunity of addressing myself to you on a subject which I expect will meet with more attention than I suppose would be paid to it by the perpetrator of the actions I am forced to complain of—the inhuman treatment imposed on the King's friends on every occasion and by every party of militia now in arms, obliges me to adopt some serious resolution to put, if possible, an end to it—the deliberate and wanton murders daily committed on them call, I should imagine, as much for your attention as they do for vengeance on my part. It is now my business to assure you, sir, that the former alone can prevent the latter.

Had I listened only to the first emotions excited by the account of Mr. Caswell's conduct in *Murdering* five men at Kingstown who were carried to him from New River; Mr. Saml. Ashe and his comrades who were put in irons for the purpose would have become the immediate victims to his

unwarrantable cruelty—fortunately for them I am a Soldier and have been taught to look on the deliberate & unnecessary shedding of blood to be repugnant to my principles as such, as the sparing the Enemies of my King in the field. I therefore determined to adopt every method I could think of to prevent the necessity which could alone justify to my own mind that extremity, to the world I am sure I should have been fully justified by the cause alone—several instances which have happened since both in that quarter and in Duplin county, have very nearly forced me to have recourse to the expedient I wish to avoid, even without previous representation, which I was at a loss how to make, as I knew not where to address you, and was determined never to have any communication with people capable of ordering such actions, & whose inhumanity gave me every reason to suppose, their answer would be the immediate occasion of the extremity I wished to avoid.

I now, Sir, call on you to use your efforts to put a stop to a proceeding which promises such additional misery to the people over whom you now preside. I fully discharge my duty in this address and shall think myself perfectly unanswerable for the consequences of its being disregarded. After allowing a reasonable time for the interposition of your authority I shall think myself called on by Justice, Duty, & I may add ultimately by every consideration of humanity, to give the people who from the most laudable principles of loyalty take arms in the King's favour, ample revenge & satisfaction for every instance of *murder* committed by any party of Militia on one of them, and for this purpose I shall not hesitate to deliver over to them those Prisoners who from character or situation are most likely to gratify them in those sentiments, and produce the effect I ardently wish for, of preventing a repition of those barbarities, however I persuade myself there will be no necessity for having recourse to these means as it will be with the utmost regret I shall aggravate the miseries to which all countries are liable when the seat of war. My wish ever is to soften them as much as is consistent with my duty & in this I know my own wishes to coincide with the intentions of my superiors.

I am, Sir,

Your most Obed. Servant,

J. H. CRAIG,
Major 82d Regmt., Commandg. at Wilmington.

(c) Governor Burke to Major Craig

STATE of NORTH CAROLINA, JUNE 27th, 1781.

SIR:

Your letter of the 20th instant to my predecessor in office, came to my hands and I am now to return you an Answer.

Being entirely uninformed of the executions you allude to I am unable to say whether they ought to be denominated Murders or not, but I will venture to affirm that if they were and wanton and unnecessary, or contrary to the Laws and Rights of War they were not tollerated by the

Government of this State, nor shall such ever be approved by me.

In several parts of the country, the war has, unhappily kindled the most fierce and vindictive animosity between the People who adhere to the Government of Great Britain and those who resolved at all hazards to oppose what they deemed an unconstitutional exercise of power, very lamentable effects have always been apprehended from this disposition and as the best means for preventing them, a resolution was very early taken to remove out of the State those People together with their property who could not reconcile themselves to the Established Government and this resolution was in part executed but the Legislature was afterwards prevailed on by the Entreaties of those very people to dispense in a great measure with the further Execution. The Animosity still continues and on some Occasions when the people have been obliged to take arms has produced reciprocal violences and bloodshed which are entirely unauthorized by the Magistrates of the State, and as much reprobated by them as they can be by his Brittanic Majesty's Officers.

To this cause may probably be attributed the acts of which you complain and whether it has produced more violence on the one side than the other might probably prove a very unpleasant and unsatisfactory Enquiry, but it is certain that many people have been killed by those whom you are pleased to call the King's friends where nothing could be assigned as provocation or excuse.

Duty and Inclination conspire in determining me to use my utmost Efforts for checking and, if possible, entirely preventing those practices which, tho occasioned by the war, are no way necessary for, nor in my opinion conducive to its happy termination. To this restitution your letter could not contribute, for the evil was already perceived and threats have no influence on my Conduct.

With respect to the particular behaviour of General Caswell I shall only say that the Laws reach every officer of this State and so far as it may depend on me they shall be enforced on all for the prevention of offenses against the Law of nations as well as the municipal Law.

I cannot see the Justice of your present Treatment of Mr. Samuel Ashe and his comrades nor of the future measures which you threaten them with. I believe they do not live in the parts of the Country which are infected with the animosity above mentioned nor can I learn that they them-

selves or any of their Connections have even countenanced such pratices as you complain of and which are unauthorized and unapproved by this Government so far as they come within the description above mentioned, &c. Should you therefore continue your treatment of those citizens or listen to any Emotions which may dictate any measures against them on the ground of retaliation which you refer to, I shall find myself under the unhappy necessity of taking Similar measures against British Prisoners, tho all such measures are utterly repugnant to my disposition.

The delivering over of such Prisoners as from Character or Situation are most likely to gratify the Vengeance of those enraged People to whom you allude which you are pleased to say you will not hesitate to do so is conformable to no pratice that know of among *Civilized* Nations, and should you in any instance put this Threat in execution, the Effect will be very different from what you expect, for altho we should Abhor the following of the Example of our Indian Savage Neighbors in delivering over Prisoners to be tortured at the pleasure of a fierce and vengeful kindred, yet the example of a nation so polite and celebrated as Great Britain would meet with more respect, and we should probably imitate it with peculiar advantages should our humanity be obliged to give way to public utility.

I wish to be favored with your ultimate resolution on this subject because there are at present some Prisoners in my Power to whom I am much disposed to grant some Indulgences which are requested, but which must be delayed until I know the result of your determination.

I concur, Sir, in your wish to mitigate as much as possible the Miseries Incident to War, and am of opinion that clemency and humanity should in every Instance prevail most liberally except where incompatible with Indispensable public utility.

I perceive the letters to my Predecessor are not directed to him in his Official Character tho on an Official Subject, as I can hold no Correspondence with the Subjects of his Brittanic Majesty or other Enemies of the United States except in my Official Character none will be opened but such as those addressed to me as Governor. This, Sir, it will be necessary to observe should I be favored with any future address.

I have the honor to be,

Your Obd. Ser.

THOS. BURKE.

Questions

1. What is the substance of General Ramsey's request? What is the situation that he describes, and what does he ask for?
2. Describe the war in the American backcountry. How was the character of the war different there than in the major colonial cities?
3. What is Governor Burke's response to Major Craig? How does the governor define his position, and what does he instruct Craig to do?

Questions for Further Thought

1. Documents 6-7 and 6-8 are derived from federal pension records. How reliable is this source of information? Can you think of any reasons why these accounts might be biased? What other sources of information might provide additional and unique perspectives on the Revolutionary War?
2. While we commonly think of the colonial War of Independence as a revolutionary war, is it fair to characterize it as a civil war as well? Explain your answer.
3. The documents in this section illuminate different aspects of warfare in the late eighteenth century. What do we learn about the savagery of warfare? How does this compare with Governor Burke's (Document 6-10) understanding of "civilized warfare"?
4. Assess the different reasons for fighting given by Paine and by the authors of the other accounts in this section. Was the colonial motivation for war simple or complex? How do issues of race, gender, and geography figure in how one experienced the war?

Republicanism Defined and Challenged

The American Revolution did more than transform the British Empire; by creating a new understanding of republican citizenship, it introduced new pressures for social change and forced the citizens of the newly independent states to grapple with new issues. Documents 6-11 and 6-12 illustrate the struggle between the two competing ideals—submission of the virtuous citizen to the "common good" and the freedom of the individual to pursue self-interest—that marked the war years and led to numerous efforts to regulate prices and equalize the burdens of citizenship.

The Revolution also shook the old notion that church and state had coordinate roles to play in governing. The rationalist ideals of the Enlightenment, and increasing religious pluralism resulting from immigration and the Great Awakening, had produced increasing resentment of state churches. While in New England the prorevolutionary Congregational Church remained established into the nineteenth century, in states where the Church of England had been a prop to royal authority the issue of whether to replace it was resolved by declaring religious faith and practice to be subject solely to the individual conscience (Document 6-13). Finally, while many slaveholding Americans identified the Revolutionary cause with their "liberty" to own slaves, many others were troubled by what they saw as slavery's affront to the deepest values of that Revolution. Thus the Revolution brought the issue of slavery onto the public stage, where it would remain for close to a century (Document 6-14).

6-11　Boston Women Support Price Control (1777)

Abigail Adams

Financing the Patriots' war effort produced a range of problems including disagreements over how to control prices and thus prevent greedy self-interest from overwhelming public virtue (see text pp. 200–202). Given the active role women had played in earlier economic boycotts (Documents 5-7 and 5-11) and were taking in the war effort (Document 6-7 and text p. 190), it seems logical that women would have participated in any program to regulate prices. Such an effort occurred in Massachusetts in 1777. As the following letter of July 31, 1777, from Abigail Adams to her husband, John, shows, what some Boston women did to achieve price regulation proved most intriguing.

Source: Charles F. Adams, ed., *Letters of Mrs. Adams, the Wife of John Adams*, 4th ed. (Boston, 1848), 84–85.

31 July, 1777

I have nothing new to entertain you with, unless it is an account of a new set of mobility, which has lately taken the lead in Boston. You must know that there is a great scarcity of sugar and coffee, articles which the female part of the state is very loth to give up, especially whilst they consider the scarcity occasioned by the merchants having secreted a large quantity. There had been much rout and noise in the town for several weeks. Some stores had been opened by a number of people, and the coffee and sugar carried into the market, and dealt out by pounds. It was rumored that an eminent, wealthy, stingy merchant (who is a bachelor) had a hogshead of coffee in his store, which he refused to sell to the committee under six shillings per pound. A number of females, some say a hundred, some say more, assembled with a cart and trucks, marched down to the warehouse, and demanded the keys, which he refused to deliver. Upon which, one of them seized him by his neck, and tossed him into the cart. Upon his finding no quarter, he delivered the keys, when they tipped up the cart and discharged him; then opened the warehouse, hoisted out the coffee themselves, put it into the truck, and drove off.

It was reported, that he had personal chastisement among them; but this, I believe was not true. A large concourse of men stood amazed, silent spectators of the whole transaction.

Questions

1. What exactly did these women do? Did they do it on their own?
2. Would Gouverneur Morris (Document 6-1) have been surprised by what happened in Boston? Why or why not?
3. Compare the actions these Boston women took with the actions described in Documents 5-7, 5-11, and 6-7. Does it appear that as the Patriot movement progressed into war, women acted more independently? Why or why not?

6-12   Philadelphia Militiamen Seek to Protect Their Rights (1779)

The militiamen of the American Revolution often justifiably complained that they were not being supported adequately (see text pp. 200–201). Just as Continental troops were not always willing merely to accept their plight, militiamen could demand that they and their families be treated fairly. Militiamen certainly did so in Philadelphia in 1779 during their campaign to regulate prices and to deal with persons who were less than fully committed to the war. As part of their campaign to support the war and receive economic justice, in May 1779 a Philadelphia militia company sent the following memorial to Pennsylvania's president and the Supreme Executive Council (the council was the equivalent of the governor in other states).

Source: Samuel Hazard, ed., *Pennsylvania Archives*, 1st ser. (Philadelphia, 1853), 7: 392–394.

The Memorial and Petition of the first company of Philadelphia Militia Artillery. . . .

To His Excellency Joseph Reed, Esquire, President, and the Honorable Supreme Executive Council of the Commonwealth of Pennsylvania.

Humbly Sheweth,

That your Petitioners and Memorialists, again call'd out in defence of this State, being ever willing to exert ourselves in behalf of the United States, and this in particular, and to support as much as in us lies, the Virtuous Cause of Freedom and Independency, have once more chearfully stepped forth in obedience to the Laws of our Country, to act in a Military Capacity.

Nevertheless, we humbly beg leave to represent to your Excellency and this Honorable Board, the Circumstances and Grievances attending ourselves and many of our worthy fellow Countreymen, who having uniformly conducted themselves hitherto, are with us, Still determined to exert their utmost Efforts.

In the Month of July, 1776, We were first call'd forth to . . . endeavor to repel the force of a formidable British and Hessian Army then landed, or landing, on Staten Island. We chearfully attended the call, and associated to stem the Current of their violent Determinations to destroy and ravage this Country; at the same time leaving our families at every risque of distress and hardships, and at the mercy of the disaffected, Inimical, or self Interested; and, we might presume to say, the most Obnoxious part of the Community. Upon the return of most of us, (for some died, were killed by accident, or taken prisoners) We found every necessary and convenience of life greatly enhanced in price, and ourselves Caluminated and despised; as having justly merited our loss of Business, etc., by being too forward in takeing an Active part, and bearing Arms. But it was at that time borne with patience, in expectation of redress.

In the month of December following, when the British Army were attempting by crossing the Jersey State to take possession of this City, we were exhorted . . . to turn out again and support the Army of his Excellency, General Washington, with the most Solemn assurance that those who turn'd out might expect to receive satisfaction and redress in the premises, and Delinquents proportionally pay for their refusal. We, with a number of virtuous Citizens and Countrymen, rushed forth, notwithstanding the Inclemency of the Season, and the Services then perform'd, thro' the Assistance of Divine Providence, and the abilities of our Excellent Commander in Chief in the Defeat of the British and Hessian forces at Trenton and Princeton, are too recent to be recapitulated, and will remain a lasting Memorial of Virtue, Prudence, and Success.

After a Series of Hardships unusual to Citizens in private life, and not common to Soldiers in the Field, we return'd, and found those persons we left behind had again taken Advantage of our Absence, and enormously advanced the prices on every thing; this was encreasing the distress of the Associators [i.e. militia], who were treated at the same time with Indignity and Contempt. We had Arms in our hands, and knew the use of them; but instead of avenging ourselves, or retaliating on our Innate and Worse of Enemies, we patiently waited the Interference of the Legislative Authority. We were amused by the promises of Fines, Penalties, etc., on the Delinquents and that the Virtuous, Voluntary Militia would be put on a respectable Footing; but we cannot help observing, that the Militia are Viewed in the most disrespectful light, and few of the Fines then mentioned, or afterwards enacted, but what were artfully evaded so as not to comply with the true End and Intention of such Imposition.

The Spring, and part of the Summer in the year 1777, pass'd without any Material Circumstances respecting the Militia, except the Law in that Clause provided whereby it was enacted, that Substitutes might be allow'd in Case the rightful Persons did not appear. By this Law, the Designing or disaffected Secur'd themselves by hiring Substitutes, many of whom were not worthy of the Charge as not being Citizens; others deserted, whilst their Employers, by staying behind, were reaping advantage at our Expence, and amassing Fortunes.

Your Petitioners, apart of the Sufferers, (and some of them among the foremost) were, in September and part of October, in the year 1777, in public Service as Militia, station'd at Billingsport, while many of our wives and families were in this City, then in possession of the Enemy. Several have lost their All; and when we return'd (as we thought) happily to the City last year, Shortly every Article of life or Convenience was rais'd upon us, Eight, ten, or twelve fold at least; and many of us are at a loss to this day what Course or Station of Life to adopt to Support ourselves and Families.

The Honorable House of Assembly during their last session, have been pleas'd to Enact a Supplement to the Militia Law impowering heavy Fines upon Delinquents not forming in Militia, or, when call'd out on service, which we are Convinced was expected to answer the purpose Intended; but when we consider that Men in these Exorbitant Times can acquire more by Monopolizeing, or by an under Trade, in one Day, than will defray all their Expences of Fines or Penalties in a whole year, We humbly presume the Midling and poor will still bear the Burden, and either be totally ruin'd by heavy Fines, or Risque the starving of their Families, whilst themselves are fighting the Battles of those who are Avariciously intent on Amassing Wealth by the Destruction of the more virtuous part of the Community.

These weighty Circumstances being duly considered, Your Petitioners most humbly pray your Excellency and this Honorable Board to state the Facts, and use your Interest with the Honorable House of Assembly at their next Session; either to enact a Law whereby every Delinquent, not turning out in Militia when Legally call'd forth, may be fined in proportion to his Estate; or, otherwise, take of[f] all the Fines and Penalties, and leave it to the Militia who obey the Call to Compell every able bodied Man to join them in some Station, lest when the Militia are call'd forth, by leaving such numbers of Disaffected in their Rear, they, by pursuing their usual Methods, render our Situation worse than making us prisoners of War.

And your Petitioners and Memorialists, as in Duty Bound, will Ever Pray.

Signed at Fort Mifflin, May 12th, 1779.

Questions

1. What rights did the militiamen believe they had?
2. How accurate is it to say that the militiamen embraced the republican ideal as it is described in the textbook (pp. 199–201)?
3. Does the memorial support the analysis and predictions that Gouverneur Morris (Document 6-1) made in 1774? Why or why not?
4. Does the memorial support or challenge the views of Peter Oliver (Document 5-8) about the ordinary people of America? Why or why not?

6-13   Virginia Statute of Religious Freedom (1786)

As the Patriots waged war against Britain to attain political freedom as a nation, they had, as many of the documents in this set illustrate, to deal with the fact that some Patriots wanted greater freedom at home. This quest for greater freedom could be seen clearly where religion was concerned (see text pp. 206–207). One of the landmarks on the road to true religious freedom in the republic was the Virginia statute of religious liberty, which is reprinted in full here. Thomas Jefferson, who authored the law, considered its enactment one of the three principal achievements of his life.

Source: William W. Hening, ed., *The Statutes at Large of Virginia*, 12: 84–86.

I. WHEREAS Almighty God hath created the mind free; that all attempts to influence it by temporal punishments or burthens, or by civil incapacitations, tend only to beget habits of hypocrisy and meanness, and are a departure from the plan of the Holy author of our religion, who being Lord both of body and mind, yet chose not to propagate it by coercions on either, as was in his Almighty power to do; that the impious presumption of legislators and rulers, civil as well as ecclesiastical, who being themselves but fallible and uninspired men, have assumed dominion over the faith of others, setting up their own opinions and modes of thinking as the only true and infallible, and as such endeavouring to impose them on others, hath established and maintained false religions over the greatest part of the world, and through all time; that to compel a man to furnish contributions of money for the propagation of opinions which he disbelieves, is sinful and tyrannical; that even the forcing him to support this or that teacher of his own religious persuasion, is depriving him of the comfortable liberty of giving his contributions to the particular pastor, whose morals he would make his pattern, and whose powers he feels most persuasive to righteousness, and is withdrawing from the ministry those temporary rewards, which proceeding from an approbation of their personal conduct, are all additional incitement to earnest and unremitting labours for the instruction of mankind; that our civil rights have no dependence on our religious opinions, any more than our opinions in physics or geometry; that therefore the proscribing any citizen as unworthy the public confidence by laying upon him an incapacity of being called to offices of trust and emolument, unless he profess or renounce this or that religious opinion, is depriving him injuriously of those privileges and advantages to which in common with his fellow-citizens he has a natural right; that it tends only to corrupt the principles of that religion it is meant to encourage, by bribing with a monopoly of worldly honours and emoluments, those who will externally profess and conform to it; that though indeed these are criminal who do not withstand such temptation, yet neither are those innocent who lay the bait in their way; that to suffer the civil magistrate to intrude his powers into the field of opinion, and to restrain the profession or propagation of principles on supposition of their ill tendency, is a dangerous fallacy, which at once destroys all religious liberty, because he being of course judge of that tendency will make his opinions the rule of judgment, and approve or condemn the sentiments of others only as they shall square with or differ from his own; that it is time enough for the rightful purposes of civil government, for its officers to interfere when principles break out into overt acts against peace and good order; and finally, that truth is great and will prevail if left to herself, that she is the proper and sufficient antagonist to error, and has nothing to fear from the conflict, unless by human interposition disarmed of her natural weapons, free argument and debate, errors ceasing to be dangerous when it is permitted freely to contradict them:

II. *Be it enacted by the General Assembly,* That no man shall be compelled to frequent or support any reli-

gious worship, place, or ministry whatsoever, nor shall be enforced, restrained, molested, or burthened in his body or goods, nor shall otherwise suffer on account of his religious opinions or belief; but that all men shall be free to profess, and by argument to maintain, their opinion in matters of religion, and that the same shall in no wise diminish, enlarge, or affect their civil capacities.

III. And though we well know that this assembly elected by the people for the ordinary purposes of legislation only, have no power to restrain the acts of succeeding assemblies, constituted with powers equal to our own, and that therefore to declare this act to be irrevocable would be of no effect in law; yet we are free to declare, and do declare, that the rights hereby asserted are of the natural rights of mankind, and that if any act shall be hereafter passed to repeal the present, or to narrow its operation, such act will be an infringement on natural right.

Questions

1. Does the wording of this statute truly guarantee absolute religious freedom? Why or why not?
2. Does this statute echo the Declaration of Independence in any important ways? If so, how?
3. Why did Thomas Jefferson, as well as many Americans at the time, believe that an "established church" undermined civil society and obstructed good government? Do you agree with Jefferson's argument?

6-14   On the Slave Trade (1790)

Benjamin Franklin

Among the most important consequences of the Revolution was a heightened concern with purging American society of what many regarded as the discrepancies between the ideals invoked to justify the Revolution and actual practice. Of these discrepancies, none was more glaring than the presence of slavery in a land boasting of its devotion to liberty. Gradual emancipation laws began to be passed by northern states, where the institution was relatively unimportant, and, beginning in 1784 with the establishment of the Pennsylvania Abolition Society, an organized antislavery movement took shape. In 1789 the Pennsylvania Society presented an anti–slave trade petition to the new federal Congress. The petition met with violent attacks by congressmen from the South, who declared the institution divinely ordained and criticism of it dangerous and subversive. Benjamin Franklin was chairman of the society at the time, and the petition was presented over his signature. Outraged by the southern arguments, he penned the following piece; it was to be the last writing of his life, which ended less than a month later.

Source: John Bigelow, ed., *The Works of Benjamin Franklin* (New York: G. P. Putnam's Sons, 1904), 12: 187–192.

March 23, 1790.

To the Editor of the Federal Gazette:

SIR:—Reading last night in your excellent paper the speech of Mr. Jackson in Congress against their meddling with the affairs of slavery, or attempting to mend the condition of the slaves, it put me in mind of a similar one made about one hundred years since by Sidi Mehemet Ibrahim, a member of the Divan of Algiers, which may be seen in Martin's account of his consulship, anno 1687. It was against granting the petition of the sect called *Erika,* or Purists, who prayed for the abolition of piracy and slavery as being unjust. Mr. Jackson does not quote it; perhaps he has not seen it. If, therefore, some of its reasonings are to be found in his eloquent speech, it may only show that men's interests and intellects operate and are operated on with surprising similarity in all countries and climates, whenever they are under similar circumstances. The African's speech, as translated, is as follows:

Allah Bismillah, etc.   God is great, and Mahomet is his Prophet

Have these *Erika* considered the consequences of granting their petition? If we cease our cruises against the Christians, how shall we be furnished with the commodities their countries produce, and which are so necessary for us? If we forbear to make slaves of their people, who in this hot climate are to cultivate our lands? Who are to perform the common labors of our city, and in our families? Must we not then be our own slaves? And is there not more compassion and more favor due to us as Mussulmen than to these Christian dogs? We have now above fifty thousand slaves in and near Algiers. This number, if not kept up by fresh supplies, will soon diminish, and be gradually annihilated. If we then cease taking and plundering the infidel ships, and making slaves of the seamen and passengers, our lands will become of no value for want of cultivation; the rents of houses in the city will sink one half; and the revenue of government arising from its share of prizes be totally destroyed! And for what? To gratify the whims of a whimsical sect, who would have us not only forbear making more slaves, but even manumit those we have.

But who is to indemnify their masters for the loss? Will the state do it? Is our treasury sufficient? Will the *Erika* do it? Can they do it? Or would they, to do what they think justice to the slaves, do a greater injustice to the owners? And if we set our slaves free, what is to be done with them? Few of them will return to their countries; they know too well the greater hardships they must there be subject to; they will not embrace our holy religion; they will not adopt our manners; our people will not pollute themselves by intermarrying with them. Must we maintain them as beggars in our streets, or suffer our properties to be the prey of their pillage? For men accustomed to slavery will not work for a livelihood when not compelled. And

what is there so pitiable in their present condition? Were they not slaves in their own countries?

Are not Spain, Portugal, France, and the Italian states governed by despots, who hold all their subjects in slavery, without exception? Even England treats its sailors as slaves; for they are, whenever the government pleases, seized, and confined in ships of war, condemned not only to work, but to fight, for small wages, or a mere subsistence, not better than our slaves are allowed by us. Is there condition then made worse by their falling into our hands? No; they have only exchanged one slavery for another, and I may say a better; for here they are brought into a land where the sun of Islamism gives forth its light, and shines in full splendor, and they have an opportunity of making themselves acquainted with the true doctrine, and thereby saving their immortal souls. Those who remain at home have not that happiness. Sending the slaves home then would be sending them out of light into darkness.

I repeat the question, What is to be done with them? I have heard it suggested that they may be planted in the wilderness, where there is plenty of land for them to subsist on, and where they may flourish as a free state; but they are, I doubt, too little disposed to labor without compulsion, as well as too ignorant to establish a good government, and the wild Arabs would soon molest and destroy or again enslave them. While serving us, we take care to provide them with every thing, and they are treated with humanity. The laborers in their own country are, as I am well informed, worse fed, lodged, and clothed. The condition of most of them is therefore already mended, and requires no further improvement. Here their lives are in safety. They are not liable to be impressed for soldiers, and forced to cut one another's Christian throats, as in the wars of their own countries. If some of the religious mad bigots, who now tease us with their silly petitions, have in a fit of blind zeal freed their slaves, it was not generosity, it was not humanity, that moved them to the action; it was the conscious burthen of a load of sins, and a hope, from the supposed merits of so good a work, to be excused from damnation.

How grossly are they mistaken to suppose slavery to be disallowed by the Alcoran! Are not the two precepts, to quote no more, *"Master, treat your slaves with kindness; Slaves, serve your masters with cheerfulness and fidelity,"* clear proofs to the contrary? Nor can the plundering of infidels be in that sacred book forbidden, since it is well known from it, that God has given the world, and all that it contains, to his faithful Mussulmen, who are to enjoy it of right as fast as they conquer it. Let us then hear no more of this detestable proposition, the manumission of Christian slaves, the adoption of which would, by depreciating our lands and houses, and thereby depriving so many good citizens of their properties, create universal discontent, and provoke insurrections, to the endangering of government and producing general confusion. I have therefore no doubt but this wise council will prefer the comfort and happiness of a whole nation of true believers to the whim of a few *Erika*, and dismiss their petition.

The result was, as Martin tells us, that the Divan came to this resolution: "The doctrine that plundering and enslaving the Christians is unjust, is at best *problematical*; but that it is the interest of this state to continue the practice, is clear; therefore let the petition be rejected."

And it was rejected accordingly.

And since like motives are apt to produce in the minds of men like opinions and resolutions, may we not, Mr. Brown, venture to predict, from this account, that the petitions to the Parliament of England for abolishing the slave trade, to say nothing of other legislatures, and the debates upon them will have a similar conclusion? I am, sir, your constant reader and humble servant,

HISTORICUS.

Questions

1. Consider the manner in which Franklin makes his argument in this essay. What does it tell you about the basic beliefs of those who, like Franklin, represented the "Age of Reason"?
2. Why does Franklin make the primary "spokesman" of his piece a Muslim?
3. What does this piece tell you about how proslavery politicians justified retaining the slave trade in a nation "conceived in liberty"?

Questions for Further Thought

1. What was so revolutionary about the American Revolution? Was the Revolution more than a political rebellion? To what extent was the Revolution a social upheaval as well?
2. How did the revolutionary generation of Americans define the "republic" that they created? Do you think that the Boston women (Document 6-11), Philadelphia's militiamen (Document 6-12), Thomas Jefferson (Document 6-13), and Benjamin Franklin (Document 6-14) agreed on what "republicanism" meant?
3. At the same time that some came to conclude that the institution of slavery contradicted the republican ideals of the American Revolution, other Americans moved to make the institution more durable (Document 6-14). How did Americans, especially those in the southern states, justify slavery as contributing to the public good? In what ways did slavery contradict republican principles?

CHAPTER 7

The New Political Order,
1776–1800

★　　　★　　　★

Creating New Institutions, 1776–1786

The American Revolution involved two different struggles; the first was to gain independence from Great Britain, and the second was to determine the principles on which America's new political institutions should be built. For Patriots who argued that America should put more real power into the hands of the common people, the Virginia Declaration of Rights (Document 7-1) took on special importance. Conversely, many Revolutionary leaders, such as John Adams, worried that democracy in the hands of the common man would itself be a threat to liberty and therefore advocated a "mixed government," similar to that of the mother country but without its monarchical features. A few intrepid women, namely Abigail Adams (see text pp. 214–216), stepped forward to argue for or claim what they believed were their rights as well. Worries over what the future would hold were not confined to the privileged. Native Americans had ample cause to be concerned that American independence would allow European settlers, hitherto bottled up by British restrictions, to surge westward (Document 7-2). Indeed, the new Confederation government was preoccupied with developing an effective system for opening up the region west of the Appalachians to white settlement.

Contention among Americans sharpened during the economic crisis of the post-Revolutionary years. Economic disruption and staggering indebtedness, both public and private, hit many people hard but was especially burdensome to city artisans and small farmers, who increasingly sought relief. Because the Confederation government was small and weak, citizens generally sought that relief from their individual states in the form of debt moratoriums and the issuance of paper money. In relatively democratic states such as Pennsylvania, representatives of western farmers used their new political power to attack what they viewed as the "special privilege" of the monied classes of places such as Philadelphia (Document 7-3). In less democratic states such as Massachusetts, aggrieved farmers such as Daniel Shays took matters into their own hands, evoking for many the danger of mob rule (Document 7-4). To many Americans, the republican experiment seemed increasingly in peril.

7-1   The Virginia Declaration of Rights (1776)

The people of Great Britain and its colonies could look back to the Magna Carta of 1215 as an example of a written guarantee of basic political rights. Moreover, England adopted a Bill of Rights in 1689, and many of the colonies passed laws that amounted to bills of rights. Thus, it was logical that a number of the new Patriot-led governments would formulate statements of what they considered basic rights. The fifth Virginia revolutionary convention was the first to act. Its Declaration of Rights, which was written principally by George Mason and was issued on June 12, 1776, offered a bold vision of how Virginia's—and America's—political system should be built and what that system should do. The democratically inclined men among those who drafted new state constitutions often copied sections of this declaration verbatim.

Source: Francis N. Thorpe, ed., *The Federal and State Constitutions . . . of the United States* (Washington, D.C.: U.S. Government Printing Office, 1909), 7: 3812–3814.

A declaration of rights made by the representatives of the good people of Virginia, assembled in full and free convention; which rights do pertain to them and their posterity, as the basis and foundation of government.

SECTION 1. That all men are by nature equally free and independent, and have certain inherent rights, of which, when they enter into a state of society, they cannot, by any compact, deprive or divest their posterity; namely, the enjoyment of life and liberty, with the means of acquiring and possessing property, and pursuing and obtaining happiness and safety.

SEC. 2. That all power is vested in, and consequently derived from, the people; that magistrates are their trustees and servants, and at all times amenable to them.

SEC. 3. That government is, or ought to be, instituted for the common benefit, protection, and security of the people, nation, or community; of all the various modes and forms of government, that is best which is capable of producing the greatest degree of happiness and safety, and is most effectually secured against the danger of maladministration; and that, when any government shall be found inadequate or contrary to these purposes, a majority of the community hath an indubitable, inalienable, and indefeasible right to reform, alter, or abolish it, in such manner as shall be judged most conducive to the public weal.

SEC. 4. That no man, or set of men, are entitled to exclusive or separate emoluments or privileges from the community, but in consideration of public services; which, not being descendible, neither ought the offices of magistrate, legislator, or judge to be hereditary.

SEC. 5. That the legislative and executive powers of the State should be separate and distinct from the judiciary; and that the members of the two first may be restrained from oppression, by feeling and participating the burdens of the people, they should, at fixed periods, be reduced to a private station, return into that body from which they were originally taken, and the vacancies be supplied by frequent, certain, and regular elections, in which all, or any part of the former members, to be again eligible, or ineligible, as the laws shall direct.

SEC. 6. That elections of members to serve as representatives of the people, in assembly, ought to be free; and that all men, having sufficient evidence of permanent common interest with, and attachment to, the community, have the right of suffrage, and cannot be taxed or deprived of their property for public uses, without their own consent, or that of their representives so elected, nor bound by any law to which they have not, in like manner, assembled, for the public good.

SEC. 7. That all power of suspending laws, or the execution of laws, by any authority, without consent of the representatives of the people, is injurious to their rights, and ought not to be exercised.

SEC. 8. That in all capital or criminal prosecutions a man hath a right to demand the cause and nature of his accusation, to be confronted with the accusers and witnesses, to call for evidence in his favor, and to a speedy trial by an impartial jury of twelve men of his vicinage, without whose unanimous consent he cannot be found guilty; nor can he be compelled to give evidence against himself; that no man be deprived of his liberty, except by the law of the land or the judgment of his peers.

SEC. 9. That excessive bail ought not to be required, nor excessive fines imposed, nor cruel and unusual punishments inflicted.

SEC 10. That general warrants, whereby an officer or messenger may be commanded to search suspected places without evidence of a fact committed, or to seize any person or persons not named, or whose offence is not particularly described and supported by evidence, are grievous and oppressive, and ought not to be granted.

SEC. 11. That in controversies respecting property, and in suits between man and man, the ancient trial by jury is preferable to any other, and ought to be held sacred.

SEC. 12. That the freedom of the press is one of the great bulwarks of liberty, and can never be restrained but by despotic governments.

SEC. 13. That a well-regulated militia, composed of the body of the people, trained to arms, is the proper, natural, and safe defence of a free State; that standing armies, in time of peace, should be avoided, as dangerous to liberty; and that in all cases the military should be under strict subordination to, and governed by, the civil power.

SEC. 14. That the people have a right to uniform government; and, therefore, that no government separate from, or independent of the government of Virginia, ought to be erected or established within the limits thereof.

SEC. 15. That no free government, or the blessings of liberty, can be preserved to any people, but by a firm adherence to justice, moderation, temperance, frugality, and virtue, and by frequent recurrence to fundamental principles.

SEC. 16. That religion, or the duty which we owe to our Creator, and the manner of discharging it, can be directed only by reason and conviction, not by force or violence; and therefore all men are equally entitled to the free exercise of religion, according to the dictates of conscience; and that it is the mutual duty of all to practice Christian forbearance, love, and charity towards each other.

Questions

1. According to the Virginia Declaration of Rights, where does legitimate power come from?
2. According to this declaration, what responsibilities does government have?
3. Compare the Virginia Declaration of Rights with the American Declaration of Independence (see text pp. D-1–D-2). To what extent did Thomas Jefferson draw upon the Virginia Declaration as he framed the American Declaration?

7-2   Pachgantschihilas Warns about the Long Knives (1781)

John Heckewelder

John Heckewelder, a Moravian, was born in England in 1743 and moved with his parents to Pennsylvania when he was eleven. As an adult he became an evangelist to the native Americans. In 1818, a year after his death, his *An Account of the History, Manners, and Customs of the Indian Nations* was published. In it he recounted and quoted the close of a 1781 speech delivered by Pachgantschihilas, a noted war chief of the Delaware. Pachgantschihilas was addressing a group of native Americans living in western Pennsylvania who had embraced Christianity and were called Moravian Indians.

When Pachgantschihilas spoke of the *long knives*, he used the term to refer to white people because some white soldiers used swords—literally, long knives. Heckewelder's account of Pachgantschihilas's thoughts and of subsequent events is reprinted here and should be compared with the ideals for western development described in the text (p. 220).

Source: Memoirs of the Historical Society of Pennsylvania (1876), 12: 80–81.

I have given here only a brief specimen of the charges which they exhibit against the white people. There are men among them, who have by heart the whole history of what took place between the whites and the Indians, since the former first came into their country; and relate the whole with ease and with an eloquence not to be imitated. On the tablets of their memories they preserve this record for posterity. I, at one time, in April, 1781, was astonished when I heard one of their orators, a great chief of the Delaware nation, go over this ground, recapitulating the most extraordinary events which had before happened, and concluding in these words: "I admit that there are good white men, but they bear no proportion to the bad; the bad must be the strongest, for they rule. They do what they please. They enslave those who are not of their colour, although created by the same Great Spirit who created us. They would make slaves of us if they could, but as they cannot do it, they kill us! There is no faith to be placed in their words. They are not like the Indians, who are only enemies, while at war, and are friends in peace. They will say to an Indian, 'my friend! my brother!' They will take him by the hand, and at the same moment destroy him. And so you (addressing himself to the Christian Indians) will also be treated by them before long. Remember! that this day I have warned you to beware of such friends as these. I know the *long knives*; they are not to be trusted."

Eleven months after this speech was delivered by this prophetic chief, ninety-six of the same Christian Indians, about sixty of them women and children, were murdered at the place where these very words had been spoken, by the same men he had alluded to, and in the same manner that he had described.

Questions

1. Does Heckewelder seem interested in assuring that the native Americans receive justice? Why or why not?

2. Would Pachgantschihilas say that the Americans believe that the ideals expressed in the Virginia Declaration of Rights (Document 7-1) apply to native Americans? Why or why not?

3. Would Pachgantschihilas say that the Americans believe that the ideals expressed in the Declaration of Independence about the people's equality and "unalienable rights" (see text p. D-1) apply to native Americans? Why or why not?

4. Given Pachgantschihilas's analysis, in what ways, if at all, were native Americans involved in what Carl Becker has called the conflict over "who should rule at home" (see text p. 212)?

7-3   On Democracy, Banks, and Paper Money (1786)

William Finlay

If the Revolution was about not only "home rule" but about "who should rule at home," the issue was framed most starkly in Pennsylvania. While most of the revolutionary states simply adapted their old governmental institutions to independence, the Keystone State threw out its old assembly, dominated by well-to-do eastern Quakers, and substituted a new one based on a greatly broadened suffrage and a reapportionment of representation that shifted power sharply toward the Scots-Irish settlers of the west. As a result, a swarm of new men surged into positions of leadership, bringing with them many of the resentments that had animated the Paxton Boys (Document 4-10). In the 1780s, the representatives of the western farmers primarily sought debt relief and state issuance of paper money to lower the cost of debt repayment. Their most powerful adversary was Robert Morris, the Philadelphia financier whose Bank of North America wished to maintain "sound money" and refused to accept the state's paper money at its face value. When the western-dominated assembly deprived Morris's bank of its charter, Morris sought without success to have it restored. Morris's leading opponent was William Finlay, a Scots-Irish westerner and former weaver. Finlay's remarks illustrate both the motives of the westerners and their own understanding of what the Revolution was about—an understanding very different from that of Morris, or James Madison (Document 7-7).

Source: Mathew Carey, ed., *Debates and Proceedings of the General Assembly of Pennsylvania on the Memorials Praying a Repeal or Suspension of the Law Annulling the Charter of the Bank* (Philadelphia: Carey and Co., Seddon and Pritchard, 1786), 64–65, 67–71, 86–87, 129–130.

Mr. Finlay: . . . All governments being instituted for the good of the society to which they belong, the supreme legislative power of every community necessarily possesses a power of repealing every law inimical to the public safety. But the government of Pennsylvania being a democracy, the bank is inconsistent with the bill of rights thereof, which says, that government is not instituted for the emolument of any man, family, or set of men. Therefore, this institution being a monopoly, and having a natural tendency, by affording the means, to promote the spirit of monopolizing, is inconsistent with not only the frame but the spirit of our government. If the legislature may mortgage, or, in other words, charter away portions of either the privileges or powers of the state—if they may incorporate bodies for the sole purposes of gain, with the power of making byelaws, and of enjoying an emolument of privilege, profit, influence, or power,—and cannot disannul their own deed, and restore to the citizens their right of equal protection, power, privilege, and influence,—the consequence is, that some foolish and wanton assembly may parcel out the commonwealth into little aristocracies, and so overturn the nature of our government without remedy.

This institution is inconsistent with our laws—our habits—our manners.—Our laws and habits countenance long credits, and afford slow methods for recovering debts. They subject our real estates to alienation, and to be sold for debts. They divide our estates, both real and personal, more equally among our heirs, than the laws or habits of any other country I know of. We are too unequal in wealth to render a perfect democracy suitable to our circumstances: yet we are so equal in wealth, power, &c. that we have no counterpoise sufficient to check or control an institution of such vast influence and magnitude. We have no kingly prerogative—no wealthy companies of merchants incorporated—no hereditary nobles, with vastly great estates and numerous dependents—no feudal laws to support family dignity, by keeping landed estates undivided. What security, then, can we purpose to ourselves against the eventual influence of such wealth, conducted under the direction of such a boundless charter? . . .

. . . [I]n the present state of our commerce, the bank facilitates both public and private ruin. The balance of trade being constantly against us, commerce with us has contracted a different meaning from what it has in Europe. There it is founded on the produce and manufactures of the respective countries, for which the merchant finds a foreign market, and in lieu of which he brings a suitable return. From the excess of the exports, the nation is enriched. With us it may, with more propriety, be styled importation than commerce: and this importation, carried on to too great a degree before the revolution, is greatly facilitated by the bank. . . .

. . . From those vast importations, the number of our dealing people was increased. The bank gave the means of purchasing foreign cargoes—the access was easy—but the credit short.—The hasty day of payment approached—hence the numerous tribe of brokers arose. The involved debtor went from friend to friend for the assistance of credit—from broker to broker for costly supplies of cash—until ruin overwhelmed him with confusion and woe: and he who was, or appeared to be, a capital dealer, fell. Like a mighty oak in the woods, he crushed many by his fall. Thus of late, the cry of private ruin in this city, has not only been heard by our sister states—but by foreign nations. Thus hath the state been drained of what money was circulating within it, and the means of supporting the revenues and credit thereof been taken away: no doubt there has been a concurrence of other causes. The imprudence of the unfortunate is often assigned as one cause: and no doubt it was: but experience forbids to set down the unfortunate always as fools or knaves. Many who had fair and honest prospects, or who assisted with their credit those who had, finding every usual means of extricating themselves cut off by the inundation of foreign goods, have, whilst possessed of honest principles and competent sagacity, sunk in the common ruin. . . .

The way for individuals or nations to get rich, is not to have artificial difficulties laid in the way of paying their debts; but to contract few of them. The debts must be paid: and the bank collects the money to a point, where it can be easier found in large sums for exportation, then in any other manner: and those little shifts, which depend on personal sagacity or integrity, are fit only for a plausible colouring for refusing to supply those who are not favourites; and the more effectually discover how well it is calculated to promote the monopolizing of trade. What security have we that its assistance will not be partially exerted for this purpose?

This institution is itself a monopoly—being incorporated a great trading company—and having a right to turn ten millions of dollars into trade, if the president and directors please—or to lay out that amount upon land. So, by taking advantage of a scarcity of money, which they have it so much in their power to occasion, they may become sole lords of the soil. If they may monopolize trade—if they may monopolize the soil—why not the government too? Doubtless they may. . . .

This institution I believe to be inimical to the emission and credit of paper money. . . .

. . . Though I do not say that any direct attack was made upon it by the directors of the bank—as I do not blame them for not receiving it—yet it was evidently opposed through the influence of that institution. In the eighth general assembly, the directors wrote to the house, dissuading them from the emission they were about to make, giving their opinion that it would not do, and offering a loan. The prophecying its fate, by those who were supposed to have the power to blast it, had the desired effect; and the emission was dropped. When the funding bill was going through the late house, could those who were interested in, or dependent on, the bank, do more than they did, to prevent the emission, and to discourage the people, already rendered suspicious by former events? Did not the friends of the bank, in that house, predict that it would be three or four for one, as soon as emitted? Did not the gentlemen of this house who are interested in the bank, endeavour at our last session, to have it all called in? Have they not afterwards complained of its not purchasing the necessaries of life? Did not one gentleman tell us it was from two and a half to five per cent. below par? I must answer, that instances of the kind have not struck my observation. . . .

. . . It brightens our prospects of prosperous days. The public creditor has been relieved by it. The moneyless farmer has with it paid his taxes, which had accumulated for years past. It has brought into circulation the little hard money that remained. Our treasury is kept busy receiving it, and as busy paying it away. Who refuses the paper money from us? None—for the comptroller general is kept employed almost night and day—people hurry him so that they may get it. . . .

Mr. R. Morris: . . . I proceed to examine the arguments adduced by a gentleman, for whose understanding and abilities I have great respect; and who generally supports what he undertakes to defend, not only with strength of reasoning, but manages it with candour. I cannot, however, help observing, that he has deviated more from that candid line of conduct in this debate, than I have ever known him to do before. . . .

I agree that in all governments, supreme power must be lodged somewhere. In ours, the assembly has the sole right of granting charters—but no right to take them away. The power there goes on a different principle: and so it does in all except arbitrary governments. In Great Britain, the sovereign grants charters, but he cannot take them away; the laws of the land have pointed out another mode of annulling them. . . .

. . . This gentleman says, let us examine our government—It is a democracy, and gives to all men equal rights: and agrarian laws[1] may not be incompatible with the spirit of it: but we are not yet arrived at the period when such laws would be proper. I trust this member has better principles than to advocate so wicked a measure as a general division of property. . . .

Mr. Finlay: . . . [T]he opportunity it gives me of offering a short but true picture of the situation of many of my constituents. Living as they do, in a new settlement, after having encountered the accumulated woods of ages, and beasts ravenous by nature, and rendered still more so by the unbounded extent of their range, they had scarcely made openings round their abodes—they had not banished the beasts of prey—when men more fierce, more cruel than the beasts, desolated their new raised dwellings, and spread destruction far and wide. Now, when they are returned, and feebly repairing the ruins of their dreary wastes, they find themselves in debt to the state for the very lands in defending which many of them lost their dearest friends and all their wealth. They endeavour—they strive with arduous diligence to pay the state its due: and, to be able to call the lands their own, they sell the last cow and sheep, to procure a little money (for nothing but cows and sheep will find money there). I myself have been urged to take the last cow—to take any thing they had, in order to secure their lands. They raise the last shilling they are able—and plead, as if for life, that we may add a few dollars to the scanty sum; . . .

We are one great family: and the laws are our common inheritance. They are general rules, and common in their nature. No man has a greater claim of special privilege for his £100,000 than I have for my £5. No. The laws are a common property. The legislature are entrusted with the distribution of them. This house will not—this house has no right, no constitutional power to give monopolies of legal privilege—to bestow unequal portions of our common inheritance on favourites.

This bank, the charter of which has been dissolved, and is now endeavoured to be renewed again, was truly an extraordinary creature. None like it does, I believe—none like it ever did exist in any nation: and surely such a being will never be restored—will never be created again by the legislature of this state. If we should restore it, we would have no security but in the moderation of the directors and stockholders: but who will answer—who can be responsible for future men—future times—and future events? . . .

---

[1]*Agrarian laws:* Laws forcing a redistribution of landed property. Morris here is accusing Finlay of attacking private property in the name of democracy.

Questions

1. Compare William Finlay's remarks with the Virginia Declaration of Rights (Document 7-1). Are Finlay and the authors of Virginia's declaration in agreement on the means and ends of good government? If not, where do they disagree, and why?

2. Why does William Finlay, like many settlers in the American backcountry, have such a problem with the Bank of North America? Why does Finlay believe that the bank represents a real threat to democracy? Is his argument believable? Explain your answer.

3. Conversely, Robert Morris clearly believes that Finlay's attacks on the bank threaten the foundations of Republican liberty. Why? Is *his* argument believable? Explain your answer.

7-4 Condemnation of Shays's Rebellion (1787)

Isaac Backus

Isaac Backus (1724–1806) was a leader of the "Separate Baptists" of New England. A fierce opponent of the established Congregational Church, he was devoted to the Revolutionary cause, which he hoped would bring both disestablishment and a revival of public virtue. The turmoil of the 1780s, however, appalled him. As an opponent of the "Standing Order," Backus was critical both of the luxurious lifestyles of rich merchants, and of the hard dealings of creditors and the "order of lawyers." While sympathetic to the plight of debtor farmers, he feared the consequences for the new experiment in self-government of Daniel Shays's 1786 rebellion and the rebels' demand for an expanded volume of paper currency. He set forth his opposition to Shays, and the reasoning behind it, in the following pamphlet.

Source: Isaac Backus, "An Address to the Inhabitants of New-England, Concerning the Present Bloody Controversy Therein" (Boston: S. Hall, 1787).

AN ADDRESS, &C.

My dear Countrymen,

Our fathers came to this land for purity and liberty in the worship of God; but now many have drawn their swords against each other, about the affairs of wordly gain, whereby an exceeding dark cloud is brought over us. Instead of being the light of the world, and the pillar and ground of the truth, as those are that obey Him who is the fountain of *light* and *love;* what a stumbling-block are we to other nations, who have their eyes fixed upon us? Permit me therefore to lay before you a few thoughts, which I hope may be serviceable in this dark season. If we were as well agreed about the way of relief, as we are about the cause of our present distress, a happy deliverance would soon appear; as the following facts will shew.

From March to July, last year, the *order of lawyers*[1] in our government, was exposed in the Boston papers, in a very striking manner; and in the two following months many people arose in arms against our executive courts, in the counties of Hampshire, Berkshire, Worcester, Middlesex and Bristol. Hereupon the town of Boston met, and sent an address to all the other towns in the Massachusetts, earnestly requesting that a redress of grievances might be fought for in a constitutional orderly way only; and pledg-

---

[1]*Order of lawyers:* Because lawyers were profiting so much from court actions against debtors, a wave of anti-lawyer sentiment swept interior New England, where attorneys were spoken of in terms similar to that of a religious order—a damning comparison to a Baptist such as Backus. Among the grievances leading to Shays's Rebellion were charges in the spring of 1786 that court fees had reached exorbitant levels.

ing themselves to join their endeavours with the country, in that way, to obtain a redress of any such grievances as really existed. Hereby they intended to have the people stirred up to send in an account of their real grievances to the General Court at Boston; and after many such accounts had been laid before them, they published an address to the people, November 14, 1786, wherein they say,

"We feel in common with our neighbours the scarcity of money; but is not this scarcity owing to our own folly? At the close of the war, there was no compliant of it; since that time, our fields have yielded their increase, and Heaven has showered its blessings on us, in uncommon abundance; but are we not constrained to allow, that immense sums have been expended, for what is of no value, for the gewgaws imported from Europe, and the more pernicious produce of the West-Indies; and the dread of a paper currency impedes the circulation of what remains: It is said however, that such a currency would give us present relief; but like the pleasure of sin, it would be but for a season; and like that too, it would be a reproach to the community, and would produce calamities without end.— Without a reformation of manners, we can have little hope to prosper in our publick or private concerns.—As the difficulty in paying debts increased, a disregard to honesty, justice and good faith, in publick and private transactions, became more manifest.—Some persons have artfully affected to make a distinction between the government and people, as though their interest were different and even opposite; but we presume, the good sense of our constituents will discern the deceit and falsity of those insinuations. Within a few months the authority delegated to us will cease, and all citizens will be equally candidates in a future election.—Many who disapprove insurrections against the government, neglect to afford their aid, in suppressing them; but to stand still, inactive spectators in such case, is like a man who when his house is in flames, should stand with folded arms, and console himself with this, that he did not set it on fire."

This view of the cause of our distress, perhaps will not be denied by a single person; but the measures which have been taken since, have moved many to declare their sorrow that we ever revolted from Great-Britain. But I am so far from any such thought, that I fully agree with our General Court, that a paper currency would produce calamities without end. For by it the Court of Britain have been enabled to carry blood and slavery round the world, and to load the nation with a debt of more than two hundred millions sterling, above a third of which was in attempts to bind us in all cases whatsoever; and so to rob us both of manhood and Christianity. For to have our choice governed by reason, is essential to manhood; and to have it governed by revelation, is essential to Christianity. . . . Thus God's immutable plan of government determines the *choice* of the worst of men, without the least excuse for their *wickedness.* John xix. 11. Acts ii. 22, 23. And if these plain truths were duly regarded, peace would soon take place among us. For our Legislature truly say,

"Within a few months the authority delegated to us will cease, and all the citizens will be equally candidates in a future *election.*" This is the true nature of our Constitution; and the command of God is, *Submit yourselves to every ordinance of man for the Lord's sake. . . .*

The way wherein teachers have kept up these evils so long in the world, has been by insisting upon it, that *self-determination* in the *will of man* is essential to moral agency. This doctrine, and the doctrine of purgatory, is now carried further in London and in Boston, than it is in Rome. Which is so opposite to the doctrine of Christ, that he says, *I came down from heaven, not to do mine own will, but the will of him that sent me. If ye keep my commandments, ye shall abide in my love; even as I have kept my father's commandments, and abide in his love.* John vi. 38. xv. 10. And in this way only can we make our *calling and election sure,* and escape the *error of the wicked.* 2 Peter i. 3—11. iii. 17, 18. And that all who are in authority may protect and encourage such a quiet and peaceable life, in all godliness and honesty, is my earnest prayer.

ISAAC BACKUS.

Boston, March 28, 1787.

Questions

1. How does Isaac Backus's position on "paper money" compare with that of William Finlay (Document 7-3)?

2. What role, according to Backus, does religion play in republican governance? Do you think that his view was common in postwar America? How do Backus's religious views influence his position on paper money?

3. Rather than armed insurrection (Shays's Rebellion), what does Backus argue is the proper way for Massachusetts debtors to redress their grievances? Do you think his solution is realistic?

Questions for Further Thought

1. Why were issues related to money and debt so volatile in postwar America?
2. Daniel Shays and William Finlay (Document 7-3) represented similar interests in the emerging United States, but their approaches to redressing their grievances were decidedly different. How do their differing approaches reflect the unstable politics of the new United States?
3. What in the Virginia Declaration of Rights (Document 7-1) foreshadowed the future destruction of the Indian nations? Taking a broader view, what consequences of the Revolution sped up the destruction of the native American cultures (Document 7-2)?

The Constitution of 1787

The deficiencies of the government based on the Articles of Confederation became increasingly apparent during the 1780s. Despite its success in dealing with the issues arising from western lands, the weak Confederation government was hamstrung by the states' continuing insistence on retaining their sovereignty. Moreover, the turmoil within the states, illustrated not only by Shays's Rebellion but by attempts to use state governments in the interests of debtors against creditors, increasingly convinced many analysts that the states themselves were unable to preserve either domestic order or the rights of property (Document 7-5). A number of Revolutionary political leaders, convinced that something needed to be done, both to bolster the power of the Confederation and to rein in the more radical element in the states, called a convention to meet in 1787 to discuss revisions to the Articles—a convention that instead produced an entire new Constitution.

The proposed new national charter was immediately hotly controversial. Many people feared that imposing a powerful new federal government on top of the existing state governments would result in a new tyranny like that of the hated British. Arguing that republics needed to be small in order to stay in touch with the people, "Antifederalists" such as George Clinton of New York vehemently opposed ratification (Document 7-6). In response, James Madison, Alexander Hamilton, and John Jay wrote a series of essays known as *The Federalist*. In *The Federalist*, No. 10, Madison argued that the very size of the new federal government would protect the people from the tyranny of special interests, who could more easily capture a state (Document 7-7). Others objected to the proposed Constitution because it lacked explicit protections for individual rights; the promise that a Bill of Rights would be added by amendment thus became critical to the final ratification of the charter (Document 7-8). The Constitution was adopted by a hairbreadth. The issues raised during the debate would continue to embroil the new federal government well into the nineteenth century, and indeed up to the time of the Civil War.

7-5   A Warning to the Delegates about Leveling (1787)

Elbridge Gerry

Shays's Rebellion (see text pp. 221–222) horrified most Americans. It seemed to demonstrate how impotent the federal government was and how easily the Union might slip into chaos. However, for many Americans Shays's Rebellion also signaled the need to reassess the nature of the American experiment with democracy. That certainly was the case for Elbridge Gerry, a delegate from Massachusetts to the Constitutional Convention. Gerry, a prominent Massachusetts Patriot, had signed the Declaration of Independence and served in the Confederation Congress. On May 31, 1787, during the Constitutional Convention's deliberations about allowing the people to elect members of the U.S. Senate directly, Gerry told his fellow delegates what Shays's Rebellion meant to him.

Source: Max Farrand, ed., *The Records of the Federal Convention of 1787*, rev. ed., 1: 48, 50. Copyright © 1911 by Yale University Press. Reprinted by permission.

Mr Gerry. The evils we experience flow from the excess of democracy. The people do not want virtue; but are the dupes of pretended patriots. In Massts. it has been fully confirmed by experience that they are daily misled into the most baneful measures and opinions by the false reports circulated by designing men, and which no one on the spot can refute. One principal evil arises from the want of due provision for those employed in the administration of Governnt. It would seem to be a maxim of democracy to starve the public servants. He mentioned the popular clamour in Massts. for the reduction of salaries and the attack made on that of the Govr. though secured by the spirit of the Constitution itself. He had he said been too republican

heretofore: he was still however republican, but had been taught by experience the danger of the levilling spirit. . . .

Mr Gerry [said he] did not like the election by the people. The maxims taken from the British constitution were often fallacious when applied to our situation which was extremely different. Experience he said had shewn that the State Legislatures drawn immediately from the people did not always possess their confidence. He had no objection however to an election by the people if it were so qualified that men of honor and character might not be unwilling to be joined in the appointments. He seemed to think the people might nominate a certain number out of which the State legislatures should be bound to choose.

Questions

1. According to Gerry, what kind of problems produced the dissatisfaction that burst forth in Shays's Rebellion?
2. According to Gerry, who caused Shays's Rebellion?
3. If democracy is defined as allowing the average person to exercise real political power, would you describe Gerry as a supporter of democracy? Why or why not?

7-6   An Attack on the Proposed Federal Constitution (1787)

George Clinton

The adoption of the proposed new constitution of the Philadelphia Convention was by no means a foregone conclusion. Having repudiated the authority of a remote government a little more than a decade earlier, many delegates were strongly opposed to accepting subordination to a new one. Many, too, feared that the new national charter would fundamentally alter the political balance of power to their disadvantage. Among the leading Antifederalists (as they were unfairly dubbed) was Governor George Clinton of New York, who wrote several letters under the pseudonym "Cato" attacking the proposal as dangerous to the liberties of the people. In the following letter he set forth one of the strongest arguments against the proposed new federal government, one that James Madison felt necessary to address in his famous *The Federalist,* No. 10 (Document 7-7).

Source: Morton Borden, ed., *The Antifederalist Papers* (East Lansing: Michigan State University Press, 1965), 36–39.

. . . The recital, or premises on which the new form of government is erected, declares a consolidation or union of all the thirteen parts, or states, into one great whole, under the form of the United States, for all the various and important purposes therein set forth. But whoever seriously considers the immense extent of territory comprehended within the limits of the United States, together with the variety of its climates, productions, and commerce, the difference of extent, and number of inhabitants in all; the dissimilitude of interest, morals, and politics, in almost every one, will receive it as an intuitive truth, that a consolidated republican form of government therein, can never *form a perfect union, establish justice, insure domestic tranquility, promote the general welfare, and secure the blessings of liberty to you and your posterity,* for to these objects it must be directed. This unkindred legislature therefore, composed of interests opposite and dissimilar in their nature, will in its exercise, emphatically be like a house divided against itself.

The governments of Europe have taken their limits and form from adventitious circumstances, and nothing can be argued on the motive of agreement from them; but these adventitious political principles have nevertheless produced effects that have attracted the attention of philosophy, which have established axioms in the science of politics therefrom, as irrefragable as any in Euclid. It is natural, says Montesquieu, *to a republic to have only a small territory, otherwise it cannot long subsist: in a large one, there are men of large fortunes, and consequently of less moderation; there are too great deposits to trust in the hands of a single subject; an ambitious person soon becomes sensible that he may be happy, great, and glorious by oppressing his fellow citizens, and that he might raise himself to grandeur, on the ruins of his country. In large republics, the public good is sacrificed to a thousand views; in a small one, the interest of the public is easily perceived, better understood, and more within the reach of every citizen; abuses have a less extent, and of course are less protected.* He also shows you, that the duration of the republic of Sparta was owing to its having continued with the same extent of territory after all its wars; and that the ambition of Athens and Lacedemon to command and direct the union, lost them their liberties, and gave them a monarchy.

From this picture, what can you promise yourselves, on the score of consolidation of the United States into one government? Impracticability in the just exercise of it, your freedom insecure, even this form of government limited in its continuance, the employments of your country disposed of to the opulent, to whose contumely you will continually be an object. You must risk much, by indispensably placing trusts of the greatest magnitude, into the hands of individuals whose ambition for power, and aggrandizement, will oppress and grind you. Where, from the vast extent of your territory, and the complication of interests, the science of government will become intricate and perplexed, and too mysterious for you to understand and observe; and by which you are to be conducted into a monarchy, either limited or despotic; the latter, Mr. Locke remarks, *is a government derived from neither nature nor compact.*

Political liberty, the great Montesquieu again observes, *consists in security, or at least in the opinion we have of security;* and this *security,* therefore, or the *opinion,* is best obtained in moderate governments, where the mildness of the laws, and the equality of the manners, beget a confidence in the people, which produces this security, or the opinion. This moderation in governments depends in a great measure on their limits, connected with their political distribution.

The extent of many of the states of the Union, is at this time almost too great for the superintendence of a republican form of government, and must one day or other revolve into more vigorous ones, or by separation be reduced into smaller and more useful, as well as moderate ones. You have already observed the feeble efforts of Massachusetts against their insurgents; with what difficulty did they quell that insurrection; and is not the province of Maine at this moment on the eve of separation from her? The reason of these things is, that for the security of the *property* of the community—in which expressive term Mr. Locke makes life, liberty, and estate, to consist—the wheels of a republic are necessarily slow in their operation. Hence, in large free republics, the evil sometimes is not only begun, but almost completed, before they are in a situation to turn the current into a contrary progression. The extremes are also too remote from the usual seat of government, and the laws, therefore, too feeble to afford protection to all its parts, and insure *domestic tranquility* without the aid of another principle. If, therefore, this state [New York], and that of North Carolina, had an army under their control, they never would have lost Vermont, and Frankland, nor the state of Massachusetts suffered an insurrection, or the dismemberment of her fairest district; but the exercise of a principle which would have prevented these things, if we may believe the experience of ages, would have ended in the destruction of their liberties.

Will this consolidated republic, if established, in its exercise beget such confidence and compliance, among the citizens of these states, as to do without the aid of a standing army? I deny that it will. The malcontents in each state, who will not be a few, nor the least important, will be exciting factions against it. The fear of a dismemberment of some of its parts, and the necessity to enforce the execution of revenue laws (a fruitful source of oppression) on the extremes and in the other districts of the government, will incidentally and necessarily require a permanent force, to be kept on foot. Will not political security, and even the opinion of it, be extinguished? Can mildness and moderation exist in a government where the primary incident in its exercise must be force? Will not violence destroy confidence, and can equality subsist where the extent, policy, and practice of it will naturally lead to make odious distinctions among citizens?

The people who may compose this national legislature from the southern states, in which, from the mildness of the climate, the fertility of the soil, and the value of its productions, wealth is rapidly acquired, and where the same causes naturally lead to luxury, dissipation, and a passion for aristocratic distinction; where slavery is encouraged, and liberty of course less respected and protected; who know not what it is to acquire property by their own toil, nor to economize with the savings of industry—will these men, therefore, be as tenacious of the liberties and interests of the more northern states, where freedom, independence, industry, equality and frugality are natural to the climate

and soil, as men who are your own citizens, legislating in your own state, under your inspection, and whose manners and fortunes bear a more equal resemblance to your own?

It may be suggested, in answer to this, that whoever is a citizen of one state is a citizen of each, and that therefore he will be as interested in the happiness and interest of all, as the one he is delegated from. But the argument is fallacious, and, whoever has attended to the history of mankind, and the principles which bind them together as parents, citizens, or men, will readily perceive it. These principles are, in their exercise, like a pebble cast on the calm surface of a river—the circles begin in the center, and are small, active and forcible, but as they depart from that point, they lose their force, and vanish into calmness.

The strongest principle of union resides within our domestic walls. The ties of the parent exceed that of any other. As we depart from home, the next general principle of union is amongst citizens of the same state, where acquaintance, habits, and fortunes, nourish affection, and attachment. Enlarge the circle still further, and, as citizens of different states, though we acknowledge the same national denomination, we lose in the ties of acquaintance, habits, and fortunes, and thus by degrees we lessen in our attachments, till, at length, we no more than acknowledge a sameness of species. Is it, therefore, from certainty like this, reasonable to believe, that inhabitants of Georgia, or New Hampshire, will have the same obligations towards you as your own, and preside over your lives, liberties, and property, with the same care and attachment? Intuitive reason answers in the negative. . . .

CATO

Questions

1. Why did George Clinton believe that the new federal Constitution was unworkable and that it would be unable to secure its stated ends?
2. Politicians of this era sought to legitimize their positions by citing the authority of eminent political philosophers. Which authorities does Clinton use to this end?
3. What is Clinton's greatest fear about the course of the American experiment in self-government? What is the primary lesson he draws from Shays's Rebellion? What lessons does he draw from history in general?
4. How does Clinton believe that regional differences will impede the ability of the federal government to function? Based on your general knowledge of United States history, how accurate was Clinton in his predictions?

7-7   The Federalist, No. 10 (1787)

James Madison

As Document 7-6 demonstrates, advocates of the proposed federal Constitution faced a difficult task, especially in obtaining the ratification of the crucial state of New York. In an effort to respond to Antifederalists such as George Clinton, three Federalists—James Madison, Alexander Hamilton, and John Jay—wrote a series of essays in late 1787 and early 1788 explaining the reasoning behind the charter. While most historians generally agree that these essays, now collectively known as *The Federalist,* probably did not play a major role in convincing New Yorkers to accept the Constitution, scholars and jurists generally consider them indispensable to understanding the thinking of the men who framed it. The most famous of these essays, No. 10, was written by Madison in response to Clinton's argument (Document 7-6) and is widely regarded as the most insightful analysis of the nature of the American political system ever written. The essay is reprinted here in its entirety.

Source: New-York Daily Advertiser, 22 November 1787.

TO THE PEOPLE OF THE STATE OF NEW-YORK.

Among the numerous advantages promised by a well constructed Union, none deserves to be more accurately developed than its tendency to break and control the violence of faction. The friend of popular governments, never finds himself so much alarmed for their character and fate, as when he contemplates their propensity to this dangerous vice. He will not fail therefore to set a due value on any plan which, without violating the principles to which he is attached, provides a proper cure for it. The instability, injustice and confusion introduced into the public councils, have in truth been the mortal diseases under which popular governments have every where perished; as they continue to be the favorite and fruitful topics from which the adversaries to liberty derive their most specious declamations. The valuable improvements made by the American Constitutions on the popular models, both ancient and modern, cannot certainly be too much admired; but it would be an unwarrantable partiality, to contend that they have as effectually obviated the danger on this side as was wished and expected. Complaints are every where heard from our most considerate and virtuous citizens, equally the friends of public and private faith, and of public and personal liberty; that our governments are too unstable; that the public good is disregarded in the conflicts of rival parties; and that measures are too often decided, not according to the rules of justice, and the rights of the minor party; but by the superior force of an interested and overbearing majority. However anxiously we may wish that these complaints had no foundation, the evidence of known facts will not permit us to deny that they are in some degree true. It will be found indeed, on a candid review of our situation, that some of the distresses under which we labor, have been erroneously charged on the operation of our governments; but it will be found, at the same time, that other causes will not alone account for many of our heaviest misfortunes; and particularly, for that prevailing and increasing distrust of public engagements, and alarm for private rights, which are echoed from one end of the continent to the other. These must be chiefly, if not wholly, effects of the unsteadiness and injustice, with which a factious spirit has tainted our public administration.

By a faction I understand a number of citizens, whether amounting to a majority or minority of the whole, who are united and actuated by some common impulse of passion, or of interest, adverse to the rights of other citizens, or to the permanent and aggregate interests of the community.

There are two methods of curing the mischiefs of faction: the one, by removing its causes; the other, by controling its effects.

There are again two methods of removing the causes of faction: the one by destroying the liberty which is essential to its existence; the other, by giving to every citizen the same opinions, the same passions, and the same interests.

It could never be more truly said than of the first remedy, that it is worse than the disease. Liberty is to faction, what air is to fire, an aliment without which it instantly expires. But it could not be a less folly to abolish liberty, which is essential to political life, because it nourishes faction, than it would be to wish the annihilation of air, which is essential to animal life, because it imparts to fire its destructive agency.

The second expedient is as impracticable, as the first would be unwise. As long as the reason of man continues fallible, and he is at liberty to exercise it, different opinions will be formed. As long as the connection subsists between his reason and his self-love, his opinions and his passions will have a reciprocal influence on each other; and the former will be objects to which the latter will attach themselves. The diversity in the faculties of men from which the rights of property originate, is not less an insuperable obstacle to a uniformity of interests. The protection of these faculties is the first object of Government. From the protection of different and unequal faculties of acquiring property, the possession of different degrees and kinds of property immediately results: and from the influence of these on the sentiments and views of the respective proprietors, ensues a division of the society into different interests and parties.

The latent causes of faction are thus sown in the nature of man; and we see them every where brought into different degrees of activity, according to the different circumstances of civil society. A zeal for different opinions concerning religion, concerning Government, and many other points, as well of speculation as of practice; an attachment to different leaders ambitiously contending for pre-eminence and power; or to persons of other descriptions whose fortunes have been interesting to the human passions, have in turn divided mankind into parties, inflamed them with mutual animosity, and rendered them much more disposed to vex and oppress each other, than to co-operate for their common good. So strong is this propensity of mankind to fall into mutual animosities, that where no substantial occasion presents itself, the most frivolous and fanciful distinctions have been sufficient to kindle their unfriendly passions, and excite their most violent conflicts. But the most common and durable source of factions, has been the various and unequal distribution of property. Those who hold, and those who are without property, have ever formed distinct interests in society. Those who are creditors, and those who are debtors, fall under a like discrimination. A landed interest, a manufacturing interest, a mercantile interest, a monied interest, with many lesser interests, grow up of necessity in civilized nations, and divide them into different classes, actuated by different sentiments and views. The regulation of these various and interfering interests forms the principal task of modern Legislation, and involves the spirit of party and faction in the necessary and ordinary operations of Government.

No man is allowed to be a judge in his own cause; because his interest would certainly bias his judgment, and, not improbably, corrupt his integrity. With equal, nay with greater reason, a body of men, are unfit to be both judges and parties, at the same time; yet, what are many of the most important acts of legislation, but so many judicial determinations, not indeed concerning the rights of single persons, but concerning the rights of large bodies of citizens; and what are the different classes of legislators, but advocates and parties to the causes which they determine? Is a law proposed concerning private debts? It is a question

to which the creditors are parties on one side, and the debtors on the other. Justice ought to hold the balance between them. Yet the parties are and must be themselves the judges; and the most numerous party, or, in other words, the most powerful faction must be expected to prevail. Shall domestic manufactures be encouraged, and in what degree, by restrictions on foreign manufactures? are questions which would be differently decided by the landed and the manufacturing classes; and probably by neither, with a sole regard to justice and the public good. The apportionment of taxes on the various descriptions of property, is an act which seems to require the most exact impartiality; yet there is perhaps no legislative act in which greater opportunity and temptation are given to a predominant party, to trample on the rules of justice. Every shilling with which they over-burden the inferior number, is a shilling saved to their own pockets.

It is in vain to say, that enlightened statesmen will be able to adjust these clashing interests, and render them all subservient to the public good. Enlightened statesmen will not always be at the helm: Nor, in many cases, can such an adjustment be made at all, without taking into view indirect and remote considerations, which will rarely prevail over the immediate interest which one party may find in disregarding the rights of another, or the good of the whole.

The inference to which we are brought, is, that the *causes* of faction cannot be removed; and that relief is only to be sought in the means of controling its *effects*.

If a faction consists of less than a majority, relief is supplied by the republican principle, which enables the majority to defeat its sinister views by regular vote: It may clog the administration, it may convulse the society; but it will be unable to execute and mask its violence under the forms of the Constitution. When a majority is included in a faction, the form of popular government on the other hand enables it to sacrifice to its ruling passion or interest, both the public good and the rights of other citizens. To secure the public good, and private rights, against the danger of such a faction, and at the same time to preserve the spirit and the form of popular government, is then the great object to which our enquiries are directed: Let me add that it is the great desideratum, by which alone this form of government can be rescued from the opprobrium under which it has so long labored, and be recommended to the esteem and adoption of mankind.

By what means is this object attainable? Evidently by one of two only. Either the existence of the same passion or interest in a majority at the same time, must be prevented; or the majority, having such co-existent passion or interest, must be rendered, by their number and local situation, unable to concert and carry into effect schemes of oppression. If the impulse and the opportunity be suffered to coincide, we well know that neither moral nor religious motives can be relied on as an adequate control. They are not found to be such on the injustice and violence of individuals, and lose their efficacy in proportion to the number combined together; that is, in proportion as their efficacy becomes needful.

From this view of the subject, it may be concluded, that a pure Democracy, by which I mean, a Society, consisting of a small number of citizens, who assemble and administer the Government in person, can admit of no cure for the mischiefs of faction. A common passion or interest will, in almost every case, be felt by a majority of the whole; a communication and concert results from the form of Government itself; and there is nothing to check the inducements to sacrifice the weaker party, or an obnoxious individual. Hence it is, that such Democracies have ever been spectacles of turbulence and contention; have ever been found incompatible with personal security, or the rights of property; and have in general been as short in their lives, as they have been violent in their deaths. Theoretic politicians, who have patronized this species of Government, have erroneously supposed, that by reducing mankind to a perfect equality in their political rights, they would, at the same time, be perfectly equalized and assimilated in their possessions, their opinions, and their passions.

A Republic, by which I mean a Government in which the scheme of representation takes place, opens a different prospect, and promises the cure for which we are seeking. Let us examine the points in which it varies from pure Democracy, and we shall comprehend both the nature of the cure, and the efficacy which it must derive from the Union.

The two great points of difference between a Democracy and a Republic are, first, the delegation of the Government, in the latter, to a small number of citizens elected by the rest: secondly, the greater number of citizens, and greater sphere of country, over which the latter may be extended.

The effect of the first difference is, on the one hand to refine and enlarge the public views, by passing them through the medium of a chosen body of citizens, whose wisdom may best discern the true interest of their country, and whose patriotism and love of justice, will be least likely to sacrifice it to temporary or partial considerations. Under such a regulation, it may well happen that the public voice pronounced by the representatives of the people, will be more consonant to the public good, than if pronounced by the people themselves convened for the purpose. On the other hand, the effect may be inverted. Men of factious tempers, of local prejudices, or of sinister designs, may by intrigue, by corruption or by other means, first obtain the suffrages, and then betray the interests of the people. The question resulting is, whether small or extensive Republics are most favorable to the election of proper guardians of the public weal; and it is clearly decided in favor of the latter by two obvious considerations.

In the first place it is to be remarked that however small the Republic may be, the Representatives must be raised to a certain number, in order to guard against the cabals of a few; and that however large it may be, they must be limited to a certain number, in order to guard against the confusion of a multitude. Hence the number of Representatives in the two cases, not being in proportion to that of the Constituents, and being proportionally greatest in the small Republic, it follows, that if the proportion of fit characters, be not less, in the large than in the small Republic, the former will present a greater option, and consequently a greater probability of a fit choice.

In the next place, as each Representative will be chosen by a greater number of citizens in the large than in the small Republic, it will be more difficult for unworthy candidates to practise with success the vicious arts, by which elections are too often carried; and the suffrages of the people being more free, will be more likely to centre on men who possess the most attractive merit, and the most diffusive and established characters.

It must be confessed, that in this, as in most other cases, there is a mean, on both sides of which inconveniencies will be found to lie. By enlarging too much the number of electors, you render the representative too little acquainted with all their local circumstances and lesser interests; as by reducing it too much, you render him unduly attached to these, and too little fit to comprehend and pursue great and national objects. The Federal Constitution forms a happy combination in this respect; the great and aggregate interests being referred to the national, the local and particular, to the state legislatures.

The other point of difference is, the greater number of citizens and extent of territory which may be brought within the compass of Republican, than of Democratic Government; and it is this circumstance principally which renders factious combinations less to be dreaded in the former, than in the latter. The smaller the society, the fewer probably will be the distinct parties and interests composing it; the fewer the distinct parties and interests, the more frequently will a majority be found of the same party; and the smaller the number of individuals composing a majority, and the smaller the compass within which they are placed, the more easily will they concert and execute their plans of oppression. Extend the sphere, and you take in a greater variety of parties and interests; you make it less probable that a majority of the whole will have a common motive to invade the rights of other citizens; or if such a common motive exists, it will be more difficult for all who feel it to discover their own strength, and to act in unison with each other. Besides other impediments, it may be remarked, that where there is a consciousness of unjust or dishonorable purposes, communication is always checked by distrust, in proportion to the number whose concurrence is necessary.

Hence it clearly appears, that the same advantage, which a Republic has over a Democracy, in controling the effects of faction, is enjoyed by a large over a small Republic—is enjoyed by the Union over the States composing it.

Does this advantage consist in the substitution of Representatives, whose enlightened views and virtuous sentiments render them superior to local prejudices, and to schemes of injustice? It will not be denied, that the Representation of the Union will be most likely to possess these requisite endowments. Does it consist in the greater security afforded by a greater variety of parties, against the event of any one party being able to outnumber and oppress the rest? In an equal degree does the encreased variety of parties, comprised within the Union, encrease this security. Does it, in fine, consist in the greater obstacles opposed to the concert and accomplishment of the secret wishes of an unjust and interested majority? Here, again, the extent of the Union gives it the most palpable advantage.

The influence of factious leaders may kindle a flame within their particular States, but will be unable to spread a general conflagration through the other States: a religious sect, may degenerate into a political faction in a part of the Confederacy; but the variety of sects dispersed over the entire face of it, must secure the national Councils against any danger from that source: a rage for paper money, for an abolition of debts, for an equal division of property, or for any other improper or wicked project, will be less apt to pervade the whole body of the Union, than a particular member of it; in the same proportion as such a malady is more likely to taint a particular county or district, than an entire State.

In the extent and proper structure of the Union, therefore, we behold a Republican remedy for the diseases most incident to Republican Government. And according to the degree of pleasure and pride, we feel in being Republicans, ought to be our zeal in cherishing the spirit, and supporting the character of Federalists.

Questions

1. According to Madison, what causes "factions" to develop?
2. According to Madison, why are factions dangerous?
3. Given his assessment of how factions develop, can Madison be called an economic determinist? Why or why not?
4. If one believes in a democratic-style republic, why, according to Madison, is it logical to want to have a physically large nation? Do you agree or disagree? Why?
5. On the basis of *The Federalist,* No. 10, would you describe Madison as a democrat? Why or why not?

7-8   Virginia Proposes Amendments to the Constitution (1788)

As indicated in the textbook (pp. 222–224), Americans who opposed the Constitution created in 1787 were afraid that it was designed to produce rule by the elite and that the elite would establish a tyranny. Opponents of the proposed Constitution, who were cleverly and misleadingly labeled "Antifederalists" by its supporters (see text pp. 226–227), considered the fact that the proposed Constitution lacked a Bill of Rights an especially dangerous sign. In the hard-fought battles that ended in the adoption of the Constitution, persons who styled themselves Federalists were able to succeed only by promising to amend the document to include a Bill of Rights (see text p. 230). The following statement issued by the Virginia Ratifying Convention on June 27, 1788, explains the rationale of advocates for a Bill of Rights. It also provides the fullest single list of the kinds of changes—amendments—most Antifederalists wanted.

Source: Jonathan Elliot, ed., *Debates in the Several State Conventions on the Adoption of the Federal Constitution . . . in 1787,* 2d. ed. (1881), 3: 657–661.

Mr. WYTHE reported, from the committee appointed, such *amendments* to the proposed Constitution of government for the United States as were by them deemed necessary to be recommended to the consideration of the Congress which shall first assemble under the said Constitution, to be acted upon according to the mode prescribed in the 5th article thereof; and he read the same in his place, and afterwards delivered them in at the clerk's table, where the same were again read, and are as follows:

—"That there be a declaration or bill of rights asserting, and securing from encroachment, the essential and unalienable rights of the people, in some such manner as the following:—

"1st. That there are certain natural rights, of which men, when they form a social compact, cannot deprive or divest their posterity; among which are the enjoyment of life and liberty, with the means of acquiring, possessing, and protecting property, and pursuing and obtaining happiness and safety.

"2d. That all power is naturally invested in, and consequently derived from, the people; that magistrates therefore are their *trustees* and *agents*, at all times amenable to them.

"3d. That government ought to be instituted for the common benefit, protection, and security of the people; and that the doctrine of non-resistance against arbitrary power and oppression is absurd, slavish, and destructive to the good and happiness of mankind.

"4th. That no man or set of men are entitled to separate or exclusive public emoluments or privileges from the community, but in consideration of public services, which not being descendible, neither ought the offices of magistrate, legislator, or judge, or any other public office, to be hereditary.

"5th. That the legislative, executive, and judicial powers of government should be separate and distinct; and, that the members of the two first may be restrained from oppression by feeling and participating the public burdens, they should, at fixed periods, be reduced to a private station, return into the mass of the people, and the vacancies be supplied by certain and regular elections, in which all or any part of the former members to be eligible or ineligible, as the rules of the Constitution of government, and the laws, shall direct.

"6th. That the elections of representatives in the legislature ought to be free and frequent, and all men having sufficient evidence of permanent common interest with, and attachment to, the community, ought to have the right of suffrage; and no aid, charge, tax, or fee, can be set, rated, or levied, upon the people without their own consent, or that of their representatives, so elected; nor can they be bound by any law to which they have not, in like manner, assented, for the public good.

"7th. That all power of suspending laws, or the execution of laws, by any authority, without the consent of the representatives of the people in the legislature, is injurious to their rights, and ought not to be exercised.

"8th. That, in all criminal and capital prosecutions, a man hath a right to demand the cause and nature of his accusation, to be confronted with the accusers and witnesses, to call for evidence, and be allowed counsel in his favor, and to a fair and speedy trial by an impartial jury of his vicinage, without whose unanimous consent he cannot be found guilty, (except in the government of the land and naval forces;) nor can he be compelled to give evidence against himself.

"9th. That no freeman ought to be taken, imprisoned, or disseized of his freehold, liberties, privileges, or franchises, or outlawed, or exiled, or in any manner destroyed, or deprived of his life, liberty, or property, but by the law of the land.

"10th. That every freeman restrained of his liberty is entitled to a remedy, to inquire into the lawfulness thereof, and to remove the same, if unlawful, and that such remedy ought not to be denied nor delayed.

"11th. That, in controversies respecting property, and in suits between man and man, the ancient trial by jury is one of the greatest securities to the rights of the people, and to remain sacred and inviolable.

"12th. That every freeman ought to find a certain remedy, by recourse to the laws, for all injuries and wrongs he may receive in his person, property, or character. He ought to obtain right and justice freely, without sale, completely and without denial, promptly and without delay; and that all establishments or regulations contravening these rights are oppressive and unjust.

"13th. That excessive bail ought not to be required, nor excessive fines imposed, nor cruel and unusual punishments inflicted.

"14th. That every freeman has a right to be secure from all unreasonable searches and seizures of his person, his papers, and property; all warrants, therefore, to search suspected places, or seize any freeman, his papers, or property, without information on oath (or affirmation of a person religiously scrupulous of taking an oath) of legal and sufficient cause, are grievous and oppressive; and all general warrants to search suspected places, or to apprehend any suspected person, without specially naming or describing the place or person, are dangerous, and ought not to be granted.

"15th. That the people have a right peaceably to assemble together to consult for the common good, or to instruct their representatives; and that every freeman has a right to petition or apply to the legislature for redress of grievances.

"16th. That the people have a right to freedom of speech, and of writing and publishing their sentiments; that the freedom of the press is one of the greatest bulwarks of liberty, and ought not to be violated.

"17th. That the people have a right to keep and bear arms; that a well-regulated militia, composed of the body of the people trained to arms, is the proper, natural, and safe defence of a free state; that standing armies, in time of peace, are dangerous to liberty, and therefore ought to be avoided, as far as the circumstances and protection of the community will admit; and that, in all cases, the military should be under strict subordination to, and governed by, the civil power.

"18th. That no soldier in time of peace ought to be quartered in any house without the consent of the owner, and in time of war in such manner only as the law directs.

"19th. That any person religiously scrupulous of bearing arms ought to be exempted, upon payment of an equivalent to employ another to bear arms in his stead.

"20th. That religion, or the duty which we owe to our Creator, and the manner of discharging it, can be directed only by reason and conviction, not by force or violence; and therefore all men have an equal, natural, and unalienable right to the free exercise of religion, according to the dictates of conscience, and that no particular religious sect or society ought to be favored or established, by law, in preference to others."

AMENDMENTS TO THE CONSTITUTION

"1st. That each state in the Union shall respectively retain every power, jurisdiction, and right, which is not by this Constitution delegated to the Congress of the United States, or to the departments of the federal government.

"2d. That there shall be one representative for every thirty thousand, according to the enumeration or census mentioned in the Constitution, until the whole number of representatives amounts to two hundred; after which, that number shall be continued or increased, as Congress shall direct, upon the principles fixed in the Constitution, by apportioning the representatives of each state to some greater number of people, from time to time, as population increases.

"3d. When the Congress shall lay direct taxes or excises, they shall immediately inform the executive power of each state, of the quota of such state, according to the census herein directed, which is proposed to be thereby raised; and if the legislature of any state shall pass a law which shall be effectual for raising such quota at the time required by Congress, the taxes and excises laid by Congress shall not be collected in such state.

"4th. That the members of the Senate and House of Representatives shall be ineligible to, and incapable of holding, any civil office under the authority of the United States, during the time for which they shall respectively be elected.

"5th. That the journals of the proceedings of the Senate and House of Representatives shall be published at least once in every year, except such parts thereof, relating to treaties, alliances, or military operations, as in their judgment, require secrecy.

"6th. That a regular statement and account of the receipts and expenditures of public money shall be published at least once a year.

"7th. That no commercial treaty shall be ratified without the concurrence of two thirds of the whole number of the members of the Senate; and no treaty ceding, contracting, restraining, or suspending, the territorial rights or claims of the United States, or any of them, or their, or any of their rights or claims to fishing in the American seas, or navigating the American rivers, shall be made, but in cases of the most urgent and extreme necessity; nor shall any such treaty be ratified without the concurrence of three fourths of the whole number of the members of both houses respectively.

"8th. That no navigation law, or law regulating commerce, shall be passed without the consent of two thirds of the members present, in both houses.

"9th. That no standing army, or regular troops, shall be raised, or kept up, in time of peace, without the consent of two thirds of the members present, in both houses.

"10th. That no soldier shall be enlisted for any longer term than four years, except in time of war, and then for no longer term than the continuance of the war.

"11th. That each state respectively shall have the power to provide for organizing, arming, and disciplining its own militia, whensoever Congress shall omit or neglect to provide for the same. That the militia shall not be subject to martial law, except when in actual service, in time of war, invasion, or rebellion; and when not in the actual service of the United States, shall be subject only to such fines, penalties, and punishments, as shall be directed or inflicted by the laws of its own state.

"12th. That the exclusive power of legislation given to Congress over the federal town and its adjacent district, and other places, purchased or to be purchased by Congress of any of the states, shall extend only to such regulations as respect the police and good government thereof.

"13th. That no person shall be capable of being President of the United States for more than eight years in any term of sixteen years.

"14th. That the judicial power of the United States shall be vested in one Supreme Court, and in such courts of admiralty as Congress may from time to time ordain and establish in any of the different states. The judicial power shall extend to all cases in law and equity arising under treaties made, or which shall be made, under the authority of the United States; to all cases affecting ambassadors, other foreign ministers, and consuls; to all cases of admiralty and maritime jurisdiction; to controversies to which the United States shall be a party; to controversies between two or more states, and between parties claiming lands under the grants of different states. In all cases affecting ambassadors, other foreign ministers, and consuls, and those in which a state shall be a party, the Supreme Court shall have original jurisdiction; in all other cases before mentioned, the Supreme Court shall have appellate jurisdiction, as to matters of law only, except in cases of equity, and of admiralty, and maritime jurisdiction, in which the Supreme Court shall have appellate jurisdiction both as to law and fact, with such exceptions and under such regulations as the Congress shall make: but the judicial power of the United States shall extend to no case where the cause of action shall have originated before the ratification of the Constitution, except in disputes between states about their territory, disputes between persons claiming lands under the grants of different states, and suits for debts due to the United States.

"15th. That, in criminal prosecutions no man shall be restrained in the exercise of the usual and accustomed right of challenging or excepting to the jury.

"16th. That Congress shall not alter, modify, or interfere in the times, places, or manner of holding elections for senators and representatives, or either of them, except when the legislature of any state shall neglect, refuse, or be disabled, by invasion or rebellion, to prescribe the same.

"17th. That those clauses which declare that Congress shall not exercise certain powers, be not interpreted, in any manner whatsoever, to extend the powers of Congress; but that they be construed either as making exceptions to the specified powers where this shall be the case, or otherwise, as inserted merely for greater caution.

"18th. That the laws ascertaining the compensation of senators and representatives for their services, be postponed, in their operation, until after the election of representatives immediately succeeding the passing thereof; that excepted which shall first be passed on the subject.

"19th. That some tribunal other than the Senate be provided for trying impeachments of senators.

"20th. That the salary of a judge shall not be increased or diminished during his continuance in office, otherwise than by general regulations of salary, which may take place on a revision of the subject at stated periods of not less than seven years, to commence from the time such salaries shall be first ascertained by Congress."

Questions

1. Do the Virginia Convention's proposed amendments show that that state was trying to live up to the Virginia Declaration of Rights (Document 7-1)? Why or why not?

2. Compare these proposed amendments with the Bill of Rights adopted in 1791 (see text pp. D-12–D-14). If Virginia's proposed amendments had been adopted, would the Constitution have been radically different? Why or why not?

3. Given what you know from Documents 7-5 through 7-7 and from the textbook, which of the amendments would the Federalists have accepted fairly readily? Why? Which of the amendments would they adamantly have *refused* to accept? Why?

Questions for Further Thought

1. Can you identify points of consensus between the Federalist (Document 7-7) and Antifederalist (Document 7-6) positions? What did men like James Madison and George Clinton understand the ends of government to be, and what arguments did they put forth?

2. After the ratification of the Constitution and the quick passage of the Bill of Rights, public opposition to the new government of the United States virtually disappeared. Given the heated nature of the ratification debates, how can we explain this sudden show of unanimity? Did both the Federalists and Antifederalists get everything that they wanted? Did the Bill of Rights ameliorate all Antifederalist fears?

3. Given that the U.S. Constitution is still in effect, were Madison's assumptions in *The Federalist,* No. 10, correct (Document 7-7)? Do you think that the U.S. government has endured because of—or in spite of—the political science of James Madison?

The Political Divisions of the 1790s

With the adoption of the Constitution and the addition of a Bill of Rights, America's political problems changed but did not disappear. The financial difficulties that had bedeviled the Confederation government still existed. Alexander Hamilton—talented, ambitious, and aristocratically inclined—was determined to confront these problems boldly. First, Hamilton successfully worked to restore the public credit in a way that would ally the interests of the states and "monied men" with those of the federal government—but at the expense of small taxpayers (Document 7-9). Having gotten his way on public credit, Hamilton next strove to create a national financial institution, the Bank of the United States. In so doing, he argued for a "loose" interpretation of the Constitution that would greatly increase the federal government's power. Thomas Jefferson and James Madison, however, fought the bank proposal, presenting as a counterargument a "strict" interpretation of the Constitution that forbade the Congress to do anything not explicitly authorized by the charter. These positions reflected fundamentally different visions of what America was and should become.

As the fight over the course the government should follow became more heated, it extended into foreign policy and deepened political divisions. The eruption of the French Revolution in 1789 was enthusiastically received by Jefferson's supporters, who increasingly took the name "Republican"; but the revolution's excesses and radical assaults on religion horrified Hamilton's faction; these men, who retained the name "Federalist," saw the new nation's economic future as dependent on good relations with Great Britain, France's enemy. While George Washington (Document 7-10) counseled a policy of aloofness from the contentions of Europe, British and especially French interests increasingly sought influence, adding hysteria over foreign "subversion" to domestic strife. The Federalists, in control of the government, went to great lengths to stifle their opponents, passing the Alien and Sedition Acts in 1798 (Document 7-11). In response, Madison and Jefferson briefly sought, in the Virginia and Kentucky Resolutions, to reassert state sovereignty against what they saw as a tyrannical federal government.

In the end, though, the contest between Federalists and Jeffersonian Republicans was decided in the electoral arena; in the presidential contest of 1800, Jefferson emerged triumphant. His victory was notable in that it proved that power in the new nation could be transferred peacefully and without serious reprisals against the losers; indeed, in his 1801 inaugural address (Document 7-12), Jefferson stressed the common interest of all parties in preserving and advancing the American experiment in republican government.

7-9   Report on Public Credit (1790)

Alexander Hamilton

As early as 1781, Alexander Hamilton, demonstrating his admiration for British institutions and economic policies, said that "a national debt if it is not excessive will be to us a national blessing, it will be [a] powerfull cement of our union." When he became the nation's first secretary of the treasury in 1789, he tried to implement his ideals by devising innovative financial policies to overcome the fiscal problems that had helped undermine the Confederation government. The intricacies of those policies are clearly analyzed in the textbook (pp. 230–233). Document 7-9, which consists of sections of

Hamilton's "Report on Public Credit" (1790), explains his view on public credit, including his position concerning a national debt.

Source: Harold C. Syrett, ed., *The Papers of Alexander Hamilton* (New York: Columbia University Press, 1962), 6: 65–71, 106.

Treasury Department, January 9, 1790.
[Communicated on January 14, 1790]
[To the Speaker of the House of Representatives]
The Secretary of the Treasury, in obedience to the resolution of the House of Representatives . . . has . . . applied himself to the consideration of a proper plan for the support of the Public Credit, with all the attention which was due to the authority of the House, and to the magnitude of the object.

In the discharge of this duty, he has felt . . . a deep and solemn conviction of the momentous nature of the truth contained in the resolution under which his investigations have been conducted, "That an *adequate* provision for the support of the Public Credit, is a matter of high importance to the honor and prosperity of the United States."

With an ardent desire that his well-meant endeavors may be conducive to the real advantage of the nation, and with the utmost deference to the superior judgment of the House, he now respectfully submits the result of his enquiries and reflections, to their indulgent construction.

In the opinion of the Secretary, the wisdom of the House, in giving their explicit sanction to the proposition which has been stated, cannot but be applauded by all, who will seriously consider, and trace through their obvious consequences, these plain and undeniable truths.

That exigencies are to be expected to occur, in the affairs of nations, in which there will be a necessity for borrowing.

That loans in times of public danger, especially from foreign war, are found an indispensable resource, even to the wealthiest of them.

And that in a country, which, like this, is possessed of little active wealth, or in other words, little monied capital, the necessity for that resource, must, in such emergencies, be proportionably urgent.

And as on the one hand, the necessity for borrowing in particular emergencies cannot be doubted, so on the other, it is equally evident, that to be able to borrow upon *good terms*, it is essential that the credit of a nation should be well established.

For when the credit of a country is in any degree questionable, it never fails to give an extravagant premium, in one shape or another, upon all the loans it has occasion to make. Nor does the evil end here; the same disadvantage must be sustained upon whatever is to be bought on terms of future payment.

From this constant necessity of *borrowing* and *buying dear*, it is easy to conceive how immensely the expences of a nation, in a course of time, will be augmented by an unsound state of the public credit.

To attempt to enumerate the complicated variety of mischiefs in the whole system of the social œconomy, which proceed from a neglect of the maxims that uphold public credit, and justify the solicitude manifested by the House on this point, would be an improper intrusion on their time and patience.

In so strong a light nevertheless do they appear to the Secretary, that on their due observance at the present critical juncture, materially depends, in his judgment, the individual and aggregate prosperity of the citizens of the United States; their relief from the embarrassments they now experience; their character as a People; the cause of good government.

If the maintenance of public credit, then, be truly so important, the next enquiry which suggests itself is, by what means it is to be effected? The ready answer to which question is, by good faith, by a punctual performance of contracts. States, like individuals, who observe their engagements, are respected and trusted: while the reverse is the fate of those, who pursue an opposite conduct. . . .

While the observance of that good faith, which is the basis of public credit, is recommended by the strongest inducements of political expediency, it is enforced by considerations of still greater authority. There are arguments for it, which rest on the immutable principles of moral obligation. And in proportion as the mind is disposed to contemplate, in the order of Providence, an intimate connection between public virtue and public happiness, will be its repugnancy to a violation of those principles.

This reflection derives additional strength from the nature of the debt of the United States. It was the price of liberty. The faith of America has been repeatedly pledged for it, and with solemnities, that give peculiar force to the obligation. There is indeed reason to regret that it has not hitherto been kept; that the necessities of the war, conspiring with inexperience in the subjects of finance, produced direct infractions; and that the subsequent period has been a continued scene of negative violation, or non-compliance. But a diminution of this regret arises from the reflection, that the last seven years have exhibited an earnest and uniform effort, on the part of the government of the union, to retrieve the national credit, by doing justice to the creditors of the nation; and that the embarrassments of a defective constitution, which defeated this laudable effort, have ceased.

From this evidence of a favorable disposition, given by the former government, the institution of a new one, cloathed with powers competent to calling forth the resources of the community, has excited correspondent expectations. A general belief, accordingly, prevails, that the credit of the United States will quickly be established on the firm foundation of an effectual provision for the existing debt. . . .

It cannot but merit particular attention, that among ourselves the most enlightened friends of good government are those, whose expectations are the highest.

To justify and preserve their confidence; to promote the encreasing respectability of the American name; to answer the calls of justice; to restore landed property to its due value; to furnish new resources both to agriculture and commerce; to cement more closely the union of the states; to add to their security against foreign attack; to establish public order on the basis of an upright and liberal policy. These are the great and invaluable ends to be secured, by a proper and adequate provision, at the present period, for the support of public credit.

To this provision we are invited, not only by the general considerations, which have been noticed, but by others of a more particular nature. It will procure to every class of the community some important advantages, and remove some no less important disadvantages. . . .

But these good effects of a public debt are only to be looked for, when, by being well funded, it has acquired an *adequate* and *stable* value. Till then, it has rather a contrary tendency. The fluctuation and insecurity incident to it in an unfunded state, render it a mere commodity, and a precarious one. As such, being only an object of occasional and particular speculation, all the money applied to it is so much diverted from the more useful channels of circulation, for which the thing itself affords no substitute: So that, in fact, one serious inconvenience of an unfunded debt is, that it contributes to the scarcity of money.

This distinction which has been little if at all attended to, is of the greatest moment. It involves a question immediately interesting to every part of the community; which is no other than this—Whether the public debt, by a provision for it on true principles, shall be rendered a *substitute* for money; or whether, by being left as it is, or by being provided for in such a manner as will wound those principles, and destroy confidence, it shall be suffered to continue, as it is, a pernicious drain of our cash from the channels of productive industry. . . .

Persuaded as the Secretary is, that the proper funding of the present debt, will render it a national blessing: Yet he is so far from acceding to the position, in the latitude in which it is sometimes laid down, that "public debts are public benefits," a position inviting to prodigality, and liable to dangerous abuse,—that he ardently wishes to see it incorporated, as a fundamental maxim, in the system of public credit of the United States, that the creation of debt should always be accompanied with the means of extinguishment. This he regards as the true secret for rendering public credit immortal. And he presumes, that it is difficult to conceive a situation, in which there may not be an adherence to the maxim. At least he feels an unfeigned solicitude, that this may be attempted by the United States, and that they may commence their measures for the establishment of credit, with the observance of it.

Questions

1. According to Hamilton, why is it essential for a nation to have good public credit?
2. According to Hamilton, what has to be done to ensure that the United States will have sound public credit?
3. Hamilton makes an open appeal to patriotism. Do you find it effective? Why or why not?

7-10   Farewell Address (1796)

George Washington

Foreign aid, especially the direct military aid that resulted from the French Alliance, proved essential to winning American independence. That alliance, however, was made when France was still a monarchy. When the French Revolution transformed France into a republic and then plunged that nation into war, the U.S. government faced a dilemma. Should the United States, a weak nation, honor its alliance with a France that was fundamentally different from the country that had entered into the Alliance of 1778? As the textbook authors indicate (pp. 236–239), the country split over the issue, and President Washington and the Federalist-dominated Congress chose to embrace neutrality. In taking that position, President Washington revealed his Federalist party leanings. Still, his emphasis on keeping America out of harm's way also reflected his view on the foreign policy guidelines that the young, still militarily weak nation should follow. In his 1796 farewell address, which also included extensive comments on "the baneful effects of the spirit of [political] parties," President Washington clearly spelled out his views on foreign policy.

Source: James D. Richardson, ed., *A Compilation of the Messages and Papers of the Presidents* (Washington, D.C.: U.S. Government Printing Office, 1896–1899), 1: 205–216 passim.

Observe good faith and justice toward all nations. Cultivate peace and harmony with all. Religion and morality enjoin this conduct. And can it be that good policy does not equally enjoin it? It will be worthy of a free, enlightened, and at no distant period a great nation to give to mankind the magnanimous and too novel example of a people always guided by an exalted justice and benevolence. Who can doubt that in the course of time and things the fruits of such a plan would richly repay any temporary advantages which might be lost by a steady adherence to it? . . .

In the execution of such a plan nothing is more essential than that permanent, inveterate antipathies against particular nations and passionate attachments for others should be excluded, and that in place of them just and amicable feelings toward all should be cultivated. The nation which indulges toward another an habitual hatred or an habitual fondness is in some degree a slave. It is a slave to its animosity or to its affection, either of which is sufficient to lead it astray from its duty and its interest. . . .

As avenues to foreign influence in innumerable ways, such attachments are particularly alarming to the truly enlightened and independent patriot. How many opportunities do they afford to tamper with domestic factions, to practice the arts of seduction, to mislead public opinion, to influence or awe the public councils! Such an attachment of a small or weak toward a great and powerful nation dooms the former to be the satellite of the latter. Against the insidious wiles of foreign influence (I conjure you to believe me, fellow-citizens) the jealousy of a free people ought to be *constantly* awake, since history and experience prove that foreign influence is one of the most baneful foes of republican government. But that jealousy, to be useful, must be impartial, else it becomes the instrument of the very influence to be avoided, instead of a defense against it. Excessive partiality for one foreign nation and excessive dislike of another cause those whom they actuate to see danger only on one side, and serve to veil and even second the arts of influence on the other. Real patriots who may resist the intrigues of the favorite are liable to become suspected and odious, while its tools and dupes usurp the applause and confidence of the people to surrender their interests.

The great rule of conduct for us in regard to foreign nations is, in extending our commercial relations to have with them as little *political* connection as possible. So far as we have already formed engagements let them be fulfilled with perfect good faith. Here let us stop.

Europe has a set of primary interests which to us have none or a very remote relation. Hence she must be engaged in frequent controversies, the causes of which are essentially foreign to our concerns. Hence, therefore, it must be unwise in us to implicate ourselves by artificial ties in the ordinary vicissitudes of her politics or the ordinary combinations and collisions of her friendships or enmities.

Our detached and distant situation invites and enables us to pursue a different course. If we remain one people, under an efficient government, the period is not far off when we may defy material injury from external annoyance; when we may take such an attitude as will cause the neutrality we may at any time resolve upon to be scrupulously respected; when belligerent nations, under the impossibility of making acquisitions upon us, will not lightly hazard the giving us provocation; when we may choose peace of war, as our interest, guided by justice, shall counsel.

Why forego the advantages of so peculiar a situation? Why quit our own to stand upon foreign ground? Why, by interweaving our destiny with that of any part of Europe, entangle our peace and prosperity in the toils of European ambition, rivalship, interest, humor, or caprice?

It is our true policy to steer clear of permanent alliances with any portion of the foreign world, so far, I mean, as we are now at liberty to do it; for let me not be understood as capable of patronizing infidelity to existing engagements. I hold the maxim no less applicable to public than to private affairs that honesty is always the best policy. I repeat, therefore, let those engagements be observed in their genuine sense. But in my opinion it is unnecessary and would be unwise to extend them.

Taking care always to keep ourselves by suitable establishments on a respectable defensive posture, we may safely trust to temporary alliances for extraordinary emergencies.

Harmony, liberal intercourse with all nations are recommended by policy, humanity, and interest. But even our commercial policy should hold an equal and impartial hand, neither seeking nor granting exclusive favors or preferences; consulting the natural course of things; diffusing and diversifying by gentle means the streams of commerce, but forcing nothing; establishing with powers so disposed, in order to give trade a stable course, to define the rights of our merchants, and to enable the Government to support them, conventional rules of intercourse, the best that present circumstances and mutual opinion will permit, but temporary and liable to be from time to time abandoned or varied as experience and circumstances shall dictate; constantly keeping in view that it is folly in one nation to look for disinterested favors from another; that it must pay with a portion of its independence for whatever it may accept under that character; that by such acceptance it may place itself in the condition of having given equivalents for nominal favors, and yet of being reproached with ingratitude for not giving more. There can be no greater error than to expect or calculate upon real favors from nation to nation. It is an illusion which experience must cure, which a just pride ought to discard.

In offering to you, my countrymen, these counsels of an old and affectionate friend I dare not hope they will make the strong and lasting impression I could wish—that they will control the usual current of the passions or prevent our nation from running the course which has hitherto marked the destiny of nations. But if I may even flatter myself that they may be productive of some partial benefit, some occasional good—that they may now and then recur to moderate the fury of party spirit, to warn against the mischiefs of foreign intrigue, to guard against the impos-tures of pretended patriotism—this hope will be a full recompense for the solicitude for your welfare by which they have been dictated.

How far in the discharge of my official duties I have been guided by the principles which have been delineated the public records and other evidences of my conduct must witness to you and to the world. To myself, the assurance of my own conscience is that I have at least believed myself to be guided by them.

In relation to the still subsisting war in Europe my proclamation of the 22d of April, 1793, is the index to my plan. Sanctioned by your approving voice and by that of your representatives in both Houses of Congress, the spirit of that measure has continually governed me, uninfluenced by any attempts to deter or divert me from it.

After deliberate examination, with the aid of the best lights I could obtain, I was well satisfied that our country, under all the circumstances of the case, had a right to take, and was bound in duty and interest to take, a neutral position. Having taken it, I determined as far as should depend upon me to maintain it with moderation, perseverance, and firmness. . . .

The inducements of interest for observing that conduct will best be referred to your own reflections and experience. With me a predominant motive has been to endeavor to gain time to our country to settle and mature its yet recent institutions, and to progress without interruption to that degree of strength and consistency which is necessary to give it, humanly speaking, the command of its own fortunes. . . .

Questions

1. What foreign policy guidelines does President Washington recommend for the United States?
2. Are Washington's reasons for following those guidelines convincing? Why or why not?
3. What does Washington mean when he says that "a free people ought to be *constantly* awake"? Do you agree or disagree with his assertion? If your answer is yes, is his advice on this point as applicable today as it was in 1796? Why or why not?

7-11   The Sedition Act (1798)

As the analysis in the textbook makes clear (pp. 239–241), President Washington was in some measure undoubtedly correct when he spoke of "the baneful effects of the spirit of [political] parties." One baneful effect was the way in which the Federalist party responded to its declining popularity in the late 1790s, when it was faced with the prospect of becoming a minority party. In an effort to retain power, leading Federalists trampled on the rights of their political opponents and precipitated a major political crisis. This crisis was evidenced and symbolized by the passage of the Alien and Sedition Acts of 1798. The Sedition Act, which is reprinted here, was seen as a direct assault on the Bill of Rights and thus provoked a sharp response.

Source: United States, *Statutes at Large*, 1: 596–597.

An Act in addition to the act, entitled "An act for the punishment of certain crimes against the United States."

SEC. 1. *Be it enacted . . .* , That if any persons shall unlawfully combine or conspire together, with intent to oppose any measure or measures of the government of the United States, which are or shall be directed by proper authority, or to impede the operation of any law of the United States, or to intimidate or prevent any person holding a place or office in or under the government of the United States, from undertaking, performing or executing his trust or duty; and if any person or persons, with intent as aforesaid, shall counsel, advise or attempt to procure any insurrection, riot, unlawful assembly, or combination, whether such conspiracy, threatening, counsel, advice, or attempt shall have the proposed effect or not, he or they shall be deemed guilty of a high misdemeanor, and on conviction, before any court of the United States having jurisdiction thereof, shall be punished by a fine not exceeding five thousand dollars, and by imprisonment during a term not less than six months nor exceeding five years; and further, at the discretion of the court may be holden to find sureties for his good behaviour in such sum, and for such time, as the said court may direct.

SEC. 2. That if any person shall write, print, utter, or publish, or shall cause or procure to be written, printed, uttered or published, or shall knowingly and willingly assist or aid in writing, printing, uttering or publishing any false, scandalous and malicious writing or writings against the government of the United States, or either house of the Congress of the United States, or the President of the United States, with intent to defame the said government, or either house of the said Congress, or the said President or to bring them, or either of them, into contempt or disrepute; or to excite against them, or either or any of them, the hatred of the good people of the United States, or to stir up sedition within the United States, or to excite any unlawful combinations therein, for opposing or resisting any law of the United States, or any act of the President of the United States, done in pursuance of any such law, or of the powers in him vested by the constitution of the United States, or to resist, oppose, or defeat any such law or act, or to aid, encourage or abet any hostile designs of any foreign nation against the United States, their people or government, then such person, being thereof convicted before any court of the United States having jurisdiction thereof, shall be punished by a fine not exceeding two thousand dollars, and by imprisonment not exceeding two years.

SEC. 3. That if any person shall be prosecuted under this act, for the writing or publishing any libel aforesaid, it shall be lawful for the defendant, upon the trial of the cause, to give in evidence in his defence, the truth of the matter contained in the publication charged as a libel. And the jury who shall try the cause, shall have a right to determine the law and the fact, under the direction of the court, as in other cases.

SEC. 4. That this act shall continue to be in force until March 3, 1801, and no longer. . . .

Questions

1. Compare the Sedition Act with the First Amendment to the Constitution (see text p. D-12). Does the Sedition Act violate the First Amendment? Why or why not?
2. Does Section 3 of the Sedition Act offer special protection for those who comment on politics? Why or why not?
3. What is the significance of the fact that the Sedition Act passed by a Federalist-dominated Congress would expire on March 3, 1801? (*Hint:* Read the headnote to Document 7-12.) What does this tell you about the Federalists who championed the Sedition Act?

7-12   First Inaugural Address (1801)

Thomas Jefferson

The 1800 presidential election was the first one marked by especially vicious mudslinging (see text pp. 240–241). However, by that time it was clear that the vision associated with the Republican party headed by Thomas Jefferson had gained ascendancy. The Federalist party was in fact disintegrating. Ironically, when a mix-up among the Republicans unexpectedly threw the election into the House of Representatives, Alexander Hamilton championed Thomas Jefferson, his longtime rival, rather than let Aaron Burr become president. Hamilton opposed Burr in part because he considered Burr a scoundrel. However, Hamilton also supported Jefferson because he believed that Jefferson as president would follow a more moderate course than would Jefferson as Republican party leader. The first proof of how perceptive Hamilton was became clear on March 4, 1801, when Jefferson delivered his stunning first inaugural address, which is reprinted here in full. In 1801, as in the Declaration of Independence of 1776, Jefferson defined the American republic as a government based on both majority rule and minority rights, with laws that treated citizens equally and respected their liberty.

Source: James D. Richardson, ed., *A Compilation of the Messages and Papers of the Presidents* (Washington, D.C.: U.S. Government Printing Office, 1913), 1: 309–312.

Friends and Fellow-Citizens.

Called upon to undertake the duties of the first executive office of our country, I avail myself of the presence of that portion of my fellow-citizens which is here assembled to express my grateful thanks for the favor with which they have been pleased to look toward me, to declare a sincere consciousness that the task is above my talents, and that I approach it with those anxious and awful presentiments which the greatness of the charge and the weakness of my powers so justly inspire. A rising nation, spread over a wide and fruitful land, traversing all the seas with the rich productions of their industry, engaged in commerce with nations who feel power and forget right, advancing rapidly to destinies beyond the reach of mortal eye—when I contemplate these transcendent objects, and see the honor, the happiness, and the hopes of this beloved country committed to the issue and the auspices of this day, I shrink from the contemplation, and humble myself before the magnitude of the undertaking. Utterly, indeed, should I despair did not the presence of many whom I here see remind me that in the other high authorities provided by our Constitution I shall find resources of wisdom, of virtue, and of zeal on which to rely under all difficulties. To you, then, gentlemen, who are charged with the sovereign functions of legislation, and to those associated with you, I look with encouragement for that guidance and support which may enable us to steer with safety the vessel in which we are all embarked amidst the conflicting elements of a troubled world.

During the contest of opinion through which we have passed the animation of discussions and of exertions has sometimes worn an aspect which might impose on strangers unused to think freely and to speak and to write what they think; but this being now decided by the voice of the nation, announced according to the rules of the Constitution, all will, of course, arrange themselves under the will of the law, and unite in common efforts for the common good. All, too, will bear in mind this sacred principle, that though the will of the majority is in all cases to prevail, that will to be rightful must be reasonable; that the minority possess their equal rights, which equal law must protect, and to violate would be oppression. Let us, then, fellow-citizens, unite with one heart and one mind. Let us restore to social intercourse that harmony and affection without which liberty and even life itself are but dreary things. And let us reflect that, having banished from our land that religious intolerance under which mankind so long bled and suffered, we have yet gained little if we countenance a political intolerance as despotic, as wicked, and capable of as bitter and bloody persecutions. During the throes and convulsions of the ancient world, during the agonizing spasms of infuriated man, seeking through blood and slaughter his long-lost liberty, it was not wonderful that the agitation of the billows should reach even this distant and peaceful shore; that this should be more felt and feared by some and less by others, and should divide opinions as to measures of safety. But every difference of opinion is not a difference of principle. We have called by different names brethren of the same principle. We are all Republicans, we are all Federalists. If there be any among us who would wish to dissolve this Union or to change its republican form, let them stand undisturbed as monuments of the safety with which error of opinion may be tolerated where reason is left free to combat it. I know, indeed, that some honest men fear that a republican government can not be strong, that this Government is not strong enough; but would the honest patriot, in the full tide of successful experiment, abandon a government which has so far kept us free and firm on the theoretic and visionary fear that this Government, the world's best hope, may by possibility want energy to preserve itself? I trust not. I believe this, on the contrary, the strongest Government on earth. I believe it the only one where every man, at the call of the law, would fly to the standard of the law, and would meet invasions of the public order as his own personal concern. Sometimes it is said that man can not be trusted with the government of himself. Can he, then, be trusted with the government of others? Or have we found angels in the forms of kings to govern him? Let history answer this question.

Let us, then, with courage and confidence pursue our own Federal and Republican principles, our attachment to union and representative government. Kindly separated by nature and a wide ocean from the exterminating havoc of one quarter of the globe; too high-minded to endure the degradations of the others; possessing a chosen country, with room enough for our descendants to the thousandth and thousandth generation; entertaining a due sense of our equal right to the use of our own faculties, to the acquisitions of our own industry, to honor and confidence from our fellow-citizens, resulting not from birth, but from our actions and their sense of them; enlightened by a benign religion, professed, indeed, and practiced in various forms, yet all of them inculcating honesty, truth, temperance, gratitude, and the love of man; acknowledging and adoring an overruling Providence, which by all its dispensations proves that it delights in the happiness of man here and his greater happiness hereafter—with all these blessings, what more is necessary to make us a happy and a prosperous people? Still one thing more, fellow-citizens—a wise and frugal Government, which shall restrain men from injuring one another, shall leave them otherwise free to regulate their own pursuits of industry and improvement, and shall not take from the mouth of labor the bread it has earned. This is the sum of good government, and this is necessary to close the circle of our felicities.

About to enter, fellow-citizens, on the exercise of duties which comprehend everything dear and valuable to you, it is proper you should understand what I deem the essential principles of our Government, and consequently those which ought to shape its Administration. I will compress them within the narrowest compass they will bear, stating the general principle, but not all its limitations. Equal and exact justice to all men, of whatever state or persuasion, religious or political; peace, commerce, and honest friendship with all nations, entangling alliances with none; the support of the State governments in all their rights, as the most competent administrations for our domestic concerns and the surest bulwarks against antirepublican tendencies; the preservation of the General Government in its whole constitutional vigor, as the sheet anchor of our peace at home and safety abroad; a jealous care of the right of election by the people—a mild and safe corrective of abuses which are lopped by the sword of revolution where peaceable remedies are unprovided; absolute acquiescence in the decisions of the majority, the vital principle of republics, from which is no appeal but to force, the vital principle and immediate parent of despotism; a well-disciplined militia, our best reliance in peace and for the first moments of war, till regulars may relieve them; the supremacy of the civil over the military authority; economy in the public expense, that labor may be lightly burthened; the honest payment of our debts and sacred preservation of the public faith; encouragement of agriculture, and of commerce as its handmaid; the diffusion of information and arraignment of all abuses at the bar of the public reason; freedom of religion; freedom of the press, and freedom of person under the protection of the habeas corpus, and trial by juries impartially selected. These principles form the bright constellation which has gone before us and guided our steps through an age of revolution and reformation. The wisdom of our sages and blood of our heroes have been devoted to their attainment. They should be the creed of our political faith, the text of civic instruction, the touchstone by which to try the services of those we trust; and should we wander from them in moments of error or of alarm, let us hasten to retrace our steps and to regain the road which alone leads to peace, liberty, and safety.

I repair, then, fellow-citizens, to the post you have assigned me. With experience enough in subordinate offices to have seen the difficulties of this the greatest of all, I have learnt to expect that it will rarely fall to the lot of imperfect man to retire from this station with the reputation and the favor which bring him into it. Without pretensions to that high confidence you reposed in our first and greatest revolutionary character, whose preeminent services had entitled him to the first place in his country's love and destined for him the fairest page in the volume of faithful history, I ask so much confidence only as may give firmness and effect to the legal administration of your affairs. I shall often go wrong through defect of judgment. When right, I shall often be thought wrong by those whose positions will not command a view of the whole ground. I ask your indulgence for my own errors, which will never be intentional, and your support against the errors of others, who may condemn what they would not if seen in all its parts. The approbation implied by your suffrage is a great consolation to me for the past, and my future solicitude will be to retain the good opinion of those who have bestowed it in advance, to conciliate that of others by doing them all the good in my power, and to be instrumental to the happiness and freedom of all.

Relying, then, on the patronage of your good will, I advance with obedience to the work, ready to retire from it whenever you become sensible how much better choice it is in your power to make. And may that Infinite Power which rules the destinies of the universe lead our councils to what is best, and give them a favorable issue for your peace and prosperity.

Questions

1. According to Jefferson, why might some observers misread the presidential election of 1800? Do you agree with his observations? Why or why not?
2. According to Jefferson, what is the "sacred principle" of American constitutional government?
3. Did the members of the Federalist party have good reason to applaud Jefferson for his proclamation of that sacred principle? Why or why not?
4. According to Jefferson, what were "the essential principles of our Government"? Would Alexander Hamilton (Document 7-9) generally agree or disagree with Jefferson's assertions? Why or why not?

Questions for Further Thought

1. Do these documents support or challenge the analysis offered by James Madison in *The Federalist*, No. 10 (Document 7-7)? Why or why not?
2. On the basis of the documents produced by Hamilton (7-9), Jefferson (7-12), and Washington (7-10), what term—political ideologue or political pragmatist—would you apply to each of these men? Why did you assign those terms?
3. On the basis of the documents produced by Hamilton (7-9), Jefferson (7-12), and Washington (7-10), would you call any of those men a political idealist? Why or why not?
4. For this question, on the basis of your father's occupation, translate your socioeconomic status into its 1790s American equivalent. (Remember that in the United States of the 1790s, virtually all married women managed a household or otherwise worked in the home, in the fields, or at the same occupation as their spouses.) Considering the information and arguments presented in these documents, would you, had you lived in the America of the 1790s, have supported a loose or a strict interpretation of the Constitution? Why?

CHAPTER 8

Westward Expansion and a New Political Economy, 1790–1820

★   ★   ★

Westward Expansion

From its inception, the United States controlled vast territories stretching westward to the Mississippi River. By 1790 farming settlements extended into the western parts of New York, Pennsylvania, and Georgia, crossing or skirting the Appalachian Mountains into parts of Tennessee and Kentucky. The lure of the West was strong among land speculators and farmer-settlers, but Indian nations west of the Appalachians—the Miami, Shawnee, Creek, Cherokee, Chickasaw, and Choctaw, among others—remained strong and resisted American encroachment. Under Presidents George Washington and Thomas Jefferson, a more orderly, sophisticated policy to promote Indian removal was developed (Documents 8-1 and 8-2); but warfare east of the Mississippi, notably with the Creek and the Shawnee leader Tecumseh (Document 8-6), continued through the War of 1812.

The character of western settlement varied considerably by latitude. The earliest western lands to be settled were in Kentucky and Tennessee, where yeomen farmers from the Chesapeake and the southern backcountry began extending settlements even before the Revolution (Document 8-3). To the south, in the future states of Alabama, Mississippi, and Louisiana, a very different sort of westward expansion took hold as southern planters, eager to profit from a lucrative new crop, cotton, snapped up the most suitable lands and settled them with slaves, many of whom were imported directly from Africa before Congress closed American ports to the transatlantic slave trade in 1808 (Document 8-4). To the north, New Englanders pressed westward from their overcrowded towns and stony farms into western New York and northern Ohio, carrying their distinctive culture along with them.

Life in the West was rude and isolated (Document 8-3). The barrier formed by the Appalachians made trade and communication with the settled East difficult and costly. The Mississippi River and its tributaries, notably the Ohio, afforded the best outlets, and the major early western trading towns—Cincinnati, Louisville, Pittsburgh, Saint Louis, and New Orleans—hugged their banks. However, downstream river traffic flowed away from major markets, and upstream traffic was difficult before the advent of the river steamboat in 1817. Accordingly, early western settlers were forced to live largely from their own produce and local exchange. The expansion of commerce in the West would await the "transportation revolution" of the years following 1820 (see Chapter 10).

8-1   Proposed Indian Policy for the New Republic (1789)

Henry Knox

The period of the Confederation saw increasing tension between American settlers and the native peoples living between the Appalachian Mountains and the Mississippi River. Americans insisted that the Treaty of 1783 with Great Britain gave the American states property rights to western lands under the right of conquest. European settlers and land speculators were eager to exploit these lands but faced mounting Indian resistance. While the states ceded control of the Northwest Territory to the Confederation government, state governments continued to control western lands in the South, allowing whites to run roughshod over the indigenous inhabitants.

Worried about frontier instability and fearful of the financial, human, and moral cost of warfare with the Indians, George Washington and his secretary of war, Henry Knox (1750–1806), sought to develop a more orderly and, they thought, more humane approach to Indian affairs. Knox set forth his view of the general principles to be followed by the United States in the following 1789 message.

Source: Henry Knox to George Washington, July 7, 1789, in *American State Papers, Class II: Indian Affairs* (Washington: Gales and Seaton, 1832), 1: 52–54.

GEN. KNOX, SECRETARY OF WAR,
TO THE PRESIDENT OF THE UNITED STATES,
IN CONTINUATION.

The report of the 23d of May, 1789, on the treaties at fort Harmar, by the Governor of the Western Territory, and the paper Number 1, of the Indian Department, contain such a general statement of the circumstances relative to the Indian tribes, within the limits of the United States, northwest of the Ohio, as will probably render their situation sufficiently understood.

The numbers two, three, and four, comprehend a general view of the nations south of the Ohio.

But the critical situation of affairs between the State of Georgia and the Creek nation, requires a more particular consideration. In discussing this subject, it will appear that the interest of all the Indian nations south of the Ohio, as far as the same may relate to the whites, is so blended together as to render the circumstance highly probable, that, in case of a war, they may make it one common cause.

Although each nation or tribe may have latent causes of hatred to each other, on account of disputes of boundaries and game, yet when they shall be impressed with the idea that their lives and lands are at hazard, all inferior disputes will be accommodated, and an union as firm as the six Northern nations may be formed by the Southern tribes.

Their situation, entirely surrounded on all sides, leads naturally to such an union, and the present difficulties of the Creeks and Cherokees may accelerate and complete it. Already the Cherokees have taken refuge from the violence of the frontier people of North Carolina within the limits of the Creeks, and it may not be difficult for a man of Mr. McGillivray's abilities to convince the Choctaws and Chickasaws that their remote situation is their only present protection; that the time must shortly arrive when their troubles will commence.

In addition to these causes, impelling to a general confederacy, there is another, of considerable importance—the policy of the Spaniards. The jealousy that Power entertains of the extension of the United States, would lead them into considerable expense to build up, if possible, an impassable barrier. They will, therefore, endeavor to form and cement such an union of the Southern Indians.

Mr. McGillivray has stated that Spain is bound by treaty to protect the Creeks in their hunting grounds. Although it may be prudent to doubt this assertion for the present, yet it is certain that Spain actually claims a considerable part of the territory ceded by Great Britain to the Unites States.

These circumstances require due weight in deliberating on measures to be adopted respecting the Creeks.

Although the case of the Creeks will be subject of legislative discussion and decisions, it may be supposed that, after due consideration, they will, in substance, adopt one or the other of the following alternatives, to wit:

1. That the national dignity and justice require that the arms of the Union should be called forth in order to chastise the Creek nation of Indians, for refusing to treat with the United States on reasonable terms, and for their hostile invasion of the State of Georgia; or,

2. That it appears to the Congress of the United States that it would be highly expedient to attempt to quiet the hostilities between the State of Georgia and the Creek Nation of Indians, by an amicable negotiation, and for that purpose there be a bill brought in to authorize the President of the United States to appoint three commissioners to repair to the State of Georgia, in order to conclude a peace with the said Creek nation and other nations of Indians to the southward of the Ohio, within the limits of the United States.

Supposing that any measure similar to either of the said alternatives should be adopted, it may be proper to examine into the manner which they are to be executed.

The most effectual mode of reducing the Creeks to submit to the will of the United States, and to acknowledge the validity of the treaties stated to have been made by the nation with Georgia, would be by an adequate army, to be raised and continued until the objects of the war should be accomplished.

When the force of the Creeks is estimated, and the probable combinations they might make with the other Indian nations, the army ought not to be calculated at less than 5,000 men. . . .

The following observations, resulting from a general view of the Indian department, are suggested with the hope, that some of them might be considered as proper principles to be interwoven in a general system, for the government of Indian affairs.

It would reflect honor on the new Government, and be attended with happy effects, were a declarative law to be passed, that the Indian tribes possess the right of the soil of all lands within their limits, respectively, and that they are not to be divested thereof, but in consequence of fair and bona fide purchases, made under the authority, or with the express approbation, of the United States.

As the great source of all Indian wars are disputes about their boundaries, and as the United States are, from the nature of the government, liable to be involved in every war that shall happen on this or any other account, it is highly proper that their authority and consent should be considered as essentially necessary to all measures for the consequences of which they are responsible.

No individual State could, with propriety, complain of invasion of its territorial rights. The independent nations and tribes of Indians ought to be considered as foreign nations, not as the subjects of any particular State. Each individual State, indeed, will retain the right of pre-emption of all lands within its limits, which will not be abridged; but the general sovereignty must possess the right of making all treaties, on the execution or violation of which depend peace or war.

Whatever may have been the conduct of some of the late British colonies, in their separate capacities toward the Indians, yet the same cannot be charged against the national character of the United States.

It is only since they possess the powers of sovereignty, that they are responsible for their conduct.

But, in future, the obligations of policy, humanity, and justice, together with that respect which every nation sacredly owes to its own reputation, unite in requiring a noble, liberal, and disinterested administration of Indian affairs.

Although the disposition of the people of the States, to emigrate into the Indian country, cannot be effectually prevented, it may be restrained and regulated.

It may be restrained, by postponing new purchases of Indian territory, and by prohibiting the citizens from intruding on the Indian lands.

It may be regulated, by forming colonies, under the direction of Government, and by posting a body of troops to execute their orders.

As population shall increase, and approach the Indian boundaries, game will be diminished, and new purchases may be made for small considerations. This has been, and probably will be, the inevitable consequence of cultivation.

It is, however, painful to consider, that all the Indian tribes, once existing in those States now the best cultivated and most populous, have become extinct. If the same causes continue, the same effects will happen; and, in a short period, the idea of an Indian on this side the Mississippi will only be found in the page of the historian.

How different would be the sensation of a philosophic mind to reflect, that, instead of exterminating a part of the human race by our modes of population, we had persevered, through all difficulties, and at last had imparted our knowledge of cultivation and the arts of the aboriginals of the country, by which the source of future life and happiness had been preserved and extended. But it has been conceived to be impracticable to civilize the Indians of North America. This opinion is probably more convenient than just.

That the civilization of the Indians would be an operation of complicated difficulty; that it would require the highest knowledge of the human character, and a steady perseverance in a wise system for a series of years; cannot be doubted. But to deny that, under a course of favorable circumstances, it could not be accomplished, is to suppose the human character under the influence of such stubborn habits as to be incapable of melioration or change—a supposition entirely contradicted by the progress of society, from the barbarous ages to its present degree of perfection.

While it is contended that the object is practicable, under a proper system, it is admitted, in the fullest force, to be impracticable, according to the ordinary course of things, and that it could be effected in a short period.

Were it possible to introduce among the Indian tribes a love for exclusive property, it would be a happy commencement of the business.

This might be brought about by making presents, from time to time, to the chiefs or their wives, of sheep and other domestic animals; and if, in the first instance, persons were appointed to take charge, and teach the use of them, a considerable part of the difficulty would be surmounted.

In the administration of the Indians, every proper expedient that can be devised to gain their affections, and attach them to the interest of the Union, should be adopted. The British Government had the practice of making the Indians presents of silver medals and gorgets, uniform clothing, and a sort of military commission. The possessors retained an exclusive property to these articles; and the Southern Indians are exceedingly desirous of receiving similar gifts from the United States, for which they would willingly resign those received from the British officers. The policy of gratifying them cannot be doubted.

Missionaries, of excellent moral character, should be appointed to reside in their nation, who should be well supplied with all the implements of husbandry, and the necessary stock for a farm.

These men should be made the instruments to work on the Indians; presents should commonly pass through their hands, or by their recommendations. They should, in no degree, be concerned in trade, or the purchase of lands, to rouse the jealousy of the Indians. They should be their friends and fathers.

Such a plan, although it might not fully effect the civilization of the Indians, would most probably be attended with the salutary effect of attaching them to the interest of the United States.

It is particularly important that something of this nature should be attempted with the Southern nations of Indians, whose confined situation might render them proper subjects for the experiment.

The expense of such a conciliatory system may be considered as a sufficient reason for rejecting it; . . .

All which is humbly submitted to the President of the United States.   H. KNOX
WAR OFFICE, *July 7*, 1789.

Questions

1. Whom did Secretary of War Knox blame for the conflicts on the frontier—settlers or natives?
2. What is Knox's plan to reduce the Creek and other eastern tribes to "the will of the United States"? Would you classify his proposals as "humane"?
3. What, according to Knox, is the major stumbling block to the Indians' peaceful incorporation into U.S. society?

8-2   Message to Congress (January 18, 1803)

Thomas Jefferson

Thomas Jefferson (1743–1826), the third president of the United States, was one of the leading intellectual figures in the early republic. Jefferson's republican belief in the United States as a nation of independent yeomen farmers called for new lands for settlement. He shared the prevailing view that the barrier represented by native Americans had to be removed one way or another. In the following message to Congress, Jefferson described the peaceful means by which he hoped to induce the Indians to sell their lands to the United States.

Source: James D. Richardson, ed., *A Compilation of the Messages and Papers of the Presidents* (Washington, D.C.: U.S. Government Printing Office, 1908), 1: 352–353.

The Indian tribes residing within the limits of the United States have for a considerable time been growing more and more uneasy at the constant diminution of the territory they occupy. . . . and the policy has long been gaining strength with them of refusing absolutely all further sale on any condition. . . . In order peaceably to counteract this policy of theirs and to provide an extension of territory which the rapid increase of our numbers will call for, two measures are deemed expedient. First. To encourage them to abandon hunting, to apply [themselves] to the raising [of] stock, to agriculture, and domestic manufacture, and thereby prove to themselves that less land and labor will maintain them . . . better than in their former mode of living. The extensive forests necessary in the hunting life will then become useless, and they will see advantage in exchanging them for the means of improving their farms and of increasing their domestic comforts. Secondly. To multiply trading houses among them, and place within their reach those things which will contribute more to their domestic comfort than the possession of extensive but uncultivated wilds. . . . In leading them thus to agriculture, to manufactures, and civilization; in bringing together their and our sentiments, and in preparing them ultimately to participate in the benefits of our Government, I trust and believe we are acting for their greatest good. . . . In one quarter this is particularly interesting . . . on the Mississippi . . . it is [desirable] to possess a respectable breadth of country . . . so that we may present as firm a front on that as on our eastern border. We possess what is below the Yazoo, and can probably acquire a certain breadth from the Illinois and Wabash to the Ohio; but between the Ohio and Yazoo the country all belongs to the Chickasaws, the most friendly tribe within our limits, but the most decided against the alienation of lands. The portion of their country most important for us is exactly that which they do not inhabit. Their settlements are not on the Mississippi, but in the interior country. They have lately shown a desire to become agricultural, and this leads to the desire of buying implements and comforts. In the strengthening and gratifying of these wants I see the only prospect of planting on the Mississippi itself the means of its own safety. Duty has required me to submit these views to the judgment of the Legislature, but as their disclosure might embarrass and defeat their effect, they are committed to the special confidence of the two Houses.

Questions

1. The United States claimed sovereignty over the native American nations but recognized the Indians' ownership of the lands they traditionally occupied. How did Jefferson propose to overcome this difficulty?
2. Why did Jefferson believe that native Americans would be better off with less land?
3. Why did Jefferson want his plans for the Indians—plans he said were "for their greatest good"—kept secret?

8-3 A Pioneer Woman in Post-Revolutionary Kentucky (1840s)

Jane Stevenson

In the 1840s and 1850s a young Presbyterian minister, John D. Shane (1812–1864), began conducting interviews with the by-then-elderly generation of pioneer European settlers in the Ohio Valley. Among the oldest of his interviewees was a woman, Jane Stevenson, who had been born in 1750; she was past ninety when he recorded her story sometime in the early 1840s. After Shane died in 1864 his notebooks were acquired by Lyman Draper (1815–1891), a major collector and disseminator of lore about the early American West. The following interview, with editorial additions by Shane and Draper (in brackets), follows Stevenson's travels from her birthplace in the Shenandoah Valley, first to the Greenbriar Valley of what is now West Virginia and then over the Wilderness Road into Kentucky. Stevenson's account is striking for its depiction of the rudeness and violence of life on the frontier, especially in the confrontation between settlers and Indians; the difficulty of travel; and the effort to build familiar institutions in a new country.

Source: Elizabeth A. Perkins, *Border Life: Experience and Memory in the Revolutionary Ohio Valley* (Chapel Hill: University of North Carolina Press, 1998), 196–200.

Jane Stevenson, wife of Samuel Stevenson, was born Nov. 15—1750, in Augusta County, Virginia.

The first fort I ever was in, a little girl was taken out of it, but from July to November older than me. She was but 7 years old. And was 7 years gone; untill (sic) Brocade's campaign [Draper: Bouquet's Campaign]. We walked out and got some haws. They, some of the company, pulled down the limbs, and handed us some of the haws. I wouldn't go any farther. And when I came, went into another cabin, wouldn't go into Mammy's, she would know I had been out. Presently the alarm came. They had gone about 200 yards further, and the Indians took them.

Where we lived was about 35 miles from Staunton. No Lexington then. The country was newly settled. Where Crawford was killed, was some 15 miles from Providence Meeting-house, down towards Staunton. Old Mr. John Brown preached there then. The men carried their guns to meeting, as regular as the congregation met. At Providence Meeting-house. The woman was told, bonie Alex.? Crawford was killed. Well said she, and indeed [Shane: Mr. C? or M? the lady or man who told her?] M [blank] he must take better care next time. This was a year or two after my mother was killed. I was only 9 or 10 then.

I was forted from the time I was 7 years old, 1757, and was never rid of the Indians till I moved to this place.

Carr's Creek was in about 7 miles of us. We were on the Calf-pasture. Mother was killed when I was about 8 years old. Mr. Crawford lived higher up towards Staunton than the Calf-pasture.

The settlement on Carr's Creek was taken twice [Draper: Carr's Creek Massacres]. The first time it was taken, Aunt escaped in the woods. Had but 2 children then, and while she escaped that way, the rout of the Indians was down the river.

The second time it was taken, I had an uncle and a cousin killed. This Aunt and her 3 children, were taken prisoners and carried to the towns. Two of the children died there. The remaining child was brought in at the treaty following Brocade's Campaign [Draper: Bouquet's]. Aunt wasn't brought in, and Uncle went out that same fall and brought her, but didn't get home till next March.

In less than 3 hours, in 2 hours, they killed and took 63 [Draper: Carr's Creek Massacre, 1763]. They no doubt had the ground all spied out. What they would do they knew. And then they came in like race horses. One Jim Milligan, who got away from them at the Ghanty [Draper: Gantey] Mountains, said the Indians there had 450 prisoners; that he had counted as they passed along. These, besides what they had killed, and a parcel, who at the time were before, in a hunting company.

Two little boys, Jimmy Woods & Jimmy McClung were taken—they went to Staunton when they got back, and had their ears recorded.

The year the Indians took Carr's Creek settlement [Draper: 1763] a second time, they were greatly bad. Almost seemed as if they thought they would make their way

to Williamsburgh that year. Shot the cows mightily with bows and arrows.

Simon Girty was from Virginia. He and old John Craig were schoolmates together in Virginia.

We moved to Greenbriar in 1775. The year after the battle of the Point. [Two sentences are struck out here.] There were but one or two families that were not dutch and half-dutch, in that whole settlement. [Shane: what settlement?] But never was a settlement of kinder people. They were great for dancing and singing. 1. William Hamilton. 2. Samuel McClung.

The hard winter was such in Virginia, as well as here.

When I started to Kentucky, I was 100 miles back from Daddy's. My father came from Ireland, when he was a boy. But then he lived on the frontier long before he was married.

John McKinney, the schoolmaster, came out with us. He was nearly killed at the Battle of the Point. We brought him out. We waited on the road a week or so, after we had left Greenbriar, for another family. Were about 2 weeks ? getting to Blackamore's station.

We never travelled a Sunday, but one in Powell's Valley, about 5 miles till we came to a beautiful clear spring of water. It must have been 70 miles we travelled in Powell's valley, for we kept all that way down till we crossed at Cumberland ford.

The morning before we came to the ford of Clinch, (Blackamore's station was 10 miles beyond that,) these murders were committed. A mother and 4 children; in sight of the fort too. The husband was in the field, but escaped. A girl about half-grown, and 3 little boys tomahawked and scalped, who were talking while their brains were boiling out. The grandmother asked them if they saw their little brother? What had become of him? Said they didn't know. These were dutch people. We staid there good part of a day. Their Aunt sat on a stump, in sight of the fort, and cried all day.

Went by Blackamore's Station next day, and didn't see the smoke of a chimney after that we go to Boonesborough.

The pretty springs of water, and the woods, rendered Powell's Valley so exceedingly beautiful, I could have stopped very freely in it. A rock road all the way down, and mountains to one side of us.

Just before we got to the foot of the Cumberland Mountain, the company three-quarters of a mile ahead of us, had all their horses stolen. They could do nothing better than just turn their feather beds loose. They could do nothing with them. About their cattle? We never saw any Indians, and were not interrupted.

I was almost afraid coming down Cumberland Mountain. The place was narrow and rocky. Stood up on either side, not broader than a house. Woods more beautiful in Cumberland Valley than any other place.

We come to Lexington in October. [Draper: 1779?] It had been settled the previous April. There were every sort of people there, and that was what took us away. We had no notion of raising our children among that sort of people. Frances McConnell was the first man I knew when I got to Lexington. I had known the McConnell's in Pennsylvania.

We went down to McConnell's station second April 1780. It was not settled till the day we went there. It took its name from Frances McConnell, and lay between Frances and William McConnell's places, & about between 1 & 1¼ miles from Lexington. Right where Royall's mill now is—on the rail-road. There was a grave yard there. James, Frances, and William McConnell, were cousins to Alexander and John McConnell.

Robert Edmiston, from Pennsylvania. Daniel Campbell, from Pennsylvania. William Hadden. John Brookey. All Presbyterians I think. All at the station were presbyterians, except two Mooneys, and they were raised presbyterians. John Nutt, Matthew Harper, John Stevenson, killed or taken at the Blue Licks from McConnell's station. [Shane: These 3.]

First summer we came out, Daddy stood sentry, while we milked. Things came on sooner that spring than ever I knew them. In the winter we were crowded. It was the continental war going on. (Safe for to be among Indians.) But as soon as warm weather came on, they put back.

Mr. Brookey didn't come out till the winter following. 1780–81. The first of March 1781, John Brookey went out to cut the first log to build his house. The Indians thought to take him. In the spring they would rather have a prisoner than a scalp. They shot him through the shoulder, and it came out in the hollow of his back. He was a very round shouldered man, and the bullet holes were 15 inches between the places. There was no doctor at the station. But he was taken care of and fed and nursed, on just what we had, and in 4 weeks was able to pick up an axe and hew. I was out, bringing in a pail of water, when I saw the Indians after Brookey. A parcel of children were out at the time; some here, some there. Some got in, and some hid in hollow logs. One so near the passing Indian, who didn't see him, that the boy could see his gun was empty. (lock down.)

The company from Lexington went out in a few minutes, (they heard the gun) and set their dogs on them. They had stripped, and left their clothes behind, in coming up to catch Brookey. Their things were all gotten; and one indian was wounded. The Indians had gotten within 60 yards of the fort. When Brookey's tree had fallen, he heard a stick crack, and looking around, saw that the Indians had almost gotten between him and the fort.

After the first campaign to Ohio had gone out, John Haggin was in it, (this after Brookey's affair I think,)—one David Hunter determined to go the other side of the river, as a place of more secure safety. Before getting off however he had a dream—that either the women & children, or that he himself would be killed. Henderson. He came down to bid us goodbye, and seemed to stay and stay. He started, and was shot, just in the hollow, about half way between McConnell's station and Lexington.

One Mitchell, was the first that I knew killed by the Indians on the Wilderness road. That was in 1776. When they got back to the first stations on Powell's valley, in June? 1776, they found the place all deserted, and every thing standing, even to the milk-pails on the stumps, as if they had been abruptly forsaken. Mitchell was killed just on this side of the Cumberland Mountain.

[Jane Stevenson's husband, Samuel, apparently speaks up now] Benjamin Blackburn, William Elliott, and Samuel Stevenson, (my father) came out in April, and got back I think in June. Took Billy Campbell with them, whom they got at one Jimmy Gilmore's, over the Kentucky river. Campbell was a wheelwright by trade. He took a parcel of buffalo horns in a bag, to make spoons of. Daddy and Billy Elliott spelled him so as to enable him to get his bag in, by walking & letting him ride some. Blackburn was so stiff with fear, we could hardly get him along. Had to light his pipe for him two or three times a day.

Moses McElwaine, (so says Samuel Stevenson) was never taken but the once, (He has a son now living over in Ohio, back of Urbana) that was in 1779. Cartwright the surveyor was with him. This was in Clarke. One McCormick, that had known him when a boy in Ireland, was a trader among the Indians, and sent McIlvaine back. McCormick afterwards came with the company to the attack on Riddle's station, to avoid the imputation that he favored the Americans, and had sent away McElwaine. But said he never unloaded his gun.

Cartwright told McElwaine he had better not speak so loud, the Indians might be about. He thought there was no danger, untill his horse was shot under him. The horse fell on his leg. One of the Indians was going to kill him, but the other prevented, and showed the horse was holding his foot. He paid the Indian. McCormick afterwards came in, and he paid him.

Daniel Barton was taken over on North Elkhorn, a little beyond Georgetown, at the same time that Samuel Hodge was killed. That day, 12 months, to the very day, from the time he was taken, he returned.

White was killed at Todd's station, down on South Elkhorn, the day we left Lexington to go to McConnell's station. The boy, his son, that was with him, went to go home to his friends in Virginia, through the Wilderness, but took sick and died somewhere on the way, perhaps at Augusta, Virginia. Mrs. Blanchard, a daughter of that Mr. White.

Robert or Charles Knox, started to go on foot up to Lexington, and was killed before he got there. He lived at the upper, we at the lower end of the station, so I didn't see him when he started. He was shot in the thigh. The Indians took him off a piece, but found he could not travel, and shot him. We had moved down to McConnell's station but about a week.

Alexander McConnell had been out to kill a deer, and had skinned and swung it up. He then came in and borrowed a chestnut dun horse, having a white main and tail, of William McConnell, and went out to bring it in. Five Indians were on the look out. This horse was shot from under him, but fell on his leg, the one indian wanted to kill him but the other indian showed that only the horse was on his leg.—This was Thursday to Tuesday he was gone.—McConnell couldn't kill the indian that had saved his life twice. He was the other side of the log.—He got the indians cappo, blue, (in the night, & he wanted to be dark) and set his gun, and pipe, and tomahawk down.—I heard him tell the story many times, and he never varied a word of it.—Tuesday evening, about sundown, he came in. His wife ran out to meet him, but they had to carry her in, she fainted away, overjoyed.

They had killed the horse, and cut off the main and tail to dye for moccasin purposes, &c. They could make it any color, almost, they pleased.—He shot the two guns first. Then shot the others alternately, and both indians fell into the fire, and flared up the ashes and light.—It is said the place where this happened, was never improved, till some 4 or 5 years ago, and that then they discovered the guns. This somewhere a little below Limestone.

We raised 4 crops, and then moved out. That was in 1784. 80–81–82–83.

The first meeting house was built in 1785. Mr. Rankin gave us time about with Lexington. He preached at first out here in private houses. At Capt. William McConnell's. (No kin to the McConnell's at McConnell's station. This William McConnell moved to St. Louis a great while ago.) Here. McElvain's, & Samuel Kelly's. He came in the fall, and the next spring we raised the house. Elders—This Capt. McConnell, Samuel Kelly, Hugh Campbell, (moved afterwards to Missouri) and another.

Was 17 days in the harvest, and every day in the river. When a young woman. Swam the Cowpasture, 300 yards wide, many a time on my back.

[Shane:] Mr. Trabue of Scott Co., Ky., obtained of "Aunt Jane," information, such as was necessary in order to obtain a pension.

Questions

1. Jane Stevenson's childhood and young womanhood coincided with the French and Indian War and the American Revolution. How did those wars shape her experience on the frontier?
2. What characteristics of her fellow settlers does Stevenson typically find worthy of remark?
3. In reading this interview, what do you think Stevenson took the most pride in having achieved in her life?

8-4   The Slaveholders' Frontier: Moving to Mississippi (1808–1809)

Leonard Covington

Jane Stevenson fits closely the stereotype of the early western pioneer, but the early-nineteenth-century frontier also attracted well-heeled emigrants with commercial concerns. Southern slaveholders in particular were eager to take up lands in the lower Mississippi Valley, where the yields were much higher than in the older, increasingly exhausted tobacco lands of the Chesapeake, and where new and lucrative crops such as sugar and especially cotton were viable. One such slaveholder was Leonard Covington (1768–1813) of Calvert County, Maryland, along Chesapeake Bay south of Annapolis. Covington, a military officer and former member of Congress, was deeply in debt; his traditional crops of tobacco and wheat were losing their profitability, and exports of both were suffering from Jefferson's Embargo Act (see text p. 259). Accordingly, he began to make plans to move to the vicinity of Natchez, Mississippi—a move previously made by his brother Alexander. Covington discussed the move in a series of letters to Alexander and others, extracts from which follow.

Source: John R. Commons et al., *A Documentary History of American Industrial Society* (Cleveland: The Arthur H. Clark Co., 1910), 2: 201–208.

(a) Extract from a Letter from Aquasco, Md., Aug. 17, 1808, to Alexander Covington in Mississippi

I find that I can dispose of my Calvert lands, but for the present forbear to do so until every information and advice is received which I hold to be necessary for enabling me to mature my plans upon a [basis(?)] at once extended and profitable. Let me therefore beg your thoughts and reflections, upon the following points particularly, and in general such other information as you may deem useful to my purpose. You have never been circumstantial as to the manner and terms of hiring your people. It would certainly be material to the owner of slaves, whether their treatment in many respects was such as would be desirable, and in what manner the payments for hirelings were made; if in advance, or punctually at the months end. Whether the slaves were well fed; and only compelled to work from "sun to sun." It is possible that so much labor may be required of hirelings and so little regard may be had for their constitutions as to render them in a few years, not only unprofitable, but expensive. In your case, who pays the doctor, abides the loss from death or running away? Do the negroes in that country generally look as happy and contented as with us, and do they as universally take husbands and wives and as easily rear their young as in Maryland? Would your negroes, think you, willingly return to Maryland? Are they satisfied with the change and with their treatment. Is the culture of cotton much easier, and a more certain crop? than our tobacco? Is there any probability that you will have any better market for your cotton than we shall have for our tobacco should our differences with Europe terminate in a war? Will this not depend upon the progress of manufactures in this country? Is the expense of making a cotton crop, where a man has hands of his own, considerable? What seems to be the current price of horses, cattle, &c., &c. The expense of clothing must be less than in a more northern climate. On lands of the U.S., such as you would like to purchase, what would be the probable expense of rough buildings and clearing for a small crop, say for ten or twelve hands? What time would such a preparation take? Fruit—is it abundant and well flavored, &c., &c? What seems to be the usual fare or allowance for working negroes, where a planter has a good many, from ten to 20, for example? Have you any sudden or great changes from heat to cold, and do you suffer as much from droughts or violent falls of rain as with us? I have a thousand more questions in my head, but pushed for time just now, must hope that you will say everything that I could ask, not forgetting politicks, the state of religion, if there be much amongst you. As to dealings generally, are the folks pretty punctual, or is there much use for lawyers? Have you found the summer sun more intolerable than in this climate? Has the thermometer been at a greater degree of heat than 85 or 86, what we experience about the latter end of June?

(b) Extract from a Letter from Aquasco, Aug. 7, 1808, to Capt. Jas. T. Magruder, Washington, Miss.

I am sorry that the prices and titles of land seem for the present in some measure to obstruct your plans, but it appears to me that your time cannot be illy spent under your existing arrangement, and possibly a purchase of lands, under existing circumstances could not be made to so great advantage as when the public office for the sale of lands shall be established, and as when the political horizon shall have been cleared of its present gloomy bodements. You mention that cash is scarce and cannot be had for produce (Cotton). I should think that this consideration alone would decide the preference in favor of your present plan of hiring your negroes, to that of cultivating the soil at your own expense and risk, if indeed the wages for hirelings are regularly and promptly paid up, (but of this neither of you have given particulars) and if the treatment in all respects to the slaves are such as we ought to wish for. Indeed I am extremely anxious to be informed of all these particular matters, and to have your full opinion and advice as to the propriety of my removing to that country, for I seriously assure (tho' I know you will be started at the assurance) you that I am at this moment earnestly employed in making arrangements to that end. I am now negotiating for the sale of the whole of my Calvert lands, with a full view to an investment and settlement in your country. Our friend Rawlings and myself have certainly got our affairs in such a train that I really think it probable that we shall set out this fall, and winter in the lower part of Kentucky, but possibly we may be delayed until the following spring. I will briefly give you the reasons which have moved me to the desire and resolution above advised you of, and again repeat my request that you will both favor me with your opinion and advice. In the first place, I find it will be extremely difficult, if not impossible, for me to meet all my pecuniary engagements, and to sink the debt incurred for the purchase of my lands. The interest upon 5 or 6 thousand dollars, under our present and apparent future commercial embarrassments, is really of itself not a slight matter, then no other means are to be found for its extinction than the uncertain and fluctuating one of a tobacco crop, which I verily believe has seen very much its best days. Add to this consideration the little chance I should have of adding to my property with my present prospect for a growing and large family, which must necessarily begin to be very expensive, and again, should a war with G. Britain terminate our present political disputes with that nation, I cannot but dread the predatory incursions which their naval superiority could enable them to make, when my little all would be entirely exposed to their merciless depredations, and, lastly, the negroes which I contemplate to take with me (amounting to 25, out of which 19 may be hired or worked to advantage) at the prices you have hired yours at, will be infinitely more productive in my expectations of compassing about $3000., and your advice will bear me out in it, I have it in contemplation to carry out with me some 10 or 15 families who are urgent in their requests for me to enlist them in my service of clearing and cultivating such lands as I may make purchase of. I mean not to defray their expenses; this they can do themselves (such men as Billy Watson, J. Letchworth, H. Watson, etc., etc.) but they want a conductor and some place to settle upon when they shall have reached their place of destination with exhausted pockets and anxious minds. With a view to the permanence of my plans, I have to beg that you will cause your people (several of them at least) to write favorable accounts of their situation, and of the country, etc., etc. Sam is now in the hire of W. B. Ellis, but I still have hopes that some means will be found to forward him to you. At any rate, should I be with you the next Spring, something to your satisfaction shall be done.

(c) Extract of a Letter from Feb. 15, 1809, to Alexander Covington

. . . The times are tough, but in other respects the good folks jog on as usual. The following is a list of my people, [i.e. slaves] such as go and such as stay:

FOR MISSISSIPPI				FOR AQUASCO			
Watt	32	Tom	36	Nick	50	Ned	24
Bess	24	Salisbury	32	Jack	22	Tabs	22
Dick	17	Moses	15	Bob	34	Nancy	46
Phill	12	Major	10	Pegg	20	Betsy	18
Dyche	35	Carolina	19	Isaac	10	Grace	5
Sal	10	Tom	5	Kitty	6	Charles	6
Pool	6	Nick	5	Charles	3	Nell	2
Hanna	1	Rachel	22	Henry	2 mos.	Christy	32
Ben	3	John	1	Flora	5	Nell	30
Jenny	26	Eliza	3	Nick	30	Dine	26
Nat	1	Jim	11	Nancy	5	Sophia	2
Rachel	11	Clem	9	Lucy	34	Joe	1
Tom	7	Cesar	5	Fanny		Moll	
Dasy	3	Cilla	12				
Bessie	11	George	9				
Flora	5						

Questions

1. When discussing a move, what characteristics of the Natchez region most concern Covington? What characteristics interest him less?
2. What does Covington expect to do when he and his force arrive in Natchez?
3. From the evidence of these letters, would you describe Covington as someone who cares about his slaves? Why or why not?

Questions for Further Thought

1. When Henry Knox set out to reform Indian policy on the frontier, he had in mind Jane Stevenson and her fellow settlers as much as he did the Shawnee. Would he agree with the settlers about the roots of frontier disorder?
2. Henry Knox was a Federalist; Thomas Jefferson was a Republican. How do you think each man's party stance affected his views about the place of the Indian in the future West?
3. Both Jane Stevenson and Leonard Covington sought to recreate on the frontier a society they knew back home, but they had very different societies in mind. Were their aspirations potentially in conflict? Consider this especially with respect to the Missouri controversy (Chapter 9).

The Republicans' Political Revolution

After the republican tide swept Thomas Jefferson to victory in the presidential election of 1800, the Federalists' concern with establishing the authority and effectiveness of the federal government was replaced by Jefferson's own efforts at paring back government power. Jefferson determined that government, and the monied interests he believed the federal government to have been serving under Hamilton's policies, threatened to exploit the productive elements of society for the benefit of bondholders, bureaucrats, and others who lived off money instead of labor. Jefferson's opposing philosophy, reflected in his *Notes on the State of Virginia* (begun in 1780), espoused that the independent yeoman farmer was the true source of civic virtue in a republic. By the time of his second inaugural address in 1805, Jefferson was boasting of the progress he had made in relieving the burdens of small farmers, making it easier for them to maintain the "independence" of their households (Document 8-5).

Jefferson also began to focus the attention of federal policy on the interior of the continent, away from the traditional orientation of the states toward Europe. Jefferson's decentralized agrarian republic needed cheap land for its expanding population (Document 8-6); it also needed to control trade routes into the interior, most importantly the Mississippi River, to assure its citizens the ability to establish their independence through trade. A feared threat to American commerce on the Mississippi from Napoleonic France led to the Louisiana Purchase in 1803. Eager to establish control of the nation's new dominion, Jefferson sent his personal secretary, Meriwether Lewis, and army officer William Clark to explore the interior and establish alliances with Indian tribes beyond the reach of American military control (Document 8-7).

While the Louisiana Purchase removed France as a threat to Jeffersonian policy, Great Britain continued to pose grave problems. On the Atlantic, the British Royal Navy opposed American efforts to trade with Napoleonic France and regularly impressed sailors on American ships into its service. Jefferson's response, a trade embargo launched in 1807, devastated eastern commerce and revived the moribund Federalist Party. In the West, Britain continued to deal with native American peoples such as the Creek in the Southeast and the Western Confederacy established by the Shawnee Tecumseh and his brother Tenkswatawa, who were seeking to repel the tide of European settlers and revitalize native culture (Document 8-8). These conflicts—with the British on the high seas and with native Americans in the West—culminated in the War of 1812. While the war was a success in the West, where Tecumseh and the Creek were routed, the British ruled in the East, burning Washington, devastating commerce, and impelling disaffected New Englanders to threaten secession.

The war was essentially a stalemate, and so was the Treaty of Ghent that ended it in 1814. However, a stunning victory at New Orleans provided America a rallying point, and the years following saw both the effective settlement of most outstanding disputes with Britain and the clearance of native Americans from most territory east of the Mississippi. The Battle of New Orleans became a legend, with the western settler as its hero (Document 8-9). For the remainder of the nineteenth century, the United States would turn its back on the Atlantic and its face toward the West.

8-5 Second Inaugural Address (March 4, 1805)

Thomas Jefferson

Thomas Jefferson served as secretary of state in George Washington's first administration and became a leading critic of Treasury Secretary Alexander Hamilton's plans for national economic development and a strong central government. As President Washington came to rely increasingly on Hamilton's advice, Jefferson resigned from the cabinet in 1793 and with his fellow Virginian James Madison formed the Democratic-Republican party to oppose the Hamilton-Washington Federalist party. Narrowly beaten by the Federalist candidate John Adams in the election of 1796, Jefferson won decisively in the "Revolution of 1800."

Jefferson's "revolution," which swept Federalists from federal office, left many of the accomplishments of the Federalist era intact, including the Bank of the United States. But Jefferson's firm belief in limited government produced significant changes in the income and expenditures of the federal government. After his sweeping victory in 1804 (with only token Federalist opposition) Jefferson reviewed in his second inaugural address the success of his first administration in eliminating internal taxes and explained why, even with the prospect of a budget surplus, he believed that a tax on imports should be maintained.

Source: James D. Richardson, ed., *A Compilation of the Messages and Papers of the Presidents, 1789–1908* (Washington, D.C.: U.S. Government Printing Office, 1908), 1: 378–382.

At home, fellow-citizens, you best know whether we have done well or ill. The suppression of unnecessary offices, of useless establishments and expenses, enabled us to discontinue our internal taxes. These, covering our land with officers and opening our doors to their intrusions, had already begun that process of domiciliary vexation which once entered is scarcely to be restrained from reaching successively every article of property and produce. . . .

The remaining revenue on the consumption of foreign articles is paid chiefly by those who can afford to add foreign luxuries to domestic comforts, being collected on our seaboard and frontiers only, and incorporated with the transactions of our mercantile citizens, it may be the pleasure and the pride of an American to ask, What farmer, what mechanic, what laborer ever sees a tax gatherer of the United States? These contributions enable us to support the current expenses of the Government, to fulfill contracts with foreign nations, to extinguish the native right of soil [to buy Indian lands] within our limits, to extend those limits, and to apply such a surplus to our public debts as places at a short day their final redemption, and that redemption once effected the revenue thereby liberated may, by a just repartition of it among the States and a corresponding amendment of the Constitution, be applied *in time of peace* to rivers, canals, roads, arts, manufactures, education, and other great objects within each State. . . .

Contemplating the union of sentiment now manifested so generally as auguring harmony and happiness to our future course, I offer to our country sincere congratulations. With those, too, not yet rallied to the same point the disposition to do so is gaining strength; facts are piercing through the veil drawn over them, and our doubting brethren will at length see that the mass of their fellow-citizens with whom they can not yet resolve to act as to principles and measures, think as they think and desire what they desire; that our wish as well as theirs is that the public efforts may be directed honestly to the public good, that peace be cultivated, civil and religious liberty unassailed, law and order preserved, equality of rights maintained, and that state of property, equal or unequal, which results to every man from his own industry or that of his father's. When satisfied of these views it is not in human nature that they should not approve and support them. In the meantime let us cherish them with patient affection, let us do them justice, and more than justice, in all competitions of interest, and we need not doubt that truth, reason, and their own interest will at length prevail, will gather them into the fold of their country, and will complete that entire union of opinion which gives to a nation the blessing of harmony and the benefit of all its strength.

Questions

1. Describe Jefferson's distinction between "internal taxes" and tariff duties on "foreign luxuries." Why did he consider the first bad and the second good?

2. When the national debt was paid off, Jefferson proposed to maintain the tariff on foreign luxuries—for what purposes?

3. Who were Jefferson's "doubting brethren," and why did he think they needed to be reassured that he would maintain "that state of property, equal or unequal, which results to every man from his own industry or that of his father's"?

8-6 Congressional Resolution on Western Lands (1800)

Wealthy speculators and poor farmer-settlers competed for control of western lands. Because speculators tended to be comfortable with the political processes through which land sales took place, they held the upper hand in this competition (see text pp. 248–250). But the demands of yeomen farmers for access to western lands created political pressure that could not be ignored by eastern politicians. As a groundswell of popular support built for Thomas Jefferson and his Democratic-Republican party, Congress passed the Land Act of 1800, which sharply reduced the minimum acreage offered for sale and provided liberal credit terms for the purchase of land (see text p. 256). In a series of resolutions Congress authorized the drafting of a new land act.

Source: Annals of the Congress of the United States, 1789–1824 (Washington, D.C.: U.S. Government Printing Office, 1799–1800), 6th Cong., 1st sess., 537–538.

The House resolved itself into a Committee of the Whole . . . to inquire whether any, and, if any, what, alterations are necessary in the laws providing for the sale of the lands of the United States Northwest of the Ohio; and, after some time spent therein, the Committee rose and reported several resolutions . . . as follows:

Resolved, That all the townships directed to be sold, either in quarter townships or in tracts of one mile square, by the act "providing for the sale of the lands of the United States, in the Territory Northwest of the river Ohio, and above the mouth of Kentucky river," shall be subdivided into half sections, containing, as nearly as may be, three hundred and twenty acres each: the additional expense of surveying to be paid by the purchasers, at the rate of three dollars per tract.

Resolved, That all the said lands shall be offered for sale at public sale, in tracts of three hun[d]red and twenty acres as above directed: *Provided,* That the same shall not be sold under the price of two dollars per acre, and that the sale shall be at the following places, to wit:

All the lands contained in the seven first ranges of townships, and north of the same, shall be offered for sale at Pittsburg[h].

All the lands contained in the eight next ranges of townships, shall be offered for sale at Marietta.

All the lands lying west of the fifteen first ranges of townships, and east of the Sciota river, shall be offered for sale at Chilicothe.

All the lands lying below the Great Miami shall be offered for sale at Cincinnati.

Resolved, That one or more land offices shall be opened in the Northwestern Territory, and that every person be permitted to locate and purchase at the rate of two dollars per acre, one or more of the half sections that shall not have been sold at public sale.

Resolved, That the payments for lands purchased either at public or private sale . . . shall be made in the following manner, and under the following conditions, viz:

1st. At the time of purchase, every purchaser shall deposit one-twentieth part of the amount of purchase money; to be forfeited, if, within three months, one-fourth of the purchase-money, including the said twentieth part, is not paid.

2d. One-fourth of the purchase-money to be paid as aforesaid, within three months, and the other three-fourths in three equal payments, within two, three, and four years, respectively, after the date of purchase.

3d. No interest to be charged in case of punctual payment; but interest at the rate of six per cent, a year, to be charged from the date of purchase, on any part of the purchase-money which shall not have been paid at the times, respectively, when the same shall have become due.

4th. A discount at the rate of eight per cent. a year, to be allowed on any of the three last payments, which shall be paid before the same shall have become due.

5th. If any tract shall not be completely paid [for] within one year after the date of the last payment, the tract to be sold in such manner as shall be provided by law; and after paying the balance due to the United States, including interest, the surplus, if any, to be returned to the original purchaser.

Ordered, That a bill or bills be brought in pursuant to the said resolutions. . . .

Questions

1. How much money did a farmer need to buy a farm under the terms of this proposed legislation?
2. Did some parts of the proposed legislation clearly favor speculators? Explain why.
3. Why did Congress specify the locations for all land sales? Whose interest did this provision serve?

8-7   The Journals of the Lewis and Clark Expedition (1804–1806)

Shortly after completing the Louisiana Purchase, President Jefferson commissioned two army captains, William Clark (the younger brother of the Revolutionary War hero George Rogers Clark) and Meriwether Lewis (Jefferson's personal secretary) to explore the new American territory. In the spring of 1804 Lewis and Clark led an expedition of twenty-five men up the Missouri River to present-day central North Dakota; in the spring of 1805 they followed the Missouri and Columbia Rivers west to the Pacific. The following spring they returned to their point of departure at St. Louis. In their journals the two men recorded a journey of discoveries as they encountered new flora and fauna, as well as a rich variety of native American cultures. In the following passages Lewis relates his encounter with the Shoshone in what is now Idaho, all the while recording careful observations on the strategic situation of the United States in the region.

Source: Gary E. Moulton and Thomas W. Dunlay, eds., *The Journals of the Lewis and Clark Expedition* (Lincoln: University of Nebraska Press, 1988), 5: 87–89, 91–92, 102–103.

Wednesday, August 14th

. . . [T]he game which they principally hunt is the Antelope which they pursue on horseback and shoot with their arrows. this animal is so extreemly fleet and dureable that a single horse has no possible chance to overtake them or run them down. the Indians are therefore obliged to have recorce to stratagem when they discover a herd of the Antelope they seperate and scatter themselves to the distance of five or six miles in different directions around them generally selecting some commanding eminence for a stand; some one or two now pursue the herd at full speed over the hills valleys gullies and the sides of precipices that are tremendious to view. thus after runing them from five to six or seven miles the fresh horses that were in the waiting head them and drive them back persuing them as far or perhaps further quite to the other extreem of the hunters who now in turn pursue on their fresh horses thus (finally) worrying the poor animal down and finally killing them with their arrows. forty or fifty hunters will be engaged for half a day in this manner and perhaps not kill more than two or three Antelopes. they have but few Elk or black tailed deer, and the common red deer they cannot take as

they secrete themselves in the brush when pursued, and they have only the bow and arrow wich is a very slender dependence for killing any game except such as they can run down with their horses. I was very much entertained with a view of this indian chase; it was after a herd of about 10 Antelope and about 20 hunters. it lasted about 2 hours and considerable part of the chase in view from my tent. about 1 A.M. the hunters returned had not killed a single Antelope, and their horses foaming with sweat. my hunters returned soon after and had been equally unsuccessfull. I now directed McNeal to make me a little paist with the flour and added some berries to it which I found very pallateable.

The means I had of communicating with these people was by way of Drewyer who understood perfectly the common language of jestication or signs which seems to be universally understood by all the Nations we have yet seen. it is true that this language is imperfect and liable to error but is much less so than would be expected. the strong parts of the ideas are seldom mistaken.

I now prevailed on the Chief to instruct me with rispect to the geography of his country. this he undertook very cheerfully, by delineating the rivers on the ground. but I soon found that his information fell far short of my expectation or wishes. he drew the river on which we now are to which he placed two branches just above us, which he shewed me from the openings of the mountains were in view; he next made it discharge itself into a large river which flowed from the S. W. about ten miles below us, then continued this joint stream in the same direction of this valley or N. W. for one days march and then enclined it to the West for 2 more days march, here he placed a number of heeps of sand on each side which he informed me represented the vast mountains of rock eternally covered by snow through which the river passed. that the perpendicular and even juting rocks so closely hemned in the river that there was no possibilyte of passing along the shore; that the bed of the river was obstructed by sharp pointed rocks and the rapidity of the stream such that the whole surface of the river was beat into perfect foam as far as the eye could reach. that the mountains were also inaccessible to man or horse. he said that this being the state of the country in that direction that himself nor none of his nation had ever been further down the river than these mountains. I then enquired the state of the country on either side of the river but he could not inform me. he said there was an old man of his nation a days march below who could probably give me some information of the country to the N. W. and refered me to an old man then present for that to the S. W.— the Chief further informed me that he had understood from the persed nosed Indians who inhabit this river below the rocky mountains that it ran a great way toward the seting sun and finally lost itself in a great lake of water which was illy taisted, and where the white men lived. . . . I can discover that these people are by no means friendly to the Spaniard their complaint is, that the Spaniards will not let them have fire arms and amunition, that they put them off by telling them that if they suffer them to have guns they will kill each other, thus leaving them defenceless and an easy prey to their bloodthirsty neighbours to the East of them, who being in possession of fire arms hunt them up and murder them without rispect to sex or age and plunder them of their horses on all occasions. they told me that to avoid their enemies who were eternally harrassing them that they were obliged to remain in the interior of these mountains at least two thirds of the year where the[y] suffered as we then saw great heardships for the want of food sometimes living for weeks without meat and only a little fish roots and berries. but this added Cameahwait, with his ferce eyes and lank jaws grown meager for the want of food, would not be the case if we had guns, we could then live in the country of buffaloe and eat as our enimies do and not be compelled to hide ourselves in these mountains and live on roots and berries as the bear do. we do not fear our enimies when placed on an equal footing with them. I told them that the Minnetares Mandans & Recares of the Missouri had promised us to desist from making war on them & that we

would indeavou to find the means of making the Minnetares of fort d Prarie or as they call them Pahkees desist from waging war against them also. that after our finally returning to our homes towards the rising sun whitemen would come to them with an abundance of guns and every other article necessary to their defence and comfort, and that they would be enabled to supply themselves with these articles on reasonable terms in exchange for the skins of the beaver Otter and Ermin so abundant in their country. they expressed great pleasure at this information and said they had been long anxious to see the whitemen that traded guns; and that we might rest assured of their friendship and that they would do whatever we wished them. . . .

. . . Drewyer who had had a good view of their horses estimated them at 400. most of them are fine horses. indeed many of them would make a figure of the South side of James River or the land of fine horses.— I saw several with spanish brands on them, and some mules which they informed me that they had also obtained from the Spaniards. I also saw a bridle bit of spanish manufactary, and sundry other articles which I have no doubt were obtained from the same source. notwithstanding the extreem poverty of those poor people they are very merry they danced again this evening untill midnight. each warrior keep one ore more horses tyed by a cord to a stake near his lodge both day and night and are always prepared for action at a moments warning. they fight on horseback altogether. I observe that the large flies are extreemly troublesome to the horses as well as ourselves. . . .

Friday, August 16th 1805.
I sent Drewyer and Shields before this morning in order to kill some meat as neither the Indians nor ourselves had any thing to eat. . . . after the hunters had been gone about an hour we set out. we had just passed through the narrows when we saw one of the spies comeing up the level plain under whip, the chief pawsed a little and seemed somewhat concerned. I felt a good deel so myself and began to suspect that by some unfortunate accedent that perhaps some of there enimies had straggled hither at this unlucky moment; but we were all agreeably disappointed on the arrival of the young man to learn that he had come to inform us that one of the whitemen had killed a deer. in an instant they all gave their horses the whip and I was taken nearly a mile before I could learn what were the tidings; as I was without [s]tirrups and an Indian behind me the jostling was disagreeable. I therefore reigned up my horse and forbid the indian to whip him who had given him the lash at every jum for a mile fearing he should loose a part of the feast. the fellow was so uneasy that he left me the horse dismounted and ran on foot at full speed, I am confident a mile. when they arrived where the deer was which was in view of me they dismounted and ran in tumbling over each other like a parcel of famished dogs each seizing and tearing away a part of the intestens which had been previously thrown out by Drewyer who killed it; the seen was such

when I arrived that had I not have had a pretty keen appetite myself I am confident I should not have taisted any part of the venison shortly. each one had a piece of some discription and all eating most ravenously. some were eating the kidnies the melt and liver and the blood running from the corners of their mouths, others were in a similar situation with the paunch and guts but the exuding substance in this case from their lips was of a different discription. one of the last who attracted my attention particularly had been fortunate in his allotment or reather active in the division, he had provided himself with about nine feet of the small guts one end of which he was chewing on while with his hands he was squezzing the contents out at the other. I really did not untill now think that human nature ever presented itself in a shape so nearly allyed to the brute creation. I viewed these poor starved divils with pity and compassion I directed McNeal to skin the deer and reserved a quarter, the ballance I gave the Chief to be divided among his people; they devoured the whole of it nearly without cooking. . . .

Questions

1. Is the daily life of the western Indians as depicted in Lewis's journal entries what you expected? What challenges did both the Indians and the explorers face on the plains?

2. What were the goals of the Lewis and Clark expedition? What information from Document 8-7 do you think that Thomas Jefferson was particularly interested in?

3. What do we learn about the balance of power in the West from the journals?

8-8   Speech to Tecumseh and the Prophet (1811) and Report to the Secretary of War (1814)

William Henry Harrison

William Henry Harrison would be elected president of the United States in 1840 largely because of his reputation as an Indian fighter. His nickname, "Tippecanoe," celebrated his victory over the followers of chief Tecumseh and his brother Tenskwatawa (the Prophet) at the Battle of Tippecanoe on November 7, 1811 (see text pp. 259–262). As governor of the Indiana Territory, Harrison carried out the Democratic-Republican policy of divesting native Americans of their land (see Document 8-2). Tecumseh and Tenskwatawa formed a coalition to resist this policy of piecemeal dispossession. As Harrison warned in his speech to Tecumseh and the Prophet, he had assembled an army of seasoned Indian fighters. He soon moved them to Tippecanoe Creek near the hostile Indian encampment called Prophetstown. Convinced by the Prophet that they were invincible, the Indians swept into the American camp in the predawn darkness. But Harrison's men held their ground, formed a defensive line, and soon turned the Indians back with heavy losses.

Tecumseh's people abandoned Prophetstown (which Harrison subsequently burned) and, fighting in small bands, made war on settlers across the Northwest. During the War of 1812 Tecumseh joined forces with the British. At the Battle of the Thames on October 5, 1813 (see text p. 263), Harrison's forces decisively defeated the Indians and their British allies and killed Tecumseh. In his letter to the secretary of war, Harrison summarized the Democratic-Republican Indian policy and his successes in implementing it.

Source: Benjamin Drake, *Life of Tecumseh* (Cincinnati: E. Morgan & Co., 1841; facsimile reprint, New York: Arno Press and New York Times, 1969).

(a) Harrison to Tecumseh and the Prophet, June 24, 1811

Brothers,—Listen to me. I speak to you about matters of importance, both to the white people and yourselves; open your ears, therefore, and attend to what I shall say.

Brothers, this is the third year that all the white people in this country have been alarmed at your proceedings; you threaten us with war, you invite all the tribes in the north and west of you to join against us. . . .

Brothers, our citizens are alarmed, and my warriors are preparing themselves; not to strike you, but to defend themselves and their women and children. You shall not surprise us as you expect to do; you are about to undertake a vary rash act; as a friend, I advise you to consider well of it. . . . Do you really think that the handful of men that you have about you, are able to contend with the Seventeen Fires [the seventeen states then composing the United States], or even that the whole of the tribes united, could contend against the Kentucky Fire alone?

Brothers, I am myself of the long knife fire; as soon as they hear my voice, you will see them pouring forth their swarms of hunting shirt men, as numerous as the musquetoes [*sic*] on the shores of the Wabash; brothers, take care of their stings.

(b) Harrison to the Secretary of War, March 22, 1814

I received instruction from President Jefferson, shortly after his first election, to make efforts for extinguishing the Indian claims upon the Ohio, below the mouth of the Kentucky river, and to such other tracts as were necessary to connect and consolidate our settlements. It was at once determined, that the community of interests in the lands among the Indian tribes, which seemed to be recognized by the treaty of Greenville, should be objected to. . . . Care was taken . . . to place the title to such tracts as might be desireable to purchase . . . upon a footing that would facilitate the procuring of them, by getting the tribes who had no claim themselves, and who might probably interfere, to recognize the titles of those who were ascertained to posses [*sic*] them.

This was particularly the case with regard to the lands watered by the Wabash, which were declared to be the property of the Miamis, with the exception of the tract occupied by the Delawares on White river, which was to be considered the joint property of them and the Miamis. This arrangement was very much disliked by Tecumseh, and the banditti that he had assembled at Tippecanoe. He complained loudly, as well of the sales that had been made, as of the principle of considering a particular tribe as the exclusive proprietors of any part of the country, which he said the Great Spirit had given to all his red children. . . .

The question of the title to the lands south of the Wabash, has been thoroughly examined; every opportunity was afforded to Tecumseh and his party to exhibit their pretensions [land claims], and they were found to rest upon no other basis than that of their being the common property of all the Indians.

Questions

1. Why did Harrison expect his image of "swarms of hunting shirt men" to intimidate Tecumseh and the Prophet?
2. By what means did Harrison intend to extinguish native American land claims along the Ohio River?
3. Why did Tecumseh protest against these methods and organize resistance to them?

8-9   The Hunters of Kentucky (1822)

Samuel Woodworth and Noah Ludlow

In New Orleans in 1822 Noah Ludlow put to music the poem "The Hunters of Kentucky" by Samuel Woodworth and first performed what soon became an enormously popular song. The song celebrated Andrew Jackson's victory over the British at the Battle of New Orleans in 1815 (see text pp. 264–265). The victory had been a stunning one: the Americans emerged from battle virtually unscathed, whereas the British were nearly destroyed with hundreds dead and more than a thousand wounded or missing. As the historian John William Ward observed, the standard infantryman's weapon was the smooth bore musket. Riflemen in Jackson's army functioned as sharpshooters and played a minor role in the battle. Nevertheless, the prowess of the Kentucky riflemen became an essential part of popular representations of Jackson's victory; the success of

Ludlow's song demonstrated the legend's popular appeal. The third verse refers to the British major general Sir Edward Pakenham, who died in the battle.

Source: Samuel Woodworth and Noah Ludlow, "The Hunters of Kentucky" (1882), in John William Ward, *Andrew Jackson: Symbol for an Age* (New York: Oxford University Press, 1953), 217–218.

1. Ye gentlemen and ladies fair,
       Who grace this famous city,
   Just listen if you've time to spare,
       While I rehearse a ditty;
   And for the opportunity
       Conceive yourselves quite lucky,
   For 'tis not often that you see
       A hunter from Kentucky
   O Kentucky, the hunters of Kentucky!
   O Kentucky, the hunters of Kentucky!

2. We are a hardy, free-born race,
       Each man to fear a stranger;
   Whate'er the game we join in chase,
       Despising toil and danger,
   And if a daring foe annoys,
       Whate'er his strength and forces,
   We'll show him that Kentucky boys
       Are alligator horses.
           Oh Kentucky, etc.

3. I s'pose you've read it in the prints,
       How Packenham attempted
   To make Old Hickory Jackson wince,
       But soon his scheme repented;
   For we with rifles ready cock'd,
       Thought such occasion lucky,
   And soon around the gen'ral flock'd
       The Hunters of Kentucky.
           Oh Kentucky, etc.

4. You've heard, I s'pose how New-Orleans
       Is fam'd for wealth and beauty,
   There's girls of ev'ry hue it seems,
       From snowy white to sooty.
   So Packenham he made his brags,
       If he in fight was lucky,
   He'd have their girls and cotton bags,
       In spite of old Kentucky.
           Oh Kentucky, etc.

5. But Jackson he was wide awake,
       And was not scar'd at trifles,
   For well he knew what aim we take
       With our Kentucky rifles.
   So he led us down to Cypress swamp,
       The ground was low and mucky,
   There stood John Bull in martial pomp
       And here was old Kentucky.
           Oh Kentucky, etc.

6. A bank was rais'd to hide our breasts,
       Not that we thought of dying,
   But that we always like to rest,
       Unless the game is flying.
   Behind it stood our little force,
       None wished it to be greater,
   For ev'ry man was half a horse,
       And half an alligator.
           Oh Kentucky, etc.

7. They did not let our patience tire,
       Before they showed their faces;
   We did not choose to waste our fire,
       So snugly kept our places.
   But when so near we saw them wink,
       We thought it time to stop 'em,
   And 'twould have done you good I think,
       To see Kentuckians drop 'em.
           Oh Kentucky, etc.

8. They found, at last, 'twas vain to fight,
       Where *lead* was all the *booty*,
   And so they wisely took to flight,
       And left *us* all our *beauty*.
   And now if danger e'er annoys,
       Remember what our trade is,
   Just send for us Kentucky boys,
       And we'll protect ye, ladies.
           Oh Kentucky, etc.

Questions

1. According to the song's lyrics, what attributes did the hunters of Kentucky possess that accounted for Jackson's victory?
2. Ludlow stated in his reminiscences, *Dramatic Life as I Found It*, that he made the fifth verse the dramatic focus of his performance. Why did he choose that particular verse?
3. Contrast the American victory at New Orleans as it was celebrated in Ludlow's song with the humiliating British capture of Washington, D.C. How were regional sources of patriotism expressed in the lyrics of "The Hunters of Kentucky"?

Questions for Further Thought

1. What roles did native tribes play in the imperial struggles that lingered on the North American continent?
2. Was the sort of frontiersman celebrated in "The Hunters of Kentucky" the sort of person Jefferson had in mind as the ideal inhabitant of his "Empire of Liberty"?
3. Based on your reading of these documents (8-5 through 8-9), was the "Empire of Liberty" truly a land of liberty for all, or was it in many respects more like a traditional empire?

The Capitalist Commonwealth

While Jefferson's overriding preoccupation was with expanding the territorial reach of the United States in the West, others were pressing for economic expansion. Given Jeffersonian hostility to the use of federal power to encourage economic growth, most initiatives along these lines came from private businessmen and from local and state governments. Merchants pressed to expand their trade and, especially after the lapsing of the First Bank of the United States in 1811, state banks proliferated. As markets began to expand, entrepreneurs began to set up rural factories, and merchants organized networks of "outworkers" making mass quantities of goods such as shoes for wide distribution. This style of rural industrialization complemented the dominant agricultural society but laid the groundwork for the larger factories and urban concentrations of industry that would soon develop (Document 10-2).

State governments sought to expand their economies and provide opportunities for their citizens by encouraging private enterprise to form banks, large-scale manufacturing firms, and transportation companies. They did so not through subsidies but through conferring special privileges, notably corporate charters, which commonly included limited liability of shareholders from corporate debts, monopoly privileges, and state powers such as eminent domain (the right to force the sale of property for public purposes) (Document 8-10). Such grants of special privilege were criticized as "unrepublican" but were defended as a means of enlisting private enterprise to serve the public good without burdening taxpayers or dangerously expanding government power.

These developments proceeded without involvement from the federal executive branch or the Congress; the Supreme Court, though, was a different story. Controlled by Federalists, notably Chief Justice John Marshall, the chief contribution of the Court was to establish the supremacy of the judiciary over the Congress in legal interpretation, the supremacy of the Constitution and the federal government over state laws, and the supremacy of property rights over legislative interference (Documents 8-11 and 8-12). In so doing, the Marshall Court laid the groundwork for the creation of a *national* economy in which businessmen could move freely in search of opportunities, corporations could operate across state lines, and firms located anywhere could do business in safety everywhere. Modern industrial America would be built on these foundations.

8-10   The Virtues and Drawbacks of Chartered Banks (1816)

Mathew Carey

Mathew Carey (1760–1839) was born in Ireland; in his youth he became an ardent Irish nationalist, and briefly had to flee to Paris, where he met Benjamin Franklin and the Marquis de Lafayette. Returning to Ireland, Carey set up shop as a radical journalist but in 1784 had to flee again, this time to Philadelphia. There he established the *Pennsylvania Herald*, which took the side of Robert Morris's faction in state politics (Document 7-3 was edited and published by Carey); he later attached himself to the party of Alexander Hamilton. Carey subsequently became wealthy and prominent, but his chief importance lay in his advocacy of the use of government to foster private enterprise and thus a broad, balanced economic prosperity. His son, Henry C. Carey, became the most prominent "political economist" in Jacksonian America and one of the foremost theorists for the Whig Party. In the following letter to a group of bank directors, Carey discusses both the benefits and drawbacks of one element of the so-called commonwealth system: the liberal chartering of private banks.

Source: Herman E. Kroos, ed. *Documentary History of Banking and Currency in the United States* (New York: Chelsea House Publishers, 1969), 1: 477–480.

March 22, 1816

Gentlemen,

The facility afforded by the banks of converting into money the notes created by the extraordinary degree of business that took place at this period, gave life and activity to trade, commerce, and manufactures. Industry, in all its various shapes and forms, prospered in the highest degree. Never was there a community in a more enviable state.

To produce this effect, another cause combined, to which little attention has been paid. In the year 1814, the legislature of Pennsylvania incorporated about forty banks throughout the state. Of these above thirty had gone into operation. They had discounted freely. And thus the country merchants were enabled to provide themselves with their notes to very large amounts. They therefore not only pretty generally discharged their old engagements, but paid for a considerable portion of their new purchases. Hence larger sums were received in Philadelphia at this period, than ever before in the same space of time.

This prosperous state of affairs created and extended a spirit of speculation, one of those mushroom plants, easily engendered, and prone to rise rapidly to destructive luxuriance. The importers, as I have already stated, profited more by this state of things, than any other class of men. And though they sold at enormous profits, yet how high soever their merchandize was disposed of in the first instance, it rose in the hands of every person who successively purchased, till it reached its ultimate destination, the palace or the cot of the consumer.

Such was the state of affairs throughout the first epoch. There was an immensity of goods for sale. There was an immense demand. Every man engaged in business throve. The banks gave every facility to trade, and promoted a rapid circulation and distribution of property.

While the community was "in the full tide of successful experiment," a sudden panic was excited, as if a general bankruptcy impended. The continuance of the suspension of specie payments by the banks, and the depreciation of the variety of foreign notes which were poured into the city from the westward and southward, excited the first alarm. There was a loud clamour against the cheapness of bank notes, and the rise in the price of almost every thing else.

Whether the Directors of the banks were the first to feel the terror, or were infected with the disorder from abroad, I cannot discover. Suffice it to say, that the panic was sensibly felt at the boards: and the necessity of applying an immediate and powerful remedy, was insisted on, and appeared to be admitted as incontrovertible.

Directors of banks, like other public bodies, are mere men. The votes of the stockholders, and of the legislature, which transform a number of common citizens into bank directors, and invest them with the transcendent powers which the boards possess, confer to title to infallibility. They are, experience proves, as prone to error as their fellow citizens. And were other proofs wanting, I am clear this case would remove all doubt on the subject.

Among the most extraordinary and at times the most ruinous of the errors and follies of mankind, is the propensity to fly from one extreme to its diametrical opposite. Thus the world has seen decided atheists become grossly superstitious—the superstitious became atheistical—violent monarchists become outrageous republicans—furious republicans become strenuous monarchists—and gross sensualists become rigid ascetics. To this rule I know but one marked exception. No man devoured by sordid avarice, has ever become prodigal, or even liberal.

The banks of Philadelphia fell into the error which I have stated above.—From a system whose leading feature was liberality, they almost instantaneously vibrated to one, of which retrenchment was the distinctive characteristic. The actual evils, real or supposed, and those dreadful ones which were gloomily anticipated, were traced to the cheapness of money. All the evils, present or future, were grossly exaggerated.—Such of them as were not imaginary, would have speedily subsided, had they been left to themselves. But unfortunately a determination was formed to apply a violent remedy to a disorder, whose existence to any considerable extent was not clearly established, and which a mild regimen would have radically removed in a short space of time. The empirical plan adopted was to make money scarce by a sudden and violent curtailment of discounts.

That the banks during the last year, greatly erred, is indisputable. They are caught on the horns of a dilemma, from which it is impossible to escape. Either the liberal system pursued in the first epoch, was extreme prodigality, or the retrenchment of the second was starvation and suffocation to the trade, commerce, industry, enterprise, and prosperity of the city. The two plans were diametrically opposite. Both could not possibly be right. Either, pursued steadily, might have been so. But considering the two in connexion, as forming component parts of one system, both were most extravagantly and ruinously wrong.

Had the banks in the first epoch, restrained their discounts within somewhat narrower limits, the spirit of speculation would not have been fostered or encouraged to the length it proceeded. Prices in that case would not have risen so high. And further—the banks would not have found it necessary in the second epoch to have made the heavy reductions of discounts to which they had recourse.—It is perfectly obvious that the prices would not then have probably fallen at all; or, if they did, it would have been in a small degree. And thus trade, commerce, industry, and prosperity would have maintained *"the even tenor of their way,"* without any of those violent ebbs and flows, those rapid elevations and precipitous descents, which are so destructive to happiness, to independence, and to morals.

This, gentlemen, is a most serious view of the subject. To suppose that you can reflect on it without extreme regret, would, I hope, be doing you great injustice. To have been instrumental in producing so much evil, even without a shadow of sinister intention, must, to every man, not destitute of humanity or sensibility, be a source of lasting, although unavailing regret. It is a melancholy part of the lot of mankind, that error and folly very frequently produce as much ill, and suffer as much punishment, as actual guilt. And thus it is that the system pursued, whose origin may be fairly ascribed to mere error, has inflicted as much irreparable injury on our citizens, and has produced as much mischief, as it could have done, had it arisen from wicked intentions.

The error, and its consequences, may be made to produce some good to compensate for a part of the ills to which it has given rise. It may, and I hope will, teach in the most energetic language the high and paramount duty that directors of banks owe the community, to proceed with care and caution, and to preserve a steady and systematic career. That these are indispensable requisites in the management of banks must be self-evident to every man who considers how much of the fortunes and happiness of a trading community, depends, especially in a time of scarcity of money, upon their operations. It is a most serious and awful truth, that at such a period, they are literally masters, in a very great degree, of the destinies of those of their debtors not in tolerably independent circumstances. They may at pleasure reduce some to bankruptcy, by abrupt requisitions for the amount of their debts; and may by undue accommodations enable others to make great fortunes out of the distresses of the public. To sum up the whole in a few words. When money is plenty, banks are servants, and useful servants, of the community. They then court business. They entice men to use their capital. When money is scarce, they withdraw it, and become absolute masters of their fellow citizens.

Questions

1. What does Carey see as the benefit to the "commonwealth" of numerous chartered banks?
2. What are the drawbacks to numerous chartered banks? To what does he attribute the problems resulting from banking expansion?
3. Would Carey agree with William Finlay (Document 7-3) that banks are dangerous in a republican society? Why or why not?

8-11   Decision in *Fletcher v. Peck* (1810)

John Marshall

In January 1801, in one of his last acts as president, John Adams appointed the staunchly Federalist John Marshall of Virginia Chief Justice of the United States. Marshall presided over the Supreme Court for the next thirty-four years until his death in 1835. Marshall's significance is difficult to overemphasize (see text pp. 272–275): he shaped the direction of the Supreme Court as the guarantor of national capitalism. The fact that he did so in the era of the Democratic-Republican "Virginia Dynasty"—that is, during the presidencies of Thomas Jefferson, James Madison, and James Monroe— makes this achievement truly remarkable. During most of Marshall's tenure he presided over a Court majority that had been appointed by Jefferson, Madison, and Monroe. Eventually Marshall was the only remaining Federalist appointee. Nevertheless, Marshall shaped the direction of the Court, repeatedly carrying a majority of the justices with him in a series of landmark decisions, including *Fletcher v. Peck* (1810). In his decision, Marshall acknowledged the corruption that tainted a Georgia land grant, but he relied on a strict construction of Article I, section 10, of the Constitution (protecting "obligation of Contracts") to strike down a law passed by the state of Georgia.

Source: Fletcher v. Peck, 6 Cranch 87 (1810), in Joseph P. Cotton, Jr., ed., The Constitutional Decisions of John Marshall (New York: P. D. Commanger, 1905; facsimile reprint, New York: Da Capo Press, 1969), 1: 243–250.

In this case the [Georgia] legislature may have had ample proof that the original grant was obtained by practices which can never be too much reprobated, and which would have justified its abrogation so far as respected those to whom crime was imputable. But the grant, when issued, conveyed an estate in fee-simple to the grantee, clothed with all the solemnities which law can bestow. This estate was transferable; and those who purchased parts of it were not stained by that guilt which infected the original transaction. . . . Their situation was the same, their title was the same, with that of every other member of the community who holds land by regular conveyances from the original patentee. . . .

The validity of this rescinding act [by the Georgia legislature] . . . might well be doubted, were Georgia a single

sovereign power. But Georgia cannot be viewed as a single unconnected, sovereign power, on whose legislature no other restrictions are imposed than may be found in its own constitution. She is a part of a large empire; she is a member of the American Union; and that Union has a constitution the supremacy of which all acknowledge, and which imposes limits to the legislatures of the several states, which none claim a right to pass. The constitution of the United States declares that no state shall pass any bill of attainder, *ex post facto* law, or law impairing the obligation of contracts.

Does the case now under consideration come within this prohibitory section of the constitution? . . .

Since . . . in fact, a grant is a contract executed, the obligation of which still continues, and since the constitution uses the general term contract . . . it must be construed to comprehend the latter as well as the former. . . .

Whatever respect might have been felt for the state sovereignties, it is not to be disguised that the framers of the constitution viewed, with some apprehension, the violent acts which might grow out of the feelings of the moment; and that the people of the United States, in adopting that instrument, have manifested a determination to shield themselves and their property from the effects of those sudden and strong passions to which men are exposed. The restrictions on the legislative power of the states are obviously founded in this sentiment; and the constitution of the United States contains what may be deemed a bill of rights for the people of each state. . . .

It is, then, the unanimous opinion of the court, that, in this case, the estate having passed into the hands of a purchaser for a valuable consideration, without notice, the state of Georgia was restrained, either by general principles, which are common to our free institutions, or by the particular provisions of the constitution of the United States, from passing a law whereby the estate of the plaintiff in the premises so purchased could be constitutionally and legally impaired and rendered null and void.

Questions

1. In Marshall's view, why did the framers of the Constitution place restrictions on state legislatures?
2. The passage of the Constitution cited by Marshall appears in Article I, section 10. Locate that passage in the Constitution (see text p. D-9). Do you agree with Marshall's interpretation of its meaning?
3. How did Marshall's decision help lay the foundation for national capitalism?

8-12   Argument for the Plaintiff in *Dartmouth College v. Woodward* (1818)

Daniel Webster

In addition to his distinguished political career, Daniel Webster (1782–1852) established himself as an influential and financially successful constitutional lawyer. When the New Hampshire legislature circumvented a colonial charter establishing Dartmouth College by attempting to make the college a state institution, Webster defended his alma mater (and the inviolability of contracts) before the Supreme Court (see text p. 275). The Court agreed with Webster, endorsing a static view of property that protected established property rights for the next two decades. In this case, Dartmouth College was the plaintiff and William Woodward (the college's treasurer, who had been directed by state law to report to a new board of trustees) was the defendant.

Source: Rev. B. F. Tefft, ed., *The Speeches of Daniel Webster* (New York: Lincoln Centenary Association, n.d. [186?]), 11–59 passim.

The charter of 1769 created and established a corporation, to consist of twelve persons, and no more; to be called the "Trustees of Dartmouth College." . . . The charter, or letters patent, then proceed to create such a corporation . . . to have perpetual existence, as such corporation, and with power to hold and dispose of lands and goods, for the use of the college with all the ordinary powers of corporations. They are in their discretion to apply the funds and property of the college to the support of the president, tutors, ministers, and other officers of the college. . . .

No funds are given to the college by this charter. A corporate existence and capacity are given to the trustees, with the privileges and immunities which have been mentioned, to enable the founder and his associates the better to manage the funds which they themselves had contributed, and such others as they might afterwards obtain.

After the institution thus created and constituted had existed, uninterruptedly and usefully, nearly fifty years, the legislature of New Hampshire passed the acts in question.

The first act makes the twelve trustees under the charter, and nine other individuals, to be appointed by the governor and council, a corporation, by a new name; and to this new corporation transfers all the *property, rights, powers, liberties, and privileges* of the old corporation; with further power to establish new colleges and an institute, and to apply all or any part of the funds to these purposes; subject to the power and control of a board of twenty-five overseers, to be appointed by the governor and council.

The second act makes further provisions for executing the objects of the first, and the last act authorizes the defendant, the treasurer of the plaintiffs, to retain and hold their property, against their will.

If these acts are valid, the old corporation is abolished, and a new one created. . . . It will be contended by the plaintiffs, that these acts are not valid . . . because they are repugnant . . . to the tenth section of the first article of the constitution of the United States. The material words of that section are: "No state shall pass any bill of attainder, *ex post facto* law, or law impairing the obligation of contracts."

The object of these most important provisions in the national constitution has often been discussed. . . . It has already been decided in this court, that a *grant* is a contract, within the meaning of this provision; and that a grant by a state is also a contract, as much as the grant of an individual. In Fletcher *v.* Peck, this court says: ". . . A grant, in its own nature, amounts to an extinguishment of the right of the grantor, and implies a contract not to reassert that right. . . . The restrictions on the legislative power of the states are obviously founded in this sentiment; and the constitution of the United States contains what may be deemed a bill of rights for the people of each state."

It has also been decided that a grant by a state before the revolution is as much to be protected as a grant since. . . . This court, then, does not admit the doctrine that a legislature can repeal statutes creating private corporations. . . . And because charters of incorporation are of the nature of contracts, they cannot be altered or varied but by consent of the original parties. . . .

The case before the court is not of ordinary importance, or of every-day occurrence. It affects not this college only, but every college. . . . They have all a common principle of existence, the inviolability of their charters. It will be a dangerous, a most dangerous experiment, to hold these institutions subject to the rise and fall of popular parties, and the fluctuations of political opinions. If the franchise may be at any time taken away, or impaired, the property, also, may be taken away, or its use perverted. . . . Party and faction will be cherished in the places consecrated to piety and learning. These consequences are neither remote nor possible only. They are certain and immediate.

Questions

1. In what ways did the New Hampshire legislature change Dartmouth College's charter?
2. What constitutional argument did Webster employ to defend the original charter?
3. In Webster's view, why should colleges such as Dartmouth be privately controlled and therefore beyond the reach of "party and faction"?

Questions for Further Thought

1. The preceding three documents all deal not only with government power but also with *limits* on government power. What do the authors believe governments—specifically *state* governments—should and should not do?
2. Compare the vision of a future America shared by Carey, Marshall, and Webster with that of Thomas Jefferson, especially as seen in Documents 8-5 and 10-1. Would Jefferson be comfortable with the country they were trying to create?
3. Do you think William Finlay (Document 7-3) would fully agree with the views of these authors? What are the implications of their views for democratic rule?

CHAPTER 9

The Quest for a Republican Society, 1790–1820

★   ★   ★

Democratic Republicanism

During the first half-century of American independence, the citizenry of the United States struggled to work out the implications of the republican experiment they had launched in 1776. At first their society and political system looked much like it had in colonial times, with a clearly defined elite governing and ordinary folk deferring to their rule. But revolutionary ideals of equality, coupled with the vast expansion of economic opportunity resulting from the opening of the West, eroded the hold of traditional elites and enhanced popular hostility toward the lingering remnants of privilege. One result of this process was a movement to broaden the franchise. Ironically, while the right to vote was increasingly extended to all adult white men regardless of wealth, it was sometimes actually narrowed with respect to race and gender; "democracy" was defined as being for white males only (Document 9-1).

One reason for confining the public sphere of politics to men was fear of the implications of republican ideology for relations between the sexes. Not only did republican women such as Abigail Adams question their subordination, but a wave of romantic sentimentalism challenged patriarchal control of wives and children in the name of romantic love. Marriages became increasingly "companionate." In a society in which middle-class and even upper-class children were increasingly expected to make their own way in the world without support from traditional family privilege, parents opted to have fewer children and to prepare them more assiduously for their independence. In this new, republican world, mothers were increasingly assigned the task of preparing virtuous citizens and self-controlled, self-reliant progeny (Document 9-2). This conception of women's "separate sphere" was considerably more spacious than patriarchal domination had been; among other things, it fostered the notion that republican mothers needed education just as fathers did (Document 9-3). In the future, however, women would increasingly find their separate sphere far from equal.

9-1   Universal (White) Manhood Suffrage? The New York State Constitutional Convention of 1821

Prior to the early nineteenth century, all the American states had maintained some sort of property-holding or taxpaying qualification for voting. At that time, though, a wave of constitutional conventions began removing these qualifications and throwing open the right to vote to all adult white men. The previous restrictions had sometimes permitted propertied free African Americans to vote; since few blacks could qualify, white men were not terribly concerned. But universal suffrage would open the floodgates, especially to blacks, and many of the most ardent supporters of universal white suffrage wanted to replace class restrictions with racial ones. Thus when the state of New York called a constitutional convention to consider broadening the suffrage, the delegates spent a great deal of time debating whether or not to restrict it by race. The debate offered plenty of ironies: the leading proponent of racial disfranchisement, Samuel Young, was a prominent Bucktail and advocate of universal white suffrage—a contradiction noted by the conservative Judge Platt, who wished to see blacks and whites remain on equal footing. In the end, the delegates accepted a compromise proposal under which property requirements were removed for whites but retained for blacks.

Source: Merrill D. Peterson, ed., *Democracy, Liberty, and Property: The State Constitutional Conventions of the 1820s* (Indianapolis: Bobbs-Merrill Company, 1966), 215–217, 223, 225–226, 228, 230, 233.

MR. ROSS: . . . That all men are free and equal, according to the usual declarations, applies to them only in a state of nature, and not after the institution of civil government; for then many rights, flowing from a natural equality, are necessarily abridged, with a view to produce the greatest amount of security and happiness to the whole community. On this principle the right of suffrage is extended to white men only. But why, it would probably be asked, are blacks to be excluded? I answer, because they are seldom, if ever, required to share in the common burthens or defence of the state. There are also additional reasons; they are a peculiar people, incapable, in my judgment, of exercising that privilege with any sort of discretion, prudence, or independence. They have no just conceptions of civil liberty. They know not how to appreciate it, and are consequently indifferent to its preservation.

Under such circumstances, it would hardly be compatible with the safety of the state, to entrust such a people with this right. It is not thought advisable to permit aliens to vote, neither would it be safe to extend it to the blacks. We deny to minors this right, and why? Because they are deemed incapable of exercising it discreetly, and therefore not safely, for the good of the whole community.—Even the better part of creation, as my honorable friend from Oneida (Mr. N. Williams,) stiles them, are not permitted to participate in this right. No sympathies seemed to be awakened in their behalf, nor in behalf of the aborigines, the original and only rightful proprietors of our soil—a

people altogether more acute and discerning, and in whose judicious exercise of the right I should repose far more confidence than in the African race. . . . The truth is, this exclusion invades no inherent rights, nor has it any connection at all with the question of slavery. The practice of every state in the union, is to make such exceptions, limitations, and provisions in relation to the elective privilege, under their respective constitutions, as are deemed to be necessary or consistent with public good—varied in each according to the existing circumstances under which they are made. It must therefore necessarily rest on the ground of expediency. And, sir, I fear that an extension to the blacks would serve to invite that kind of population to this state, an occurrence which I should most sincerely deplore. The petition presented in their behalf, now on your table, in all probability has been instigated by gentlemen of a different colour, who expect to control their votes. But whether this be so or not, next the blacks will claim to be represented by persons of their own colour, in your halls of legislation. And can you consistently refuse them? It would be well to be prepared for such a claim. . . .

R. CLARKE: . . . But it is said these people are incapable of exercising the right of suffrage judiciously; that they will become the tools and engines of aristocracy, and set themselves up in market, and give their votes to the highest bidder; that they have no will or judgment of their own, but will follow implicitly the dictates of the purse-proud aristocrats of the day, on whom they depend for bread. This may be true to a certain extent; but, sir, they are not the only ones who abuse this privilege; and if this be a sufficient reason for depriving any of your citizens of their just rights, go on and exclude also the many thousands of white fawning, cringing sycophants, who look up to their more wealthy and more ambitious neighbours for direction at the polls, as they look to them for bread. But although most of this unfortunate class of men may at present be in this dependent state, both in body and mind, yet we ought to remember, that we are making our constitution, not for a day, nor for a year, but I hope for many generations; and there is a redeeming spirit in liberty, which I have no doubt will eventually raise these poor, abused, unfortunate people, from their present degraded state, to equal intelligence with their more fortunate and enlightened neighbours. . . .

COL. YOUNG: . . . The gentleman who had just sat down had adverted to the declaration of independence to prove that the blacks are possessed of "certain unalienable rights." But is the right of voting a natural right? If so, our laws are oppressive and unjust. A natural right is one that is born with us. No man is born twenty-one years old, and of course all restraint upon the natural right of voting, during the period of nonage, is usurpation and tyranny. This confusion arises from mixing natural with acquired rights. The right of voting is adventitious. It is resorted to only as a means of securing our natural rights.

In forming a constitution, we should have reference to the feelings, habits, and modes of thinking of the people. The gentleman last up has alluded to the importance of regarding public sentiment. And what is the public sentiment in relation to this subject? Are the negroes permitted to a participation to social intercourse with the whites! Are they elevated to public office! No, sir—public sentiment forbids it. This they know; and hence they are prepared to sell their votes to the highest bidder. In this manner you introduce corruption into the very vitals of the government. . . .

The minds of the blacks are not competent to vote. They are too much degraded to estimate the value, or exercise with fidelity and discretion that important right. It would be unsafe in their hands. Their vote would be at the call of the richest purchaser. If this class of people should hereafter arrive at such a degree of intelligence and virtue, as to inspire confidence, then it will be proper to confer this privilege upon them. At present emancipate and protect them; but withhold that privilege which they will inevitably abuse. Look to your jails and penitentiaries. By whom are they filled? By the very race, whom it is now proposed to clothe with the power of deciding upon your political rights.

If there is that natural, inherent right to vote, which some gentlemen have urged, it ought to be further extended. In New-Jersey, females were formerly allowed to vote; and on that principle, you must admit *negresses* as well as *negroes* to participate in the right of suffrage. Minors, too, and aliens must no longer be excluded, but the "era of good feelings" be commenced to earnest. . . .

MR. PLATT . . . The gentleman from Saratoga, who, as chairman of the committee, reported this proviso, (Mr. Young,) has exultingly told us, that ours is the only happy country where freemen acknowledge no distinction of ranks—where real native genius and merit can emerge from the humblest conditions of life, and rise to honours and distinction. It sounded charmingly in our replication cars, and I have but one objection to it, which is that, unfortunately for our patriotic pride, it is not true. . . . The gentleman from Saratoga, (Mr. Young,) began his philipic in favour of universal suffrage, by an eulogium on liberty and equality, in our happy state. And what then? Why, the same gentleman concluded by moving a resolution, in substance, that 37,000 of our free black citizens, and their posterity, for ever, shall be degraded by our constitution, below the common rank of freeman—that they never shall emerge from their humble condition—that they shall never assert the dignity of human nature, but shall ever remain a degraded caste in our republic. . . .

As a republican statesman, I protest against the principle of inequality contained in this proviso. As a man and a father, who expects justice for himself and his children, in this world; and as a Christian, who hopes for mercy in the world to come; I can not, I dare not, consent to this unjust proscription. . . .

Questions

1. What do Mr. Ross and Colonel Young fear would be the consequences for both blacks and the state if New York gave blacks the franchise?
2. Colonel Young draws a distinction between "natural" and "acquired" rights. What do you think of his argument? Do you agree or disagree?
3. In their debate over universal suffrage for New York, how do the participants draw distinctions between whites and blacks? What are some similarities?

9-2   The Mother's Book (1831)

Lydia Maria Child

Lydia Maria Child (1802–1880) was born in Medford, Massachusetts, and married a prominent Boston lawyer. She was best known as a leading abolitionist agitator, but she also enjoyed a successful career as a writer of fiction, juvenile literature, and works on domestic economy. Her most widely read work, *The Mother's Book* (1831), explained to women in middle-class households how the mother's role in child rearing had assumed vast new meaning and significance. In Child's view, an internalized sense of self-restraint represented the central object of the "affectionate rationalist" approach to child rearing (see text pp. 288–289): children should not be whipped into obedience, they should be instructed in a manner that encouraged them to wish to be obedient. In this passage, Child explored the means by which this moral education could be accomplished.

Source: Lydia Maria Child, *The Mother's Book* (Boston: Carter and Hendee, 1831).

I once saw a mother laugh very heartily at the distressed face of a kitten, which a child of two years old was pulling backward by the tail. At last, the kitten, in self-defense, turned and scratched the boy. He screamed, and his mother ran to him, kissed the wound, and beat the poor kitten, saying all the time, "Naughty kitten, to scratch John!" . . .

This little incident, trifling as it seems, no doubt had important effects on the character of the child. . . .

In the first place, the child was encouraged in cruelty, by seeing that it gave his mother amusement. . . .

In the next place, the kitten was struck for defending herself; this was injustice to the injured animal, and a lesson of tyranny to the boy. In the third place, striking the kitten because she had scratched him, was teaching him retaliation . . . the influence upon him is, that it is right to injure when we are injured. . . .

The mind of a child is not like that of a grown person . . . it is a vessel empty and pure—always ready to receive, and always receiving.

Every look, every movement, every expression, does something toward forming the character of the little heir to immortal life. . . .

The rule, then, for developing good affections in a child is, that he never be allowed to see or feel the influence of bad passions, even in the most trifling things; and in order to effect this, you must drive evil passions from your own heart. Nothing can be real that has not its home *within* us. The only sure way, as well as the easiest, to *appear* good, is to *be* good.

It is not possible to indulge anger, or any other wrong feeling, and conceal it entirely. If not expressed in words, a child *feels* the baneful influence. Evil enters into his soul, as the imperceptible atmosphere he breathes enters into his lungs: and the beautiful little image of God is removed farther and farther from his home in heaven.

Questions

1. What moral lessons were drawn from the "trifling" incident of the child pulling the cat's tail?

2. Do you agree with Child's premise that a child's mind is "a vessel empty and pure"?

3. Consider the new authority and responsibility of the middle-class mother. How, in Child's view, should a mother develop "good affections" in a child's mind?

9-3   The Education of Republican Women (1798)

Benjamin Rush

Benjamin Rush (1745–1813) studied medicine in Philadelphia and the University of Edinburgh. He returned to Philadelphia in 1769 to practice medicine and advance American republican values. For Rush, republicanism implied a host of social and moral reforms as Americans distinguished their society from that of monarchical Great Britain. Here he advocates improved education for young women to prepare them to be republican mothers (see text pp. 285–287). Rush addressed his remarks on female education to "The Visitors of the Young Ladies' Academy in Philadelphia, 28th July, 1787." The essay was first published in 1798.

Source: Benjamin Rush, *Essays Literary, Moral, and Philosophical* (Philadelphia, 1798; reprint, Schenectady, N.Y.: Union College Press, 1988), 44–54.

The first remark that I shall make upon this subject, is, that female education should be accommodated to the state of society, manners, and government of the country, in which it is conducted.

This remark leads me at once to add, that the education of young ladies, in this country, should be conducted upon principles very different from what it is in Great Britain, and in some respects, different from what it was when we were part of a monarchical empire.

There are several circumstances in the situation, employments, and duties of women in America, which require a peculiar mode of education. . . .

The equal share that every citizen has in the liberty, and the possible share he may have in the government of our country, make it necessary that our ladies should be qualified to a certain degree by a peculiar and suitable education, to concur in instructing their sons in the principles of liberty and government. . . .

Vocal music should never be neglected, in the education of a young lady, in this country. Besides preparing her to join in that part of public worship which consists in psalmody, it will enable her to soothe the cares of domestic life. The distress and vexation of a husband—the noise of a nursery, and, even, the sorrows that will sometimes intrude into her own bosom, may all be relieved by a song, where sound and sentiment unite to act upon the mind. . . .

The attention of our young ladies should be directed, as soon as they are prepared for it, to the reading of history—travels—poetry—and moral essays. These studies are accommodated, in a peculiar manner, to the present state of society in America, and when a relish is excited for them, in early life, they subdue that passion for reading novels, which so generally prevails among the fair sex. . . . As yet the intrigues of a British novel, are . . . foreign to our manners. . . . Let it not be said, that the tales of distress, which fill modern novels, have a tendency to soften the female heart into acts of humanity. The fact is the reverse of this. The abortive sympathy which is excited by the recital of imaginary distress, blunts the heart to that which is real; and, hence, we sometimes see instances of young ladies, who weep away a whole forenoon over the criminal sorrows of a fictitious Charlotte . . . turning with disdain at three o'clock from the sight of a beggar, who solicits in feeble accents or signs, a small portion only of the crumbs which fall from their fathers' tables. . . .

It should not surprize us that British customs, with respect to female education have been transplanted into our American schools and families. . . . It is high time to awake from this servility—to study our own character—to examine the age of our country—and to adopt manners in every thing, that shall be accommodated to our state of society, and to the forms of our government. In particular it is incumbent upon us to make ornamental accomplishments yield to principles and knowledge, in the education of our women. . . . The influence of female education would be still more extensive and useful in domestic life. The obligations of gentlemen to qualify themselves by knowledge and industry to discharge the duties of benevolence, would be encreased [*sic*] by marriage; and the patriot—the hero—and the legislator, would find the sweetest regard of their toils, in the approbation and applause of their wives. Children would discover the marks of maternal prudence and wisdom in every station of life; for it has been remarked that there have been few great or good men who have not been blessed with wise and prudent mothers. . . . I know that the elevation of the female mind, by means of moral, physical and religious truth, is considered by some men as unfriendly to the domestic character of a woman. But this is a prejudice of little minds, and springs from the same spirit which opposes the general diffusion of knowledge among the citizens of our republic. If men believe that ignorance is favourable to the government of the female sex, they are certainly deceived; for a weak and ignorant woman will always be governed with the greatest difficulty. . . . It will be in our power, LADIES, to correct the mistakes and practice of our sex upon these subjects, by demonstrating, that the female temper can only be governed by reason, and that the cultivation of reason in women, is alike friendly to the order of nature, and to private as well as public happiness.

Questions

1. Why did Rush want to discourage young American women from reading novels?
2. What did he mean when he insisted that "ornamental accomplishments" must "yield to principles and knowledge"?
3. In what ways would the proper education of women promote republican virtue?

Questions for Further Thought

1. In Documents 9-1 through 9-3, we see a range of opinions expressed about the relationship between republican society and republican government. Did Americans in the early nineteenth century have a clear model for the republican society that they were trying to create, or were they fumbling in the dark? How did Americans define a republican society as opposed to a monarchical society?
2. Where does the notion of equality fit into the larger constellation of republican ideals—particularly in regard to race, class, and gender differences in the new republic, as expressed in Documents 9-1 through 9-3?
3. At the New York State Constitutional Convention (Document 9-1) and in Lydia Maria Child's and Benjamin Rush's advice books (Documents 9-2 and 9-3), the different voices draw strong connections between private (personal) virtue and public virtue. Why, in a republic, was the inner state of each individual so important? Do you think that these nineteenth-century arguments are still valid in the twenty-first century?

Slavery and Aristocratic Republicanism in the South

The influence of democratic republicanism on American society was felt in all regions of the nation. However, in one region—the South—this influence was fundamentally altered in its effects by the dominance of plantation slavery. The explosive westward expansion of the nation's first half-century was not confined to the northern states. Aided by both the invention of the cotton gin and the voracious demands of British and American factories for southern cotton, planters surged halfway across the continent in search of their own vision of American opportunity. By 1819, however, slaveholders' understanding of republicanism was starting to clash with that of the free whites of the North—a conflict appearing in sharp relief at the time of the Missouri controversy (Documents 9-4 and 9-5).

At the heart of that conflict, of course, was slavery; southern planters sought their fortunes either by dragging their slaves behind them into expanding western territory or by purchasing additional slave labor from dealers operating a new, lucrative trade in human flesh (Document 9-6). These new cotton plantations were thoroughly efficient, albeit brutal, business enterprises that kept refining their operations until the Civil War (Document 9-7). Along with the expansion of the plantation came the development of a distinctly African American culture among the slaves—a mix of African customs and newer adoptions such as evangelical Christianity—that provided an important source of dignity and, when the time was right, collective action (Document 9-8).

Nonslaveholding white southerners, as well, suffered from the influence of the slave plantation. The slaveholding interest dominated political life, and the plantation economy retarded the sort of economic development that was so sharply expanding opportunity in the Free States. Most nonslaveholders accepted the existing order, but it produced a society whose republicanism was of a very different sort than that seen elsewhere in the United States—one whose consequences would haunt the South long after the end of slavery.

9-4   The Missouri Controversy I: The Benefits of Slavery Extension (1819)

Richard Mentor Johnson

In 1819 a proposal to authorize the people of Missouri to organize their territory as a new state sparked the first major sectional crisis in the history of the young republic, when New York representative James Tallmadge suggested that the state be required to begin the gradual emancipation of its slaves. The debate over Missouri raged for two years. Northerners asserted that Congress had the clear right to govern the territories and to impose conditions on prospective states, including the constitutional requirement of a "republican form of government." Southerners, for their part, insisted that "states' rights" required recognizing the sovereignty of local (white) people in determining their own institutions and were horrified at the implication that slavery was "unrepublican." Indeed, to white southerners slavery provided the very foundation for white equality, without which a republic could not be viable. The case for this position was made by Richard Mentor Johnson (1780–1850), an ardent Jeffersonian Republican then serving as U.S. senator from Kentucky.

Source: Annals of the Congress of the United States, 1789–1824 (Washington, D.C.: U.S. Government Printing Office, 1819–1820), 16th Cong., 1st sess., 345–359.

. . . Can gentlemen sincerely believe that the cause of humanity will be promoted by still confining this population [i.e., slaves] within such limits, as that their relative numbers will oppose everlasting obstacles to their emancipation? Upon the most extensive principles of philanthropy, I say, let them spread forth with the growing extent of our nation. I am sure I plead the cause of humanity. I advocate the best interests of the sons of bondage, when I entreat you to give them room to be happy; and so disperse them as that, under the auspices of Providence, they may one day enjoy the rights of man, without convulsing the empire or endangering society. . . .

There is no just cause for irritation on this subject. We should suppress our feelings, when they threaten to transport us beyond the bounds of reason. Early habits beget strong prejudices, and under a heavy burden of them we all labor. But it becomes us to bring them to one common altar, and consume them together. Before we compel our brother to pluck the mote from his eye, it will be wise to take the beam from our own. On this occasion I cannot omit to mention my own feelings on a former occurrence. When I first came to Congress, it was with mingled emotions of horror and surprise that I saw citizens from the non-slaveholding States, as they are called—yes, and both branches of our National Legislature—riding in a coach and four, with a white servant seated before, managing the reins, an-

other standing behind the coach, and both of these white servants in livery. Is this, said I to myself, the degraded condition of the citizen, on whose voice the liberties of a nation may depend? I could not reconcile it with my ideas of freedom; because, in the State where I received my first impressions, slaves alone were servile. All white men there are on an equality, and every citizen feels his independence. We have no classes—no patrician or plebeian rank. Honesty and honor form all the distinctions that are felt or known. Whatever may be the condition of a citizen with us, you must treat him as an equal. This I find is not so in every part of the non-slaveholding States, especially in your populous cities, where ranks and distinctions, the precursors of aristocracy, already begin to exist. They whose business it is to perform menial offices in other States, are as servile as our slaves in the West. Where is the great difference betwixt the conditions of him who keeps your stable, who blacks your boots, who holds your stirrups, or mounts behind your coach when you ride, and the slave who obeys the command of his master? There may be a nominal difference; but it would be difficult to describe its reality. In the one case it is called voluntary, because it is imposed by its own necessity, and in the other involuntary, because imposed by the will of another. Whatever difference there may be in the principle, the effects upon society are the same. The condition, in some respects, is in favor of the slave. He is supplied with food and clothing; and in the hour of sickness he finds relief. No anxious cares, in relation to age and infirmity, invade his breast. He fears no duns [demands for payment]: careless of the pressure of the times, he dreads not the coercion of payment, nor feels the cruelty of that code which confines the white servant in prison, because the iron hand of poverty has wrested from him the means of support for his family. Though slavery still must be confessed a bitter draught, yet where the stamp of nature marks the distinction, and when the mind, from early habit, is moulded to the condition, the slave often finds less bitterness in the cup of life than most white servants. What is the condition of many, who are continually saluting our ears with cries of want, even in this city? Men, women, boys, girls, from infancy to old age, craving relief from every passenger. Are they slaves? No. Among the slaves are no beggars; no vagrants; none idle for want of employ, or crying for want of bread. Every condition of life has its evils; and most evils have some palliative; though perhaps none less than those of white menials. Yet, sir, none are more lavish

of their censures against slaveholders than those lordlings with livery servants of their own complexion. . . .

I never could stand having white servants dressed in livery. No, sir, when the honest laborer, the mechanic, however poor, or whatever his employment, visits my house, it matters not what company is there, he must sit with me at my board, and receive the same treatment as the most distinguished guest; because in him I recognise a fellow citizen and an equal.

The condition of the slave is but little understood by those who are not the eye-witnesses of his treatment. His sufferings are greatly aggravated in their apprehension. The general character of the slaveholding community can no more be determined, nor should they be any more stigmatized, by a particular instance of cruelty to a slave, than the character of the non-slaveholding community by a particular instance of cruelty in a parent towards his child, a guardian to his ward, or a master to his apprentice. No man among us can be cruel to his slave without incurring the execration of the whole community.

Questions

1. What does Johnson mean when he suggests that the westward extension of slavery might encourage its demise?
2. According to Johnson, in what ways did the enslavement of blacks encourage equality among whites?
3. On what did Johnson base his claim that slaves found "less bitterness in the cup of life than most white servants"?

9-5   The Missouri Controversy II: The Blight of Slavery (1819)

Daniel Raymond

Daniel Raymond (1786–1849) was born in New Haven, Connecticut, but at the time of the Missouri controversy was a member of the Baltimore bar. A former Federalist, Raymond was much enamored of the economic ideas of Alexander Hamilton and, like his older contemporary Mathew Carey (Document 8-10), believed that the government should take a hand in developing the economic capacities of the people. Raymond's ideas, like Carey's, helped provide the theoretical underpinnings for the later Whig Party. It was Raymond's insistence on the links between broad-based economic prosperity and republican liberty that led him to join the Missouri controversy on the antislavery side. To Raymond, slavery was not simply an affront to humanity; it was also an impediment to the development of a prosperous and truly egalitarian republic—and he saw evidence for this position in the relative stagnation of the slaveholding South. Unlike Richard Mentor Johnson, Raymond was beginning to see slavery—and the South—not as bulwarks of the republic but as threats to it. In the following treatise, he gave voice to many of the deeper fears for the future of American (white) liberty that underlay the exalted moral and constitutional arguments of the antislavery side.

Source: Daniel Raymond, *The Missouri Question* (Baltimore: Schaeffer and Maund, 1819), 3–5, 8–9, 18–21, 23, 30–34.

THERE is no subject so interesting and important to the real lovers of their country, as that of slavery, because there is none which involves the happiness, prosperity and glory of our country in so great a degree—none attended with so many difficulties in remidying. It is admitted by all parties, slave-holders or not, that slavery is the greatest curse our country is afflicted with—it is a foul stain upon our national escutcheon—A canker which is corroding the moral and political vitals of our country. There is but one voice on this subject, and that is the voice of condemnation, as an enormous, and an alarming evil.

But although there is such an union of sentiment, as to the existence and nature of the evil, there is a vast diversity of opinion as to the remedy to be applied, for its correction or its cure.

The true policy of every wise legislator is to consider his country immortal, and to legislate for it as if it were to exist forever; but unfortunately, most legislators act as though they thought their country as short lived as themselves, and instead of adopting a policy, which is to look prospectively to future generations and centuries; they adopt a policy which looks only to themselves and to the present race. Unless the fruits of a policy are to be gathered by themselves, they think it unworthy their attention. This is eminently the case in the Southern States, in regard to their policy towards their slaves. They reprobate slavery as the eldest and greatest curse, and *at the same time* adopt measures *calculated* to increase and perpetuate it to the latest generations. They affect to despise the traitor, but they *love* the treason. This may appear to be a bold charge, but I trust, I shall be able to make it good; which, if I do not, I shall be very ready to retract.

A writer in the Federal Gazette of the 23d Nov. under the signature of PHOCION, says, "since the establishment of our independence, every state has engaged in the humane work of freeing our country from this curse, or where this could not be done with safety to the state or advantage to the slaves, in ameliorating their condition." This writer speaks the general sentiment of the southern public on this subject; but I trust I shall show before I conclude, that the southern states, Maryland excepted, not only have not done any thing towards freeing our country from this curse; but that they have on the contrary done and are doing all in their power, both to magnify the *curse* beyond all calculation, and to perpetuate it to the latest ages. That under the policy they are now persuing, the evil will continue to increase in a geometrical ratio, and that there can be no hope of its ever being ameliorated—nay farther, that *the policy* they are now pursuing, and *the policy* they wish the United States to adopt, will not only magnify and perpetuate the evil in the present slave holding states, but will extend it in all its horrors over a vast and boundless tract of country. I allude to the policy of permitting the new states west of the Mississippi, to become slave holding states. And here I will observe, that if the admission of slaves into the western world, would diminish the

evil in the old slave states, I would say, *let them be admitted.* But I believe, I shall be able to prove upon the soundest principles of political æconomy, that the admission of slaves into those western states, so far from diminishing the evil in the old states, will have directly the contrary effect—that it will be the very means of preventing the southern states from ever ridding themselves of that *curse*. I shall also endeavour to free myself from the charge which Phocion brings against the eastern writers and eastern presses, of "upbraiding their neighbours, when they can suggest no remedy for the evil for which they upbraid them."

The idea, however, that this curse is to be increased and perpetrated through all succeeding generations, is very appalling, and our southern politicians either refrain from looking at so forbidding a picture, or they cast about for some remedy, which they flatter themselves, may mitigate its horrors. I shall attempt to show that they have not yet devised any plan that can in the smallest perceptible degree, effect their purpose, and that their policy is in fact increasing and perpetuating that evil upon their posterity. Slavery is a poisonous plant of vigorous and rapid growth—plant but a scion in any soil, and it will soon spread forth its pestiferous branches, overshadowing, choaking and finally destroying every thing within the sphere of its influence. . . .

The first proposition which I will lay down, is *That in our country, a free black population does not increase by procreation so fast by nearly 50 per cent in twenty years, as a white population in a non slave holding state.*

2. *That a free black population does not increase so fast by procreation as a slave population.*

3. *That the white population in a slave state, does not increase so fast by at least 30 or 40 per cent. in twenty years, as the same population does in a state where there are none, or but few slaves.*

4. *That a slave population increases by procreation, faster than the white population in a slave state.*

And 5. (As a corollary from the foregoing propositions) *that in proportion as you restrain the increase of a slave population, you promote the increase of the white population;* and then the question for politicians to decide, arises, to wit: Whether that policy is best which promotes the increase of a free white population, by restraining the increase of a slave population, or that which promotes the increase of a slave population, by restraining the increase of a free white population. And can there be any doubt upon this question? Does that man live and breathe the air of this free country, who would dare to say, that a legislature ought to hesitate for a moment, in adopting that policy which would promote the increase of a white population, rather than of a black slave population? If there be such a man, he is a disgrace to his species. . . .

From all these estimates, it is clear, that the white population in a slave state, does not increase so fast as the white population in a non slave holding state, nor is this difference a small one. It is at a moderate calculation a difference of from 40 to 60 per cent. in 20 years. The difference is 86 per cent. against Maryland, 74 against Virginia, 68 against North Carolina, and 35 per cent. against South Carolina. This is certainly a matter of no trifling consideration. The great end of government in our country, is to promote the increase of our species, especially the free portion of them; and any cause, whatever it be, that prevents their increase, ought to be removed. There can be no doubt that slavery is the primary cause of the white population in the southern states, not increasing so fast as in the northern. I admit there may, and doubtless are at present, other immediate causes to be found in the manners, customs and habits of the people; but this difference in the manners, customs and habits of the people, is traceable to slavery as the primary cause. If the southern people are less industrious, less enterprising, less provident, it is because they are and have been cursed with slavery. It is an old maxim, that idleness is the parent of vice and dissipation, but there is nothing which so much conduces to idleness in a white population as slavery.—May it not then be said that slavery is a poisonous plant which takes deep root in any soil, and shoots forth its vigorous branches in all directions, blasting, withering, and ultimately destroying every goodly plant. Is it not in fact that *bohun upas* which has been supposed to exist only in the imagination of fanciful travellers?

The reasons why the white population does not increase so fast in a slave state, as in a state where there are no slaves, are neither doubtful nor mysterious. They are apparent to the most superficial observer. It is a self-evident axiom, that population or the increase of population must be limited to the means of subsistence. . . . If all the product of the earth be consumed by slaves, a white population cannot subsist; and whatever portion of the product of the earth be consumed by slaves, in the same proportion will the means of subsistence be taken from a white population, and in the same proportion will the increase of the white population be limited or restrained. In other words, every slave in the world, especially in our country occupies the place of a free man. Nay he does much more than this, or I will show hereafter that no country can be the nature of things contain or support so many human beings where slavery exists, as it would do if there was no slavery.

In all countries the great mass of the population is poor and obliged to depend upon manual labour for the subsistence of themselves and families. This is as much the case in the slave states, as in those where there are no slaves—A large portion of the white population in the southern states, are neither slave owners nor land owners, and are as much dependant on the labor of their lands for subsistence as the eastern people. But where slavery abounds they have no market for their labour—they cannot obtain employment. How then are they to raise families? Besides, it is in slave states a disgrace for white people to labour—the labourer is reduced to the level of slaves. . . .

I have said that no country can support as many human beings where slavery exists, as it would do if there was no slavery. We have already seen that population is always restrained and kept down to the means of subsistence. The means of subsistence depends upon the industry of man—the earth yielding more or less abundantly, in proportion to the labour bestowed upon it. It is ordained of God that it shall be so. There certainly needs no argument to prove that slaves are less industrious, and less faithful in their labours, than a free white population who labour for their own benefit, and reap that which they sow, universal experience proves that this is the case. It follows then that slaves will never produce the means of subsistence so abundantly as free whites, and of course so many of them cannot subsist in the same country.

The most important proposition still remains to be examined, which is, *that a slave population increases faster than the white population in a slave state.* A most momentous and alarming proposition this! one which portends more mischief, misery, insurrection, bloodshed and desolation to our country and our race, than any the imagination can conceive, provided the present policy of the southern states in regard to their slaves is still pursued. Who can tell what is to be the issue of this, and where it is to end? If the slave population, increase faster than the white, it will ere long be the most numerous, and not only the most numerous, but vastly the most numerous. And shall ten men be in subjection to one, or will a thousand quietly remain in bondage to an hundred? Such things cannot be—it was not intended by Him who made the black man as well as the white, that such things should be. We may put far off the evil day, but it will surely come upon us or our posterity.—The day of desolation and wrath is sure to overtake us, unless we avert it by a timely reformation of our policy. . . .

The reason then why a slave population increases faster than the white in a slave state, is because their means of subsistence are more abundant. The slaves usually belong to men of wealth, who have the means of supplying them with food, and whose interest it is that the slaves should multiply as fast as possible, at least it is their interest so long as there is a demand for slaves, and the increase of the slaves will always be proportionate to the demand. The greater and more extensive the market, therefore the faster they will increase. They are raised as an article of traffic, the same as cattle and horses and the market regulates the increase of the one in the same manner that it does the other. If the market would justify it, we should see masters promoting the increase of their slaves, treating their breeding slaves with the same care, and nursing their offspring with the same attention and tenderness, that they now bestow upon their breeding mares and their foals. When this comes to be the case we shall find that the slave population will double at least every fifteen or twenty years, and there is nothing wanting to make this the case but an extensive demand and a high market. . . .

The main question still remains to be discussed. That question is the policy of admitting slavery into the new states hereafter to be formed beyond the Mississippi. A more momentous question has never been agitated in Congress—a more momentous question has never been agitated in this country since the declaration of independence. I am aware of its importance—I am aware of the interest it excites in the southern states—I am aware of its delicacy—of the angry feelings it has already produced, and being aware of all these things, I would wish to treat the subject if possible, in a manner calculated to assuage these feelings, and produce reflection and calculation in the thinking part of the community, rather than abuse or evil thinking of these gentlemen who differ with them in opinion, as being actuated with disposition to do a thing either unjust, unconstitutional, or impolitic.

This question naturally divides itself into two branches, 1st, What effect upon those new states will the introduction of slavery produce? 2d, What effect will it produce upon the old slave holding states? In other words, will either the old states or the new, be benefitted by such introduction, or will both be prejudiced by it? I purposely leave out all consideration of the slaves themselves in the discussion of this question. I am willing to discuss it like a politician, without any regard to the iniquity, morality, or injustice, which it may involve. If I show that the introduction of slavery into these states will not only prejudice the new states but the old ones also, I shall expect the southern gentlemen to join heart and hand with the northern, in preventing so great a curse. I expect to be able to do this.

As it regards the first branch of this question, I believe there is very little difference of opinion between the northern and southern gentlemen. It is generally admitted that slavery is a curse to any state, and of course it would be a curse to these new states. The calculations and observations which have been already made, are, I think, sufficient to satisfy any man whose mind is not impervious to the power of argument, of the truth of this fact. Slavery would restrain the increase of the white population in those states which is of itself sufficient to satisfy any man of its injurious tendency, who does not think a slave a more valuable member of society, than a free white citizen. I shall therefore take it for granted, that the introduction of slavery into those states would be a curse to them, and proceed to examine the second branch of the question, to wit: *what effect would the introduction of slavery into these new states have upon the old slave states*. If I show that it would have no good effect—that it would not is the smallest degree alleviate the evil of slavery in those states—I shall show all that will be necessary to secure the cordial co-operation of every honest man in preventing its introduction. It is true there are men who would have slavery introduced into those states for their own individual profit, even though they knew the ruin of the states, both old and new, in the next generation, would be the consequence.—But I hope and trust there are not many, if any such men in Congress. . . .

. . . Suppose then 50,000 slaves were to be annually exported to the western country, would that number in the smallest degree diminish the number in the old states?—not one whit. If that were the case, we should see the planters then using as great exertion to increase their annual product of slaves, as they now are to increase their annual product of sugar and cotton—and we should find that the slaves would re-produce their number every fifteen years. This would be establishing the slave trade in our country with a vengeance. The old states would become a second Africa, overspreading the world with pestilence, misery, and desolation. It is therefore I think plain reasoning a *priori*, that the old slave states would derive no benefit from introducing slaves into the new. . . .

Questions

1. Raymond accuses southern political leaders of failing to do what they *know* to be best for the country. What case does he make? Is he right?
2. Would you say that Raymond would agree with those who were already suggesting that the South was falling short of being truly republican?
3. To what extent was Raymond worried about the presence of *slaves* in Missouri, and to what extent was he worried about the presence of *blacks*?

9-6   Forced Migration to the Cotton South: The Narrative of Charles Ball (1837)

As the cotton boom began to consume the Lower (or Deep) South at the beginning of the nineteenth century, a large and lucrative domestic slave trade sprang up to supply slaves from Virginia and Maryland to the expanding plantations of the Cotton Belt.

Among those caught up in the trade was Charles Ball, a slave in Calvert County, Maryland (Leonard Covington's home county; see Document 8-4), whose master sold him to a trader in the year 1805. Ball was moved, first to central South Carolina, and then to frontier Georgia, before escaping and returning to his family in Maryland. Later recaptured, he escaped again, settling near Philadelphia in the 1830s. There his story was recorded by a sympathetic abolitionist who rendered Ball's narrative in genteel nineteenth-century language and embellished the story with numerous anecdotes about southern society obtained from other sources. For this and other reasons, the veracity of the narrative was sharply attacked at the time by proslavery apologists; however, modern scholars have confirmed that those parts of the narrative dealing with Ball's own experience are consistent with what is known about the times and places he visited. Used with care (as with all the other documents reproduced in this collection), Ball's story provides an extraordinary glimpse at life in the Old South at a critical moment in its development. The excerpts reproduced below recount Ball's sale to the trader in 1805, the conditions of his journey to South Carolina, and his observations of the land and the people along his route.

Source: Charles Ball, *Slavery in the United States: A Narrative of the Life and Adventures of Charles Ball, a Black Man . . .* (New York: John S. Taylor, 1837), 35–39, 41, 44, 50–51, 67–68, 71–73, 79–83.

. . . My master kept a store at a small village on the bank of the Patuxent river, called B——, although he resided at some distance on a farm. One morning he rose early, and ordered me to take a yoke of oxen and go to the village, to bring home a cart which was there, saying he would follow me. He arrived at the village soon after I did, and took his breakfast with his store-keeper. He then told me to come into the house and get my breakfast. Whilst I was eating in the kitchen, I observed him talking earnestly, but lowly, to a stranger near the kitchen door. I soon after went out, and hitched my oxen to the cart, and was about to drive off, when several men came round about me, and amongst them the stranger whom I had seen speaking with my master. This man came up to me, and, seizing me by the collar, shook me violently, saying I was his property, and must go with him to Georgia. At the sound of these words, the thoughts of my wife and children rushed across my mind, and my heart died away within me. I saw and knew that my case was hopeless, and that resistance was vain, as there were near twenty persons present, all of whom were ready to assist the man by whom I was kidnapped. I felt incapable of weeping or speaking, and in my despair I laughed loudly. My purchaser ordered me to cross my hands behind, which were quickly bound with a strong cord; and he then told me that we must set out that very day for the south. I asked if I could not be allowed to go to see my wife and children, or if this could not be permitted, if they might not have leave to come to see me; but was told that I would be able to get another wife in Georgia.

My new master, whose name I did not hear, took me that same day across the Patuxent, where I joined fifty-one other slaves, whom he had bought in Maryland. Thirty-two of these were men, and nineteen were women. The women were merely tied together with a rope, about the size of a bed cord, which was tied like a halter round the neck of each; but the men, of whom I was the stoutest and strongest, were very differently caparisoned. A strong iron collar was closely fitted by means of a padlock round each of our necks. A chain of iron, about a hundred feet in length, was passed through the hasp of each padlock, except at the two ends, where the hasps of the padlocks passed through a link of the chain. In addition to this, we were handcuffed in pairs, with iron staples and bolts, with a short chain, about a foot long, uniting the handcuffs and their wearers in pairs. In this manner we were chained alternately by the right and left hand; and the poor man, to whom I was thus ironed, wept like all infant when the blacksmith, with his heavy hammer, fastened the ends of the bolts that kept the staples from slipping from our arms. For my own part, I felt indifferent to my fate. It appeared to me that the worst had come, that could come, and that no change of fortune could harm me.

After we were all chained and handcuffed together, we sat down upon the ground; and here reflecting upon the sad reverse of fortune that had so suddenly overtaken me, and the dreadful suffering which awaited me, I became weary of life, and bitterly execrated the day I was born. It seemed that I was destined by fate to drink the cup of sorrow to the very dregs, and that I should find no respite from misery but in the grave. I longed to die, and escape from the hands of my tormentors; but even the wretched privilege of destroying myself was denied me; for I could not shake off my chains, nor move a yard without the consent of my master. Reflecting in silence upon my forlorn condition, I at length concluded that as things could not become worse—and as the life of man is but a continued round of changes, they must, of necessity, take a turn in my favour at some future day. I found relief in this vague and indefinite hope, and when we received orders to go on board the scow, which was to transport us over the Patuxent, I marched down to the water with a firmness of purpose of which I did not believe myself capable, a few minutes before.

We were soon on the south side of the river, and taking up our line of march, we travelled about five miles that evening, and stopped for the night at one of those miserable public houses, so frequent in the lower parts of Maryland and Virginia, called *"ordinaries."*

Our master ordered a pot of mush to be made for our supper; after despatching which, we all lay down on the naked floor to sleep in our handcuffs and chains. The women, my fellow-slaves, lay on one side of the room; and the men who were chained with me, occupied the other. I slept but little this night, which I passed in thinking of my wife and little children, whom I could not hope ever to see again. I also thought of my grandfather, and of the long nights I had passed with him, listening to his narratives of the scenes through which he had passed in Africa. . . .

From this time, to the end of our journey southward, we all slept, promiscuously, men and women, on the floors of such houses as we chanced to stop at. We had no clothes except those we wore, and a few blankets; the larger portion of our gang being in rags at the time we crossed the Potomac. Two of the women were pregnant; the one far advanced—and she already complained of inability to keep pace with our march; but her complaints were disregarded. We crossed the Rappahannock at Port Royal, and afterwards passed through the village of Bowling Green; a place with which I became better acquainted in after times; but which now presented the quiet so common to all the small towns in Virginia, and indeed in all the southern states. . . .

In Virginia, it appeared to me that the slaves were more rigorously treated than they were in my native place. It is easy to tell a man of colour who is poorly fed, from one who is well supplied with food, by his personal appearance. A half-starved negro is a miserable looking creature. His skin becomes dry, and appears to be sprinkled over with whitish husks, or scales; the glossiness of his face vanishes, his hair loses its colour, becomes dry, and when stricken with a rod, the dust flies from it. These signs of bad treatment I perceived to be very common in Virginia; many young girls who would have been beautiful, if they had been allowed enough to eat, had lost all their prettiness through mere starvation; their fine glossy hair had become of a reddish colour, and stood out round their heads like long brown wool. . . .

As I advanced southward, even in Virginia, I perceived that the state of cultivation became progressively worse. Here, as in Maryland, the practice of the best farmers who cultivate grain, of planting the land every alternate year in corn, and sowing it in wheat or rye in the autumn of the same year in which the corn is planted, and whilst the corn is yet standing in the field, so as to get a crop from the same ground every year, without allowing it time to rest or recover, exhausts the finest soil in a few years, and in one or two generations reduces the proprietors to poverty. Some, who are supposed to be very superior farmers, only plant the land in corn once in three years; sowing it in wheat or rye as in the former case; however, without any covering of clover or other grass to protect it from the rays of the sun. The culture of tobacco prevails over a large portion of Virginia, especially south of James river, to the exclusion of almost every other crop, except corn. This destructive crop ruins the best land in a short time; and in all the lower parts of Maryland and Virginia the traveller will see large old family mansions, of weather-beaten and neglected appearance, standing in the middle of vast fields of many hundred acres, the fences of which have rotted away, and have been replaced by a wattled work in place of a fence, composed of short cedar stakes driven into the ground, about two feet apart, and standing about three feet above the earth, the intervals being filled up by branches cut from the cedar trees, and worked into the stakes horizontally, after the manner of splits in a basket. . . .

As we approached the Yadkin river, the tobacco disappeared from the fields, and the cotton plant took its place, as an article of general culture. We passed the Yadkin by a ferry, on Sunday morning; and on the Wednesday following, in the evening, our master told us we were in the state of South Carolina. We staid this night in a small town called Lancaster; and I shall never forget the sensations which I experienced this evening, on finding myself in chains, in the state of South Carolina. From my earliest recollections, the name of South Carolina had been little less terrible to me than that of the bottomless pit. In Maryland, it had always been the practice of masters and mistresses, who wished to terrify their slaves, to threaten to sell them to South Carolina; where, it was represented, that their condition would be a hundred fold worse than it was in Maryland. I had regarded such a sale of myself, as the greatest of evils that could befall me, and had striven to demean myself in such manner, to my owners, as to preclude them from all excuse for transporting me to so horrid a place. At length I found myself, without having committed any crime, or even the slightest transgression, in the place and condition, of which I had, through life, entertained the greatest dread. I slept but little this night, and for the first time felt weary of life. . . .

. . . Early in the morning, our master called us up; and distributed to each of the party, a cake made of corn meal, and a small piece of bacon. On our journey, we had only eaten twice a day, and had not received breakfast until about nine o'clock; but he said this morning meal was given to welcome us to South Carolina. He then addressed us all, and told us we might now give up all hope of ever returning to the places of our nativity; as it would be impossible for us to pass through the states of North Carolina and Virginia, without being taken up and sent back. He further advised us to make ourselves contented, as he would take us to Georgia, a far better country than any we had seen; and where we would be able to live in the greatest abundance. About sunrise we took up our march on the road to Columbia, as we were told. Hitherto our master had not offered to sell any of us, and had even refused to stop to talk to any one on the subject of our sale, although he had several times been addressed on this point, before we reached Lancaster; but soon after we departed from this village, we were overtaken on the road by a man on horseback, who accosted our driver by asking him if his *niggers* were for sale. The latter replied, that he believed he would not sell any yet, as he was on his way to Georgia, and cotton being now much in demand, he expected to obtain high prices for us from persons who were going to settle in the new purchase. He, however, contrary to his custom, ordered us to stop, and told the stranger he might look at us, and that he would find us as fine a lot of hands, as were ever imported into the country—that we were all prime property, and he had no doubt would command his own prices in Georgia.

The stranger, who was a thin, weather-beaten, sunburned figure, then said, he wanted a couple of breeding-wenches, and would give as much for them as they would bring in Georgia—that he had lately heard from Augusta, and that *niggers* were not higher there than in Columbia and, as he had been in Columbia the week before, he knew what *niggers* were worth. He then walked along our line, as we stood chained together, and looked at the whole of us—then turning to the women, asked the prices of the two pregnant ones. Our master replied, that these were two of the best breeding-wenches in all Maryland—that one was twenty-two, and the other only nineteen—that the first was already the mother of seven children, and the other of four—that he had himself seen the children at the time he bought their mothers—and that such wenches would be cheap at a thousand dollars each; but as they were not able to keep up with the gang, he would take twelve hundred dollars for the two. The purchaser said this was too much, but that he would give nine hundred dollars for the pair. This price was promptly refused; but our master, after some consideration, said he was willing to sell a bargain in these wenches, and would take eleven hundred dollars for them, which was objected to on the other side; and many faults and failings were pointed out in the merchandise. After much bargaining, and many gross jests on the part of the stranger, he offered a thousand dollars for the two; and said he would give no more. He then mounted his horse, and moved off; but after he had gone about one hundred yards, he was called back; and our master said, if he would go with him to the next blacksmith's shop on the road to Columbia, and pay for taking the irons off the rest of us, he might have the two women. . . .

The landlord assured my master that at this time slaves were much in demand, both in Columbia and Augusta; that purchasers were numerous and prices good; and that the best plan of effecting good sales would be to put up each *nigger*, separately, at auction, after giving a few days' notice, by an advertisement, in the neighbouring country. Cotton, he said, had not been higher for many years, and as a great many persons, especially young men, were moving off to the new purchase in Georgia, prime hands were in high demand, for the purpose of clearing the land in the new country—that the boys and girls, under twenty, would bring almost any price at present, in Columbia, for the purpose of picking the growing crop of cotton, which promised to be very heavy; and as most persons had planted more than their hands would be able to pick, young *niggers,* who would soon learn to pick cotton, were prime articles in the market. As to those more advanced in life, he seemed to think the prospect of selling them at an unusual price, not so good, as they could not so readily become expert cotton-pickers—he said further, that from some cause, which he could not comprehend, the price of rice had not been so good this year as usual; and that he had found it cheaper to purchase rice to feed his own *niggers* than to provide them with corn, which had to be brought from the upper country. He therefore, advised my master, not to drive us towards the rice plantation of the low country. My master said he would follow his advice, at least so far as to sell a portion of us in Carolina, but seemed to be of opinion that his prime hands would bring him more money in Georgia, and named me, in particular, as one who would be worth, at least, a thousand dollars, to a man who was about making a settlement, and clearing a plantation in the new purchase. . . . For several days past, I had observed that in the country through which we travelled, little attention was paid to the cultivation of any thing but cotton. Now this plant was almost the sole possessor of the fields. It covered the plantations adjacent to the road, as far as I could see, both before and behind me, and looked not unlike buckwheat before it blossoms. I saw some small fields of corn, and lots of sweet potatoes, amongst which the young vines of the water-melon were frequently visible. The improvements on the plantations were not good. There were no barns, but only stables and sheds, to put the cotton under, as it was brought from the field. Hay seemed to be unknown in the country, for I saw neither hay-stacks nor meadows; and the few fields that were lying fallow, had but small numbers of cattle in them, and these were thin and meagre. We had met with no flocks of sheep of late, and the hogs that we saw on the road-side, were in bad condition. The horses and mules that I saw at work in the cotton-fields, were poor and badly harnessed, and the half-naked condition of the negroes, who drove them, or followed with the hoe, together with their wan complexions, proved to me that they had too much work, or not enough food. We passed a cotton-gin this morning, the first that I ever saw; but they were not at work with it. We also met a party of ladies and gen-tlemen on a journey of pleasure, riding in two very hand-some carriages, drawn by sleek and spirited horses, very different in appearance from the moving skeletons that I had noticed drawing the ploughs in the fields. The black drivers of the coaches were neatly clad in gay-coloured clothes, and contrasted well with their half-naked brethren, a gang of whom were hoeing cotton by the road-side, near them, attended by an overseer in a white linen shirt and pantaloons, with one of the long negro whips in his hand.

I observed that these poor people did not raise their heads, to look either at the fine coaches and horses then passing, or at us; but kept their faces steadily bent towards the cotton-plants, from among which they were removing the weeds. I almost shuddered at the sight, knowing, that I myself was doomed to a state of servitude, equally cruel and debasing, unless, by some unforeseen occurrence, I might fall into the hands of a master of less inhumanity of temper than the one who had possession of the miserable creatures before me.

It was manifest, that I was now in a country, where the life of a black man was no more regarded than that of an ox, except as far as the man was worth the more money in the market. On all the plantations that we passed, there was a want of live stock of every description, except slaves, and they were deplorably abundant. . . .

Questions

1. Compare Ball's experience with what you know about the experience of Leonard Covington's slaves (Document 8-4). All in all, how would you characterize the impact on slaves of this sort of westward movement?
2. Why do you think Ball regarded "the name of South Carolina" as "little less terri-ble . . . than that of the bottomless pit"?
3. How would you characterize the whites depicted in these excerpts? Do they fit your prior understandings of the character of southern slaveholders?

9-7   Slave Management on a Mississippi Plantation (1852)

Frederick Law Olmsted

In the years before the Civil War, a number of journalists traveled through the South, reporting their observations on the lives and labors of slaves and their masters. The keenest of these observers was Frederick Law Olmsted, who first journeyed through the South in 1852 on a commission from the *New York Times*. In the following excerpt Olmsted describes an extremely large cotton plantation in Mississippi. The basic prin-ciples of its organization, notably the use of labor in highly regimented gangs, were de-veloped in the early nineteenth century, when cotton became, for the first time, the major staple crop of the slave South. While Olmsted made his observations much later, near the close of the slave-plantation era, his comments on the plantation system and its operations were so acute that they bear examination here.

Source: Frederick Law Olmsted, *A Journey in the Back Country* (New York: Mason Brothers, 1860; reprint, Williamstown, Mass.: Corner House Publishers, 1972), 72–83.

SLAVE MANAGEMENT ON THE LARGEST SCALE

The estate I am now about to describe, was situated upon a tributary of the Mississippi, and accessible only by occa-sional steamboats; even this mode of communication being frequently interrupted at low stages of the rivers. The slaves upon it formed about one twentieth of the whole population of the county, in which the blacks considerably out-number the whites. . . .

The property consisted of four adjoining plantations, each with its own negro-cabins, stables and overseer, and each worked to a great extent independently of the others, but all contributing their crop to one [cotton] gin-house and warehouse, and all under the general superintendence of a bailiff or manager, who constantly resided upon the estate, and in the absence of the owner, had vice-regal power over the overseers, controlling, so far as he thought fit, the economy of all the plantations. . . .

. . . The overseers were superior to most of their class, and, with one exception, frank, honest, temperate and industrious, but their feelings toward negroes were such as naturally result from their occupation. They were all married, and lived with their families, each in a cabin or cottage, in the hamlet of the slaves of which he had especial charge. Their wages varied from $500 to $1,000 a year each. . . .

. . . Of course, to secure their own personal safety and to efficiently direct the labor of such a large number of ignorant, indolent, and vicious negroes, rules, or rather habits and customs, of discipline, were necessary, which would in particular cases be liable to operate unjustly and cruelly. It is apparent, also, that, as the testimony of negroes against them would not be received as evidence in court, that there was very little probability that any excessive severity would be restrained by fear of the law. A provision of the law intended to secure a certain privilege to slaves, was indeed disregarded under my own observation, and such infraction of the law was confessedly customary with one of the overseers, and was permitted by the manager, for the reason that it seemed to him to be, in a certain degree, justifiable and expedient under the circumstances, and because he did not like to interfere unnecessarily in such matters.

In the main, the negroes appeared to be well taken care of and abundantly supplied with the necessaries of vigorous physical existence. A large part of them lived in commodious and well-built cottages, with broad galleries in front, so that each family of five had two rooms on the lower floor, and a loft. The remainder lived in log-huts, small and mean in appearance, but those of their overseers were little better, and preparations were being made to replace all of these by neat boarded cottages. Each family had a fowl-house and hog-sty (constructed by the negroes themselves), and kept fowls and swine, feeding the latter during the summer on weeds and fattening them in the autumn on corn *stolen* (this was mentioned to me by the overseers as if it were a matter of course) from their master's corn-fields. I several times saw gangs of them eating the dinner which they had brought, each for himself, to the field, and observed that they generally had plenty, often more than they could eat, of bacon, corn-bread, and molasses. The allowance of food is weighed and measured under the eye of the manager by the drivers, and distributed to the head of each family weekly: consisting of—for each person, 3 pounds of pork, 1 peck [8 quarts] of meal; and from January to July, 1 quart of molasses. Monthly, in addition, 1 pound tobacco, and 4 pints salt. No drink is ever served but water, except after unusual exposure, or to ditchers working in water, who get a glass of whisky at

night. All hands cook for themselves after work at night, or whenever they please between nightfall and daybreak, each family in its own cabin. Each family had a garden, the products of which, together with eggs, fowls and bacon, they frequently sold, or used in addition to their regular allowance of food. Most of the families bought a barrel of flour every year. The manager endeavored to encourage this practice, and that they might spend their money for flour instead of liquor, he furnished it to them at rather less than what it cost him at wholesale. There were many poor whites within a few miles who would always sell liquor to the negroes, and encourage them to steal, to obtain the means to buy it of them. These poor whites were always spoken of with anger by the overseers, and they each had a standing offer of much more than the intrinsic value of their land, from the manager, to induce them to move away. . . .

Near the first quarters we visited there was a large blacksmith's and wheelwright's shop, in which a number of mechanics were at work. Most of them, as we rode up, were eating their breakfast, which they warmed at their fires. Within and around the shop there were some fifty plows which they were putting in order. The manager inspected the work, found some of it faulty, sharply reprimanded the workmen for not getting on faster, and threatened one of them with a whipping for not paying closer attention to the directions which had been given him. He told me that he once employed a white man from the North, who professed to be a first-class workman, but he soon found he could not do nearly as good work as the negro mechanics on the estate, and the latter despised him so much, and got such high opinions of themselves in consequence of his inferiority, that he had been obliged to discharge him in the midst of his engagement.

HOURS OF LABOR

Each overseer regulated the hours of work on his own plantation. I saw the negroes at work before sunrise and after sunset. At about eight o'clock they were allowed to stop for breakfast, and again about noon, to dine. The length of these rests was at the discretion of the overseer or drivers, usually, I should say, from half an hour to an hour. There was no rule.

OVERSEERS

The number of hands directed by each overseer was considerably over one hundred. The manager thought it would be better economy to have a white man over every fifty hands, but the difficulty of obtaining trustworthy overseers prevented it. Three of those he then had were the best he had ever known. He described the great majority as being passionate, careless, inefficient men, generally intemperate, and totally unfitted for the duties of the position.

The best overseers, ordinarily, are young men, the sons of small planters, who take up the business temporarily, as a means of acquiring a little capital with which to purchase negroes for themselves.

PLOW-GIRLS

The plowing, both with single and double mule teams, was generally performed by women, and very well performed, too. I watched with some interest for any indication that their sex unfitted them for the occupation. Twenty of them were plowing together, with double teams and heavy plows. They were superintended by a male negro driver, who carried a whip, which he frequently cracked at them, permitting no dawdling or delay at the turning; and they twitched their plows around on the head-land, jerking their reins, and yelling to their mules, with apparent ease, energy, and rapidity. Throughout the Southwest the negroes, as a rule, appear to be worked much harder than in the eastern and northern slave States. I do not think they accomplish as much daily, as agricultural laborers at the North usually do, but they certainly labor much harder, and more unremittingly. They are constantly and steadily driven up to their work, and the stupid, plodding, machine-like manner in which they labor, is painful to witness. This was especially the case with the hoe-gangs. One of them numbered nearly two hundred hands (for the force of two plantations was working together), moving across the field in parallel lines, with a considerable degree of precision. I repeatedly rode through the lines at a canter, with other horsemen, often coming upon them suddenly, without producing the smallest change or interruption in the dogged action of the laborers, or causing one of them to lift an eye from the ground. A very tall and powerful negro

walked to and fro in the rear of the line, frequently cracking his whip, and calling out, in the surliest manner, to one and another, "Shove your hoe, there! shove your hoe!" But I never saw him strike any one with the whip.

DISCIPLINE

The whip was evidently in constant use, however. There were no rules on the subject, that I learned; the overseers and drivers punished the negroes whenever they deemed it necessary, and in such manner, and with such severity, as they thought fit. "If you do n't work faster," or "If you do n't work better," or "If you do n't recollect what I tell you, I will have you flogged," are threats which I have often heard. I said to one of the overseers, "It must be very disagreeable to have to punish them as much as you do?" "Yes, it would be to those who are not used to it—but it's my business, and I think nothing of it. Why, sir, I would n't mind killing a nigger more than I would a dog." I asked if he had ever killed a negro? "Not quite," he said, but overseers were often obliged to. Some negroes are determined never to let a white man whip them, and will resist you, when you attempt it; of course you must kill them in that case. Once a negro, whom he was about to whip in the field, struck at his head with a hoe. He parried the blow with his whip, and drawing a pistol tried to shoot him, but the pistol missing fire he rushed in and knocked him down with the butt of it. At another time a negro whom he was punishing, insulted and threatened him. He went to the house for his gun, and as he was returning, the negro, thinking he would be afraid of spoiling so valuable a piece of property by firing, broke for the woods. He fired at once, and put six buck-shot into his hips. He always carried a bowie-knife, but not a pistol.

Questions

1. Does the plantation Olmsted describes more resemble a great landed estate or a modern factory?
2. Do you think the treatment of slaves on this plantation was typical of cotton plantations in the South? Would it apply to plantations growing other crops, such as rice, sugar, or tobacco?
3. Olmsted is seeking to be an "objective" reporter here. Can you determine from this passage his own views of slavery?

9-8   Religion in the Quarters (1832)

Nat Turner

Among the major influences shaping the culture of American slaves in the early nineteenth century was their widespread adoption of evangelical Protestant Christianity. Christianity, as the "masters' religion," had made little headway among slaves before evangelical preachers such as the Reverend James Ireland (Document 4-7) began making special appeals to them. The demonstrative conversion experiences characteristic of camp meetings such as that at Cane Ridge (Document 9-9) resembled in some ways African beliefs in spirit possession. More importantly, though, evangelicals preached the equality of all human beings before God and declared that social status counted for nothing in the scales of salvation. To be sure, white evangelicals drew back quickly from the more radical implications of this stance, but the slaves took it to heart and created their own distinctive brand of Christianity—a faith that has lain at the core of the African American cultural experience ever since. To some degree it helped slaves accommodate to their situation by counseling patience until the Lord should call his children out of Egypt. But what would happen if God in fact called? In that case, slave religion could take the faithful in unexpected directions—as it did with Nat Turner, who in 1831 led the greatest slave rebellion of the antebellum era (text pp. 399–400). The following is his own account, dictated in his jail cell.

Source: Kenneth S. Greenberg, ed., *The Confessions of Nat Turner and Related Documents* (Boston: Bedford/St. Martin's, 1996), 44–48.

Agreeable to his own appointment, on the evening he was committed to prison, with permission of the jailer, I visited NAT on Tuesday the 1st November, when, without being questioned at all, he commenced his narrative in the following words:—

Sir,—You have asked me to give a history of the motives which induced me to undertake the late insurrection, as you call it—To do so I must go back to the days of my infancy, and even before I was born. I was thirty-one years of age the 2d of October last, and born the property of Benj. Turner, of this county. In my childhood a circumstance occurred which made an indelible impression on my mind, and laid the ground work of that enthusiasm, which has terminated so fatally to many, both white and black, and for which I am about to atone at the gallows. It is here necessary to relate this circumstance—trifling as it may seem, it was the commencement of that belief which has grown with time, and even now, sir, in this dungeon, helpless and forsaken as I am, I cannot divest myself of. Being at play with other children, when three or four years old, I was telling them something, which my mother overhearing, said it had happened before I was born—I stuck to my story, however, and related somethings which went, in her opinion, to confirm it—others being called on were greatly astonished, knowing that these things had happened, and caused them to say in my hearing, I surely would be a prophet, as the Lord had shewn me things that had happened before my birth. And my father and mother strengthened me in this my first impression, saying in my presence, I was intended for some great purpose, which they had always thought from certain marks on my head and breast—[a parcel of excrescences which I believe are not at all uncommon, particularly among negroes, as I have seen several with the same. In this case he has either cut them off or they have nearly disappeared]—My grandmother, who was very religious, and to whom I was much attached—my master, who belonged to the church, and other religious persons who visited the house, and whom I often saw at prayers, noticing the singularity of my manners, I suppose, and my uncommon intelligence for a child, remarked I had too much sense to be raised, and if I was, I would never be of any service to any one as a slave—To a mind like mine, restless, inquisitive and observant of every thing that was passing, it is easy to suppose that religion was the subject to which it would be directed, and although this subject principally occupied my thoughts—there was nothing that I saw or heard of to which my attention was not directed—The manner in which I learned to read and write, not only had great influence on my own mind, as I acquired it with the most perfect ease, so much so, that I have no recollection whatever of learning the alphabet—but to the astonishment of the family, one day, when a book was shewn me to keep me from crying, I began spelling the names of different objects—this was a source of wonder to all in the neighborhood, particularly the blacks—and this learning was constantly improved at all opportunities—when I got large enough to go to work, while employed, I was reflecting on many things that would present themselves to my imagination, and whenever an opportunity occurred of looking at a book, when the school children were getting their lessons, I would find many things that the fertility of my imagination had depicted to me before; all my time, not devoted to my master's service, was spent either in prayer, or in making experiments in casting different things in moulds made of earth, in attempting to make paper, gunpowder, and many other experiments, that although I could not perfect, yet convinced me of its practicability if I had the means. I was not addicted to stealing in my youth, nor have ever been—Yet such was the confidence of the negroes in the neighborhood, even at this early period of my life, in my superior judgment, that they would often carry me with them when they were going on any roguery, to plan for them. Growing up among them, with this confidence in my superior judgment, and when this, in their opinions, was perfected by Divine inspiration, from the circumstances already alluded to in my infancy, and which belief was ever afterwards zealously inculcated by the austerity of my life and manners, which became the subject of remark by white and black.—Having soon discovered to be great, I must appear so, and therefore studiously avoided mixing in with society, and wrapped myself in mystery, devoting my time to fasting and prayer—By this time, having arrived to man's estate, and hearing the scriptures commented on at meetings, I was struck with that particular passage which says: "Seek ye the kingdom of Heaven and all things shall be added unto you." I reflected much on this passage, and prayed daily for light on this subject—As I was praying one day at my plough, the spirit spoke to me, saying "Seek ye the kingdom of Heaven and all things shall be added unto you. ["] *Question*—what do you mean by the Spirit. *Ans.* The Spirit that spoke to that prophets in former days—and I was greatly astonished, and for two years prayed continually, whenever my duty would permit—and then again I had the same revelation, which fully confirmed me in the impression that I was ordained for some great purpose in the hands of the Almighty. Several years rolled round, in which many events occurred to strengthen me in this my belief. At this time I reverted in my mind to the remarks made of me in my childhood, and the things that had been shewn me—and as it had been said of me in my childhood by those by whom I had been taught to pray, both white and black, and in whom I had the greatest confidence, that I had too much sense to be raised, and if I was, I would never be of use to any one as a slave. Now finding I had arrived to man's estate, and was a slave, and these revelations being made known to me, I began to direct my attention to this great object, to fulfil the purpose for which, by this time, I felt assured I was intended. Knowing the influence I had obtained over the minds of my fellow servants, (not by the means of conjuring and such like tricks—for to them I always spoke of such things with contempt) but by the communion of the Spirit whose revelations I often communicated to them, and they believed and said my wisdom came from God. I now began to prepare them for my purpose, by telling them something was about to happen that would terminate in fulfilling the great promise that had been made to me—About this time I was placed under an overseer, from whom I ran away—and after remaining in the woods thirty days, I returned, to the astonishment of the negroes on the plantation, who thought I had made my escape to some other part of the country, as my father had done before. But the reason of my return was, that the Spirit appeared to me and said I had my wishes directed to the things of this world, and not

to the kingdom of Heaven, and that I should return to the service of my earthly master—"For he who knoweth his Master's will, and doeth it not, shall be beaten with many stripes, and thus have I chastened you." And the negroes found fault, and murmured against me, saying that if they had my sense they would not serve any master in the world. And about this time I had a vision—and I saw white spirits and black spirits engaged in battle, and the sun was darkened—the thunder rolled in the Heavens, and blood flowed in streams—and I heard a voice saying, "Such is your luck, such you are called to see, and let it come rough or smooth, you must surely bare it." I now withdrew myself as much as my situation would permit, from the intercourse of my fellow servants, for the avowed purpose of serving the Spirit more fully—and it appeared to me, and reminded me of the things it had already shown me, and that it would then reveal to me the knowledge of the elements, the revolution of the planets, the operation of tides, and changes of the seasons. After this revelation in the year 1825, and the knowledge of the elements being made known to me, I sought more than ever to obtain true holiness before the great day of judgment should appear, and then I began to receive the true knowledge of faith. And from the first steps of righteousness until the last, was I made perfect; and the Holy Ghost was with me, and said, "Behold me as I stand in the Heavens"—and I looked and saw the forms of men in different attitudes—and there were lights in the sky to which the children of darkness gave other names than what they really were—for they were the lights of the Saviour's hands, stretched forth from east to west, even as they were extended on the cross on Calvary for the redemption of sinners. And I wondered greatly at these miracles, and prayed to be informed of a certainty of the meaning thereof—and shortly afterwards, while laboring in the field, I discovered drops of blood on the corn as though it were dew from heaven—and I communicated it to many, both white and black, in the neighborhood—and I then found on the leaves in the woods hieroglyphic characters, and numbers, with the forms of men in different attitudes, portrayed in blood, and representing the figures I had seen before in the heavens. And now the Holy Ghost had revealed itself to me, and made plain the miracles it had shown me—For as the blood of Christ had been shed on this earth, and had ascended to heaven for the salvation of sinners, and was now returning to earth again in the form of dew—and as the leaves on the trees bore the impression of the figures I had seen in the heavens, it was plain to me that the Saviour was about to lay down the yoke he had borne for the sins of men, and the great day of judgment was at hand. About this time I told these things to a white man, (Etheldred T. Brantley) on whom it had a wonderful effect—and he ceased from his wickedness, and was attacked immediately with a cutaneous eruption, and blood oozed from the pores of his skin, and after praying and fasting nine days, he was healed, and the Spirit appeared to me again, and said, as the Saviour had been baptized so should we be also—and when the white people would not let us be baptised by the church, we went down into the water together, in the sight of many who reviled us, and were baptised by the Spirit— After this I rejoiced greatly, and gave thanks to God. And on the 12th of May, 1828, I heard a loud noise in the heavens, and the Spirit instantly appeared to me and said the Serpent was loosened, and Christ had laid down the yoke he had borne for the sins of men, and that I should take it on and fight against the Serpent, for the time was fast approaching when the first should be last and the last should be first. *Ques.* Do you not find yourself mistaken now? *Ans.* Was not Christ crucified. And by signs in the heavens that it would make known to me when I should commence the great work—and until the first sign appeared, I should conceal it from the knowledge of men—And on the appearance of the sign, (the eclipse of the sun last February) I should arise and prepare myself, and slay my enemies with their own weapons. And immediately on the sign appearing in the heavens, the seal was removed from my lips, and I communicated the great work laid out for me to do, to four in whom I had the greatest confidence. (Henry, Hark, Nelson, and Sam)—It was intended by us to have begun the work of death on the 4th July last—Many were the plans formed and rejected by us, and it affected my mind to such a degree, that I fell sick, and the time passed without our coming to any determination how to commence—Still forming new schemes and rejecting them, when the sign appeared again, which determined me not to wait longer. . . .

Questions

1. What attracted Nat Turner to the "calling" of a slave preacher?
2. What can you deduce from this passage about the relationship of Turner and his fellow slave Christians to the whites around them?
3. In what ways does Turner compare himself to Jesus Christ?

Questions for Further Thought

1. Historians have been sharply divided over the character of the nineteenth-century South, with some describing it as "aristocratic" and others viewing it as essentially similar to the larger American society but with a peculiarly nasty twist. Considering these documents and those in the preceding section, how different would you say the South was from the Northeast at this time?
2. Daniel Raymond calls slavery a "poisonous plant . . . overshadowing, choking, and finally destroying every thing within the sphere of its influence." By this he meant far more than its effects on African American slaves. What were the larger effects of slavery on the American landscape, and why did people like Raymond fear its expansion?
3. Prior to the American Revolution, slavery was common to all the colonies. By 1820, those states north of the Ohio River and the Mason-Dixon Line had either abolished it or committed themselves to its ultimate extinction. Accordingly, discussions of the relative merits of slavery and free labor increasingly involved comparisons of North and South. What regional stereotypes do you see coming into play in these discussions?

Protestant Christianity as a Social Force

The so-called Great Awakening of the eighteenth century had introduced to America the variant of Protestant Christianity we call *evangelicalism*—a form of Christian faith that stressed emotion over doctrinal correctness, judged people less by their social station or their education than by the genuineness of their "call," and demanded of all believers that they work to share the "good news" with others. In the years following the Revolution, massive social change, most especially the surge of white settlers into the

West, brought on a countermovement to bring order to the new societies. A new evangelizing institution, the camp meeting, brought thousands together in massive displays of religious fervor. While many outside observers were appalled or bemused by the reported excesses of these revivals, they introduced a new order to the frontier, recruiting large numbers of souls into local congregations (Document 9-9). While older churches had been organized from the top down, the newer congregations were voluntary societies that joined together into a new kind of church, the *denomination*. Denominations existed less to enforce orthodoxy than to organize missionary efforts to combat what they feared was the rampant infidelity and social chaos accompanying geographic and economic expansion. In time, religious folk began to organize across denominational lines, creating a "benevolent empire" of national organizations. These denominations and agencies printed newspapers, Bibles, books, and tracts; spread them across the nation through the postal system and their networks of local affiliates; and deployed armies of missionaries both at home and abroad. In so doing, they played a major role in tying Americans together into a national community (Document 9-10).

Thanks to both revival enthusiasm and organizational genius, evangelical precepts increasingly pervaded American life; biblical themes and rhetoric shaped the ways in which Americans understood their world and discussed it with each other. Evangelicals were pleased at this development but wished to go much further. While they were happy to live in a land without an established church, they nonetheless believed that public, as well as private, life should be dominated by their own understanding of Christian principles and sought to use their organizational skills and their hold on public opinion to Christianize politics (Document 9-11). Theirs was hardly a pluralistic vision of the promise of America, for it shut out not only non-Christians but Roman Catholics as well. But it also made the evangelical mission one of saving society as well as individuals. If Americans were in fact a new chosen people of God, their country needed to conform to God's will—a notion that in the hands of a Frederick Douglass, an Abraham Lincoln, or a Martin Luther King would become a powerful force for change.

9-9   Defending the Revival at Cane Ridge, Kentucky (1802)

Reverend George Baxter

The meeting held at Cane Ridge, Kentucky, in August 1801 was the signature event of the Second Great Awakening. Originally meant to be an outdoor communion service of the sort that frontier Presbyterians had brought from their homelands in Scotland and Ireland, it drew hosts of settlers from far and wide to camp in the vicinity. Thousands experienced conversion, often accompanied by spectacular emotional and physical displays. Cane Ridge quickly became nationally notorious for the behavior of those attending. More orthodox Calvinist ministers expressed grave concern at the proceedings, especially given the accounts of sensuous singing and dancing and reports of sexual excesses, which suggested that the revival was at best a mass delusion and at worst the product of demonic possession. A distinguished eastern Presbyterian, Reverend George Baxter, the principal of Washington Academy in Virginia (now Washington and Lee University), traveled to the area in the fall of 1801 to assess the aftermath of the revival and to assure his skeptical colleagues that it was in fact the work of the Holy Spirit.

Source: W. W. Woodward, ed., *Increase of Piety, or the Revival of Religion in the United States of America . . .* (Philadelphia: W. W. Woodward, 1802), 57–66.

In the older settlement of Kentucky the revival made its first appearance among the Presbyterians last spring; the whole of that country about a year before was remarkable for vice and dissipation; and I have been credibly informed that a decided majority of the people were professed infidels. During the last winter appearances were favourable among the *Baptists,* and great numbers were added to their churches: early in the spring, the ministrations of the Presbyterian Clergy began to be better attended than they had been for many years before. Their worshipping assemblies became more solemn, and the people after they were dismissed shewed a strange reluctance at leaving the place: they generally continued some time in the meeting-house—in singing or in religious conversation. Perhaps about the last of May or the first of June the awakenings became general in some congregations, and spread through the country in every direction with amazing rapidity. I left that country about the first of November, at which time this revival in connexion with the one on Cumberland had covered the whole state, excepting a small settlement which borders on the waters of Green-river, in which no Presbyterian ministers are settled; and I believe very few of any denomination. The power with which this revival has spread; and its influence in moralizing the people, are difficult for you to conceive of, and more difficult for me to describe. I had heard many accounts and seen many letters respecting it before I went to that country; but my expectations though greatly raised were much below the reality of the work. The congregations, when engaged in worship, presented scenes of solemnity superior to what I had ever seen before; and in private houses it was no uncommon thing to hear parents relate to strangers the wonderful things which God had done in their neighbourhoods, whilst a large circle of young people would be in tears. On my way to Kentucky I was told by settlers on the road, that the character of Kentucky travellers was entirely changed, and that they were now as distinguished for sobriety as they had formerly been dissoluteness; and indeed I found Kentucky the most moral place I had ever been in; a profane expression was hardly heard; a religious awe seemed to pervade the country; and some Deistical characters had confessed that from whatever cause the revival might originate, it certainly made the people better.—Its influence was not less visible in promoting a friendly temper; nothing could appear more amiable than that undissembled benevolence which governs the subjects of this work: I have often wished that the mere politician or Deist could observe with impartiality their peaceful and amicable spirit. He would certainly see that nothing could equal the religion of JESUS, for promoting even the temporal happiness of society—some neighbourhoods visited by the revival had been formerly notorious for private animosities; and many petty law-suits had commenced on that ground. When the parties in these quarrels were impressed with religion, the first thing was to send for their antagonists; and it was often very affect-

ing to see their meeting. Both had seen their faults, and both contended that they ought to make concessions, till at last they were obliged to request each other to forbear all mention of the past, and to act as friends and brothers for the future. Now sir, let modern philosophists talk of reforming the world by banishing Christianity and introducing their licentious systems. The blessed gospel of our God and Saviour is shewing what it can do.

Some circumstances have concurred to distinguish the Kentucky revival from most others, of which we have had any account, I mean the largeness of the assemblies of sacramental occasions.

The length of the time they continued on the ground in devotional exercises. And the great numbers who have fallen down under religious impressions,—on each of these particulars I shall make some remarks.

With respect to the largeness of the assemblies. It is generally supposed that at many places there were not fewer than 8, 10, or 12 thousand people—at a place called Cane Ridge meeting-house, many are of opinion there were at least 20 thousand, there were 140 waggons which came loaded with people, besides other wheel carriages. Some persons had come 200 miles. The largeness of these assemblies was an inconvenience—they were too numerous to be addressed by one speaker, it therefore became necessary for several ministers to officiate at the same time at different stands: this afforded an opportunity to those who were but slightly impressed with religion to wander to and fro between the different places of worship which created an appearance of confusion, and gave ground to such as were unfriendly to the work to charge it with disorder. Another cause also conduced to the same effect; about this time the people began to fall down in great numbers under serious impressions: this was a new thing among Presbyterians; it excited universal astonishment, and created a curiosity which could not be restrained when people *fell* even during the most solemn parts of divine service; those who stood near were so extremely anxious to see how they were affected, that they often crouded about them so as to disturb the worship.—But these causes of disorder were soon removed; different sacraments were appointed on the same Sabbath, which divided the people; and the falling down became so familiar as to excite no disturbance.

In October I attended three Sacraments, at each there were supposed to be 4 or 5 thousand people, and every thing was conducted with strict propriety; when persons fell, those who were near took care of them, and every thing continued quiet until the worship was concluded.

The length of time that people continue at the places of worship, is another important circumstance of the Kentucky revival; at Cane Ridge they met on Friday and continued till Wednesday evening, night and day without intermission, either in public or private exercises of devotion; and with such earnestness that heavy showers of rain were not sufficient to disperse them. On other Sacramental occasions they generally continued on the ground until Monday or Tuesday evening; and had not the preachers been exhausted and obliged to retire, or had they chosen to prolong the worship they might have kept the people any length of time they pleased, and all this was, or might have been done, in a country where less than twelve months before the Clergy found it difficult to detain the people during the usual exercises of the Sabbath. The practice of camping on the ground was introduced, partly by necessity, and partly by inclination; the assemblies were generally too large to be received by any common neighbourhood; every thing indeed was done which hospitality and brotherly kindness could do, to accommodate the people; public and private houses were opened, and free invitations given to all persons who wished to retire. Farmers gave up their meadows before they were mown to supply the horses; yet notwithstanding all this liberality it would have been impossible in many cases, to have accommodated the whole assemblies with private lodgings: but besides the people were unwilling to suffer any interruption in their devotions; and they formed an attachment to the place where they were continually seeing so many careless sinners receiving their first impressions, and so many Deists constrained to call on the formerly despised name of JESUS; they conceived a sentiment like what Jacob felt in Bethel. "Surely the Lord is in this place," "This is none other than the house of God, and this is the gate of heaven."

The number of persons who have fallen down under serious impressions in this revival, is another matter worthy of attention, and on this I shall be more particular, as it seems to be the principal cause why this work should be more suspected of enthusiasm than some other revivals.

At Cane Ridge Sacrament it is generally supposed not less than 1000 persons fell prostrate to the ground, among whom were many infidels. At one sacrament which I attended, the number that fell was thought to be more than 300. Persons who fall, are generally such as had manifested symptoms of the deepest impressions for some time previous to the event. It is common to see them shed tears plentifully for about an hour.

Immediately before they become totally powerless they are seized with a general tremor and sometimes, though not often, they utter one or two piercing shrieks in the moment of falling; persons in this situation are affected in different degrees; sometimes when unable to stand or sit they have the use of their hands and can converse with perfect composure. In other cases they are unable to speak, the pulse becomes weak, and they draw a difficult breath about once in a minute: in some instances their extremities become cold, and pulsation, breathing, and all the signs of life forsake them for nearly an hour; persons who have been in this situation have uniformly avowed that they felt no bodily pain, that they had the entire use of their reason and reflection, and when recovered, they could relate every thing that had been said or done near them, or which could possibly fall within their observation. From this it appears that their falling is neither common fainting, nor a nervous action. In-

deed this strange phenomenon appears to have taken every possible turn to baffle the conjectures of those who are not willing to consider it a supernatural work. Persons have sometimes fallen on their way from public worship; and sometimes after they arrived at home, and in some cases when they were pursuing their common business on their farms, or when retired for secret devotion. It was above observed that persons generally are seriously affected for some time previous to their falling; in many cases however, it is otherwise. Numbers of thoughtless sinners have fallen as suddenly as if struck with lightening. Many professed Infidels, and other vicious characters, have been arrested in this way, and sometimes at the very moment when they were uttering blasphemies against the work.

At the beginning of the revival in Shelby county the appearances, as related to me by eye-witnesses, were very surprising indeed. The revival had before this spread with irresistible power through the adjacent counties: and many of the pious had attended distant sacraments with great benefit. These were much engaged, and felt unusual freedom in their addresses at the throne of grace, for the outpouring of the divine Spirit at the approaching sacrament in Shelby. The Sacrament came on in September. The people, as usual, met on Friday: but all were languid, and the exercises went on heavily. On Saturday and Sunday morning it was no better, at length the communion service commenced, everything was still lifeless; whilst the minister of the place was speaking at one of the tables, without any unusual animation, suddenly there were several shrieks from different parts of the assembly; instantly persons fell in every direction; the feelings of the pious were suddenly revived, and the work progressed with extraordinary power, till the conclusion of the solemnity: this phenomenon of falling is common to all ages, sexes and characters; and when they fall they are differently exercised. Some pious people have fallen under a sense of ingratitude and hardness of heart, and others under affecting manifestations of the love and goodness of GOD. Many thoughtless persons under legal convictions, have obtained comfort before they arose. But perhaps the most numerous class consists of those who fall under distressing views of their guilt, who arise with the same fearful apprehensions, and continue in that state for some days, perhaps weeks, before they receive comfort. I have conversed with many who fell under the influence of comfortable feelings, and the account they gave of their exercises while they lay entranced was very surprising. I know not how to give you a better idea of them than by saying that in many cases they appeared to surpass the dying exercises of Dr. Finley: their minds appeared wholly swallowed up in contemplating the perfections of Deity, as illustrated in the plan of salvation, and whilst they lay apparently senseless, and almost lifeless, their minds were more vigorous and their memories more retentive and accurate than they had ever been before. I have heard men of respectability assert that their manifestations of gospel truth were so clear as to require some caution when they began to speak, less they should use language which might induce their hearers to suppose they had seen those things with their bodily eyes; but at the same time they had seen no image nor sensible representation, nor indeed any thing besides the old truths contained in the Bible.

Among those whose minds were filled with the most delightful communications of divine love, I but seldom observed any thing ecstatic. Their expressions were just and rational, they conversed with calmness and composure, and on their first recovering the use of speech, they appeared like persons recovering from a violent disease which had left them on the borders of the grave. I have sometimes been present when persons who fell under the influence of convictions obtained relief before they arose; in these cafes it was impossible not to observe how strongly the change in their minds was depicted in their countenances, instead of a face of horror and despair, they assumed one open, luminous, serene and expressive of all the comfortable feelings of religion. As to those who fall down under legal convictions and continue in that state, they are not different from those who receive convictions in other revivals, excepting that their distress is more severe. Indeed extraordinary power is the leading characteristic of this revival; both saints and sinners have more striking discoveries of the realities of another world, than I have ever known on any other occasion.

I trust I have said enough on this subject to enable you to judge how far the charge of enthusiasm is applicable to it. Lord Lyttleton in his letter on the conversion of St. Paul observes, (I think justly) that enthusiasm is a vain self-righteous spirit, swelled with self-sufficiency and disposed to glory in its religious attainments. If this be a good definition there has been perhaps as little enthusiasm in the Kentucky revival as in any other, never have I seen more genuine marks of that humility which disclaims the merit of its own duties, and looks to the Lord Jesus Christ as the only way of acceptance with God, I was indeed highly pleased to find that Christ was all and all in their religion, as well as in the religion of the gospel. Christians in their highest attainments seemed most sensible of their entire dependance on divine grace, and it was truly affecting to hear with what agonizing anxiety awakened sinners enquired for Christ, as the only physician who could give them any help.—Those who call these things enthusiasm ought to tell us what they understand by the spirit of christianity. In fact, sir, this revival operates as our Saviour promised the Holy Spirit should when sent into the world, it convinces of sin, of righteousness, and of judgment, a strong confirmation to my mind, both that the promise is divine, and that this is a remarkable fulfilment of it. It would be of little avail to object to all this, that probably the professions of many were counterfeited, such as objection would rather establish what it meant to destroy, for where there is no reality, there can be no counterfeit, and besides when the general tenor of a work is such as to dispose the more insincere professors to counterfeit what is right, the work itself must be genuine; but as an eye-witness in the café, I may be permitted to declare that the professions of those under religious convictions were generally marked with such a degree of engagedness and feeling as wilful hypocrisy could hardly assume—the language of the heart when deeply impressed is very distinguishable from the language of affection. Upon the whole, sir, I think the revival in Kentucky among the most extraordinary that have ever visited the church of Christ, and, all things considered, peculiarly adapted to the circumstances of that country. Infidelity was triumphant, and religion at the point of expiring. Something of an extraordinary nature seemed necessary to arrest the attention of a giddy people, who were ready to conclude that Christianity was a fable, and futurity a dream. This revival has done it; it has confounded infidelity, awed vice into silence, and brought numbers beyond calculation, under serious impressions.

Whilst the Blessed Saviour was calling home his people, and building up his church in this remarkable way, opposition could not be silent—At this I hinted above; but it is proper to observe, that the clamorous opposition which assailed the work at its commencement has been in a great measure borne down before it. A large proportion of those who have fallen, were at first opposers, and their example has taught others to be cautious, if it has not taught them to be wise. . . .

Questions

1. What evidence does Reverend Baxter cite as proof of the good and lasting effects of the Cane Ridge revival? Could the facts he states be interpreted differently?

2. Reverend Baxter goes to great lengths to defend the "devotional exercises" and extreme religious "enthusiasm" that set the Cane Ridge camp meeting apart from other frontier revivals. Why do you think he feels the need to do so? Who might be skeptical of the goings-on at Cane Ridge, and why?

3. What challenges did the frontier camp meeting pose to its organizers? From a logistical and organizational standpoint, how did a camp meeting work?

9-10   The Formation of the American Home Missionary Society (1826)

The American Home Missionary Society was founded in New York City in 1826 as a product of a "Plan of Union" that united Congregationalists and Presbyterians in an effort to send ministers west with the growing stream of settlers. Although national in its aspirations, the society focused its efforts in western New York State. Along the course of the Erie Canal, eastern merchants and capitalists transformed towns such as Utica, Syracuse, and Rochester into manufacturing centers while evangelical ministers fanned the flames of revivalism during the Second Great Awakening. In the following passage the founders of the American Home Missionary Society set out their society's mission.

Source: Address of the American Home Missionary Society to the Christian Public (New York: Vanderpool, 1826).

Since the commencement of the present century . . . Christians of different names have been brought under a practical conviction—that in their design to preach the gospel to every creature, there is a need of extended co-operation. Sectional partialities have accordingly been overcome, the great brotherhood of the churches has been recognized, and distant portions of Christendom have consented to commune together. . . .

In the midst of the progress of this state of things, the American Home Missionary Society has had its origins. . . .

Composed . . . as it is of those who are united in their belief of essential doctrines, and who do not greatly differ in their views of church government, and the qualifications for admission to the sacraments of Christianity, it is to be expected . . . that [the Society] . . . will assist in the support of only such ministers as hold a regular standing in the several ecclesiastical connexions represented in the Society, or are in doctrinal agreement and friendly correspondence with the same. By the employment of such missionaries, it is the object of this Society to occupy . . . the ground that otherwise would remain destitute of an evangelical ministry, and to assist feeble congregations in all parts of the United States, which, on these principles, shall desire its aid in the support of settled pastors. . . .

In connexion with this national object, let it be considered that the Congregationalists, and Presbyterians of different names, who are already represented in this Society, are probably the largest denominations of Christians in the United States.—Let it be considered also that other denominations may hereafter make this Society the channel through which to convey their contributions to the destitute, and its founders can hardly be charged with presumption in having given to it the style of *National Institution*. . . .

It remains only to state, that the location of this Society has been chosen in reference to the great national object which it contemplates. The city of New-York possesses peculiar advantages as the seat of this Institution. Its site is central, in that portion of the country which at present will be expected to furnish the principal resources of the Society, and its intercourse with all parts of the United States is constant. Here the necessary means can be more conveniently collected, and information more readily received, than in any other place. It is the heart of the land; and the God of nature seems to have designed that the channels through which this city derives its wealth from every line of the continent, should in return, be channels of mercy, through which the knowledge that saves is to be conveyed to the farthest limits of the nation.

Questions

1. How did the founders of the American Home Missionary Society propose to advance the evangelical goals of the Second Great Awakening?
2. Why did the founders of the society seek a "national" organization that could overcome "sectional partialities"?
3. Why did the society's founders make New York City their headquarters? What did they mean when they said that God intended the channels of commerce to serve also as "channels of mercy"?

9-11   The Duty of Christian Freemen to Elect Christian Rulers (1828)

Ezra Stiles Ely

A Presbyterian clergyman in Philadelphia, Ezra Stiles Ely (1786–1861) strongly supported the Sabbatarian reforms of the Second Great Awakening, which urged Americans to respect the Sabbath by opposing all secular activities on Sundays. When the Pennsylvania state senate refused to grant an act of incorporation to the American Sunday School Union, an interdenominational society devoted to the Sabbatarian movement, Ely published extracts from a sermon he had delivered the previous Fourth of July calling on Christians to unite to elect devout Christians to public office.

Source: Ezra Stiles Ely, *The Duty of Christian Freemen to Elect Christian Rulers* (Philadelphia: W. F. Gettes, 1828), 6–14.

God, my hearers, requires a Christian faith, a Christian profession, and a Christian practice of all our public men; and we as Christian citizens ought, by the publication of our opinions, to require the same.

. . . . Since it is the duty of all our rulers to serve the Lord and kiss the Son of God, it must be most manifestly the duty of all our Christian fellow-citizens to honour the Lord Jesus Christ and promote christianity by electing and supporting as public officers the friends of our blessed Saviour. Let it only be granted, that Christians have the same rights and privileges in exercising the elective franchise, which are here accorded to Jews and Infidels, and we ask no other evidence to show, that those who prefer a Christian ruler, may unite in supporting him, in preference to any one of a different character. It shall cheerfully be granted, that every citizen is eligible to every office, whatever may be his religious opinions and moral character; and that every one may constitutionally support any person whom he may *choose*; but it will not hence follow, that he is without accountability to his Divine Master for his choice; or that he may lay aside all his Christian principles and feelings when he selects his ticket and presents it at the polls. "*In all* thy ways acknowledge him," is a maxim which should dwell in a Christian's mind on the day of a public election as much as on the Sabbath; and which should govern him when conspiring with others to honour Christ, either at the Lord's table, or in the election of a Chief Magistrate. In elucidating the duty of private Christians in relation to the choice of their civil rulers, it seems to me necessary to remark,

That every Christian who has the right and the opportunity of exercising the elective franchise ought to do it. Many pious people feel so much disgust at the manner in which elections are conducted, from the first nomination to the closing of the polls, that they relinquish their right of voting for years together. But if all *pious* people were to conduct thus, then our rulers would be wholly elected by the *impious*. If all *good men* are to absent themselves from

elections, then the *bad* will have the entire transaction of our public business. . . .

I propose, fellow-citizens, a new sort of union, or, if you please, a *Christian party in politics*, which I am exceedingly desirous all good men in our country should join: not by *subscribing a constitution* and the formation of a new society, to be added to the scores which now exist; but by adopting, avowing, and determining to act upon, truly religious principles in all civil matters. I am aware that the true Christians of our country are divided into many different denominations; who have, alas! too many points of jealousy and collision; still, a union to a very great extent, and for the most valuable purposes is not impracticable. For,

All Christians, of all denominations, may, and ought to, agree in determining, that they will never wittingly support for any public office, any person whom they know or believe to sustain, at the time of his proposed election, a bad moral character. In this, thousands of moralists, who profess no experimental acquaintance with Christianity, might unite and co-operate with *our Christian party*. And surely, it is not impossible, nor unreasonable for all classes of Christians to say within themselves, no man that we have reason to think is a liar, thief, gambler, murderer, debauchee, spendthrift, or openly immoral person in any way, shall have our support at any election. REFORMATION should not only be allowed, but encouraged; for it would be requiring too much to insist upon it, that a candidate for office *shall always have sustained an unblemished moral character*, and it would be unchristian not to forgive and support one who has proved his repentance by recantation and a considerable course of new obedience.

Some of the best men were once vile; but they have been washed from their sins. Present good moral character should be considered as essential to every candidate for the post of honour. In this affair I know we are very much dependent on testimony, and that we may be deceived; especially in those controverted elections in which all manner of falsehoods are invented and vended, wholesale and retail, against some of the most distinguished men of our country: but after all, we must exercise our candour and best discretion, as we do in other matters of belief. We must weigh evidence, and depend most on those who appear the most competent and credible witnesses. It will be natural for us to believe a man's neighbours and acquaintances in preference to strangers. When we have employed the lights afforded us for the illumination of our minds, we shall feel peace of conscience, if we withhold our vote from every one whom we believe to be an immoral man.

Come then, fellow Christians, and friends of good morals in society, let us determine thus far to unite; for thus far we may, and ought to, and shall unite, if we duly weigh the importance of a good moral character in a ruler. Let no love of *the integrity of a party* prevent you from striking out the name of every dishonest and base man from your ticket. You have a right to choose, and you glory in your freedom: make then your own election: and when all good *men* act on this principle it will not be a vain thing. Candidates then, must be moral men, or seem to be, or they will not secure an election. . . .

All who profess to be Christians of any denomination ought to agree that they will support no man as a candidate for any office, who is not professedly friendly to Christianity, and a believer in divine Revelation. We do not say that true or even pretended Christianity shall be made a constitutional test of admission to office; but we do affirm that Christians may in their elections lawfully prefer the avowed friends of the Christian religion to Turks, Jews, and Infidels. . . . While every religious system is tolerated in our country, and no one is established by law, it is still possible for me to think, that the friend of Christianity will make a much better governor of this commonwealth or President of the United States, than the advocate of Theism or Polytheism. . . . If three or four of the most numerous denominations of Christians in the United States, the Presbyterians, the Baptists, the Methodists and Congregationalists for instance, should act upon this principle, our country would never be dishonoured with an *avowed infidel* in her national cabinet or capitol. . . . Let a man be of good moral character, and let him profess to believe in and advocate the Christian religion, and we can all support him. At one time he will be a Baptist, at another an Episcopalian, at another a Methodist, at another a Presbyterian of the American, Scotch, Irish, Dutch, or German stamp, and always a friend to our common Christianity. . . .

Let us elect men who dare to acknowledge the Lord Jesus Christ for their Lord in their public documents. Which of our Presidents has ever done this? It would pick no infidel's pocket, and break no Jew's neck, if our President should be so singular as to let it be known, that he is a *Christian* by his Messages, and an advocate for the Deity of Christ by his personal preference. . . .

We are a Christian nation: we have a right to demand that all our rulers in their conduct shall conform to Christian morality; and if they do not, it is the duty and privilege of Christian freemen to make a new and a better election.

May the Lord Jesus Christ for ever reign in and over these United States, and call them peculiarly his own. *Amen.*

Questions

1. How does Ely define a "good moral character"?
2. In Ely's view, what were the limitations of the existing system of party politics? How could voters determine a candidate's moral character?
3. How did Ely deal with the First Amendment's separation of church and state?

Questions for Further Thought

1. At the same time that Americans set out to create a republican society, they also, in the first few decades of the nineteenth century, transformed the United States into a fundamentally Christian nation. What parallels can you draw between republicanism and Pietism or evangelical Christianity? How were they mutually supportive? Can you think of any instances where the two value systems might have come in conflict?
2. In Document 9-11, Ezra Stiles Ely called upon all Christians to cast their votes according to their faith. How does this square with the constitutional separation of church and state? Would it be fair to say that in the early nineteenth century, many Americans believed the separation of religion and politics was not the same thing?

3. One of the most noted aspects of the United States in the early nineteenth century was the rapid proliferation of volunteer organizations. As reflected in Documents 9-9 through 9-11, how did Americans organize themselves as Christians in the new republic, and what relationship did these religious organizations have to the rest of civil society?

CHAPTER **10**

The Economic Revolution, 1820–1860

★　　　★　　　★

The Rise of Manufacturing

At first it seemed unlikely that the United States would become an industrial nation. Only one nation in the world—Great Britain—had progressed very far toward industrialization at the beginning of the nineteenth century, and its factories owed much of their success to the cheap labor resulting from widespread poverty. Blessed with large amounts of land (once the Indian population was dealt with) and relatively few people, Americans such as Thomas Jefferson expected the nation to remain agricultural; indeed, since they saw factories and industrial cities as teeming with mobs of poor, dependent people, they hoped that such "unrepublican" institutions would remain far from their shores (Document 10-1). Other Americans, though, such as Tench Coxe, contended that properly carried on, manufacturing could complement agriculture and bolster the nation's wealth and the welfare of all Americans (Document 10-2).

The emergence of the textile industry depended on several factors: entrepreneurs with access to capital, an abundant source of cheap labor, and a reliable source of energy. In New England, wealthy merchants Francis Cabot Lowell and Nathan Appleton successfully invested in a number of textile factories powered by waterwheels. They obtained their work force by hiring young women from New England farms to work temporarily at their mills while living in well-supervised boardinghouses. At least initially, these factory jobs were quite attractive to young women, who found in them a means of escaping the drudgery of the farm, an opportunity to enjoy some freedom between childhood and marriage, and a means of accumulating some money (Document 10-3). The paternalism of what was called the Waltham plan also seemed to offer a "republican" American alternative to the specter of pauper labor that haunted industrial Great Britain and Thomas Jefferson alike (Document 10-4).

The industrial revolution was more than simply a new way to organize labor, though. By the early nineteenth century the skilled craftsmen of the Northeast were creating what perhaps was the most advanced culture of innovation in the world. Rather than perceiving machines as threats to traditional ways of life, Americans welcomed them as aids to personal and national prosperity, and were eager to gain and apply the skills needed to invent more and better machines. The resulting economic progress stirred the admiration of foreign observers, who saw the American working-man as leading his country into the front rank of industrial powers (Document 10-5).

10-1   Notes on the State of Virginia, Query XIX (1780)

Thomas Jefferson

In 1780 Thomas Jefferson, then governor of Virginia, received a set of twenty-two questions from François Marbois, secretary of the French legation to the United States, seeking intelligence about the thirteen new "nations" for his government. After responding to Marbois's queries, however, Jefferson continued to elaborate on them; the work we now know as the *Notes on the State of Virginia* was revised several times before the now-standard version appeared some twenty years after Jefferson began work on the project. Beginning as a simple factual report, the *Notes* became a classic meditation on the character of the New World and of the new society that Jefferson himself was helping to bring into being. His response to Query XIX, concerning "the present state of manufactures, commerce, interior and exterior trade," is an especially striking example that offers both an economic and a philosophical argument against the prospects for manufacturing in the new nation.

Source: Thomas Jefferson, *Notes on the State of Virginia*, Frank Sufleton, ed. (London and New York: Penguin Books, 1999), 170–171.

THE PRESENT STATE OF MANUFACTURES COMMERCE, INTERIOR AND EXTERIOR TRADE?

Manufactures

We never had an interior trade of any importance. Our exterior commerce has suffered very much from the beginning of the present contest. During this time we have manufactured within our families the most necessary articles of cloathing. Those of cotton will bear some comparison with the same kinds of manufacture in Europe; but those of wool, flax and hemp are very coarse, unsightly, and unpleasant: and such is our attachment to agriculture, and such our preference for foreign manufactures, that be it wise or unwise, our people will certainly return as soon as they can, to the raising raw materials, and exchanging them for finer manufactures than they are able to execute themselves.

The political oeconomists of Europe have established it as a principle that every state should endeavour to manufacture for itself: and this principle, like many others, we transfer to America, without calculating the difference of circumstance which should often produce a difference of result. In Europe the lands are either cultivated, or locked up against the cultivator. Manufacture must therefore be resorted to of necessity not of choice, to support the sur-

plus of their people. But we have an immensity of land courting the industry of the husbandman. Is it best then that all our citizens should be employed in its improvement, or that one half should be called off from that to exercise manufactures and handicraft arts for the other? Those who labour in the earth are the chosen people of God, if ever he had a chosen people, whose breasts he has made his peculiar deposit for substantial and genuine virtue. It is the focus in which he keeps alive that sacred fire, which otherwise might escape from the face of the earth. Corruption of morals in the mass of cultivators is a phaenomenon of which no age nor nation has furnished an example. It is the mark set on those, who not looking up to heaven, to their own soil and industry, as does the husbandman, for their subsistance, depend for it on the casualties and caprice of customers. Dependance begets subservience and venality, suffocates the germ of virtue, and prepares fit tools for the designs of ambition. This, the natural progress and consequence of the arts, has sometimes perhaps been retarded by accidental circumstances: but, generally speaking, the proportion which the aggregate of the other classes of citizens bears in any state to that of its husbandmen, is the proportion of its unsound to its healthy parts, and is a good-enough barometer whereby to measure its degree of corruption. While we have land to labour then, let us never wish to see our citizens occupied at a work-bench, or twirling a distaff. Carpenters, masons, smiths, are wanting in husbandry: but, for the general operations of manufacture, let our work-shops remain in Europe. It is better to carry provisions and materials to workmen there, than bring them to the provisions and materials, and with them their manners and principles. The loss by the transportation of commodities across the Atlantic will be made up in happiness and permanence of government. The mobs of great cities add just so much to the support of pure government, as sores do to the strength of the human body. It is the manners and spirit of a people which preserve a republic in vigour. A degeneracy in these is a canker which soon eats to the heart of its laws and constitution.

Questions

1. How does Jefferson reason that Americans will leave manufacturing to the Europeans? What assumptions about American society lead him to this conclusion?
2. Why does Jefferson believe that an agricultural society—specifically, a society made up of yeoman farmers—was the only socioeconomic foundation for a republic? Why do you think Jefferson believed that a society of manufacturers "suffocates the germ of virtue"?
3. How do you think Jefferson formed his opinions about the evils of manufacturing? What might he have seen or experienced that might explain this revulsion?

10-2   Cotton Cultivation and Textile Factories (1810)

Tench Coxe

A native of Philadelphia, Tench Coxe (1755–1824) studied at the College of Philadelphia (which later became the University of Pennsylvania) before working in his father's countinghouse. A strong supporter of the Constitution, Coxe held a number of minor government offices during the presidencies of George Washington and Thomas Jefferson. He had his greatest influence, however, as a writer on economics. Coxe emphasized what he viewed as a harmony of interests between a small but growing manufacturing sector and the dominant agricultural interest. He advocated a modest tariff on imported manufactures and firmly opposed commercial restrictions between states. Coxe was also one of the first to see the full economic implications of the cotton gin and increased cultivation of cotton in the South. In a report drafted for Jefferson's treasury secretary, Albert Gallatin, Coxe noted the emergence of a cotton textile industry in the Northeast and tied its future growth to the cultivation of cotton on southern plantations.

Source: A Statement of the Arts and Manufactures of the United States of America, for the Year 1810: Digested and Prepared by Tench Coxe, Esquire, of Philadelphia (Philadelphia: A. Cornman, 1814).

It is a fact of great importance. . . . on the subject of the relation of manufactures to the landed interest, that none of the productions of the earth, whether of *natural growth* or *the fruits of cultivation*, in the middle, northern and eastern states, which can be considered as "raw materials," are now exported in an *unmanufactured* condition to foreign markets. . . .

Until the late revolution in the cultivation of cotton, by which it was converted, through the strenuous excitements of the friends of manufactures, from a petty object in little fields and gardens, into an article of extensive cultivation among the planters and farmers, there was no redundant [surplus] raw materials for the manufacture of cloths and stuffs, for apparel and furniture, in the United States. There is at this time no other redundant raw material.

The green seed cotton was the best adapted to the general quality and situation, and to the climate of the southern states. But its cultivation, though perfectly pleasant and easy, was very much restrained by the extraordinary difficulty of separating it from the seeds. This operation required so much manual industry, as greatly to impede the manufacture, and of course, for the time, to prevent an extensive cultivation. In the year 1793 *the invaluable . . . gin* was invented by a citizen of the United States [in a note Coxe identified "Mr. Eli Whitney, of Connecticut"], and was so improved and perfected, as to render it easy, it is said to separate the seeds from one hundred million of pounds weight of cotton wool by the employment of three or four hundred persons, although it is alleged that it would require three hundred thousand persons to effect the same by hand. . . . By employing this machinery, every vicinity can easily and expeditiously prepare its cotton for the manufacturing cards . . . to any extent, that the world could require, were it to clothe itself entirely in cotton manufactures. Thus has been added, by our own invention, to the machinery *to facilitate the manufacture of a staple production of our soil*, a single improvement movable by water, steam, cattle or hand, which has set loose these immense powers of agriculture, *to produce cotton wool*. . . .

The water spinners of cotton, in one of the states, have represented . . . that they can make eighty-two pounds and one half of yarn by each spindle in every year. But the owners of other spinning mills deem it unsafe to calculate upon more than fifty-two pounds of yarn per annum for each spindle. . . . At the lowest of the rates, the United States, had they 1,160,000 spindles, could work up into yarn the sixty-four millions of pounds weight of cotton, which are the maximum of our exportation, in a single year. . . . Sixty-four millions of pounds of cotton . . . would produce about 50,000,000 pounds of cotton yarn, and with the labor . . . of about 58,000 persons . . . one eighth part ought to be adult males. The remaining seven eighths, might be women and children. This employment of less than *an hundredth part of* our white population of 1810 would be no inconvenience to agriculture or commerce.

. . . If the weaving of this be executed, as may be done with perfect ease, by the employment of 100,000 women (less than one sixth of our adult females) with *the fly shuttle*, during *one half* of each working day in the year, the quantity of cloth by the Rhode Island rule of four yards for every pound, would amount to about 200,000,000 of yards. This quantity of cotton cloth, at one third of a dollar per yard, would be worth about 67,000,000 dollars.

There is yet another operation, which can be effected by labor-saving means, and by a process superceding the labor of many hands. Machinery is now in actual operation in the United States, for printing cotton and linen cloths, by engraving rollers of copper, moved by water. Ten thousand yards have been printed, with ease in a single day, by one man and two boys, with these rollers. . . . Similar means are in constant use for staining and dying cotton and linen cloths of one colour, in the same expeditious manner, so as to make them fit for a greater variety of apparel and furniture. Were these operations to be performed, upon the whole quantity of cotton goods estimated in this statement, they would add seven or eight millions to their value, and would require but 50 or 60,000 men and children. . . . The total addition to the original value of our cotton crop alone would be at a rate, far exceeding the value of our exports of American growth. . . . A quantity of cotton wool equal to all that is now produced by the civilized and uncivilized nations of the world, could be raised on a very small portion of our southern soil.

Such are the benefits, which agriculture and the country at large may derive from the manufacture of *our only redundant raw material*. The states of Rhode Island and Massachusetts have expelled all doubts about the practicability of the cotton operations. With the smallest territory in the United States, Rhode Island has already attained and introduced into her vicinity a cotton branch of our manufactures as valuable, as the cotton branch of any country in Europe was, at the time of the formation of our present constitution.

Questions

1. Coxe wanted the United States to spin, weave, and print the cotton it cultivated rather than export it raw. Why?
2. From Coxe's perspective, why was it important that manufactures be linked to the "landed interest"?
3. Why did Coxe emphasize that cotton manufacturers needed to employ relatively few men and that cotton cultivation required only a small amount of southern land?

10-3   A Mill Worker Describes Her Work and Life (1844)

A majority of the workers in the early years of the textile industry were young women from New England farm families (see text pp. 319–320). The women mill hands in Lowell, Massachusetts, published their own poetry and other compositions in *The Lowell Offering*. The following letters, written by a worker identified only as "Susan," were published in 1844.

Source: The Lowell Offering (June and August 1844), 169–172, 237–240, in Stanley I. Kutler, ed., *Looking for America: The People's History*, 2d ed. (New York: Norton, 1979), 1: 260–265.

Dear Mary:

In my last I told you I would write again, and say more of my life here; and this I will now attempt to do.

I went into the mill to work a few days after I wrote to you. It looked very pleasant at first, the rooms were so light, spacious, and clean, the girls so pretty and neatly dressed, and the machinery so brightly polished or nicely painted. The plants in the windows, or on the overseer's bench or desk, gave a pleasant aspect to things. You will wish to know what work I am doing. I will tell you of the different kinds of work.

There is, first, the carding-room, where the cotton flies most, and the girls get the dirtiest. But this is easy, and the females are allowed time to go out at night before the bell rings—on Saturday night at least, if not on all other nights. Then there is the spinning-room, which is very neat and pretty. In this room are the spinners and doffers. The spinners watch the frames; keep them clean, and the threads mended if they break. The doffers take off the full bobbins, and put on the empty ones. They have nothing to do in the long intervals when the frames are in motion, and can go out to their boarding-houses, or do any thing else that they like. In some of the factories the spinners do their own doffing, and when this is the case they work no harder than the weavers. These last have the hardest time of all— or can have, if they choose to take charge of three or four looms, instead of the one pair which is the allotment. And they are the most constantly confined. The spinners and dressers have but the weavers to keep supplied, and then their work can stop. The dressers never work before breakfast, and they stay out a great deal in the afternoons. The drawers-in, or girls who draw the threads through the harnesses, also work in the dressing-room, and they all have very good wages—better than the weavers who have but the usual work. The dressing-rooms are very neat, and the frames move with a gentle undulating motion which is really graceful. But these rooms are kept very warm, and are disagreeably scented with the "sizing," or starch, which stiffens the "beams," or unwoven webs. There are many plants in these rooms, and it is really a good green-house for them. The dressers are generally quite tall girls, and must have pretty tall minds too, as their work requires much care and attention.

I could have had work in the dressing-room, but chose to be a weaver; and I will tell you why. I disliked the closer air of the dressing-room, though I might have become accustomed to that. I could not learn to dress so quickly as I could to weave, nor have work of my own so soon, and should have had to stay with Mrs. C. two or three weeks before I could go in at all, and I did not like to be "lying upon my oars" so long. And, more than this, when I get well learned I can have extra work, and make double wages, which you know is quite an inducement with some.

Well, I went into the mill, and was put to learn with a very patient girl—a clever old maid. I should be willing to be one myself if I could be as good as she is. You cannot think how odd every thing seemed to me. I wanted to laugh at every thing, but did not know what to make sport of first. They set me to threading shuttles, and tying weaver's knots, and such things, and now I have improved so that I can take care of one loom. I could take care of two if I only had eyes in the back part of my head, but I have not got used to "looking two ways of a Sunday" yet.

At first the hours seemed very long, but I was so interested in learning that I endured it very well; and when I went out at night, the sound of the mill was in my ears, as of crickets, frogs, and jewsharps [small musical instrument; it twangs], all mingled together in strange discord. After that it seemed as though cotton-wool was in my ears, but now I do not mind it at all. You know that people learn to sleep with the thunder of Niagara in their ears, and a cotton mill is no worse, though you wonder that we do not have to hold our breath in such a noise.

It makes my feet ache and swell to stand so much, but I suppose I shall get accustomed to that too. The girls generally wear old shoes about their work, and you know nothing is easier; but they almost all say that when they have worked here a year or two they have to procure shoes a size or two larger than before they came. The right hand, which is the one used in stopping and starting the loom, becomes larger than the left; but in other respects the factory is not detrimental to a young girl's appearance. Here they look delicate, but not sickly; they laugh at those who are much exposed, and get pretty brown; but I, for one, had rather be brown than pure white. I never saw so many pretty looking girls as there are here. Though the number of men is small in proportion there are many marriages here, and a great deal of courting. I will tell you of this last sometime.

You wish to know minutely of our hours of labor. We go in at five o'clock; at seven we come out to breakfast; at half-past seven we return to our work, and stay until half-past twelve. At one, or quarter-past one four months in the year, we return to our work, and stay until seven at night. Then the evening is all our own, which is more than some laboring girls can say, who think nothing is more tedious than a factory life.

When I first came here, which was the last of February, the girls ate their breakfast before they went to their work. The first of March they came out at the present breakfast hour, and the twentieth of March they ceased to "light up" the rooms, and come out between six and seven o'clock.

You ask if the girls are contented here: I ask you, if you know of *any one* who is perfectly contented. Do you remember the old story of the philosopher, who offered a field to the person who was contented with his lot; and when one claimed it, he asked him why, if he was so perfectly satisfied, he wanted his field. The girls here are not contented; and there is no disadvantage in their situation which they do not perceive as quickly, and lament as loudly, as the sternest opponents of the factory system do. They would scorn to say they were contented, if asked the question; for it would compromise their Yankee spirit—their pride, penetration, independence, and love of "freedom and equality" to say that they were *contented* with such a life as this. Yet, withal, they are cheerful. I never saw a happier set of beings. They appear blithe in the mill, and out of it. If you see one of them, with a very long face, you may be sure that it is because she has heard bad news from home, or because her beau has vexed her. But, if it is a Lowell trouble, it is because she has failed in getting off as many "sets" or "pieces" as she intended to have done; or because she had a sad "break-out," or "break-down," in her work, or something of that sort.

You ask if the work is not disagreeable. Not when one is accustomed to it. It tried my patience sadly at first, and does now when it does not run well; but, in general, I like it very much. It is easy to do, and does not require very violent exertion, as much of our farm work does.

You also ask how I get along with the girls here. Very well indeed. . . .

Dear Mary: . . .
The mill girls are the prettiest in the city. You wonder how they can keep neat. Why not? There are no restrictions as to the number of pieces to be washed in the boarding-house. And, as there is plenty of water in the mill, the girls can wash their laces and muslins and other nice things themselves, and no boarding woman ever refuses the con-

veniences for starching and ironing. You say too that you do not see how we can have so many conveniences and comforts at the price we pay for board. You must remember that the boarding-houses belong to the companies, and are let to the tenants far below the usual city rent—sometimes the rent is remitted. Then there are large families, so that there are the profits of many individuals. The country farmers are quite in the habit of bringing their produce to the boarding-houses for sale, thus reducing the price by the omission of the market-man's profit. So you see there are many ways by which we get along so well.

You ask me how the girls behave in the mill, and what are the punishments. They behave very well while about their work, and I have never heard of punishments, or scoldings, or anything of that sort. Sometimes an overseer finds fault, and sometimes offends a girl by refusing to let her stay out of the mill, or some deprivation like that; and then, perhaps, there are tears and pouts on her part, but, in general, the tone of intercourse between the girls and overseers is very good—pleasant, yet respectful. When the latter are fatherly sort of men the girls frequently resort to them for advice and assistance about other affairs than their work. Very seldom is this confidence abused; but, among the thousands of overseers who have lived in Lowell, and the tens of thousands of girls who have in time been here, there are legends still told of wrong suffered and committed. "To err is human," and when the frailties of humanity are exhibited by a factory girl it is thought of for worse than are the errors of any other persons.

The only punishment among the girls is dismission from their places. They do not, as many think, withhold their wages; and as for corporal punishment—mercy on me! To strike a female would cost any overseer his place. If the superintendents did not take the affair into consideration the girls would turn out [go on strike], as they did at the Temperance celebration, "Independent day;" and if they didn't look as pretty, I am sure they would produce as deep an impression. . . .

Do you wish to hear anything more about the overseers? Once for all, then, there are many very likely intelligent public-spirited men among them. They are interested in the good movements of the day; teachers in the Sabbath schools; and some have represented the city in the State Legislature. They usually marry among the factory girls, and do not connect themselves with their inferiors either. Indeed, in almost all the matches here the female is superior in education and manner, if not in intellect, to her partner.

The overseers have good salaries, and their families live very prettily. I observe that in almost all cases the mill girls make excellent wives. They are good managers, orderly in their households, and "neat as waxwork." It seems as though they were so delighted to have houses of their own to take care of, that they would never weary of the labor and the care. . . .

Questions

1. What appears to be the purpose of Susan's letters to Mary?
2. How does Susan describe the work environment?
3. What does she consider the advantages and disadvantages of working in the mill?

10-4 Morals of Manufactures (1837)

Harriet Martineau

Harriet Martineau (1802–1876) joined a steady stream of British and European visitors to the United States in the early nineteenth century. She published her observations about society in America after a two-year stay from 1834 to 1836. Martineau enthusiastically embraced the radical social implications of the Industrial Revolution and saw in the United States a brave social experiment in human equality. An ardent feminist and abolitionist, Martineau noted that the subordination of women and slaves in the United States contradicted the egalitarian principles enunciated in the Declaration of Independence. But she saw signs of future progress emerging in New England's new industrial order. The Waltham plan (see text pp. 319–320) offered young American women of modest means an alternative to domestic service; the factory system also suggested to Martineau the manner in which the United States could protect itself from the ills of poverty that infected industrial society in Britain.

Source: Harriet Martineau, *Society in America* (London: Saunders and Otley, 1837; reprint, New York: AMS Press, 1966), 2: 355–358.

The morals of the female factory population may be expected to be good when it is considered of what class it is composed. Many of the girls are in the factories because they have too much pride for domestic service. Girls who are too proud for domestic service as it is in America, can hardly be low enough for any gross immorality; or to need watching; or not to be trusted to avoid the contagion of evil example. To a stranger, their pride seems to take a mistaken direction, and they appear to deprive themselves of a respectable home and station, and many benefits, by their dislike of service: but this is altogether their own affair. They must choose for themselves their way of life. But the reasons of their choice indicate a state of mind superior to the grossest dangers of their position.

I saw a bill fixed up in the Waltham mill which bore a warning that no young lady who attended dancing-school that winter should be employed: and that the corporation had given directions to the overseer to dismiss any one who should be found to dance at the school. I asked the meaning of this; and the overseer's answer was, "Why, we had some trouble last winter about the dancing-school. It must, of course, be held in the evening, as the young folks are in the mill all day. They are very young, many of them; and they forget the time, and everything but the amusement, and dance away till two or three in the morning. They are unfit for their work the next day; or, if they get properly through their work, it is at the expense of their health. So we have forbidden the dancing-school; but, to make up for it, I have promised them that, as soon as the great new room at the hotel is finished, we will have a dance once a-fortnight. We shall meet and break up early; and my wife and I will dance; and we will all dance together."

I was sorry to see one bad and very unnecessary arrangement, in all the manufacturing establishments. In England, the best friends of the poor are accustomed to think it the crowning hardship of their condition that solitude is wholly forbidden to them. It is impossible that any human being should pass his life as well as he might do who is never alone. . . . The silence, freedom and collectedness of solitude are absolutely essential to the health of the mind. . . . In the dwellings of the English poor, parents and children are crowded into one room. . . . All wise parents above the rank of poor, make it a primary consideration so to arrange their families as that each member may, at some hour have some place where he may enter in, and shut his door, and feel himself alone. If possible, the sleeping places are so ordered. In America, where space is of far less consequence . . . these same girls have no private apartments, and sometimes sleep six or eight in a room, and even three in a bed. This is very bad. . . .

Now are the days when these gregarious habits should be broken through. . . . If the change be not soon made, the American factory population, with all its advantages of education and of pecuniary sufficiency, will be found, as its numbers increase, to have been irreparably injured by its subjection to a grievance . . . to which poverty exposes artisans in old countries.

Questions

1. Why did the young women at Waltham prefer factory work to domestic service?
2. Why is Martineau concerned about the "morals" of industrial employment?
3. What social dangers does Martineau think will result from the absence of solitude in the new industrial order?

10-5   The American System of Manufactures (1854)

Joseph Whitworth

At London's Great (or "Crystal Palace") Exhibition of 1851, widely regarded as the first world's fair, the British sought to demonstrate their technological supremacy in the world. However, the American exhibit quickly indicated that Britain's cousins across the water were rapidly coming to the fore. Moreover, as the exhibit of Samuel Colt's machine-made revolvers attested, Americans had developed their own distinctive technological style, which was soon dubbed "the American system of manufactures." Several years later, the British government sent investigators to America, including Joseph Whitworth (1803–1887), the world's leading manufacturer of machine tools, to assess the progress made by American manufacturers. The conclusion of Whitworth's 1854 report to Parliament contains the following observations on the environmental characteristics he believed made Americans such an innovative people.

Source: "Special Report of Mr. Joseph Whitworth," in Nathan Rosenberg, ed., *The American System of Manufactures* (Edinburgh: Edinburgh University Press, 1969), 387–389.

NEW YORK INDUSTRIAL EXHIBITION, SPECIAL REPORT OF MR. JOSEPH WHITWORTH. PRESENTED TO THE HOUSE OF COMMONS BY COMMAND OF HER MAJESTY, IN PURSUANCE OF THEIR ADDRESS OF FEBRUARY 6, 1854. LONDON: PRINTED BY HARRISON AND SON.

Conclusions

The parts of the United States which I visited form, geographically, a small portion of their extended territory, but they are the principal seats of manufactures, and afford ample opportunities for arriving at general conclusions. I could not fail to be impressed, from all that I saw there, with the extraordinary energy of the people, and their peculiar aptitude in availing themselves to the utmost of the immense natural resources of the country.

The details which I have collected in this report show, by numerous examples, that they leave no means untried to effect what they think it is possible to accomplish, and they have been signally successful in combining large practical results with great economy in the methods by which these results are secured.

The labouring classes are comparatively few in number, but this is counter-balanced by, and indeed may be regarded as one of the chief causes of, the eagerness with which they call in the aid of machinery in almost every department of industry. Wherever it can be introduced as a substitute for manual labour, it is universally and willingly resorted to; of this the facts stated in my report contain many conclusive proofs, but I may here specially refer, as examples, to plough making, where eight men are able to finish thirty per day; to door making, where twenty men make 100 panelled doors per day; to last making, the process of which is completed in 1½ minutes; to sewing by machinery, where one woman does the work of 20; to net making, where one woman does the work of 100. It is this condition of the labour market, and this eager resort to machinery whenever it can be applied, to which, under the guidance of superior education and intelligence, the remarkable prosperity of the United States is mainly due. That prosperity is frequently attributed to the possession of a soil of great natural fertility, and it is doubtless true that in certain districts the alluvial deposits are rich and the land fruitful to an extraordinary degree; but while traversing many hundred miles of country in the Northern States, I was impressed with the conviction that the general character of the soil there was the reverse of fertile.

It is not for a moment denied that the natural resources of the United States are immense, that the products of the soil seem capable of being multiplied and varied to almost any extent, and that the supplies of minerals appear to be nearly unlimited.

The material welfare of the country, however, is largely dependent upon the means adopted for turning its natural resources to the best account, at the same time that the calls made upon human labour are reduced as far as practicable.

The attention paid to the working of wood, some details connected with which I have included in the report, is a striking illustration of this. The early settlers found in the forests which they had to clear an unlimited supply of material, which necessity compelled them to employ in every possible way, in the construction of their houses, their furniture, and domestic utensils, in their implements of labour, and in their log-paved roads.

Wood thus became with them a universal material, and work-people being scarce, machinery was introduced as far as possible to supply the want of hands. The character thus given to one branch of manufactures has gradually extended to others. Applied to stone-dressing, for example, one man is enabled, as I have shown, to perform as much work as twenty masons by hand. So great again are the improvements effected in spinning machinery, that one man can attend to a mule containing 1,088 spindles, each spinning 3 hanks, or 3,264 hanks in the aggregate per day. In Hindoostan, where they still spin by hand, it would be extravagant to expect a spinner to accomplish one hank per day; so that in the United States we find the same amount of manual labour, by improved machinery, doing more than 3,000 times the work. But a still more striking comparison between hand and machine labour may be made in the case of lace making in England. Lace of an ordinary figured pattern used to be made 'on the cushion' by hand, at the rate of about three meshes per minute. At Nottingham, a machine attended by one person will now produce lace of a similar kind at the rate of about 24,000 meshes per minute; so that one person can, by the employment of a machine, produce 8,000 times as much work as one lace maker by hand.

The results which have been obtained in the United States, by the application of machinery wherever it has been practicable to manufactures, are rendered still more remarkable by the fact, that combinations to resist its in-troduction there are unheard of. The workmen hail with satisfaction all mechanical improvements, the importance and value of which, as releasing them from the drudgery of unskilled labour, they are enabled by education to understand and appreciate. With the comparatively superabundant supply of hands in this country, and therefore a proportionate difficulty in obtaining remunerative employment, the working classes have less sympathy with the progress of invention. Their condition is a less favourable one than that of their American brethren for forming a just and unprejudiced estimate of the influence which the introduction of machinery is calculated to exercise on their state and prospects. I cannot resist the conclusion, however, that the different views taken by our operatives and those of the United States upon this subject are determined by other and powerful causes, besides those dependent on the supply of labour in the two countries. The principles which ought to regulate the relations between the employer and the employed seem to be thoroughly understood and appreciated in the United States, and while the law of limited liability affords the most ample facilities for the investment of capital in business, the intelligent and educated artizan is left equally free to earn all that he can, by making the best use of his hands, without let or hindrance by his fellows.

It may be that the working classes exhibit an unusual independence of manner, but the same feeling insures the due performance of what they consider to be their duty with less supervision than is required where dependence is to be placed upon uneducated hands.

It rarely happens that a workman who possesses peculiar skill in his craft is disqualified to take the responsible position of superintendent, by the want of education and general knowledge, as is frequently the case in this country. In every State in the Union, and particularly in the north, education is, by means of the common schools, placed within the reach of each individual, and all classes avail themselves of the opportunities afforded. The desire of knowledge so early implanted is greatly increased, while the facilities for diffusing it are amply provided through the instrumentality of an almost universal press. No taxation of any kind has been suffered to interfere with the development of this powerful agent for promoting the intelligence of the people, and the consequence is, that where the humblest labourer can indulge in the luxury of his daily paper, everybody reads, and thought and intelligence penetrate through the lowest grades of society. The benefits which thus result from a liberal system of education and a cheap press to the working classes of the United States can hardly be over-estimated in a national point of view; but it is to the co-operation of both that they must undoubtedly be ascribed. For if, selecting a proof from among the European States, the condition of Prussia be considered, it will be found that the people of that country, as a body, have not made that progress which, from the great attention paid to the education of all classes, might have been anticipated; and this must certainly be ascribed to the restrictions laid upon the press, which have so materially impeded the general advancement of the people. Wherever education and an unrestricted press are allowed full scope to exercise their united influence, progress and improvement are the certain results, and among the many benefits which arise from their joint co-operation may be ranked most prominently the value which they teach men to place upon intelligent contrivance; the readiness with which they cause new improvements to be received, and the impulse which they thus unavoidably give to that inventive spirit which is gradually emancipating man from the rude forms of labour, and making what were regarded as the luxuries of one age to be looked upon in the next as the ordinary and necessary conditions of human existence.

signed   JOSEPH WHITWORTH

Questions

1. How does Joseph Whitworth explain the rapid development of manufacturing in the United States? What factors does he believe are the most important?
2. How does Whitworth reason that the existence of a free press in the United States explains why America's workingmen embrace machinery? Do you agree?
3. How, according to Whitworth, do English and American workers compare with each other? Why does Whitworth believe that American laborers perceive machinery as a positive good rather than a threat?

Questions for Further Thought

1. Contrary to Thomas Jefferson's hopes (Document 10-1), in the first half of the nineteenth century American entrepreneurs transformed the United States into a vibrant manufacturing nation. How can we explain Jefferson's lack of foresight?
2. From your reading of the text, was Jefferson against all manufacturing? Do you see evidence that his ideas influenced the social organization of manufacturing in the early nineteenth century (see especially Document 10-3)? If so, in what ways?
3. To Thomas Jefferson, industrial technology was the enemy of republican values. To the workingmen described by Joseph Whitworth, technology was a friend. What accounts for the difference in their attitudes?

The Expansion of Markets

The developing factory system was made possible by an ever-broadening national market, and in turn encouraged its further extension. Trade expanded first within regions and then, more gradually, between regions. The rise in manufacturing and the growth of cities and towns increased the demand for surplus agricultural produce, and farmers responded by abandoning less productive lands in the East for fertile virgin lands in the West. As westward expansion proceeded, though, the burgeoning population of the interior needed better means of transportation to the outside. In response, a "transportation revolution" developed new means of tying producers and consumers together: the turnpike, the steamboat, the canal, and the railroad. Railroads showed special promise; not only were they more flexible and reliable than water transportation, but they offered promoters great and small the opportunity to carve out economic empires that would sprawl across the continent (Document 10-6). The West in particular fired the imaginations of men who dreamed of creating great cities like Chicago on top of swampland and prairie. Many of these schemes failed, and indeed many of them were designed to swindle the gullible (Document 10-7), but the "boosters" of the West, working through both private enterprises and state undertakings such as canals, knitted the continental interior into an emerging national market and laid the groundwork for the mighty cities and industries of the post–Civil War Midwest.

10-6   Western Railroads (1845)

Jesup W. Scott

Jesup W. Scott (1798–1873) was born in Connecticut and spent his early manhood in South Carolina, but in 1830 he moved to Ohio, where he became a journalist and land speculator. Caught up in the great land boom of the 1830s, he made—and lost—a fortune before settling into life as a real estate dealer and editor of the *Toledo Blade*. In his own time, Scott was best known for his grand vision of economic empire in the Midwest. While others still saw the promise of the West as Jeffersonian utopia, Scott envisioned networks of railroads linking together mighty metropolises, including "the future great city of the world," Toledo. While Scott's prophetic talents obviously had their limits, his writings offer us a glimpse into the mind of a typical western booster, a type of American whose imaginings, however extravagant, would ultimately transform the Midwest into an urban-industrial giant.

Source: Jesup W. Scott, "The Western Railroad Movement," *Hunt's Merchants' Magazine* 12 (1845): 323–330.

THE WESTERN RAILROAD MOVEMENT.

. . . For a time, nearly all the railroads in the country were under the ban of public opinion, almost as much as speculations in corner lots. The tide is evidently again turning in favor of these improvements. It is not, however, a blind or headlong impulse, like that which existed in 1836. It looks back calmly on the past, discriminates what has been wisely done, from what has been done in the spirit of wild speculation, and is ready to embark with caution in new enterprises. In selecting routes for these expensive iron ways, there was, of course, at the commencement, a wide field for the exercise of a well-informed judgment. The country, in all its length and breadth, was open for a choice. Some were so strongly pointed out by the finger of nature, that he who ran might read. Such was the route from New York to Philadelphia and Baltimore, and that between Utica and Albany. These completed, it was plain that the great commercial city of Boston should be connected with the lake region. Yankee enterprise said, and it was done. The commercial and manufacturing towns of New England have already access to lake Erie by locomotive engines. Soon the great commercial emporium, New York, will link herself to this chain. Will this stop at Buffalo, or will it pass westward, and become the great road between New England and the Mississippi? No sane man can doubt that it will be continued, some day, to the center of the great western valley. The practical question now to

be answered is—can any part of it be made now, with a fair prospect of paying interest?

We believe there is a portion of it which should be constructed without delay; and we will briefly give our reasons for this belief. The location, between Buffalo and the west end of lake Erie, is painfully directed by the commercial towns on its souther shore, and the uniform level of that shore. From Toledo westward, the indications of nature are not less plain. The shortest route across the Michigan peninsula, that will approach lake Michigan, and admit a continuous line to the Mississippi at its great eastern bend, near the mouth of Rock river, is the natural route, against which no competition can be successfully maintained. It should be connected, either in its main line or by branches, with Michigan city and Chicago. From Toledo to Michigan city, 186 miles, and to the west line of Indiana, 220 miles, the line has been surveyed by competent engineers, and found highly favorable. If it were continued to the Mississippi, the whole length of railroad from Toledo to the Mississippi would be less than 370 miles. The portion from Toledo to the west line of Indiana is that which would pay best; and, as we believe, warrant the outlay of money necessary to complete it without delay. It would encounter no successful competition, in winter or summer; whereas that between Buffalo and Toledo would have a large portion of travel and trade diverted by the steamers on the lake, for some five months every year. The counties through which this road would pass are admirably adapted to the growth of wheat; and although they are at present but partially settled, such is the ease with which a large portion (being openings and prairies) could be improved, that the construction of the railroad would itself nearly fill it with settlers, and cause it to produce a large surplus of wheat before the work should be completed. A district of country, equal to 40 miles in breadth, lying on both sides of this road for, say 180 miles, might be safely calculated on to use it for its exports and imports. This district alone has an area of 7,200 square miles—about equal to the state of Massachusetts. With an average population equal to that of Ohio in 1840, it would contain 270,000 inhabitants. We believe it would contain that number by the time the work could be completed, if entered on within one year. This route would take all the travel, summer and winter, between the country eastward of Toledo and a vast extent of country lying westward, northwestward, and southwestward of its western termination. Much of the travel between the southwestern states, Louisiana, Mississippi, Arkansas, and the northeastern states, may be expected to take this route, until a more direct road is made from St. Louis to Toledo. This travel is now large, and no intelligent man need be told that the summer migrations of the people of the lower Mississippi country may be relied on, with a moral certainty of a regular increase. In the winter, a railroad between Toledo and Chicago would take all the travel and trade of the whole Wisconsin and Iowa, and the north half of Illinois, in the intercourse of these extensive regions with the Atlantic states. It would also draw largely from the peninsula of Michigan. In five years, Wisconsin, Iowa, and the north half of Illinois, will have a population of at least 700,000, being nearly equal to that of Massachusetts. Can it be possible that this road, well built and well managed, would not be profitable? Its construction would be cheap. . . . What would be its probable income when brought into operation? By that time it would command the business and travel of not less than 1,000,000 people living westward of Toledo, eight or nine months of the year, in all their intercourse with the east. During the period of navigation on lake Michigan, say three or four months of the year, the number depending on it could scarcely be 500,000. The country on which this population is settled and settling is not excelled in natural resources, and it is undeniably receiving more immigrants than any other great section. In seven years its numbers will be doubled. The road will then have the winter trade and travel of 2,000,000 living westward of Toledo, and the summer business of half that number. . . .

Of the character of the country along the line it may be well to particularize. In Ohio, about one-half the line is through openings, and the other half through timbered land. Both are well adapted to the growth of wheat, and contain an abundant supply of timber for the construction of the road. Through Indiana, the line traverses an almost uninterrupted chain of prairies, along, or near the route, in its whole extent, of sizes convenient for cultivating the entire surface, and of a productiveness to yield a large surplus for exportation. Many of these prairies are already reclaimed, and the whole will soon be under cultivation.

The water power, for durability and ease of management, is excelled nowhere, in proportion to its magnitude, and it is very abundant after the waters of the St. Josephs, of Michigan, are reached. Everywhere in this region, the productive wheat crop may be converted into flour in the neighborhood where it is grown. For 30 miles along the same portion of the line, are extensive beds of iron ore. These are now wrought to some extent, and eventually must add considerable to the resources of the country. It is stated by Joseph Orr, president of the Indiana road, in his address to the stockholders, that during the season of 1837, insurance on goods shipped from Buffalo to the head of lake Michigan, taking the average of a number of receipts which he had compared, cost $12.50 per ton. This would pay the freight on a railroad 416 miles long, at the rate of 3 cents per mile per ton. He truly says: "No thoroughfare now projected, is more rational in its character, or will be more general in its benefit—none uniting more natural advantages, or combining more interest. Nor is there any, in the vast extent of line, more direct. All others, natural or artificial, must be circumscribed in their usefulness by the close of navigation."

The charters given by Ohio and Indiana are of the most liberal character. The first in its operations would be perpetual, the last is to continue seventy-five years, with a right reserved to the state to buy out the stockholders after thirty-five years, by paying the cost with 18 percent interest. Five years were given in Indiana to complete the road in that state. Such an opportunity as these charters hold out for an investment which must be exceedingly profitable, would, in Europe, or the Eastern States, be seized with avidity. As a project, it stands out bold and strong, before any other of the kind in this country. Let the reader place himself before a large map of the United States, and first fixing his eyes on the 40th parallel of latitude, south of lake Michigan, let it then survey all the country north of that parallel, and west of that longitude, and it will take in nearly one-fourth of our entire country. What other route, during the fall, winter, and spring months, can the travel of this great region take to the commercial and manufacturing states eastward, than the railroad under consideration? It has no other: for it would be preposterous to suppose it would go by way of New Orleans, and not at all probable that it would go down to St. Louis, and thence by the national road. But if the prospects of profit from this road were small instead of large on its completion, there are persons enough interested in its construction to make it politic to build it without delay. How deeply the owners of the railroad from Buffalo to Boston and New York are interested, needs buy few words to illustrate. In winter, almost every traveller passing eastward on it, would be a passenger added to the whole line of travel from Buffalo to

Boston or New York; and a great portion passing west, will have come over those eastern roads from those great marts of trade. The next Congress will probably make a large appropriation for the Cumberland road.

That road has a strong tendency to draw travel from the broad west to Baltimore and Philadelphia; and the farther it is continued west, the wider is the sweep of country which it will control. New York and Boston have a great stake in securing the winter, spring, and fall travel and trade of the great valley. With a railroad from Buffalo to the Mississippi, above the mouth of Rock river, and a branch of this road from Elkhast county, Indiana, to St. Louis, Boston and New York, would control the trade of the best part of the great valley, during the entire year. They would then have no dull season of winter; but their public houses at all seasons would be full of merchants and business men from the west and south. We say south, for, with these roads completed, the Louisiana, Mississippi, Arkansas, and Texas travel would, to a great extent, come this way. If a railroad were made as straight as practicable from Toledo to St. Louis, its length would not exceed 440 miles. Branching at Elkhast, its length would not be over 465 miles. This will be its best route, because it would pass so far from the Wabash and Erie canal as not to interfere with its business. Indeed, it would be about midway between that canal and the Illinois canal and river, and thus be out of the way of rivalry, and at the same time have its length increased on the whole line but 25 miles. Supposing Alton to be taken in its route, by either course, and the increase of distance over the most direct route will not exceed 20 miles, and that over a level country, where locomotives may go 25 miles an hour.

This, then, is the great plan to be carried out in the future. But the link between the west end of lake Erie and the navigable waters of the Illinois river, is that which should be first constructed; and the time for it to be commenced with a certainty of success has arrived. . . .

. . . To the feasibility of the route, no serious objection can be urged. The shore is nearly a uniform elevation above the lake—so that the road might be almost perfectly horizontal. The main cost of its superstructure would be the erection of bridges, for which abundant material of timber and stone exist on the spot.

But we feel that enough, and more than enough has been said in favor of this link of the great iron chain that is to grapple the west to the east. We will, therefore, return to the main subject of this article—the railroad across the base of the peninsula of Michigan. The water route from lake Erie to the head of lake Michigan has been regularly opened to the keels of commerce but little more than ten years; yet it has become one of the greatest thoroughfares in the nation. About three large steamers a day, including propellers, besides a great fleet of sailing vessels, have found full employment in plying between lake Erie and Chicago the past season; and every year is adding a large per centage to the business of the preceding year. To the

friends of the proposed railroad, it is a question of extreme interest, whether a large portion of this great and increasing business may not be diverted from its circuitous water channel, and be made to roll across the isthmus that separates lake Erie from the head of lake Michigan. The following reasons in favor of this diversion seem to possess no little strength. The railroad connecting Albany and Boston is 200 miles long, although these cities are but 140 miles apart in a straight line. The distance by water between them is 450 miles. Between Toledo and the south end of lake Michigan is 200 miles, and by water between the same points 750 miles. Our railroad will be straight, with trifling exceptions, through its whole length; that of Boston and Albany loses by a deviation from a straight line 60 miles in 200. The Massachusetts road has cost upwards of $40,000 per mile, with grades of 82 feet to the mile. The Toledo road, made as good, would cost but one-third as much with a grade of 32 feet to the mile, and not over two-fifths as much with a grade of 20 feet to the mile. The road connecting Boston and Albany was built with a view of transacting the travel and transportation business between these points, in successful competition with the water route; and also with the expectation that the 200 mile railroad from Albany would, to some extent, divert the western trade from the 145 mile water route to New York. The 200 mile railway has competed successfully with the 450 mile water route from Boston to Albany. Even flour (one of the heaviest articles in proportion to its value) has given the railroad the preference. Of the 244,984 barrels passing, in 1844, from Albany to Boston, 151,721 barrels passed over the railroad. How would it have been, if the distance had been 300 miles greater—the cost of the railroad three-fifths less—and the power of traction required two-thirds less? Unless the object of Massachusetts in extending a railroad to Albany was utterly European, a railroad from Toledo to the west line of Indiana, near the south end of lake Michigan, will control the business now passing around from the head of that lake to lake Erie. The central railroad of Michigan in its business of the last year affords a practical, but faint illustration of the profits to be expected from this. That road extends 100 miles—from Detroit to Marshall. The western section was in operation only after the 10th of August. If we suppose the average length run during the year, to have been 100 miles, and the cost of that 100 miles what such a road could now be built for—say $1,000,000—the clear income (as stated by Governor Barry) of $121,750, would give a dividend for the year of over 12 per cent. The board of internal improvement of Michigan estimate the receipts of the road, for 1845, at $275,000. If the expense bears the same proportion to receipts as in 1844, the clear income will be $158,000 or nearly 16 per cent on a capital of $1,000,000. Now, this central railroad of Michigan does but little more than the business of the country through which it passes; having as yet not been pushed far enough toward lake Michigan to compete, to any great extent in summer, with the Chicago steamers. The country west of Toledo, and near the line of the proposed railway, is not less fertile than that traversed by the central railroad, and the obstruction to an easy grade and cheap construction are much less, and more easily overcome. But its great advantage is the control it will hold of the entire fall and winter business of northern Illinois and the whole of Wisconsin, during the long season of suspended and highly dangerous navigation of lake Michigan. If, in addition to this, it can be made to enter into successful competition with the lake route in summer, in the carriage of passengers and freight—thereby securing the immense business now centering in Michigan city, Chicago, and other ports at the end of lake Michigan, how strong beyond any other road, become its claims on the attention of men who wish to invest in railroad stock. The certainty, that all the goods on lake Erie, moving on their way to the country west and southwest of Chicago, would find the cost of transport on this road smaller than the insurance around the lakes, would seem to render it certain that, besides salt, no up freights would be carried by water; and in consequence that down freights would have to pay the loss and profit on the upward voyage. This would materially enhance the price of down freights by water, and thus give the railroad an additional advantage in the competition. With a heavy T or H rail, and a grade of not over 20 feet to the mile, we believe that competition may be made overwhelmingly successful.

Questions

1. At the opening of his article, Scott refers to the fact that in the mid-1830s, railroad construction across the nation had suddenly ground to a halt. Why had public opinion shifted against railroad projects at this time?

2. In what ways, according to Scott, do the building of railroads spur local development? Is his account accurate, or do you think that he paints too optimistic a picture?

3. From Scott's piece of western boosterism and your reading of the text, what role did government—whether local, state, or national—play in the building of the railroads? What challenges did railroad entrepreneurs encounter, and how did they overcome these difficulties? Why was railroad construction such a risky enterprise?

10-7   A Satire on Western Boosterism (1845)

If hope sprang eternal in the imagination of a Jesup Scott (Document 10-6), the consequences of such imaginings burned many another soul caught up in western speculation. In 1845, in the eastern Whig journal *The American Review,* an anonymous writer penned a satirical first-person account of what he claimed were his own bruising encounters with western boosters such as Scott. But the following essay does more than illustrate the rampant fraud and excess of the time; like Scott's article, it vividly captures the boundless optimism stirring the western entrepreneurs of that era.

Source: "'Commercial Delusions'—Speculations," *The American Review* 2 (October 1845): 347, 349–357.

. . . Down to 1834, the emigration to the West had been steadily increasing, and was of a beneficial and healthy character; for thus far all became actual settlers. From this time forward it was of a mixed character. Actual, bonâ fide settlers still thronged the thoroughfares and crowded the government land-offices: others went to purchase for their own future use, or for the benefit of their children; but a great majority were speculators who expected to make large gains by buying tracts of land at low prices, holding them until the surrounding country should be partially settled and improved, and then selling at advanced rates. . . .

That was the era of imaginary villages. We once saw a party of surveyors in midwinter laying out a village on the ice. The spot of ground, a marsh or swamp, with a small stream creeping lazily through it, was so low and wet that it could only be traversed by boats in summer. The proprietor had failed in business in one of the Eastern States, and found himself with a debt of thousands on his shoulders and no apparent means of paying for it. He was a "'cute Yankee," and of course turned speculator. He bought two or three hundred acres of this swamp, caused a survey to be made, then a village map showing the usual proportion of streets and squares, all named after presidents and generals of note. His next step was to visit his creditors, and offer them "village property at reduced prices," in payment of their claims. The creditors, not expecting much, were highly delighted of course, and willingly took each a few "lots," and gave him acquittances. Some were even more liberal than this, and paid the proprietor considerable sums in cash for additional lots. Thus he got rid of his debts, and found himself provided with money to commence business on a larger scale. We believe he is still out of the penitentiary.

The mania for speculation in village property at that time is unaccountable; it was so great, so universally prevalent, that one can hardly trust to his own knowledge and recollection on the subject. Common sense was entirely thrown aside in the calculations of village and city-makers, and impossibilities were deemed feasible of execution. On all the rivers village plots were found staked out at intervals of two or three miles; not only every inland county, but every remote township, had its village, and often scores of them, in which land was sold by the foot and inch, at prices varying from one hundred to twenty thousand dollars per acre—the land the while worth barely the government price of one dollar and a quarter. Each of these places were to be *cities,* and had some remarkable advantages that were possessed by none other, which must bring in a large population. So thought the "operators." There is not in all probability coin and bullion enough on this continent, if brought together, to purchase a mile in width on each side of the Maumee river, for twenty miles from its mouth, at the prices demanded for it in 1836; and this is only one point in the "great West" out of thousands equally rich and promising.

The method of operating was simple, and but little money was required to get up a respectable village on paper. About two hundred acres of land was necessary, which, if purchased of the government, must be paid for in cash, at ten shillings the acre; if bought of second hands, from three to ten dollars per acre was sufficient, and one-half of this would be in most cases secured by mortgage on the whole plot. Then a surveyor would be employed to divide the land into lots of about three rods by ten, leaving streets between every second tier, and others running at right angles, and stakes were then driven into the ground making the divisions. Afterwards came the "map," drawn with precision and care, and the more splendidly executed the better; next the erection of a few buildings, generally of logs or loose boards, except one which must be large and

gaudily painted, as it was to be "the Hotel." All this required but little money, and now the operator was ready for business. He would circulate the maps over the country, and write puffs for publication in the newspapers, wherein was duly heralded "great sales of village property"—"flourishing village in the centre of a rich and growing country"—"on the great thoroughfare between the East and the West"—"emigration rapidly pouring in"—and much more, set forth with all the flourish of Western eloquence. . . .

As a pendant to the foregoing remarks, and as illustrative in some measure of the experience of hundreds, we have furnished to our hands by one who it seems has "suffered some," a chapter in his history.

MY FIRST SPECULATION

In the height of the fever for land speculations in the renowned era of 1835, a very verdant young gentleman—since grown a trifle wiser—might have been seen one fair morning preparing for a journey to the "great west," where riches, even mines of wealth, were to be had for the asking, where villages and *eke* cities grew up into perfect being, like Jonah's gourd, in a night. My neighbor Dickens, an honest, plodding carpenter, had emigrated but a few months before, with hardly a sous in his pocket, leaving behind divers mementos in the hands of his friends with his name attached, and which, by a pleasant legal fiction, were made to represent a certain amount in dollars and cents. His anxious friends had now received intelligence that he had founded a city, and that by selling corner and other "city lots," he had become worth at least half a million dollars. Now our quondam neighbor never enjoyed any especial reputation for acuteness or sagacity, and the apparent ease with which he had slipped into a fortune operated with the force and speed of an electrical battery upon his old acquaintance.

But this was not all the evidence we had "bearing upon the case," as gentlemen of the legal school are wont to say. One Timothy Jenkins, a fiddling village tailor, and withal a very great "loafer," having a soul above buttons, had also some twelve months previous left the circle of his numerous admirers, without even the ceremony of an adieu—going off, indeed, between two days—and he too, it was ascertained, had made a fortune. In fact, he had become a nabob, lived like a gentleman, and was in a fair way, ere long, to represent his enlightened fellow-citizens in the National Legislature, if he did not conclude to accept in lieu the more dignified, but less profitable post of Governor of the Northwestern Territory. . . .

Besides these tangible evidences, we had other proofs of Western wealth. The newspapers—and they are always to be credited—were filled with glowing accounts of the construction of railroads and canals without number (as certain Indiana and Illinois bond-holders will no doubt well recollect)—of boundless immigration—of towns suddenly arising full grown, armed with all the civic strength of mayors, aldermen and police—and, most captivating of all, of vast individual wealth suddenly acquired. There was no resisting the temptation; the idea of saving pennies and shillings in the old-fashioned slow-and-sure way, appeared sufficiently ridiculous, after it was once well authenticated that thousands could be made in a single operation any day before dinner. . . .

Embarking on a steamboat, I found its decks crowded with keen-eyed, thin-visaged, anxious-looking gentlemen, all like myself bound to the land of promise. . . . Descending to the spacious cabin, I soon found game more worthy of notice. There the sound of "dollars—dollars," in thousands, again met my ear; all were discussing the flattering prospects of the "great West;" choice locations were spoken of in the most positive terms; great cities and towns were named, of whose existence I had no previous knowledge; banks, railways and canals were discussed, as means of accumulating wealth, and every man seemed to be the owner of one. "What a wonderful country!" was my internal ejaculation; "yes! what a wonderful people!"

A portly good-looking man of middle age was seated at a table listening with apparent unconcern to the conversation around him. His appearance attracted my attention. . . . I resolved to make his acquaintance and obtain his advice as to the best mode of investing my small means. . . . Gradually narrowing down the circle of his encomiastic remarks, he proved, conclusively, that the State of Illinois was the very seat and center of the West, and one spot in particular, he declared, after mature reflection, *must* inevitably become the metropolis of that favored country. The city of Franklin, he continued, was to be the West what New York is to the East, and New Orleans to the South.

Notwithstanding a dubious smile on the faces of a few quiet elderly gentlemen who had been listeners to this harangue, I was convinced by the evident sincerity and candor of the speaker. I ventured to inquire where the city was situated. The surprise he manifested at my ignorance somewhat disconcerted me, but he condescended to inform me that it was near the center of the State, and the geographical center of ——— County. Here he unrolled a spacious map representing that city in sections, blocks and lots. It was a beautiful lithograph, the first I had examined, on which streets, squares and public buildings were laid down with the most captivating conspicuousness. Here was the ground for "St. Paul's Church," evidently an extensive Park; on an opposite corner was "University Square;" here figured the "North American Bank," and there the "market house" and the "town hall." Railroads and canals on this map seemed innumerable and all centered in the city of Franklin. . . .

Such glowing descriptions increased my impatience. The steamer moved quite too slow. The white villages that decked the shore of the Lake seemed beckoning to me to "come and buy." "How could one," said I, "live so long without real estate!". . . .

I inquired if I could not through his assistance get hold of a little property in the city of Franklin, it being my aim to make a permanent investment. . . . In half an hour he had my thousand dollars safe in his pocket; I, a deed—duly "signed, sealed and delivered,"—conveying to me "Lots 500 and 501, on National Avenue in the City of Franklin," bound by what other squares, parks, or streets I do not now recollect. And it was conveyed not only to me, but to my "heirs forever." The phrase added something to my posthumous importance.

I was now a "freeholder," an owner of "Real Estate."—"Blessed be all deeds of conveyance!" said I, gloating over the fair, smooth paper and writing, on and by which the delightful transfer was effected.—"What will my dear mother say, heaven bless her!—yes, and how shall I be envied by all my cousins and kinsfolk at home! Did they not predict that I would lose all my careful earnings? Will I not show them a few things yet?"—All the evening of this auspicious day I paced the deck of the steamer, ruminating upon my present good fortune and future consequence. For I was able to look beyond a few years—a *very* few, as it was not necessary to consider a great many vanished. I saw myself a man of substance and standing. In due time, I was an alderman—in the city of Franklin, finally, a mayor. I was looked up to by all of my name, as the "head of their house." I was the owner of blocks of buildings, stores, warehouses, and offices—had a handsome rent-roll—kept an open hall, feasted my friends, knew the finest carriage in the city as mine, and was conscious of much stock in banks. At last, I died:—"For we must all go," said I—'omnes eodem cogimur'—repeating a solemn line from Flaccus:—

> 'Omnium
> Versatur urna serius, ocius,'—

I added, from the same melancholy poet, 'every one kicks the bucket finally!'" But I went off highly respected, and all the city journals—very numerous then in Franklin—recorded the demise of "a wealthy and munificent Father of the City" gone to glory! . . .

. . . In this idea, among others, I was indulging, when the boat—an old one—put in unexpectedly at Toledo, to caulk up a leak and take in wood.

Here the conversation all turned on the growth of Toledo, and other amazing cities adorning the Maumee. That river, indeed, was expected to rival the Nile—which, in the matter of mud and bulrushes, it does. Our boat was visited at once by the possessors of city property at various points up the shore. One smooth-faced gentleman—with the exception of a wen on one side of his nose—set forth such advantages of a particular point, where "*he* hadn't much interest, but a *friend of his* something," as to induce several to transfer themselves to another boat—a small "half-pony power" affair, which plied up the Maumee—"in general," the Captain said, "as far as it *could git,* more or less!" I was of that fortunate number. Such a chance to make a purchase, equal, if not superior, to that already achieved, was not to be lost. It was a sultry day. The interest of the shores was exhausted in the first half-mile. Books I had none. Newspapers were unknown in that region. . . .

By means of a rickety skiff, three at a time were deposited on a lubricated log, tilted down from the swampy bank into the water. My confidence in the owner of lots was somewhat diminished. Still, I and one or two others followed him, valise in hand, as with map sticking out from my pocket behind, he made his way through a mile and a-half of marshy grounds, —*very rich,* as he said—till we came to a bend in the river where some twenty acres were just being cleared, half of it lying level with the Maumee. "This is the spot, gentlemen," said he, mounting a log: "a most desirable locality. No great city can ever rise between Toledo and this point (which is undoubtedly true!) it is the head of navigation on the Maumee, as you experienced by your boat being stopped—a *very* little below here—and as to these low lands, a slight draining, gentlemen,"—Here, by a flourish of his lithograph, the eloquent expositor of rising towns, slipping off, slumped standing into a habitation of the "green gentry"—of whom there were a hoarse acre or two on each side—forming, as the speculator next to me said, the finest example of a proprietor "*locum tenens.*" Helping him out, I concluded "not to purchase," and made "the *best* of my way" (and wretched enough it was) back through the woods for Toledo, which I reached the next day about noon—immediately taking a chance steamer for my original landing-place, Detroit. . . .

I visited all those mighty cities on the West shore of Lake Erie; Brest, Havre, and a score of others, whose names have fled from my memory. Tacitus, in describing the destruction by fire of a town in Gaul, used the sententious words: "Between a great city and none, but a single night intervened." I might in another sense make the same observation of these mighty towns. A survey, and the making of a map, and the work was done to your hands. Buildings, streets, and inhabitants, were absolute superfluities. Some of them were without a single house, others were in a morass, made life-like only by the hum of musquitoes, and the evening song of multitudinous frogs; others again were under water, or in a dense forest. A pleasant sight for an innocent purchaser, on his first visit to his landed acquisitions! But my faith in my steamboat-friend was great; I never doubted the value of *my* purchase;—although the specimens I had seen were enough to shatter the nerves of an elephant. Longing to set foot on my own ground, I equipped myself, speculator-fashion, with a Canadian pony—an ugly obstinate, crabbed rascal as ever a man bestrode, a pair of capacious saddlebags, a pocket map, and a Mackinaw blanket, set out for Illinois and the city of Franklin. . . .

I pass over all the incidents of the journey, many of which were amusing to me, but might not be so to the reader. I must not forget, however, to mention one remarkable fact: every river on the route, large enough to bear up a canoe, had a village on either bank, every six or seven miles. Moreover, at each one was the actual head of navigation, beyond which no steamer or other craft could possibly pass. This imparted a peculiar value to each point. Another fact quite as singular I discovered. Every village, taken by itself was uncommonly healthy; no one ever died *there*—that was certain; but the next village was sickly, and always would be—at least so I was informed again and again by many a poor fellow, upon whom the "fever and ague" had plainly exerted their utmost ingenuity. I also found that village and city property grew more valuable the further it was removed from the business and population of the East. . . .

I passed through Michigan City, then in its infancy, but possessing a mayor and city council—through Chicago, where land was valued at about as high a price per foot as it was in Broadway or Wall Street, "water lots" especially—through Romeo and Juliette, and countless lesser cities. . . .

At last I reached ———— county and in "hot haste" for the aforesaid city. I very naturally looked forward to my arrival with no small degree of interest. In the first place I was in need of rest and repose; my "accommodations" had been none of the best, on the route, and there I imagined I should find a good hotel and an obliging host, and, in virtue of my proprietorship, thought it very likely I should receive some extra attentions. Then again I was anxious to see the character of the town, the mode of building, and to become acquainted with my future neighbors. I had made up my mind to assume an air of dignity, as became a freeholder. I made due inquiries as I entered the limits of the county, cautiously and modestly at first, but at last with agitation and vehemence. I was informed that there was no such city, town or village in the county! My hair fairly rose on end, like "quills upon the fretful porcupine." I perused my deed of conveyance again and again. There it was, plainly, in black and white, "the city of Franklin"—"lots 500 and 501 on National Avenue." I traversed the county in all directions, wearied every traveler with my inquiries, disturbed the inmates of every log hut, and got myself kicked out of one or two for my impetuosity of manner. It was labor lost. In the language of the region, I was "done for"—"diddled." Civic honors!—rent roll!—blocks of buildings! Alas! My dreams had fled—so had my money. My obliging friend of the steamboat was a man of imagination, as well as profound morality; the city existed *on his map.* "The scoundrel!" said I, "let me catch him again!"—But instead of my catching him he had evidently caught me—something of a difference as I found. One thing I did catch—the fever-and-ague. I took it at a log-house, in the vicinity of a "slight swamp"—as the owner of the shantee called a three mile morass—and had it a trifle over nine weeks. The ghost of my father wouldn't have known me!

This was my *first speculation*. It may be imagined in what mood I traveled after this adventure, but it cannot well be imagined why, after this lesson, I continued the pleasing game of getting rich without labor. The result of my gains as a speculator may be expressed by a cipher, or any number of them together, as $0,000, etc. I returned "a sadder, but a wiser man," the owner of eighty acres of wild land, and in debt eleven thousand dollars!

Questions

1. What is the point of the *American Review* satire? What is the moral or lesson that the author is trying to convey?
2. From your reading of the *American Review* satire, what do you learn about the tactics of western land swindlers? How did these con men dupe easterners into purchasing worthless tracts of land? What language did they use, and what ideals and values did they appeal to?
3. How much of the *American Review* satire do you think is myth, and how much is reality? What aspects of the West does the author illuminate?

Questions for Further Thought

1. What do Jesup W. Scott's article (Document 10-6) and the *American Review* satire (Document 10-7) reveal about the American Dream in the first half of the nineteenth century? Many Americans viewed the West as a land of opportunity; how accurate do you think these visions were?
2. What role did the settlement and development of the West play in the larger story of the growth of the United States during the nineteenth century? Why was westward expansion so important to so many? What effects did the development of the West have in the East, and vice versa?
3. Compare the society depicted by Scott and The *American Review* satirist with Thomas Jefferson's vision of the West as an "Empire of Liberty." Would Jefferson have been happy with how his vision turned out?

Changes in the Social Structure

The Industrial Revolution reshaped the social structure and social values of the northeastern United States. The emergence of both a business class and a wage-earning class revealed a striking and, to many, disturbing gap between the rich and the poor (see text pp. 333–337). For the business class it seemed clear that the expanding American economy offered a wide field of opportunity for those with the discipline and diligence to work hard, although risks were high and danger lurked for those who were either unwary or tempted by quick, speculative roads to riches. Both the opportunities and the anxieties evoked were addressed by a new breed of self-help literature (Document 10-8).

The gap between the rich (and the newly emergent middle class) and the laboring poor also revealed social problems that were troubling to the business class. Workingmen no longer lived in the household and under the supervision of a master. These masterless men increasingly resided in neighborhoods separate from the residential areas occupied by the business class (see text p. 337). Workingmen also frequented saloons that catered to their class exclusively. The question of how to assure social stability in a newly fragmented society was the era's major problem; this was an unwanted and potentially dangerous consequence of economic progress. Through benevolent reform and an evangelical Protestantism that stressed the individual conversion experience (Document 10-9), the business class worked to erect new standards of social order compatible with the individual autonomy that was characteristic of industrial society. Of all the era's moral reforms, temperance (Document 10-10) reached the widest audience and achieved the greatest success across class lines (see text pp. 337–341).

10-8 Advice for Businessmen (1856)

Freeman Hunt

Freeman Hunt (1804–1858) was born in Quincy, Massachusetts, but was orphaned at an early age. Learning the printer's trade, he worked for a succession of newspapers and advanced rapidly thanks to both his skill and his pen. From 1828 on, he published a succession of newspapers and magazines. In 1839 he established the journal with which he is most closely identified, *Hunt's Merchants' Magazine,* which he edited until his death in 1858. Through his magazine, Hunt became one of the foremost spokesmen for the emerging business culture of the nation. In 1856 he compiled a number of his short pieces, along with some written by others, into a collection of maxims he entitled *Worth and Wealth.* In a society in which success and failure were never far apart, Hunt provided both reassurance and a vision of the businessman as a new kind of hero.

Source: Freeman Hunt, *Worth and Wealth* (New York: Stringer and Townsend, 1856). Also available in Merle Curti et al., eds., *American Issues: The Social Record,* 4th ed. (Philadelphia and New York: Lippincott, 1941), 1: 258–259.

A man of business should be able to fix his attention on details, and he ready to give every kind of argument a hearing. This will not encumber him, for he must have been practised before-hand in the exercise of his intellect, and be strong in principles. One man collects materials together, and there they remain, a shapeless heap; another, possessed of method, can arrange what he has collected; but such a man as I would describe, by the aid of principles, goes farther, and builds with his materials.

He should be courageous. The courage, however, required in civil affairs, is that which belongs rather to the able commander than the mere soldier. But any kind of courage is servicable.

Besides a stout heart, he should have a patient temperament, and a vigorous but disciplined imagination; and then he will plan boldly, and with large extent of view, execute calmly, and not be stretching out his hand for things not yet within his grasp. He will let opportunities grow before his eyes until they are ripe to be seized. He will think steadily over possible failure, in order to provide a remedy or a retreat. There will be the strength of repose about him.

He must have a deep sense of responsibility. He must believe in the power and vitality of truth, and in all he does or says, should be anxious to express as much truth as possible.

His feeling of responsibility and love of truth will almost inevitably endow him with diligence, accuracy, and discreetness—those commonplace requisites for a good man of business, without which all the rest may never come to be "translated into action." . . .

Almost every merchant has been rich, or at least prosperous, at some point of his life; and if he is poor now, he can see very well how he might have avoided the disaster which overthrew his hopes. He will probably see that his misfortunes arose from neglecting some of the following rules:—

Be industrious. Everybody knows that industry is the fundamental virtue in the man of business. But it is not every sort of inidustry which tends to wealth. Many men work hard to do a great deal of business, and, after all, make less money than they would if they did less. Industry should be expended in seeing to all the details of business—in the careful finishing up of each separate undertaking, and in the maintainance of such a system will keep everything under control.

Be economical. This rule, also, is familiar to everybody. Economy is a virtue to be practised every hour in a great city. It is to practiced in pence as much as in pounds. A shilling a day saved, amounts to an estate in the course of a life. Economy is especially important in the outset of life, until the foundations of an estate are laid. Many men are poor all their days, because, when their necessary expenses were small, they did not seize the opportunity to save a small capital, which would have changed their fortunes for the whole of their lives.

Stick to the business in which you are regularly employed. Let speculators make their thousands in a year or day; mind your own regular trade, never turning from it to the right hand or the left. If you are a merchant, a professional man, or a mechanic, never buy lots or stocks unless you have surplus money which you wish to invest. Your own business you understand as well as other men; but other people's business you do not understand. Let your business be some one which is useful to the community. All such occupations possess the elements of profits in themselves, while mere speculation has no such element.

Never take great hazards. Such hazards are seldom well balanced by the prospects of profit; and if they were, the habit of mind which is induced is unfavorable, and generally the result is bad. To keep what you have, should be the first rule; to get what you can fairly, the second.

Do not be in a hurry to get rich. Gradual gains are the only natural gains, and they who are in haste to be rich, break over sound rules, fall into temptations and distress of various sorts, and generally fail of their object. There is no use in getting rich suddenly. The man who keeps his business under his control, and saves something from year to year, is always rich. At any rate, he possesses the highest enjoyment which riches are able to afford.

Never do business for the sake of doing it, and being counted a great merchant. There is often more money to be made by a small business than a large one; and that business will in the end be most respectable which is most successful. Do not get deeply in debt; but so manage as always, if possibly, to have your financial position easy, so that you can turn any way you please.

Do not love money extravagantly. We speak here merely with reference to getting rich. In morals, the inordinate love of money is one of the most degrading vices. But the extravagant desire of accumulation induces an eagerness, many times, which is imprudent, and so misses its object from too much haste to grasp it. . . .

Success in life mainly depends upon perseverance. When a man has determined to follow a certain line of business, he must at the same time learn to persevere until success crowns his efforts. He must never be cast down by the difficulties which may beset his path—for whoever conquers difficulty, conquers a weakness of his own frail nature likewise. How many men have commenced business under the most favorable auspices, and yet when a cloud has momentarily overshadowed their path, have lost all command over themselves and fled before the temporary gloom, instead of persevering on until the cloud has been dispersed, and sunshine once more smiled upon their efforts. Others, more fickle, have thought their business, in some minor departments, unworthy of their perseverance and energy, and forgetting the golden maxim that, "whatever is worth doing is worth doing well," have ceased to persevere in small matters, until sloth has entered deeply into their minds, and their whole business greatly neglected.

We are too apt to attribute success in business to good fortune, instead of great perseverance. This is a great evil, and should be eshewed, as it leads many to suppose that Dame Fortune will do that for them which they are unwilling to do for themselves.

The history of every great success in business is the history of great perseverance. By perseverance the mind is strengthened and invigorated, and the difficulty that once seemed so formidable is a second time surmounted with ease and confidence.

Energy and great perseverance are never thrown away on a good cause, or left unrewarded; and to every man of business, perseverance should be his motto, and then he may look with confidence to fortune as his reward.

Questions

1. According to Hunt, what qualities should a successful businessman possess and what rules should he follow?
2. What relationship between individual success and the community is suggested?
3. Why does Hunt warn against speculation and the pursuit of sudden wealth?

10-9   A Conversion Experience (1821)

Charles Grandison Finney   Charles Grandison Finney (1792–1875) (see text pp. 339–341) was the leading revivalist of the early nineteenth century. He was born in Connecticut, but his family moved westward to Oneida County, New York, where Finney grew up. The religious experience he describes here ended his career as a lawyer and inspired his work as a revivalist. Finney's dramatic preaching stressed the importance of the immediate acceptance of God's grace through Jesus Christ. He emphasized the individual's need to assume moral responsibility for himself or herself. Those who flocked to Finney's revivals hoped to experience God's regenerating grace in essentially the same way Finney had.

Source: Used with permission from *The Autobiography of Charles G. Finney*, condensed and edited by Helen Wessel, 13–25. Published by Bethany House Publishers, Minneapolis. Copyright 1977. All rights reserved.

On a Sunday evening in the autumn of 1821 I made up my mind that I would settle the question of my soul's salvation at once, that if it were possible I would make my peace with God. . . .

During Monday and Tuesday my convictions increased, but still it seemed as if my heart grew harder. I could not shed a tear. I could not pray. . . .

Tuesday night I had become very nervous, and in the night a strange feeling came over me as if I were about to die. I knew that if I did I would sink down to hell, but I quieted myself as best I could until morning.

At an early hour I started for the office. But just before I arrived at the office, it seemed as if an inward voice confronted me with questions like these: "What are you waiting for? Did you not promise to give your heart to God? And what are you trying to do? Are you endeavoring to work out a righteousness of your own?"

Just at this point the whole question of Gospel salvation opened to my mind in a manner most marvelous. I think I then saw, as clearly as I ever have in my life, the reality and fullness of the atonement of Christ. I saw that his work was a finished work, and that instead of having, or needing, any righteousness of my own to recommend me to God, I had to submit to the righteousness of God through Christ. Gospel salvation seemed to be an offer to be accepted, and that it was full and complete. All that was necessary on my part was my own consent to give up my sins and accept Christ. Salvation was not achieved by my own works, but was to be found entirely in the Lord Jesus Christ, who presented himself before me as my God and my Savior.

Without being distinctly aware of it, I had stopped in the street right where the inward voice seemed to arrest me. How long I remained in that position I cannot say. But after this distinct revelation had stood for some little time before my mind, the question seemed to be, "Will you accept it now, today?"

I replied, "Yes, I will accept it today, or I will die in the attempt." . . .

The thought was pressing me of the rashness of my promise that I would give my heart to God that day or die in the attempt. It seemed to me as if that was binding upon my soul, and yet I was going to break my vow. A great

sinking and discouragement came over me, and I felt almost too weak to stand upon my knees.

Just at this moment I again thought I heard someone approach me, and I opened my eyes to see whether it were so. But right there the revelation of my pride was distinctly shown to me as the great difficulty that stood in the way. An overwhelming sense of my wickedness in being ashamed to have a human being see me on my knees before God took such powerful possession of me that I cried at the top of my voice and exclaimed that I would not leave that place if all the men on earth and all the devils in hell surrounded me. "What!" I said, "such a degraded sinner as I am, on my knees confessing my sins to the great and holy God, ashamed to have any human being find me on my knees endeavoring to make my peace with my offended God!" The sin appeared awful, infinite. It broke me down before the Lord.

Just at that point this passage of scripture seemed to drop into my mind with a flood of light: "Then shall you go and pray unto me, and I will hearken to you. Then shall you seek me and find me, when you shall search for me with all your heart."

I instantly seized hold of this with my heart. I had intellectually believed the Bible before, but never had the truth been in my mind that faith was a voluntary trust instead of an intellectual state. I was as conscious of trusting at that moment in God's truthfulness as I was of my own existence. Somehow I knew that that was a passage of scripture, though I do not think I had ever read it. I knew that it was God's word, and God's voice, as it were, that spoke to me.

I cried to him, "Lord, I take Thee at Thy word. Now Thou knowest that I do search for Thee with all my heart, and that I have come here to pray to Thee; and Thou hast promised to hear me." . . .

But how was I to account for the quiet of my mind? I tried to recall my convictions, to get back again the load of sin under which I had been laboring. But all sense of sin, all consciousness of present sin or guilt, had departed from me. I said to myself, "What is this, that I cannot arouse any sense of guilt in my soul, as great a sinner as I am?" I tried in vain to make myself anxious about my present state. I was so quiet and peaceful that I tried to feel concerned about that, lest it should be a result of my having grieved the Spirit away. But take any view of it I would, I could not be anxious at all about my soul and about my spiritual state. The repose of my mind was unspeakably great. I cannot describe it in words. The thought of God was sweet to my mind, and the most profound spiritual tranquillity had taken full possession of me. This was a great mystery, but it did not distress or perplex me. . . .

[That evening] There was no fire and no light in this back room; nevertheless it appeared to me as if it were perfectly light. As I went in and shut the door after me, it seemed as if I met the Lord Jesus Christ face to face. It seemed to me that I saw him as I would see any other man. He said nothing, but looked at me in such a manner as to break me right down at his feet. It seemed to me a reality that he stood before me, and I fell down at his feet and poured out my soul to him. I wept aloud like a child and made such confessions as I could with my choked words. It seemed to me that I bathed his feet with my tears, and yet I had no distinct impression that I touched him.

I must have continued in this state for a good while, but my mind was too much absorbed with the interview to remember anything that I said. As soon as my mind became calm enough I returned to the front office and found that the fire I had made of large wood was nearly burned out. But as I turned and was about to take a seat by the fire, I received a mighty baptism of the Holy Spirit. Without any expectation of it, without ever having the thought in my mind that there was any such thing for me, without any memory of ever hearing the thing mentioned by any person in the world, the Holy Spirit descended upon me in a manner that seemed to go through me, body and soul. I could feel the impression, like a wave of electricity, going through and through me. Indeed it seemed to come in waves of liquid love, for I could not express it in any other way. It seemed like the very breath of God. I can remember distinctly that it seemed to fan me, like immense wings.

No words can express the wonderful love that was spread abroad in my heart. I wept aloud with joy and love. I literally bellowed out the unspeakable overflow of my heart. These waves came over me, and over me, and over me, one after the other, until I remember crying out, "I shall die if these waves continue to pass over me." I said, "Lord, I cannot bear any more," yet I had no fear of death. . . .

In this state I was taught the doctrine of justification by faith as a present experience. That doctrine had never taken possession of my mind. I had never viewed it distinctly as a fundamental doctrine of the Gospel. Indeed, I did not know at all what it meant in the proper sense. But I could now see and understand what was meant by the passage, "Being justified by faith, we have peace with God through our Lord Jesus Christ." I could see that the moment I believed, while up in the woods, all sense of condemnation had entirely dropped out of my mind, and that from that moment I could not feel a sense of guilt or condemnation by any effort I could make. My sense of guilt was gone, my sins were gone, and I do not think I felt any more sense of guilt than if I never had sinned.

This was just the revelation I needed. I felt myself justified by faith, and, so far as I could see, I was in a state in which I did not sin. Instead of feeling that I was sinning all the time, my heart was so full of love that it overflowed. My cup ran over with blessing and with love. I could not feel that I was sinning against God, nor could I recover the least sense of guilt for my past sins. Of this experience of justification I said nothing to anybody at the time.

Questions

1. What does Finney mean by "salvation" and "faith"?
2. What physical and psychological changes does he undergo?
3. What does the conversion experience teach him, and how is he different after it?

10-10   The Beginning of the Temperance Movement (1812)

Lyman Beecher

Lyman Beecher (1775–1863) was a pastor in both Congregational and Presbyterian churches and founded one of America's most remarkable families. A graduate of Yale College, he led parishes in New York, Connecticut, Massachusetts, and Ohio. Many of his eleven children achieved distinction, including sons Henry Ward and Edward and daughters Catharine and Harriet Beecher Stowe. He composed his autobiography by dictating it to several of his children. This selection describes his commitment to temperance reform soon after he became pastor of the Congregational Church in Litchfield, Connecticut.

Source: Reprinted by permission of the publisher from *The Autobiography of Lyman Beecher*, Volume I, ed. Barbara M. Cross (Cambridge, Mass.: The Belknap Press of Harvard University Press), 179–182. Copyright © 1961 by the President and Fellows of Harvard College. Reprinted by permission of Harvard University Press.

Soon after my arrival at Litchfield I was called to attend the ordination at Plymouth of Mr. Heart, ever after that my very special friend. I loved him as he did me. He said to me one day, "Beecher, if you had made the least effort to govern us young men, you would have had a swarm of bees about you; but, as you have come and mixed among us, you can do with us what you will."

Well, at the ordination at Plymouth, the preparation for our creature comforts, in the sitting-room of Mr. Heart's house, besides food, was a broad sideboard covered with decanters and bottles, and sugar, and pitchers of water. There we found all the various kinds of liquors then in vogue. The drinking was apparently universal. This preparation was made by the society as a matter of course. When the Consociation [of ministers] arrived, they always took something to drink round; also before public services, and always on their return. As they could not all drink at once, they were obliged to stand and wait as people do when they go to mill.

There was a decanter of spirits also on the dinnertable, to help digestion, and gentlemen partook of it through the afternoon and evening as they felt the need, some more and some less; and the sideboard, with the spillings of water, and sugar, and liquor, looked and smelled like the bar of a very active grog-shop. None of the Consociation were drunk; but that there was not, at times, a considerable amount of exhilaration, I can not affirm.

When they had all done drinking, and had taken pipes and tobacco, in less than fifteen minutes there was such a smoke you couldn't see. And the noise I can not describe; it was the maximum of hilarity. They told their stories, and were at the height of jocose talk. They were not old-fashioned Puritans. They had been run down. Great deal of spirituality on Sabbath, and not much when they got where there was something good to drink.

I think I recollect some animadversions [criticisms] were made at that time by the people on the amount of liquor drank, for the tide was swelling in the drinking habits of society.

The next ordination was of Mr. Harvey, in Goshen, and there was the same preparation, and the same scenes acted over, and then afterward still louder murmurs from the society at the quantity and expense of liquor consumed.

These two meetings were near together, and in both my alarm, and shame, and indignation were intense. 'Twas that that woke me up for the war. And silently I took an oath before God that I would never attend another ordination of that kind. I was full. My heart kindles up at the thoughts of it now.

There had been already so much alarm on the subject, that at the General Association [of ministers] at Fairfield in 1811, a committee of three had been appointed to make inquiries and report measures to remedy the evil. A committee was also appointed by the General Association of Massachusetts for the same purpose that same month, and to confer with other bodies.

I was a member of General Association which met in the year following at Sharon, June, 1812, when said committee reported. They said they had attended to the subject committed to their care; that intemperance had been for some time increasing in a most alarming manner; but that, after the most faithful and prayerful inquiry, they were obliged to confess they did not perceive that any thing could be done.

The blood started through my heart when I heard this, and I rose instanter, and moved that a committee of three be appointed immediately, to report at this meeting the ways and means of arresting the tide of intemperance.

The committee was named and appointed. I was chairman, and on the following day brought in a report, the most important paper that ever I wrote.

ABSTRACT OF REPORT.

The General Association of Connecticut, taking into consideration the undue consumption of ardent spirits, the enormous sacrifice of property resulting, the alarming increase of intemperance, the deadly effect on health, intellect, the family, society, civil and religious institutions, and especially in nullifying the means of grace and destroying souls, recommend,

1. Appropriate discourses on the subject by all ministers of Association.

2. That District Associations abstain from the use of ardent spirits at ecclesiastical meetings.

3. That members of Churches abstain from the unlawful vending, or purchase and use of ardent spirits where unlawfully sold; exercise vigilant discipline, and cease to

consider the production of ardent spirits a part of hospitable entertainment in social visits.

4. That parents cease from the ordinary use of ardent spirits in the family, and warn their children of the evils and dangers of intemperance.

5. That farmers, mechanics, and manufacturers substitute palatable and nutritious drinks, and give additional compensation, if necessary, to those in their employ. . . .

Immense evils, we are persuaded, afflict communities, not because they are incurable, but because they are tolerated; and great good remains often unaccomplished merely because it is not attempted.

Questions

1. What does this account reveal about the social uses of alcohol before the beginning of the temperance campaign?
2. Why was Beecher offended by the two ordination meetings he described?
3. According to the "Abstract," what was the problem and what measures were proposed to deal with it?

Questions for Further Thought

1. What qualities does Hunt's businessman share with Finney's converted Christian?
2. Why did reformers in the early nineteenth century prefer self-restraint to legislation that would make undesirable behavior illegal?
3. Compare Finney's account of his conversion to the Reverend George Baxter's description of the conversions at Cane Ridge (Document 9-9). What do these evangelicals see as the best evidence of genuine salvation?

CHAPTER 11

A Democratic Revolution, 1820–1844

★   ★   ★

The Rise of Popular Politics, 1820–1829

In the first generation or two following independence, political life continued to be dominated by the traditional elite. Since most Americans lived relatively settled lives in communities where they knew and trusted the "leading men," it remained customary to provide them with political support. Moreover, in a largely rural society where property-holding was widespread and generally considered a mark of independence and reliability, property requirements for voting were standard and were justified as protecting the rights of all against assaults by those who would use government to obtain special favors (Document 11-1).

However, the Revolution marked the beginning of a long-term breakdown in this traditional pattern of deference to a traditional ruling class. Constitutional reforms immediately brought fresh blood into power (Document 7-3), while the opening of the West and the expansion of new opportunities in commerce and manufacturing drew increasing numbers of Americans away from their home communities to seek their fortunes. Eager to attract new and as yet unpropertied settlers, western states offered them universal white male suffrage, and many (not all) eastern states followed suit, though not without conflict. With political office seen more as a "gift of the people" and less as an entitlement, a broader range of offices were made elective. Presidential electors, who were originally appointed by state legislatures, also came to be popularly elected, supplying voters for the first time with a direct voice in the choosing of the president.

In the meantime, the economic expansion of the nation raised a host of new political issues. While many Americans continued to fear special privilege and the use of government to further private interests, others, such as Henry Clay, began to argue that government aid to economic development, such as the use of tariffs to raise the prices of foreign imports in competition with American manufactures, would benefit all Americans (Document 11-2). Cultural conflicts growing out of the rise of the evangelicals (Document 9-11), and later from increased immigration, likewise spilled over into politics. These new political concerns cut across community lines and could not be contained by the old deferential politics. Instead, a new class of professional politicians, epitomized by Martin Van Buren, began to develop the modern mass political party; operating at first in the states, they mobilized armies of local workers and voters to "campaign" for party control of government policy and patronage jobs (Document 11-3). During the administration of President John Quincy Adams, increasing polarization between Adams's National Republican supporters and the Democratic-Republican (soon Democratic) supporters of Andrew Jackson allowed Van Buren, a Jackson supporter, to extend his organization to the national level. The result was not only a victory for Jackson in the election of 1828, but the first great national victory for the new mass electorate.

11-1   An Argument against Universal Suffrage (1821)

James Kent

Thomas Jefferson's characterization of John Quincy Adams's presidential policies as the "splendid government of an aristocracy" and Adams's criticism of democracy (see text pp. 351–353) illustrate the divergence of political ideology that was central to the age of democratic revolution. In an increasingly commercial society the agricultural simplicity of the early republic faded, and critics of democracy warned that the foundations of republican liberty could be eroded by poor men seeking equality with the wealthy. James Kent (1763–1847), a New York Federalist, was a leading jurist and the author of the most influential treatise on American law in the nineteenth century. Kent expressed the antidemocratic point of view with striking clarity at the New York Constitutional Convention of 1821.

Source: Reports of the Proceedings and Debates of the Convention of 1821 Assembled for the Purpose of Amending the Constitution of the State of New York (Albany: E. and E. Hosford, 1821).

[W]e propose . . . to bow before the idol of universal suffrage. That extreme democratic principle . . . has been regarded with terror by the wise men of every age because, in every European republic, ancient and modern, in which it has been tried, it has terminated disastrously and been productive of corruption, injustice, violence, and tyranny. And dare we flatter ourselves that we are a peculiar people . . . exempted from the passions which have disturbed and corrupted the rest of mankind? . . . I wish those who have an interest in the soil to retain the exclusive possession of a branch in the legislature as a stronghold in which they may find safety through all the vicissitudes which the state may be destined . . . to experience. I wish them to be always enabled to say that their freeholds cannot be taxed without their consent. The men of no property, together with the crowds of dependents connected with great manufacturing and commercial establishments, and the motley and undefinable population of crowded ports, may, perhaps, at some future day, under skilful management, predominate in the assembly, and yet we should be perfectly safe if no

laws could pass without the free consent of the owners of the soil. . . .

The apprehended danger from the experiment of universal suffrage applied to the whole legislative department is no dream of the imagination. . . . The tendency of universal suffrage is to jeopardize the rights of property and the principles of liberty. There is a constant tendency . . . in the poor to covet and to share the plunder of the rich; in the debtor to relax or avoid the obligation of contracts; in the majority to tyrannize over the minority and trample down their rights; in the indolent and the profligate to cast the whole burdens of society upon the industrious and the virtuous. . . . We are no longer to remain plain and simple republics of farmers. . . . We are fast becoming a great nation, with great commerce, manufactures, population, wealth, luxuries, and with the vices and miseries that they engender. . . . [W]e have to apprehend the establishment of unequal and, consequently, unjust systems of taxation and all the mischiefs of a crude and mutable legislation.

Questions

1. In Kent's view, how did property qualifications protect America against "corruption, injustice, violence, and tyranny"?
2. What dangers did Kent see as the nation ceased to be composed of "simple republics of farmers"?
3. If Kent's view had prevailed, how might representative government have been structured in New York?

11-2 Speech on the Tariff (March 30–31, 1824)

Henry Clay

A native of Virginia, Henry Clay (1777–1852) migrated to Kentucky, where he established himself as a substantial slaveholding planter and lawyer. A strong nationalist and War Hawk, Clay won election to the House of Representatives in 1810 and became Speaker the following year. A candidate for president in 1824, Clay advocated what he called the "American System" (see text pp. 330–351) and later played a leading role in building the Whig opposition to Andrew Jackson.

Clay's American System envisioned an integrated national economy in which a protective tariff would encourage domestic manufacturing while it generated revenues to support federally financed harbors, canals, and other major internal improvements. Clay was largely successful in his immediate aim: the Tariff of 1824, raising rates, passed. But his larger goal of harnessing the federal government to the development of the national economy fell victim to sectional rivalry and to a democratic critique of the special privilege enjoyed by established elites in the mainstream of economic development.

In the following extracts from Clay's two-day-long speech of March 1824 in the House of Representatives he explained why he believed it was in the nation's interest to impose a tariff on imports to protect domestic manufacturing.

Source: Annals of the Congress of the United States, 1789–1824 (Washington, D.C.: U.S. Government Printing Office), 18th Cong., 1st sess. (1824), 1962–2001.

And what is this tariff? It seems to have been regarded as a sort of monster, huge and deformed; a wild beast, endowed with tremendous powers of destruction, about to be let loose among our people, if not to devour them, at least to consume their substance. But let us calm our passions, and deliberately survey this alarming, this terrific being. The sole object of the tariff is to tax the produce of foreign industry, with the view of promoting American industry. The tax is exclusively levelled at foreign industry. . . .

It has been treated as an imposition of burthens upon one part of the community by design for the benefit of another; as if, in fact, money were taken from the pockets of one portion of the people and put into the pockets of another. But, is that a fair representation of it? No man pays the duty assessed on the foreign article by compulsion, but voluntarily; and this voluntary duty, if paid, goes into the common exchequer, for the common benefit of all. . . . According to the opponents of the domestic policy, the proposed system will force capital and labor into new and reluctant employments; we are not prepared, in consequence of the high price of wages, for the successful establishment of manufactures, and we must fail in the experiment. We have seen that the existing occupations of our society, those of agriculture, commerce, navigation, and the learned professions, are overflowing with competitors, and that the want of employment is severely felt. Now what does this bill propose? To open a new and extensive field of business, in which all that choose may enter. There is no compulsion upon any one to engage in it. An option only is given to industry, to continue in the present unprofitable pursuits, or to embark in a new and promising one. The effect will be to lessen the competition in the old branches of business and to multiply our resources for increasing our comforts and augmenting the national wealth. The alleged fact of the high price of wages is not admitted. The truth is, that no class of society suffers more, in the present stagnation of business, than the laboring class. That is a necessary effect of the depression of agriculture, the principal business of the community. The wages of able-bodied men vary from five to eight dollars per month; and such has been the want of employment, in some parts of the Union, that instances have not been unfrequent, of men working merely for the means of present subsistence. . . . We are now, and ever will be, essentially, an agricultural people. Without a material change in the fixed habits of the country, the friends of this measure desire to draw to it, as a powerful auxiliary to its industry, the manufacturing arts. The difference between a nation with, and without the arts, may be conceived, by the difference between a keelboat and a steam-boat, combatting the rapid torrent of the Mississippi. How slow does the former ascend, hugging the sinuosities of the shore, pushed on by her hardy and exposed crew, now throwing themselves in vigorous concert on their oars, and then seizing the pendant boughs of over-hanging trees: she seems hardly to move; and her scanty cargo is scarcely worth the transportation! With what ease is she not passed by the steam-boat, laden with the riches of all quarters of the world, with a crowd of gay, cheerful, and protected passengers, now dashing into the midst of the current, or gliding through the eddies near the shore. . . . The adoption of the restrictive system, on the part of the United States, by excluding the produce of foreign labor, would extend the consumption of American produce, unable, in the infancy and unprotected state of the arts, to sustain a competition with foreign fabrics. Let our arts breathe under the shade of protection; let them be perfected as they are in England, and we shall then be ready, as England now is said to be, to put aside protection, and to enter upon the freest exchanges. . . .

Other and animating considerations invite us to adopt the policy of this system. Its importance, in connexion with the general defence in time of war, cannot fail to be duly estimated. Need I recal [*sic*] to our painful recollection the sufferings, for the want of an adequate supply of absolute

necessaries, to which the defenders of their country's rights and our entire population were subjected during the late war [the War of 1812]? Or to remind the committee of the great advantage of a steady and unfailing source of supply, unaffected alike in war and in peace? Its importance, in reference to the stability of our Union, that paramount and greatest of all our interests, cannot fail warmly to recommend it, or at least to conciliate the forbearance of every patriot bosom. Now our people present the spectacle of a vast assemblage of jealous rivals, all eagerly rushing to the sea-board, jostling each other in their way, to hurry off to glutted foreign markets the perishable produce of their labor. The tendency of that policy, in conformity to which this bill is prepared, is to transform these competitors into friends and mutual customers; and, by the reciprocal exchanges of their respective productions, to place the confederacy upon the most solid of all foundations, the basis of common interest. . . .

Even if the benefits of the policy were limited to certain sections of our country, would it not be satisfactory to behold American industry, wherever situated, active, animated, and thrifty, rather than persevere in a course which renders us subservient to foreign industry? But these benefits are twofold, direct, and collateral, and in the one shape or the other, they will diffuse themselves throughout the Union. All parts of the Union will participate, more or less, in both. As to the direct benefit, it is probable that the North and the East will enjoy the largest share. But the West and the South will also participate in them. . . . And where the direct benefit does not accrue, that will be enjoyed of supplying the raw material and provisions for the consumption of artisans. . . . I appeal to the South—to the high-minded, generous, and patriotic South—with which I have so often co-operated. . . . Of what does it complain? A possible temporary enhancement [i.e., price increase] in the objects of consumption. Of what do we complain? A total incapacity, produced by the foreign policy, to purchase, at any price, necessary foreign objects of consumption. In such an alternative, inconvenient only to it, ruinous to us, can we expect too much from Southern magnanimity? . . .

Questions

1. How does Clay explain the importance to an agricultural nation of the "manufacturing arts"?
2. According to Clay, how would a protective tariff promote a "common interest" across the nation?
3. How did Clay answer the South's complaint that the benefits of the tariff went primarily to the manufacturing sector in the Northeast?

11-3   The Beginnings of Grass-Roots Democracy (1830)

Amos Kendall   Amos Kendall (1789–1869) was born on a poor farm in western Massachusetts. With the support his family could offer and his own ambitious efforts he was graduated from Dartmouth College in 1811, studied law, and in 1814 sought brighter prospects in the West. Kendall settled in Kentucky, where he briefly tutored the sons of Henry Clay before establishing himself as a lawyer and newspaper editor. In 1816 he moved to the state capital, Frankfort, to take charge of the influential *Argus of Western America* and was soon joined by coeditor Francis P. Blair (see text p. 355 and Document 11-10). Kendall and Blair supported Clay in the presidential election of 1824 but helped carry Kentucky for Jackson in 1828. After Jackson's victory, Kendall moved to Washington and became one of the most influential of the new president's informal "Kitchen Cabinet"; Kendall was the principal author of Jackson's Bank Veto Message (see Document 11-4). In 1830, with Jackson's political support, Kendall founded the Washington, D.C., *Globe* and called Blair east to be its editor. Sustained by a patronage position in the Treasury Department, Kendall became a powerful dispenser of Democratic patronage as postmaster general (1835–1840). In the following extracts from private letters written by Kendall in Washington to Blair in Kentucky, Kendall examines the altered political landscape that produced Jackson's victory and assesses its significance for the future.

Source: Francis P. Blair Papers, Princeton University, Princeton, New Jersey.

AMOS KENDALL TO FRANCIS P. BLAIR,
JANUARY 28, 1830:

The Democratic ascendancy in our state can only be maintained by diminishing the power of lawyers. I can think of no way so effectual to do that as to induce our farmers and mechanics to take a part in the *nomination* of candidates as well as their election. Now, our lawyers, big and little, thrust themselves out and forestall the field, and no modest farmer or mechanic dare come in competition with their pretentions. If the people could be made sensible of the wrong and injury done them by these upstarts, they would be ready to apply the remedy. . . . Let meetings of the democratic Jackson men be called in each militia company of the county on the same day. . . . By such means, the people would take the government into their own hands and send to the Legislature sounder men and better politicians. The Lawyers would not attend all these company meetings and an entire class of politicians would spring up opposed to them. . . .

By this plan the town aristocracies and the influence of rich men in the country would be measurably disarmed.

AMOS KENDALL TO FRANCIS P. BLAIR,
AUGUST 27, 1830:

There is to be a new paper here entitled the "American Statesman and Workingmen's Advocate" devoted to Mr. [Henry] Clay. It will be a poor concern; but the factious object is seen by the title. . . I am not sorry to see the efforts made to organize the workingmen. If Mr. Clay shall succeed in teaching them their strength, they will hurl him and all the factious lawyers out of power and almost out of sight. They are whetting a razor to cut their own throat. I would rejoice to see the *real* workingmen take a decisive stand in politics and place more of themselves in public office. Besides, their notions in relation to the U.S. Bank and many other matters are not very congenial to the objects of H. Clay. I know his only object is to *use* them; but he ought to remember the old proverb—"Do not meddle with edge-tools."

Questions

1. Why did Kendall (himself a lawyer) think it was important for farmers and mechanics to take part in the *nomination* as well as the election of political candidates?
2. In Kendall's view, how would this grass-roots involvement displace the "town aristocracies"?

3. Why did Kendall feel confident that Clay's efforts to "*use*" the workingmen would backfire?

Questions for Further Thought

1. Kent (Document 11-1) and Clay (Document 11-2) were both responding to the rising importance of manufactures in the United States. Based on these documents, what were the political implications of that impact?
2. Kent's elitist views, like those of the Federalist party, had to make way for the democratic revolution described by Kendall (Document 11-3). Compare the tone and content of Kent's and Clay's speeches. In what ways was Clay better equipped than Kent to meet the demands of that revolution?
3. Consider the relationship between politics and economic interest. In what ways would you expect Kendall's description of grass-roots democratic politics to affect Clay's comprehensive economic agenda?

The Presidency of Andrew Jackson, 1829–1837

Andrew Jackson entered the White House in 1829 determined to reverse what he saw as a dangerous alliance of federal government power with the forces of special privilege. An advocate of limited government, he sought to block enactment of Henry Clay's American System and to dismantle those elements of it (protective tariffs, the Bank of the United States) that were already in place. Yet in order to achieve his goals, he had to take a traditionally weak office and expand its power. Jackson used his control of federal patronage to build a strong party organization loyal to him. He pressed for tariff reduction; when South Carolina denied the right of the federal government to collect tariffs within the state, he firmly asserted the supremacy of the federal government and his right to use military force against a state to enforce federal law. Above all, Jackson went to war with the Second Bank of the United States, which he and his followers regarded as a grant of extensive public powers to a small, well-heeled band of eastern capitalists, who in turn used it for their own self-interest rather than the public good (Documents 11-4 and 11-5; compare Document 7-3). Although his goals were similar to those of Jefferson (compare Document 8-5), he pursued them by means that greatly (and, to some, dangerously) extended executive power; he vetoed the proposed rechartering of the Bank, and after his triumphant re-election in 1832, withdrew federal deposits from the Bank in defiance of Congress.

Jackson also moved to accelerate the removal of the remaining Indian peoples east of the Mississippi to new "Indian Territories" far to the west. In the South, states were seeking to extend their authority over territory held by the so-called Five Civilized Tribes (the Cherokee, Chickasaw, Choctaw, Creek, and Seminole) who insisted instead that they were sovereign peoples. Jackson sided with his white constituents and their insistence on states' rights against even the Cherokee, who had developed a sophisticated government and literature (Document 11-6). In 1830 he obtained passage of the Indian Removal Act, and he began to use both cajolery and military force to drive Indian tribes westward—a process that culminated after his administration in the infamous Trail of Tears.

11-4 Bank Veto Message (1832)

Andrew Jackson

The first Bank of the United States had been established at the behest of President Washington's treasury secretary, Alexander Hamilton, and was rechartered for a twenty-year period in 1816 during the Era of Good Feeling. The Bank had become a political issue after the Panic of 1819, when the question of the country's monetary policy suddenly became associated with financial collapse and economic depression. The bank issue had for some years generated factional political divisions at the state level, and Jackson entered the presidency opposed to the existing structure and policies of the Second Bank of the United States. He also found himself in an intense personal struggle with the Bank's president, Nicholas Biddle. When Congress approved an extended charter for Biddle's bank, Jackson vetoed the legislation (see text p. 359). Jackson made his veto message the opening shot in a campaign to destroy the Bank, a war that became the defining event of his presidency (see text p. 360). In the following extracts from his veto message Jackson explains why he viewed the Bank as an undemocratic concentration of economic power and a threat to the republic.

Source: James D. Richardson, ed., *A Compilation of the Message and Papers of the Presidents* (Washington, D.C.: U.S. Government Printing Office, 1896–1899), 2: 576–591.

The bill "to modify and continue" the act entitled "An act to incorporate the subscribers to the Bank of the United States" was presented to me on the 4th July instant. Having considered it with that solemn regard to the principles of the Constitution which the day was calculated to inspire, and come to the conclusion that it ought not to become a law, I herewith return it to the Senate, in which it originated, with my objections.

A bank of the United States is in many respects convenient for the Government and useful to the people. Entertaining this opinion, and deeply impressed with the belief that some of the powers and privileges possessed by the existing bank are unauthorized by the Constitution, subversive of the rights of the States, and dangerous to the liberties of the people, I felt it my duty at an early period of my Administration to call the attention of Congress to the practicability of organizing an institution combining all its advantages and obviating these objections. I sincerely regret that in the act before me I can perceive none of these modifications of the bank charter which are necessary, in my opinion, to make it compatible with justice, with sound policy, or with the Constitution of our country. . . .

But this act does not permit competition in the purchase of this monopoly [the bank]. It seems to be predicated on the erroneous idea that the present stockholders have a prescriptive right not only to the favor but to the bounty of Government. It appears that more than a fourth part of the stock is held by foreigners and the residue is held by a few hundred of our own citizens, chiefly of the richest class. For their benefit does this act exclude the whole American people from competition in the purchase of this monopoly and dispose of it for many millions less than it is worth. This seems the less excusable because some of our citizens not now stockholders petitioned that the door of competition might be opened, and offered to take a charter on terms much more favorable to the Government and country. . . .

It is to be regretted that the rich and powerful too often bend the acts of government to their selfish purposes. Distinctions in society will always exist under every just government. Equality of talents, of education, or of wealth can not be produced by human institutions. In the full enjoyment of the gifts of Heaven and the fruits of superior industry, economy, and virtue, every man is equally entitled to protection by law; but when the laws undertake to add to these natural and just advantages artificial distinction, to grant titles, gratuities, and exclusive privileges, to make the rich richer and the potent more powerful, the humble members of society—the farmers, mechanics, and laborers—who have neither the time nor the means of securing like favors to themselves, have a right to complain of the injustice of their Government. There are no necessary evils in government. Its evils exist only in its abuses. If it would confine itself to equal protection, and, as Heaven does its rains, shower its favors alike on the high and the low, the rich and the poor, it would be an unqualified blessing. In the act before me there seems to be a wide and unnecessary departure from these just principles. . . .

Many of our rich men have not been content with equal protection and equal benefits, but have besought us to make them richer by act of Congress. By attempting to gratify their desires we have in the results of our legislation arrayed section against section, interest against interest, and man against man, in a fearful commotion which threatens to shake the foundations of our Union. If we can not at once, in justice to interests vested under improvident legislation, make our Government what it ought to be, we can at least take a stand against all new grants of monopolies and exclusive privileges, against any prostitution of our Government to the advancement of the few at the expense of the many, and in favor of compromise and gradual reform in our code of laws and system of political economy. . . .

Questions

1. In his veto message, Jackson did not question the ability of the bank to regulate currency and credit. What public policy objectives does his message attempt to advance?
2. Despite the Supreme Court's decision in *McCulloch v. Maryland* (1819), Jackson insisted in his veto message that some of the "powers and privileges possessed by the existing bank are unauthorized by the Constitution." What reasons does he give for that judgment?
3. What did the "humbler members of society" rightly complain about, in Jackson's view?

11-5   Opposition to Banks and Monopoly (c. 1832)

William Leggett

William Leggett (1801–1839) was perhaps the most insightful political writer in the Jacksonian camp. He was born in New York City and briefly lived a frontier life with his parents in Illinois. In 1829 Leggett became joint owner and editor (with William Cullen Bryant) of the New York *Evening Post*. An enthusiastic and sophisticated supporter of Jackson's war against the Second Bank of the United States, Leggett developed the theoretical implications of Jacksonian antimonopoly and equal rights rhetoric. In the following editorial Leggett offers a practical description of the operations of unregulated banks and explains how bank-sponsored speculation entraps the unwary and makes honest producers the victims of financial corruption.

Source: Theodore Sedgwick Jr., ed., *A Collection of the Political Writings of William Leggett* (New York, 1840), 1: 97–101.

Our primary ground of opposition to banks as they at present exist is that they are a species of monopoly. All corporations are liable to the objection that whatever powers or privileges are given to them, are so much taken from the government of the people. Though a state legislature may possess a constitutional right to create bank incorporations, yet it seems very clear to our apprehension that the doing so is an invasion of the grand republican principle of Equal Rights—a principle which lies at the bottom of our constitution, and which, in truth, is the corner-stone of our national government. . . .

Let us trace the progress of a new banking institution. Let us imagine a knot of speculators to have possessed themselves, by certain acts of collusion, bribery, and political management, of a bank charter; and let us suppose them commencing operations under their corporate privileges. They begin by lending their capital. After that, if commercial business is active, and the demand for money urgent, they take care to put as many of their notes in circulation as possible. For awhile this does very well and the Bank realizes large profits. Every thing seems to flourish; merchants extend their operations. . . . Others, in the meanwhile, stimulated by the same appearance of commercial prosperity, borrow money (that is notes) from the bank, and embark in enterprises of a different nature. They purchase lots, build houses, set railway and canal projects on foot, and every thing goes on swimmingly. The demand for labour is abundant, property of all kinds rises in price, and speculators meet each other in the streets, and exult in their anticipated fortunes.

But by and by things take a different turn. . . . The bank now perceives that it has extended itself too far. Its notes, which, until now, circulated currently enough, begin to return in upon it in demand for specie; while, at the same time, the merchants, whom it has been all along eager to serve, now call for increased accommodations. But the bank cannot accommodate them any longer. Instead of increasing its loans, it is obliged to require payment of those which it had previously made. . . . The merchants, unable to get the amount of accommodation necessary to sustain their operations, are forced to suspend payment. . . . Then follows wider derangement. One commercial house after another becomes bankrupt, and finally the bank itself, by these repeated losses forced to discontinue its business, closes its doors, and hands over its affairs for the benefit of its creditors. . . . On investigation it is discovered, most likely, that the whole capital of the institution has been absorbed by its losses. The enormous profits which it made during the first part of its career, had been regularly withdrawn by the stockholders, and the deluded creditor has nothing but a worthless bit of engraved paper to show for the valuable consideration which he parted with for what he foolishly imagined [to be] money.

Questions

1. How does Leggett define a monopoly?
2. In Leggett's view, why do banks inevitably tend toward corruption?
3. Consider the implications of Leggett's remarks. How might the Jacksonians have protected the people from the mischief of what they "foolishly imagined money"?

11-6   On Indian Removal (1829)

Andrew Jackson and Elias Boudinot

In 1829, in his first annual message (what we now call the State of the Union Address, but in those days not delivered as a speech), President Jackson, alluding to the conflict between the Cherokee and the states of Georgia and Alabama, used the occasion to present his broader views about the "Indian problem" and its solution. Earlier in 1829, when Jackson and his secretary of war, John Eaton, had announced their position on the issue between the Cherokee and Georgia, Elias Boudinot, editor of the *Cherokee Phoenix*, set forth the Cherokee case.

Sources: James D. Richardson, ed., *A Compilation of the Messages and Papers of the Presidents, 1789–1902* (Washington, D.C.: Bureau of National Literature and Art, 1904), 2: 457–459; *Cherokee Phoenix*, 17 June 1829, reprinted in Theda Perdue, ed., *Cherokee Editor: The Writings of Elias Boudinot* (Knoxville: University of Tennessee Press, 1983), 108–109.

(a) Andrew Jackson, First Annual Message, December 8, 1829

. . . The condition and ulterior destiny of the Indian tribes within the limits of some of our States have become objects of much interest and importance. It has long been the policy of Government to introduce among them the arts of civilization, in the hope of gradually reclaiming them from a wandering life. This policy has, however, been coupled with another wholly incompatible with its success. Professing a desire to civilize and settle them, we have at the same time lost no opportunity to purchase their lands and thrust them farther into the wilderness. By this means they have not only been kept in a wandering state, but been led to look upon us as unjust and indifferent to their fate. Thus, though lavish in its expenditures upon the subject, Government has constantly defeated its own policy, and the Indians in general, receding farther and farther to the west, have retained their savage habits. A portion, however, of the Southern tribes, having mingled much with whites and made some progress in the arts of civilized life, have lately attempted to erect an independent government within the limits of Georgia and Alabama. These States, claiming to be the only sovereigns within their territories, extended their laws over the Indians, which induced the latter to call upon the United States for protection. . . .

. . . I informed the Indians inhabiting parts of Georgia and Alabama that their attempt to establish an independent government would not be countenanced by the Executive of the United States, and advised them to emigrate beyond the Mississippi or submit to the laws of those States.

Our conduct toward these people is deeply interesting to our national character. Their present condition, contrasted with what they once were, makes a most powerful appeal to our sympathies. Our ancestors found them the uncontrolled possessors of these vast regions. By persuasion and force they have been made to retire from river to river and from mountain to mountain, until some of the tribes have become extinct and others have left but remnants to preserve for awhile their once terrible names. Surrounded by the whites with their arts of civilization, which by destroying the resources of the savage doom him to weakness and decay, the fate of the Mohegan, the Narragansett, and the Delaware is fast overtaking the Choctaw, the Cherokee, and the Creek. That this fate surely awaits them if they remain within the limits of the States does not admit of a doubt. Humanity and national honor demand that every effort should be made to avert so great a calamity. It is too late to inquire whether it was just in the United States to include them and their territory within the bounds of new States, whose limits they could control. That step can not be retraced. A State can not be dismembered by Congress or restricted in the exercise of her constitutional power. But the people of those States and every State, actuated by feelings of justice and a regard of our national honor, submit to you the interesting question whether something can not be done, consistently with the rights of the States, to preserve this much-injured race.

As a means of effecting this end I suggest for your consideration the propriety of setting apart an ample district west of the Mississippi, and without the limits of any State or Territory now formed, to be guaranteed to the Indian tribes as long as they shall occupy it, each tribe having a distinct control over the portion designated for its use. There they may be secured in the enjoyment of governments of their own choice, subject to no other control from the United States than such as may be necessary to preserve peace on the frontier and between the several tribes. There the benevolent may endeavor to teach them the arts of civilization, and, by promoting union and harmony among them, to raise up an interesting commonwealth, destined to perpetuate the race and to attest the humanity and justice of this Government.

This emigration should be voluntary, for it would be as cruel as unjust to compel the aborigines to abandon the graves of their fathers and seek a home in a distant land. But they should be distinctly informed that if they remain within the limits of the States they must be subject to their laws. In return for their obedience as individuals they will

without doubt be protected in the enjoyment of those possessions which they have improved by their industry. But it seems to me visionary to suppose that in this state of things claims can be allowed on tracts of country on which they have neither dwelt nor made improvements, merely because they have seen them from the mountain or passed them in the chase. Submitting to the laws of the States, and receiving, like other citizens, protection in their persons and property, they will ere long become merged in the mass of our population. . . .

(b) Elias Boudinot, Excerpted from the *Cherokee Phoenix*, June 17, 1829

From the documents which we this day lay before our readers, there is not a doubt of the kind of policy, which the present administration of the General Government intends to pursue relative to the Indians. President Jackson has, as a neighboring editor remarks, "recognized the doctrine contended for by Georgia in its full extent." It is to be regretted that we were not undeceived long ago, while we were hunters and in our savage state. It appears now from the communication of the Secretary of War to the Cherokee Delegation, that the illustrious Washington, Jefferson, Madison and Monroe were only tantalizing us, when they encouraged us in the pursuit of agriculture and Government, and when they afforded us the protection of the United States, by which we have been preserved to this present time as a nation. Why were we not told long ago, that we could not be permitted to establish a government within the limits of any state? Then we could have borne disappointment much easier than now. The pretext of Georgia to extend her jurisdiction over the Cherokees has always existed. The Cherokees have always had a government of their own. Nothing, however, was said when we were governed by savage laws, when the abominable law of retaliation carried death in our midst, when it was a lawful act to shed the blood of a person charged with witchcraft, when a brother could kill a brother with impunity, or an innocent man suffer for an offending relative. At that time it might have been a matter of charity to have extended over us the mantle of Christian laws & regulations. But how happens it now, after being fostered by the U. States, and advised by great and good men to establish a government of regular law; when the aid and protection of the General Government have been pledged to us; when we, as dutiful "children" of the President, have followed his instructions and advice, and have established for ourselves a government of regular law; when everything looks so promising around us, that a storm is raised by the extension of tyrannical and unchristian laws, which threatens to blast all our rising hopes and expectations?

There is, as would naturally be supposed, a great rejoicing in Georgia. It is a time of "important news"— "gratifying intelligence"—"The Cherokee lands are to be obtained speedily." It is even reported that the Cherokees have come to the conclusion to sell, and move off to the west of the Mississippi—not so fast. We are yet at our homes, at our peaceful firesides . . . attending to our farms and useful occupations.

We had concluded to give our readers fully our thoughts on the subject, which we, in the above remarks, have merely introduced, but upon reflection & remembering our promise, that we will be moderate, we have suppressed ourselves, and have withheld what we had intended should occupy our editorial column. We do not wish, by any means, unnecessarily to excite the minds of the Cherokees. To our home readers we submit the subject without any special comment. They will judge for themselves. To our distant readers, who may wish to know how we feel under present circumstances, we recommend the memorial, the leading article in our present number. We believe it justly contains the views of the nation.

Questions

1. How does Jackson believe that the federal government's Indian policy to date (1829) has been counterproductive to its stated goals? What information does Jackson provide to support his position? Based on what you already know about federal Indian policy since the Confederation period, does Jackson's reasoning make sense?

2. What does Elias Boudinot argue, and how does his position concerning federal Indian policy compare with Jackson's?

3. Do you think Jackson truly believes that he is helping the Indians? Or is Jackson's rhetoric merely a cynical cover for yet another white seizure of Indian lands? Explain.

Questions for Further Thought

1. From your reading of Documents 11-4 through 11-6 as well as your understanding of the text, is it possible to piece together Jackson's position on the limits of the power of the federal government? On the one hand, Jackson used federal power to act swiftly during the Nullification Crisis and against the Second Bank of the United States (Document 11-4); on the other, Jackson claimed that the federal government could do little to curb the actions of Georgia and Alabama against the Indians (Document 11-6). Is Jackson's constitutional position consistent or contradictory? Explain.

2. Jackson was the last U.S. president to have fought in the Revolution, and the war had a formative and lasting impact on his understanding of both the power of the federal government and the uses of that power. How did Jackson understand the Revolution, and what type of society did he believe America should be? In what ways did Jackson view the Bank as undermining the goals of the Revolution as he understood them? Do you agree?

3. Like Thomas Jefferson before him and Ronald Reagan after him, Andrew Jackson ran successfully for president on a platform that promised to get the government off the backs of the people (in 1980, Reagan's campaign slogan stated that the government was the problem, not the solution). Once in office Jackson, like Jefferson and Reagan, expanded the power of the government rather than shrinking it—and all three were overwhelmingly elected to a second term of office. How can this be explained?

Class, Culture, and the Second Party System

Jackson's high-handed wielding of the powers of the presidency, as much as his actual policies, horrified many Americans, notably those who advocated Clay's American System. These opponents of "King Andrew" coalesced into an opposition political party, calling themselves "Whigs" after the eighteenth-century British opponents of royal prerogative. Whigs believed that government could best foster liberty not by attacking special privilege, but by encouraging economic development, which, like the proverbial rising tide, would lift the boats of even the humblest of Americans. They also believed that government had a critical role to play in helping foster virtue; they were among the leading advocates of expanded public education and the use of government institutions such as penitentiaries to "reform" criminals. Whigs especially attracted support from New Englanders and evangelicals who believed that the state needed to foster "Christian" morality (thereby offending Catholics, who flocked to the Democrats).

Meanwhile, by the 1830s, the progress of industrialization and urbanization had begun to generate a large laboring class in the United States. As household production was increasingly replaced by merchant-organized outwork and by factories, more and more Americans found themselves faced with the prospect of being permanent employees. Workingmen found this development disturbing, for it began to appear that Americans had thrown off rule by an aristocracy of birth only to replace it with an aristocracy of wealth (Document 11-7). In an effort to reverse what they described as their slide into "wage slavery," workers established Working Men's Parties to agitate for such reforms as the ten-hour day; by the mid-1830s, many of these parties had allied with the Democrats. Workers also formed labor unions; although employers challenged them as illegal conspiracies, these unions appealed not only to workers but to much of the public as well (Document 11-8).

The devastating depression following the financial panic of 1837 sent the early labor movement into reverse. Because it occurred on the Democrats' watch, and because the policies of Jackson and his successor, Martin Van Buren, could be blamed for it, the Whigs were provided a golden opportunity to gain power. Even though the party appealed chiefly to evangelicals and commercial interests, from the outset Whig politicians were eager to participate in the rough-and-tumble of mass politics (Document 11-9), competing with the Democrats for the workingman's vote (Documents 11-10 and 11-11). In 1840 the Whigs turned the tables on the Democrats, successfully depicting Van Buren as an "aristocrat" and their own candidate, William Henry Harrison (of Virginia gentry background), as a log-cabin-dwelling, cider-swilling man of the people. With two parties now contending to be the "people's choice," mass party politics had arrived.

11-7 Address to the Working Men of New England (1832)

Seth Luther

Seth Luther (1817?–1846), who probably was born in Providence, Rhode Island, became a strong voice for workingmen in Jacksonian America. A carpenter by trade, Luther had little formal education, but he was an avid reader of newspapers and books and became a leading figure in the fight for the ten-hour day. In the following speech, delivered to a gathering of workingmen, Luther described an American System dedicated not to expanding manufactures (see Document 11-2) but to securing the equality of men.

Source: The Globe (Washington, D.C.), May 13, 1832.

I would ask if persons not possessing one hundred and thirty four dollars in soil, are permitted to address this meeting. If so, I wish to make a few remarks. This community seems to be divided into two parties. Not Jackson men and Clay men . . . but the Aristocracy and Democracy. The term Aristocracy denotes a privileged class. Although the Constitution of the United States acknowledges no hereditary right, yet there exists among us a class well deserving the name of Aristocrats. I will mention some of their privileges. . . . Sir, this aristocracy of wealth claims the right to shut up in the Cotton Mill the almost infant child for . . . 13 or 14 hours per diem, with only 20 or 30 minutes for each meal . . . thereby depriving them of the best of all earthly good, an education. . . . Sir, we are in favor of an American System that will benefit all interests. But we are not satisfied with *the* System, whatever it may be, which enables a favored few to accumulate mountains of wealth, at the expense of our dearest interests. . . . We hear the philanthropist moaning over the fate of the Southern slave, when there are thousands of children in this State as truly slaves as the blacks of the South. . . .

Sir, we find the aristocracy in all countries, using their efforts, either directly or indirectly, to hold the poorer classes in ignorance; that they may rivet the chains of oppression more effectually. Where, Sir, is the difference in the effect between Southern measures, and measures now practiced by the Manufacturer, to accomplish this dreadful object?

Much, Sir, have we heard respecting the happiness of a manufacturing population. The Hon. H.[enry] Clay . . . draws a most beautiful picture. He has seen *one* Cotton Mill in Cincinnati. . . . He exclaims, " 'Tis a paradise!"— But . . . one of my friends remarked, if a *Cotton Mill* is paradise, it is "Paradise Lost." . . . we would presume to advise the Hon. Senator from Kentucky to . . . see . . . instead of rosy cheeks, the *pale*, the *sickly*, the *haggard*, countenance of the ragged child from six to twelve years of age. Haggard from the worse than slavish confinement in the cotton mill.

Questions

1. What does Luther mean by the "aristocracy of wealth"?
2. Why is Luther not moved by a philanthropic concern for southern slaves?
3. What is it about the factory system that Luther opposes?

11-8   Acquittal of Cordwainers of Hudson, New York, in *People v. Cooper* (1836)

In 1836 leading members of the United Society of the Journeymen Cordwainers of the City of Hudson in New York were tried by the state for engaging in a conspiracy against their employers for the purpose of demanding higher wages (see text p. 371). The following account of the trial, *People v. Cooper* (1836), was reported by the attorneys in the case.

Source: John R. Commons et al., eds., *A Documentary History of American Industrial Society* (New York: Russell & Russell, 1958), 4: 277–312.

The defendants were indicted under the statute for a combination and conspiracy to raise their wages, etc., to "the great injury of trade and commerce." They were indicted at the instance of Eli Mosier, a boss shoemaker, of the city of Hudson. . . .

The first count charges, "that the defendants, not being content to work for the usual prices, but combining to increase their wages, and the wages of other journeymen . . . did on the 15th of September, 1835, combine together with other workmen, and agree that none of them, would after that day, work at any lower prices than those mentioned in the list, to the great damage of the boss shoemakers, and the injury of trade and commerce, and against the statute."

The second count charges, "that the defendants . . . did thereby agree . . . that any member who should work for less, should be expelled from the society and . . . that any boss who should refuse to pay their rates of wages should be fined, and no member of the society would work for him until he paid his fine. . . ."

SOLOMON SHATTOCK, sworn. I am a boss shoemaker. Several of the members of the society . . . left my employ because I would not give them the wages on their list. None but Defries left the first time—the rest did not leave until afterwards. Several members of the society . . . said that if I did not pay the fine they would leave me. . . . At the time Defries left me, I was paying the prices on their list to him—but in consequence of my not giving the full price to the other men Defries left me. . . .

His Hon. Judge Wilcoxon then charged the Jury in substance as follows: . . .

If the journeymen shoemakers of the city of Hudson had a right to combine, then the Journeymen [everywhere] . . . had a right to combine and to control the labor of every mechanical State in the Union. The question for consideration was whether the controlling the labor of the country in this manner had a tendency to injure trade. For instance, in a manufacturing establishment where there were a hundred hands, and where contracts had to be performed in a given time, would not a sudden combination and refusal to work, cause the ruin of the individual? . . .

The cause was then committed to the Jury. . . . The Jury were together about 209 minutes. . . . The next morning they delivered in Court the following verdict: The Jurors find the Prisoners Not Guilty.

Questions

1. Summarize the charges brought against the journeymen cordwainers.
2. Since Defries received the wage rate demanded by the journeymen, what motivated him to leave Shattock's employ?
3. In the view of the presiding judge, why were associations of journeymen dangerous?

11-9   Set-to between the Champion Old Tip and the Swell Dutchman of Kinderhook (1836)

Edward C. Clay

Andrew Jackson's direct appeal to voters in the presidential elections of 1824, 1828, and 1832 ended the reign of "King Caucus" and left a legacy of sharply contested partisan contests for the presidency. In this Whig cartoon, the election of 1836 (see text pp. 367–368) is depicted as a fistfight between Martin Van Buren and one of his Whig opponents, William Henry Harrison of Ohio. Van Buren won in 1836 but would be defeated by Harrison in 1840. Supporting Van Buren in the cartoon are a timorous and tipsy "Amos" Kendall (see Document 11-3) and an anxious Andrew Jackson. Backing Harrison are Davy Crockett and a war veteran holding Harrison's whiskey bottle.

Source: Library of Congress, Washington, D.C.

The words in the balloons, from left to right, are as follows:

"Amos" [Kendall] character:
I begin to tremble for Matty [Martin Van Buren].
There appears to be a Surplus Fund [a surplus of federal
    revenue from land sales distributed to the states during
    the 1836 campaign]
in this Bottle, so I'll een [var. of "even"]
take a pull to raise my spirits
Oh dear.

Andrew Jackson character:
By the Eternal! what a severe
counterhit! It's bunged up Matty's
peeper, and if he don't keep his other eye
Open he'll get a Cross buttock [a wrestling move to throw
    an opponent with the thrust of a hip or buttock] He
begins to be a little queerish already
D——n his *Dutch* courage [bravery induced by drinking]!
    Amos
where's the Bottle? after this
Round put some more into him

Martin Van Buren character:
Stand by me Old Hickory
or I'm a gone chicken!

William Henry Harrison character:
Look out for your bread-basket
Matty, I'll remove the deposits
for you

Davy Crockett character:
Whoop! wake snakes! Go it
Old Tip! by the Immortals he
puts it into him as fast as a
streak of greased lightning
through a gooseberry bush
That *Cold Blooded* Kinderhooker [Van Buren's nickname:
    "Red Fox of Kinderhook" (Kinderhook, New York)]
will be rowed up Salt river or I'm a nigger!

War veteran character:
Thank Heaven
the people have a
Champion at last
who will support the
Constitution and laws
that we fought and bled
to obtain Huzza for my
old Comrade

Questions

1. This cartoon suggests that Americans had come to view the election of a president as a rough-and-tumble fight. Why would a Whig want to depict the contest in this way?

2. Examine the cartoon for its symbolic meanings. What messages are the characters meant to convey?

3. Evaluate the cartoon from the perspective of the debate over the extension of the franchise (see Documents 11-1 and 11-3). Did this depiction of electoral politics express the fears of those who opposed the eradication of property qualifications?

11-10   Protecting Domestic Industry (1842)

Francis P. Blair

By the election of 1840, the two new mass political parties—the Democrats and Whigs—had established both their organizations and their platforms. (The platforms would remain stable until the crisis of the 1850s.) At the core of the issues separating the two parties were their differing views about the relationship of government to individual liberty. Democrats generally held to the "old republican" view that government was inherently dangerous to the liberties of the people and needed to be kept well pruned. They also saw government power as intrinsically allied with the forces of private privilege. That had been Jackson's view of the "Monster Bank," and it was also the view Democrats took of Whig proposals for tariffs to "protect domestic industry." In the following passage, Francis P. Blair (1791–1876), a member of Jackson's "kitchen cabinet" and editor of Washington's Democratic party organ, the *Globe,* crafts an appeal to working-class voters by linking their own fear of employer power to the Democrats' fear of government power. While this piece is dated 1842, it is representative of attitudes established years earlier.

Source: The Globe (Washington, D.C.), 11 January 1842.

In the good old days of the Republic, when every man minded his own business and left others to take care of their own; when dependence was placed on personal exertion alone, and people did not look up to HERCULES Congress to get them out of the slough into which they had plunged by their own folly and improvidence; in those times, domestic industry was a different thing from what it is now. If we are to believe the assertions of members of Congress advocating a protective tariff, there is no other domestic industry than that employed in our great manufactories. According to their definition, tending spinning jennies in a stupendous brick building, six or seven stories high, some ten or twenty miles from home, surrounded by hundreds of strapping "operatives," from all quarters of the world, with tremendous whiskers, is your only domestic industry for the young and blooming daughters of the land.

"DOMESTIC INDUSTRY" is no longer represented by the ruddy matron sitting at her own fireside in her own home, turning the spinning wheel with one foot and rocking a chubby bantling with the other, while singing it to sleep with lullabies. . . .

"DOMESTIC INDUSTRY," according to the tariff definition, is not that of the healthy mechanic or artisan, who works for himself at his own shop, or if he goes abroad, returns home to his meals every day, and sleeps under his own roof every night; whose earnings are regulated by the wants of the community at large, not by the discretion of a penurious master; whose hours of labor depend on universal custom; who, when the sun goes down, is a freeman until he rises again; who can eat his meals in comfort, and sleep as long as nature requires. . . . Domestic industry is nothing but bondage in its most oppressive form, labor in its utmost extremity of degradation.

"DOMESTIC INDUSTRY," according to the protective tariff cant, is that which separates wives, husbands, parents and children; annihilates every domestic tie and association, and renders all domestic duties subservient to the will, not of a husband or parent, but that of an unfeeling taskmaster, to whom the sacrifice of every moment of time, and every comfort of life, is wealth and prosperity.

Questions

1. What was the meaning of "domestic industry" in tariff legislation (see Document 11-2)?
2. What ironic meanings did Blair find in the term *domestic industry*?
3. How did Blair define the "healthy mechanic"? In his view, why was the mechanic's "health" in jeopardy?

11-11   A Whig Discusses How to Appeal to the Workingman (1833)

John Scholefield

If Democrats couched their antitariff message in terms of their fear of privilege, Whigs responded by asserting a "harmony of interests" uniting employers and artisans. Such measures as protective tariffs, the Whigs contended, benefited everyone, not just industrialists. Indeed, they had to make such arguments; the Whig leadership realized that in order to be competitive the party would need to build the same sort of massive, top-to-bottom organization as the Jacksonian Democrats had. Party building required that Whig leaders engage in extensive correspondence with local political figures and learn from them how to express the Whig program in terms that ordinary voters could appreciate. In the following letter, Henry Clay is offered advice by a Philadelphia carpet manufacturer on how to appeal to the numerically powerful workingmen of that city.

Source: John Scholefield, Philadelphia, to Henry Clay, 13 November 1833, in Robert Seager II, ed., *The Papers of Henry Clay* (Lexington: University Press of Kentucky, 1985?), 666–667.

From JOHN SCHOLEFIELD

Philadelphia, November 13, 1833
[Asks if a group of Philadelphia "Manufacturers and Merchants" could honor Clay, "the Father of the American System," by greeting him in New York and escorting him to Philadelphia on his return trip to Washington. Continues:]

May I be permitted, Sir to embrace this opportunity for acquainting you with a little piece of history—partly secret—belonging to the present times?—About two weeks ago, Gen. Duff Green—alarmed at the notice you have recently attracted, and, as we understand, at an expression in your favor from the South—left Washington for New York, on a political mission. He commenced his operations at Baltimore:—got up a meeting of "Working Men," so called, at which John McLean was nominated as a candidate for the Presidency. The scheme failed. His next attempt was in our city, where he also tried to operate on the same description of persons. At a very early stage of the business, we became acquainted with his designs, and measures were accordingly taken to frustrate them. We succeeded, and consequently he was defeated: he could not even get a meeting. He then went to Trenton, Newark, and New York, for the same *avowed* purpose; and he was every where unsuccessful. Since that time, we have heard no more of him, except of his return home.—A few days ago, however, the partisans of Mr. McLean in this City, made another clandestine attempt; in a similar way, and for the same purpose; and again they have been defeated.

Now, Sir, in order to a right understanding of their movements, it is necessary to state, that the "Working Men," when well organised, constitute a considerable portion of the political strength of the city and county of Philadelphia. They have formerly been found quite available for party porpuses [sic]. At the present moment they are not very firmly bound together, not having recently moved in unison. It is evident that although many of their most influential men are decidedly of one party, they have among them political characters of every shade.

Such being the materials of which this class of our citizens is composed, a question presents itself as to the best mode of operating upon them, for the advantage of the public. The knowledge of one little secret gives us a ready answer to the question. It is simply to make them of some consequence in the world—to give them an air of importance in the eyes of others. As a body, they are very ambitious to possess some weight in society. Let this feeling be gratified, and they are content. It is for these reasons that we apprehend they may some time or other, be induced to unite for evil as well as good. And in in [sic] order to prevent the former, we must endeavour to ensure the latter. As manufacturers and mechanics, in other words, as "working men," they have a deep interest at stake in the support of "the protective system." But, Sir, many of them do not perfectly understand it; nor, in this respect, is there any other way in which a favorable and lasting impression can possibly be made upon their minds, like that which would come from the lips of the *Father* of that system. Greatly therefore should I rejoice if by any means an opportunity co[u]ld consistently be embraced for doing so much go[od]. The benefit thus to be conferred on a great pu[bl]ic cause, would be incalculable—But m[ore] of this when we have the happiness to see you here.

Questions

1. What is John Scholefield's core advice to Henry Clay? What, specifically, is his "one little secret"?
2. Do you think that Scholefield's advice is sincere or cynical—substantive advice or political spin? What do the remarks of Scholefield, a carpet manufacturer, tell us about early-nineteenth-century working-class culture in the United States?
3. From what you already know about Henry Clay, how do you think he received Scholefield's advice? How much political power did working-class Americans have at the time?

Questions for Further Thought

1. In what ways did workingmen define their interests as different from other social groups, and how did they go about trying to achieve them? How does the American working class compare with the working classes in England and Europe?
2. While many workingmen articulated their grievances in the language of the Revolution, other members of American society rejected as un-American working-class demands and organizations such as that of the Cordwainers of Hudson, New York (Document 11-8). Why was this so, and which group—working-class defenders or their detractors—do you think had the better argument?
3. Looking at the Democrats and the Whigs, which party had the better appeal to the workingman?

CHAPTER 12

The Ferment of Reform, 1820–1860

★   ★   ★

Individualism and *Communalism*

The explosion of economic opportunity that manifested itself in the industrial and market revolutions and rapid expansion into the West weakened old social restraints and obligations and encouraged new visions of an ideal social order. To many Americans, especially among the middle-class beneficiaries of what seemed to be limitless economic opportunity, the restraints and obligations of the past seemed artificial and contrived. They searched for society's "natural" foundations, seeking principles that at once would secure the autonomy of the individual and define the individual's social responsibility in terms of his or her highest interests.

Certain themes connected these enthusiastic crusades and suggest the ways in which middle-class radicalism influenced society in industrializing America. One of these themes was individualism. The faith of transcendentalist intellectuals such as Ralph Waldo Emerson and Henry David Thoreau in the power of the individual to tap directly into natural and spiritual wisdom stood in sharp contrast to the forms of deference and coercion that still pervaded American life, forms radical reformers associated with a rapidly fading age of barbarism. Individualism and self-restraint required self-reliance and a capacity to distinguish what was necessary and good from all that was frivolous and distracting. It also required the absolute freedom of the individual to seek out the truth and to act upon it (Document 12-1). It thus strongly implied—even required—radical assaults on all forms of domination, including those of masters over slaves and of men over women, whether in public or in the most intimate settings.

Related to individualism was communalism, the impulse to create communities where these radical individualist ideals could be sheltered and nurtured; Thoreau created a utopian community of one at Walden. In this regard utopian reformers followed in the footsteps of their Puritan forebears, who also saw the American "wilderness" as providing the space and freedom necessary for the creation of an ideal society. Transcendentalists established Brook Farm in Massachusetts (Document 12-2). The Shakers, a radical religious group, created communities that shunned marriage in favor of celibacy and celebrated their founder, Mother Ann Lee, as the embodiment of the female aspect of a God whose nature was both male and female (Document 12-3). In the Oneida community of upstate New York, the utopian John Humphrey Noyes sought to free men and women alike from the tyranny of exclusive marriage, and to free the pleasures of sexuality from the dangers of pregnancy and childbirth (Document 12-4). Few of these communities were able to last. Nonetheless, they served as incubators for ideas that radical reformers would take into the larger society.

12-1   Walden (1854)

Henry David Thoreau

Henry David Thoreau (1817–1862) was born and lived most of his life in Concord, Massachusetts. A graduate of Harvard, he taught for a time in Concord but soon devoted himself to the transcendentalist movement (see text pp. 382–383). His most famous works, an account of his residence at Walden Pond and the essay "On Civil Disobedience," although not widely read in his day, have become an enduring legacy of transcendentalism. In contrast to Emerson (see text pp. 380–382), whose romantic individualism stayed aloof from material conditions, Thoreau offered a subversive twist to a principal tenet of liberal capitalism: the proposition that individuals exchange labor for leisure to promote future pleasure. If the highest sphere of individual pleasure is transcendental contemplation, Thoreau reasoned, an individual should strive to exchange the least labor for the most leisure.

Source: Henry David Thoreau, *Walden or, Life in the Woods and On the Duty of Civil Disobedience* (Boston, 1854; reprint, New York: NAL Penguin, 1960).

ECONOMY

When I wrote the following pages, or rather the bulk of them, I lived alone, in the woods, a mile from any neighbor, in a house which I had built myself, on the shore of Walden Pond, in Concord, Massachusetts, and earned my living by the labor of my hands only. I lived there two years and two months. At present I am a sojourner in civilized life again. . . . It would be some advantage to live a primitive and frontier life, though in the midst of an outward civilization, if only to learn what are the gross necessaries of life and what methods have been taken to obtain them. . . . By the words, *necessary of life*, I mean whatever, of all that man obtains by his own exertions, had been from the first, or from long use has become, so important to human life that few, if any whether from savageness, or poverty, or philosophy, ever attempt to do without it. . . .

Though we are not so degenerate but that we might possibly live in a cave or a wigwam or wear skins to-day, it certainly is better to accept the advantages, though so dearly bought, which the invention and industry of mankind offer. In such a neighborhood as this, boards and shingles, lime and bricks, are cheaper and more easily obtained than suitable caves. . . .

Near the end of March, 1845, I borrowed an axe and went down to the woods by Walden Pond. . . . It is difficult to begin without borrowing, but perhaps it is the most generous course thus to permit your fellow-men to have an interest in your enterprise. . . .

I hewed the main timbers six inches square, most of the studs on two sides only, and the rafters and floor timbers on one side, leaving the rest of the bark on, so that they were just as straight and much stronger than sawed ones. Each stick was carefully mortised or tenoned by its stump, for I had borrowed other tools by this time. . . .

By the middle of April, for I made no haste in my work, but rather made the most of it, my house was framed and ready for raising. . . . At length, in the beginning of May, with the help of some of my acquaintances, rather to improve so good an occasion for neighborliness than from any necessity, I set up the frame of my house. . . . Before winter I built a chimney, and shingled the sides of my house. . . . I have thus a tight shingled and plastered house, ten feet wide by fifteen long, and eight-feet posts, with a garret and a closet, a large window on each side. . . .

One says to me, "I wonder that you do not lay up money; you love to travel." . . . But I am wiser than that. . . . I say to my friend, Suppose we try who will get there first. The distance is thirty miles; the fare ninety cents. That is almost a day's wages. . . . Well, I start now on foot, and get there before night. . . . You will in the meanwhile have earned your fare, and arrive there some time to-morrow, or possibly this evening, if you are lucky enough to get a job in season. . . .

Such is the universal law, which no man can ever outwit, and with regard to the railroad even we may say it is as broad as it is long. To make a railroad round the world available to all mankind is equivalent to grading the whole surface of the planet. Men have an indistinct notion that if they keep up this activity of joint stocks and spades long enough all will at length ride somewhere, in next to no time, and for nothing; but though a crowd rushes to the depot, and the conductor shouts "All aboard!" when the smoke is blown away and the vapor condensed, it will be perceived that a few are riding, but the rest are run over,— and it will be called, and will be, "A melancholy accident." . . .

For more than five years I maintained myself thus solely by the labor of my hands, and I found that, by working about six weeks in a year, I could meet all the expenses of living. The whole of my winters, as well as most of my summers, I had free and clear for study. . . .

As I preferred some things to others, and especially valued my freedom. . . . I did not wish to spend my time in earning rich carpets or other fine furniture, or delicate cookery, or a house in the Grecian or the Gothic style just yet. . . . In short, I am convinced, both by faith and experience that to maintain one's self on this earth is not a hardship but a pastime, if we live simply and wisely. . . .

Questions

1. Thoreau lived alone at Walden Pond, but was he isolated from society?
2. What was the purpose of Thoreau's exercise in self-sufficiency?
3. What did Thoreau mean when he wrote that railroads would produce "a melancholy accident"? Analyze this passage as a critique of industrialization.

12-2   The Blithedale Romance (1852)

Nathaniel Hawthorne

Nathaniel Hawthorne (1804–1864), a native of Salem, Massachusetts, and a graduate of Bowdoin College, lived for a year at Brook Farm. He drew on this experience and on the themes of moral reform and feminism to write the novel *The Blithedale Romance*. With Herman Melville (the two writers admired each other's work) Hawthorne explored the human isolation of individualism and the destructive capacity of moral crusades. While most reformers identified with the antislavery movement, Hawthorne and Melville distanced themselves from the certitude of moral reform (see text p. 383). In the following passage from *The Blithedale Romance*, the narrator describes the romantic idealism of the Brook Farm community and the sense of moral isolation that followed its demise.

Source: Nathaniel Hawthorne, *The Blithedale Romance* (Boston, 1852).

If ever men might lawfully dream awake, and give utterance to their wildest visions, without dread of laughter or scorn on the part of the audience—yes, and speak of earthly happiness, for themselves and mankind, as an object to be hopefully striven for, and probably attained—we . . . were those very men. We had left the rusty iron framework of society behind us. We had broken through many hindrances that are powerful enough to keep most people on the weary tread-mill of the established system, even while they feel its irksomeness almost as intolerable as we did. . . . It was our purpose—a generous one, certainly, and absurd, no doubt, in full proportion with its generosity—to give up whatever we had theretofore attained, for the sake of showing mankind the example of a life governed by other than the false and cruel principles, on which human society has all along been based. . . . We meant to lessen the laboring man's great burthen of toil, by performing our due share of it. . . . We sought our profit by mutual aid, instead of wresting it by the strong hand from an enemy, or filching it craftily from those less shrewd than ourselves. . . .

The experiment, so far as its original projectors were concerned, proved long ago a failure, first leaping into Fourierism [see text pp. 386–387], and dying, as it well deserved, for this infidelity to its own higher spirit. . . .

My subsequent life has passed—I was going to say, happily—but, at all events, tolerably enough. I am now at middle-age—well, well, a step or two beyond the midmost point. . . . I live very much at my ease, and fare sumptuously every day. . . . As regards human progress . . . let them believe in it who can, and aid in it who choose! . . . I lack a purpose. . . . I by no means wish to die. Yet, were there any cause, in this whole chaos of human struggle, worth a sane man's dying for, and which my death would benefit, then—provided, however, the effort did not involve an unreasonable amount of trouble—methinks I might be bold to offer my life. . . . Farther than that, I should be loth to pledge myself.

Questions

1. Why do you think Hawthorne chose the word *Blithedale* for his fictionalized account of Brook Farm? Do you agree with the observation of the narrator (the character Miles Coverdale) that utopian reform was "absurd . . . in full proportion with its generosity"?
2. How would you answer the question posed by Miles Coverdale in the final paragraph: In a self-interested world, is there "any cause . . . worth . . . dying for"?
3. Judging from this excerpt, what do you think Hawthorne missed most about Brook Farm?

12-3   The Shakers (1850)

Rebecca Cox Jackson

Rebecca Cox Jackson (1795–1871) was a free African American woman who renounced a relatively secure life with her husband in Philadelphia to become an itinerant Methodist preacher. During the 1830s she traveled throughout the countryside, accompanied by a younger disciple, Rebecca Perot. In 1843 the "two Rebeccas" became committed Shakers, eventually settling in the community of Watervliet, near Albany, New York (see text pp. 385–386). They remained ambiguous about Shaker isolation, however, and in 1851 they resumed their ministry in the free black community. In 1858 Jackson founded her own Shaker family in Philadelphia. In the 1840s, Jackson began to write a memoir of her religious experiences, including powerful dreams and visions.

In these passages Jackson expressed three key elements of the Shaker faith: that they received the direct guidance of the Holy Ghost; that Mother Ann Lee (the movement's founder) represented the female embodiment of a God comprising both male and female attributes; and that the millennium (the end of human time) was near at hand.

Source: Jean McMahon Humez, ed., *Gifts of Power: The Writings of Rebecca Jackson, Black Visionary, Shaker Eldress* (Amherst: University of Massachusetts Press, 1981), 220–221.

Monday evening, February 18, 1850. I was instructed concerning the atmosphere and its bounds. I saw its form—it is like the sea, which has her bounds. . . . It covered land and sea, so far above all moving things, and yet so far beneath the starry heavens. Its face is like the face of the sea, smooth and gentle when undisturbed by the wind. So is the atmosphere, when undisturbed by the power of the sun and moon. When agitated by these, it rages like the sea and sends forth its storms upon the earth. Nothing can live above it. A bird could no more live or fly above its face, than a fish can live or swim out of the water. It is always calm and serene between its face and the starry heaven. The sight, to me, was beautiful.

March 1, 1850. . . . Prayer given to me by Mother Ann Lee: "Oh God, my Everlasting Father, to Thee do I lift up my soul in prayer and thanksgiving for the gift of Thy dear Son, our Blessed Savior, who has begotten to us a living hope. And to Thee, Holy Mother Wisdom, do I lift up my soul in prayer and thanksgiving, for the gift of Thy Holy Daughter, whose blessed Spirit has led me and instructed me in this, the holy way of God, lo! these many years, and has borne with my infirmities and many shortcomings. And lo! Thou hast comforted me in all my sorrows and Thy blessed Spirit comforts me today."

Then I saw our Heavenly Parents look on me and smile, and Mother Ann gave me sweet counsel. And I was greatly strengthened in the way of God.

March 15, 1850. After I came to Watervliet . . . and saw how the Believers seemed to be gathered to themselves, in praying for themselves and not for the world, which lay in midnight darkness, I wondered how the world was to be saved, if Shakers were the only people of God on earth, and they seemed to be busy in their own concerns, which were mostly temporal. . . .

Then seeing these at ease in Zion, I cried in the name of Christ and Mother that He in mercy would do something for the helpless world. At that time, it seemed as if the whole world rested upon me. I cried to the Lord both day and night, for many months, that God would make a way that the world might hear the Gospel—that God would send spirits and angels to administer to their understanding, that they might be saved in the present tense, for I knew by revelation, that it was God's will that they should be.

Questions

1. What significance do you think Jackson attached to her vision of the atmosphere and the heavens?
2. Examine the prayer given to Jackson by Mother Ann Lee. In what ways does it deviate from the language of patriarchal religion?
3. How did Jackson's millenarianism affect her attitude toward the Shakers at Watervliet?

12-4 Male Continence (1872)

John Humphrey Noyes

John Humphrey Noyes (1811–1886) was born in Brattleboro, Vermont. After graduation from Dartmouth College he was drawn to the revivalist ministry. Noyes carried the logic of moral perfectionism (the belief that people, while living, could achieve the perfection of Christ) in a new direction, arguing that Christ had returned to earth in A.D. 70 and had established the one true Christian church. When he announced his own state of moral perfection in 1834, he broke his ties with established religion and society and began a spiritual journey that would lead him to the Christian communist and free-love community he founded at Oneida (see text pp. 387–388). In the treatise *Male Continence* he explained his theory of controlled propagation and complex marriage.

Source: John Humphrey Noyes, *Male Continence* (Oneida, N.Y., 1872).

I was married in 1838, and lived in the usual routine of matrimony till 1846. It was during this period of eight years that I studied the subject of sexual intercourse in connection with my matrimonial experience, and discovered the principle of Male Continence. And the discovery was occasioned and even forced upon me by very sorrowful experience. In the course of six years my wife went through the agonies of five births. Four of them were premature. Only one child lived. . . . After our last disappointment, I pledged my word to my wife that I would never again expose her to such fruitless suffering. I made up my mind to live apart from her, rather than break this promise. This was the situation in the summer of 1844. At that time I conceived the idea that the sexual organs have a social function which is distinct from the propagative function; and that these functions may be separated practically. I experimented on this idea, and found that the self-control which it requires is not difficult; also that my enjoyment was increased; also that my wife's experience was very satisfactory, as it had never been before; also that we have escaped the horrors and the fear of involuntary propagation. This was a great deliverance. It made a happy household. . . . In 1848, soon after our removal to Oneida, I published the new theory in a pamphlet. . . .

The pamphlet referred to embraced a general exhibition of the principles of the kingdom of heaven promised in the Bible, and for this reason it was entitled *The Bible Argument*; but the most important chapter of it was that which undertook to show *"How the sexual function is to be redeemed and true relations between the sexes are to be restored."* . . . I will now venture to reprint that notable chapter.

FROM THE BIBLE ARGUMENT, PRINTED IN 1848

The amative and propagative functions of the sexual organs are distinct from each other, and may be separated practically. . . . If amativeness is the first and noblest of the social affections, and if the propagative part of the sexual relation was originally secondary, and became paramount by the subversion of order in the fall [as had previously been shown], we are bound to raise the amative office of the sexual organs into a distinct and paramount function. . . . We insist, then, that the amative function—that which consists in a simple union of persons, making "of twain one flesh," and giving a medium of magnetic and spiritual interchange—is a distinct and independent function, as superior to the reproductive as we have shown amativeness to be to propagation. . . .

The method of controlling propagation which results from our argument is natural, healthy, favorable to amativeness, and effectual.

First, it is *natural*. The useless expenditure of seed certainly is not natural. . . . Our method simply proposes the subordination of the flesh to the spirit, teaching men to seek principally the elevated spiritual pleasures of sexual connection, and to be content with them in their general intercourse with women, restricting the more sensual part to its proper occasions. . . .

The separation of the amative from the propagative, places amative sexual intercourse on the same footing with other ordinary forms of social interchange. . . . In society trained in these principles . . . amative intercourse will have place among the "fine arts" . . . when sexual intercourse becomes an honored method of innocent and useful communion, and each is married to all.

Questions

1. How did Noyes change the "usual routine of matrimony"? How did he separate, "practically," amative from propagative sexual intercourse?
2. Assuming that amative and propagative sexual intercourse can be distinguished, how and why do you think Noyes concluded that amative intercourse would become indistinguishable from "ordinary forms of social interchange"?
3. Does sexuality separated from procreation and marriage promote equality between women and men? Why or why not?

Questions for Further Thought

1. For Thoreau and Noyes (Documents 12-1 and 12-4), and for Hawthorne in his Brook Farm days (Document 12-2), an ideal social order consisted of the free and mutually beneficial interaction of autonomous, self-restrained individuals. Under what conditions, if any, could such a society exist? What would become of the national state?
2. A central concern in these documents is the proper relationship of the individual to society. Examine each document from this perspective and consider what processes industrialization set in motion that generated this concern.
3. The word *utopian* is often used to mean "impractical." Consider, however, the significance of utopian thought and action in the transformation of social norms. Did the utopian thinkers of the nineteenth century influence the social norms of this century? In what way?

The Women's Movement

In the female-centered middle-class home, women were indeed insulated from the workplace, but their new roles as moral stewards of their families suggested new responsibilities and authority. The moral-reform movements of the early nineteenth century provided these women with a forum for the advancement of their rights as individuals and opportunities to assert equality with men in discussions of public policy. The antislavery movement projected a striking analogy between the dominion of master over slave and the dominion of man over woman (Document 12-5). As women reformers noted, all the evils of the former applied to the latter. The participation of women in public discussions of government policy implied that women deserved the full rights of citizenship, most prominently property rights and the right to vote (Document 12-6). Women made significant progress in acquiring property rights, but woman suffrage proved far more elusive. Even in reform circles the agitation for women's rights produced deep divisions. The assertion of female equality in the American Anti-Slavery Society, for example, contributed to a major schism in the ranks of abolitionists in 1840. Many male reformers—and even a number of female reformers—who embraced the equality of the races as a moral principle turned a deaf ear to advocates for women's rights. Nevertheless, perceptions of women's proper "place" began to shift, however haltingly.

12-5   Breaking Out of Women's Separate Sphere (1838)

Angelina E. Grimké

Angelina E. Grimké (1805–1879) was born in Charleston, South Carolina, and raised in a wealthy, aristocratic, conservative family. Deeply influenced by her older sister, Angelina soon rejected Charleston society, converted from Episcopalianism to Quakerism during a visit to Philadelphia, and quickly embraced moral reform (see text pp. 392–393). In 1835 she wrote to William Lloyd Garrison to express her support for abolitionism. When Garrison published the letter in his newspaper, *The Liberator,* her public reform career began. Criticism of Grimké's public opposition to slavery soon led her to advocate women's rights in conjunction with abolitionism. One of Grimké's principal opponents was Catharine Beecher (1800–1878), the daughter of prominent Congregationalist minister Lyman Beecher. Catharine Beecher was an early advocate of education for women but was also a formative figure in defining the female domestic sphere. Defending this sphere from the public activity of abolitionist women, Beecher published *An Essay on Slavery and Abolitionism, with Reference to the Duty of American Females* (1837). The following extracts are taken from Grimké's reply to Beecher.

Source: Angelina E. Grimké, *Letters to Catharine E. Beecher, in Reply to an Essay on Slavery and Abolitionism, Addressed to A. E. Grimké* (Boston, 1838; facsimile reprint, New York: Arno Press, 1969), 103–113.

I come now to that part of thy book, which is, of all others, the most important to the women of this country; thy "general views in relation to the place woman is appointed to fill by the dispensations of heaven." . . .

Thou sayest, "Heaven has appointed to one sex the *superior,* and to the other the *subordinate* station. . . ." This is an assertion without proof. Thou further sayest, that "it was designed that the mode of faining influence and exercising power should be *altogether different and peculiar.*" Does the Bible teach this? . . . Did Jesus . . . give a different rule of action to men and women? . . . I read in the Bible, that Miriam, and Deborah, and Huldah, were called to fill *public stations* in Church and State. I find Anna, the prophetess, speaking in the temple "unto all them that looked for redemption in Jerusalem." . . . I see them even standing on Mount Calvary, around his cross . . . but he never *rebuked* them; He never told them it was unbecoming *their sphere of life* to mingle in the crowds which followed his footsteps. . . .

Thou sayest . . . "make no claims, and maintain no rights, but what are the gifts of honor, rectitude and love." From whom does woman receive her *rights*? From God, or from man? . . . I understand . . . her *rights* are an integral part of her moral being; they cannot be withdrawn; they must live with her forever. Her rights lie at the foundation of all her duties; and, so long as the divine commands are binding upon her, so long must her rights continue. . . .

Thou sayest, "In this country, petitions to Congress, in reference to official duties of legislators, seem IN ALL CASES, to fall entirely without the sphere of female duty. Men are the proper persons to make appeals to the rulers whom they appoint," etc. Here I entirely dissent from thee. The fact that women are denied the right of voting for members of Congress, is but a poor reason why they should also be deprived of the right of petition. If their numbers are counted to swell the number of Representatives in our State and National Legislatures, the *very least* that can be done is to give them the right of petition in all cases whatsoever. . . . If not, they are mere slaves, known only through their masters."

Questions

1. What arguments does Grimké use to link moral reform with women's rights and political action?
2. The campaign to collect signatures on antislavery petitions to Congress was an important aspect of the abolitionist movement in the 1830s. How did that campaign raise women's rights issues?
3. How does Grimké differ with Beecher on the issue of women's rights? How does Grimké define the relationship between rights and duties?

12-6   Declaration of Sentiments and Resolutions (1848)

Elizabeth Cady Stanton

Elizabeth Cady Stanton (1815–1902) and Lucretia Mott (1793–1880) met in London at the World's Anti-Slavery Convention in 1840 (see text pp. 392–396). Stanton attended with her husband, the abolitionist Henry B. Stanton. Mott, a Quaker minister, attended as a delegate for the American Anti-Slavery Society. The convention's decision to deny recognition to women consigned Stanton and Mott to the gallery as observers, and they resolved to link the struggle against slavery with a struggle for women's rights. In 1848 they convened the first women's rights convention at Seneca Falls, New York, and Stanton drafted its famous "Declaration of Sentiments" and Resolutions, using the Declaration of Independence as a model.

Source: Elizabeth Cady Stanton, Susan B. Anthony, and Matilda Joslyn Gage, *History of Woman Suffrage* (1881–1922; reprint, New York: Arno Press and New York Times, 1969), 1: 70–73.

When, in the course of human events, it becomes necessary for one portion of the family of man to assume among the people of the earth a position different from that which they have hitherto occupied, but one to which the laws of nature and nature's God entitle them, a decent respect to the opinions of mankind requires that they should declare the causes that impel them to such a course.

We hold these truths to be self-evident: that all men and women are created equal; that they are endowed by their Creator with certain inalienable rights. . . . Whenever any form of government becomes destructive of these ends, it is the right of those who suffer from it to refuse allegiance to it, and to insist upon the institution of a new government. . . .

The history of mankind is a history of repeated injuries and usurpations on the part of man toward woman, having in direct object the establishment of an absolute tyranny over her. To prove this, let facts be submitted to a candid world.

He has never permitted her to exercise her inalienable right to the elective franchise. . . .

He has withheld from her rights which are given to the most ignorant and degraded men—both natives and foreigners. . . .

He has made her, if married, in the eye of the law, civilly dead.

He has taken from her all right in property, even to the wages she earns. . . .

After depriving her of all rights as a married woman, if single, and the owner of property, he has taxed her to support a government which recognizes her only when her property can be made profitable to it. . . .

He has denied her the facilities for obtaining a thorough education, all colleges being closed against her. . . .

He has created a false public sentiment by giving the world a different code of morals for men and women, by which moral delinquencies which exclude women from society, are not only tolerated, but deemed of little account in man. . . .

He has endeavored, in every way that he could, to destroy her confidence in her own powers, to lessen her self-respect and to make her willing to lead a dependent and abject life. . . .

Resolved, That all laws which prevent woman from occupying such a station in society as her conscience shall dictate, or which place her in a position inferior to that of man, are contrary to the great precept of nature, and therefore of no force or authority.

Resolved, That woman is man's equal—was intended to be so by the Creator, and the highest good of the race demands that she should be recognized as such. . . .

Resolved, That it is the duty of the women of this country to secure to themselves their sacred right to the elective franchise. . . .

Questions

1. Read the Declaration of Independence (see text pp. D-1–D-2) and consider the structural as well as ideological reasons why Stanton used it as a model.
2. In light of the tone and substance of Stanton's protest, why did so many male abolitionists fail to see these "self-evident" truths?
3. How are Stanton's arguments related to the interests and experiences of middle-class women?

Questions for Further Thought

1. Grimké and Stanton were both concerned with women's rights (Documents 12-5 and 12-6). How did their respective concerns with transcendentalism, moral reform, and political reform shape their arguments?
2. Use Grimké's and Stanton's arguments to describe the world they hoped to transform. By what logic were women traditionally considered subordinate to men?
3. In 1870 the Fifteenth Amendment to the U.S. Constitution prohibited states from denying the vote to black men; in 1920 the Nineteenth Amendment prohibited states from denying the vote to women. In your opinion, why did gender discrimination last fifty years longer in this arena than did racial discrimination?

Abolitionism

The moral crusade against slavery had its origin in the evangelical reforms of the Second Great Awakening. Given that each human being was understood to be a responsible moral agent in the eyes of God, abolitionists argued that the relationship of master and slave fundamentally violated Christian morality because the slave was deprived of the right to follow her conscience and the master was tempted to assert himself in place of God. Animated by the apocalyptic spirit of the age, abolitionists attacked slavery with a zeal that alarmed many northerners and outraged most white southerners (Document 12-7). In the abolitionists' view, slavery denied the essential humanity of the enslaved, a point they underscored by emphasizing the physical brutality of the system (Document 12-8). Finally, to the abolitionists, slavery was a *national* sin, not simply a southern one: the Constitution permitted slavery and even required that states without slavery return fugitive slaves to their masters. Slavery was not a problem confined to exotic corners of the nation; its influence permeated national life, and all Americans had to confront it in order to restore the ideals of the Declaration of Independence (Document 12-9).

12-7 Commencement of *The Liberator* (1831)

William Lloyd Garrison

In 1829 William Lloyd Garrison (1805–1879) broke with traditional abolitionist proposals for gradual emancipation to demand the immediate abolition of slavery in the United States (see text p. 400). Later in that year he added his voice to those of African American freedmen in the North who denounced the American Colonization Society as a thinly disguised plot to remove free blacks, not slaves, from America. In 1830 Garrison prepared to launch the Boston *Liberator* to express his new views; the paper's first number appeared on January 1, 1831. The publication of *The Liberator* in January and the bloody slave rebellion led by Nat Turner in Southampton County, Virginia, in August 1831 (see text pp. 398–400) reinforced each other in ways that unsettled northern and southern whites and prompted the supporters of Andrew Jackson to attempt to silence the abolitionist "incendiaries." The following extracts are from Garrison's opening editorial, "Commencement of *The Liberator*," in the first issue.

Source: William Lloyd Garrison, "Commencement of *The Liberator*," *Liberator*, 1 January 1831, in *Selections from the Writings and Speeches of William Lloyd Garrison* (New York: New American Library, 1969), 62–63.

In Park Street Church, on the Fourth of July, 1829, in an address on slavery, I unreflectingly assented to the popular but pernicious doctrine of gradual abolition. I seize this opportunity to make a full and unequivocal recantation, and thus publicly to ask pardon of my God, of my country, and of my brethren, the poor slaves, for having uttered a sentiment so full of timidity, injustice and absurdity. . . .

I am aware, that many object to the severity of my language; but is there not cause for severity? I will be as harsh as truth, and as uncompromising as justice. On this subject, I do not wish to think, or speak, or write, with moderation. No! no! Tell a man, whose house is on fire, to give a moderate alarm; tell him to moderately rescue his wife from the hands of the ravisher; tell the mother to gradually extricate her babe from the fire into which it has fallen; but urge me not to use moderation in a cause like the present! I am in earnest. I will not equivocate—I will not excuse—I will not retreat a single inch, AND I WILL BE HEARD. . . .

It is pretended, that I am retarding the cause of emancipation by the coarseness of my invective, and the precipitancy of my measures. The charge is not true. On this question, my influence, humble as it is, is felt at this moment to a considerable extent, and shall be felt in coming years—not perniciously, but beneficially—not as a curse, but as a blessing; and POSTERITY WILL BEAR TESTIMONY THAT I WAS RIGHT.

12-8 American Slavery as It Is (1839)

Theodore Dwight Weld

Converted to the evangelistic ministry by Charles Grandison Finney, Theodore Dwight Weld (1803–1895) moved beyond his mentor's interest in temperance to join the newly invigorated abolitionist crusade. A founding member of the American Anti-Slavery Society, Weld organized a group of antislavery ministers who toured the country preaching against the sin of slavery. Weld married Angelina Grimké (Document 12-5) in 1838 at the height of his reform career, a career that ended shortly after the abolitionist schism of 1840 (see text pp. 402–403). Weld's aim in the 1830s was the aim of abolitionism generally, to convince all who would listen that slavery was morally wrong. Evangelical abolitionists, he believed, would launch a moral reformation across the land, and the slaves would be set free. His best-known effort to produce such a moral reformation, written in collaboration with Sarah and Angelina Grimké, was *American Slavery as It Is: Testimony of a Thousand Witnesses*, which compiled documentary information, especially from southern newspapers, to support the moral argument against slavery.

Source: Theodore Dwight Weld, *American Slavery as It Is: Testimony of a Thousand Witnesses* (New York, 1839; reprint, New York: Arno Press, 1968), 60–63.

PUNISHMENTS: I. FLOGGINGS.

The slaves are terribly lacerated with whips, paddles, etc.; red pepper and salt are rubbed into their mangled flesh; hot brine and turpentine are poured into their gashes; and innumerable other tortures inflicted upon them.

We will in the first place, prove by a cloud of witnesses, that the slaves are whipped with such inhuman severity, as to lacerate and mangle their flesh in the most shocking manner, leaving permanent scars and ridges; after establishing this, we will present a mass of testimony, concerning a great variety of other tortures. The testimony, for the most part, will be that of the slaveholders themselves, and in their own chosen words. A large portion of it will be taken from the advertisements, which they have published in their own newspapers, describing by the scars on their bodies made by the whip, their own runaway slaves. To copy these advertisements *entire* would require a great amount of space, and flood the reader with a vast mass of matter irrelevant to the *point* before us; we shall therefore insert only so much of each, as will intelligibly set forth the precise point under consideration. In the column under the word "witnesses," will be found the name of the individual, who signs the advertisement, or for whom it is signed, with his or her place of residence, and the name and date of the paper, in which it appeared, and generally the name of the place where it is published. Opposite the name of each witness, will be an extract, from the advertisement, containing his or her testimony.

WITNESSES.

Mr. D. Judd, jailor, Davidson Co., Tennessee, in the "Nashville Banner," Dec. 10th, 1838.

Mr. Robert Nicoll, Dauphin st. between Emmanuel and Conception st's, Mobile, Alabama, in the "Mobile Commercial Advertiser."

Mr. Bryant Johnson, Fort Valley, Houston Co., Georgia, in the "Standard of Union," Milledgeville Ga. Oct. 2, 1838.

Mr. James T. De Jarnett, Vernon, Autauga Co., Alabama, in the "Pensacola Gazette," July, 14, 1838.

Maurice Y. Garcia, Sheriff of the County of Jefferson, La., in the "New Orleans Bee," August 14, 1838.

R. J. Bland, Sheriff of Claiborne Co, Miss., in the "Charleston (S.C.) Courier," August, 28, 1838.

Mr. James Noe, Red River Landing, La., in the "Sentinel," Vicksburg, Miss., August 22, 1837.

William Craze, jailor, Alexandria, La. in the "Planter's Intelligencer," Sept. 26, 1838.

John A. Rowland, jailor, Lumberton, North Carolina, in the "Fayetteville (N. C.) Observer," June 20, 1838.

J. K. Roberts, sheriff, Blount county, Ala., in the "Huntsville Democrat," Dec. 9, 1838.

Mr. H. Varillat, No. 23 Girod street, New Orleans—in the "Commercial Bulletin," August 27, 1838.

Mr. Cornelius D. Tolin, August, Ga., in the "Chronicle and Sentinel," Oct. 18, 1838.

W. H. Brasseale, sheriff, Blount county, Ala., in the "Huntsville Democrat," June 9, 1838.

Mr. Robert Beasley, Macon, Ga., in the "Georgia Messenger," July 27, 1837.

Mr. John Wotton, Rockville, Montgomery county, Maryland, in the "Baltimore Republican," Jan. 13, 1838.

D. S. Bennett, sheriff, Narchitoches, La., in the "Herald," July 21, 1838.

Messrs. C. C. Whitehead, and R. A. Evans, Marion, Georgia, in the Milledgeville (Ga.) "Standard of Union," June 26, 1838.

Mr. Samuel Stewart, Greensboro, Ala., in the "Southern Advocate," Huntsville, Jan. 6, 1838.

Mr. John Walker, No. 6, Banks' Arcade, New Orleans, in the "Bulletin" August 11, 1838.

Mr. Jesse Beene, Cahawba, Ala., in the "State Intelligencer," Tuskaloosa, Dec. 25, 1837.

TESTIMONY.

"Committed to jail as a runaway, a negro woman named Martha, 17 or 18 years of age, has *numerous scars of the whip* on her back."

"Ten dollars reward for my woman Siby, *very much scarred about the neck and ears by whipping.*"

"Ranaway [sic], a negro woman, named Maria, *some scars on her back occasioned by the whip.*"

"Stolen a negro woman, named Celia. On examining her back you will find *marks caused by the whip.*"

"Lodged in jail, a mulatto boy, *having large marks of the whip*, on his shoulders and other parts of his body."

"Was committed a negro boy, named Tom, is *much marked with the whip.*"

"Ranaway, a negro fellow named Dick—has *many scars* on his back from being *whipped.*"

"Committed to jail, a negro slave—his back is *very badly scarred.*"

"Committed, a mulatto fellow—his back shows *lasting impressions of the whip*, and leaves no doubt of his being a SLAVE."

"Committed to jail, a negro man—his back *much marked* by the whip."

"Ranaway, the negro slave named Jupiter—has a *fresh mark* of a cowskin on one of his cheeks."

"Ranaway, a negro man named Johnson—he has a *great many marks of the whip* on his back."

"Committed to jail, a negro slave named James—*much scarred* with a whip on his back."

"Ranaway, my man Fountain—he is marked *on the back with the whip.*"

"Ranaway, Bill—has *several* LARGE SCARS on his back from a *severe* whipping in *early* life."

"Committed to jail, a negro boy who calls himself Joe—said negro bears *marks of the whip.*"

"Ranaway, negro fellow John—from being whipped, has *scars on his back, arms, and thighs.*"

"Ranaway, a boy named Jim—with the marks of the *whip* on the small of the back, reaching round to the flank."

"Ranaway, the mulatto boy Quash—*considerably marked* on the back and other places with the lash."

"Ranaway, my negro man Billy—he has the *marks of the whip.*"

WITNESSES.	TESTIMONY.
Mr. John Turner, Thomaston, Upson county, Georgia—in the "Standard of Union," Milledgeville, June 26, 1838.	"Left, my negro man named George—has *marks of the whip very plain* on his thighs."
James Derrah, deputy sheriff, Claiborne county, Mi., in the "Port Gibson Correspondent," April 15, 1837.	"Committed to jail, negro man Toy—he has been *badly whipped.*"
S. B. Murphy, sheriff, Wilinson county, Georgia—in the Milledgeville "Journal," May 15, 1838.	"Brought to jail, a negro man named George—he has a *great many scars from the lash.*"
Mr. L. E. Cooner, Branchville Orangeburgh District, South Carolina—in the Macon "Messenger," May 25, 1837.	"One hundred dollars reward, for my negro Glasgow, and Kate, his wife. Glasgow is 24 years old—has *marks of the whip* on his back. Kate is 26—has a *scar* on her cheek, *and several marks of a whip.*"
John H. Hand, jailor, Parish of West Feliciana, La., in the St. "Francisville Journal," July 6, 1837.	"Committed to jail, a negro boy named John, about 17 years old—his back *badly marked* with the *whip*, his upper lip and chin *severely bruised.*"

Questions

1. Who are Weld's "witnesses," and why did they testify?
2. What does Weld wish the reader to conclude from the "testimony"?
3. Weld's book sold well. What qualities made it effective in portraying "slavery as it is"?

12-9   What to the Slave Is the Fourth of July? (1852)

Frederick Douglass

Born a slave on a Maryland plantation, Frederick Douglass (1817?–1895) escaped to the North as a young man. There he became a leading abolitionist speaker; having learned to read and write while a slave, he was also a powerful and eloquent writer, editing the antislavery newspaper *The North Star* in Rochester, New York. An astute reformer and political leader, Douglass became the dominant African American public figure in nineteenth-century America; his literary works, especially his autobiographies, are regarded as classics.

In 1852 the Rochester Ladies' Anti-Slavery Society invited Douglass to deliver the principal address at a Fourth of July celebration. (Because that year the holiday fell on Sunday, the celebration was actually held on July 5.) Douglass began in a conventional fashion, setting forth the case of the colonists against Great Britain and extolling the Founding Fathers. But then he veered off in a different direction entirely.

Source: John W. Blassingame, ed., *The Frederick Douglass Papers, Series One: Speeches, Debates, and Interviews,* 5 vols. (New Haven: Yale University Press, 1982), 2: 366–369, 371, 382–384, 386–388.

I leave, therefore, the great deeds of your fathers to other gentlemen whose claim to have been regularly descended will be less likely to be disputed than mine! . . .

Fellow-citizens, pardon me, allow me to ask, why am I called upon to speak here to-day? What have I, or those I represent, to do with your national independence? Are the great principles of political freedom and of natural justice, embodied in that Declaration of Independence, extended to us? and am I, therefore, called upon to bring our humble offering to the national altar, and to confess the benefits and express devout gratitude for the blessings resulting from your independence to us?

Would to God, both for your sakes and ours, that an affirmative answer could be truthfully returned to these questions! Then would my task be light, and my burden easy and delightful. For *who* is there so cold, that a nation's sympathy could not warm him? Who so obdurate and dead to the claims of gratitude, that would not thankfully acknowledge such priceless benefits? Who so stolid and selfish, that would not give his voice to swell the hallelujahs of a nation's jubilee, when the chains of servitude had been torn from his limbs? I am not that man. In a case like that, the dumb might eloquently speak, and the "lame man leap as an hart." . . .

But, such is not the state of the case. I say it with a sad sense of the disparity between us. I am not included within the pale of this glorious anniversary! Your high independence only reveals the immeasurable distance between us. The blessings in which you, this day, rejoice, are not enjoyed in common. The rich inheritance of justice, liberty, prosperity, and independence, bequeathed by your fathers, is shared by you, not by me. The sunlight that brought life and healing to you, has brought stripes of death to me. This Fourth [of] July is *yours,* not *mine. You* may rejoice, *I* must mourn. To drag a man in fetters into the grand illuminated temple of liberty, and call upon him to join in joyous anthems, were inhuman mockery and sacrilegious irony. Do you mean, citizens, to mock me, by asking me to speak to-day? If so, there is a parallel to your conduct. And let me warn you that it is dangerous to copy the example of a nation whose crimes, towering up to heaven, were thrown down by the breath of the Almighty, burying that nation in irrecoverable ruin! I can to-day take up the plaintive lament of a peeled and woe-smitten people!

"By the rivers of Babylon, there we sat down. Yea! we wept when we remembered Zion. We hanged our harps upon the willows in the midst thereof. For there, they that carried us away captive, required of us a song: and they who wasted us required of us mirth, saying, Sing us one of the songs of Zion. How can we sing the Lord's song in a strange land? If I forget thee, O Jerusalem, let my right hand forget her cunning. If I do not remember thee, let my tongue cleave to the roof of my mouth."

Fellow-citizens; above your national, tumultuous joy, I hear the mournful wail of millions! whose chains, heavy and grievous yesterday, are, to-day, rendered more intolerable by the jubilee shouts that reach them. If I do forget, If I do not faithfully remember those bleeding children of sorrow this day, "may my right hand forget her cunning, and may my tongue cleave to the roof of my mouth!" To forget them, to pass lightly over their wrongs, and to chime in with the popular theme, would be treason most scandalous and shocking, and would make me a reproach before God and the world. My subject, then fellow-citizens, is AMERICAN SLAVERY. I shall see, this day, and its popular characteristics, from the slave's point of view. Standing,

there, identified with the American bondman, making his wrongs mine, I do not hesitate to declare, with all my soul, that the character and conduct of this nation never looked blacker to me than on this 4th of July! Whether we turn to the declarations of the past, or to the professions of the present, the conduct of the nation seems equally hideous and revolting. America is false to the past, false to the present, and solemnly binds herself to be false to the future. Standing with God and the crushed and bleeding slave on this occasion, I will, in the name of humanity which is outraged, in the name of liberty which is fettered, in the name of the constitution and the Bible, which are disregarded and trampled upon, dare to call in question and to denounce, with all the emphasis I can command, everything that serves to perpetuate slavery—the great sin and shame of America! "I will not equivocate; I will not excuse;"—I will use the severest language I can command; and yet not one word shall escape me that any man, whose judgement is not blinded by prejudice, or who is not at heart a slaveholder, shall not confess to be right and just.

But I fancy I hear some one of my audience say, it is just in this circumstance that you and your brother abolitionists fail to make a favorable impression on the public mind. Would you argue more, and denounce less, would you persuade more, and rebuke less, your cause would be much more likely to succeed. But, I submit, where all is plain there is nothing to be argued. . . .

At a time like this, scorching irony, not convincing argument, is needed. O! had I the ability, and could I reach the nation's ear, I would, to-day, pour out a fiery stream of biting ridicule, blasting reproach, withering sarcasm, and stern rebuke. For it is not light that is needed, but fire; it is not the gentle shower, but thunder. We need the storm, the whirlwind, and the earthquake. The feeling of the nation must be quickened; the conscience of the nation must be roused; the propriety of the nation must be startled; the hypocrisy of the nation must be exposed; and its crimes against God and man must be proclaimed and denounced.

What, to the American slave, is your 4th of July? I answer: a day that reveals to him, more than all other days in the year, the gross injustice and cruelty to which he is the constant victim. To him, your celebration is a sham; your boasted liberty, an unholy license; your national greatness, swelling vanity; your sounds of rejoicing are empty and heartless; your denunciations of tyrants, brass fronted impudence; your shouts of liberty and equality, hollow mockery; your prayers and hymns, your sermons and thanksgivings, with all your religious parade, and solemnity, are, to him, mere bombast, fraud, deception, impiety, and hypocrisy—a thin veil to cover up crimes which would disgrace a nation of savages. There is not a nation on the earth guilty of practices, more shocking and bloody, than are the people of these United States, at this very hour.

Go where you may, search where you will, roam through all the monarchies and despotisms of the old world, travel through South America, search out every abuse, and when you have found the last, lay your facts by the side of the everyday practices of this nation, and you will say with me, that, for revolting barbarity and shameless hypocrisy, America reigns without a rival. . . .

Americans! your republican politics, not less than your republican religion, are flagrantly inconsistent. You boast of your love of liberty, your superior civilization, and your pure Christianity, while the whole political power of the nation (as embodied in the two great political parties), is solemnly pledged to support and perpetuate the enslavement of three millions of your countrymen. You hurl your anathemas at the crowned headed tyrants of Russia and Austria, and pride yourselves on your Democratic institutions, while you yourselves consent to be the mere *tools* and *bodyguards* of the tyrants of Virginia and Carolina. You invite to your shores fugitives of oppression from abroad, honor them with banquets, greet them with ovations, cheer them, toast them, salute them, protect them, and pour out your money to them like water; but the fugitives from your own land you advertise, hunt, arrest, shoot and kill. You glory in your refinement and your universal education; yet you maintain a system as barbarous and dreadful as ever stained the character of a nation—a system begun in avarice, supported in pride, and perpetuated in cruelty. You shed tears over fallen Hungary, and make the sad story of her wrongs the theme of your poets, statesmen and orators, till your gallant sons are ready to fly to arms to vindicate her cause against her oppressors; but, in regard to the ten thousand wrongs of the American slave, you would enforce the strictest silence, and would hail him as an enemy of the nation who dares to make those wrongs the subject of public discourse! You are all on fire at the mention of liberty for France or for Ireland; but are as cold as an iceberg at the thought of liberty for the enslaved of America. You discourse eloquently on the dignity of labor; yet, you sustain a system which, in its very essence, casts a stigma upon labor. You can bare your bosom to the storm of British artillery to throw off a threepenny tax on tea; and yet wring the last hard-earned farthing from the grasp of the black laborers of your country. You profess to belief "that, of one blood, God made all nations of men to dwell on the face of all the earth," and hath commanded all men, everywhere, to love one another, yet you notoriously hate, (and glory in your hatred), all men whose skins are not colored like your own. You declare, before the world, and are understood by the world to declare, that you *"hold these truths to be self evident, that all men are created equal; and are endowed by their Creator with certain inalienable rights; and that, among these are, life, liberty, and the pursuit of happiness;"* and yet, you hold securely, in a bondage which, according to your own Thomas Jefferson, *"is worse than ages of that which your fathers rose in rebellion to oppose,"* a *seventh* part of the inhabitants of your country.

Fellow-citizens! I will not enlarge further on your national inconsistencies. The existence of slavery in this country brands your republicanism as a sham, your humanity as a base pretence, and your Christianity as a lie. It destroys your moral power abroad; it corrupts your politicians at home. It saps the foundation of religion; it makes your name a hissing, and a by-word to a mocking earth. It is the antagonistic force in your government, the only thing that seriously disturbs and endangers your *Union*. It fetters your progress; it is the enemy of improvement, the deadly foe of education; it fosters pride; it breeds insolence; it promotes vice; it shelters crime; it is a curse to the earth that supports it; and yet, you cling to it, as if it were the sheet anchor of all your hopes. Oh! be warned! be warned! a horrible reptile is coiled up in your nation's bosom; the venomous creature is nursing at the tender breast of your youthful republic; *for the love of God, tear away,* and fling from you the hideous monster, and *let the weight of twenty millions crush and destroy it forever!* . . .

Allow me to say, in conclusion, notwithstanding the dark picture I have this day presented of the state of the nation, I do not despair of this country. There are forces in operation, which must inevitably work the downfall of slavery. *"The arm of the Lord is not shortened,"* and the doom of slavery is certain. I therefore, leave off where I began, with hope. While drawing encouragement from the Declaration of Independence, the great principles it contains, and the genius of American Institutions, my spirit is also cheered by the obvious tendencies of the age. Nations do not now stand in the same relation to each other that they did ages ago. No nation can now shut itself up from the surrounding world, and trot round in the same old path of its fathers without interference. The time *was* when such could be done. Long established customs of hurtful character could formerly fence themselves in, and do their evil work with social impunity. Knowledge was then confined and enjoyed by the privileged few, and the multitude walked on in mental darkness. But a change has now come over the affairs of mankind. Walled cities and empires have become unfashionable. The arm of commerce has borne away the gates of the strong city. Intelligence is penetrating the darkest corners of the globe. It makes its pathway over and under the sea, as well as on the earth. Wind, steam, and lightning are its chartered agents. Oceans no longer divide, but link nations together. From Boston to London is now a holiday excursion. Space is comparatively annihilated. Thoughts expressed on one side of the Atlantic are distinctly heard on the other.

The far off and almost fabulous Pacific rolls in grandeur at our feet. The Celestial Empire, the mystery of ages, is being solved. The fiat of the Almighty, *"Let there be Light,"* has not yet spent its force. No abuse, no outrage whether in taste, sport or avarice, can now hide itself from the all-pervading light. The iron shoe, and crippled foot of China must be seen, in contrast with nature. *Africa must rise and put on her yet unwoven garment. "Ethiopia shall stretch out her hand unto God."* In the fervent aspirations of William Lloyd Garrison, I say, and let every heart join in saying it:

God speed the year of jubilee
The wide world o'er!
When from their galling chains set free,
Th' oppress'd shall vilely bend the knee,
And wear the yoke of tyranny
Like brutes no more.
That year will come, and freedom's reign,
To man his plundered rights again
Restore.
God speed the day when human blood
Shall cease to flow!
In every clime, be understood,
The claims of human brotherhood,
And each return for evil, good,
Not blow for blow;
That day will come all feuds to end,
And change into a faithful friend
Each foe.

God speed the hour, the glorious hour,
When none on earth
Shall exercise a lordly power,
Nor in a tyrant's presence cower;
But all to manhood's stature tower,
By equal birth!
THAT HOUR WILL COME, to each, to all
And from his prison-house, the thrall
Go forth.

Until that year, day, hour, arrive,
With head, and heart, and hand I'll strive,
To break the rod, and rend the gyve,
The spoiler of his prey deprive—
So witness Heaven!
And never from my chosen post,
What'er the peril or the cost,
Be driven.

Questions

1. How does Douglass make effective use of the Declaration of Independence to confront white Americans with their shortcomings? What sort of imagery does Douglass use, and how effective do you think his speech was?

2. In what ways does Douglass indicate that all white Americans, not just white southerners, are implicated in the crime of slavery? Do you agree that slavery was a national, rather than local, sin?

3. Compare Douglass's speech to Samuel Danforth's "Errand into the Wilderness" (Document 2-9). How does each man use scriptural passages to reinforce his point? Can Douglass and Danforth be said to be pursuing similar objectives in their respective "sermons"?

Questions for Further Thought

1. Compare and contrast Frederick Douglass's speech (Document 12-9) with the rhetoric of William Lloyd Garrison (Document 12-7). How are they similar? Does Theodore Dwight Weld (Document 12-8) use a different approach to further the abolitionist cause? Which approach do you think was most effective, and why?

2. A byproduct of the Second Great Awakening, the abolitionist crusade drew much of its inspiration from evangelical Christianity. In what ways do the writings of Garrison, Weld, and Douglass (Documents 12-7 through 12-9) embody the evangelical spirit and methods of conversion? What sort of appeal did the abolitionists make, and why did they believe that they would be successful?

3. The twentieth-century conservative American politician Barry Goldwater once remarked that "extremism in defense of liberty is no vice." Others, though, have contended that extremism *is* vicious because it tends to be antidemocratic and intolerant of the give-and-take of the political process. Were abolitionists extremists? Was their extremism hurtful or helpful to their cause?

CHAPTER 13

The Crisis of the Union, 1844–1860

★   ★   ★

Manifest Destiny

For a quarter-century after the annexation of Florida in 1819, the boundaries of the United States remained the same. Although the extension of slavery into new territories had become a bone of contention between North and South in the Missouri Controversy of 1819–1821, the settlement of that crisis by the Missouri Compromise had been accepted by all. Moreover, with the rise of mass party politics, both major parties courted support from both sections and were therefore eager to keep slavery out of public debate.

But the land hunger of white North Americans continued unabated. To the southwest, American settlers had pressed beyond national borders into the newly independent nation of Mexico, where they came to dominate the northeastern province of Texas. When the Mexican central government attempted to bring the Americans under closer central rule, they rebelled and successfully established their independence (Document 13-1). Their request for annexation to the United States, however, was initially rebuffed; Texas was a slaveholding republic, and Martin Van Buren was fearful that his party would split over the issue.

Texas was not the only territory attracting the attention of Americans, however. In the early 1840s large numbers of settlers began traveling overland to the Oregon Territory; to its south, California, with its fertile valleys and great harbors, attracted both settlers and strategic interest. Back East, the heady optimism resulting from explosive economic growth and American pride in the creation of a new society fed an expansionist ideology that took the label "Manifest Destiny" (Documents 13-2 and 13-3).

With sentiment for territorial expansion rising in both North and South, southern Democrats, fearing that an independent Texas might abandon slavery and pose a threat to the security of the institution, began a new push for annexation. Whigs and many northern Democrats were virulently opposed, but the Democratic Party's 1844 convention united the party behind an expansionist candidate, James K. Polk, and a promise to pursue expansion in both Texas and Oregon. Although the antislavery

Liberty Party complicated the election, Democrats took their victory as an endorsement of vigorous pursuit of what they deemed America's Manifest Destiny.

13-1   Texas Declares Its Independence (1836)

The Adams-Onis Treaty (1819) established the Sabine River as the southwestern border between the United States and the Spanish territories in North America. Many Americans in the South and the West believed that Secretary of State John Quincy Adams, a New Englander, had conceded too much to Spain. They looked farther south to the Rio Grande and welcomed Mexican independence from Spain in 1822 because it potentially opened the Southwest to American settlers. Negotiating with Stephen Austin, Mexican authorities initially admitted about 2,000 families of American settlers. But relations between the Americans and the Mexican government were tense from the outset (see text pp. 408–409). In October 1832 and again in April 1833 the Texans held conventions that called on Mexico to reform its governance of the region. Unresolved grievances led to fighting and, in March 1836, to the Texas Declaration of Independence.

Source: Francis N. Thorpe, ed., *The Federal and State Constitutions . . . of the United States* (Washington, D.C.: U.S. Government Printing Office, 1909), 6: 3528.

When a government has ceased to protect the lives liberty and property of its people, from whom its legitimate powers are derived, and for the advancement of whose happiness it was instituted, and so far from being a guarantee for the enjoyment of those inestimable and inalienable rights, becomes an instrument in the hands of evil rulers for their oppression: When the Federal Republican Constitution of their country [Mexico], which they have sworn to support, no longer has a substantial existence, and the whole nature of their government has been forcibly changed without their consent, from a restricted federative republic, composed of sovereign states to a consolidated central military despotism in which every interest is disregarded but that of the army and the priesthood—both the eternal enemies of civil liberty, the ever-ready minions of power, and the usual instruments of tyrants: . . . the inherent and unalienable right of the people to appeal to first principles and take their political affairs into their own hands in extreme cases enjoins it as a right towards themselves and a sacred obligation to their posterity to abolish such government and create another in its stead, calculated to rescue them from impending dangers, and to secure their future welfare and happiness. . . .

The Mexican government, by its colonization laws, invited and induced the Anglo-American population of Texas to colonize its wilderness under the pledged faith of a written constitution that they should continue to enjoy that constitutional liberty and republican government to

which they had been habituated in the land of their birth, the United States of America. In this expectation they have been cruelly disappointed, in as much as the Mexican nation had acquiesced in the late changes made in the government by General Antonio Lopez de Santa Anna, who, having overturned the constitution of his country, now offers as the cruel alternative either to abandon our homes, acquired by so many privations, or submit to the most intolerable of all tyranny, the combined despotism of the sword and the priesthood. . . .

It has suffered the military commandants stationed among us to exercise arbitrary acts of oppression and tyranny; thus trampling upon the most sacred rights of the citizen and rendering the military superior to the civil power. . . .

It denies us the right of worshipping the Almighty according to the dictates of our own conscience, by the support of a national religion calculated to promote the temporal interest of its human functionaries rather than the glory of the true and living God.

It has demanded us to deliver up our arms, which are essential to our defence, the rightful property of freemen, and formidable only to tyrannical governments. . . .

These, and other grievances, were patiently borne by the people of Texas until they reached the point at which forbearance ceases to be a virtue. We then took up arms in defence of the national constitution. We appealed to our Mexican brethren for assistance. Our appeal has been made in vain. Though months have elapsed, no sympathetic response has yet been heard from the interior. We are, therefore, forced to the melancholy conclusion that the Mexican people have acquiesced in the destruction of their liberty and the substitution therefore of a Military Government—that they are unfit to be free and incapable of self-government. . . .

We therefore, the delegates with plenary powers, of the people of Texas, in solemn convention assembled, appealing to a candid world for the necessities of our condition, do hereby resolve and declare that our political connections with the Mexican Nation has forever ended; and that the people of Texas do now constitute a free sovereign and independent republic. . . .

Questions

1. Compare the Texas Declaration of Independence with the U.S. Declaration of Independence (see text pp. D-1–D-2). How are they similar? Where do they differ?
2. Texans complained of the "combined despotism of the sword and the priesthood." What did they mean?
3. Did the Americans in Texas see their revolution as one which would liberate the Mexicans from oppression? Explain why.

13-2 Texas, California, and Manifest Destiny (1845)

John L. O'Sullivan

John L. O'Sullivan (1813–1895) came from a line of Irish-American adventurers, and he carried his family's love of grand gestures into journalism, politics, and diplomacy. In 1837, at the age of twenty-three, O'Sullivan, a lawyer and Democratic Party activist, founded *The United States Magazine and Democratic Review,* which he made into a mouthpiece for Democratic Party propaganda; a vehicle for his own expansive, romantic views on the future of American democracy; and an outlet for such emerging American writers as Emerson, Hawthorne, Thoreau, and Whitman. O'Sullivan was especially obsessed with the notion that the mission of the United States was to spread the gospel of democracy across the continent; it was he who coined the term *manifest destiny* (used for the first time in the following article) to justify American expansion.

O'Sullivan later sought to practice what he preached; he became involved in efforts by private adventurers to seize Cuba and annex it to the United States, a project that ruined him financially and nearly threw him into prison. He later moved back to Europe, where he promoted the Confederate cause during the Civil War. He returned to the United States in the 1870s, broken by years spent promoting grand schemes; but his bumptious, continental vision of his country's promise fundamentally shaped the ways in which Americans understood their relationship to their neighbor countries and, later, the world.

Source: John L. O'Sullivan, "Annexation," *The United States Magazine and Democratic Review* 17 (July and August 1845): 5–10.

. . . Why, were other reasoning wanting, in favor of now elevating this question of the reception of Texas into the Union, out of the lower region of our past party dissensions, up to its proper level of a high and broad nationality, it surely is to be found, found abundantly, in the manner in which other nations have undertaken to intrude themselves into it, between us and the proper parties to the case, in a spirit of hostile interference against us, for the avowed object of thwarting our policy and hampering our power, limiting our greatness and checking the fulfilment of our manifest destiny to overspread the continent allotted by Providence for the free development of our yearly multiplying millions. This we have seen done by England, our old rival and enemy. . . .

It is wholly untrue, and unjust to ourselves, the pretence that the Annexation has been a measure of spoliation, unrightful and unrighteous—of military conquest under forms of peace and law—of territorial aggrandizement at the expense of justice, and justice due by a double sanctity to the weak. . . . If Texas became peopled with an American population, it was by no contrivance of our government, but on the express invitation of that of Mexico herself; accompanied with such guaranties of State independence, and the maintenance of a federal system analogous to our own, as constituted a compact fully justifying the strongest measures of redress on the part of those afterwards deceived in this guaranty, and sought to be enslaved under the yoke imposed by its violation. She was released, rightfully and absolutely released, from all Mexican allegiance, or duty of cohesion to the Mexican political body, by the acts and fault of Mexico herself, and Mexico alone. There never was a clearer case. It was not revolution; it was resistance to revolution; and resistance under such circumstances as left independence the necessary resulting state, caused by the abandonment of those with whom her former federal association had existed. What then can be more preposterous than all this clamor by Mexico and the Mexican interest, against Annexation, as a violation of any rights of hers, any duties of ours? . . .

California will, probably, next fall away from the loose adhesion which, in such a country as Mexico, holds a remote province in a slight equivocal kind of dependence on the metropolis. Imbecile and distracted, Mexico never can exert any real governmental authority over such a country. The impotence of the one and the distance of the other, must make the relation one of virtual independence; unless, by stunting the province of all natural growth, and forbidding that immigration which can alone develope its capabilities and fulfil the purposes of its creation, tyranny may retain a military dominion which is no government in the legitimate sense of the term. In the case of California this is now impossible. The Anglo-Saxon foot is already on its borders. Already the advance guard of the irresistible army of Anglo-Saxon emigration has begun to pour down upon it, armed with the plough and the rifle, and marking its trail with schools and colleges, courts and representative halls, mills and meeting-houses. A population will soon be in actual occupation of California, over which it will be idle for Mexico to dream of dominion. They will necessarily become independent. All this without agency of our government, without responsibility of our people—in the natural flow of events, the spontaneous working of principles, and the adaptation of the tendencies and wants of the human race to the elemental circumstances in the midst of which they find themselves placed. And they will have a right to independence—to self-government—to the possession of the homes conquered from the wilderness by their own labors and dangers, sufferings and sacrifices—a better and a truer right than the artificial title of sovereignty in Mexico a thousand miles distant, inheriting from Spain a title good only against those who have none better. Their right to independence will be the natural right of self-government belonging to any community strong enough to maintain it—distinct in position, origin and character, and free from any mutual obligations of membership of a common political body, binding it to others by the duty of loyalty and compact of public faith. This will be their title to independence; and by this title, there can be no doubt that the population now fast streaming down upon California will both assert and maintain that independence. . . .

Away, then, with all idle French talk of *balances of power* on the American Continent. There is no growth in Spanish America! Whatever progress of population there may be in the British Canadas, is only for their own early severance of their present colonial relation to the little island three thousand miles across the Atlantic; soon to be followed by Annexation, and destined to swell the still accumulating momentum of our progress. And whosoever may hold the balance, though they should cast into the opposite scale all the bayonets and cannon, not only of France and England, but of Europe entire, how would it kick the beam against the simple solid weight of the two hundred and fifty, or three hundred millions—and American millions—destined to gather beneath the flutter of the stripes and stars, in the fast hastening year of the Lord 1945!

Questions

1. Explain what John L. O'Sullivan means by the phrase "manifest destiny." By what right does O'Sullivan believe that the United States must annex Texas? Do you agree with his argument?

2. According to O'Sullivan, who is responsible for Texas's declaration of independence?

3. Why does O'Sullivan believe that California will "fall" next? For what reasons does he argue that California will inevitably declare its independence from Mexico? Why does O'Sullivan consider Mexico's title of sovereignty over California to be "artificial"?

13-3   The Importance of California (1845)

Thomas Oliver Larkin

Born in 1802, Thomas O. Larkin grew up in Lynn, Massachusetts, where his stepfather was a wealthy leather merchant. After failing at several enterprises in the East, Larkin in 1832 followed a relative to Monterey, California, where he became the leading merchant of that town, the capital of Mexico's northwestern state. Remote from central authority, its "Californio" inhabitants restive and sometimes rebellious, the region's natural wealth and strategic importance made it a center of intrigue among major powers as well as an attractive destination for American immigrants. In 1843 Larkin, who had never taken Mexican citizenship, became American consul. Eager to see California shake off Mexican rule, and fearful that it might become prey to British or French ambitions, he became an advocate of peaceful annexation, and in 1845 became a confidential agent of the U.S. government seeking to effect it. In the meantime, Larkin became the leading source of news about California to readers of the eastern press. If John L. O'Sullivan spoke romantically of "destiny," Larkin, the man in the field, spoke roughly and practically, as the following sample shows.

Source: Thomas Oliver Larkin to *Journal of Commerce,* July 1845, in George P. Hammond, ed., *The Larkin Papers: Personal, Business, and Official Correspondence of Thomas Oliver Larkin, Merchant and United States Consul in California* (Berkeley and Los Angeles: University of California Press, 1952), 3: 292–296. (*Note:* Spelling original to the document.)

California July 1845

By almost evry newspaper from the united States and many from England we find extracts and surmises respectng the sale of this country. One month England is the purchaser the next month the U. States. In the meantime the prorgress of California is onward, and would still be more so if Mexico would not send eviry few years a band of theivng soldiers and rapacous officers.

Should the supreme Governmet alow the Californias to rule there own Country they would have peace and prosperity. . . . We have now news that Mexico is fitting out an expedition of troops in Acapulco for Californa the expences to be paid by two or three English houses in Mexico who it is said are responsible for the pay for Eighteen months. . . .

The British Govermt have apponted one of her subjects (he formerly resided in N York where he owns property) Vice Consul of Californa with a salarey of 1000$ pr anum. This salay is small but as he can live on his own Rancho he has no expence in entertaining company Etc. nor does he attend to any distresed Eng seamen who may apply to him. In fact as he is much at his Country house they can not visit him unless under a heavy personal expence for horse hire.

The French Consul lives in Mont. with a Salery of over 4000$. There is not one E or French vessel dng business on this Coast nor has been for years. Ther Consul therefore have nothig to do *apparenty.* Why they are in Service there Govt best know and Uncle Sam will know to his cost.

The whole forign trade of C. in the hands of Amricans. There is now Sevn Boston Ships & Barks hire. The Am Consul has a jurisdictin of 1000 miles of Sea Coast, while the nature of the trade is such that he has barely any fees. Governmt allows no salary. The fees of this Consular is under 200$ a year, the Stationry bill about the same which is not allowed by the Dept of State.

There are many owners of large tracts of land in C. who hold them under the idea of the Country chang owners, having no preset use for thm, as the Indians tame & wild steal several thousand head of Horses yearly from the Rancho. Most of these horses are stole for food. The Indins cut up the meat in strips and dry it in the sun. While this continue Grazng of Cattle can not be profitible conducted. There is no expectiation that this Govt. will find a prevntive—nothng but the fear of the Indian for the American Settlers will prevent it. They steal but a few horse from Foreigner as there is to much danger of bng followed. Mexico may fret and treatent as much as she pleases but all her Cal Gov & Gen. give Cal land to all who apply for thm and from the nature of thigs will continue to do so. Foreignrs arring here expect to live & die in the Country, Mexican officers to remain 2 or 3 years & be shipt off by force unless they choose to marry a Native and becone a Californian, Body & Soul. This Ports in C. with the exceptin of Mazalan are the only Mexican Pacific Ports that are flourishng. All othrs are fallig & fallig fast. Here there is much advance in every thng and the Country present each year a bolder front to the world. It must change owners. Its of no use to Mexico. To hir its but a eye sore a shame and bone of Contentin. Here are many fine Ports, the land produces wheat over 100 fold. Cotten & hemp will grow here and every kind of fruit there is in New Eng—granes in abundance of the furst qualuty. Wine of many kinds are made, yet there is no faciluty of makng. Much of it will pass for Port. The Bays are full of fish, the Woods of game. Bears, and Whales can be seen from one view. The latter are offen in the way of the Boats near the Beach. Finaly there is San Francisco with its rivers. This Bay will hold all the ship in the U. S. The entranc is verry narrow between two mountains easly defended and pre-haps the most magnuficnt Harbour in the World and at present of as much use to the civilized world as if it did not exist. Some day or other this will belong to som Naval power. This every Native is prepared for. . . . Letters nor words can not express the advantag and importance of San F. to a Naval power. There is 500 to 1000 Am Whaelers with 20000 Amn Seamn in the Pacific. Half of them will be withen 20 day sail of San F. While the port belogs to Mex. its a safe place for whale ship in a war with England fran or Russian. Should one of these Native own the port and at some future day declare war aganst the U.S. what the re-sults. It require not the discruptin from the writer nor from anyone. If Congres wishes the exention[?] of the Navy, our Naval power or our commerce St F. must be obtaind, or the Origon & Cali must becone a Nation withn themsefs. Time is continualy brngng this into notice, and one of the two must soon be consumated or if the Origon dispute continues let E. take 8 degres N of the Columbia and pur-chase 8 Degres S. of 42 of Mex. and exchange.

The Origon will never be a benefit to the U. S. if Eng-land owns St. F. Vessels sometimes lay withen the bar of the Columbia 30 to 40 days waiting an opportunitey to go out. When once out they can reach St. F. in 4 days, a Steam Boat in less than two days. The time will soon arrive when by steam a person will go from the Columbia to Mont. & back in less in 4 days. For Navagation of the Columbia is of little use. A few English Vessel could prevent any vessels gong in—even if the wind allowed them. Whalers now from the N. W. pass the place for C.

The Settlers of the Origon anticipate the supplyng of California. Under present curcumstances they may. A Cali-fornia will not work if he can avoid it. The time will come, must come, when this Country is peopled by another race. This is as fully expected here as any other natual course of events. Many children have been sent to the Oahu English School to learn the Eng language to prepare them for the coming events, be the visit from John Bull or Uncle Sam. One of the two will have the Country. When once this is accomplished, the place will team with a busy race. As I before observed all fruits will grow here. Hemp, Cotten every Variuty of grain, timber from the tender Willow to Trees 17 feet in diamater. The Natives now expecting Troops from Acupulco to reconquer the Country are drillng many young men in preparation intended to sur-round the first port the Mexicans arrive at, drive away the Cattle, prevent all intercours with the Ranchos, and by this mean drive them out of C. If they can not succeed in this manner take to the mountans and worry them out.

There is no doubt but these soldiers are sent by Mexico under the instigatin of the English under the pretext that the Am are settlng in the C too fast and will one day obtain pos-sessin. In the time the C do not believe this story but give land to all that come, be they from what nation they may be.

These letter contans many facts well known to the writer and should be know to his Countrymen. Each para-graph contans matter suffcent for much thought & re-flectin and are sent to you because from your paper the writer has read many subjects respectng C. and give you his information in return.

Questions

1. Why does Larkin believe that the British and French are positioning themselves to seize California? What evidence does Larkin give to support his suspicion?

2. How does Larkin view the Indians in California? According to Larkin, what chal-lenges do the Indians pose to the settlement and development of California and what does he view as their inevitable fate?

3. How does Larkin's assessment of California compare with John L. O'Sullivan's? What economic and political potential does Larkin believe California possesses? Why is San Francisco so important?

Questions for Further Thought

1. Is it fair to say that Manifest Destiny was a fancy way for Americans to rational-ize the conquest of the West? Or, do you think that many Americans really be-lieved they had a God-given mission to "civilize" the West? What features of American culture might have contributed to this sense of mission?

2. In your opinion, was it inevitable that the United States would expand its control westward to the Pacific Ocean? Was Manifest Destiny a foregone conclusion? Based on your knowledge of the text, what rights and territories did the British, French, Russians, and Mexicans claim in the West, and why did the United States eventually get its way?

3. From your reading of Documents 13-1 through 13-3 as well as your reading of the text, what was Mexico's internal political situation in the 1830s and 1840s? How did the Americans exploit Mexico's weaknesses to its own advantage? What place did westward expansion have in domestic politics in the United States—specifically, the party rivalry between the Democrats and the Whigs?

War, Expansion, and Slavery, 1846–1850

Following his victory in the election of 1844, President James K. Polk pursued an aggressively expansionist policy. To the northwest, he ended joint American-British control of the Oregon Territory, though he agreed to dividing control along the 49th parallel rather than insisting on seizing the entire territory south of the "Fifty-Four Forty or Fight" line. Polk proved far more aggressive in the southwest against a weaker opponent, Mexico. Goading the Mexicans into providing him a pretext, Polk got Congress to declare war in May 1846. The war proved both popular (despite significant opposition from "Conscience" Whigs) and successful, resulting not only in the annexation of an enlarged Texas but in the seizure of California and New Mexico.

However, Polk's very success in pursuing the United State's Manifest Destiny immediately sharpened intersectional conflict over slavery. Mexico had abolished slavery, and many northerners were averse to seeing American power used to extend the "peculiar institution" to regions where freedom had been established. Many other white northerners, feeling that western lands should be reserved for white small farmers, not great planters (and blacks), were beginning to adhere to a new form of antislavery, the free-soil movement. If it was morally inferior to humanitarian antislavery, free soil was politically much more potent; one of its leaders, Representative David Wilmot, proposed a popular measure to bar slavery from the Mexican territories.

The 1846 Wilmot Proviso quickly became a flash point for North-South conflict, but it was soon joined by other issues, including a free-state movement in California and increasing northern resistance to enforcement of the constitutional requirement that fugitive slaves be returned to their masters. The southern champion John C. Calhoun declared free soil to be a violation of the Constitution and of states' rights (Document 13-4), and more radical white southerners threatened secession if "southern rights" were not acknowledged and protected. Antislavery spokesmen warned that to give in to what they saw as southern bullying would extend the sway in federal affairs of what they called the "Slave Power"—a southern interest hostile not simply to abolitionists but to the rights of white northerners as well (Document 13-5). The Compromise of 1850 successfully papered over the conflict; most Americans valued the Union more than they valued the principles of either antislavery northerners or southern white "fire-eaters." But the Compromise left the underlying issues intact, and they would explode later in the 1850s.

13-4   The Territories as Common Property (1847)

John C. Calhoun

John C. Calhoun of South Carolina (1782–1850), one of the so-called Great Triumvirate of antebellum American political leaders along with Henry Clay and Daniel Webster, was at once the least powerful and, in the long run, the most influential of the three. In the late 1820s, in the midst of a meteoric career that brought him to the vice presidency of the United States, he took up a crusade against protective tariffs that led to the Nullification Crisis of 1832–1833. In his later years, his national ambitions now set aside, Calhoun became preoccupied with what he saw as the threat posed by an increasingly powerful federal government—and an increasingly industrial, antislavery North—to the right of states, especially those of his native South, to govern themselves and be treated as equals in the larger Union. The most brilliant American political theorist since the Founders, he persistently sought the best defense of the South in a return to fundamental principles. When the Wilmot Proviso proposed to bar the introduction of slavery into the territories seized from Mexico by the United States, Calhoun set forth what would become the southern position.

Source: John C. Calhoun, "Speech and Resolutions on the Restriction of Slavery from the Territories," in Clyde N. Wilson and Shirley Bright Cook, eds., *The Papers of John C. Calhoun* (Columbia: University of South Carolina Press, 1998), 14: 169–176.

SPEECH AND RESOLUTIONS ON THE RESTRICTION OF SLAVERY FROM THE TERRITORIES

[In the Senate, February 19, 1847] Mr. Calhoun rose and said: Mr. President, I rise to offer a set of resolutions in reference to the various resolutions from the State legislatures upon the subject of what they call the extension of slavery, and the [Wilmot] proviso attached to the House bill, called the three million bill. What I propose before I send my resolutions to the table, is to make a few explanatory remarks.

Mr. President, it was solemnly asserted on this floor some time ago, that all parties in the non-slaveholding States had come to a fixed and solemn determination upon two propositions. One was, that there should be no further admission of any States into this Union which permitted by their constitution the existence of slavery; and the other was, that slavery shall not hereafter exist in any of the Territories of the United States; the effect of which would be to give to the non-slaveholding States the monopoly of the public domain, to the entire exclusion of the slave-holding States. Since that declaration was made, we we [*sic*] have abundant proof that there was a satisfactory foundation for it. We have received already solemn resolutions passed by seven of the non-slaveholding States—one-half of the number already in the Union, Iowa not being counted—using the strongest possible language to that effect; and no doubt in a short space of time similar resolutions will be received from all of the non-slaveholding States. But we need not go beyond the walls of Congress. The subject has been agitated in the other House, and they have set up a

bill "prohibiting the extension of slavery" (using their own language) "to any territory which may be acquired by the United States hereafter." At the same time, two resolutions which have been moved to extend the compromise line from the Rocky mountains to the Pacific, during the present session, have been rejected by a decided majority. . . .

Sir, if this state of things is to go on—if this determination, so solemnly made, is to be persisted in, where shall we stand, as far as this federal government of ours is concerned? We shall be at the entire mercy of the non-slaveholding States. Can we look to their justice and regard for our interests? I ask, can we rely on that? Ought we to trust our safety and prosperity to their mercy and sense of justice? These are the solemn questions which I put to all—this and the other side of the chamber.

Sir, can we find any hope by looking to the past[?] If we are to look to that—I will not go into the details—we will see from the beginning of this government to the present day, as far as pecuniary resources are concerned—as far as the disbursement of revenue is involved, it will be found that we have been a portion of the community which has substantially supported this government without receiving anything like a proportionate return. But why should I go beyond this very measure itself? Why go beyond this determination on the part of the non-slaveholding States, that there shall be no further addition to the slave-holding States, to prove what our condition will be?

Sir, what is the entire amount of this policy? I will not say that it is so designed. I will not say from what cause it originated. I will not say whether blind fanaticism on one side, whether a hostile feeling to slavery entertained by many not fanatical on the other, has produced it; or whether it has been the work of men, who, looking to political power, have considered the agitation of this question as the most effectual mode of obtaining the spoils of this Government. I look to the fact itself. It is a policy now openly avowed as one to be persisted in. It is a scheme, which aims to monopolize the powers of this Government and to obtain sole possession of its territories.

Now, I ask, is there any remedy? Does the Constitution afford any remedy? And if not, is there any hope? These, Mr. President, are solemn questions—not only to us, but, let me say to gentlemen from the non-slaveholding States, to them. Sir, the day that the balance between the two sections of the country—the slaveholding States and the non-slaveholding States—is destroyed, is a day that will not be far removed from political revolution, anarchy, civil war, and wide-spread disaster. The balance of this system is in the slave-holding States. They are the conservative portion—always have been the conservative portion—always will be the conservative portion; and with a due balance on their part may, for generations to come, uphold this glorious Union of ours. But if this scheme should be carried out—if we are to be reduced to a handful—if we are to become a mere ball to play the presidential game with—to count something in the Baltimore caucus—if this is to be the result—wo! wo! I say to this Union!

Now, sir, I put again the solemn question—does the Constitution afford any remedy? Is there any provision in it by which this aggressive policy—boldly avowed, as if perfectly consistent with our institutions and the safety and prosperity of the United States!—may be confronted? Is this a policy consistent with the Constitution? No, Mr. President, no! It is, in all its features, daringly opposed to the Constitution. What is it? Ours is a Federal Constitution. The States are its constituents, and not the people. The twenty-eight States—the twenty-nine States (including Iowa)—stand under this Government as twenty-nine individuals, or as twenty-nine millions of individuals would stand to a consolidated power. No, sir. It was made for higher ends. It was formed that every State as a constituent member of this Union of ours should enjoy all its advantages, natural and acquired, with greater security, and enjoy them more perfectly. The whole system is based on justice and equality—perfect equality between the members of this republic. Now can that be consistent with equality which will make this public domain a monopoly on one side—which, in its consequences, would place the whole power in one section of the Union to be wielded against the other sections of the Union? Is that equality?

How then do we stand in reference to this territorial question—this public domain of ours? Why, sir, what is it? It is the common property of the States of this Union. They are called "the territories of the United States." And what are the "United States" but the States united? Sir, these territories are the property of the States united; held jointly for their common use. And is it consistent with justice—is it consistent with equality, that any portion of the partners, outnumbering another portion, shall oust them of this common property of theirs—shall pass any law which shall proscribe the citizens of other portions of the Union from emigrating with their property to the territories of the United States? Would that be consistent—can it be consistent with the idea of a common property, held jointly for the common benefit of all? Would it be so considered in private life? Would it not be considered the most flagrant outrage in the world—one, which any court of equity would restrain by injunction, or any court of law in the world would overrule[?]

Mr. President, not only is that proposition grossly inconsistent with the Constitution, but the other, which undertakes to say that no State shall be admitted into this Union, which shall not prohibit by its constitution the existence of slaves, is equally a great outrage against the Constitution of the United States. Sir, I hold it to be a fundamental principle of our political system, that the people have a right to establish what government they may think proper for themselves; that every State about to become a member of this Union has a right to form its government as it pleases; and that, in order to be admitted there is but one qualification, and that is, that the government shall be republican. There is no express provision to that effect, but it results from that important section, which guarantees to every State in this Union a republican form of government. Now, sir, what is proposed? It is proposed, from a vague, indefinite, erroneous, and most dangerous conception of private individual liberty, to overrule this great common liberty which a people have of framing their own constitution! Sir, the right of framing self-government on the part of individuals, is not near so easily to be established by any course of reasoning, as the right of a community or State to self-government. And yet, sir, there are men of such delicate feeling on the subject of liberty—men who cannot possibly bear what they call slavery in one section of the country—although, (not so much slavery as an institution indispensable for the good of both races)—men so squeamish on this point, that they are ready to strike down the higher right of a community to govern themselves, in order to maintain the absolute right of individuals in every possible condition to govern themselves! . . .

I see my way in the Constitution. I cannot in a compromise. A compromise is but an act of Congress. It may be overruled at any time. It gives us no security. But the Constitution is stable. It is a rock. On it we can stand, and on it we can meet our friends from the non-slaveholding States. It is a firm and stable ground, on which we can better stand in opposition to fanaticism, than on the shifting sands of compromise.

Let us be done with compromises. Let us go back and stand upon the Constitution!

Well, sir, what if the decision of this body shall deny to us this high Constitutional right, not the less clear, because deduced from the entire body of the instrument, and the nature of the subject to which it relates, instead of being specially provided for? What then? I will not undertake to decide. It is a question for our constituents—the slaveholding States. A solemn and a great question. If the decision should be adverse, I trust and do believe, that they will take under solemn consideration what they ought to do. I give no advice. It would be hazardous and dangerous for me to do so. But I may speak as an individual member of that section of the Union. There is my family and connexions. There I drew my first breath. There are all my hopes. I am a planter—a cotton planter. I am a Southern man and a slaveholder—a kind and a merciful one, I trust—and none the worse for being a slaveholder. I say, for one, I would rather meet any extremity upon earth than give up one inch of our equality—one inch of what belongs to us as members of this great republic! What! acknowledged inferiority! The surrender of life is nothing to sinking down into acknowledged inferiority!

I have examined this subject largely—widely. I think I see the future. If we do not stand up as we ought, in my humble opinion, the condition of Ireland is prosperous and happy—the condition of Hindostan is prosperous and happy—the condition of Jamaica is prosperous and happy, to what the condition of the Southern States will be if now they should not stand up manfully in defence of their rights.

Mr. President, I desire that the resolutions which I now send to the table be read.

(The resolutions were read as follows:)

Resolved, That the territories of the United States belong to the several States composing this Union, and are held by them as their joint and common property.

Resolved, That Congress, as the joint agent and representative of the States of this Union, has no right to make any law, or do any act whatever, that shall directly, or by its effects, make any discrimination between the States of this Union, by which any of them shall be deprived of its full and equal right in any territory of the United States, acquired, or to be acquired.

Resolved, That the enactment of any law which should directly, or by its effects, deprive the citizens of any of the States of this Union from emigrating with their property into any of the territories of the United States, will make such discrimination, and would, therefore, be a violation of the Constitution, and the rights of the States from which such citizens emigrated, and in derogation of that perfect equality which belongs to them as members of this Union, and would tend directly to subvert the Union itself.

Resolved, That it is a fundamental principle in our political creed, that a people in forming a constitution have the unconditional right to form and adopt the Government which they may think best calculated to secure their liberty, prosperity, and happiness; and that in conformity thereto, no other condition is imposed by the Federal Constitution on a State in order to be admitted into this Union, except that its Constitution shall be republican; and that the imposition of any other by Congress would not only be in violation of the Constitution, but in direct conflict with the principle on which our political system rests.

I move that the resolutions be printed. I shall move that they be taken up tomorrow; and I do trust that the Senate will give them early attention, and an early vote upon the subject.

Questions

1. What is the substance of Calhoun's argument? Why does he believe that the southern states are being treated unfairly?
2. Calhoun says, "I see my way in the Constitution. I cannot in a compromise." What does Calhoun see wrong with compromise?
3. How does Calhoun define a federal republic?
4. Based on your reading of the text, how do you think Calhoun's colleagues in the Senate received his speech? Do you think that he changed many minds?

13-5   Defining the Constitutional Limits of Slavery (1850)

Salmon P. Chase

Born in New Hampshire and educated at Dartmouth College, Salmon P. Chase (1808–1873) studied law with President John Quincy Adams's attorney general, William Wirt, before moving west to establish himself as a successful young lawyer in Cincinnati, Ohio. Chase voted for William Henry Harrison in 1840 but soon afterward joined the fledgling abolitionist Liberty Party. Chase volunteered to be the defense attorney in a celebrated 1836 fugitive slave case involving a woman named Matilda and James G. Birney (the Liberty Party presidential candidate in 1840 and 1844), who employed her in his home. Chase lost the case, but the state supreme court ordered his argument printed, securing for Chase the title "attorney general of the fugitive slave" in antislavery circles. Chase took a leading role in the formation of the Free Soil Party in 1848 and forged a Free Soil–Democratic coalition in Ohio that elected him to the U.S. Senate (see text pp. 418–420). In the Senate Chase opposed the compromise measures crafted by Henry Clay, Daniel Webster, and Stephen Douglas. The argument he developed became the central tenet of the Republican party.

Source: Salmon P. Chase, *Union and Freedom, without Compromise. Speech of Mr. Chase of Ohio, On Mr. Clay's Compromise Resolutions* (Washington, D.C.: Buell and Blanchard, 1850).

I think, Mr. President, that two facts may now be regarded as established: First that in 1787 the national policy in respect to slavery was one of restriction, limitation, and discouragement. Second that it was generally expected that under the action of the State Governments slavery would gradually disappear from the States.

Such was the state of the country when the Convention met to frame the Constitution of the United States. . . . The framers of the Constitution acted under the influence of the general sentiment of the country. Some of them had contributed in no small measure to form that sentiment. Let us examine the instrument [the Constitution] in its light, and ascertain the original import of its language.

What, then, shall we find in it? The guaranties so much talked of? Recognition of property in men? Stipulated protection for that property in national territories and by national law? No, sir: nothing like it.

We find, on the contrary, extreme care to exclude these ideas from the Constitution. Neither the word "slave" nor "slavery" is to be found in any provision. There is not a single expression which charges the National Government with any responsibility in regard to slavery. No power is conferred on Congress either to establish or sustain it. The framers of the Constitution left it where they found it, exclusively within and under the jurisdiction of the States. Wherever slaves are referred to at all in the Constitution, whether in the clause providing for the apportionment of representation and direct taxation [Article I, section 2], or in that stipulating for the extradition of fugitive from service [the "fugitive slave" clause, Article IV, section 2], or in that restricting Congress as to the prohibition of importation or migration [Article I, section 9], they are spoken of, not as persons held as property, but as persons held to service, or having their condition determined, under State laws. We learn, indeed from the debates in the

Constitutional Convention that the idea of property in men was excluded with special solicitude. . . .

Unhappily . . . the original policy of the Government and the original principles of the Government in respect to slavery did not permanently control its action. A change occurred—almost imperceptible at first but becoming more and more marked and decided until nearly total. . . . It was natural, though it does [not] seem to have been anticipated, that the unity of the slave interest strengthened by this accession of political power, should gradually weaken the public sentiment and modify the national policy against slavery. . . . Mr. President, I have spoken freely of slave State ascendency in the affairs of this Government, but I desire not to be misunderstood. I take no sectional position. The supporters of slavery are the sectionalists. . . . Freedom is national; slavery only is local and sectional. . . .

What have been the results . . . of the subversion of the original policy of slavery restriction and discouragement . . . instead of slavery being regarded as a curse, a reproach, a blight, an evil, a wrong, a sin, we are now told that it is the most stable foundation of our institutions; the happiest relation that labor can sustain to capital; a blessing to both races . . . this is a great change, and a sad change. If it goes on, the spirit of liberty must at length become extinct, and a despotism will be established under the forms of free institutions. . . . There can be no foundation whatever for the doctrine advanced . . . that an equilibrium between the slaveholding and non-slaveholding sections of our country has been, is, and ought to be, an approved feature of our political system. . . . I shall feel myself supported by the precepts of the sages of the Revolutionary era, by the example of the founders of the Republic, by the original policy of the Government, and by the principles of the Constitution.

Questions

1. Why is Chase concerned with the history of the slavery issue? What difference did it make?

2. Locate in the Constitution (see text pp. D-7–D-10) the passages cited by Chase as referring to slaves. Do you agree with Chase that these passages were part of an original policy of "slavery restriction and discouragement"? Explain why.

3. What are the implications of Chase's conclusion that "Freedom is national; slavery . . . is . . . local"?

Questions for Further Thought

1. Compare and contrast the constitutional arguments of Calhoun (Document 13-4) and Chase (Document 13-5). Under the Constitution, was slavery a federal or a state—that is, national or local—responsibility? In your opinion, which senator makes a better case?

2. How does the emerging Republican Party's position on slavery as articulated by Chase (Document 13-5) differ from the abolitionist position as expressed by William Lloyd Garrison (Document 12-7), Theodore D. Weld (Document 12-8), and Frederick Douglass (Document 12-9)? Do you think that southerners could see these differences?

3. Why was the status of slavery in the territories of such paramount importance to both northerners and southerners? Why were southerners like Calhoun (Document 13-4) and northerners like Chase (Document 13-5) equally adamant that in the end, there could be no compromise on this one issue?

The End of the Second Party System, 1850–1858

While many Americans celebrated the Compromise of 1850 as a "final settlement" of all outstanding sectional issues, its central provisions served only to keep those issues visible. The Fugitive Slave Act of 1850, for instance, made it federal policy not simply to allow slavery in the states where it existed, but to extend the reach of the institution into the heart of the North itself (Document 13-6). In response, northern states passed more stringent "personal liberty" laws (Document 13-7), while antislavery militants increasingly turned to direct action both to free slaves and to protect fugitives from slave catchers and federal marshals (Document 13-8). Northerners saw the Fugitive Slave Act as demonstrating the lengths to which the "Slave Power," would go in attacking the liberties even of Americans in the "free states"; white southerners saw northern resistance as evidence that free-state residents refused to accept their constitutional obligations.

Meanwhile, in 1854 the issue of whether or not to allow the expansion of slavery in the western territories reasserted itself with the passage of the Kansas-Nebraska Act, which repealed the Missouri Compromise and allowed settlers in the newly organized territories of Kansas and Nebraska to determine the future of slavery there. Alarmed at what they viewed as a fresh triumph of the "Slave Power," a resurgent antislavery movement launched a new political party, the Republican Party, of unprecedentedly broad appeal. As Kansas degenerated into civil war between proslavery and antislavery factions, atrocity stories provided grist for sectional propagandists on both sides, while violence spread to the floor of the U.S. Senate itself (Document 13-9). The Supreme Court finally sought to resolve the issues in its 1857 *Dred Scott* decision (Document 13-10). However, its declaration that Congress had no constitutional right to bar slavery from the territories outraged Republicans and raised northern fears that the Court would ultimately declare slavery a *national* institution. To many northerners, it was becoming increasingly evident that the federal government had to be purged of all "Slave Power" influences—and the vehicle for doing so would be the Republican Party.

13-6   The Fugitive Slave Act of 1850

Under the Constitution (Article IV, section 2), states were obligated to surrender escaped slaves back to their owners. Growing antislavery sentiment in the North had led most states to ignore that provision, and as tensions rose, the South insisted that the northern states live up to their constitutional obligation. As part of the Compromise of 1850 Congress enacted a tougher fugitive slave statute to satisfy southern demands (see text pp. 425–427).

Source: U.S. Statutes at Large 9: 462ff.

Be it enacted by the Senate and House of Representatives of the United States of America in congress assembled, . . .

SEC. 6. *And be it further enacted,* That when a person held to service or labor in any State or Territory of the United States, has heretofore or shall hereafter escape into another State or Territory of the United States, the person or persons to whom such service or labor may be due, or his, her, or their agent or attorney, duly authorized, by power of attorney, in writing, acknowledged and certified under the seal of some legal officer or court of the State or Territory in which the same may be executed, may pursue and reclaim such fugitive person, either by procuring a warrant from some one of the courts, judges, or commissioners aforesaid, of the proper circuit, district, or county, for the apprehension of such fugitive from service or labor, or by seizing and arresting such fugitive, where the same can be done without process, and by taking, or causing such person to be taken, forthwith before such court, judge, or commissioner, whose duty it shall be to hear and determine the case of such claimant in a summary manner. . . . In no trial or hearing under this act shall the testimony of such alleged fugitive be admitted in evidence; and the certificates in this and the first [fourth] section be mentioned, shall be conclusive of the right of the person or persons in whose favor granted, to remove such fugitive to the State or Territory from which he escaped, and shall prevent all molestation of such person or persons by any process issued by any court, judge, magistrate, or other person whomsoever.

SEC. 7. *And be it further enacted,* That any person who shall knowingly and willingly obstruct, hinder, or prevent such claimant, his agent or attorney, or any person or persons lawfully assisting him, her, or them, from arresting such a fugitive from service or labor, either with or without process as aforesaid, or shall rescue, or attempt to rescue, such fugitive from service or labor, from the custody of such claimant, his or her agent or attorney, or other person or persons lawfully assisting as aforesaid, when so arrested, pursuant to the authority herein given and declared; or shall aid, abet, or assist such person so owing service or labor as aforesaid, directly or indirectly, to escape from such claimant, his agent or attorney, or other person or persons legally authorized as aforesaid; or shall harbor or conceal such fugitive, so as to prevent the discovery and arrest of such person, after notice or knowledge of the fact that such person was a fugitive from service or labor as aforesaid, shall, for either of said offences, be subject to a fine not exceeding one thousand dollars, and imprisonment not exceeding six months . . . and shall moreover forfeit and pay, by way of civil damages to the party injured by such illegal conduct, the sum of one thousand dollars, for each fugitive so lost as aforesaid. . . .

SEC. 9. *And be it further enacted,* That, upon affidavit made by the claimant of such fugitive, his agent or attorney, after such certificate has been issued, that he has reason to apprehend that such fugitive will be rescued by force from his or their possession before he can be taken beyond the limits of the State in which the arrest is made, it shall be the duty of the officer making the arrest to retain such fugitive in his custody, and to remove him to the State whence he fled, and there to deliver him to said claimant, his agent, or attorney. And to this end, the officer aforesaid is hereby authorized and required to employ so many persons as he may deem necessary to overcome such force, and to retain them in his service so long as circumstances may require. The said officer and his assistants, while so employed, to receive the same compensation, and to be allowed the same expenses, as are now allowed by law for transportation of criminals, to be certified by the judge of the district within which the arrest is made, and paid out of the treasury of the United States.

Questions

1. How does the act discourage people from helping fugitive slaves?
2. The Constitution called for the states to surrender runaways. Which people were specifically charged in the act with the enforcement of this law?
3. According to the act, whose responsibility is it to pay the expenses of slave catchers? Why was this provision included?

13-7   The Massachusetts Personal Liberty Act (1855)

Growing abolitionist sentiment led many northern states to seek ways to counteract the fugitive slave laws, first the old one of 1793 and then the stronger 1850 statute. They did this by enacting personal liberty laws, which did no more than ensure that captured runaways would receive a fair judicial hearing to see if they should be returned. The Personal Liberty Act of the Commonwealth of Massachusetts is excerpted here. Northern judges using such laws easily found ways to sabotage the Fugitive Slave Act.

Source: Massachusetts, *Acts and Resolves . . . 1855,* 924ff.

SEC. 2. The meaning of the one hundred and eleventh chapter of the Revised Statutes is hereby declared to be, that every person imprisoned or restrained of his liberty is entitled, as of right and course, to the writ of habeas corpus, except in the cases mentioned in the second section of that chapter.

SEC. 3. The writ of habeas corpus may be issued by the supreme judicial court, the court of common pleas, by any justice's court or police court of any town or city, by any court of record, or by any justice of either of said courts, or by any judge of probate; and it may be issued by any justice of the peace, if no magistrate above named is known to said justice of the peace, if no magistrate above named is known to said justice of the peace to be within five miles of the place where the party is imprisoned or restrained, and it shall be returnable before the supreme judicial court, or any one of the justices thereof, whether the court may be in session or not, and in term time or vacation. . . .

SEC. 6. If any claimant shall appear to demand the custody or possession of the person for whose benefit such writ is sued out, such claimant shall state in writing the facts on which he relies, with precision and certainty; and neither the claimant of the alleged fugitive, nor any person interested in his alleged obligation to service or labor, nor the alleged fugitive, shall be permitted to testify at the trial of the issue; and no confessions, admissions or declarations of the alleged fugitive against himself shall be given in evidence. Upon every question of fact involved in the issue, the burden of proof shall be on the claimant, and the facts alleged and necessary to be established, must be proved by the testimony of at least two credible witnesses, or other legal evidence equivalent thereto, and by the rules of evidence known and secured by the common law; and no ex parte [on behalf] deposition or affidavit shall be received in proof in behalf of the claimant, and no presumption shall arise in favor of the claimant from any proof that the alleged fugitive or any of his ancestors had actually been held as a slave, without proof that such holding was legal.

SEC. 7. If any person shall remove from the limits of this Commonwealth, or shall assist in removing therefrom, or shall come into the Commonwealth with the intention of removing or assisting in the removing therefrom, or shall procure or assist in procuring to be so removed, any person being in the peace thereof who is not "held to service or labor" by the "party" making "claim," or who has not "escaped" from the "party" making "claim," within the meaning of those words in the constitution of the United States, on the pretence that such person is so held or has so escaped, or that his "service or labor," is so "due," or with the intent to subject him to such "service or labor," he shall be punished by a fine of not less than one thousand, nor more than five thousand dollars, and by imprisonment in the State Prison not less than one, nor more than five years. . . .

SEC. 9. No person, while holding any office of honor, trust, or emolument, under the laws of this Commonwealth, shall, in any capacity, issue any warrant or other process, or grant any certificate, under or by virtue of an act of congress . . . or shall in any capacity, serve any such warrant or other process . . .

SEC. 11. Any person who shall act as counsel or attorney for any claimant of any alleged fugitive from service or labor, under or by virtue of the acts of congress mentioned in the ninth section of this act, shall be deemed to have resigned any commission from the Commonwealth that he may possess, and he shall be thereafter incapacitated from appearing as counsel or attorney in the courts of this Commonwealth. . . .

SEC. 14. Any person holding any judicial office under the constitution or laws of this Commonwealth, who shall continue, for ten days after the passage of this act, to hold the office of United States commissioner, or any office . . . which qualifies him to issue any warrant or other process . . . under the [Fugitive Slave Acts] shall be deemed to have violated good behavior, to have given reason for the loss of public confidence, and furnished sufficient ground either for impeachment or for removal by address.

SEC. 15. Any sheriff, deputy sheriff, jailer, coroner, constable, or other officer of this Commonwealth, or the police of any city or town, or any district, county, city or town officer, or any officer or other member of the volunteer militia of this Commonwealth, who shall hereafter arrest . . . any person for the reason that he is claimed or adjudged to be a fugitive from service or labor, shall be punished by fine . . . and by imprisonment.

SEC. 19. No jail, prison, or other place of confinement belonging to, or used by, either the Commonwealth of Massachusetts or any county therein, shall be used for the detention or imprisonment of any person accused or convicted of any offence created by [the Federal Fugitive Slave Act] . . . or accused or convicted of obstructing or resisting any process, warrant, or order issued under either of said acts, or of rescuing, or attempting to rescue, any person arrested or detained under any of the provisions of either of the said acts.

Questions

1. Compare this law with the Fugitive Slave Act. What is the essential difference between the two laws in how they treat the runaway slaves?
2. The 1850 Fugitive Slave Act specifically obligated state officials to enforce the law. How does the Massachusetts act get around that provision?
3. What evidence is there in the act that would lead you to believe there was strong abolitionist sentiment in Massachusetts?

13-8 Opposing Accounts of the Rescue of a Fugitive (1851)

Although personal liberty laws helped impede the enforcement of the Fugitive Slave Act, their effect was slight at best; the new federal machinery ground on and moreover was supported by large segments of public opinion, which regarded the law as the price to be paid for sectional peace and continued to see abolitionists as disruptive and potentially treasonous. Feeling increasingly beleaguered, abolitionists and free blacks living in the North sought to protect alleged fugitive slaves through direct action. One of the more famous early examples of such action was the "Jerry Rescue" of October 1851 in Syracuse, New York. The following account, from a sympathetic reporter for the *New York Tribune,* was reprinted in William Lloyd Garrison's newspaper *The Liberator.* Following the account is a hostile editorial from a New York City Whig newspaper. (Note: Earlier that year, Daniel Webster, in a speech in Syracuse, had predicted that the law would be enforced there.)

Sources: The Liberator (Boston), 10 October 1851; *National Intelligencer* (Washington, D.C.), 7 October 1851.

(a) From the New York *Tribune*: Slave Catching in Syracuse—Intense Excitement.

I.

SYRACUSE, Wednesday, Oct. 1, 1851—9 P.M.

Our city is perfectly wild with excitement. A negro man named Jerry was arrested here to-day, claimed by a man named McHenry of Missouri, as a fugitive slave. The United States Marshal, with aids from the neighboring cities congregated here, arrested Jerry and brought him before United States Commissioner Sabine. The news spread over the city,—the bells in the various churches were tolled,—and the people assembled in knots at the corners of the streets,—one general feeling pervaded every breast, that of disgust and abhorrence at the Fugitive Slave Law, and this its first foul offspring in Syracuse. Our County Fair was being held in the city, and the farmers from the surrounding country were all here. In addition, a Liberty Party Convention was called for to-day, and I notice, prominent in our streets, some of the leaders of that party.—The Court of appeals is also in session here, and have had a good opportunity to witness the feeling here to-day.

The examination of Jerry, who is a fine athletic man, commenced at the Commissioner's office about 2 o'clock, P.M. The Court room and every avenue leading to it was densely crowded. The prosecution was conducted by three lawyers, named Anderson, Loomis and Lawrence. The defence was by Hillis, Morgan and Sheldon. The Commissioner adjourned the Court for half an hour, at about half-past 2 o'clock, P.M. The adjournment had no sooner been made, than a band of negroes and others seized the alleged fugitive, rescued him from the custody of the officers, and rushed down Water and Genessee streets, through Market Square, and down Water street to Lock street, over Lock street bridge, where he was caught by the officers and taken back to the police office of Justice House. Jerry was heavily handcuffed, which prevented his successful escape this time.

In the meantime, the crowd and excitement became intense; and the feeling gained upon the people, that the Fugitive Slave Law must not be executed in Syracuse. The military companies were ordered out by the Sheriff of the county, and got under arms, and prepared for action. Only one company, however, would leave their armory, and finally they went back, and the whole military of the city refused to aid and abet in carrying Jerry back into slavery. The Commissioner resumed the examination at 5 P.M., at the police office of Justice House. The crowd outside, unable to gain admittance, became more and more excited, and the noise and confusion frequently prevented the prosecution of the examination on the inside. Stones were thrown through the windows of the room, and the crowd exhibited certain other unmistakable signs that they were decidedly hostile to the Fugitive Slave Law. About 7 P.M., the crowd outside became more and more clamorous, and stones, &c., becoming more and more frequent, the Commissioner decided to adjourn the examination until to-morrow morning, at 8 o'clock.

This was announced to the crowd by Mr. Hillis, counsel for the prisoner, but the excitement could not be allayed. The officers in charge of the fugitive soon found it necessary to board up the windows, and in so doing, they got pretty well pelted. They next tried the effect of a few shots fired over the heads of the people, but it only increased the excitement. About 9 P.M., a desperate onslaught was made, and the doors and windows of the office were broken in, the lights extinguished, and the fugitive taken from the custody of the officers, and carried away to breathe freedom and liberty in the rural districts of our delightful country. So Mr. Webster's prophecy proves false, and the Fugitive Slave Law cannot be executed in Syracuse. The agent of the claimant at the final rescue jumped from the window of the police office, on the heel path of the canal, (or into the canal, I don't know which,) where he was caught by the crowd, but he claimed to be a line-boat passenger, and the crowd believed the story, and let him go. A barrel of tar and feathers had been provided for his accommodation, and were within a convenient distance, but he escaped them by his dexterous subterfuge. I understand the Marshal from Rochester had his arm broken in the melee at the last escape, and rumor is busy reporting other injuries, none, however, of a serious nature, and I have no faith in any of the reports. Some two or three persons fell from an awning into a cellar-way, and were somewhat injured. The appearance of the police office is rather dejected, and looks some as if it had stood pretty hard fire. The general sentiment was and is against the law and its execution; and one general congratulation is passing around the streets, and from mouth to mouth, at this final issue of the attempt to kidnap a human being in the 'Central City' of the Empire State.　　　　　　　　　G.B.

[October 2, 1851]

The chief movers in the crowd appeared to be negroes, although no one could be recognized in the darkness of the night, and amid the excitement and whirl of the occasion. No one was foremost in the rescue, no one did it, and I have seen no one of our citizens this morning so unfortunate in his opinions as to condemn the act. Indeed, congratulatory remarks and smiles prevail on every countenance. No sooner do two persons meet, than one begins to grin, and the other to say, 'Where's Jerry?' The one strong sentiment in the heart of the whole city is, that the Slave Law is wrong.

(b) from the *New York Express:* Lawlessness in Syracuse

Syracuse, in this State, is a city of salt; and if there be a city in this broad Union which especially lives, thrives, or *exists* on the Federal Government of the thirty-one United States, and upon the laws, it is this Syracuse, this city of salt, salt works, and salt boilers, and that surrounding country of farmers that feed these Syracusans.

In the first place, this Federal Republic—this Government of thirty-one States, fifteen of which are slaveholding—gives this Syracuse a protective duty of twenty per cent. *ad volorem* on every bushel of salt it makes. In 1850 the imports of salt into the United States were 11,224,185 bushels; and on every bushel of that salt, mainly to aid, strengthen, and support Syracuse and such like manufacturing places, the people of these United States, and slaveholding people among them, paid a duty of twenty percent. *ad valorem.*

In the second place, the more to protect, build up, and make rich Syracuse and her salt-boilers, the State of New York levies a discriminating duty by tolls on her canals against all foreign salt, so that nearly a MONOPOLY of the sale of salt in the western and central parts of this State, and in the Lake States, is thus secured by protective LAW to Syracuse.

Nevertheless, now for some years this Syracuse has been the hot-bed of abolitionism, but especially so since the passage of the compromise bills of 1850; and one leading (so misnamed) Whig paper there, but more especially one (so called) clergyman, a Rev. Mr. May, have deliberately preached what inevitably led to the nullification of law by force. Hence, under such teachings, we have such scenes as are reported at Syracuse.

To rescue a *negro* man *against law,* a *white* man, acting *under the imperative obligations of law,* is maimed, having his right arm broken in two places!

Further comment is unnecessary. Every fact set forth above speaks trumpet-tongued for itself. All we have to add is, that beyond all question there is a very large majority of law-loving, law-abiding people in Syracuse who abhor all such enormous outrages as these. We know, of our own knowledge, at least thirty leading men there who abhor such things, if possible, more heartily than we do. Their only fault is, that they have not met the very beginnings of treason, when it was counselled in theory, with hearty fearless opposition, or that they have taken into their dwellings papers that preach treason, or endured in their pulpits preachers that represented it as of God, and godly.

Questions

1. Judging from the above accounts, who took the lead in rescuing Jerry?
2. Could this rescue have been successfully carried off *anywhere* in the North? Or was Syracuse special?
3. What accounts for the hostility of the *New York Express* editor toward the rescue? Which do you think was more reflective of public opinion in the North—the rescue itself, or this reaction to it?

13-9　The Crime against Kansas (1856)

Charles Sumner

Born in Boston and educated at Harvard, Charles Sumner (1811–1874) entered the world of New England social reform in the 1840s and moved quickly into antislavery political activity after the organization of the Free Soil Party in 1848. A political coalition of Free-Soilers and Democrats in Massachusetts sent Sumner to the U.S. Senate in 1851, replacing Daniel Webster, whose authorship of and support for the Compromise of 1850 and the Fugitive Slave Act outraged the growing antislavery sentiment in Massachusetts. Sumner's purpose in the Senate was first and foremost to fight the Slave Power, which he blamed for the outbreak of violence in Kansas (see text pp. 429–432). Sumner took the floor of the Senate over two days (May 19 and 20, 1856) to defend the free-soil settlers and denounce as barbarians the proslavery forces that were attempting to seize control of the territory. In the course of that speech, "The Crime against Kansas," Sumner made derogatory personal references to South Carolina's elderly senator, Andrew Butler, who had recently suffered a stroke. Two days later Senator Butler's nephew, Representative Preston S. Brooks of South Carolina, severely beat Sumner with a cane. Brooks became a hero in South Carolina (see text p. 407). Sumner, revered as a martyr to the cause of freedom, won reelection to the Senate until he died.

Source: Charles Sumner: His Complete Works (Lee and Shepard, 1900; reprint, New York: Negro Universities Press edition, 1969), 5: 125–126.

Mr. President,—You are now called to redress a great wrong. Seldom in the history of nations is such a question presented. Tariffs, army bills, navy bills, land bills, are important, and justly occupy your care; but these all belong to the course of ordinary legislation. . . . Far otherwise is it with the eminent question now before you, involving, as it does, Liberty in a broad Territory, and also involving the peace of the whole country, with our good name in history forevermore. . . .

The wickedness which I now begin to expose is immeasurably aggravated by the motive which prompted it. Not in any common lust for power did this uncommon tragedy have its origin. It is the rape of a virgin Territory, compelling it to the hateful embrace of Slavery; and it may be clearly traced to a depraved desire for a new Slave State, hideous offspring of such a crime, in the hope of adding to the power of Slavery in the National Government. Yes, Sir, when the whole world alike . . . is rising up to condemn this wrong . . . here in our Republic, *force*—ay, Sir, FORCE—is openly employed in compelling Kansas to this pollution, and all for the sake of political power. . . .

Before entering upon the argument, I must say something of a general character, particularly in response to what has fallen from Senators who have raised themselves to eminence on this floor in championship of human wrong: I mean the Senator from South Carolina [Mr. Butler]. . . . The Senator from South Carolina had read many books of chivalry, and believes himself a chivalrous knight, with sentiments of honor and courage. Of course he has chosen a mistress to whom he has made his vows, and who, though ugly to others, is always lovely to him,—though polluted in the sight of the world, is chaste in his sight: I mean the harlot Slavery. For her his tongue is always profuse with words. Let her be impeached in character, or any proposition be made to shut her out from the extension of her wantonness, and no extravagance of manner or hardihood of assertion is then too great for this Senator. . . .

I undertake, in the first place, to expose the CRIME AGAINST KANSAS, in origin and extent. . . . The debate [over the Kansas-Nebraska bill], which convulsed Congress, stirred the whole country. From all sides attention was directed upon Kansas, which at once became the favorite goal of emigration. The bill loudly declares that its object is "to leave the people perfectly free to form and regulate their domestic institutions in their own way"; and

its supporters everywhere challenge the determination of the question between Freedom and Slavery by a competition of emigration. . . . The populous North, stung by sense of outrage, and inspired by a noble cause, are pouring into the debatable land, and promise soon to establish a supremacy of Freedom.

Then was conceived the consummation of the Crime against Kansas. What could not be accomplished peaceably was to be accomplished forcibly. . . . The violence, for some time threatened, broke forth on the 29th of November, 1854, at the first election of a Delegate to Congress, when companies from Missouri, amounting to upwards of one thousand, crossed into Kansas, and with force and arms proceeded to vote for . . . the candidate of Slavery. . . . Five . . . times and more have these invaders entered Kansas in armed array, and thus five . . . times and more have they trampled upon the organic law of the Territory. These extraordinary expeditions are simply the extraordinary witnesses to successive, uninterrupted violence. . . . Border incursions, which in barbarous ages or barbarous lands fretted and harried an exposed people, are here renewed, with this peculiarity, that our border robbers do not simply levy blackmail and drive off a few cattle . . . they commit a succession of deeds in which . . . the whole Territory is enslaved.

Private griefs mingle their poignancy with public wrongs. I do not dwell on the anxieties of families exposed to sudden assault, and lying down to rest with the alarms of war ringing in the ears, not knowing that another day may be spared to them. . . . Our souls are wrung by individual instances. . . .

Thus was the Crime consummated. Slavery stands erect, clanking its chains on the Territory of Kansas, surrounded by a code of death, and trampling upon all cherished liberties. . . . Emerging from all the blackness of this Crime . . . I come now to the APOLOGIES which the Crime has found. . . .

With regret I come again upon the Senator from South Carolina [Butler. His speech slurred by a stroke, Butler had interjected critical comments on more than thirty occasions while Sumner spoke] who, omnipresent in this debate, overflows with rage at the simple suggestion that Kansas has applied for admission as a State, and, with incoherent phrase, discharges the loose expectoration of his speech, now upon her representative, and then upon her people. . . . [I]t is against the [free-soil majority in] . . . Kansas that sensibilities of the Senator are particularly aroused. . . .

The contest, which, beginning in Kansas, reaches us will be transferred soon from Congress to that broader stage, where every citizen is not only spectator, but actor; and to their judgment I confidently turn. To the people, about to exercise the electoral franchise, in choosing a Chief Magistrate of the Republic, I appeal, to vindicate the electoral franchise in Kansas. Let the ballot-box of the Union . . . protect the ballot-box in that Territory.

Questions

1. According to Sumner, why did the Slave Power no longer support the "popular sovereignty" solution to the question of the extension of slavery?
2. Read Sumner's comments about Senator Butler from the perspective of Representative Preston Brooks. How had Sumner challenged the honor of his uncle?
3. What is the political intent of Sumner's speech? Whom does he expect to agitate with his heated remarks? To what purpose?

13-10   The *Dred Scott* Decision (1857)

In his inaugural address on March 4, 1857, President James Buchanan announced that the constitutional issues associated with the struggle between proslavery and antislavery forces in Kansas would soon be "speedily and finally settled" by the judicial branch of the federal government. Two days later the Supreme Court announced its decision in the case of *Dred Scott v. Sandford*, which the Court had accepted for review in 1854. Scott had been the slave of Dr. John Emerson, a surgeon in the U.S. Army. While on active duty, Emerson had taken Scott to Illinois in 1834 and to the upper Louisiana Purchase territory in 1836 and then had returned to Missouri. Slavery had been excluded in Illinois by the Northwest Ordinance of 1787 and from the upper Louisiana Purchase territory by the Missouri Compromise of 1820. In his suit Scott claimed to have been freed by reason of his residence in free territory (see text pp. 433–434). The Supreme Court's decision came in nine separate decisions, two in dissent. But it was the wide-ranging opinion of Chief Justice Roger B. Taney that was popularly considered the decision of the Court. Taney had been in correspondence with Buchanan before his inaugural address. In his decision Taney endeavored to provide a final settlement to the question of slavery.

Source: Dred Scott v. Sandford, 19 How. 393 (1857).

Chief Justice Taney delivered the opinion of the Court.

The question is simply this: Can a negro, whose ancestors were imported into this country, and sold as slaves, become a member of the political community formed and brought into existence by the constitution of the United States, and as such become entitled to all the rights, and privileges, and immunities, guaranteed by that instrument to the citizen? One of which rights is the privilege of suing in a court of the United States in the cases specified in the constitution. . . .

The words "people of the United States" and "citizens" are synonymous terms, and mean the same thing.

They both describe the political body who, according to our republican institutions, form the sovereignty, and who hold the power and conduct the government through their representatives. They are what we familiarly call the "sovereign people," and every citizen is one of this people, and a constituent member of this sovereignty. The question before us is, whether the class of persons described in the plea in abatement compose a portion of this people, and are constituent members of this sovereignty? We think they are not, and that they are not included, and were not intended to be included, under the word "citizens" in the constitution, and can therefore claim none of the rights and privileges which that instrument provides for and secures to citizens of the United States. On the contrary, they were at that time considered as a subordinate and inferior class of beings, who had been subjugated by the dominant race, and, whether emancipated or not, yet remained subject to their authority, and had no rights or privileges but such as those who held the power and the government might choose to grant them. . . .

In discussing this question, we must not confound the rights of citizenship which a State may confer within its own limits, and the rights of citizenship as a member of the Union. It does not by any means follow, because he [Scott] has all the rights and privileges of a citizen of a State, that he must be a citizen of the United States. He may have all of the rights and privileges of the citizen of a State, and yet not be entitled to the rights and privileges of a citizen in any other State. For, previous to the adoption of the constitution of the United States, every State had the undoubted right to confer on whomsoever it pleased the character of citizen, and to endow him with all its rights. But this character of course was confined to the boundaries of the State, and gave him no rights or privileges in other States beyond those secured to him by the laws of nations and the comity of States. Nor have the several States surrendered the power of conferring these rights and privileges by adopting the constitution of the United States. . . .

It is very clear, therefore, that no State can, by any act or law of its own, passed since the adoption of the constitution, introduce a new member into the political community created by the constitution of the United States. It cannot make him a member of this community by making him a member of its own. And for the same reason it cannot introduce any person, or description of persons, who were not intended to be embraced in this new political family, which the constitution brought into existence, but were intended to be excluded from it.

The question then arises, whether the provisions of the constitution, in relation to the personal rights and privileges to which the citizen of a State should be entitled, embraced the negro African race, at that time in this country, or who might afterwards be imported, who had then or should afterwards be made free in any State; and to put it in the power of a single State to make him a citizen of the United States, and endue him with the full rights of citizenship in every other State without their consent? Does the constitution of the United States act upon him whenever he shall be made free under the laws of a State, and raised there to the rank of a citizen, and immediately clothe him with all the privileges of a citizen in every other State, and in its own courts?

In the opinion of the court, the legislation and histories of the times, and the language used in the declaration of independence, show, that neither the class of persons who had been imported as slaves, nor their descendants, whether they had become free or not, were then acknowledged as a part of the people, nor intended to be included

in the general words used in that memorable instrument. . . .

It is too clear for dispute, that the enslaved African race were not intended to be included, and formed no part of the people who framed and adopted this declaration; for if the language, as understood in that day, would embrace them, the conduct of the distinguished men who framed the declaration of independence would have been utterly and flagrantly inconsistent with the principles they asserted; and instead of the sympathy of mankind, to which they so confidently appealed, they would have deserved and received universal rebuke and reprobation.

We proceed . . . to inquire whether the facts relied on by the plaintiff entitled him to his freedom. . . .

The act of Congress, upon which the plaintiff relies, declares that slavery and involuntary servitude, except as a punishment for crime, shall be forever prohibited in all that part of the territory ceded by France, under the name of Louisiana, which lies north of thirty-six degrees thirty minutes north latitude and not included within the limits of Missouri. And the difficulty which meets us at the threshold of this part of the inquiry is whether Congress was authorized to pass this law under any of the powers granted to it by the Constitution; for, if the authority is not given by that instrument, it is the duty of this Court to declare it void and inoperative and incapable of conferring freedom upon anyone who is held as a slave under the laws of any one of the states.

The counsel for the plaintiff has laid much stress upon that article in the Constitution which confers on Congress the power "to dispose of and make all needful rules and regulations respecting the territory or other property belonging to the United States"; but, in the judgment of the Court, that provision has no bearing on the present controversy, and the power there given, whatever it may be, is confined, and was intended to be confined, to the territory which at that time belonged to, or was claimed by, the United States and was within their boundaries as settled by the [1783] treaty with Great Britain and can have no influence upon a territory afterward acquired from a foreign government. It was a special provision for a known and particular territory, and to meet a present emergency, and nothing more. . . .

. . . It may be safely assumed that citizens of the United States who migrate to a territory belonging to the people of the United States cannot be ruled as mere colonists, dependent upon the will of the general government, and to be governed by any laws it may think proper to impose. The principle upon which our governments rest, and upon which alone they continue to exist, is the union of states, sovereign and independent within their own limits in their internal and domestic concerns, and bound together as one people by a general government, possessing certain enumerated and restricted powers, delegated to it by the people of the several states, and exercising supreme authority within the scope of the powers granted to it, throughout the dominion of the United States. A power, therefore, in the general government to obtain and hold colonies and dependent territories, over which they might legislate without restriction, would be inconsistent with its own existence in its present form. Whatever it acquires, it acquires for the benefit of the people of the several states who created it. It is their trustee acting for them and charged with the duty of promoting the interests of the whole people of the Union in the exercise of the powers specifically granted. . . .

But the power of Congress over the person or property of a citizen can never be a mere discretionary power under our Constitution and form of government. The powers of the government and the rights and privileges of the citizen are regulated and plainly defined by the Constitution itself. And, when the territory becomes a part of the United States, the federal government enters into possession in the character impressed upon it by those who created it. It enters upon it with its powers over the citizen strictly defined and limited by the Constitution, from which it derives its own existence, and by virtue of which alone it continues to exist and act as a government and sovereignty. . . .

Upon these considerations it is the opinion of the Court that the act of Congress which prohibited a citizen from holding and owning property of this kind in the territory of the United States north of the line therein mentioned is not warranted by the Constitution and is therefore void; and that neither Dred Scott himself, nor any of his family, were made free by being carried into this territory; even if they had been carried there by the owner with the intention of becoming a permanent resident.

Questions

1. What did the Court decide about whether a slave had standing to sue in a federal court?
2. If the Court lacked jurisdiction, why do you think Chief Justice Taney went ahead and dealt with the merits? Why did he not just say: "This Court lacks jurisdiction; case dismissed"?
3. What status does Taney say slaves enjoyed at the time the Constitution was adopted?

Questions for Further Thought

1. The passage of the Fugitive Slave Act in 1850 (Document 13-6) and the Supreme Court's 1857 *Dred Scott* decision (Document 13-10) had disturbing implications for Salmon Chase's argument (Document 13-5) about the relationship of the federal government to slavery. In what ways did antislavery forces respond to these reverses?
2. In the debate over the status of slavery in the territories that shattered the Second Party System, all sides appealed to the Constitution as legitimizing the validity of their position. From your reading of Documents 13-6 through 13-10 as well as Documents 13-4 and 13-5, what were the specific constitutional issues in question, and how did the different participants in the debate argue their case?
3. Do you think that by the 1850s, northerners like Chase (Document 13-5) and Sumner (Document 13-9) and southerners like Calhoun (Document 13-4) and Taney (Document 13-10) were able to understand one another's positions concerning slavery? Had the political debate in the United States become so polarized that rational discussion on the topic of slavery was impossible?

Abraham Lincoln and the Republican Triumph, 1858–1860

By 1858 the Republican Party had effectively become the major vehicle of opposition to the still-dominant Democrats, supplanting the Whigs and the short-lived, anti-immigrant American ("Know-Nothing") Party. The Republicans, though, were an exclusively northern party; indeed, by building its appeal around opposition to the Slave Power, it was as much anti-southern as antislavery. The Democratic Party, on the other hand, spanned the two sections; while southerners dominated its councils and the administration of President James Buchanan, the party retained considerable northern support. Its foremost figure was Senator Stephen A. Douglas of Illinois, the champion of popular sovereignty in Kansas and Nebraska.

In 1858, though, Douglas was challenged for reelection by a prominent Republican lawyer, Abraham Lincoln. Though born poor and largely self-educated, Lincoln was a brilliant debater, and in his celebrated joint appearances with Douglas demonstrated that popular sovereignty was unworkable (Document 13-11). While he won reelection, Douglas's efforts to straddle the sections only excited suspicion of him in both North and South. Southerners were further inflamed the following year when a notorious antislavery bushwhacker from "Bleeding Kansas," John Brown, hoping to foment a slave revolt, launched a private invasion of Virginia (Document 13-12). In earlier times Brown would have been dismissed as an isolated fanatic, but he received backing from prominent antislavery northerners. His execution, which was declared a "martyrdom" throughout the North, convinced many white southerners that even their personal safety might be at risk if northerners controlled the federal government.

Southern disaffection with Douglas, and Douglas's increasing resistance to southern demands, led to a split in the Democratic Party in 1860. In the meantime, the Republican Party built a strong coalition tying its crusade against the Slave Power to a number of positive programs that it argued would benefit ordinary white northerners (Document 13-13). Behind Lincoln, their standard-bearer, the Republicans received less than 40 percent of the vote in the 1860 elections. But with the Democrats in disarray, and with strong Republican majorities in the populous free states, they gained a majority of electoral votes. For the first time in the history of the Republic, a presidential election had been won solely with the votes of one section, by a party whose core principle was hostility to the other section. The final conflict was now at hand.

13-11   The Lincoln–Douglas Debates (1858)

Stephen Douglas had tried to finesse the issue of slavery in the territories with his theory of popular sovereignty, by which the people could decide. But the *Dred Scott* decision seemed to cut the ground from under his argument. When Lincoln and Douglas ran for the Senate in 1858, they engaged in a series of debates (see text p. 436). At Freeport, Lincoln put the issue to him squarely, and Douglas attempted to resolve the seeming inconsistencies between the Court's ruling and his own political views.

Source: Alonzo T. Jones, ed., *Political Speeches and Debates of Abraham Lincoln and Stephen A. Douglas, 1854–1861* (Battle Creek, Mich., 1895).

LINCOLN'S OPENING SPEECH

As to the first one, in regard to the fugitive slave law, I have never hesitated to say, and I do not now hesitate to say, that I think, under the Constitution of the United States, the people of the southern states are entitled to a congressional fugitive slave law. Having said that, I have had nothing to say in regard to the existing fugitive slave law further than that I think it should be framed so as to be free from some of the objections that pertain to it, without lessening its efficiency. And inasmuch as we are not now in an agitation in regard to an alteration or modification of that law, I would not be the man to introduce it as a new subject of agitation upon the general question of slavery.

In regard to the other question of whether I am pledged to the admission of any more slave states into the Union, I state to you very frankly that I would be exceedingly sorry ever to be put in a position of having to pass upon that question. I should be exceedingly glad to know that there would never be another slave state admitted into the Union; . . . but I must add, that if slavery shall be kept out of the territories during the territorial existence of any one given territory, and then the people shall, having a fair chance and a clear field, when they come to adopt the constitution, do such an extraordinary thing as to adopt a slave constitution, uninfluenced by the actual presence of the institution among them, I see no alternative, if we own the country, but to admit them into the Union. . . .

The fourth one is in regard to the abolition of slavery in the District of Columbia. In relation to that, I have my mind very distinctly made up. I should be exceedingly glad to see slavery abolished in the District of Columbia. . . . I believe that Congress possesses the constitutional power to abolish it. Yet as a member of Congress, I should not with my present views, be in favor of *endeavoring* to abolish slavery in the District of Columbia, unless it would be upon these conditions. *First,* that the abolition should be gradual. *Second,* that it should be on a vote of the majority of qualified voters in the District, and *third,* that compensation should be made to unwilling owners. With these three conditions, I confess I would be exceedingly glad to see Congress abolish slavery in the District of Columbia, and, in the language of Henry Clay, "sweep from our Capital that foul blot upon our nation." . . .

My answer as to whether I desire that slavery should be prohibited in all the territories of the United States is full and explicit within itself, and cannot be made clearer by any comments of mine. So I suppose in regard to the question of whether I am opposed to the acquisition of any more territory unless slavery is first prohibited therein, my answer is such that I could add nothing by way of illustration, or making myself better understood, than the answer which I have placed in writing. . . .

I now proceed to propound to the Judge the interrogatories, as far as I have framed them. . . . The first one is—

Question 1. If the people of Kansas shall, by means entirely unobjectionable in all other respects, adopt a state constitution, and ask admission into the Union under it, *before* they have the requisite number of inhabitants according to the English Bill—some ninety-three thousand—will you vote to admit them? . . .

Q. 2. Can the people of a United States territory, in any lawful way, against the wish of any citizen of the United States, exclude slavery from its limits prior to the formation of a state constitution? . . .

Q. 3. If the Supreme Court of the United States shall decide that states can not exclude slavery from their limits, are you in favor of acquiescing in, adopting and following such decision as a rule of political action? . . .

Q. 4. Are you in favor of acquiring additional territory, in disregard of how such acquisition may affect the nation on the slavery question? . . .

DOUGLAS'S REPLY

In a few moments I will proceed to review the answers which he has given to these interrogatories; but in order to relieve his anxiety I will first respond to those which he has presented to me. . . .

First, he desires to know if the people of Kansas shall form a constitution by means entirely proper and unobjectionable and ask admission into the Union as a state, before they have the requisite population for a member of Congress, whether I will vote for that admission. . . . In reference to Kansas; it is my opinion, that as she has population enough to constitute a slave state, she has people enough for a free state. . . . I will not make Kansas an exceptional case to the other states of the Union. ("Sound," and "hear, hear.") I hold it to be a sound rule of universal application to require a territory to contain the requisite population for a member of Congress, before it is admitted as a state into the Union. I made that proposition in the Senate in 1856, and I renewed it during the last session, in a bill providing that no territory of the United States should form a constitution and apply for admission until it had the requisite population. . . .

The next question propounded to me by Mr. Lincoln is, can the people of a territory in any lawful way against the wishes of any citizen of the United States; [*sic*] exclude slavery from their limits prior to the formation of a state constitution? I answer emphatically, as Mr. Lincoln has heard me answer a hundred times from every stump in Illinois, that in my opinion the people of a territory can, by lawful means, exclude slavery from their limits prior to the formation of a state constitution. . . . Mr. Lincoln knew that I had answered that question over and over again. He heard me argue the Nebraska Bill on that principle all over the state in 1854, in 1855 and in 1856, and he has no excuse for pretending to be in doubt as to my position on that question. It matters not what way the Supreme Court may hereafter decide as to the abstract question whether slavery may or may not go into a territory under the Constitution, the people have the lawful means to introduce it or exclude it as they please, for the reason that slavery cannot exist a day or an hour anywhere, unless it is supported by local police regulations. . . . Those police regulations can only be established by the local legislature, and if the people are opposed to slavery they will elect representatives to that body who will by unfriendly legislation effectually prevent the introduction of it into their midst. If, on the contrary, they are for it, their legislation will favor its extension. Hence, no matter what the decision of the Supreme Court may be on that abstract question, still the right of the people to make a slave territory or a free territory is perfect and complete under the Nebraska Bill. I hope Mr. Lincoln deems my answer satisfactory on that point. . . .

The third question which Mr. Lincoln presented is, if the Supreme Court of the United States shall decide that a state of this Union cannot exclude slavery from its own limits will I submit to it? I am amazed that Lincoln should ask such a question. . . . Yes, a school boy does know better. Mr. Lincoln's object is to cast an imputation upon the Supreme Court. He knows that there never was but one man in America, claiming any degree of intelligence or decency, who ever for a moment pretended such a thing. It is true that the Washington *Union*, in an article published on the 17th of last December, did put forth that doctrine, and I denounced the article on the floor of the Senate. . . .

The fourth question of Mr. Lincoln is, are you in favor of acquiring additional territory in disregard as to how such acquisition may affect the Union on the slavery question. This question is very ingeniously and cunningly put. . . .

The Black Republican creed lays it down expressly, that under no circumstances shall we acquire any more territory unless slavery is first prohibited in the country. I ask Mr. Lincoln whether he is in favor of that proposition. Are you (addressing Mr. Lincoln) opposed to the acquisition of any more territory, under any circumstances, unless slavery is prohibited in it? That he does not like to answer. When I ask him whether he stands up to that article in the platform of his party, he turns, Yankee-fashion, and without answering it, asks me whether I am in favor of acquiring territory without regard to how it may affect the Union on the slavery question. . . . I answer that whenever it becomes necessary, in our growth and progress to acquire more territory, that I am in favor of it, without reference to the question of slavery, and when we have acquired it, I will leave the people free to do as they please, either to make it slave or free territory, as they prefer. . . . It is idle to tell me or you that we have territory enough. Our fathers supposed that we had enough when our territory extended to the Mississippi River, but a few years' growth and expansion satisfied them that we needed more, and the Louisiana territory, from the west branch of the Mississippi, to the British possessions, was acquired. Then we acquired Oregon, then California and New Mexico. We have enough now for the present, but this is a young and a growing nation. It swarms as often as a hive of bees, and as new swarms are turned out each year, there must be hives in which they can gather and make their honey.

Questions

1. Which speaker in this exchange do you think is more consistent in his arguments? Why?
2. Does it seem that Lincoln is speaking primarily to one part of the country, and Douglas to the other? Explain.
3. Does Lincoln oppose slavery completely? If not, what is his position?

13-12 The Trial of John Brown (1859)

Lincoln and the Republicans tried to reassure the South that they did not want to disturb slavery where it existed but only to halt its spread. Then came John Brown's attempt to raid the government arsenal at Harpers Ferry and trigger a massive slave rebellion (see text pp. 436–437). Although Republican leaders disavowed his action, private letters showed that he had had support from prominent abolitionists. Brown was tried and convicted of treason, and his statement before sentencing has become a classic. He was hanged on December 2, 1859, and abolitionists, as Emerson said, now had a "new saint." Slaveholders blamed Republican ideas for the raid and more than ever feared a Republican presidential victory.

Source: The Life, Trial and Execution of Captain John Brown . . . (New York: R. M. DeWitt, 1859), 94–95.

The clerk then asked Mr. Brown whether he had anything to say why sentence should not be pronounced upon him.

Mr. Brown immediately rose, and in a clear, distinct voice, said:

I have, may it please the Court, a few words to say. In the first place, I deny everything but what I have all along admitted, of a design on my part to free slaves. I intended certainly to have made a clean thing of that matter, as I did last winter when I went into Missouri, and there took slaves without the snapping of a gun on either side, moving them through the country, and finally leaving them in Canada. I designed to have done the same thing again on a larger scale. That was all I intended to do. I never did intend murder or treason, or the destruction of property, or to excite or incite the slaves to rebellion, or to make insurrection. I have another objection, and that is that it is unjust that I should suffer such a penalty. Had I interfered in the manner which I admit, and which I admit has been fairly proved—for I admire the truthfulness and candor of the greater portion of the witnesses who have testified in this case—had I so interfered in behalf of the rich, the powerful, the intelligent, the so-called great, or in behalf of any of their friends, either father, mother, brother, sister, wife, or children, or any of that class, and suffered and sacrificed what I have in this interference, it would have been all right, and every man in this Court would have deemed it an act worthy of reward rather than punishment. This Court acknowledges, too, as I suppose, the validity of the law of God. I see a book kissed, which I suppose to be the Bible, or at least the New Testament, which teaches me that all things whatsoever I would that men should do to me, I should do even so to them. It teaches me further to remember them that are in bonds as bound with them. I endeavored to act up to that instruction. I say I am yet too young to understand that God is any

respecter of persons. I believe that to have interfered as I have done, as I have always freely admitted I have done in behalf of His despised poor, is no wrong, but right. Now, if it is deemed necessary that I should forfeit my life for the furtherance of the ends of justice, and mingle my blood further with the blood of my children and with the blood of millions in this slave country whose rights are disregarded by wicked, cruel, and unjust enactments, I say let it be done. Let me say one word further. I feel entirely satisfied with the treatment I have received on my trial. Considering all the circumstances, it has been more generous than I expected. But I feel no consciousness of guilt. I have stated from the first what was my intention, and what was not. I never had any design against the liberty of any person, nor any disposition to commit treason or excite slaves to rebel or make any general insurrection. I never encouraged any man to do so, but always discouraged any idea of that kind. Let me say also in regard to statements made by some of those who were connected with me, I fear it has been stated by some of them that I have induced them to join me, but the contrary is true. I do not say this to injure them, but as regretting their weakness. Not one but joined me of his own accord, and the greater part at their own expense. A number of them I never saw, and never had a word of conversation with till the day they came to me, and that was for the purpose I have stated. Now, I am done.

While Mr. Brown was speaking, perfect quiet prevailed, and when he had finished the Judge proceeded to pronounce sentence upon him. After a few primary remarks, he said, that no reasonable doubt could exist of the guilt of the prisoner, and sentenced him to be hung in public, on Friday, the 2d of December next.

Mr. Brown received his sentence with composure.

Questions

1. Do you think Brown really meant to free so many slaves without firing a shot? If so, why did he seize the arsenal?
2. Was Brown making a legal argument, or was he appealing to a "higher authority"?
3. Does it appear to you that Brown was seeking martyrdom? Why or why not?

13-13   The Republican Party Platform of 1860

Party platforms were, and are, designed to be statements of party principle, but they have other functions as well: they bring different political factions together on the same plank, and they seek to appeal to a coalition of voters sufficiently large to give the party victory in the coming election. They seek to embrace voters with common interests while accommodating their differences and to motivate voters by setting them against a common enemy. All of these purposes were served in the construction of the Republican Party platform of 1860, which helped carry the party to victory in the most important popular presidential election in American history. It also defined, with unprecedented clarity, a distinctly *northern* vision of the nature, purpose, and future of the United States.

Source: Kirk H. Porter and Donald Bruce Johnson, eds., *National Party Platforms, 1840–1968* (Urbana: University of Illinois Press, 1970), 31–33.

Resolved, That we, the delegated representatives of the Republican electors of the United States, in Convention assembled, in discharge of the duty we owe to our constituents and our country, unite in the following declarations:

1. That the history of the nation during the last four years, has fully established the propriety and necessity of the organization and perpetuation of the Republican party, and that the causes which called it into existence are permanent in their nature, and now, more than ever before, demand its peaceful and constitutional triumph.

2. That the maintenance of the principles promulgated in the Declaration of Independence and embodied in the Federal Constitution, "That all men are created equal; that they are endowed by their Creator with certain inalienable rights; that among these are life, liberty and the pursuit of happiness; that to secure these rights, governments are instituted among men, deriving their just powers from the consent of the governed," is essential to the preservation of our Republican institutions; and that the Federal Constitution, the Rights of the States, and the Union of the States must and shall be preserved.

3. That to the Union of the States this nation owes its unprecedented increase in population, its surprising development of material resources, its rapid augmentation of wealth, its happiness at home and its honor abroad; and we hold in abhorrence all schemes for disunion, come from whatever source they may. And we congratulate the country that no Republican member of Congress has uttered or countenanced the threats of disunion so often made by Democratic members, without rebuke and with applause from their political associates; and we denounce those threats of disunion, in case of a popular overthrow of their ascendency as denying the vital principles of a free government, and as an avowal of contemplated treason, which it is the imperative duty of an indignant people sternly to rebuke and forever silence.

4. That the maintenance inviolate of the rights of the states, and especially the right of each state to order and control its own domestic institutions according to its own judgment exclusively, is essential to that balance of powers on which the perfection and endurance of our political fabric depends; and we denounce the lawless invasion by armed force of the soil of any state or territory, no matter under what pretext, as among the gravest of crimes.

5. That the present Democratic Administration has far exceeded our worst apprehensions, in its measureless subserviency to the exactions of a sectional interest, as especially evinced in its desperate exertions to force the infamous Lecompton Constitution upon the protesting people of Kansas; in construing the personal relations between master and servant to involve an unqualified property in persons; in its attempted enforcement everywhere, on land and sea, through the intervention of Congress and of the Federal Courts of the extreme pretensions of a purely local interest; and in its general and unvarying abuse of the power intrusted to it by a confiding people.

6. That the people justly view with alarm the reckless extravagance which pervades every department of the Federal Government; that a return to rigid economy and accountability is indispensable to arrest the systematic plunder of the public treasury by favored partisans; while the recent startling developments of frauds and corruptions at the Federal metropolis, show that an entire change of administration is imperatively demanded.

7. That the new dogma that the Constitution, of its own force, carries slavery into any or all of the territories of the United States, is a dangerous political heresy, at variance with the explicit provisions of that instrument itself, with contemporaneous exposition, and with legislative and judicial precedent; is revolutionary in its tendency, and subversive of the peace and harmony of the country.

8. That the normal condition of all the territory of the United States is that of freedom: That, as our Republican fathers, when they had abolished slavery in all our national territory, ordained that "no persons should be deprived of life, liberty or property without due process of law," it becomes our duty, by legislation, whenever such legislation is necessary, to maintain this provision of the Constitution against all attempts to violate it; and we deny the authority of Congress, of a territorial legislature, or of any individuals, to give legal existence to slavery in any territory of the United States.

9. That we brand the recent reopening of the African slave trade, under the cover of our national flag, aided by perversions of judicial power, as a crime against humanity and a burning shame to our country and age; and we call upon Congress to take prompt and efficient measures for the total and final suppression of that execrable traffic.

10. That in the recent vetoes, by their Federal Governors, of the acts of the legislatures of Kansas and Nebraska, prohibiting slavery in those territories, we find a practical illustration of the boasted Democratic principle of Non-Intervention and Popular Sovereignty, embodied in the Kansas-Nebraska Bill, and a demonstration of the deception and fraud involved therein.

11. That Kansas should, of right, be immediately admitted as a state under the Constitution recently formed and adopted by her people, and accepted by the House of Representatives.

12. That, while providing revenue for the support of the general government by duties upon imports, sound policy requires such an adjustment of these imports as to encourage the development of the industrial interests of the whole country; and we commend that policy of national exchanges, which secures to the workingmen liberal wages, to agriculture remunerative prices, to mechanics and manufacturers an adequate reward for their skill, labor, and enterprise, and to the nation commercial prosperity and independence.

13. That we protest against any sale or alienation to others of the public lands held by actual settlers, and against any view of the free-homestead policy which regards the settlers as paupers or suppliants for public bounty; and we demand the passage by Congress of the complete and satisfactory homestead measure which has already passed the House.

14. That the Republican party is opposed to any change in our naturalization laws or any state legislation by which the rights of citizens hitherto accorded to immigrants from foreign lands shall be abridged or impaired; and in favor of giving a full and efficient protection to the rights of all classes of citizens, whether native or naturalized, both at home and abroad.

15. That appropriations by Congress for river and harbor improvements of a national character, required for the accommodation and security of an existing commerce, are authorized by the Constitution, and justified by the obligation of Government to protect the lives and property of its citizens.

16. That a railroad to the Pacific Ocean is imperatively demanded by the interests of the whole country; that the federal government ought to render immediate and efficient aid in its construction; and that, as preliminary thereto, a daily overland mail should be promptly established.

17. Finally, having thus set forth our distinctive principles and views, we invite the co-operation of all citizens, however differing on other questions, who substantially agree with us in their affirmance and support.

Questions

1. In what ways does the Republican Party platform of 1860 express a distinctly "northern" vision of the United States? Beyond the controversy over slavery, what issues do the Republicans address, and why do you think that southerners might have objected?

2. What groups in American society did the Republicans attempt to forge into a coalition? From what you know of the election of 1860, how successful were they?

3. How does the Republican Party legitimize its reason for existence? In their platform, what authorities do the Republicans cite as the foundational principles of their party?

Questions for Further Thought

1. From a political standpoint, why was Lincoln's election to the presidency in 1860 so threatening to southerners? If Calhoun (Document 13-4) had lived to witness the election, do you think that he would have seen the Republican victory as confirming his fear of the permanent inferiority of southerners within the Union? If so, why?

2. A school of historical thought has held that the slave plantation system was approaching its natural geographic limits by the 1850s, and it would not have be-

come important in the western territories even if it had had free rein there. If so, what was the fuss about?

3. Whether in Thomas Jefferson's drafting of the Declaration of Independence, the debates at the Constitutional Convention, the Missouri Compromise (1820), or the Compromise of 1850, Americans in the North, South, and West had continually compromised on the issue of slavery to save the Union. Why, by 1860, had compromise for the Union become impossible?

CHAPTER 14

Two Societies at War, 1861–1865

★ ★ ★

Secession and Military Stalemate, 1861–1862, *and* Toward Total War

The election of Abraham Lincoln in 1860 represented a fundamental shift in the balance of power within the federal Union. For the first time in the history of the country, a president had been elected without any support from the slaveholding states; furthermore, Lincoln was the candidate of a party whose central ideology was *opposition* to the Slave Power. To be sure, Lincoln's election did not mean Republican control of the federal government: Democrats, including southern Democrats, still controlled the Congress, and the Supreme Court was still the same court that had less than four years earlier handed down the *Dred Scott* decision. But secessionists convincingly argued that the election, along with resistance to enforcement of the Fugitive Slave Act and widespread northern sympathy for John Brown, demonstrated that northerners could no longer be depended on to protect the South's "peculiar institution" (Document 14-1). South Carolina, long a hotbed of secessionist sentiment, led the way in leaving the Union, followed quickly by the rest of the Lower South: Georgia, Florida, Alabama, Mississippi, Louisiana, and Texas. In February 1861 the seven seceded states joined together as the new Confederate States of America.

Lincoln took office on March 4, 1861, determined to face down the secessionists but seeking to proceed in a manner that would not spark further defections among the states of the Upper South. The presence of a federal garrison at Fort Sumter in Charleston Harbor, however, became a flash point for Confederates who regarded it as an occupying force. Insistent on continuing the Union's sovereignty over the fort, Lincoln vowed to resupply the garrison, whereupon Confederate forces began an artillery bombardment that forced the garrison's surrender. In Lincoln's eyes, secession was now rebellion, and he called for troops to suppress it—an action that sent Arkansas, Tennessee, North Carolina, and Virginia into the Confederate camp. The Civil War had begun (Document 14-2).

At first, the war was makeshift. Although the first skirmish, the Battle of Bull Run (Manassas), was a disaster for the Union side (Document 14-3), the Confederates were scarcely able to follow up on their victory. By 1862 both sides had successfully mobilized armies, and were also mobilizing their civilian populations to support the troops (Document 14-4). Furthermore, the Confederates had found a brilliant military leader in Robert E. Lee. Thanks largely to a remarkable string of victories by Lee's Army of Northern Virginia, the Confederacy successfully held off Union invaders and even launched two counterstrikes into Union territory in the fall of 1862. To be sure, the Union was showing greater success than the Confederacy at mustering its resources. The Union government paid for the war with a balanced program of taxes, bond sales to a mass market, and a moderate issue of paper currency ("greenbacks"); the Confederacy, wedded to small and decentralized government and fearing to alienate the powerful planters, resorted to massive issues of paper money, sparking ruinous inflation. Nonetheless, many outside observers were convinced that the Confederacy would be successful in maintaining its independence and that the Union would lack the staying power to continue the struggle—an opinion bolstered by major Republican reverses in the 1862 elections.

14-1   South Carolina Secedes from the Union (1860)

Charles Memminger

The secession crisis was both a constitutional and a social problem in the eyes of white southerners (see text pp. 441–442). Secessionists believed that the election of Lincoln threatened not only their slave property but also their freedom from a coercive central government in Washington. By exaggerating the policies of northern Republicans, secessionists convinced other white southerners that Republicans were revolutionaries bent on racial amalgamation and the destruction of southern society.

On December 20, 1860, three months before Lincoln was inaugurated, the South Carolina convention passed a terse Ordinance of Secession. The prominent Charleston lawyer and politician Charles Memminger was charged with writing a detailed explanation and defense of the state's action. Memminger argued that the North was wholly to blame, that the non-slaveholding states had violated the "constitutional compact" regarding slavery. (Memminger later served as chairman of the committee that drafted the Confederate constitution and as Treasury secretary of the Confederacy.)

Sources: South Carolina State Archives, Columbia, South Carolina. Available in Henry Steele Commager and Milton Cramer, *Documents of American History,* 10th ed. (Englewood Cliffs, N.J.: Prentice-Hall, 1988), 1: 372; *Declaration of the Immediate Causes Which Induce and Justify the Secession of South Carolina from the Federal Union* (Charleston, S.C.: Evans and Cogswell, 1860).

(a) South Carolina Ordinance of Secession
December 20, 1860

An Ordinance to Dissolve the Union between the State of South Carolina and other States united with her under the compact entitled the Constitution of the United States of America:

We, the people of the State of South Carolina, in Convention assembled, do declare and ordain, and it is hereby declared and ordained, that the ordinance adopted by us in Convention, on the 23d day of May, in the year of our Lord 1788, whereby the Constitution of the United States of

America was ratified, and also all Acts and parts of Acts of the General Assembly of this State ratifying the amendments of the said Constitution, are hereby repealed, and that the union now subsisting between South Carolina and other States under the name of the United States of America is hereby dissolved.

(b) Declaration of the Immediate Causes [for] the
Secession of South Carolina

The People of the State of South Carolina, in Convention assembled, on the 2d of April, A.D., 1852, declared that the frequent violations of the Constitution of the United States, by the Federal Government, and its encroachments upon the reserved rights of the States, fully justified this State in then withdrawing from the Federal Union; but in deference to the opinions and wishes of the other slaveholding States, she forbore at that time to exercise this right. Since that time, these encroachments have continued to increase, and further forbearance ceases to be a virtue.

And now the State of South Carolina having resumed her separate and equal place among nations, deems it due to herself, to the remaining United States of America, and to the nations of the world, that she should declare the immediate causes which have led to this act.

In the year 1765, that portion of the British Empire embracing Great Britain, undertook to make laws for the government of that portion composed of the thirteen American Colonies. A struggle for the right of self-government ensued, which resulted, on the 4th July, 1776, in a Declaration by the Colonies, "that they are, and of right ought to be, FREE AND INDEPENDENT STATES; and that, as free and independent States, they have full power to levy war, conclude peace, contract alliances, establish commerce, and to do all other acts and things which independent States may of right do."

They further solemnly declared that whenever any "form of government becomes destruction of the ends for which it was established, it is the right of the people to alter or abolish it, and to institute a new government." Deeming the Government of Great Britain to have become destructive of these ends, they declared that the Colonies "are absolved from all allegiance to the British Crown, and that all political connection between them and the State of Great Britain is, and ought to be, totally dissolved."

In pursuance of this Declaration of Independence, each of the thirteen States proceeded to exercise its separate sovereignty; adopted for itself a Constitution, and appointed officers for the administration of government in all its departments—Legislative, Executive and Judicial. For purposes of defence, they united their arms and their counsels; and, in 1778, they entered into a league known as the Articles of Confederation, whereby they agreed to entrust the administration of their external relations to a common agent, known as the Congress of the United States, expressly declaring, in the first article, "that each State retains its sovereignty, freedom and independence, and every power, jurisdiction and right which is not, by this Confederation, expressly delegated to the United States in Congress assembled."

Under this Confederation the War of the Revolution was carried on, and on the 3d September, 1783, the contest ended, and a definitive Treaty was signed by Great Britain, in which she acknowledged the Independence of the Colonies in the following terms:

Article 1.—His Britannic Majesty acknowledges the said United States, viz: New Hampshire, Massachu-

setts Bay, Rhode Island and Providence Plantations, Connecticut, New York, New Jersey, Pennsylvania, Delaware, Maryland, Virginia, North Carolina, South Carolina and Georgia, to be FREE, SOVEREIGN AND INDEPENDENT STATES; that he treats them as such; and for himself, his heirs and successors, relinquishes all claims to the government, propriety and territorial rights of the same and every part thereof.

Thus were established the two great principles asserted by the Colonies, namely: the right of a State to govern itself; and the right of a people to abolish a Government when it becomes destructive of the ends for which it was instituted. And concurrent with the establishment of these principles, was the fact, that each Colony became and was recognized by the mother Country as a FREE, SOVEREIGN AND INDEPENDENT STATE.

In 1787, Deputies were appointed by the States to revise the Articles of Confederation, and on the 17th September, 1787, these Deputies recommended, for the adoption of the States, the Articles of Union, known as the Constitution of the United States.

The parties to whom this Constitution was submitted, were the several sovereign States; they were to agree or disagree, and when nine of them agreed, the compact was to take effect among those concurring; and the General Government, as the common agent, was then to be invested with their authority.

If only nine of the thirteen States had concurred, the other four would have remained as they then were—separate, sovereign States, independent of any of the provisions of the Constitution. In fact, two of the States did not accede to the Constitution until long after it had gone into operation among the other eleven; and during that interval, they each exercised the functions of an independent nation.

By this Constitution, certain duties were imposed upon the several States, and the exercise of certain of their powers were restrained, which necessarily implied their continued existence as sovereign States. But, to remove all doubt, an amendment was added, which declared that the powers of delegated to the United States by the Constitution, nor prohibited by it to the States, are reserved to the States, respectively, or to the people. On 23d May, 1788, South Carolina, by a Convention of her people, passed an Ordinance assenting to this Constitution, and afterwards altered her own Constitution, to conform herself to the obligations she had undertaken.

Thus was established, by compact between the States, a Government, with defined objects and powers, limited to the express words of the grant. This limitation left the whole remaining mass of power subject to the clause reserving it to the States or to the people, and rendered unnecessary any specification of reserved rights.

We hold that the Government thus established is subject to the two great principles asserted in the Declaration of

Independence; and we hold further, that the mode of its formation subjects it to a third fundamental principle, namely: the law of compact. We maintain that in every compact between two or more parties, the obligation is mutual; that the failure of one of the contracting parties to perform a material part of the agreement, entirely releases the obligation of the other; and that where no arbiter is provided, each party is remitted to his own judgment to determine the fact of failure, with all its consequences.

In the present case, that fact is established with certainty. We assert, that fourteen of the States have deliberately refused for years past to fulfill their constitutional obligations, and we refer to their own Statutes for the proof.

The Constitution of the United States, in its 4th Article, provides as follows:

No person held to service or labor in one State, under the laws thereof, escaping into another shall, in consequence of any law or regulation therein, be discharged from such service or labor, but shall be delivered up, on claim of the party to whom such service or labor may be due.

This stipulation was so material to the compact, that without it that compact would not have been made. The greater number of the contracting parties held slaves, and they had previously evinced their estimate of the value of such a stipulation by making it a condition in the Ordinance for the government of the territory ceded by Virginia, which now composes the States north of the Ohio river.

The same article of the Constitution stipulates also for rendition by the several States of fugitives from justice from the other States.

The General Government, as the common agent, passed laws to carry into effect these stipulations of the States. For many years these laws were executed. But an increasing hostility on the part of the non-slaveholding States to the Institution of Slavery has led to a disregard of their obligations, and the laws of the General Government have ceased to effect the objects of the Constitution. The States of Maine, New Hampshire, Vermont, Massachusetts, Connecticut, Rhode Island, New York, Pennsylvania, Illinois, Indiana, Michigan, Wisconsin and Iowa, have enacted laws which either nullify the Acts of Congress or render useless any attempt to execute them. In many of these States the fugitive is discharged from the service or labor claimed, and in none of them has the State Government complied with the stipulation made in the Constitution. The State of New Jersey, at an early day, passed a law in conformity with her constitutional obligation; but the current of anti-slavery feeling has led her more recently to enact laws which render inoperative the remedies provided by her own law and by the laws of Congress. In the State of New York even the right of transit for a slave has been denied by her tribunals; and the States of Ohio and Iowa have refused to surrender to justice fugitives charged with murder, and with inciting servile insurrection in the State of Virginia. Thus the consti-

tutional compact has been deliberately broken and disregarded by the non-slaveholding States, and the consequence follows that South Carolina is released from her obligation.

The ends for which this Constitution was framed are declared by itself to be "to form a more perfect union, establish justice, insure domestic tranquility, provide for the common defence, promote the general welfare, and secure the blessings of liberty to ourselves and our posterity."

These ends it endeavored to accomplish by a Federal Government, in which each State was recognized as an equal, and had separate control over its own institutions. The right of property in slaves was recognized by giving to free persons distinct political rights, by giving them the right to represent, and burthening them with direct taxes for three-fifths of their slaves; by authorizing the importation of slaves for twenty years; and by stipulating for the rendition of fugitives from labor.

We affirm that these ends for which this Government was instituted have been defeated, and the Government itself has been made destructive of them by the action of the non-slaveholding States. Those States have assumed the right of deciding upon the propriety of our domestic institutions; and have denied the rights of property established in fifteen of the States and recognized by the Constitution; they have denounced as sinful the institution of slavery; they have permitted the open establishment among them of societies, whose avowed object is to disturb the peace and to eloign [take away] the property of the citizens of other States. They have encouraged and assisted thousands of our slaves to leave their homes; and those who remain, have been incited by emissaries, books and pictures to servile insurrection.

For twenty-five years this agitation has been steadily increasing, until it has now secured to its aid the power of the Common Government. Observing the *forms* of the Constitution, a sectional party has found within that article establishing the Executive Department, the means of subverting the Constitution itself. A geographical line has been drawn across the Union, and all the States north of that line have united in the election of a man to the high office of President of the United States whose opinions and purposes are hostile to slavery. He is to be entrusted with the administration of the Common Government, because he has declared that that "Government cannot endure permanently half slave, half free," and that the public mind must rest in the belief that Slavery is in the course of ultimate extinction.

This sectional combination for the subversion of the Constitution, has been aided in some of the States by elevating to citizenship persons, who, by the Supreme Law of the land, are incapable of becoming citizens; and their votes have been used to inaugurate a new policy, hostile to the South, and destructive to its peace and safety.

On the 4th of March next, this party will take possession of the Government. It has announced, that the South shall be excluded from the common Territory; that the Judicial Tribunals shall be made sectional, and that a war must be waged against slavery until it shall cease throughout the United States.

The Guaranties of the Constitution will then no longer exist; the equal rights of the States will be lost. The slave-holding States will no longer have the power of self-government, or self-protection, and the Federal Government will have become their enemy.

Sectional interest and animosity will deepen the irritation, and all hope of remedy is rendered vain, by the fact that public opinion at the North has invested a great political error with the sanctions of a more erroneous religious belief.

We, therefore, the people of South Carolina, by our delegates, in Convention assembled appealing to the Supreme Judge of the world for the rectitude of our intentions, have solemnly declared that the Union heretofore existing between this State and the other States of North America, is dissolved, and that the State of South Carolina has resumed her position among the nations of the world, as a separate and independent State; with full power to levy war, conclude peace, contract alliances, establish commerce, and to do all other acts and things which independent States may of right do.

Questions

1. What similarities are there in tone and wording between the two South Carolina documents and the American Declaration of Independence (see text pp. D-1–D-2)?
2. On what three fundamental principles does Memminger rest his argument?
3. It is often said that the Confederate states seceded to protest an overweening federal government. What (or who) is the principal target of the "Declaration of Causes," and why?

14-2   The Crisis at Fort Sumter (April 1861)

Mary Chesnut

When South Carolina seceded from the United States on December 20, 1860, the construction of Fort Sumter, on an island in Charleston harbor, was not complete and the fort had not yet been occupied by federal troops. On December 26, however, the federal commander in Charleston, Major Robert Anderson, consolidated his forces (fewer than a hundred men) at the new fort. Anderson's force could not be easily defeated, but it also could not be easily reenforced or resupplied. On March 1, 1861, General P. G. T. Beauregard assumed command of Confederate forces at Charleston; on March 4 Lincoln became president of the United States. Throughout the month of March the crisis at Fort Sumter grew increasingly tense (see text pp. 443–444). On April 6 Lincoln announced a "humanitarian" effort to resupply the fort. On April 9 the Confederate president, Jefferson Davis, ordered Beauregard to capture the fort. The Confederate bombardment began on April 12 at 4:30 A.M. Anderson surrendered on April 14, and on April 15 Lincoln called on the states to send 75,000 troops to suppress the insurrection. The Civil War had begun.

The wife of James C. Chesnut, a wealthy planter and prominent southern politician, Mary Chesnut (see "American Voices" in Chapter 13 of the textbook, p. 427), began her diary as the war clouds gathered and ended it when the Confederacy collapsed under the pressure of the advancing Union armies. Surrounded by the leaders of the Confederate cause, Mary Chesnut epitomized the aristocratic southern lady: charming in manners, clever in conversation, and modest in deferring to the public life of the men around her. In her diary, however, she revealed her independent cast of mind and deep misgivings about the Confederate cause.

Source: C. Vann Woodward, ed., *Mary Chesnut's Civil War* (New Haven and London: Yale University Press, 1981), 35–53 passim.

March 26, 1861. Charleston. Yesterday we came down here by rail, as the English say. . . .

March 31, 1861 . . . At church today, saw one of the peculiar local traits—old Negro maumeys going up to the communion in their white turbans.

Being the Lord's table—so-called. Even there—black, white, and brown, separate according to caste. . . .

No war yet, thank God. . . .

There stands Fort Sumter . . . and thereby hangs peace or war. . . .

April 6, 1861. The plot thickens. The air is red-hot with rumors. The mystery is to find out where these utterly groundless tales originate. . . .

April 7, 1861 . . . [Former] Governor [John Laurence] Manning walked in, bowed gravely, and seated himself by me.

Again he bowed low, in mock heroic style and, with a grand wave of his hand said, "Madame, your country is invaded."

When I had breath to speak, I asked, "What does he mean?"

"He means this. There are six men-of-war outside of the bar. . . . Governor [Francis Wilkinson] Pickens and [General P. G. T.] Beauregard are holding a council of war."

Mr. [James C.] Chesnut then came in. He confirmed the story.

[Louis Trezevant] Wigfall next entered in boisterous spirits. . . .

In any stir or confusion, my heart is apt to beat so painfully. Now the agony was so stifling—I could hardly see or hear. The men went off almost immediately. And I crept silently to my room, where I sat down to a good cry.

Mrs. Wigfall came in, and we had it out on the subject of civil war. We solaced ourselves with dwelling on all its known horrors, and then we added what we had a right to expect, with Yankees in front and negroes in the rear.

"The slave-owners must expect a servile insurrection, of course," said Mrs. Wigfall, to make sure that we were unhappy enough. . . . Ammunition wagons rumbling along the streets all night. Anderson burning blue lights—signs and signals for the fleet outside, I suppose.

Today at dinner there was no allusion to things as they stand in Charleston Harbor. There was an undercurrent of intense excitement. . . . In earnest, [former] Governor Means rummaged a sword and red sash from somewhere and brought it for Colonel Chesnut, who has gone to demand the surrender of Fort Sumter.

And now, patience—we must wait.

Why did that green goose Anderson go into Fort Sumter? Then everything began to go wrong. . . .

April 12, 1861. Anderson will not capitulate. . . .

I do not pretend to go to sleep. How can I? If Anderson does not accept terms—at four—the orders are—he shall be fired upon.

I count four—St. Michael chimes. I begin to hope. At half-past four, the heavy booming of a cannon.

I sprang out of bed. And on my knees—prostrate—I prayed as I never prayed before.

There was a sound of stir all over the house—pattering of feet in the corridor—all seemed hurrying one way. I put on my double gown and a shawl and went, too. It was to the housetop.

The shells were bursting. In the dark I heard a man say "waste of ammunition."

I knew my husband was rowing about in a boat somewhere in that dark bay. And that the shells were roofing it over—bursting toward the fort. If Anderson was obstinate—he [Chesnut] was to order the forts on our side to open fire. Certainly fire had begun. The regular roar of the cannon—there it was. And who could tell what each volley accomplished of death and destruction. . . .

April 13, 1861 . . . Not by one word or look can we detect any change in the demeanor of these negro servants. Laurence sits at our door, as sleepy and as respectful and as profoundly indifferent. So are they all. They carry it too far. You could not tell that they hear even the awful row that is going on in the bay, though it is dinning in their ears night and day. And people talk before them as if they were chairs and tables. And they make no sign. Are they stolidly stupid or wiser than we are, silent and strong, biding their time? . . .

April 15, 1861. I did not know that one could live such days of excitement. . . .

And so we took Fort Sumter.

Questions

1. Unlike the men around her, Chesnut appears to be fearful of war. Why?
2. Does Chesnut seem confident and comfortable as part of the slave-holding elite? Explain why or why not.
3. Why are the slaves quiet and subdued during the bombardment of Fort Sumter?

14-3   A British Reporter Witnesses the First Battle of Bull Run (July 1861)

William Howard Russell

William Howard Russell, a special correspondent for the London *Times,* began his career in journalism in the early 1840s when he began publishing reports on events in Ireland. Russell wrote in a style that appeared to be unbiased, objective, and illuminating. When he covered the Crimean War, many of his letters to the London *Times* were also published in American newspapers. As civil war loomed on the horizon in the United States, Russell—now well known to Americans as a war correspondent—arrived in New York in March 1861. In April and June he toured the South, arriving in Charleston shortly after the fall of Fort Sumter. His southern tour ended in Washington, D.C., in July as the North and the South prepared for the first battle of the war. Russell's coverage of the Union defeat at Bull Run (see text pp. 446–448) angered many in the North, and the pro-Confederate sympathies of the London *Times* caused President Lincoln to deny Russell any special privileges. Without the ability to write the firsthand reports that had made him famous, Russell soon returned to England, where he published the diary of his American journey.

Source: William Howard Russell, *My Diary North and South* (London, 1863; reprinted, edited by Eugene H. Berwanger, New York: Knopf, 1988), 257–277.

July 20th. The great battle which is to arrest rebellion, or to make it a power in the land, is no longer distant or doubtful. [General Irvin] McDowell has completed his reconnaissance of the country in front of the enemy and General [Winfield] Scott anticipates that he will be in possession of Manassas tomorrow night. All the statements of officers concur in describing the Confederates as strongly entrenched along the line of Bull's Run covering the railroad. . . . July 21st. . . . I swallowed a cup of tea and a morsel of bread . . . got a flask of light Bordeaux, a bottle of water, a paper of sandwiches, and having replenished my small flask with brandy, stowed them all away in the bottom of the gig . . . and thus through the deserted city we proceeded [across the Potomac into Virginia]. . . . [About] nine o'clock . . . I thought I heard . . . the well-known boom of a gun, followed by two or three in rapid succession. . . . "They are at it! We shall be late! Drive on as fast as you can!" . . . the sounds which came upon the breeze, and the fights which met our eyes, were in terrible variance with the tranquil character of the landscape. The woods far and near echoed to the roar of cannon, and then frayed lines of blue smoke marked the spots whence came the muttering sound of rolling musketry; the white puffs of smoke burst high above the tree tops, and the gunners' rings from shell and howitzer marked the fire of the artillery. . . .

On the hill beside me there was a crowed of civilians on horseback and in all sorts of vehicles, with a few of the fairer, if not gentler sex. A few officers and some soldiers . . . from the regiments in reserve, moved about among the spectators and pretended to explain the movements of the troops below, of which they were profoundly ignorant. . . .

Loud cheers suddenly burst from the spectators as a man dressed in the uniform of an officer . . . galloped along the front . . . shouting at the top of his voice. . . . "We've whipped them on all points," he cried. "We have taken all their batteries. They are retreating as fast as they can, and we are after them". . . . I had ridden between three and a half and four miles [further] . . . when my attention was attracted by loud shouts in advance. . . . My first impression was that the wagons were returning for fresh supplies of ammunition. But every moment the crowd increased, drivers and men cried out with the most vehement gestures, "Turn back! Turn back! We are whipped". . . . A[n] . . . officer . . . confirmed the report that the whole army was in retreat and that the Federals were beaten on all points. . . . All these things took place in a few seconds. I got up out of the road into a cornfield, through which men were hastily walking or running, their faces streaming with perspiration, and generally without arms, and worked my way for about half a mile or so . . . against an increasing stream of fugitives, the ground being strewed with coats, blankets, firelocks, cooking tins, caps, belts, bayonets. . . . [Then] the dreaded cry, "The cavalry! cavalry are coming!" rang through the crowd, and looking back to Centreville I perceived coming down the hill, between me and the sky, a number of mounted men, who might at a hasty glance be taken for horsemen in the act of sabering the fugitives. In reality they were soldiers and civilians with, I regret to say, some officers among them. . . . [To a] fellow who shouting out, "Run! run!" as loud as he could beside me . . . I said, "What on earth are you running for? What are you afraid of?" He was in the roadside below me, and at once turning on me exclaimed, "I'm not afraid of you," presented his piece and pulled the trigger so instantaneously, that had it gone off I could not have swerved from the ball. As the scoundrel deliberately drew up to examine the [gun] . . . I judged it best not to give him another chance and spurred on through the crowd. . . .

And I continued through the wood till I got a clear space in front on the road, along which a regiment of infantry was advancing towards me. They halted ere I came up, and with leveled firelocks arrested the men on horses and the carts and wagons galloping towards them, and blocked the road to stop their progress. . . . [A] soldier pointed his firelock at my head from the higher ground on which he stood . . . and sung out, "Halt! Stop—or I fire!" . . . Bowing to the officer who was near me, I said . . . "I am a civilian going to Washington; will you be kind enough to look at this pass, specially given to me by Gen-

eral Scott." The officer looked at it . . . [a]nd with a cry of "Pass that man!" . . . I . . . very leisurely . . . got out on the road. . . . July 22nd. I awoke from a deep sleep this morning, about six o'clock. The rain was falling in torrents . . . but louder than all came a strange sound . . . I saw a steady stream of men covered with mud, soaked through with rain, who were pouring irregularly, without any semblance of order up Pennsylvania Avenue towards the Capitol. A dense steam of vapour rose from the multitude. . . . Many of them were without knapsacks, crossbelts, and firelocks. Some had neither greatcoats nor shoes, others were covered with blankets. . . . I ran down stairs and asked an "officer" . . . where the men were coming from. "Where from? Well, sir, I guess we're all coming out of Verginny as far as we can, and pretty well whipped too."

Questions

1. In what ways would an orderly retreat from Bull Run have differed from the scenes described by Russell?
2. How did the inexperience of the troops contribute to the confusion of the retreat?
3. What do you think the federal forces learned from the defeat at Bull Run?

14-4   The Work of the United States Sanitary Commission (1864)

The United States Sanitary Commission represented the largest and most successful volunteer wartime activity in the North (see text p. 452). The commission's founders intended to bring modern methods of sanitation to the treatment of sick and wounded soldiers and thereby avoid the devastating health problems that had plagued British and French troops during the Crimean War (1854–1856). In June 1861 the United States Sanitary Commission received official recognition from the War Department as a civilian agency supporting the Army Medical Bureau.

Sharply critical of traditional army methods, Sanitary Commission inspectors visited military encampments to direct latrine construction, food preparation, and the design of hospitals. Sanitary Commission activities dominated the home-front activities of northern women. Hundreds of volunteers organized "sanitary fairs" in northern cities to raise funds to supply soldiers with medical supplies, fresh fruits and vegetables, and nurses and doctors to assist in the care and evacuation of the wounded. Although the intrusion of civilians into military matters disturbed some commanders, the commission's popularity among the troops and its influence with Congress assured the success of its efforts.

Source: [Linus P. Brockett], *The Philanthropic Results of the War in America: Collected from Official and Other Authentic Sources, by an American Citizen* (New York: Sheldon & Co., 1864), 32–42, 89–91.

The proclamation of the President [following the fall of Fort Sumter] . . . evoked the patriotic and earnest sympathies of the women of the nation, as well as those of the sterner sex. Everywhere fair hands were at work, and fair brows grew grave with thought, of what could be done for those who were going forth to fight the nation's battles. With the characteristic national fondness for organization, Ladies' Aid and Relief Societies were formed everywhere. One, "The Soldiers' Aid Society," at Cleveland, Ohio, bearing the date April 20, 1861, only five days after the President's proclamation; another at Philadelphia, "The Ladies' Aid Society," adopting its constitution on the 26th of April, and a third, "The Woman's Central Association of Relief, of New York," on the 30th of the same month. By the middle of May there were hundreds of these associations formed. As yet, however, they hardly knew what was to be done, or how, when, and where to do it. . . . The Woman's Central Association of Relief had among its officers some gentlemen of large experience in sanitary science, and of considerable knowledge of military hygiene, and they wisely gave a practical turn to its labors from the first. . . . Other organizations of gentlemen were attempting by . . . similar measures, to render assistance to the Government. . . . Fraternizing with each other . . . these associations resolved to send a joint delegation to Washington. . . .

On the 18th of May, 1861 . . . representatives of these . . . associations drew up and forwarded to the Secretary of War a communication setting forth the propriety of creating an organization which should unite the duties and labors of [these] associations, and co-operate with the Medical Bureau of the War Department . . . in securing the welfare of the army. For this purpose they asked that a mixed commission of civilians, military officers, and medical men, might be appointed by the Government, charged with the duty of methodizing and reducing to practical service the already active but undirected benevolence of the people. . . .

The President and Secretary of War were not at first disposed to look with any great favor upon this plan, which they regarded rather as a sentimental scheme concocted by women, clergymen, and humane physicians, than as one whose practical workings would prove of incalculable benefit to the army. . . . [But] when the Acting Surgeon-General asked for it, as a needed adjuvant to the Medical Bureau, likely soon to be overwhelmed by its new duties, they finally decided, though reluctantly, to permit its organization.

Accordingly the Secretary of War, on the 9th of June, decided on the creation of . . . "The United States Sanitary Commission." . . . After the Government had established its own permanent hospitals . . . a considerable number of the supplies were furnished by the Sanitary Commission. The value of these supplies furnished by private hands . . . has been carefully ascertained . . . [and] could not have been less in value than $2,200,000.

One of these hospitals, now under the charge of the Government, originated in the philanthropic spirit of the citizens of . . . Philadelphia. . . . After the great battles before Washington, in the summer of 1862 [the Second Battle of Bull Run], trains, freighted with the wounded, poured into Philadelphia, and no provisions having been made for their quiet and speedy transfer to the hospitals, most of which were at considerable distance, they were temporarily placed in churches. . . . The citizens of the vicinity, a large portion of them mechanics, laboring by day in the busy manufactories of that vicinity, were greatly distressed at witnessing this suffering, and resolved . . . to erect near the station-house a hospital for the temporary accommodation of sick and wounded soldiers. A landowner generously gave them the use of some vacant lots . . . others contributed lumber, furniture, heating apparatus, bath-tubs, and some, money. One poor Irishman wheeled a half-worn stove to the new hospital. "He had nothing else to give," he said, "and must do something for the sogers." The hospital was erected, and furnished with five hundred beds in fifteen days. . . .

The feeling of sympathy and patriotism which has actuated the masses of the people, manifested itself in numberless instances of thoughtfulness and tenderness, even from classes, among whom it was hardly to be looked for.

Questions

1. Why do you think the president and the secretary of war were initially leery of civilian involvement in aiding sick and wounded soldiers?
2. Even if these volunteer activities were not absolutely necessary to the Union cause, were they important in maintaining home-front morale? Explain why or why not.
3. What class of people did the writer of this document expect to respond to the Sanitary Commission's philanthropic appeal? Why?

Questions for Further Thought

1. Why wasn't the Union better prepared for war (Documents 14-2 and 14-3)? Considering the North's overwhelming superiority in resources and manpower, how can the Confederate victories in the war's first years be explained?

2. Why do you think that William Howard Russell's London *Times* article on the First Battle of Bull Run (Document 14-3) angered Lincoln so much? Why was Lincoln so concerned with how the foreign—and specifically, the European—press reported the war?

3. The passages from Mary Chesnut's diary of 1861 (Document 14-2) are striking in the way in which they speak of the slaves. What presuppositions about the nature of slaves underlie both these passages and the "Declaration of Immediate Causes" (Document 14-1)?

4. How might women's efforts during the war—especially in organizations like the United States Sanitary Commission (Document 14-4)—have helped the Union solve its problems of war mobilization? Was there a difference in this regard between northern and southern women?

The Turning Point: 1863

As the war progressed, its character and aims underwent fundamental change. Most important, for the Union it became not simply a war to quell a rebellion but a war to end slavery. At first Lincoln was careful to avoid addressing the issue of slavery. He had a conception of his own powers as president and commander in chief that limited his authority to enforcing the law and upholding federal authority. Moreover, he was eager to keep the remaining slave states in the Union, hoped to entice seceded slave states back in, and needed to pay heed to a northern white public opinion that was hardly as much opposed to slavery as he, let alone the Radical Republicans to his left.

The stalemate of 1861–1862, however, convinced more and more northerners that winning the war required more than strictly military means. Slavery was a major prop to Confederate power, and it soon became apparent that the slaves themselves regarded Union troops, and the missionaries that came in their wake, as "liberators" (Document 14-5). Given the racism prevalent among white Union soldiers, much of that grateful admiration was misplaced. Nonetheless, increasing numbers of northerners began to endorse the notion that at least a threatened strike against slavery might end the war more quickly and appeal to those slaves itching to forward insurrection within the Confederacy. Accordingly, on September 22, 1862, Lincoln issued a carefully worded preliminary Emancipation Proclamation (Document 14-6), which was followed by the formal proclamation on January 1, 1863. The Confederacy reacted with outrage, and Lincoln's move also stirred hostility in the North: the Republicans suffered major reverses in the fall elections of 1862, and the shift in war aims, along with resentment at the inequities of war mobilization, led to serious riots in New York City in July 1863 (Document 14-7). But the character of the war had shifted irreversibly; slaves increasingly undercut the Confederacy by fleeing to Union lines, with many of the men enlisting in the Union army to fight for their own and their people's freedom.

In the meantime, the Union's advantages in war mobilization made themselves felt. The Union naval blockade tightened; the army of Ulysses S. Grant scored a major strategic victory in the West at Vicksburg, breaking the Confederacy's supply lines to

Texas and Mexico. Robert E. Lee's string of brilliant victories finally ended at Gettysburg (Document 14-8). By the end of the year the Confederate cause was still potent, but it was now clearly on the defensive.

14-5   A Northern Black Woman Teaches Contrabands in South Carolina (1862)

Charlotte Forten

In November 1861 federal gunboats forced the evacuation of the Confederate defenders of the Sea Islands region of South Carolina (between Charleston and Savannah on the Atlantic coast). The Sea Islands became a federal base in the Atlantic blockade of southern commerce. Confederate soldiers left the islands, as did the wealthy planters and their families. The slaves remained, sensing that the enemies of their masters would be their friends. With the federal government now in control of about 10,000 "contrabands" (see text pp. 458–459) and some of the most productive cotton land in the South, the future development of the plantations and the fate of the laborers attracted immediate attention. The Treasury Department took control of the plantations and appointed superintendents to direct their operations. Northern abolitionists sent teachers into the region to educate the former slaves and prove them worthy of emancipation. One of the teachers was Charlotte Forten (1838–1914) of Philadelphia. For generations the Fortens had been abolitionist leaders in the black community. Charlotte Forten had taught in the nonsegregated public schools of Salem, Massachusetts, before visiting the Sea Islands. Her light complexion and northern ways raised suspicions at first, but she deemed her labors on the islands a success. From her journal she drafted a narrative of her experience to share with her friends. One friend, the poet John Greenleaf Whittier, arranged to have the piece published in the *Atlantic Monthly* in May and June 1864.

Source: Charlotte Forten, "Life on the Sea Islands," *Atlantic Monthly* 13 (May 1864 and June 1864), 587–596, 666–676, in *Two Black Teachers during the Civil War* (New York: Arno Press and New York Times, 1969).

It was on the afternoon of a warm, murky day late in October that our steamer, the United States, touched the landing at Hilton head. A motley assemblage had collected on the wharf,—officers, soldiers, and "contrabands" of every size and hue: black was, however, the prevailing color. . . . It is wonderful with what ease they carry all sorts of things on their heads,—heavy bundles of wood, hoes and rakes, everything, heavy or light, that can be carried in the hands; and I have seen a woman, with a bucketful of water on her head, stoop down to take up another in her hand, without spilling a drop from either. We noticed that the people had much better taste in selecting materials for dresses than we had supposed. They do not generally like gaudy colors, but prefer neat, quiet patterns. They are, however, very fond of all kinds of jewelry. I once asked the children in school what their ears were for. "To put rings in," promptly replied one of the little girls.

These people are exceedingly polite in their manner towards each other, each new arrival bowing, scraping his feet, and shaking hands with the others, while there are constant greetings, such as, "Huddy? How's yer lady?" ("How d' ye do? How's your wife?"). The hand-shaking is performed with the greatest possible solemnity. There is never the faintest shadow of a smile on anybody's face during this performance. The children, too, are taught to be very polite to their elders, and it is the rarest thing to hear a disrespectful word from a child to his parent, or to any grown persons. They have really what the New-Englanders call "beautiful manners" . . . .

In the evenings, the children frequently come in to sing and shout for us. These "shouts" are very strange,—in truth, almost indescribable. It is necessary to hear and see in order to have any clear idea of them. The children form a ring, and move around in a kind of shuffling dance, singing all the time. Four or five stand apart, and sing very energetically, clapping their hands, stamping their feet and rocking their bodies to and fro. These are the musicians, to whose performance the shouters keep perfect time. . . . We cannot determine whether it has a religious character or not. Some of the people tell us that it has, others, that it has not. But as the shouts of the grown people are always in connection with their religious meetings, it is probable that they are the barbarous expression of religion, handed down to them from their African ancestors, and destined to pass away under the influence of Christian teachings. . . . Prince, a large black boy from a neighboring plantation, was the principal shouter among the children. . . . His performances were most amusing specimens of Ethiopian gymnastics. Amaretta . . . a cunning, kittenish little creature of only six years old, had a remarkably sweet voice. . . .

Daily the long-oppressed people of these islands are demonstrating their capacity for improvement in learning and labor. What they have accomplished in one short year exceeds our utmost expectations. . . . An old freedman said to me one day, "De Lord make me suffer long time, Miss. 'Peared like we nebber was gwine to get troo. But now we's free. He bring us all out right at las'." In their darkest hours they have clung to Him, and we know He will not forsake them.

Questions

1. What does Forten find most surprising about the people of the Sea Islands?
2. What strengths and weaknesses does she discern in the culture she encounters?
3. At the very moment of emancipation why does Forten feel the need to demonstrate the African Americans' "capacity for improvement in learning and labor"?

14-6   The Preliminary Emancipation Proclamation (1862)

Abraham Lincoln

President Lincoln issued the preliminary Emancipation Proclamation on September 22, 1862, ensuring that a Union victory would mean an end to slavery (see text pp. 459–460). In theory the proclamation was a bold action, but its practical effects were limited. Although under tremendous pressure from some Republicans to abolish slavery, Lincoln still hoped for a compromise with slaveholders that would end the war.

Source: U.S. Statutes at Large, 12 (1862): 1268–1269.

That on the first day of January, A.D. 1863, all persons held as slaves in any State or designated part of a state the people whereof shall then be in rebellion against the United States shall be then, thenceforward, and forever free; and the executive government of the United States, including the military and naval authority thereof, will recognize and maintain the freedom of all such persons and will do no act or acts to repress such persons, or any of them, in any efforts they may make for their actual freedom.

That the executive will on the first day of January aforesaid, by proclamation, designate the States and parts of States, if any, in which the people thereof, respectively, shall then be in rebellion against the United States.

Questions

1. Which geographic areas were affected by the Proclamation? Why do you think Lincoln limited the scope of the Proclamation?
2. What steps did the Proclamation require the Union military forces to take?
3. A distinguished historian once characterized this document as having "all the moral grandeur of a bill of lading" (a document certifying that goods have been loaded for shipment). What do you think he meant by that?

14-7 The New York City Draft Riots (July 1863)

Anna Elizabeth Dickinson

When the Union instituted conscription in 1863, it allowed men to avoid the draft if they could provide a substitute or pay a $300 fee—more than half an average worker's annual income. Democratic opponents of Lincoln exploited resentment over the high fee to win support from recent immigrants and the urban poor. In July 1863 riots against the draft exploded in New York City. The following description of the riots is by Anna Dickinson, who was involved in the antislavery and women's rights movements. Her account is no exaggeration; the rioting was finally suppressed on the fourth day by troops from the Army of the Potomac.

Source: Anna Elizabeth Dickinson, *What Answer?* (Boston, 1868), 242–259.

On the morning of Monday, the thirteenth of July, began this outbreak, unparalleled in atrocities by anything in American history, and equalled only by the horrors of the worst days of the French Revolution. Gangs of men and boys, composed of railroad *employees*, workers in machine-shops, and a vast crowd of those who lived by preying upon others, thieves, pimps, professional ruffians,— the scum of the city,—jail-birds, or those who were running with swift feet to enter the prison-doors, began to gather on the corners, and in streets and alleys where they lived; from thence issuing forth they visited the great establishments on the line of their advance, commanding their instant clos[ing] and the companionship of the workmen,—many of them peaceful and orderly men,—on pain of the destruction of one and a murderous assault upon the other, did not their orders meet with instant compliance.

A body of these, five or six hundred strong, gathered about one of the enrolling-offices in the upper part of the city, where the draft was quietly proceeding, and opened the assault upon it by a shower of clubs, bricks, and paving-stones torn from the streets, following it up by a furious rush into the office. Lists, records, books, the drafting-wheel, every article of furniture or work in the room was rent in pieces, and strewn about the floor or flung into the street; while the law officers, the newspaper reporters,—who are expected to be everywhere,—and the few peaceable spectators, were compelled to make a hasty retreat through an opportune rear exit, accelerated by the curses and blows of the assailants.

A safe in the room, which contained some of the hated records, was fallen upon by the men, who strove to wrench open its impregnable lock with their naked hands, and, baffled, beat them on its iron doors and sides till they were stained with blood, in a mad frenzy of senseless hate and fury. And then, finding every portable article destroyed,— their thirst for ruin growing by the little drink it had had,— and believing, or rather hoping, that the officers had taken refuge in the upper rooms, set fire to the house, and stood watching the slow and steady lift of the flames, filling the air with demoniac shrieks and yells, while they waited for the prey to escape from some door or window, from the merciless fire to their merciless hands. One of these, who was on the other side of the street, courageously stepped forward, and, telling them that they had utterly demolished all they came to seek, informed them that helpless women and little children were in the house, and besought them to extinguish the flames and leave the ruined premises; to disperse, or at least to seek some other scene.

By his dress recognizing in him a government official, so far from hearing or heeding his humane appeal, they set upon him with sticks and clubs, and beat him till his eyes were blind with blood, and he—bruised and mangled— succeeded in escaping to the handful of police who stood helpless before this howling crew, now increased to thousands. With difficulty and pain the inoffensive tenants escaped from the rapidly spreading fire, which, having devoured the house originally lighted, swept across the neighboring buildings till the whole block stood a mass of burning flames. The firemen came up tardily and reluctantly, many of them of the same class as the miscreants who surrounded them, and who cheered at their approach, but either made no attempt to perform their duty, or so feeble and farcical a one, as to bring disgrace upon a service they so generally honor and ennoble.

At last, when there was nothing more to accomplish, the mob, swollen to a frightful size, including myriads of wretched, drunken women, and the half-grown, vagabond boys of the pavements, rushed through the intervening streets, stopping cars and insulting peaceable citizens on their way, to an armory where were manufactured and stored carbines and guns for the government. In anticipation of the attack, this, earlier in the day, had been fortified by a police squad capable of coping with an ordinary crowd of ruffians, but as chaff before fire in the presence of these murderous thousands. Here, as before, the attack was begun by a rain of missiles gathered from the streets; less fatal, doubtless, than more civilized arms, but frightful in the ghastly wounds and injuries they inflicted. Of this no notice was taken by those who were stationed within; it was repeated. At last, finding they were treated with contemptuous silence, and that no sign of surrender was offered, the crowd swayed back,—then forward,—in a combined attempt to force the wide entrance-doors. Heavy hammers and sledges, which had been brought from forges and workshops, caught up hastily as they gathered the mechanics into their ranks, were used with frightful violence to beat them in,—at last successfully. The foremost assailants began to climb the stairs, but were checked, and for the moment driven back by the fire of the officers, who at last had been commanded to resort to their revolvers. A half-score fell wounded; and one, who had been acting in some sort as their leader,—a big, brutal, Irish ruffian,—dropped dead. . . .

Late in the afternoon a crowd which could have numbered not less than ten thousand, the majority of whom were ragged, frowzy, drunken women, gathered about the Orphan Asylum for Colored Children,—a large and beautiful building, and one of the most admirable and noble charities of the city. When it became evident, from the menacing cries and groans of the multitude, that danger, if not destruction, was meditated to the harmless and inoffensive inmates, a flag of truce appeared, and an appeal was made in their behalf, by the principal, to every sentiment of humanity which these beings might possess,—a vain appeal! Whatever human feeling had ever, if ever, filled these souls was utterly drowned and washed away in the tide of rapine and blood in which they had been steeping themselves. The few officers who stood guard over the doors, and manfully faced these demoniac legions, were beaten down and flung to one side, helpless and stunned, whilst the vast crowd rushed in. All the articles upon which they could seize—

beds, bedding, carpets, furniture,—the very garments of the fleeing inmates, some of these torn from their persons as they sped by—were carried into the streets, and hurried off by the women and children who stood ready to receive the goods which their husbands, sons, and fathers flung to their care. The little ones, many of them, assailed and beaten; all,—orphans and care-takers,—exposed to every indignity and every danger, driven on to the street,—the building was fired. This had been attempted whilst the helpless children—some of them scarce more than babies—were still in their rooms. . . .

By far the most infamous part of these cruelties was that which wreaked every species of torture and lingering death upon the colored people of the city,—men, women, and children, old and young, strong and feeble alike. Hundreds of these fell victims to the prejudice fostered by public opinion, incorporated in our statute-books, sanctioned by our laws, which here and thus found legitimate outgrowth and action. . . .

It was absurd and futile to characterize this new Reign of Terror as anything but an effort on the part of Northern rebels to help Southern ones, at the most critical moment of the war,—with the State militia and available troops absent in a neighboring Commonwealth,—and the loyal people unprepared. These editors [of Democratic newspapers] and their coadjutors, men of brains and ability, were of that most poisonous growth,—traitors to the Government and the flag of their country,—renegade Americans. Let it, however, be written plainly and graven deeply, that the tribes of savages—the hordes of ruffians—found ready to do their loathsome bidding, were not of native growth, nor American born. . . .

Questions

1. According to Dickinson, what kinds of people made up the mobs?
2. Why did the mob attack blacks, including black children?
3. Why were the police and firemen so ineffective in stopping the riots and arson?

14-8   The Gettysburg Address (1863)

Abraham Lincoln

The Battle of Gettysburg in July 1863 was the bloodiest of the Civil War. But the costly Union victory strengthened northern resolve and ended any hopes the Confederacy had of winning foreign recognition (see text pp. 460–463). Later that year, in a speech dedicating a cemetery at Gettysburg, Abraham Lincoln helped define the modern concept of the American nation.

Source: Roy P. Basler et al., eds., *The Collected Works of Abraham Lincoln* (New Brunswick, N.J.: Rutgers University Press, 1953), 7: 23.

Four score and seven years ago our fathers brought forth on this continent, a new nation, conceived in Liberty, and dedicated to the proposition that all men are created equal.

Now we are engaged in a great civil war, testing whether that nation, or any nation so conceived and so dedicated, can long endure. We are met on a great battlefield of that war. We have come to dedicate a portion of that field, as a final resting place for those who here gave their lives that that nation might live. It is altogether fitting and proper that we should do this.

But, in a larger sense, we can not dedicate—we can not consecrate—we can not hallow—this ground. The brave men, living and dead, who struggled here, have consecrated it, far above our poor power to add or detract. The world will little note, nor long remember what we say here, but it can never forget what they did here. It is for us the living, rather, to be dedicated here to the unfinished work which they who fought here have thus far so nobly advanced. It is rather for us to be here dedicated to the great task remaining before us—that from these honored dead we take increased devotion to that cause for which they gave the last full measure of devotion—that we here highly resolve that these dead shall not have died in vain—that this nation, under God, shall have a new birth of freedom—and that government of the people, by the people, for the people, shall not perish from the earth.

Questions

1. Why did Lincoln say in 1863 that the United States had been founded on the "proposition that all men are created equal"?
2. Why did Lincoln want to tie the Union's cause so closely to that of the Founders? Was Lincoln attempting to redefine the Union cause with the Gettysburg Address? If so, in what way?
3. Lincoln concluded his address with the thought "that this nation, under God, shall have a new birth of freedom." What type of freedom did he mean?

Questions for Further Thought

1. Many historians have argued that at this point the Civil War changed character and became a struggle over fundamentally different issues than it had been concerned with before. Given these documents, would you agree? What or who was responsible?
2. Compare the preliminary Emancipation Proclamation (Document 14-6) to the Gettysburg Address (Document 14-8). The two were separated by just little more than a year in time, yet their spirit is strikingly different. How?
3. As Document 14-7 shows, the turning point of the war was accompanied by considerable turmoil in the North. Were the two connected by more than coincidence? If so, how?

The Union Victorious, 1864–1865

The war was hardly finished by the beginning of 1864. While the Confederacy could no longer hope to score a knockout punch, it had plenty of reason to hope it could simply outlast the Union side. Ulysses Grant's Virginia campaign of 1864 produced unprecedented Union advances in a theater that had seen previous commanders squander their opportunities, but his casualty rate was appalling. By fall Grant had pressed Lee's army to the outskirts of Petersburg, where both sides settled into grim, ugly trench warfare. War-weariness was a real threat to continuation of the war; 1864 was an election year, and the Democrats were gearing up to run against the "Republican war."

On September 2, though, a major break came for the Union when William Tecumseh Sherman's western army captured the then-small but strategic rail center of

Atlanta; the lift to Union morale led to Republican victory in the fall elections. By the end of the year, the principal western Confederate army had disintegrated at Nashville and Sherman had completed his legendary march to the sea, "making Georgia howl." The Confederate cause was now in such desperate straits that some leaders, including Jefferson Davis and Robert E. Lee, began to endorse proposals to arm and free slaves, suggestions that stirred violent opposition (Document 14-9). While some African Americans were enlisted in the Confederate army after being voluntarily freed by their masters, they were too few and too late. By April 1865 Sherman had swept through the Carolinas meeting little resistance, threatening Lee's rear, while Grant's forces had out-flanked Lee, forcing him to abandon Richmond and Petersburg and retreat to Appomattox Court House, where he surrendered on April 9. The Confederacy was no more.

With the end of the Confederacy came the effective end of slavery in its former territory (Document 14-10), although, ironically, slavery continued in the Union slave states until the ratification of the Thirteenth Amendment late in 1865.

14-9   Confederates Debate Emancipation (1863–1864)

After the critical Confederate defeats at Gettysburg and Vicksburg in 1863, with Emancipation now Union policy and African Americans flocking to Union colors, some Confederates began to think the previously unthinkable: that in order to attain independence, the Confederacy might have to enlist blacks in its own army. The ensuing debate got louder as the Confederate position deteriorated, and especially after President Jefferson Davis in November 1864 suggested the possibility of emancipation as a reward for service. In March 1865, after intervention by General Robert E. Lee, the Confederate Congress finally passed legislation permitting the enlistment of slaves, but without changing their status. Although the army recognized the impossibility of arming slaves, the most it could do was require that masters grant freedom to any slaves they sent into service. Few were recruited in the scant month remaining before Appomattox. Thus the debate was fatally inconclusive for the Confederacy; but it laid bare some of the basic contradictions underlying the Confederate cause.

Source: Robert F. Durden, *The Gray and the Black: The Confederate Debate on Emancipation* (Baton Rouge: Louisiana State University Press, 1972), 30–32, 97–99, 124–125, 141–142.

(a) Excerpts from the Jackson *Mississippian*, Reprinted in Montgomery (AL) *Weekly Mail*, September 9, 1863

EMPLOYMENT OF NEGROES IN THE ARMY.
. . . We must either employ the negroes ourselves, or the enemy will employ them against us. While the enemy retains so much of our territory, they are, in their present avocation and status, a dangerous element, a source of weakness. They are no longer negative characters, but subjects of volition as other people. They must be taught to know that this is peculiarly the country of the black man—that in no other is the climate and soil so well adapted to his nature and capacity. He must further be taught that it is his duty, as well as the white man's, to defend his home with arms, if need be.

We are aware that there are persons who shudder at the idea of placing arms in the hands of negroes, and who are not willing to trust them under any circumstances. The negro, however, is proverbial for his faithfulness under kind treatment. He is an affectionate, grateful being, and we are persuaded that the fears of such persons are groundless.

There are in the slaveholding States four millions of negroes, and out of this number at least six hundred thousand able-bodied men capable of bearing arms can be found. Lincoln proposes to free and arm them against us. There are already fifty thousand of them in the Federal ranks. Lincoln's scheme has worked well so far, and if no[t] checkmated, will most assuredly be carried out. The Confederate Government must adopt a counter policy. It must thwart the enemy in this gigantic scheme, at all hazards, and if nothing else will do it—if the negroes cannot be made effective and trustworthy to the Southern cause in no other way, we solemnly believe it is the duty of this Government to forestall Lincoln and proceed at once to take steps for the emancipation or liberation of the negroes itself. Let them be declared free, placed in the ranks, and told to fight for their homes and country.

We are fully sensible of the grave importance of the question, but the inexorable logic of events has forced it upon us. We must deal with it, then, not with fear and trembling—not as timid, time-serving men—but with a boldness, a promptness and a determination which the exigency requires, and which should ever characterize the action of a people resolved to sacrifice everything for liberty. It is true, that such a step would revolutionize our whole industrial system—that it would, to a great extent, impoverish the country and be a dire calamity to both the negro and the white race of this and the Old World; but better this than the loss of the negroes, the country and liberty.

If Lincoln succeeds in arming our slaves against us, he will succeed in making them our masters. He will reverse the social order of things at the South. Whereas, if he is checkmated in time, our liberties will remain intact; the land will be ours, and the industrial system of the country still controlled by Southern men.

Such action on the part of our Government would place our people in a purer and better light before the world. It would disabuse the European mind of a grave error in regard to the cause of our separation. It would prove to them that there were higher and holier motives which actuated our people than the mere love of property. It would show that, although slavery is one of the principles that we started to fight for, yet it falls far short of being the chief one; that, for the sake of our liberty, we are capable of any personal sacrifice; that we regard the emancipation of slaves, and the consequent loss of property as an evil infinitely less than the subjugation and enslavement of ourselves; that it is not a war exclusively for the privilege of holding negroes in bondage. It would prove to our soldiers, three-fourths of whom never owned a negro, that it is not "the rich man's war and the poor man's fight," but a war for the most sacred of all principles, for the dearest of all rights—the right to govern ourselves. It would show them that the rich man who owned slaves was not willing

to jeopardize the precious liberty of the country by his eagerness to hold on to his slaves, but that he was ready to give them up and sacrifice his interest in them whenever the cause demanded it. It would lend a new impetus, a new enthusiasm, a new and powerful strength to the cause, and place our success beyond a peradventure. It would at once remove all the odium which attached to us on account of slavery, and bring us speedy recognition, and, if necessary, intervention.

We sincerely trust that the Southern people will be found willing to make any and every sacrifice which the establishment of our independence may require. Let it never be said that to preserve slavery we were willing to wear the chains of bondage ourselves—that the very avarice which prompted us to hold on to the negro for the sake of the money invested in him, riveted upon us shackles more galling and bitter than ever a people yet endured. Let not slavery prove a barrier to our independence. If it is found in the way—if it proves an insurmountable obstacle to the achievement of our liberty and separate nationality, away with it! Let it perish. We must make up our minds to one solemn duty, the first duty of the patriot, and that is, to save ourselves from the rapacious North, WHATEVER THE COST. . . .

(b) Charleston *Mercury,* November 3, 1864

Usurpation is ever prolific. When the Confederacy, by the Confederate Congress, claimed omnipotence over the States and its citizens, including the officers of the States in its military resources, by the Conscription Law, any one conversant with human nature must have known that this might not be the end of its usurpations. A Constitution is like a dyke keeping out the sea. Cut it and the influx of waters must be endless. This usurpation was soon followed by the Direct Tax Act, by which the Confederate Government claimed to be omnipotent and consolidated, in its taxing, as it was, by the Conscription Law, in its military powers. We are now at a third stage of its usurpations, soon to [be] accomplished, if not promptly met by the States—*the power to emancipate our slaves.*

. . . Now, if there was any single proposition that we thought was unquestionable in the Confederacy it was this—that the States, and the States alone, have the *exclusive* jurisdiction and mastery over their slaves. To suppose that any slaveholding country [*i.e.,* state] would voluntarily leave it to any other power than its own, to emancipate its slaves, is such an absurdity, that we did not believe a single intelligent man in the Confederacy could entertain it. Still less could we believe that after what had taken place under the United States, with respect to slavery in the Southern States, it was possible that any pretension to emancipate slaves could be set up for the Confederate States. It was because the exclusion of slaves from our Territories by the Government of the United States, *looked to their emancipation,* that we resisted it. The power to exercise it was never claimed by that Government. The mere agitation in the Northern States to effect the emancipation of our slaves largely contributed to our separation from them. And now, before a Confederacy which we established to put at rest forever all such agitation is four years old, we find the proposition gravely submitted that the Confederate Government should emancipate slaves in the States. South Caroline, acting upon the principle that she and she alone had the power to emancipate her slaves, has passed laws prohibiting their emancipation by any of her citizens, unless they are sent out of the State; and no free person of color already free, who leaves the State, shall ever afterwards enter it. She has laws now in force, prohibiting free negroes, belonging either to the Northern States, or to European powers, from entering the State, and by the most rigid provisions, they are seized and put into prison should they enter it. These were her rights, under the Union of the United States, recognized and protected by the Government of the United States, and acquiesced in by all foreign nations. And, now, here, it is proposed that the Government of the Confederate States, not only has the right to seize our slaves and to make them soldiers, but to emancipate them in South Carolina, and compel us to give them a home amongst us. We confess, that our indignation at such pretensions is so great, that we are at a loss to know how to treat them. To argue against them, is self-stultification. They are as monstrous as they are insulting.

The pretext for this policy is, that we want soldiers in our armies. This pretext is set up by the *Enquirer* in the face of the fact disclosed by the President of the Confederate States, that two-thirds of our soldiers, now in the army, are absentees from its ranks. The *Enquirer* is a devout upholder of President Davis and the Administration. It does not arraign the Government for such a state of things. It passes over the gross mismanagement which has produced them; and cries out, that negroes are wanted to fill the ranks of our armies. . . . It is vain to attempt to blink the truth. The freemen of the Confederate States must work out their own redemption, or they must be the slaves of their own slaves. The statesmanship, which looks to any other source for success, is contemptible charlatanry. It is worse—it is treachery to our cause itself. Assert the right in the Confederate Government to emancipate slaves, and it is stone dead. . . .

(c) "Sydney" (a nonslaveholder), in the Macon *Telegraph and Confederate*, November 19, 1864

. . . Now there is [*sic*] in the Confederacy one or two hundred thousand able bodied negroes not engaged in agriculture. Many of them [are] refugees from the country overrun, and they consume just as much as if they were in the army and can be very well spared. While thousands of poor white men that have nothing but their country to defend, have bled and died, their families are left to the cold charities of the world. The rich planters can stay at home undisturbed, and if it is hinted [that] cuffey [the Negro] is wanted to help defend his country and property we see a great howl set up about it, and more fuss made than if 1000 white men were sacrificed. Try to hide it as much as we may, yet the question of negro slavery was the great leading cause of this war, and but for it we would have been recognized long ago by foreign powers, but in that particular the world is against us, and so we will remain until this war shall have placed it upon a basis too firm to be questioned.

Then why may not the negro help to establish the only government that looks to the Christianizing of the African and placing him in a condition far above his fellow countrymen in any part of the world, if the exigency demands men to the extent above referred to, in God's name, do not sacrifice every white man in the Confederacy in preference to taking a few negroes from their fondling masters. . . .

(d) Rep. Henry C. Chambers (MS) in Confederate House of Representatives, November 10, 1864

. . . Sir, on what motive is he to fight our battles? He is after all a human being, and acts upon motives. Will you offer him his freedom? The enemy will offer him his freedom, and also as a deserter, immunity from military service. Will you offer him the privilege of return home to his family, a freeman, after the war? That you dare not do, remembering it was the free negroes of St. Domingo, who had been trained to arms, that excited the insurrection of the slaves. And the enemy would meet even that offer with the promise of a return free to his Southern home and the right of property in it. The amount of it all is, that in despair of achieving our independence with our own right arms, we turn for succor to the slave and implore him to establish our freedom and fix slavery upon himself, or at least upon his family and his race, forever. He, at least, after the expiration of his term of service, is to be banished to Liberia or other inhospitable shore, for the States could never permit an army of negroes to be returned home, either free or slave. . . .

. . . Sir, this scheme, if attempted, will end in rapid emancipation and colonization—colonization in the North by bringing up the slaves by regiments and brigades to the opportunity of escape to the enemy; emancipation and colonization abroad to those who render service to us for a specified period. I argue on the presumption that nothing of the kind will be attempted without the consent of the States, whether as to employing them on the promise of freedom, or as to returning them free and disciplined to their old homes. By means of the power of impressment or purchase, this Government could not safely be permitted, without the consent of the States, to inaugurate a system of emancipation that might end in the abolition of the institution, nor do I suppose that the President designed the contrary. In suggesting freedom as the motive to be offered to the slave, he performed a simple official duty, leaving to Congress if it adopted the suggestion, to provide by law all the conditions it might be proper to impose.

In any aspect of the case, this is a proposition to subvert the labour system, the social system and the political system of our country. Better, far, to employ mercenaries from abroad, if dangerous and impracticable expedients are to be attempted, and preserve that institution which is not only the foundation of our wealth but the palladium of our liberties. Make the experiment, of course, with negro troops as the last means to prevent subjugation; but when we shall be reduced to the extremity of exclaiming to the slave, "help us, or we sink," it will already have become quite immaterial what course we pursue! . . .

Questions

1. Some historians have argued that the existence of this debate demonstrates that a fundamental change had occurred in Confederate, as well as Union, war aims after the turning point of the war. Do you agree?
2. On what grounds does the writer in the Charleston *Mercury* oppose the emancipation and arming of the slaves? What does his position reveal about the nature of the Confederacy and its ability to take united action for its own self-preservation?
3. Both the Jackson *Mississippian* and the Macon *Telegraph and Confederate* allude to divisions among southern whites—specifically, between slaveholders and non-slaveholders—and suggest that arming slaves might restore white solidarity. How?
4. For what reasons does the author writing in the Jackson *Mississippian* believe that the slaves, once freed, will fight for the South?

14-10   A Freedman Writes to His Former Master (1865)

Jourdon Anderson

The unsettling effect of the Civil War on southern society enabled thousands of African Americans to flee to freedom in the North. Jourdon Anderson, for instance, left his master in Tennessee well before the end of the war and started a more profitable and fulfilling life in Ohio. The eloquence of Anderson's letter reveals much about the meaning of freedom to former slaves.

Source: Lydia Maria Child, ed., *The Freedmen's Book* (Boston, 1865), 265–267.

Dayton, Ohio, August 7, 1865

To My Old Master, Colonel P. H. Anderson,
Big Spring, Tennessee

Sir: I got your letter and was glad to find you had not forgotten Jourdon, and that you wanted me to come back and live with you again, promising to do better for me than anybody else can. I have often felt uneasy about you. I thought the Yankees would have hung you long before this for harboring Rebs they found at your house. I suppose they never heard about your going to Col. Martin's to kill the Union soldier that was left by his company in their stable. Although you shot at me twice before I left you, I did not want to hear of your being hurt, and am glad you are still living. It would do me good to go back to the dear old home again and see Miss Mary and Miss Martha and Allen, Esther, Green, and Lee. Give my love to them all, and tell them I hope we will meet in the better world, if not in this. I would have gone back to see you all when I was working in the Nashville hospital, but one of the neighbors told me Henry intended to shoot me if he ever got a chance.

I want to know particularly what the good chance is you propose to give me. I am doing tolerably well here; I get $25 a month, with victuals and clothing, have a comfortable home for Mandy (the folks here call her Mrs. Anderson), and the children, Milly, Jane and Grundy, go to school and are learning well; the teacher says Grundy has a head for a preacher. They go to Sunday-School, and Mandy and me attend church regularly. We are kindly treated; sometimes we overhear others saying, "Them colored people were slaves" down in Tennessee. The children feel hurt when they hear such remarks, but I tell them it was no disgrace in Tennessee to belong to Col. Anderson. Many darkies would have been proud, as I used to was, to call you master. Now, if you will write and say what wages you will give me, I will be better able to decide whether it would be to my advantage to move back again.

As to my freedom, which you say I can have, there is nothing to be gained on that score, as I got my free-papers in 1864 from the Provost-Marshal-General of the Department of Nashville. Mandy says she would be afraid to go back without some proof that you are sincerely disposed to treat us justly and kindly—and we have concluded to test your sincerity by asking you to send us our wages for the time we served you. This will make us forget and forgive old scores, and rely on your justice and friendship in the future. I served you faithfully for thirty-two years and Mandy twenty years. At $25 a month for me, and $2 a week for Mandy, our earnings would amount to $11,680. Add to this the interest for the time our wages has been kept back and deduct what you paid for our clothing and three doctor's visits to me, and pulling a tooth for Mandy, and the balance will show what we are in justice entitled

to. Please send the money by Adams Express, in care of V. Winters, esq. Dayton, Ohio. If you fail to pay us for faithful labors in the past we can have little faith in your promises in the future. We trust the good Maker has opened your eyes to the wrongs which you and your fathers have done to me and my fathers, in making us toil for you for generations without recompense. Here I draw my wages every Saturday night, but in Tennessee there was never any pay day for the negroes any more than for the horses and cows. Surely there will be a day of reckoning for those who defraud the laborer of his hire.

In answering this letter please state if there would be any safety for my Milly and Jane, who are now grown up and both good-looking girls. You know how it was with poor Matilda and Catherine. I would rather stay here and starve and die if it comes to that than have my girls brought to shame by the violence and wickedness of their young master. You will also please state if there has been any schools opened for the colored children in your neighborhood, the great desire of my life now is to give my children an education, and have them form virtuous habits.

P.S.—Say howdy to George Carter, and thank him for taking the pistol from you when you were shooting at me.

From your old servant,
Jourdon Anderson

Questions

1. What does Anderson's letter indicate about the nature of black-white relationships in the South?
2. What specific aspects of his freedom does Anderson value the most?
3. To what extent is Anderson being humorous, or even sarcastic? How can you tell?

14-11 Second Inaugural Address (1865)

Abraham Lincoln

Abraham Lincoln's reelection in 1864 demonstrated the desire of northerners to continue the war until the Confederacy was totally defeated and had yielded to all northern war aims. In his second inaugural address in March 1865, Lincoln presented the "causes" of a war that was in its fourth year and suggested that the Almighty had imposed "this terrible war" on the nation as punishment for the evils of slavery. Lincoln's reflections are reminiscent of the classic Puritan jeremiad (see Document 2-9) and Frederic Douglass's "What to the Slave Is the Fourth of July?" speech (Document 12-9).

Source: James D. Richardson, ed., *A Compilation of the Messages and Papers of the Presidents* (Washington, D.C.: U.S. Government Printing Office, 1896–1899), 6: 276ff.

At this second appearing to take the oath of the presidential office, there is less occasion for an extended address than there was at the first. Then a statement, somewhat in detail, of a course to be pursued, seemed fitting and proper. Now, at the expiration of four years, during which public declarations have been constantly called forth on every point and phase of the great contest which still absorbs the attention, and engrosses the energies of the nation, little that is new could be presented. The progress of our arms, upon which all else chiefly depends, is as well known to the public as to myself; and it is, I trust, reasonably satisfactory and encouraging to all. With high hope for the future, no prediction in regard to it is ventured.

On the occasion corresponding to this four years ago, all thoughts were anxiously directed to an impending civil-war. All dreaded it—all sought to avert it. While the inaugural address was being delivered from this place, devoted altogether to *saving* the Union without war, insurgent agents were in the city seeking to *destroy* it without war—seeking to dissolve the Union, and divide effects, by negotiation. Both parties deprecated war; but one of them would *make* war rather than let the nation survive; and the other would *accept* war rather than let it perish. And the war came.

One eighth of the whole population were colored slaves, not distributed generally over the Union, but localized in the Southern part of it. These slaves constituted a peculiar and powerful interest. All knew that this interest was, somehow, the cause of the war. To strengthen, perpetuate, and extend this interest was the object for which the insurgents would rend the Union, even by war; while the government claimed no right to do more than to restrict the territorial enlargement of it. Neither party expected for the war, the magnitude, or the duration, which it has already attained. Neither anticipated that the *cause* of the conflict might cease with, or even before, the conflict itself should cease. Each looked for an easier triumph, and a result less fundamental and astounding. Both read the same Bible, and pray to the same God; and each invokes His aid against the other. It may seem strange that any men should dare to ask a just God's assistance in wringing their bread from the sweat of other men's faces; but let us judge not that we be not judged. The prayers of both could not be answered; that of neither has been answered fully. The Almighty has His own purposes. "Woe unto the world because of offences! for it must needs be that offences come; but woe to that man by whom the offence cometh!" If we shall suppose that American Slavery is one of those offences which, in the providence of God, must needs come, but which, having continued through His appointed time, He now wills to remove, and that He gives to both North and South, this terrible war, as the woe due to those by whom the offence came, shall we discern therein any departure from those divine attributes which the believers in a Living God always ascribe to Him? Fondly do we hope—fervently do we pray—that this mighty scourge of war may speedily pass away. Yet, if God wills that it continue, until all the wealth piled by the bond-man's two hundred and fifty years of unrequited toil shall be sunk, and until every drop of blood drawn with the lash, shall be paid by another drawn with the sword, as was said three thousand years ago, so still it must be said "the judgments of the Lord, are true and righteous altogether."

With malice toward none; with charity for all; with firmness in the right, as God gives us to see the right, let us strive on to finish the work we are in; to bind up the nation's wounds; to care for him who shall have borne the battle, and for his widow, and his orphan—to do all which may achieve and cherish a just, and a lasting peace, among ourselves, and with all nations.

Questions

1. What is Lincoln saying about the treatment of African Americans in the United States?

2. In this speech, does Lincoln view the Civil War and slavery as a tragedy, a sin, or a crime?

3. Which do you think Lincoln is emphasizing in this speech, the extraordinarily radical statement about race relations in America or the "with malice toward none" passage?

Questions for Further Thought

1. Compare Lincoln's second inaugural address (Document 14-11) to Douglass's "What to the Slave Is the Fourth of July?" speech (Document 12-9). Both speeches introduce a biblical quotation at a critical moment. Why?

2. A school of historical thinking has held that the Civil War was a "needless tragedy" and that slavery would have ended eventually without the slaughtering of 600,000 people. Given what you have read, would you agree?

3. One historian has described the end of the Civil War as the "moment of truth" for southern slaveholders, when their illusions about themselves and "their people" were exposed for what they were. What illusions do you see in these documents?

CHAPTER 15

Reconstruction, 1865–1877

★   ★   ★

Presidential Reconstruction

Planning for Reconstruction began to take shape in December 1863, when President Lincoln laid out his ideas in a presidential proclamation. His pronouncement opened a debate that became the central issue in American politics for more than a decade. The power struggle that followed led to a collision between the executive and legislative branches of government, the displacement of presidential Reconstruction by congressional Reconstruction, and the first impeachment of a president of the United States.

Reconstruction involved fundamental questions. To begin with, who had the primary responsibility for Reconstruction—the president or Congress? Believing that rebuilding the Union was simply a matter of suppressing "rebels" under presidential war powers, Lincoln's successor, Andrew Johnson, took the early initiative, establishing provisional governments that would purge secessionists from southern leadership, repudiate secession and Confederate debts, and recognize the end of slavery (Document 15-1). Beyond these measures Johnson was unwilling to go: a former southern slaveholder himself, he had no sympathy for blacks; in addition, as a southern Democrat he was firmly devoted to states' rights. Although Johnson was satisfied with these measures, northerners were hearing increasingly alarming reports that white southerners were refusing to recognize their defeat; engaging in brutal reprisals against blacks, northern whites, and southern unionists; and enacting "black codes" that appeared to be backdoor attempts to restore slavery (Documents 15-2 and 15-3). A rising tide of northern outrage pushed the Republican-dominated Congress toward the views of the Republicans' Radical wing; in 1866, over the violent opposition of President Johnson, Congress undertook an unprecedented extension of federal power. With the Civil Rights Act of 1866 (Document 15-4) and the Fourteenth Amendment, Congress declared for the first time that federal citizenship was not restricted by race, and guaranteeing to all citizens the "equal protection of the laws," even if it required federal intervention into the affairs of a state. The outcome of the Civil War was beginning to force fundamental changes in the constitutional character of the American political system, with profound consequences for subsequent American history.

15-1   Plan of Reconstruction (1865)

Andrew Johnson

As the Civil War came to an end, Lincoln's successor, Andrew Johnson, moved quickly to implement his plan for Reconstruction, which differed little from Lincoln's plan (see text pp. 478–479). Johnson acted largely on his own, without much consultation with Congress. In particular, he ignored Congress's demand for a harsher policy toward the former Confederate states.

On May 29, 1865, President Johnson set forth his plan in two presidential proclamations. In the first he promised amnesty to all rebels who would swear an oath of future loyalty, except for certain high-ranking officials and officers of the Confederacy, who had to petition for a presidential pardon.

In the second proclamation, which appears below, Johnson announced the creation of a provisional government for North Carolina. After appointing William W. Holden, a North Carolina Unionist who had opposed secession, as the provisional governor, Johnson described the means by which that state could be restored to the Union. Johnson intended this plan to serve as a model for the other seceded states, hoping that all could be restored before Congress reconvened in December.

Johnson's approach to Reconstruction was very different from that proposed by the Wade-Davis bill (see text p. 478), which stipulated that more than 50 percent of the voters who were qualified in 1860 in each southern state had to be able to prove their past loyalty and swear future loyalty to the Union. Johnson and Congress also differed about allowing former Confederate leaders to participate in Reconstruction and in government. Presidents Lincoln and Johnson envisioned temporary disqualification; Congress favored permanent exclusion.

Source: James D. Richardson, ed., *A Compilation of the Messages and Papers of the Presidents* (Washington, D.C.: U.S. Government Printing Office, 1896–1899), 6: 312–313.

Whereas the fourth section of the fourth article of the Constitution of the United States declares that the United States shall guarantee to every State in the Union a republican form of government and shall protect each of them against invasion and domestic violence; and

Whereas the President of the United States is by the Constitution made Commander in Chief of the Army and Navy, as well as chief civil executive officer of the United States, and is bound by solemn oath faithfully to execute the office of President of the United States and to take care that the laws be faithfully executed; and

Whereas the rebellion which has been waged by a portion of the people of the United States against the properly constituted authorities of the Government . . . and

Whereas it becomes necessary and proper to carry out and enforce the obligations of the United States to the people of North Carolina in securing them in the enjoyment of a republican form of government:

Now, therefore, in obedience to the high and solemn duties imposed upon me by the Constitution of the United States and for the purpose of enabling the loyal people of said State to organize a State government whereby justice may be established, domestic tranquillity insured, and loyal citizens protected in all their rights of life, liberty, and property, I, Andrew Johnson, President of the United States and Commander in Chief of the Army and Navy of the United States, do hereby appoint William W. Holden provisional governor of the State of North Carolina, whose duty it shall be, at the earliest practicable period, to prescribe such rules and regulations as may be necessary and proper for convening a convention composed of delegates to be chosen by that portion of the people of said State who are loyal to the United States, and no others, for the purpose of altering or amending the constitution thereof, and with authority to exercise within the limits of said State all the powers necessary and proper to enable such loyal people of the State of North Carolina to restore said State to its constitutional relations to the Federal Government and to present such a republican form of State government as will entitle the State to the guaranty of the United States therefor and its people to protection by the United States against invasion, insurrection, and domestic violence: *Provided*, That in any election that may be hereafter held for choosing delegates to any State convention as aforesaid no person shall be qualified as an elector or shall be eligible as a member of such convention unless he shall have previously taken and subscribed the oath of amnesty as set forth in the President's proclamation of May 29, A.D. 1865, and is a voter qualified as prescribed by the constitution and laws of the State of North Carolina in force immediately before the 20th day of May, A.D. 1861, the date of the so-called ordinance of secession; and the said convention, when convened, or the legislature that may be thereafter assembled, will prescribe the qualification of electors and the eligibility of persons to hold office under the constitution and laws of the State—a power the people of the several States composing the Federal Union have rightfully exercised from the origin of the Government to the present time.

And I do hereby direct—

. . . That the military commander of the department and all officers and persons in the military and naval service aid and assist the said provisional governor in carrying into effect this proclamation; and they are enjoined to abstain from in any way hindering, impeding, or discouraging the loyal people from the organization of a State government as herein authorized. . . .

Questions

1. According to President Johnson, what was his authority for this proclamation? Who was to be in charge of the process?
2. What steps did Johnson prescribe for restoring civil government in North Carolina?
3. Under Johnson's plan, would freedmen be able to vote? (*Hint:* See the section starting "*Provided.*")

15-2   Report on Conditions in the South (1865)

Carl Schurz

By December 1865, when Congress was gathering in Washington for a new session, Johnson had declared that all the Confederate states but Texas had met his requirements for restoration. Newly elected senators and congressmen from the former Confederacy had arrived to take seats in Congress.

Johnson's efforts to restore the South stalled. Congress exercised its constitutional authority to deny seats to delegations from the South and launched an investigation into conditions there. In response to a Senate resolution requesting "information in relation to the States of the Union lately in rebellion," Johnson painted a rosy picture: "In 'that portion of the Union lately in rebellion' the aspect of affairs is more promising than, in view of all the circumstances, could well have been expected. The people throughout the entire south evince a laudable desire to renew their allegiance to the government, and to repair the devastations of war by a prompt and cheerful return to peaceful pursuits. An abiding faith is entertained that their actions will conform to their professions, and that, in acknowledging the supremacy of the Constitution and the laws of the United States, their loyalty will be unreservedly given to the government, whose leniency they cannot fail to appreciate, and whose fostering care will soon restore them to a condition of prosperity. It is true, that in some of the States the demoralizing effects of war are to be seen in occasional disorders, but these are local in character, not frequent in occurrence, and are rapidly disappearing as the authority of civil law is extended and sustained."

Johnson's message to the Senate was accompanied by a report from Major General Carl Schurz. Among the subjects on which Schurz reported were whether southern whites had accepted defeat and emancipation, and whether ex-slaves and southern Unionists were safe in the South and were receiving fair treatment. Schurz's report was apparently largely ignored by President Johnson, who had assigned him to make the report but was not happy with what he said.

Schurz went to considerable lengths to get an accurate reading of attitudes in the South. He tried to get a representative sample of people to interview in his three-month tour of portions of South Carolina, Georgia, Alabama, Mississippi, and Louisiana and gathered documentary evidence as well as interviews. Then he tried to analyze his findings carefully and make recommendations on the basis of those findings. Clearly, he believed that Reconstruction in the South involved more than the restoration of civil government.

Source: U.S. Congress, Senate, 39th Cong., 1st sess., 1865, Ex. Doc. No. 2, 1–5, 8, 36–39, 41–44.

SIR: . . . You informed me that your "policy of reconstruction" was merely experimental, and that you would change it if the experiment did not lead to satisfactory results. To aid you in forming your conclusions upon this point I understood to be the object of my mission, . . .

CONDITION OF THINGS IMMEDIATELY AFTER THE CLOSE OF THE WAR

In the development of the popular spirit in the south since the close of the war two well-marked periods can be distinguished. The first commences with the sudden collapse of the confederacy and the dispersion of its armies, and the second with the first proclamation indicating the "reconstruction policy" of the government. . . . When the news of Lee's and Johnston's surrenders burst upon the southern country the general consternation was extreme. People held their breath, indulging in the wildest apprehensions as to what was now to come. . . . Prominent Unionists told me that persons who for four years had scorned to recognize them on the street approached them with smiling faces and both hands extended. Men of standing in the political world expressed serious doubts as to whether the rebel States would ever again occupy their position as States in the Union, or be governed as conquered provinces. The public mind was so despondent that if readmission at some future time under whatever conditions had been promised, it would then have been looked upon as a favor. The most uncompromising rebels prepared for leaving the country. The masses remained in a state of fearful expectancy. . . .

Such was, according to the accounts I received, the character of that first period. The worst apprehensions were gradually relieved as day after day went by without bringing the disasters and inflictions which had been vaguely anticipated, until at last the appearance of the North Carolina proclamation substituted new hopes for them. The development of this second period I was called

upon to observe on the spot, and it forms the main subject of this report.

RETURNING LOYALTY

. . . [T]he white people at large being, under certain conditions, charged with taking the preliminaries of "reconstruction" into their hands, the success of the experiment depends upon the spirit and attitude of those who either attached themselves to the secession cause from the beginning, or, entertaining originally opposite views, at least followed its fortunes from the time that their States had declared their separation from the Union. . . .

I may group the southern people into four classes, each of which exercises an influence upon the development of things in that section:

1. Those who, although having yielded submission to the national government only when obliged to do so, have a clear perception of the irreversible changes produced by the war, and honestly endeavor to accommodate themselves to the new order of things. Many of them are not free from traditional prejudice but open to conviction, and may be expected to act in good faith whatever they do. This class is composed, in its majority, of persons of mature age—planters, merchants, and professional men; some of them are active in the reconstruction movement, but boldness and energy are, with a few individual exceptions, not among their distinguishing qualities.

2. Those whose principal object is to have the States without delay restored to their position and influence in the Union and the people of the States to the absolute control of their home concerns. They are ready, in order to attain that object, to make any ostensible concession that will not prevent them from arranging things to suit their taste as soon as that object is attained. This class comprises a considerable number, probably a large majority, of the professional politicians who are extremely active in the reconstruction movement. They are loud in their praise of

the President's reconstruction policy, and clamorous for the withdrawal of the federal troops and the abolition of the Freedmen's Bureau.

3. The incorrigibles, who still indulge in the swagger which was so customary before and during the war, and still hope for a time when the southern confederacy will achieve its independence. This class consists mostly of young men, and comprises the loiterers of the towns and the idlers of the country. They persecute Union men and negroes whenever they can do so with impunity, insist clamorously upon their "rights," and are extremely impatient of the presence of the federal soldiers. A good many of them have taken the oaths of allegiance and amnesty, and associated themselves with the second class in their political operations. This element is by no means unimportant; it is strong in numbers, deals in brave talk, addresses itself directly and incessantly to the passions and prejudices of the masses, and commands the admiration of the women.

4. The multitude of people who have no definite ideas about the circumstances under which they live and about the course they have to follow; whose intellects are weak, but whose prejudices and impulses are strong, and who are apt to be carried along by those who know how to appeal to the latter. . . .

FEELING TOWARDS THE SOLDIERS AND THE PEOPLE OF THE NORTH

. . . [U]pon the whole, the soldier of the Union is still looked upon as a stranger, an intruder—as the "Yankee," "the enemy." . . .

It is by no means surprising that prejudices and resentments, which for years were so assiduously cultivated and so violently inflamed, should not have been turned into affection by a defeat; nor are they likely to disappear as long as the southern people continue to brood over their losses and misfortunes. They will gradually subside when those who entertain them cut resolutely loose from the past and embark in a career of new activity on a common field with those whom they have so long considered their enemies. . . . [A]s long as these feelings exist in their present strength, they will hinder the growth of that reliable kind of loyalty which springs from the heart and clings to the country in good and evil fortune.

SITUATION OF UNIONISTS

. . . It struck me soon after my arrival in the south that the known Unionists—I mean those who during the war had been to a certain extent identified with the national cause—were not in communion with the leading social and political circles; and the further my observations extended the clearer it became to me that their existence in the south was of a rather precarious nature. . . . Even Governor [William L.] Sharkey, in the course of a conversation I had with him in the presence of Major General Osterhaus, ad-

mitted that, if our troops were then withdrawn, the lives of northern men in Mississippi would not be safe. . . . [General Osterhaus said]: "There is no doubt whatever that the state of affairs would be intolerable for all Union men, all recent immigrants from the north, and all negroes, the moment the protection of the United States troops were withdrawn." . . .

NEGRO INSURRECTIONS AND ANARCHY

. . . [I do] not deem a negro insurrection probable as long as the freedmen were assured of the direct protection of the national government. Whenever they are in trouble, they raise their eyes up to that power, and although they may suffer, yet, as long as that power is visibly present, they continue to hope. But when State authority in the south is fully restored, the federal forces withdrawn, and the Freedmen's Bureau abolished, the colored man will find himself turned over to the mercies of those whom he does not trust. If then an attempt is made to strip him again of those rights which he justly thought he possessed, he will be apt to feel that he can hope for no redress unless he procure it himself. If ever the negro is capable of rising, he will rise then. . . .

There is probably at the present moment no country in the civilized world which contains such an accumulation of anarchical elements as the south. The strife of the antagonistic tendencies here described is aggravated by the passions inflamed and the general impoverishment brought about by a long and exhaustive war, and the south will have to suffer the evils of anarchical disorder until means are found to effect a final settlement of the labor question in accordance with the logic of the great revolution.

THE TRUE PROBLEM—DIFFICULTIES AND REMEDIES

In seeking remedies for such disorders, we ought to keep in view, above all, the nature of the problem which is to be solved. As to what is commonly termed "reconstruction," it is not only the political machinery of the States and their constitutional relations to the general government, but the whole organism of southern society that must be reconstructed, or rather constructed anew, so as to bring it in harmony with the rest of American society. The difficulties of this task are not to be considered overcome when the people of the south take the oath of allegiance and elect governors and legislatures and members of Congress, and militia captains. That this would be done had become certain as soon as the surrenders of the southern armies had made further resistance impossible, and nothing in the world was left, even to the most uncompromising rebel, but to submit or to emigrate. It was also natural that they should avail themselves of every chance offered them to resume control of their home affairs and to regain their influence in the Union. But this can hardly be called the first step towards the solution of the true problem, and it is a fair question to ask, whether the hasty gratification of their desire to resume such control would not create new embarrassments.

The true nature of the difficulties of the situation is this: The general government of the republic has, by proclaiming the emancipation of the slaves, commenced a great social revolution in the south, but has, as yet, not completed it. Only the negative part of it is accomplished. The slaves are emancipated in point of form, but free labor has not yet been put in the place of slavery in point of fact. And now, in the midst of this critical period of transition, the power which originated the revolution is expected to turn over its whole future development to another power which from the beginning was hostile to it and has never yet entered into its spirit, leaving the class in whose favor it was made completely without power to protect itself and to take an influential part in that development. The history of the world will be searched in vain for a proceeding similar to this which did not lead either to a rapid and violent reaction, or to the most serious trouble and civil disorder. It cannot be said that the conduct of the southern people since the close of the war has exhibited such extraordinary wisdom and self-abnegation as to make them an exception to the rule.

In my despatches from the south I repeatedly expressed the opinion that the people were not yet in a frame of mind to legislate calmly and understandingly upon the subject of free negro labor. And this I reported to be the opinion of some of our most prominent military commanders and other observing men. It is, indeed, difficult to imagine circumstances more unfavorable for the development of a calm and unprejudiced public opinion than those under which the southern people are at present laboring. The war has not only defeated their political aspirations, but it has broken up their whole social organization. . . .

In which direction will these people be most apt to turn their eyes? Leaving the prejudice of race out of the question, from early youth they have been acquainted with but one system of labor, and with that one system they have been in the habit of identifying all their interests. They know of no way to help themselves but the one they are accustomed to. . . .

It is certain that every success of free negro labor will augment the number of its friends, and disarm some of the prejudices and assumptions of its opponents. I am convinced one good harvest made by unadulterated free labor in the south would have a far better effect than all the oaths that have been taken, and all the ordinances that have as yet been passed by southern conventions. But how can such a result be attained? The facts enumerated in this report, as well as the news we receive from the south from day to day, must make it evident to every unbiased observer that unadulterated free labor cannot be had at present, unless the national government holds its protective and controlling hand over it. . . . One reason why the southern people are so slow in accommodating themselves to the new order of things is, that they confidently expect soon to be permit-

ted to regulate matters according to their own notions. Every concession made to them by the government has been taken as an encouragement to persevere in this hope, and, unfortunately for them, this hope is nourished by influences from other parts of the country. Hence their anxiety to have their State governments restored *at once*, to have the troops withdrawn, and the Freedmen's Bureau abolished, although a good many discerning men know well that, in view of the lawless spirit still prevailing, it would be far better for them to have the general order of society firmly maintained by the federal power until things have arrived at a final settlement. Had, from the beginning, the conviction been forced upon them that the adulteration of the new order of things by the admixture of elements belonging to the system of slavery would under no circumstances be permitted, a much larger number would have launched their energies into the new channel, and, seeing that they could do "no better," faithfully co-operated with the government. It is hope which fixes them in their perverse notions. That hope nourished or fully gratified, they will persevere in the same direction. That hope destroyed, a great many will, by the force of necessity, at once accommodate themselves to the logic of the change. If, therefore, the national government firmly and unequivocally announces its policy not to give up the control of the free-labor reform until it is finally accomplished, the progress of that reform will undoubtedly be far more rapid and far less difficult than it will be if the attitude of the government is such as to permit contrary hopes to be indulged in. . . .

IMMIGRATION [AND CAPITAL]

[The south would benefit] from immigration of northern people and Europeans. . . . The south needs capital. But capital is notoriously timid and averse to risk. . . . Capitalists will be apt to consider—and they are by no means wrong in doing so—that no safe investments can be made in the south as long as southern society is liable to be convulsed by anarchical disorders. No greater encouragement can, therefore, be given to capital to transfer itself to the south than the assurance that the government will continue to control the development of the new social system in the late rebel States until such dangers are averted by a final settlement of things upon a thorough free-labor basis.

How long the national government should continue that control depends upon contingencies. It ought to cease as soon as its objects are attained; and its objects will be attained sooner and with less difficulty if nobody is permitted to indulge in the delusion that it will cease *before* they are attained. This is one of the cases in which a determined policy can accomplish much, while a half-way policy is liable to spoil things already accomplished. . . .

NEGRO SUFFRAGE

It would seem that the interference of the national authority in the home concerns of the southern States would be rendered less necessary, and the whole problem of political and social reconstruction be much simplified, if, while the masses lately arrayed against the government are permitted to vote, the large majority of those who were always loyal, and are naturally anxious to see the free labor problem successfully solved, were not excluded from all influence upon legislation. In all questions concerning the Union, the national debt, and the future social organization of the south, the feelings of the colored man are naturally in sympathy with the views and aims of the national government. While the southern white fought against the Union, the negro did all he could to aid it; while the southern white sees in the national government his conqueror, the negro sees in it his protector; while the white owes to the national debt his defeat, the negro owes to it his deliverance; while the white considers himself robbed and ruined by the emancipation of the slaves, the negro finds in it the assurance of future prosperity and happiness. In all the important issues the negro would be led by natural impulse to forward the ends of the government, and by making his influence, as part of the voting body, tell upon the legislation of the States, render the interference of the national authority less necessary.

As the most difficult of the pending questions are intimately connected with the status of the negro in southern society, it is obvious that a correct solution can be more easily obtained if he has a voice in the matter. In the right to vote he would find the best permanent protection against oppressive class-legislation, as well as against individual persecution. The relations between the white and black races, even if improved by the gradual wearing off of the present animosities, are likely to remain long under the troubling influence of prejudice. It is a notorious fact that the rights of a man of some political power are far less exposed to violation than those of one who is, in matters of public interest, completely subject to the will of others. . . .

In discussing the matter of negro suffrage I deemed it my duty to confine myself strictly to the practical aspects of the subject. I have, therefore, not touched its moral merits nor discussed the question whether the national government is competent to enlarge the elective franchise in the States lately in rebellion by its own act; I deem it proper, however, to offer a few remarks on the assertion frequently put forth, that the franchise is likely to be extended to the colored man by the voluntary action of the southern whites themselves. My observation leads me to a contrary opinion. Aside from a very few enlightened men, I found but one class of people in favor of the enfranchisement of the blacks: it was the class of Unionists who found themselves politically ostracised and looked upon the enfranchisement of the loyal negroes as the salvation of the whole loyal element. But their numbers and influence are sadly insufficient to secure such a result. The masses are strongly opposed to colored suffrage; anybody that dares to advocate it is stigmatized as a dangerous fanatic; nor do I deem it probable that in the ordinary course of things prejudices will wear off to such an extent as to make it a popular measure. . . .

DEPORTATION OF THE FREEDMEN

. . . [T]he true problem remains, not how to remove the colored man from his present field of labor, but how to make him, where he is, a true freeman and an intelligent and useful citizen. The means are simple: protection by the government until his political and social status enables him to protect himself, offering to his legitimate ambition the stimulant of a perfectly fair chance in life, and granting to him the rights which in every just organization of society are coupled with corresponding duties.

CONCLUSION

I may sum up all I have said in a few words. If nothing were necessary but to restore the machinery of government in the States lately in rebellion in point of form, the movements made to that end by the people of the south might be considered satisfactory. But if it is required that the southern people should also accommodate themselves to the results of the war in point of spirit, those movements fall far short of what must be insisted upon. . . .

Questions

1. Why did Schurz recommend keeping the Freedmen's Bureau and the army in the South? How did that differ from what Johnson wanted?

2. Why did Schurz suggest that it might be wise to give African Americans in the South the vote?

3. What does Schurz say about the Unionists in the South? About the emergence of a free labor system?

15-3   The Mississippi Black Codes (1865)

As Carl Schurz reported, after the Civil War whites in the South sought a system of race relations in which African Americans would be clearly subordinate to whites and would constitute a readily accessible and controllable work force (see text p. 479).

Immediately after the Civil War southern whites wrote or revised vagrancy laws and the old slave codes as a means of establishing the system of race relations they wanted. Below is one of their most famous attempts to codify race relations, the Black Codes passed by the Mississippi legislature.

The Mississippi codes gave blacks rights they had not had before and clearly acknowledged that chattel slavery had ended. The codes recognized the right of African Americans to own property, though not in incorporated towns or cities. (Before the Civil War there were black property owners in Mississippi and even a few black slaveholders, but their legal standing was not clear.) The 1865 codes also recognized marriages among blacks as legal.

Not all the southern states passed comprehensive Black Codes, and some codes were much less stringent than those of Mississippi. South Carolina's codes differed in that they restricted blacks to buying property in cities or towns.

The creators of the codes drew their ideas from the world in which they lived. Slavery had just ended very abruptly, and the ravages of war were ever present. The men who drafted these codes used the old slave codes from the South, vagrancy laws from the North and the South, laws for former slaves in the British West Indies, and antebellum laws for free blacks. They were also aware that most northern states had laws that discriminated against African Americans and that very few northern states allowed African Americans to vote.

Most of these codes and similar measures were declared void by the Union army officials who were stationed in the former Confederate states. Subsequently, during Reconstruction, the rights of African Americans were greatly expanded (see text pp. 484–485).

Source: Laws of Mississippi, 1865, pp. 82ff.

---

1.   CIVIL RIGHTS OF FREEDMEN IN MISSISSIPPI

... That all freedmen, free negroes, and mulattoes may sue and be sued ... may acquire personal property ... and may dispose of the same in the same manner and to the same extent that white persons may: [but no] freedman, free negro, or mulatto ... [shall] rent or lease any lands or tenements except in incorporated cities or towns, in which places the corporate authorities shall control the same. ...

All freedmen, free negroes, or mulattoes who do now and have herebefore lived and cohabited together as husband and wife shall be taken and held in law as legally married, and the issue shall be taken and held as legitimate for all purposes; that it shall not be lawful for any freedman, free negro, or mulatto to intermarry with any white person; nor for any white person to intermarry with any freedman, free negro, or mulatto; and any person who shall so intermarry, shall be deemed guilty of felony, and on conviction thereof shall be confined in the State peni-

tentiary for life; and those shall be deemed freedmen, free negroes, and mulattoes who are of pure negro blood, and those descended from a negro to the third generation, inclusive, though one ancestor in each generation may have been a white person. ...

[F]reedmen, free negroes, and mulattoes are now by law competent witnesses ... in civil cases [and in criminal cases where they are the victims]. ...

All contracts for labor made with freedmen, free negroes, and mulattoes for a longer period than one month shall be in writing, and in duplicate. ... and said contracts shall be taken and held as entire contracts, and if the laborer shall quit the service of the employer before the expiration of his term of service, without good cause, he shall forfeit his wages for that year up to the time of quitting.

... Every civil officer shall, and every person may, arrest and carry back to his or her legal employer any freedman, free negro, or mulatto who shall have quit the service of his or her employer before the expiration of his or term of service without good cause; and said officer and person shall be entitled to receive for arresting and carrying back every deserting employee aforesaid the sum of five dollars. . . .

. . . If any person shall persuade or attempt to persuade, entice, or cause any freedman, free negro, or mulatto to desert from the legal employment of any person before the expiration of his or her term of service, or shall knowingly employ any such deserting freedman, free negro, or mulatto, or shall knowingly give or sell to any such deserting freedman, free negro, or mulatto, any food, raiment, or other thing, he or she shall be guilty of a misdemeanor. . . .

2. MISSISSIPPI APPRENTICE LAW

. . . It shall be the duty of all sheriffs, justices of the peace, and other civil officers of the several counties in this State, to report to the probate courts of their respective counties semi-annually, at the January and July terms of said courts, all freedmen, free negroes, and mulattoes, under the age of eighteen, in their respective counties, beats or districts, who are orphans, or whose parent or parents have not the means or who refuse to provide for and support said minors; . . . the clerk of said court to apprentice said minors to some competent and suitable person, on such terms as the court may direct, having a particular care to the interest of said minor: *Provided*, that the former owner of said minors shall have the preference when, in the opinion of the court, he or she shall be a suitable person for that purpose. . . .

. . . In the management and control of said apprentice, said master or mistress shall have the power to inflict such moderate corporal chastisement as a father or guardian is allowed to inflict on his or her child or ward at common law: *Provided*, that in no case shall cruel or inhuman punishment be inflicted. . . .

3. MISSISSIPPI VAGRANT LAW

. . . That all rogues and vagabonds, idle and dissipated persons, beggars, jugglers, or persons practicing unlawful games or plays, runaways, common drunkards, common night-walkers, pilferers, lewd, wanton, or lascivious persons, in speech or behavior, common railers and brawlers, persons who neglect their calling or employment, misspend what they earn, or do not provide for the support of themselves or their families, or dependents, and all other idle and disorderly persons, including all who neglect all lawful business, habitually misspend their time by frequenting houses of ill-fame, gaming-houses, or tippling shops, shall be deemed and considered vagrants, under the provisions of this act, and upon conviction thereof shall be fined not exceeding one hundred dollars . . . and be imprisoned at the discretion of the court, not exceeding ten days.

. . . All freedmen, free negroes and mulattoes in this State, over the age of eighteen years, found on the second Monday in January, 1866, or thereafter, with no lawful employment or business, or found unlawfully assembling themselves together, either in the day or night time, and all white persons so assembling themselves with freedmen, free negroes or mulattoes, or usually associating with freedmen, free negroes or mulattoes, on terms of equality, or living in adultery or fornication with a freed woman, free negro or mulatto, shall be deemed vagrants, and on conviction thereof shall be fined in a sum not exceeding, in the case of a freedman, free negro or mulatto, fifty dollars, and a white man two hundred dollars, and imprisoned at the discretion of the court, the free negro not exceeding ten days, and the white man not exceeding six months. . . .

4. PENAL LAWS OF MISSISSIPPI

. . . That no freedman, free negro or mulatto, not in the military service of the United States government, and not licensed so to do by the board of police of his or her county, shall keep or carry fire-arms of any kind, or any ammunition, dirk or bowie knife. . . .

. . . Any freedman, free negro, or mulatto committing riots, routs, affrays, trespasses, malicious mischief, cruel treatment to animals, seditious speeches, insulting gestures, language, or acts, or assaults on any person, disturbance of the peace, exercising the function of a minister of the Gospel without a license from some regularly organized church, vending spirituous or intoxicating liquors, or committing any other misdemeanor, the punishment of which is not specifically provided for by law, shall, upon conviction thereof in the county court, be fined not less than ten dollars, and not more than one hundred dollars, and may be imprisoned at the discretion of the court, not exceeding thirty days. . . .

. . . If any freedman, free negro, or mulatto, convicted of any of the misdemeanors provided against in this act, shall fail or refuse for the space of five days, after conviction, to pay the fine and costs imposed, such person shall be hired out by the sheriff or other officer, at public outcry, to any white person who will pay said fine and all costs, and take said convict for the shortest time.

Questions

1. What was the intent of these laws?
2. Who was charged with enforcing them? ("Every civil officer shall, and every person may, arrest and carry back to his or her legal employer. . . .") Who was considered a "person"? Who was not a "person"?
3. How were vagrants defined? Were these laws based on the assumption that the only vagrants were African Americans? What restrictions were placed on the freedom of expression of African Americans? What restrictions were placed on their freedom of association? On whites in Mississippi?

15-4   The Civil Rights Act of 1866

When Congress reconvened in December 1865, it blocked President Johnson's attempts to restore the South quickly. It extended the life of the Freedmen's Bureau over the president's veto and passed another landmark law, the Civil Rights Act of 1866, again over the president's veto (see text p. 484). This act made African Americans citizens and countered the 1857 *Dred Scott* decision, in which the Supreme Court had declared that no African American who was descended from a slave was or could ever be a citizen.

Doubts about the constitutionality and permanence of the Civil Rights Act of 1866 prompted Congress to pass the Fourteenth Amendment (see text pp. 484–485 and D-17). Ratified in 1868, this amendment for the first time constitutionally defined citizenship and some of the basic rights of citizenship; it also embraced the Republican program for Reconstruction.

Source: U.S. Statutes at Large, 14 (1868?), 27ff.

An Act to protect all Persons in the United States in their Civil Rights, and furnish the Means of their Vindication.

Be it enacted, That all persons born in the United States and not subject to any foreign power, excluding Indians not taxed, are hereby declared to be citizens of the United States; and such citizens, of every race and color, without regard to any previous condition of slavery or involuntary servitude, except as a punishment for crime whereof the party shall have been duly convicted, shall have the same right, in every State and Territory in the United States, to make and enforce contracts, to sue, be parties, and give evidence, to inherit, purchase, lease, sell, hold, and convey real and personal property, and to full and equal benefit of all laws and proceedings for the security of person and property, as is enjoyed by white citizens, and shall be subject to like punishment, pains, and penalties, and to none other, any law, statute, ordinance, regulation, or custom, to the contrary notwithstanding. SEC. 2. *And be it further enacted,* That any person who, under color of any law, statute, ordinance, regula-

tion, or custom, shall subject, or cause to be subjected, any inhabitant of any State or Territory to the deprivation of any right secured or protected by this act, or to different punishment, pains, or penalties on account of such person having at any time been held in a condition of slavery or involuntary servitude, except as a punishment for crime whereof the party shall have been duly convicted, or by reason of his color or race, than is prescribed for the punishment of white persons, shall be deemed guilty of a misdemeanor, and, on conviction, shall be punished by fine not exceeding one thousand dollars, or imprisonment not exceeding one year, or both, in the discretion of the court. SEC. 3. *And be it further enacted,* That the district courts of the United States, . . . shall have, exclusively of the courts of the several States, cognizance of all crimes and offences committed against the provisions of this act, and also, concurrently with the circuit courts of the United States, of all causes, civil and criminal, affecting persons who are denied or cannot enforce in the courts or judicial tribunals of the State or locality where they may be any of the rights secured to them by the first section of this act. . . .

SEC. 4. *And be it further enacted,* That the district attorneys, marshals, and deputy marshals of the United States, the commissioners appointed by the circuit and territorial courts of the United States, with powers of arresting, imprisoning, or bailing offenders against the laws of the United States, the officers and agents of the Freedmen's Bureau, and every other officer who may be specially empowered by the President of the United States, shall be, and they are hereby, specially authorized and required, at the expense of the United States, to institute proceedings against all and every person who shall violate the provisions of this act, and cause him or them to be arrested and imprisoned, or bailed, as the case may be, for trial before such court of the United States or territorial court as by this act has cognizance of the offence. . . .

SEC. 8. *And be it further enacted,* That whenever the President of the United States shall have reason to believe that offences have been or are likely to be committed against the provisions of this act within any judicial district, it shall be lawful for him, in his discretion, to direct the judge, marshal, and district attorney of such district to attend at such place within the district, and for such time as he may designate, for the purpose of the more speedy arrest and trial of persons charged with a violation of this act; and it shall be the duty of every judge or other officer, when any such requisition shall be received by him, to attend at the place and for the time therein designated.

SEC. 9. *And be it further enacted,* That it shall be lawful for the President of the United States, or such person as he may empower for that purpose, to employ such part of the land or naval forces of the United States, or of the militia, as shall be necessary to prevent the violation and enforce the due execution of this act.

SEC. 10. *And be it further enacted,* That upon all questions of law arising in any cause under the provisions of this act a final appeal may be taken to the Supreme Court of the United States.

Questions

1. What was the intent of the Civil Rights Act?
2. Who was responsible for enforcing this law, and what powers might they use? Was it necessary to wait until the law was violated before officers of the law could act?
3. According to the Fourteenth Amendment, who is a citizen of the United States? What rights does the amendment say citizens have? What does "equal protection of the laws" mean?

Questions for Further Thought

1. Compare and contrast President Johnson's description of conditions in the South (Document 15-1) with that of General Schurz (Document 15-2). Which do you find to be more accurate? Why?
2. What did Johnson and Schurz say about relations between blacks and whites?
3. Compare the Mississippi Black Codes (Document 15-3) with the Civil Rights Act of 1866 (Document 15-4). Why do you think Congress believed that it had to pass the Civil Rights Act and then adopt the Fourteenth Amendment?

Radical Reconstruction

When only Tennessee ratified the Fourteenth Amendment (and was readmitted to the Union), Congressional Republicans, strengthened by their victories in the 1866 congressional elections, passed the Reconstruction Acts. These laws forced unreconstructed former Confederate states to meet Republican conditions for readmission, including granting African American men the vote. While these measures were called radical by their detractors (and this phase of Reconstruction referred to as "radical Reconstruction"), these measures actually fell far short of what some in Congress desired

(Document 15-5). They fell even further short of the hopes of women's rights advocates that the vote might be extended to them as well as blacks—a frustration that seriously split the movement, but led ultimately to the creation of a new, and ultimately successful, woman suffrage movement (Document 15-6).

During Reconstruction African Americans obtained a number of civil and political rights, most especially in the realm of politics. While no former Confederate state was controlled by blacks, a large group of African American politicians surged into prominence, seeking to use government power to help constituents who previously had not even been regarded as citizens (Document 15-7). While many of these new political rights were lost in the years following Reconstruction, other gains, especially in social and economic realms, were more enduring. At the insistence of the freed slaves, planters dismantled much of the old slave regime, replacing gang labor and the old slave quarters with a new system of individual plots worked by families for shares of the crops. Black marriages were formalized, and African Americans gained control over their family lives. They pursued education, built new institutions such as the black church, and began to acquire property. While white racism and white landlord power raised enormous barriers to black advancement, through the years increasing (though still small) numbers of African Americans became property holders (Document 15-8).

15-5   Black Suffrage and Land Redistribution (1867)

Thaddeus Stevens

The Radical Republicans, including Congressman Thaddeus Stevens of Pennsylvania, believed that besides the vote, freedmen would need an economic basis for controlling their lives (see text pp. 485–486). Below are excerpts from the remarks of Thaddeus Stevens and from a bill in which he proposed to alter the South drastically.

Source: Congressional Globe, 3 January 1867, 252; 19 March 1867, 203.

ON BLACK SUFFRAGE

Unless the rebel States, before admission, should be made republican in spirit, and placed under the guardianship of loyal men, all our blood and treasure will have been spent in vain. I waive now the question of punishment which, if we are wise, will still be inflicted by moderate confiscations. . . . Impartial suffrage, both in electing the delegates and ratifying their proceedings, is now the fixed rule. There is more reason why colored voters should be admitted in the rebel States than in the Territories. In the States they form the great mass of the loyal men. Possibly with their aid loyal governments may be established in most of those States. Without it all are sure to be ruled by traitors; and loyal men, black and white, will be oppressed, exiled, or murdered. There are several good reasons for the passage of this bill. In the first place, it is just. I am now confining my argument to negro suffrage in the rebel States. Have not loyal blacks quite as good a right to choose rulers and make laws as rebel whites? In the second place,

it is a necessity in order to protect the loyal white men in the seceded States. The white Union men are in a great minority in each of those States. With them the blacks would act in a body; and it is believed that in each of said States, except one, the two united would form a majority, control the States, and protect themselves. Now they are the victims of daily murder. . . .

Another good reason is, it would insure the ascendency of the Union party. . . . I believe . . . that on the continued ascendency of that party depends the safety of this great nation. If impartial suffrage is excluded in the rebel States, then every one of them is sure to send a solid rebel representative delegation to Congress, and cast a solid rebel electoral vote. They, with their kindred Copperheads of the North, would always elect the President and control Congress. While slavery sat upon her defiant throne, and insulted and intimidated the trembling North, the South frequently divided on questions of policy between Whigs and Democrats, and gave victory alternately to the sections. Now, you must divide them between loyalists, without regard to color, and disloyalists, or you will be the perpetual vassals of the free-trade, irritated, revengeful South. . . . I am for negro suffrage in every rebel State. If it be just, it should not be denied; if it be necessary, it should be adopted; if it be a punishment to traitors, they deserve it.

BILL ON LAND REDISTRIBUTION

Whereas it is due to justice, as an example to future times, that some proper punishment should be inflicted on the people who constituted the "confederate States of America," both because they, declaring an unjust war against the United States for the purpose of destroying republican liberty and permanently establishing slavery, as well as for the cruel and barbarous manner in which they conducted said war, in violation of all the laws of civilized warfare, and also to compel them to make some compensation for the damages and expenditures caused by said war: Therefore,

Be it enacted by the Senate and House of Representatives of the United States of America in Congress assembled, That all the public lands belonging to the ten States that formed the government of the so-called "confederate States of America" shall be forfeited by said States and become forthwith vested in the United States. . . .

That out of the lands thus seized and confiscated the slaves who have been liberated by the operations of the war and the amendment to the Constitution or otherwise, who resided in said "confederate States" on the 4th day of March, A.D. 1861, or since, shall have distributed to them as follows, namely: to each male person who is the head of a family, forty acres; to each adult male, whether the head of a family or not, forty acres; to each widow who is the head of a family, forty acres—to be held by them in fee-simple, but to be inalienable for the next ten years after they become seized thereof. . . .

That out of the balance of the property thus seized and confiscated there shall be raised, in the manner hereinafter provided, a sum equal to fifty dollars, for each homestead, to be applied by the trustees hereinafter mentioned toward the erection of buildings on the said homesteads for the use of said slaves; and the further sum of $500,000,000, which shall be appropriated as follows, to wit: $200,000,000 shall be invested in United States six per cent securities; and the interest thereof shall be semi-annually added to the pensions allowed by law to pensioners who have become so by reason of the late war; $300,000,000, or so much thereof as may be needed, shall be appropriated to pay damages done to loyal citizens by the civil or military operations of the government lately called the "confederate States of America." . . .

That in order that just discrimination may be made, the property of no one shall be seized whose whole estate on the 4th day of March, A.D. 1865, was not worth more than $5,000, to be valued by the said commission, unless he shall have voluntarily become an officer or employé in the military or civil service of the "confederate States of America," or in the civil or military service of some one of said States. . . .

Questions

1. On what grounds did Stevens justify granting African American men the vote?
2. What did Stevens want to do with land confiscated in the South?
3. Why do you think Congress rejected Stevens's land confiscation and redistribution proposal? Do you think that if Congress had adopted the proposal, it would have made a difference in the history of the South or the United States? Why or why not?

15-6 The Fourteenth Amendment and Woman Suffrage (1873, 1875)

As noted in the text (p. 488), not only did the Fourteenth and Fifteenth amendments ignore the demands of the women's rights movement for equal access to the ballot box, but the Fourteenth Amendment introduced the word "male" for the first time into the U.S. Constitution. Nonetheless, many suffragists continued to believe that the newly formalized and broadened definition of American citizenship established by the Fourteenth Amendment could be used to gain women the vote through a judicial ruling. In 1872 a number of suffragists, including Susan B. Anthony, voted in the presidential election; Anthony was indicted and brought to trial, providing her the opportunity she sought to make her case (Document 15-6a). Anthony was blocked from making her appeal, but another suffragist, Virginia Minor of Missouri, sued the official who blocked her from the ballot box and saw her case reach the Supreme Court. The Court's decision (Document 15-6b), handed down in 1875, effectively ended all hopes that gender relations as well as race relations had been "reconstructed" by the Fourteenth Amendment, and strengthened the movement for a constitutional woman suffrage amendment. Furthermore, by effectively separating the right to vote from fundamental citizenship rights, the Court also helped set the stage for the later movement to use "color-blind" laws to disfranchise African Americans.

Sources: Ruth Barnes Moynihan, Cynthia Russett, and Laurie Crumpacker, eds., *Second to None: A Documentary History of American Women* (Lincoln: University of Nebraska Press, 1993), 2: 16–19; *Minor v. Happersett,* 88 U.S. 162, in Linda Kerber and Jane Sherron DeHart, eds., *Women's America: Refocusing the Past,* 5th ed. (New York: Oxford University Press, 2000), 245–246.

(a) I Stand Before You Under Indictment (1873)

Friends and Fellow-Citizens:—I stand before you under indictment for the alleged crime of having voted at the last presidential election, without having a lawful right to vote. It shall be my work this evening to prove to you that in thus doing, I not only committed no crime, but instead simply exercised my citizen's right, guaranteed to me and all United States citizens by the National Constitution beyond the power of any State to deny.

Our democratic-republican government is based on the idea of the natural right of every individual member thereof to a voice and a vote in making and executing the laws. We assert the province of government to be to secure the people in the enjoyment of their inalienable rights. We throw to the winds the old dogma that government can give rights. No one denies that before governments were organized each individual possessed the right to protect his own life, liberty and property. When 100 or 1,000,000 people enter into a free government, they do not barter away their natural rights; they simply pledge themselves to protect each other in the enjoyment of them through prescribed judicial and legislative tribunals. They agree to abandon the methods of brute force in the adjustment of their differences and adopt those of civilization. Nor can you find a word in any of the grand documents left us by the fathers which assumes for government the power to create or to confer rights. The Declaration of Independence, the United States Constitution, the constitutions of the several States and the organic laws of the Territories, all alike propose to *protect* the people in the exercise of their God-given rights. Not one of them pretends to bestow rights.

All men are created equal, and endowed by their Creator with certain inalienable rights. Among these are life, liberty and the pursuit of happiness. To secure these, governments are instituted among men, deriving their just powers from the consent of the governed.

Here is no shadow of government authority over rights, or exclusion of any class from their full and equal enjoyment. Here is pronounced the right of all men, and "consequently," as the Quaker preacher said, "of all women," to a voice in the government. And here, in this first paragraph of the Declaration, is the assertion of the natural right of all to the ballot; for how can "the consent of the governed" be given, if the right to vote be denied? Again:

Whenever any form of government becomes destructive of these ends, it is the right of the people to alter or abolish it, and to institute a new government, laying its foundations on such principles, and organizing its powers in such form, as to them shall seem most likely to effect their safety and happiness.

Surely the right of the whole people to vote is here clearly implied; for however destructive to their happiness this government might become, a disfranchised class could neither alter nor abolish it, nor institute a new one, except by the old brute force method of insurrection and rebellion. One-half of the people of this nation today are utterly powerless to blot from the statute books an unjust law, or to write there a new and just one. The women, dissatisfied as they are with this form of government, that enforces taxation without representation—that compels them to obey laws to which they never have given their consent—that imprisons and hangs them without a trial by a jury of their peers—that robs them, in marriage, of the custody of their own persons, wages and children—are this half of the people who are left wholly at the mercy of the other half, in direct violation of the spirit and letter of the declarations of the framers of this government, every one of which was based on the immutable principle of equal rights to all. By these declarations, kings, popes, priests, aristocrats, all were alike dethroned and placed on a common level, politically, with the lowliest born subject or serf. By them, too, men, as such, were deprived of their divine right to rule and placed on a political level with women. By the practice of these declarations all class and caste distinctions would be abolished, and slave, serf, plebeian, wife, woman, all alike rise from their subject position to the broader platform of equality.

The preamble of the Federal Constitution says:

We, the people of the United States, in order to form a more perfect union, establish justice, insure domestic tranquillity, provide for the common defence, promote the general welfare and secure the blessings of liberty to ourselves and our posterity, do ordain and establish this Constitution for the United States of America.

It was we, the people, not we, the white male citizens, nor we, the male citizens; but we, the whole people, who formed this Union. We formed it not to give the blessings of liberty but to secure them; not to the half of ourselves and the half of our posterity, but to the whole people—women as well as men. It is downright mockery to talk to women of their enjoyment of the blessings of liberty while they are denied the only means of securing them provided by this democratic-republican government—the ballot. . . .

For any State to make sex a qualification, which must ever result in the disfranchisement of one entire half of the people, is to pass a bill of attainder, an ex post facto law, and is therefore a violation of the supreme law of the land. By it the blessings of liberty are forever withheld from women and their female posterity. For them, this government has no just powers derived from the consent of the governed. For them this government is not a democracy; it is not a republic. It is the most odious aristocracy ever established on the face of the globe. An oligarchy of wealth, where the rich govern the poor; an oligarchy of learning, where the educated govern the ignorant; or even an oligarchy of race, where the Saxon rules the African, might be endured; but this oligarchy of sex which makes father, brothers, husband, sons, the oligarchs over the mother and sisters, the wife and daughters of every household; which ordains all men sovereigns, all women subjects—carries discord and rebellion into every home of the nation. . . . The moment you deprive a person of his right to a voice in the government, you degrade him from the status of a citizen of the republic to that of a subject. It matters very little to him whether his monarch be an individual tyrant, as is the Czar of Russia, or a 15,000,000 headed monster, as here in the United States; he is a powerless subject, serf or slave; not in any sense a free and independent citizen. . . .

Though the words persons, people, inhabitants, electors, citizens, are all used indiscriminately in the national and State constitutions, there was always a conflict of opinion, prior to the war, as to whether they were synonymous terms, but whatever room there was for doubt, under the old regime, the adoption of the Fourteenth Amendment settled that question forever in its first sentence:

All persons born or naturalized in the United States, and subject to the jurisdiction thereof, are citizens of the United States, and of the State wherein they reside.

The second settles the equal status of all citizens:

No State shall make or enforce any law which shall abridge the privileges or immunities of citizens of the United States; nor shall any State deprive any person of life, liberty or property without due process of law, or deny to any person within its jurisdiction the equal protection of the laws.

The only question left to be settled now is: Are women persons? I scarcely believe any of our opponents will have the hardihood to say they are not. Being persons, then, women are citizens, and no State has a right to make any new law, or to enforce any old law, which shall abridge their privileges or immunities. Hence, every discrimination against women in the constitutions and laws of the several States is today null and void, precisely as is every one against negroes.

Is the right to vote one of the privileges or immunities of citizens? I think the disfranchised ex-rebels and ex-State prisoners all will agree that it is not only one of them, but the one without which all the others are nothing. Seek first the kingdom of the ballot and all things else shall be added, is the political injunction. . . .

If once we establish the false principle that United States citizenship does not carry with it the right to vote in every State in this Union, there is no end to the petty tricks and cunning devices which will be attempted to exclude one and another class of citizens from the right of suffrage. It will not always be the men combining to disfranchise all women; native born men combining to abridge the rights of all naturalized citizens, as in Rhode Island. It will not always be the rich and educated who may combine to cut off the poor and ignorant; but we may live to see the hardworking, uncultivated day laborers, foreign and native born, learning the power of the ballot and their vast majority of numbers, combine and amend State constitutions so as to disfranchise the Vanderbilts, the Stewarts, the Conklings and the Fentons. It is a poor rule that won't work more ways than one. Establish this precedent, admit the State's right to deny suffrage, and there is no limit to the confusion, discord, and disruption that may await us. There is and can be but one safe principle of government—equal rights to all. Discrimination against any class on account of color, race, nativity, sex, property, culture, can but embitter and disaffect that class, and thereby endanger the safety of the whole people. Clearly, then, the national government not only must define the rights of citizens, but must stretch out its powerful hand and protect them in every State of this Union.

(b) *Minor v. Happersett* (1875)

MR. CHIEF JUSTICE MORRISON R. WAITE DELIVERED THE OPINION OF THE COURT:

The question is presented in this case, whether, since the adoption of the fourteenth amendment, a woman, who is a citizen of the United States and of the State of Missouri, is a voter in that State, notwithstanding the provision of the constitution and laws of the State, which confine the right of suffrage to men alone. . . . The argument is, that as a woman, born or naturalized in the United States and subject to the jurisdiction thereof, is a citizen of the United States and of the State in which she resides, she has the right of suffrage as one of the privileges and immunities of her citizenship, which the State cannot by its laws or constitution abridge.

There is no doubt that women may be citizens. They are persons, and by the fourteenth amendment "all persons born or naturalized in the United States and subject to the jurisdiction thereof" are expressly declared to be "citizens of the United States and of the State wherein they reside." But, in our opinion, it did not need this amendment to give them that position . . . sex has never been made one of the elements of citizenship in the United States. In this respect men have never had an advantage over women. The same laws precisely apply to both. The fourteenth amendment did not affect the citizenship of women any more than it did of men . . . Mrs. Minor . . . has always been a citizen from her birth, and entitled to all the privileges and immunities of citizenship.

If the right of suffrage is one of the necessary privileges of a citizen of the United States, then the constitution and laws of Missouri confining it to men are in violation of the Constitution of the United States, as amended, and conse-

quently void. The direction question is, therefore, presented whether all citizens are necessarily voters.

The Constitution does not define the privileges and immunities of citizens. For that definition we must look elsewhere. In this case we need not determine what they are, but only whether suffrage is necessarily one of them.

It certainly is nowhere made so in express terms. The United States has no voters in the States of its own creation. The elective officers of the United States are all elected directly or indirectly by state voters. . . . it cannot for a moment be doubted that if it had been intended to make all citizens of the United States voters, the framers of the Constitution would not have left it to implication. . . .

It is true that the United States guarantees to every State a republican form of government. . . . No particular government is designated as republican, neither is the exact form to be guaranteed, in any manner especially designated. . . . When the Constitution was adopted . . . all the citizens of the States were not invested with the right of suffrage. In all, save perhaps New Jersey, this right was only bestowed upon men and not upon all of them. . . . Under these circumstances it is certainly now too late to contend that a government is not republican, within the meaning of this guaranty in the Constitution, because women are not made voters. . . . If suffrage was intended to be included within its obligations, language better adapted to express that intent would most certainly have been employed. . . .

. . . For nearly ninety years the people have acted upon the idea that the Constitution, when it conferred citizenship, did not necessarily confer the right of suffrage. If uniform practice long continued can settle the construction of so important an instrument as the Constitution of the United States confessedly is, most certainly it has been done here. Our province is to decide what the law is, not to declare what it should be.

We have given this case the careful consideration its importance demands. If the law is wrong, it ought to be changed; but the power for that is not with us. . . . No argument as to woman's need of suffrage can be considered. We can only act upon her rights as they exist. . . .

Questions

1. What case does Anthony make for treating voting as an "inalienable right"?
2. What does Anthony see as the consequence of denying that the right to vote is intrinsic to citizenship? Is her view prophetic?
3. Compare the reasoning of Anthony and of Chief Justice Waite on the question of whether the right to vote is one of the "privileges and immunities" of citizenship. What sorts of evidence do they cite?

15-7　An Advocate of Federal Aid for Land Purchase (1868)

Richard H. Cain

With the enactment of the Reconstruction Act of 1867, the cast of political leadership in the South dramatically changed. One good example of the new men rising to prominence was Richard H. Cain (1825–1887). Born in Virginia of African American and Cherokee parents, Cain was raised in Ohio, attending Wilberforce University and becoming a minister in the African Methodist Episcopal (A.M.E.) Church. After spending the Civil War as pastor of a Brooklyn church, he went south in 1865 as a missionary; reorganizing the Emmanuel A.M.E. Church of Charleston, South Carolina, Cain built it into the largest A.M.E. congregation in the state and used it as a political base. He was a delegate to the South Carolina constitutional convention of 1868; served as a state senator from 1868 to 1870; unsuccessfully sought the Republican nomination for lieutenant governor in 1872; and served in the U.S. House of Representatives from 1873 to 1875 and again from 1877 to 1879. Cain left South Carolina in 1880 and spent the remainder of his life as a bishop and college president in the A.M.E. Church.

Like many successful African American preachers, Cain was an astute businessman, eager to lend his services to build up the black community. Like many other black politicians, he saw the issue of land for the freedmen as paramount. An early advocate of redistribution of confiscated lands à la Thaddeus Stevens (Document 15-5), at the constitutional convention Cain advocated petitioning the federal government to appropriate $1 million to finance land purchases by the freedmen. When his proposal was attacked by C. P. Leslie, a white Republican delegate, Cain defended it with the following remarks.

Source: Proceedings of the Constitutional Convention of South Carolina (Charleston: Denny and Perry, 1868), 378–382.

. . . Mr. CAIN. I offer this resolution with good intentions. I believe there is need of immediate relief to the poor people of the State. I know from my experience among the people, there is pressing need of some measures to meet the wants of the utterly destitute. The gentleman says it will only take money out of the Treasury. Well that is the intention. I do not expect to get it anywhere else. I expect to get the money, if at all, through the Treasury of the United States, or some other department. It certainly must come out of the Government. I believe such an appropriation would remove a great many of the difficulties now in the State and do a vast amount of good to poor people. It may be that we will not get it, but that will not debar us from asking. It is our privilege and right. Other Conventions have asked from Congress appropriations. Georgia and other States have sent in their petitions. One has asked for $30,000,000 to be appropriated to the Southern States. I do not see any inconsistency in the proposition presented by myself.

Mr. C. P. LESLIE. Suppose I should button up my coat and march up to your house and ask you for money or provisions, when you had none to give, what would you think of me?

Mr. CAIN. You would do perfectly right to run the chance of getting something to eat. This is a measure of relief to those thousands of freed people who now have no lands of their own. I believe the possession of lands and homesteads is one of the best means by which a people is made industrious, honest and advantageous to the State. I believe it is a fact well known, that over three hundred thousand men, women and children are homeless, landless. The abolition of slavery has thrown these people upon their own resources. How are they to live? I know the philosopher of the New York *Tribune* says, "root hog or die;" but in the meantime we ought to have some place to root. My proposition is simply to give the hog some place to root. I believe if the proposition is sent to Congress, it will certainly receive the attention of our friends. I believe the whole country is desirous to see that this State shall return to the Union in peace and quiet, and that every inhabitant of the State shall be made industrious and profitable to the State. I am opposed to this Bureau system. I want a system adopted that will do away with the Bureau, but I cannot see how it can be done unless the people have homes. As long as people are working on shares and contracts, and at the end of every year are in debt, so long will they and the country suffer. But give them a chance to buy lands, and they become steady, industrious men. That is the reason I desire to bring this money here and to assist them to buy lands. It will be the means of encouraging them to industry if the petition be granted by Congress. It will be the means of meeting one of the great wants of the present among the poor. It will lay the foundation for the future prosperity of the country as no other measure will at this time, because it will bring about a reconciliation in the minds of thousands of these helpless people, which nothing else can. This measure, if carried out, will bring capital to the State and stimulate the poor to renewed efforts in life, such as they never had before. Such a measure will give to the landholders relief from their embarrassments financially, and enable them to get fair compensation for their lands. It will relieve the Government of the responsibility of taking care of the thousands who now are fed at the Commissaries and fostered in laziness. I have gone through the country and on every side I was besieged with questions: How are we to get homesteads, to get lands? I desire to devise some plan, or adopt some measure by which we can dissipate one of the arguments used against us, that the African race will not work. I do not believe the black man hates work any more than the white man does. Give these men a place to work, and I will guarantee before one year passes, there will be no necessity for the Freedman's Bureau, or any measure aside from those measures which a people may make in protecting themselves.

But a people without homes become wanderers. If they possess lands they have an interest in the soil, in the State, in its commerce, its agriculture, and in everything pertaining to the wealth and welfare of the State. If these people had homes along the lines of railroads, and the lands were divided and sold in small farms, I will guarantee our railroads will make fifty times as much money, banking systems will be advanced by virtue of the settlement of the people throughout the whole State. We want these large tracts of land cut up. The land is productive, and there is nothing to prevent the greatest and highest prosperity. What we need is a system of small farms. Every farmer owning his own land will feel he is in possession of something. It will have a tendency to settle the minds of the people in the State and settle many difficulties. In the rural districts now there is constant discontent, constant misapprehension between the parties, a constant disregard for each other. One man won't make an engagement to work, because he fears if he makes a contract this year, he will be cheated again as he thinks he was last year. We have had petitions from planters asking the Convention to disabuse the minds of the freedmen of the thought that this Convention has any lands at its disposal, but I do desire this Convention to do something at least to relieve the wants of these poor suffering people. I believe this measure, if adopted and sent to Congress, will indicate to the people that this Convention does desire they shall possess homes and have relief.

Some of my friends say that the sum is too small, and ask why I do not make it more. I made it a million, because I thought there would be more probability of getting one

million than five. It might be put into the hands of the Bureau, and I am willing to trust the Bureau. . . .

I do not desire to have a foot of land in this State confiscated. I want every man to stand upon his own character. I want these lands purchased by the government, and the people afforded an opportunity to buy from the government. I believe every man ought to carve out for himself a character and position in this life. I believe every man ought to be made to work by some means or other, and if he does not, he must go down. I believe if the same amount of money that has been employed by the Bureau in feeding lazy, worthless men and women, had been expended in purchasing lands, we would to-day have no need of the Bureau. Millions upon millions have been expended, and it is still going on *ad infinitum*. I propose to let the poor people buy these lands, the government to be paid back in five years time. It is one of the great cries of the enemies of reconstruction, that Congress has constantly fostered laziness. I want to have the satisfaction of showing that the freedmen are as capable and willing to work as any men on the face of the earth. This measure will save the State untold expenses. I believe there are hundreds of persons in the jail and penitentiary cracking rock to-day who have all the instincts of honesty, and who, had they an opportunity of making a living, would never have been found in such a place. I think if Congress will accede to our request, we shall be benefited beyond measure, and save the State from taking charge of paupers, made such by not having the means to earn a living for themselves.

I can look to a part of my constituency, men in this hall, mechanics, plasterers, carpenters, engineers, men capable of doing all kind of work, now idle because they cannot find any work in the city. Poverty stares them in the face, and their children are in want. They go to the cotton houses, but can find no labor. They are men whose honesty and integrity has never been called in question. They are suffering in consequence of the poverty-stricken condition of the city and State. I believe the best measure is to open a field where they can labor, where they can take the hoe and the axe, cut down the forest, and make the whole land blossom as the Garden of Eden, and prosperity pervade the whole land.

Now, the report of Major General Howard gives a surplus of over seven millions in the Freedman's Bureau last year. Out of that seven millions I propose we ask Congress to make an appropriation of one million, which will be properly distributed and then leave several millions in that Department, my friend from Barnwell notwithstanding.

I think there could be no better measure for this Convention to urge upon Congress. If that body should listen to our appeal, I have no doubt we shall be benefited. This measure of relief, it seems to me, would come swiftly. It is a swift messenger that comes in a week's time after it is passed; so that in the month of February or March the people may be enabled to go to planting and raising crops for the ensuing year. One gentleman says it will take six months or a year, but I hope, with the assistance of the Government, we could accomplish it in less time.

Mr. C. P. LESLIE. Did you ever see the Government do anything quick?

Mr. R. H. CAIN. They make taxes come quick. If this measure is carried out, the results will be that we will see all along our lines of railroad and State roads little farms, log cabins filled with happy families, and thousands of families coming on the railroads with their products. There will also spring up depots for the reception of cotton, corn and all other cereals. Prosperity will return to the State, by virtue of the people being happy, bound to the Government by a tie that cannot be broken. The taxes, that are so heavy now that men are compelled to sell their horses, will be lightened. I want to see the State alive, to hear the hum of the spindle and the mills! I want to see cattle and horses, and fowls, and everything that makes up a happy home and family. I want to see the people shout with joy and gladness. There shall then be no antagonism between white men and black men, but we shall all realize the end of our being, and realize that we are all made to dwell upon the earth in peace and happiness. The white man and the black man may then work in harmony, and secure prosperity to all coming generations. . . .

Questions

1. What arguments does Cain make in favor of his proposal? To what present policies, especially of the Freedmen's Bureau, does he object?
2. In certain respects, Cain's proposal can be characterized as *conservative*. How? Would you agree, or not?
3. How would you characterize Cain's intentions toward the *whites* of South Carolina?

15-8 Statistics on Black Ownership (1870–1910)

During Reconstruction the lives of African Americans improved significantly, largely as a result of their own efforts. When Reconstruction ended, many of those gains were lost, particularly in the areas of civil and political rights. Still, African Americans continued to improve themselves. As the statistics below indicate, African Americans after 1870 increasingly joined the ranks of farm owners and homeowners.

Source: Loren Schweninger, *Black Property Owners in the South, 1790–1915*, 164, 170, 174, 180. Copyright 1990 by the Board of Trustees of the University of Illinois. Used with permission of the University of Illinois Press.

(a) Black Farm Owners in the South, 1870–1910: Total Number and Percentage of Owners (Black and White)

State	1870		1890		Percentage of increase, 1870–1890	1900		Percentage of increase, 1890–1900	1910		Percentage of increase, 1900–1910
	Total	Percentage	Total	Percentage		Total	Percentage		Total	Percentage	
Alabama	1,152	1.3	8,847	13	668	14,110	15	59	17,047	15	21
Arkansas	1,203	5.2	8,004	24	565	11,941	25	49	14,660	23	23
Florida	596	3.5	4,940	38	729	6,551	48	33	7,286	50	11
Georgia	1,367	1.4	8,131	13	495	11,375	14	40	15,698	13	38
Louisiana	1,107	1.8	6,685	18	504	9,378	16	40	10,681	19	14
Mississippi	1,600	1.9	11,526	13	620	20,973	16	82	24,949	15	19
North Carolina	1,628	2.2	10,494	26	545	16,834	31	60	20,707	32	23
South Carolina	3,062	4.0	13,075	21	327	18,970	22	45	20,356	21	7
Tennessee	1,301	2.2	6,378	23	390	9,414	28	48	10,698	28	14
Texas	839	1.8	12,513	26	1,391	20,139	31	61	21,182	30	5
Virginia	860	1.0	13,678	43	1,490	26,527	59	94	32,168	67	21

(b) Black Homeowners* in the South, 1870–1910: Total Number and Percentage of Owners (Black and White)

State	1870		1890		1910	
	Total	Percentage	Total	Percentage	Total	Percentage
Alabama	215	4.3	6,898	11	16,714	17
Arkansas	56	5.3	3,840	17	9,802	27
Florida	46	3.7	5,709	28	13,581	22
Georgia	232	2.9	11,874	12	22,544	16
Louisiana	639	5.7	7,917	11	16,160	16
Mississippi	138	4.5	5,430	11	13,783	20
North Carolina	199	5.6	9,516	15	19,627	26
South Carolina	312	4.8	8,026	11	12,730	15
Tennessee	187	3.0	8,285	16	16,070	23
Texas	27	1.0	8,367	22	20,443	26
Virginia	409	3.3	16,210	20	24,405	27

*Excludes farm homes

Questions

1. Which state(s) had the greatest increase in black farm owners? In black homeowners?
2. What do the tables reveal about African Americans in the South in an era when they were systematically oppressed by whites?
3. How can you explain this evidence of the success of African Americans in the South in the late nineteenth century?

Questions for Further Thought

1. Compare Cain's argument on land reform (Document 15-7) to that of Thaddeus Stevens (Document 15-5). To what degree does Cain, like Stevens, see land redistribution as a means of punishing "rebels"? What does each man see as the proper role of the federal government in "reconstructing" the South?
2. Susan B. Anthony's argument (Document 15-6a) rests on an analogy between the status of women in the pre-Reconstruction United States and the status of African Americans. How well does that analogy work?
3. In view of the preceding documents, just how "radical" would you say radical Reconstruction really was? Bear in mind the meaning of the word *radical*—to desire change not on the surface of society, but *at its roots*.

The Undoing of Reconstruction

Northern support for Reconstruction was never reliable. Because most white northerners feared that President Johnson's program threatened to undo the Union victory and place Confederates back in the saddle (Document 15-9a), they preferred the program of congressional Republicans. However, they were at best only slightly more liberal in their racial views than were southerners, and over time northerners were increasingly receptive to southern white arguments that blacks were not to be trusted to govern (Document 15-9b).

Most southern whites, of course, opposed congressional Reconstruction from the outset, though the vehemence of the opposition fluctuated. The animosity of southern whites toward Reconstruction, Republicans, and African Americans intensified when elections were contested or when sensitive issues were placed before the public. The Ku Klux Klan was especially active during such times (Document 15-10), despite legislation passed against it.

The final undoing of Reconstruction came in the mid-1870s. A serious economic crisis struck the nation in 1873, plunging it into depression. New, economic issues, such as unemployment, labor conflict, and monetary policy, increasingly took precedence over the aging agenda of the sectional conflict, while northern lack of sympathy for blacks became increasingly important in shaping federal policy toward the South (Document 15-11). At the same time, southern whites got bolder, organizing paramilitary organizations to carry elections by whatever means were necessary. In such states as Mississippi and South Carolina, the end of Reconstruction resulted not so much from an election as from a white counterrevolution (Document 15-12).

15-9   The Rise and Fall of Northern Support for Reconstruction (1868, 1874)

Thomas Nast

Evidence of broad northern support for the Republican program could be found in many places other than the ballot box. Illustrations from *Harper's Weekly,* such as the one in the text (p. 485) and the one here from 1868 titled "This Is a White Man's Government," reflected popular attitudes in the North in the 1860s. However, northern support for Reconstruction began to erode as early as 1868 and was exhausted by

1874 (see text pp. 495–499), the year the second *Harper's Weekly* illustration presented here appeared. Both cartoons shown here on pages 367 and 368 are by Thomas Nast.

The first cartoon satirizes the Democratic Party in 1868, with its platform rejecting the Congressional Reconstruction Acts as "unconstitutional, null, and void." Nathan Bedford Forrest—the Confederate general who became the first Grand Wizard of the Ku Klux Klan—is represented in the center, while to his right stands an Irish immigrant, depicted (as was common in Nast cartoons) as a barbaric hoodlum. The third figure (to Forrest's left) is the Democratic candidate for President in 1868, Governor Horatio Seymour—depicted here as the prosperous associate of New York financiers. This unholy alliance unites in what to Nast were the characteristic Democratic Party activities of racial oppression and treason, illustrated by scenes from the New York Draft riots (see Document 14-7) and the postwar South, and by their trampling on the prostrate form of a black Union soldier.

The second cartoon shows a sharp shift in opinion on the part of both Nast and his audience. The cartoon illustrates a derisive news account of the black-majority South Carolina House of Representatives, reprinted from the white conservative *Charleston News*. In 1868 the views of the *News* would have been dismissed as "disloyal" by Nast's employer, *Harper's Weekly;* by 1874 the magazine was allowing those views a respectful hearing, and its famous cartoonist was giving them his stamp of approval. Why?

Sources: Thomas Nast, "This Is a White Man's Government," *Harper's Weekly,* 5 September 1868; Thomas Nast, "Colored Rule in a Reconstructed State," *Harper's Weekly,* 14 March 1874. Art courtesy the Research Libraries, New York Public Library.

Questions

1. Note the picture of African Americans presented here and in the illustration on text page 485. Contrast that with the portrayal of government by southern whites.
2. Compare the portrayal of African Americans in the last illustration with that in the earlier illustrations.
3. What do you think accounts for the change?

(a) This Is a White Man's Government (1868)

(b) Colored Rule in a Reconstructed State (1874)

COLORED RULE IN A RECONSTRUCTED (?) STATE.—[See Page 242.]

(THE MEMBERS CALL EACH OTHER THIEVES, LIARS, RASCALS, AND COWARDS.)

COLUMBIA. "You are Aping the lowest Whites. If you disgrace your Race in this way you had better take Back Seats."

15-10   A Fool's Errand. By One of the Fools (1879)

Albion W. Tourgee

A native of Ohio, Albion Winegar Tourgee (1838–1905) was working as a school-teacher in New York when the Civil War began. In April 1861 he joined the 27th New York Regiment and was wounded at the first battle of Bull Run. He returned to the army in July 1862 as a lieutenant in the 105th Ohio Regiment. Captured in 1863 at Murfreesboro, he returned to Ohio through a prisoner exchange and then rejoined his regiment to fight at Chickamauga, Lookout Mountain, and Missionary Ridge. Twice charged with insubordination, Tourgee resigned his commission in December 1863 and returned to Ohio to study law. By the fall of 1865 he had relocated, as a "carpet-bagger" (see text p. 489), in Greensboro, North Carolina. In 1868, under the electoral rule imposed under radical Reconstruction (see text pp. 490–491), Tourgee won election as a judge on the state superior court. He served there for six years, finding ample opportunity to defend the rights of freedmen and denounce the atrocities of the Ku Klux Klan. When his tenure on the court ended, President Grant appointed him pension agent at Raleigh, from which office he continued his battle with the Klan and with redeemer Democrats (see text pp. 494–495). By the summer of 1879 he had had enough and moved north with his family, making Mayville, New York, his home by 1881. In the novel *A Fool's Errand*, published in the year of his departure from North Carolina, Tourgee described his experiences during Reconstruction through the character Colonel Comfort Servosse, whom he depicted as "the Fool."

Source: [Albion W. Tourgee], *A Fool's Errand. By One of the Fools* (New York: Fords, Howard, & Hulbert, 1878), 182–192.

It was in the winter of 1868–69 . . . when it was said that already Reconstruction had been an approved success, [and] the traces of the war been blotted out . . . a little company of colored men came to the Fool one day; and one of them, who acted as spokesman said,—

"What's dis we hear, Mars Kunnel [Master Colonel], bout de Klux?"

"The what?" he asked.

"De Klux—de Ku-Kluckers dey calls demselves."

"Oh! The Ku-Klux, Ku-Klux-Klan . . . you mean."

"Yes: dem folks what rides about at night a-pesterin' pore colored people, an' pretendin' tu be jes from hell, or some of de battle-fields ob ole Virginny."

"Oh, that's all gammon [humbug]! There is nothing in the world in it,—nothing at all. . . ."

"You don't think dey's ghostses, nor nothing' ob dat sort?" asked another.

"Think! I know they are not."

"So do I," growled one of their number who had not spoken before, in a tone . . . that . . . drew the eyes of the Fool upon him at once.

"So your mind's made up on that point too, is it Bob?" he asked laughingly.

"I know dey's not ghosts, Kunnel. I wish ter God dey was!" was the reply.

"Why, what do you mean, Bob?" asked the colonel in surprise.

"Will you jes help me take off my shirt, Jim?" said Bob . . . as he turned to one of those with him. . . .

"What d'ye tink ob dat, Kunnel?"

"My God!" exclaimed the Fool, starting back in surprise and horror. "What does this mean, Bob?"

"Seen de Kluckers, sah," was the grimly-laconic answer.

The sight which presented itself to the Fool's eyes was truly terrible. . . . The whole back was livid and swollen, bruised as if it had been brayed in a mortar. Apparently, after having cut the flesh with closely-laid welts and furrows, sloping downward from the left side towards the right, with the peculiar skill . . . which could only be obtained through the abundant opportunity for severe . . . flagellation which prevailed under . . . slavery, the operator had changed his position, and scientifically cross-checked the whole. . . . "Nobody but an ole oberseer ebber dun dat, Kunnel." . . . When his clothing had been resumed, he sat down and poured into the wondering ears of the Fool this story:—

BOB'S EXPERIENCE.

"Yer see, I'se a blacksmith at Burke's Cross-Roads. I've been thar ever since a few days arter I heer ob de surrender. I rented an ole house dar, an' put up a sort of shop . . . an' went to work. . . .

"Long a while back—p'raps five er six month—I refused ter du some work fer Michael Anson or his boy, 'cause they'd run up quite a score at de shop, an' allers put me off when I wanted pay. . . . Folks said I waz gettin' too smart fer a nigger, an' sech like; but I kep right on; tole em I waz a free man . . . an' I didn't propose ter do any man's work fer noffin'. Most everybody hed somefin' ter say about it; but it didn't seem ter hurt my trade very much. . . . When ther come an election, I sed my say, did my own votin', an' tole de other colored people dey waz free, an' hed a right ter du de same. Thet's bad doctrine up in our country. . . . Dey don't mind 'bout . . . our votin', so long ez we votes ez day tell us. Dat' dare idea uv liberty fer a nigger.

"Well, here a few weeks ago, I foun' a board stuck up on my shop one mornin', wid dese words on it:—

"'BOB MARTIN,—You're gettin' too dam smart! The white folks round Burke's Cross-Roads don't want any sech smart niggers round thar. You'd better git, er you'll hev a call from the

"'K.K.K.'

. . . [Y]esterday . . . my ole 'ooman . . . tuk part ob de chillen into bed wid her; an' de rest crawled in wid me. . . . I kinder remember hearin' de dog bark, but I didn't mind it; an', de fust ting I knew, de do' was bust in. . . . Dar was 'bout tirty of 'em standin' dar in de moonlight, all dressed in black gowns thet come down to ther boots, an' some sort of high hat on, dat come down ober der faces. . . . Den dey tied me tu a tree, an' done what you've seen. Dey tuk my wife an' oldes' gal out of de house, tore de close right about off 'em, an' abused 'em shockin' afore my eyes. After tarin' tings up a heap in de house, dey rode off, tellin' me dey reckoned I's larn to be 'spectful to white folks here-arter. . . .

"Why have you not complained of this outrage to the authorities?" . . . asked [the Fool] after a moment.

"I tole Squire Haskins an' Judge Thompson what I hev tole you," answered Bob.

"And what did they say?"

"Dat dey couldn't do noffin' unless I could sw'ar to the parties." . . .

There was a moment's silence. Then the colored man asked,—

"Isn't dere no one else, Kunnel, dat could do any ting? Can't de President or Congress do somefin'? De gov'ment sot us free, an' it 'pears like it oughtn't to let our old masters impose on us in no sech way now. . . . We ain't cowards. We showed dat in de wah. I'se seen darkeys go whar de white troops wa'n't anxious to foller 'em, mor'n once."

"Where was that, Bob?"

"Wal, at Fo't Wagner, for one."

"How did you know about that?"

"How did I know 'bout dat? Bress yer soul, Kunnel, I was dar!"

Questions

1. Tourgee, thinly disguised as Comfort Servosse in the novel, depicted himself as "the Fool." Why?

2. Could the president or Congress have acted in ways that they did not to suppress the Ku Klux Klan? Describe the measures you think would have been necessary.

3. Were equal rights for blacks and the restoration of civil government in the South compatible? Explain why or why not.

15-11   President Grant Refuses to Aid Republicans in Mississippi (1875)

As one of three southern states with a black-majority population, one whose black voters were well organized, Mississippi should logically have remained secure for the Republicans. However, in the state election year of 1875, white Democrats launched a campaign of systematic violent intimidation of black and Republican voters. Against the massive mobilization of white "Rifle Clubs," the state government of Governor Adelbert Ames was helpless, and in September Ames sent President Grant a desperate plea for federal troops. Grant and his attorney general, Edwards Pierrepont, turned down Ames's request; Pierrepont's letter to Ames of September 14, quoting Grant, was subsequently released to the press (Document 15-11a). Thanks to a catastrophic decline in Republican votes and blatant ballot-box stuffing, Democrats "redeemed" the state in a landslide. One of the few survivors of the Democratic onslaught, African American Congressman John R. Lynch, wrote some years later of a postelection encounter with President Grant, who explained to him the political considerations behind his abandonment of Mississippi Republicans (Document 15-11b).

Sources: New York Times, 17 September 1875, 1; John Roy Lynch, *The Facts of Reconstruction* (New York: Neale Publishing Co, 1913), 150–153.

(a) Pierrepont's Letter of Refusal

DEPARTMENT OF JUSTICE,
WASHINGTON, Sept. 14, 1875.

To Gov. Ames, Jackson, Miss.:

This hour I have had dispatches from the President. I can best convey to you his ideas by extracts from his dispatch: "The whole public are tired out with these annual Autumnal outbreaks in the South, and the great majority are ready now to condemn any interference on the part of the Government. I heartily wish that peace and good order may be restored without issuing the proclamation; but if it is not the proclamation must be issued, and if it is I shall instruct the commander of the forces to have *no child's play.* If there is a necessity for military interference, there is justice in such interference as shall deter evil-doers. . . . I would suggest the sending of a dispatch (or better, a private messenger,) to Gov. Ames, urging him to strengthen his own position by exhausting his own resources in restoring order before he receives Government aid. He might accept the assistance offered by the citizens of Jackson and elsewhere. . . . Gov. Ames and his advisors can be made perfectly secure. As many of the troops in Mississippi as he deems necessary may be sent to Jackson. If he is betrayed by those who offer assistance, he will be in a position to defeat their ends and punish them."

You see by this the mind of the President, with which I and every member of the Cabinet who has been consulted are in full accord. You see the difficulties—you see the responsibilities which you assume. We cannot understand why you do not strengthen yourself in the way the President suggests, nor do we see why you do not call the Legislature together, and obtain from them whatever powers, money, and arms you need. The Constitution is explicit that the Executive of the State can call upon the President for aid in suppressing "domestic violence" only "when the Legislature cannot be convened," and the law expressly says: "In case of an insurrection in any State against the Government thereof, it shall be lawful for the President, on application of the Legislature of such State, or of the Executive, when the Legislature cannot be convened, to call," &c. It is the plain meaning of the Constitution and laws when taken together that the Executive of the State may call upon the President for military aid to quell "domestic violence" only in case of an insurrection in any State against the Government thereof when the Legislature can-

not be called together. You make no suggestions even that there is any insurrection against the Government of the State, or that the Legislature would not support you in any measures you might propose to preserve the public order. I suggest that you take all lawful means and all needed measures to preserve the peace by the forces in your own State, and let the country see that the citizens of Mississippi, who are largely favorable to good order, and who are largely Republican, have the courage and the manhood to fight for their rights and to destroy the bloody ruffians who murder the innocent and inoffending freedmen. Everything is in readiness. Be careful to bring yourself strictly within the Constitution and the laws, and if there is such resistance to your State authorities as you cannot, by all the means at your command, suppress, the President will swiftly aid you in crushing those lawless traitors to human rights.

Telegraph me on receipt of this, and state explicitly what you need. Very respectfully yours,

EDWARDS PIERREPONT, Attorney General.

(b) Grant's Subsequent Explanation

. . . I then informed the President that there was another matter about which I desired to have a short talk with him, that was the recent election in Mississippi. After calling his attention to the sanguinary struggle through which we had passed, and the great disadvantages under which we labored, I reminded him of the fact that the Governor, when he saw that he could not put down without the assistance of the National Administration what was practically an insurrection against the State Government, made application for assistance in the manner and form prescribed by the Constitution, with the confident belief that it would be forthcoming. But in this we were, for some reason, seriously disappointed and sadly surprised. The reason for this action, or rather non-action, was still an unexplained mystery to us. For my own satisfaction and information I should be pleased to have the President enlighten me on the subject.

The President said that he was glad I had asked him the question, and that he would take pleasure in giving me a frank reply. He said he had sent Governor Ames' requisition to the War Department with his approval and with instructions to have the necessary assistance furnished without delay. He had also given instructions to the Attorney-General to use the marshals and the machinery of the Federal judiciary as far as possible in coöperation with the War Department in an effort to maintain order and to bring about a condition which would insure a peaceable and fair election. But before the orders were put into execution a committee of prominent Republicans from Ohio had called on him. (Ohio was then an October State,—that is, her elections took place in October instead of November.) An important election was then pending in that State. This committee, the President stated, protested against having the requisition of Governor Ames honored. The committee, the President said, informed him in a most emphatic way that if the requisition of Governor Ames were honored, the Democrats would not only carry Mississippi,—a State which would be lost to the Republicans in any event,—but that Democratic success in Ohio would be an assured fact. If the requisition were not honored it would make no change in the result in Mississippi, but that Ohio would be saved to the Republicans. The President assured me that it was with great reluctance that he yielded,—against his own judgment and sense of official duty,—to the arguments of this committee, and directed the withdrawal of the orders which had been given the Secretary of War and the Attorney-General in that matter.

This statement, I confess, surprised me very much.

"Can it be possible," I asked, "that there is such a prevailing sentiment in any State in the North, East or West as renders it necessary for a Republican President to virtually give his sanction to what is equivalent to a suspension of the Constitution and laws of the land to insure Republican success in such a State? I cannot believe this to be true, the opinion of the Republican committee from Ohio to the contrary notwithstanding. What surprises me more, Mr. President, is that you yielded and granted this remarkable request. That is not like you. It is the first time I have ever known you to show the white feather. Instead of granting the request of that committee, you should have rebuked the men,—told them that it is your duty as chief magistrate of the country to enforce the Constitution and laws of the land, and to protect American citizens in the exercise and enjoyment of their rights, let the consequences be what they may; and that if by doing this Ohio should be lost to the Republicans it ought to be lost. In other words, no victory is worth having if it is to be brought about upon such conditions as those,—if it is to be purchased at such a fearful cost as was paid in this case."

"Yes," said the President, "I admit that you are right. I should not have yielded. I believed at the time that I was making a grave mistake. But as presented, it was duty on one side, and party obligation on the other. Between the two I hesitated, but finally yielded to what was believed to be party obligation. If a mistake was made, it was one of the head and not of the heart. That my heart was right and my intentions good, no one who knows me will question. If I had believed that any effort on my part would have saved Mississippi I would have made it, even if I had been convinced that it would have resulted in the loss of Ohio to the Republicans. But I was satisfied then, as I am now, that Mississippi could not have been saved to the party in any event and I wanted to avoid the responsibility of the loss of Ohio, in addition. This was the turning-point in the case. . . ."

Questions

1. Do you think that Grant was correct in his argument against federal intervention? Was there really nothing that the federal government and the national Republican Party could have done to "save" Mississippi?
2. Had Governor Ames convened the Mississippi legislature to deal with "the bloody ruffians," how successful do you think he would have been?
3. What does Grant's decision illuminate about how Republicans, and many people in the North, had come to view the South and the progress of Reconstruction—especially in the Deep South—by the mid-1870s?

15-12   Plan of the Campaign (1876)

Martin W. Gary

The Mississippi Plan of 1875 proved so successful in "redeeming" that state in 1875 that it attracted attention from white Democrats in the other southern states still under Republican rule. In South Carolina—like Mississippi a black-majority state—white "Conservatives" created a paramilitary organization called the Red Shirts. The chief organizer of the campaign to overthrow the Republicans, an upcountry lawyer and politician named Martin W. Gary, prepared the following "Plan of the Campaign," which in revised form was sent out to all county Conservative organizations. The "rules" in italics were omitted in the printed version. Like the "Mississippi Plan," Gary's plan was successful in ousting the Republican regime in the state, although the Conservative victory was only ratified when President Hayes withdrew federal troops from the state as part of the Compromise of 1877.

Source: Francis Butler Simkins and Robert Hilliard Woody, *South Carolina during Reconstruction* (Chapel Hill: University of North Carolina Press, 1932), 564–569.

1. That every Democrat in the Townships must be put upon the Roll of the Democratic Clubs. Nolens volens.

2. That a Roster must be made of every *white* and of *every negro* voter in the Townships and *returned immediately* to the Country Executive Committee.

3. *That the Democratic Military Clubs are to be armed with rifles and pistols and such other arms as they may command. They are to be divided into two companies, one of the old men the other of the young; an experienced captain or commander to be placed over each of them. That each Company is to have a 1st and 2nd Lieutenant. That the number of ten privates is to be the unit of organization. That each Captain is to see that his men are well armed and provided with at least thirty rounds of ammunition. That the Captain of the young men is to provide a Baggage wagon, in which three days rations for the horses and three days rations for the men are to be stored on the day before the election in order that they may be prepared at a moments notice to move to any point in the County when ordered by the Chairman of the Executive Committee.*

ELECTION

4. We must get the three Commissioners of Election, who are appointed by the Governor, as favorable to us as possible, and we must demand that at least one reliable Democrat is on the Commission and he must endeavor to get to be Chairman of the Commission, and the clerk that is allowed them must be a Democrat if we can possibly bring it about.

5. We must have at least one half of the managers of Election Democrats and as many more as we can get. We must have the Chairman of the Board of Managers a Democrat by all means. Also all the clerks to the managers of Precincts must be Democrats.

6. We must have a duplicate of the result of the Election made out for the benefit of the Executive Committee so soon as the ballots are counted and forwarded at once by a courier, on the night of the Election. There must be a Committee who shall keep watch and guard over the ballot boxes to prevent the Radicals from tampering with them in any way.

7. We must send a committee with a duplicate of the Election to Columbia in order to see to it that the State Canvassers do not perpetrate any fraud upon us after the Election is held, and . . . that the Clerk of the Court files a copy of the returns of Election in accordance with Law.

8. *There must be at least two hundred select men, chosen from the different Clubs, to go to Columbia in the event of a refusal to seat the Democratic members elected, to compel and enforce their rights to be seated at all hazards.*

9. Every Democrat must be at the polls by five o'clock in the morning of the election, carry his dinner with him and stay there until the votes are counted, unless the exigencies require him elsewhere.

10. It shall be the duty of each club to provide transportation to old and helpless voters and assist them to the Polls, and at the same time see to it that all Democrats turn out and vote.

11. Every Democrat must be on the alert on the day of Election to see that negroes under age do not vote and that those who are properly entitled to vote do not repeat, and if they should discover that squads should leave the precincts and go in the direction of another precinct, they must follow them and challenge their vote at the next precinct.

12. Every Democrat must feel honor bound to control the vote of at least one negro, by intimidation, purchase, keeping him away or as each individual may determine, how he may best accomplish it.

13. We must attend every Radical meeting that we hear of whether they meet at night or in the day time. Democrats must go in as large numbers as they can together, and well armed, behave at *first* with great courtesy and assure the ignorant negroes that you mean them no harm and so soon as their *leaders* or speakers begin to speak and make false statements of facts, tell them *then* and *there* to their faces, that they are liars, thieves and rascals, and are only trying to mislead the ignorant negroes and if you get a chance get upon the platform and address the negroes.

14. In speeches to negroes you must remember that *argument* has no effect upon them: They can only be influenced by their *fears,* superstition and cupidity. Do not attempt to flatter and persuade them. Tell them plainly of our wrongs and grievances, perpetrated upon us, by their rascally leaders. Prove to them that we can carry the election without them and if they coöperate with us, it will benefit them more than it will us. Treat them so as to show

them, you are the superior race, and that their natural position is that of subordination to the white man.

15. Let it be generally known that if any blood is shed, houses burnt, votes repeated, ballot boxes stuffed, false counting of votes, or any acts on their part that are in violation of *Law* and *Order!* that we will hold the leaders of the *Radical Party personally responsible,* whether they were present at the time of the commission of the offense or crime or not; beginning *first* with the white men, second the mulatto men and third with the black leaders. This should be proclaimed from one end of the country to the other, so that *every Radical* may know it, as the *certain, fixed* and *unalterable determination* of every Democrat in this county.

16. *"Never threaten a man individually if he deserves to be threatened, the necessities of the times require that he should die. A dead Radical is very harmless—a threatened Radical or one driven off by threats from the scene of his operations is often very troublesome, sometimes dangerous, always vindictive."* . . .

21. *In the month of September we ought to begin to organize negro clubs, or pretend that we have organized them and write letters from different parts of the County giving the facts of organization out from prudential reasons, the names of the negroes are to be withheld. Those who join are to be taken on probation and are not to be taken into full fellowship, until they have proven their sincerity by voting our ticket.*

22. In the nomination of candidates we should nominate those who will give their time, their money, their brains, their energies and if necessary lay down their lives to carry this election. Any attempt to run independent candidates must be prevented at any risk.

23. There should not be any assessment for money to carry on the campaign, before the month of October, when the cotton crop begins to mature and our people have an opportunity of raising money by its sale.

24. In voting for or nominating candidates for County, State or Federal offices, we must give the preference to native born *white South Carolinians* over Carpet baggers.

25. The watch word of our Campaign should be "fight the Devil with fire." That we are in favor of local self government, home rule by home folks and that we are determined to drive the carpet baggers from this State at all hazards. . . .

28. In all processions the clubs must parade with banners, mottoes, etc. and keep together so as to make an imposing spectacle.

29. Every club must be uniformed in a red shirt and they must be sure and wear it upon all public meetings and particularly on the day of election. . . .

30. Secrecy should shroud all of transactions. Let not your left hand know what your right does. . . .

33. Any member of the Party who fails to vote the ticket must be read out of the Party.

Questions

1. Is this a plan for a political or a military campaign? Explain the difference.
2. What distinguishes the provisions in italics from those in regular typeface?
3. What are Gary's attitudes toward blacks? Does he regard them as citizens to be persuaded of the justice of his cause?

Questions for Further Thought

1. Compare and contrast northern and southern views of blacks (Documents 15-9a, 15-9b, and 15-10). How are they the same? How are they different? What impact did the northern view of blacks have on the progress of Reconstruction?
2. Why did the Radical Republican program (Document 15-5) for reconstruction fail? After years of promises, why did the Republican Party in particular, and northerners in general, turn their backs on the freedmen and leave them to the mercy of their former masters in the South (Documents 15-11 and 15-12)?
3. If the Republican Party had pressed ahead with Reconstruction, do you think that it could have achieved its goals? Or was Albion Tourgee correct in calling the effort to reform the post–Civil War South "a fool's errand" (Document 15-10)?